Shelly and Cashman

COMPUTER FUNDAMENTALS for an Information Age

Hossein

Shelly and Cashman Books

Computer Fundamentals for an Information Age
Workbook and Study Guide to accompany Computer Fundamentals for an Information Age
Introduction to BASIC Programming
Introduction to BASIC Programming Workbook and Study Guide
Introduction to Computers and Data Processing
Student Workbook and Study Guide to accompany Introduction to Computers and Data Processing
Introduction to Computer Programming Structured COBOL
Advanced Structured COBOL: Program Design and File Processing
Business Systems Analysis and Design
Computer Programming RPG II
Introduction to Computer Programming ANSI COBOL
ANSI COBOL Workbook — Testing and Debugging Techniques and Exercises
Advanced ANSI COBOL Disk/Tape Programming Efficiencies
Introduction to Computer Programming RPG
Introduction to Flowcharting and Computer Programming Logic
Introduction to Computer Programming IBM System/360 Assembler Language
IBM System/360 Assembler Language Workbook Core Dump Analysis and Debugging Techniques
IBM System/360 Assembler Language Disk/Tape Advanced Concepts
DOS Utilities Sort/Merge Multiprogramming
OS Job Control Language
DOS Job Control For Assembler Language Programmers
DOS Job Control for COBOL Programmers
Introduction to Computer Programming IBM System/360 PL/I

COMPUTER FUNDAMENTALS for an Information Age

Gary B. Shelly
Educational Consultant
Brea, California

&

Thomas J. Cashman, CDP, B.A., M.A.
Long Beach City College
Long Beach, California

ANAHEIM PUBLISHING COMPANY, INC.
2632 Saturn St., P. O. Box 9600, Brea, CA 92622
(714) 993-3700

ISBN 0-88236-125-2

Printed in the United States of America

10987654321

Table of Contents

Chapter One

An Introduction To Computers

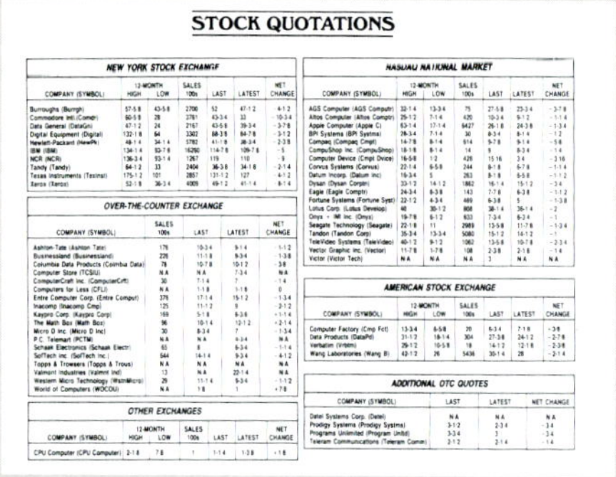

STOCK QUOTATIONS

NEW YORK STOCK EXCHANGE

COMPANY (SYMBOL)	12-MONTH HIGH	LOW	SALES 100s	LAST	LATEST	NET CHANGE
Burroughs (Burrgh)	57-5 8	43-5 8	2700	52	47-1 2	-4-1 2
Commodore Intl.(Comdr)	60-5 8	28	3761	43-3 4	33	-10-3 4
Data General (DataGn)	47-1 2	24	2167	43-5 8	39-3 4	-3-7 8
Digital Equipment (Digital)	132-1 8	64	3302	68-3 8	64-7 8	-3-1 2
Hewlett-Packard (HewPk)	48-1 4	34-1 4	5782	41-1 8	38-3 4	-2-3 8
IBM (IBM)	134-1 4	93-7 8	16260	114-7 8	109-7 8	-5
NCR (NCR)	136-3 4	93-1 4	1267	119	110	-9
Tandy (Tandy)	64-1 2	33	2404	36-3 8	34-1 8	-2-1 4
Texas Instruments (Texinst)	175-1 2	101	2857	131-1 2	127	-4-1 2
Xerox (Xerox)	52-1 8	36-3 4	4009	49-1 2	41-1 4	-8-1 4

OVER-THE-COUNTER EXCHANGE

COMPANY (SYMBOL)	SALES 100s	LAST	LATEST	NET CHANGE
Ashton-Tate (Ashton Tate)	176	10-3 4	9-1 4	-1-1 2
Businessland (Businessland)	226	11-1 8	9-3 4	-1-3 8
Columbia Data Products (Colmbia Data)	78	10-7 8	10-1 2	-3 8
Computer Store (TCSIU)	N A	N A	7-3 4	N A
ComputerCraft Inc. (ComputerCrft)	30	7-1 4	7	-1 4
Computers for Less (CFL)	N A	1-1 8	1-1 8	0
Entre Computer Corp. (Entre Comput)	376	17-1 4	15-1 2	-1-3 4
Inacomp (Inacomp Cmp)	125	11-1 2	9	-2-1 2
Kaypro Corp. (Kaypro Corp)	169	5-1 8	6-3 8	+1-1 4
The Math Box (Math Box)	96	10-1 4	12-1 2	+2-1 4
Micro D Inc. (Micro D Inc)	30	8-3 4	7	-1-3 4
P.C. Telemart (PCTM)	N A	N A	4-3 4	N A
Schaak Electronics (Schaak Electr)	65	8	6-3 4	-1-1 4
SofTech Inc. (SofTech Inc.)	544	14-1 4	9-3 4	-4-1 2
Topps & Trowsers (Topps & Trous)	N A	N A	N A	N A
Valmont Industries (Valmnt Ind)	13	N A	22-1 4	N A
Western Micro Technology (WstnMicro)	29	11-1 4	9-3 4	-1-1 2
World of Computers (WOCOU)	N A	1 8	1	+7 8

OTHER EXCHANGES

COMPANY (SYMBOL)	12-MONTH HIGH	LOW	SALES 100s	LAST	LATEST	NET CHANGE
CPU Computer (CPU Computer)	2-1 8	7 8	1	1-1 4	1-3 8	+1 8

NASDAQ NATIONAL MARKET

COMPANY (SYMBOL)	12-MONTH HIGH	LOW	SALES 100s	LAST	LATEST	NET CHANGE
AGS Computer (AGS Computr)	32-1 4	13-3 4	75	27-5 8	23-3 4	-3-7 8
Altos Computer (Altos Comptr)	25-1 2	7-1 4	420	10-3 4	9-1 2	-1-1 4
Apple Computer (Apple C)	63-1 4	17-1 4	6427	26-1 8	24-3 8	-1-3 4
BPI Systems (BPI Systms)	28-3 4	7-1 4	30	8-3 4	8-1 4	-1 2
Compaq (Compaq Cmpt)	14-7 8	8-1 4	614	9-7 8	9-1 4	-5 8
CompuShop Inc. (CompuShop)	18-1 8	8-1 4	14	9	8-3 4	-1 4
Computer Device (Cmpt Dvice)	16-5 8	1 2	428	15 16	3 4	-3 16
Corvus Systems (Corvus)	22-1 4	6-5 8	244	8-1 8	6-7 8	-1-1 4
Datum Incorp. (Datum Inc)	16-3 4	5	263	8-1 8	6-5 8	-1-1 2
Dysan (Dysan Corptn)	33-1 2	14-1 2	1862	16-1 4	15-1 2	-3 4
Eagle (Eagle Comptr)	24-3 4	6-3 8	143	7-7 8	6-3 8	-1-1 2
Fortune Systems (Fortune Syst)	22-1 2	4-3 4	489	6-3 8	5	-1-3 8
Lotus Corp. (Lotus Develop)	40	30-1 2	808	38-1 4	36-1 4	-2
Onyx + IMI Inc. (Onyx)	19-7 8	6-1 2	633	7-3 4	6-3 4	-1
Seagate Technology (Seagate)	22-1 8	11	2989	13-5 8	11-7 8	-1-3 4
Tandon (Tandon Corp)	35-3 4	13-3 4	5080	15-1 2	14-1 2	-1
TeleVideo Systems (TeleVideo)	40-1 2	9-1 2	1062	13-5 8	10-7 8	-2-3 4
Vector Graphic Inc. (Vector)	11-7 8	1-7 8	108	2-3 8	2-1 8	-1 4
Victor (Victor Tech)	N A	N A	N A	3	N A	N A

AMERICAN STOCK EXCHANGE

COMPANY (SYMBOL)	12-MONTH HIGH	LOW	SALES 100s	LAST	LATEST	NET CHANGE
Computer Factory (Cmp Fct)	13-3 4	6-5 8	20	6-3 4	7-1 8	+3 8
Data Products (DataPd)	31-1 2	18-1 4	304	27-3 8	24-1 2	-2-7 8
Verbatim (Vrbtm)	29-1 2	10-5 8	18	14-1 2	12-1 8	-2-3 8
Wang Laboratories (Wang B)	42-1 2	26	5436	30-1 4	28	-2-1 4

ADDITIONAL OTC QUOTES

COMPANY (SYMBOL)	LAST	LATEST	NET CHANGE
Datel Systems Corp. (Datel)	N A	N A	N A
Prodigy Systems (Prodigy Systms)	3-1 2	2-3 4	-3 4
Programs Unlimited (Program Unltd)	3-3 4	3	-3 4
Teleram Communications (Teleram Comm)	2-1 2	2-1 4	-1 4

Chapter Two

Evolution of the Computer Industry

Objectives

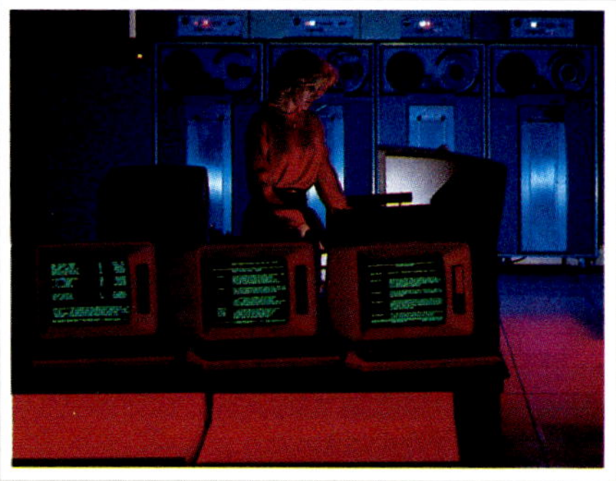

Chapter Three

Processing Data On a Computer

Objectives

Chapter Four

Interactive and Batch Processing Systems

Chapter Five

Input to the Computer

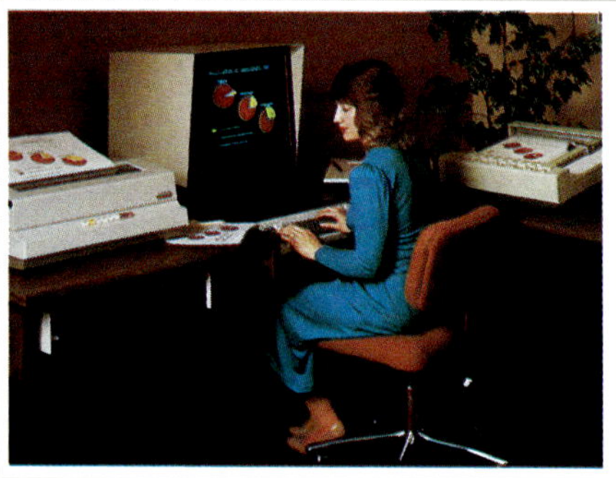

Chapter Six

Obtaining Output From the Computer

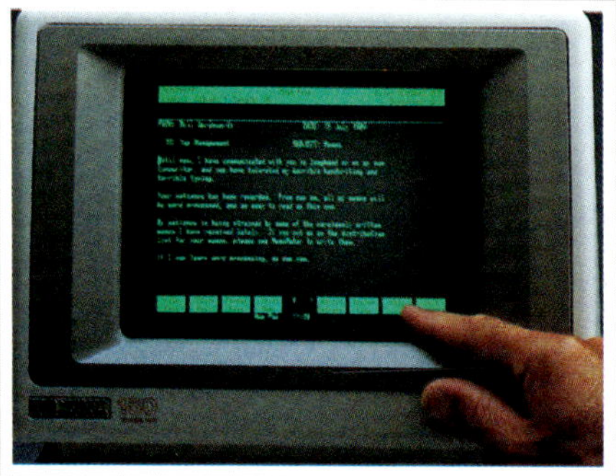

Chapter Seven

User Interface with Information Systems

Chapter Eight

Processor Unit and Data Representation

Chapter Nine

Auxiliary Storage

Chapter Ten

File Organization And Data Base

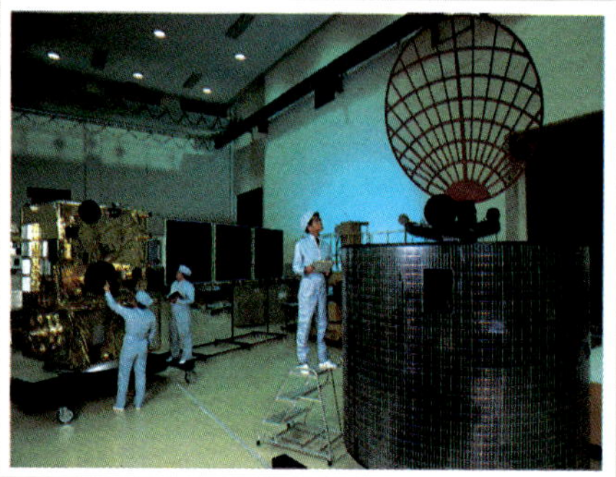

Chapter Eleven

Data Communications

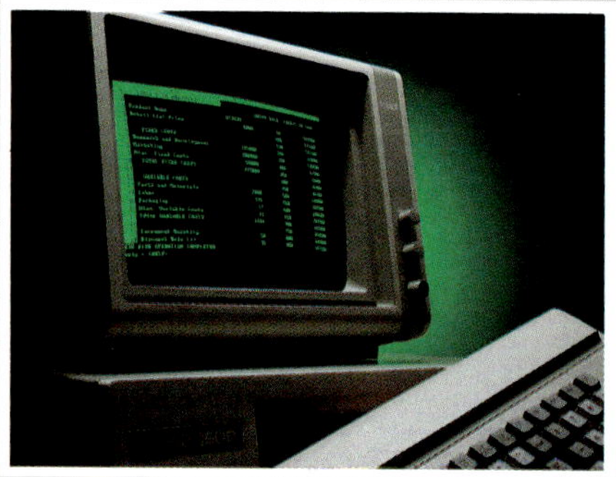

Chapter Twelve

Application Software

Chapter Thirteen

Programming Languages

Chapter Fourteen

Operating Systems and Systems Software

Chapter Fifteen

Systems Analysis And Design

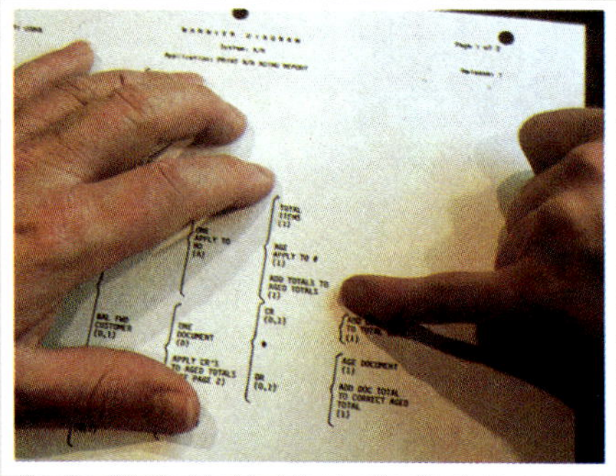

Chapter Sixteen

Program Design, Coding, And Implementation

Chapter Seventeen

Careers and the Computer Industry

Chapter Eighteen

Computers in Our Society

Appendix A

Programming in BASIC

Appendix B

Number Systems

Index/Glossary

PREFACE

Many people refer to this era in history as the age of high technology, the age of information processing . . . the age of the computer! Whatever term is used, it is now recognized that an understanding of the computer, how it works, how it processes data to produce useful information, and how it can be used as a tool in the home, in school, and in our work environment is a necessary part of the general education for all who live and work in this information processing age.

This textbook is designed to be used in the **introductory course in computers and information processing** as taught throughout the country. Its purpose is to provide an introduction to the fundamentals of computers and information processing for general education, business, and computer science students so that they may be able to understand what a computer is, how it operates, and when a computer should be applied to the solution of personal, business, and scientific problems.

The development of this textbook

In the past few years, the types of computers, the number of computers, and the way in which computers are used has changed dramatically. The personal computer is no longer just an intriguing device used by the computer hobbyist, but is an integral part of the information processing environment. Integrated software with electronic spreadsheet, data base, graphics, and word processing capabilities are no longer just interesting topics of conversation. Software of this type has changed the way tasks in the world of business are being accomplished. A modern computer textbook must lead to a thorough understanding of this new world of information processing.

As a result of our research, five goals were set for this book: 1) The book should reflect state-of-the-art technology; 2) The book should reflect modern, up-to-date applications of computers in all areas of use; 3) The personal computer should be treated, as it is now treated in industry, as an integral part of the information processing industry; 4) The book should allow the student to see and understand the business, industrial, and scientific areas in which the computer is used; 5) The textbook should move from an overview of a subject area to a detailed examination of the subject area.

Textbook approach

The first significant approach taken in the development of this textbook was the recognition that the personal computer is an integral part of the information processing industry. Thus, the use and application of the personal computer is discussed throughout the textbook in the same detail as minicomputers and mainframes. Many of the illustrations utilize the personal computer to demonstrate important processing concepts, while others illustrate processing concepts using minicomputers and mainframes. It is important to recognize that this is not a personal computer book. Instead, this is a textbook devoted to teaching students about the full range of computers and the processing concepts associated with each.

It was further decided in the development of this textbook that computer hardware and software should not be treated as individual units of study. Instead, the approach is to integrate these concepts throughout the text. For example, in Chapter 1, the student is provided with an overview of the basic concepts of information processing. This chapter includes material on the need for information processing; the basic components of a personal computer; software concepts; how a personal computer processes data using an electronic spreadsheet application; a tour of a large computer center; the information center; and the use of the computer and application software.

Chapter 2 contains a discussion of the evolution of the electronic computer industry. The purpose of this chapter is not to merely identify various types of computer hardware and their announcement dates. The intent is to capture for the student the excitement, growth, and problems that the information processing profession has faced as it emerged to become one of the world's largest industries. This chapter includes not only a discussion of significant announcements in computer hardware and software, but also includes information intended to make the student aware of important social issues related to this new technology.

In Chapter 3, students are presented with the concepts of fields, records, and files and the importance of data relationships, together with a more detailed discussion of the types of processing that can occur on a computer. Included are diagrams of basic input operations, arithmetic operations, comparing operations, and operations requiring auxiliary storage. The basic concepts of both sequential and random retrieval of data, and updating files are also explained. Sample illustrations that include the use of both personal computers, minicomputers, and mainframes provide a further in-depth understanding of computers.

Chapter 4 presents the student with an explanation of the flow of data in both interactive and batch processing systems. To assist the student in evaluating when a computer should be used, a number of specific criteria are identified. Diagrams illustrating the steps that occur when processing large volumes of data, sorting, selecting, and summarizing, and other uses of the computer are contained in this chapter.

Chapter 5 provides an in-depth discussion of the input portion of the information processing cycle. Emphasis is placed upon input in interactive and batch environments, reflecting state-of-the-art input operations that are currently implemented in industry. Important characteristics and types of computer terminals are reviewed in the context of the input function. Specialized input operations such as optical character reading and point-of-sale terminals are also discussed.

Chapter 6 is devoted to an analysis of the output function of the information processing cycle, including the latest developments in printing technology as applied to personal computers. Printers used with large computers are also illustrated and explained. Because of the widespread use of business graphics, a thorough coverage of this output function is included. The chapter concludes with a review of specialized output devices.

Chapter 7 treats the very important topic of user interface with information systems. This topic is seldom covered in an introductory textbook but is extremely important. The chapter answers the question, How does a user communicate and interact with a computer? from both a software and hardware point of view. Software interface includes the use of menus and submenus, error messages, and other interaction that the user might have with the computer. Hardware interface includes a detailed discussion of the mouse and vocal input as forms of user interface. Topics such as icons and query languages are also explained. Upon completion of this chapter, the students should be aware of the experiences that will occur when they interact with a computer.

Chapter 8 explains how data is stored in main computer memory. Both the ASCII code and EBCDIC are explained. The elements of a computer instruction on a machine language level and the basic steps that occur when a machine language instruction is executed are covered. This chapter also presents an explanation of the advantages of the 16-bit and 32-bit computer as compared to the 8-bit computer.

In Chapter 9, the use of auxiliary storage is explained. With the widespread use of the floppy disk and hard disks for personal computers, careful coverage is included of these subjects. Other topics include magnetic tape and magnetic disk auxiliary storage devices and media as utilized with large computers.

File and data base management systems are widely used on computers of all types, ranging from personal computers to mainframes. Chapter 10 covers the basic concepts of file and data base management systems. The important subject of data communications is covered in Chapter 11. Special emphasis is placed upon the use of local area networks. After studying this material, the student will have gained an insight into how data communications takes place and how networks are established to use computers and data communications together.

Subsequent chapters are concerned with the important topics of applications software, including a detailed analysis of electronic spreadsheet, spelling checker, file management, and personal financial management software; programming languages; operating systems as applied to both personal computers and large computers; and program design. A chapter is included on systems analysis and design which is intended to provide the student with an overview of this important area of study.

The concluding chapters are designed to point out to the student some of the jobs which are available in the information processing industry, as well as the structure of the industry itself. In addition, an analysis of the social issues associated with the world of high technology, including such issues as national data banks, computer crime, software piracy, and the more general question, Will computers contribute to the quality of life? will be explored.

Many beginning courses introduce students to the principles and concepts of computer programming by requiring the students to write and execute a number of programs. Because of the wide usage of BASIC, Appendix A has been included in the text for those instructors desiring to teach BASIC programming.

With millions of personal computers being sold, it is extremely important that students be taught to program a computer correctly in their first course, for if students are poorly taught or develop their own programming techniques, these habits will carry over to subsequent classes. It is well recognized by computer professionals and knowledgeable computer educators that structured design and structured programming form the basis of good programming methodology. All sample programs in this textbook illustrate and teach the principles of good structured design and structured programming using the BASIC language.

Teachers are strongly urged to teach proper documentation and programming style in the introductory class and require students to complete programs in a professional manner.

Student learning aids

At the conclusion of each chapter, a comprehensive summary is provided. Review questions are included to serve as the basis for testing one's knowledge of the concepts presented in the chapter.

To encourage students to analyze and evaluate controversial issues in the subject of information processing, a series of questions presenting issues is included at the end of each chapter. The questions relate to the material presented in the chapter. Teachers are urged to include a discussion of these issues as a part of the classroom activity, probing into these issues with students to assist in developing critical thinking about important issues in information processing. Research projects are also included as a part of each chapter.

The workbook and study guide and computer projects

For additional student activities, a Workbook and Study Guide which accompanies this textbook is available. The material in the workbook is designed to further enhance the instructional materials in each chapter. Each chapter in the workbook includes a chapter review, key words with definitions, matching, true/false and multiple choice self-tests, and other types of projects designed to assist the student in mastering the material in the textbook. Most students entering an introductory course desire to interact with the computer as rapidly as possible. In addition, there is a great need to expose students to the operation of personal computers and computer terminals from the user's viewpoint. To meet both of these needs, the Workbook and Study Guide contains a series of computer projects which simulate typical uses of the computer in an interactive environment. For example, there are projects to introduce the student to electronic spreadsheet applications and word processing. There are projects that simulate the activities of a bank teller and an airline reservation clerk. These projects have been very successful in motivating students and producing an exciting classroom environment. It is recommended that the projects be used, beginning with the first week of instruction. The projects have been written in BASIC, and the source listings are provided free of charge in the Instructor's Guide for the Workbook and Study Guide. They may be used by schools using Computer Fundamentals for an Information Age.

Acknowledgements

A project of this size does not happen without the help of many people. We would like to thank the users of our previous textbooks who have supplied us with information relative to what they would like to see in an introductory textbook. In addition, over 400 companies supplied us with pictures and source material. Without them, this book would not have been produced.

The production of the book required the help of true professionals. Ms. Sue Davis served as color consultant. Mr. Max Loftin of Quality Graphics accepted the challenge of providing quality separations and stripping in a very limited period of time so that the latest developments could be included in the textbook. Bob Rochelle, Tim Dorf, and the press crews at R. R. Donnelley and Sons provided their usual professional services.

Our colleagues at Anaheim Publishing Company — Mrs. Marilyn Martin, Mr. Michael Broussard, and Mr. Kenneth Russo — accepted the challenge of producing a truly unique and exciting textbook. The quality of their work is reflected in the final product. We thank them very much. Terry Humphries did a superior job in developing the support material for this book, and Steve Forsythe did likewise in developing the Workbook and accompanying software. Their contributions are immeasurable.

For their support and understanding, we dedicate this book to Val Martin and the Martin family; Kathleen Shelly and Philipp, Konrad, and Hans; and Merilyn Cashman and the Cashman family.

Gary B. Shelly
Thomas J. Cashman

Picture Credits

The pictures contained in this book are courtesy of the following organizations. We are most appreciative of their cooperation.

3M Figures 1-38, 5-18, 8-26 (10), 9-26
3M (Alvin Upitis Photographer) Figure 9-24
ACCO International, Inc. Figure 17-1
Adage Inc. Figures 2-38, 4-16, 5-42
Allied Corporation Figure 8-25
Amcodyne, (Copyright 1983 David Bluebaugh) Figure 9-18
American Telephone and Telegraph Company Figures 2-36, 2-41, 6-33 (left), 8-26 (9), 15-1
Anchor Hocking Corp. Figure 9-32
Apple Computer Inc. Figures 1-6, 1-35, 7-8, 9-3, 17-4
Avnet, Inc. (© Clint Clemens 1984) Cover
Bell & Howell Company Figure 2-27
Burroughs Corporation Figure 8-26 (4)
Byte Magazine Figure 6-28
Caere Corporation Figures 5-26, 5-29
CalComp Sanders, Inc. Figures 1-17, 1-20
Callan Data Systems Figure 5-15
Candle Corporation Figure 14-1
Carl Howard Figure 2-2
Cincinnati Milacron Inc. Figure 2-35
Commodore Ltd. Figure 2-28
Computer Memories, Inc. Figure 9-17
Computervision Corporation Figures 4-17, 5-43, 17-3
Consolidated Foods, Inc. Figures 5-32, 5-38
Control Data Corporation Figures 1-13, 1-19, 1-20, 2-33, 7-12
Corning Glass Works Figure 11-19
Corvus Systems, Inc. Figure 5-17
Dartmouth College News Service Figure 2-21
Data General Corporation Figure 17-12
DatagraphiX Figure 6-19
Dataproducts Corporation Figures 6-4, 6-13, 6-18
Department of the Navy Figure 2-15
Dysan Corporation Figure 9-14
Eagle Computer, Inc. Figures 12-1, 15-2
Epson America, Inc. Figure 1-32, 6-6
Evans & Sutherland Figures 1-44, 6-33 (right), 6-36
Exxon Office Systems Company Figure 1-41
Facit-Dataroyal Figure 6-12
Firestone Tire & Rubber Company Figure 1-43
Formation Inc. Figure 1-40
Goodyear Tire & Rubber Company Figure 1-2
Gould Inc. Figures 1-12, 1-45, 2-39, 17-13
Greyhound Corporation Figure 11-7
Grumman Corporation Figure 1-7
Harris Corporation - Data Communications Division Figure 5-15
Hayes Microcomputer Products Inc. Figures 11-4, 11-5
Hewlett-Packard Company Figures 2-34, 6-14, 6-17, 6-20, 7-1, 18-2
Honeywell Inc. Figures 4-1, 17-11
Honeywell Information Systems, Inc. Figure 4-15
Houston Instruments of Bausch & Lomb Figures 5-41, 6-41
ITT Courier Terminal Systems, Inc. Figures 1-1, 17-2
Informatics General Corporation Figures 6-2, 17-9
Intecolor Corporation Figures 6-1, 8-1
Integrated Software (ISSCO Graphics) Figures 6-35, 15-3
Intel Corporation Figures 2-26, 8-26 (6)
Intergraph Corporation Figure 6-34
Internal Revenue Service Figure 5-7
International Business Machines Corporation (IBM) Figures 1-3, 1-27, 1-34, 1-39, 2-11, 2-12, 2-18, 2-19, 2-20, 2-30, 2-32, 5-10, 5-33, 5-36, 6-30, 6-31, 6-37, 7-7, 8-26, 11-11
International Business Machines Corporation (IBM) Thomas Way, Photographer Figure 9-35
Intertec Diversified Systems, Inc. Figures 1-14, 1-20, 5-12
Iomega Corporation Figure 9-19
Iowa State University Figure 2-3
Kaypro Corporation Figure 1-33
Koala Technologies Corporation Figure 1-28
Lear Sigler, Inc. 5-40
Lockheed Corporation Figure 9-25
Lundy Electronics & Systems, Inc. Figure 5-31
M/A—COM, Inc. Figure 11-9
MDS Trivex Figure 17-15
Management Science America, Inc. Figures 1-21, 4-19, 17-6
McDonnell Douglas Automation Company (MCAUTO) Figures 1-18, 6-17
Mini-Computer Business Applications, Inc. (MCBA) Figures 10-1, 16-1
Modular Computer Systems, Inc. (MODCOMP) Figures 1-16, 1-20
Mohawk Data Sciences Corporation Figures 5-25, 13-1
Mountain Computer, Inc. Figure 1-29
NABU Manufacturing Corporation Figure 1-30
NCR Corporation 5-37
NCR Comten, Inc. Figures 1-26, 8-20
NEC Corporation Figures 1-15, 1-20, 2-29, 2-37, 11-1, 11-10, 17-14
NEC Home Electronics Figure 6-38
NNC Electronics Figure 9-27
National Semiconductor Corporation Figures 2-25, 8-26 (7), 5-39, 17-8
Onyx Systems, Inc. Figure 9-15
Otrona Advanced Systems Corporation Figures 1-36, 5-11
Panasonic Industrial Co. Figure 11-6
Paradyne Corporation Figures 2-23, 3-1, 5-1, 18-1
Pertec Computer Corporation Figures 1-42, 9-6
Planning Research Corporation (Copyright Steve Uzzell) Figure 2-42
Prime Computer, Inc. Figure 17-10
Princeton University Figure 2-5
Printacolor Corporation Figure 6-15
Protocol Computers, Inc. Figure 1-25
Racal-Milgo, Inc. Figures 1-14, 1-20, 4-14, 11-17, 17-16
Radio Shack, A Division of Tandy Corporation Figures 1-31, 1-37, 2-31, 6-9, 6-40, 17-17
Rexon Business Machines Corporation Figure 9-21
SAS Institute, Inc. Figure 6-32
Scientia Figure 6-25
Siltec Corporation, Frank Wing Photographer Figure 8-26 (1, 2, and 3)
Sperry Univac, A Division of Sperry Corporation Figures 2-8, 5-24
Squibb Corporation Figures 2-40, 6-11
Storage Technology Corporation Figures 9-1, 8-26 (5)
Sydis, Inc. Figure 5-19
TEC Figures 5-8, 5-16
Texas Instruments, Inc. Figure 7-13
Times Fiber Communications, Inc. Figures 11-18, 11-29
Tomy Corporation Figure 9-22
United Press International Figures 2-4, 2-7
United Telecommunications, Inc. Figure 1-24
University of Pennsylvania Figure 2-6
Wang Laboratories, Inc. Figure 5-9
Wyle Laboratories Figure 4-13
Xerox Corporation Figure 7-11

Acknowledgements

The following organizations donated materials used for research and photographs for use in the book. We thank them.

3M Company; ACCO International, Inc.; ACT (North America) Inc.; ASAP Systems, Inc.; AT&T Information Systems; AT&T Technolgies; Adage Inc.; Alden Electronics, Inc.; Allied Corp.; Alloy Engineering Co., Inc.; Altos Computer Systems; Amcodyne Inc.; Amdahl Communication Systems Division Corp.; Amdax Corp.; American District Telegraph Co.; American Laser Systems, Inc.; American Telephone and Telegraph Co.; Amperex Electronic Corp.; Anacomp Inc.; Anchor Hocking Corp.; Ann Arbor Terminals, Inc.; Ansul Fire Protection; Apollo Computer Inc.; Apple Computer Inc.; Application Development Systems, Inc.; Applicon Inc.; Applied Data Research, Inc.; Arktronics Corporation; Artificial Intelligence Corp.; Ask Computer Systems, Inc.; Association for Computing Machinery (ACM); Atari Inc.; Auto-trol Technology Corp.; Avnet, Inc.; Aydin Corp.; Azurdata, Inc.; BASF; BGS Systems, Inc.; BMS Computer Inc.; BOW Industries, Inc.; Baker Industries, Inc.; BancTec, Inc.; Bank of America; Bankers Box; Basics and Beyond, Inc.; Battelle Columbus Laboratories; Battelle Memorial Institute; Bell and Howell Company; Benson; Billings Computer Corp.; Blackhawk Computer System; Boise Cascade Corp.; Bruning; Bunker Ramo Information Systems; Burlington Industries, Inc.; Burroughs Corp.; Byte Magazine; CMS Software Systems Inc.; COSMIC — University of Georgia; CPT Corp.; CTS Corp.; CTSI Corp.; Caere Corp.; CalComp Sanders, Inc.; Callan Data Systems; Candle Corp.; Canon U.S.A., Inc.; Cap-Cap Corp.; CardioData Corp.; Carl Howard Productions; Canon U.S.A., Inc.; Century Data Systems, Inc.; Chrislin Industries, Inc.; Chromatics; Cincinnati Milacron Inc.; Cincom Systems, Inc.; Codata; Cognitronics Corp.; Columbia Data Products, Inc.; Com/Tech Systems, Inc.; Commodore Ltd.; Compaq Computer Corp.; Compre Comm, Inc.; Compression Labs, Inc.; CompuScan Inc.; Compumax Associates, Inc.; Computax Inc.; Computer Consoles, Inc.; Computer Memories, Inc.; Computer Power Products; Computer Power Systems Corp.; Computer Sciences Corp.; Computervision Corp.; Conrac Corp.; Consolidated Foods Corp.; Continuous Expression Processor, Inc.; Control Data Corp.; Cooper Industries, Inc.; Corning Glass Works; Corvus Systems, Inc.; Cray Research, Inc.; Cromemco, Inc.; Cullinet Software; Cynthia Peripheral Corp.; DICOMED Corp.; Danyl Corp.; Dartmouth College News Service; Data General Corp.; Data Systems Design; Data Systems of Baton Rouge, Inc.; DataMed Research; Database Design, Inc.; Datacopy Corp.; Datacq Corp.; DatagraphiX, Inc.; Datametrics Corp.; Datapoint Corp.; Dataproducts Corp.; Datasouth Computer Corp.; Datec Inc.; Denver Software Co.; Department of the Navy; Devoke Co.; Diebold, Inc.; Digi-Log Circuits Co.; DigiTec (United Systems Corp.); Digital Design and Development, Inc.; Digital Equipment Corp.; Digital Graphic Systems, Inc.; Digital Researach, Inc.; Digital Systems Corp.; Distributed Logic Corp.; Dow Jones and Co., Inc.; Drivetec; Durango Systems, Inc.; Dysan Corp.; ECS Microsystems; EG&G, Inc.; EG&G Reticon; Eagle Computer, Inc.; Eaton Corp.; Educational Testing Service; Eichner Systems, Inc.; Elbit Computers Ltd.; Electro General Corp.; Electronic Associates, Inc.; Electronic Data Systems Corp.; Electronic Specialists, Inc.; Engineered Data Products, Inc.; Engineer ing Computer Services; Engineering Technology Inc.; Epson America, Inc.; Evans & Sutherland; Executive Planning, Inc.; Exxon Corp.; Exxon Office Systems Co.; Facit-Dataroyal; Ferox Microsystems Inc.; Financial Software, Inc.; Firestone Tire & Rubber Co.; Fischer & Porter Co.; Formation Inc.; Foxboro Co.; Franklin Computer Corp.; Fujitsu Microelectronics; Future Computing Inc.; GRiD Systems Corp.; GTE Telenet Communications Corp.; Gandalf Technologies Inc.; Gates Energy Products, Inc.; General Electric Co.; General Electric Information Services Co.; General Motors Corp.; General Terminal Corp.; Gerber Systems Technology, Inc.; Goodyear Tire & Rubber Co.; Gould Inc.; Grafcon Corp.; Greyhound Corp.; Grumman Corp.; HEI Corp.; HEXCO, Inc.; Hagen Systems Inc.; Harris Corp.; Harvard University Laboratory for Computer Graphics and Spatial Analysis; Hayes Microcomputer Products, Inc.; Hewlett-Packard Company; Honeywell Inc.; Honeywell Information Systems Inc.; Houston Instrument of Bausch & Lomb; International IPAC Group, Inc.; ITI Electronics, Inc.; ITT Courier Terminal Systems, Inc.; Iconica Inc.; Informatics General Corp.; Information Automation Inc.; Information Builders, Inc.; Infotron Systems; Inmac; Innovation Data Processing; Innovative Computer Products; Input-Ez Corp.; Intecolor Corporation; Integral Data Systems, Inc.; Integrated Business Systems; Integrated Material Control; Integrated Software Systems Corp.; Intel Corp. Intelligent Systems Corp.; Interactive Systems Corp.; Interface Mechanisms, Inc.; Intergraph Corp.; Intermetrics Inc.; Internal Revenue Service; International Business Machines Corp. (IBM); International Data Base Systems, Inc.; International Mathematical and Statistical Libraries, Inc.; Intertec Diversified Systems, Inc.; Iomega Corp.; Iowa State University; Johnson and Johnson; Jones/Hosplex Systems, Inc.; Kaye Instruments Inc.; Kaypro Corp.; Koala Technologies Corp.; Kronos, Inc.; Kyros Corp.; LINC Resources; Lanier Business Products Inc.; Laredo Systems, Inc.; Lear Sigler, Inc.; Leggett & Platt, Inc.; Lemcom Systems Inc.; Lexidata Corp.; Lexor Corp.; Lockheed Corp.; Lotus Development Corporation; Lundy Electronics and Systems, Inc.; M. Bryce and Associates, Inc.; M/COM/DDC, Inc.; MCI Mail; MDCR, Inc.; MDS Trivex, Inc.; MSI Data Corp.; MSP Inc.; Management Science America, Inc.; Management Sciences, Inc.; Marion Corp.; Marketing Information Services; Martin Marietta Data Systems; McCormack & Dodge Corp.; McDonnell Douglas Automation Co. (MCAUTO); Media Systems Technology, Inc.; Megatest Corp.; Meilin Safe Co.; Mercator Business Systems; Merit Machinery, Inc.; Micro Business Software, Inc.; Micro D (Micro Distributors); Micropro International Corp.; Microsoft Corp.; Miltope Corp.; Mini-Computer Business Applications, Inc. (MCBA); Minitab Project; Modular Computer Systems, Inc. (MODCOMP); Mohawk Data Sciences Corp.; Morino Associates, Inc.; Morrow Computer and Electronic Design; Morton Thiokol, Inc.; Motorola Inc.; Mountain Computer, Inc.; Muirhead Vactric Components, Ltd.; NABU Manufacturing Corp.; NASA; NCR Comten, Inc.; NCR Corp.; NEC America, Inc.; NEC Corp.; NEC Home Electronics; NEC Information Systems, Inc.; National Controls, Inc.; National Micronetics, Inc.; National Semiconductor Corp.; Navtel; Nestar Systems Inc.; Network Systems Corp.; Nicolet Zeta Corp.; Nixdorf Computer Corp.; Norsk Data; North Star Computers, Inc.; Northern Telecom Inc.; Novation, Inc.; Numeritronix, Inc.; OAK Industries Inc.; OSM Computer Corp.; Olympia USA Inc.; Omation Corp.; Omnidata; Onyx Systems, Inc.; Optelecom, Inc.; Optical Systems Design, Inc.; Optipro Inc.; Otrona Advanced Systems Corp.; PCD Systems, Inc.; Pacific Software Services Co.; Panasonic Industrial Co.; Paradyne Corp.; Performance Systems Inc.; Periphonics Corp.; Perkin Elmer; Pertec Computer Corp.; Philip Morris Inc.; Pilgrim Electric Co.; Pitney Bowes; Planning Research Corp.; Powertec, Inc.; Prime Computers, Inc.; Princeton University; Printacolor Corp.; Protocol Computers, Inc.; Quality Micro Systems, Inc.; Quarterdeck Office Systems; Questronics Inc.; RCA Corp.; RCA Microcomputer; Racal-Milgo, Inc.; Racal-Telesystems, Inc.; Radio Shack, A Division of Tandy Corp.; Rana Systems; Raytheon Co.; Rexon Business Machines Corp.; Ring King Visibles, Inc.; Rixon Inc.; Rockwell International Corp.; Rolm Corp.; Royal Seating Corp.; S & H Computer Systems, Inc.; SAS Institute, Inc.; Sanders Associates, Inc.; Sanyo Business Systems Corp.; Scan-Data Corp.; Scan-Optics, Inc.; Schlage Electronics; Schlumberger Ltd.; Schwab Safe Co.; Scientia, Inc.; Scientific Atlanta; Scientific Calculations, Inc.; Scientific Micro Systems, Inc.; Scope, Inc.; Shaffstall Systems Co.; Shugart Associates; Sideral Computer Corp.; Sigma Systems Inc.; Simplan Systems, Inc.; Sinclair Research Ltd.; Softool Corp.; Software Application of North America, Inc.; Software Results Corp.; Solidstate Controls, Inc.; Source Telecomputing Corp.; Sperry Univac, A Division of Sperry Corp.; Squibb Corp.; Sterling Software Marketing; Storage Technology Corp.; Structural Programming Inc.; Summagraphics Corp.; Sundstrand Corp.; Superior Electric Co.; Swanson Analysis Systems, Inc.; Sydis Inc.; Sydney Dataproducts; Synergistics, Inc.; Syntrex Inc.; Systel Inc.; System Support Software Inc.; Systems Plus, Inc.; T-bar Inc.; TEC, Inc.; TRW Inc.; TRW-Fujitsu Co.; Tandem Computers Inc.; Tandon Corp.; Tape Research, Inc.; Tate Architectural Products, Inc.; Telautograph Corp.; Teleram; Teletype Corp.; Televideo Systems, Inc.; Terak Corp.; Termiflex Corp.; Tesseract Corp.; Texas Instruments, Inc.; Three Rivers Computer Corp.; Threshold Technology Inc.; Tiffany Stand and Furniture Co.; Timeplex, Inc.; Times Fiber Communications, Inc.; Tomy Corp.; Toor Furniture Corp.; Topaz, Inc.; Travenol Laboratories, Inc.; Trilogy Systems Corporation; Ultra-Violet Products, Inc.; United Press International; United Telecommunications, Inc.; University of Pennsylvania; Upjohn Co.; VeSoft; Vector General, Inc.; Vector Graphic, Inc.; Ven-Tel Inc.; Vermont Research Corp.; Versatec; Video Technology (U. S.) Inc.; Wabash DataTech, Inc.; Wallace Computer Services, Inc.; Wang Laboratories; Gerald M. Weinberg and Associates; Western Electric Co.; Western Union; Westinghouse Electric Corp.; Wilson Jones Co.; Wintek Corp.; Wismer Associates, Inc.; Woodbury Business Forms, Inc.; Wormald U. S., Inc.; Wyle Laboratories; Xerox Corp.

Chapter One

An Introduction To Computers

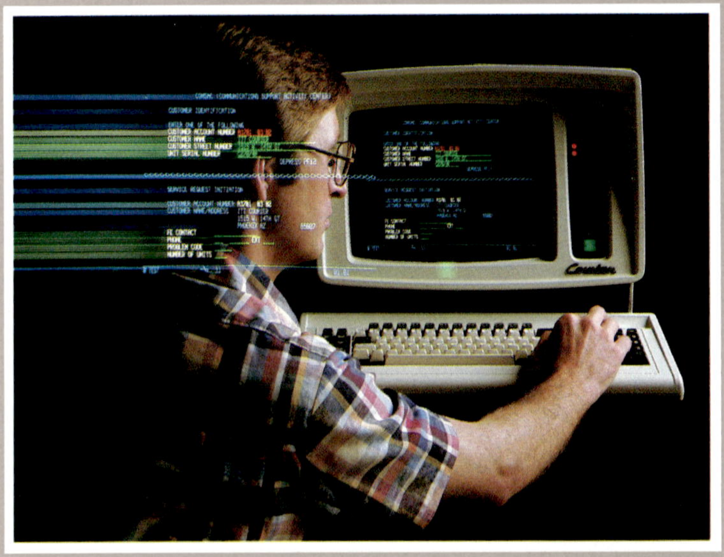

Objectives

- ☐ Explain what a computer is and how it processes data to produce output information
- ☐ Identify the input, process, output, and storage elements of the information processing cycle and explain each element
- ☐ Explain the use of the input, processor, output, and storage units of both personal computers and large computers
- ☐ Define the roles played by personnel in the information systems department
- ☐ State how computers are used in the modern world and describe user needs, personal computer use and software, information center, and the use of a centralized computer
- ☐ Distinguish the different sizes and types of computers

An Introduction To Computers

Chapter One

Approximately twenty years ago, Dr. John Kemeny of Dartmouth College said, "Knowing how to use a computer will be as important as reading and writing." At the time, most people did not believe such a statement would ever be true. Few people had access to a computer. Many had never seen a computer. To some, the computer was a scientific curiosity used by scientists and mathematicians. To others, the computer was a machine used to produce thousands of paychecks and business reports for the largest companies and governmental agencies. Most people felt the computer was such a complex piece of machinery that only individuals specially trained in computer technology could operate one.

Today, the validity of Dr. Kemeny's prediction is apparent. The number of computer systems has increased dramatically since 1964. Small computer systems called **microcomputers,** or **personal computers,** have made computing available to almost everyone in society. The manner in which computers are used has changed as well. Thousands of households now have computers which are used for such varying activities as playing games, keeping track of home finances, and writing letters. Computers are used in elementary schools to teach reading and in universities to serve as research tools. Color screens generated from computer processing are used for communication in all areas of business and government (Figure 1-1).

Because of the widespread use and availability of computer systems, it is now apparent that knowledge of computers and their applications is "as important as reading and writing." It is the intent of this book to present the material needed to gain that knowledge.

Figure 1-2 The microcomputer chip below contains electronic circuits to perform the functions of a computer.

What is a computer?

The most obvious question concerning the explosive growth of the computer is, "What is a computer?" A **computer** is an electronic device, operating under the control of instructions stored in its own memory unit, which can accept and store data, perform arithmetic and logical operations on that data without human intervention, and produce output from the processing. This definition encompasses many devices. For example, the microcomputer chip shown in Figure 1-2 fulfills the definition of a computer. More generally, however, the computer can take many forms and will usually include not only the microcomputer chip, but also devices which will make data available for processing and devices on which the information produced from the computer processing can be made available for use by people. For example, in Figure 1-3 on the next two pages, the computer user enters data on a keyboard and views information on a color CRT screen.

Figure 1–3 The personal computers shown in this picture use a keyboard as an input device and a CRT screen and a printer as output devices. The IBM PCjr in the foreground uses a color CRT screen while the IBM Personal Computer in the background uses a monochrome (one color) display screen.

What does a computer do?

Although the results of computer processing can indeed be marvelous, such as controlling the flight path of the space shuttle, or keeping track of millions of credit card customers, or allowing a user to perform thousands of calculations at the touch of a button, computers are capable of performing only a small number of specific operations. These operations include:

1. **Input operations**, which allow data to be entered into the computer for processing.
2. **Arithmetic operations**, which involve performing addition, subtraction, multiplication, and division calculations.
3. **Logical operations**, which allow the computer to compare data and determine if one value is less than, equal to, or greater than another value.
4. **Output operations**, which make information generated from the processing on the computer available for use.
5. **Storage operations**, which include electronically storing data on an external device for future reference.

Even though these operations seem very basic, and in fact not very powerful, it is through the ability of the computer to perform them very quickly and reliably that the power of a computer is derived. In the computer, the various operations occur through the use of electronic circuits contained on small chips such as shown in Figure 1–2. Since these electronic circuits rarely fail and the data flows along these circuits at close to the speed of light, processing can be accomplished in billionths of a second.

Data and information processing

The operations which are carried out by a computer all require access to data. **Data** is the numbers, words, and phrases which are suitable for processing in some manner on a computer to produce **information**. Information produced by the processing of data can be used for whatever functions are required by the user.

The example in Figure 1–4 illustrates the use of a computer to produce varied information from data. The processing occurs as follows:

1. The data contained on the sales invoice includes the name and address of the buyer, the date, the buyer's phone number, the sales terms, shipping instructions, purchase order number, and salesperson. In addition, the quantity, product number, description, and unit price of each item purchased is contained on the sales invoice. The gross amount, discount percentage, net amount, and totals are also contained on the invoice.
2. The data on the sales invoice is entered into the computer by the person using the computer.
3. From the data entered into the computer, information is generated in three different forms:
   a. The daily sales are illustrated through the use of a colored bar chart. Each day of the week is represented by a different color bar on the chart.
   b. The monthly sales are shown in a monthly sales report. The total sales for each week ending date are displayed, together with the total sales for the month.

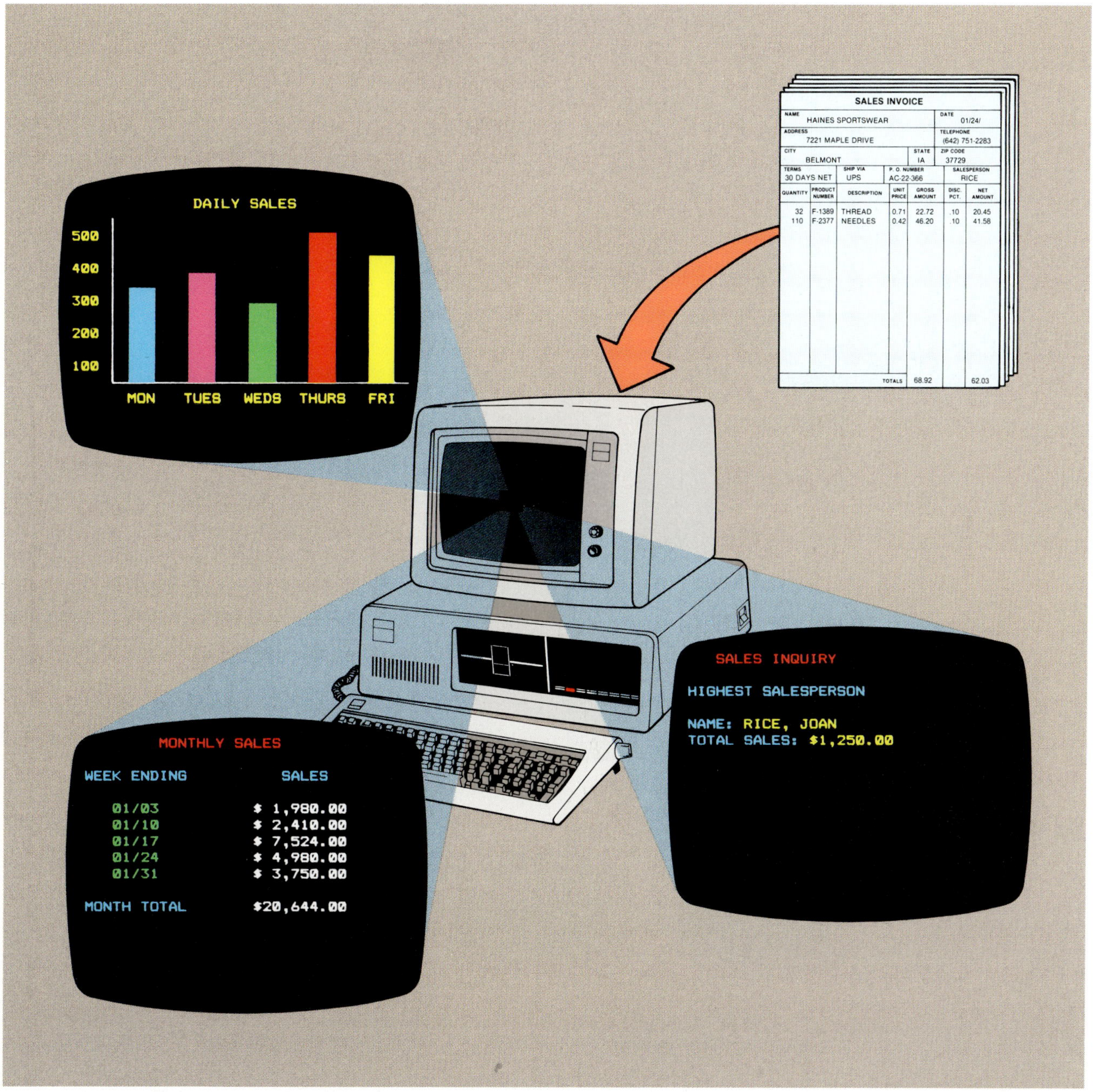

c. A sales inquiry is performed to determine which salesperson generated the most sales in the month. In this example, Joan Rice had total sales of $1,250.00, which was the highest for the month.

Figure 1–4 The data contained on the sales invoices is entered into the computer. After the data is processed, information in the form of a graph, a report, and a specific request (an inquiry) is produced.

The key to this example is to realize that from a single set of data, such as the sales data on the invoices, information in many different forms can be produced by computer processing. Even more important, it should be understood that this information would be extremely difficult, costly, and time-consuming to obtain without the use of a computer. The production of information by processing data on a computer is called **information processing**, or sometimes **electronic data processing**. With the increased need of business and society for information of all kinds, the use of the computer to produce this information is indispensable.

THE COMPONENTS OF A COMPUTER

Processing data on a computer is performed by specific units (Figure 1-5). These units, which are called the **computer hardware**, are:

1. Input units.
2. Processor unit.
3. Output units.
4. Auxiliary storage units.

Each of these units is explained in the following sections.

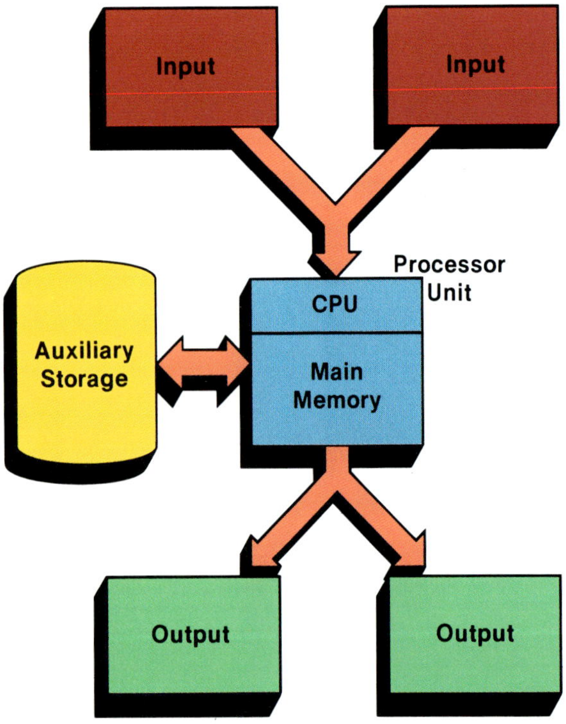

Figure 1-5 A basic computer is composed of input units from which data is entered into the computer; the processor unit which stores data and processes the stored data; the auxiliary storage units which save data for future processing; and the output units on which the results of the processing are made available.

Input units

Input units are used to enter data into a computer. A commonly used input unit is the keyboard, on which the operator manually keys the input data (Figure 1-6). As the data is keyed, it is placed in the main memory of the computer.

Processor unit

The **processor unit** of a computer is composed of two distinct parts: main memory and the central processing unit (Figure 1-5). **Main memory** consists of components which electronically store data, including letters of the alphabet, numbers, and special characters such as decimal points or dollar signs. When data is entered into a computer from an input unit, it is stored in main memory. When a computer processes this data, instructions directing the processing are required. These instructions are also stored in main memory.

The **central processing unit (CPU)** contains the electronic circuits which actually cause processing to occur by interpreting and executing the instructions to the computer, and controlling the input, output, and storage operations of the computer.

Output units

Output from a computer can be presented in many forms, varying from a printed report to color graphics. In those environments where the computer is used for business applications or business-related personal applications, the two most commonly found output units are the **printer** and the television-like screen called a **cathode ray**

tube, or **CRT** (Figure 1–6).

Auxiliary storage units

Main memory on the computer is used to store instructions and data while the instructions are being executed and the data is being processed. In most applications, however, these instructions and data must be stored elsewhere when they are not being used because main memory is not large enough to store the instructions and data for all applications at one time. **Auxiliary storage units** are used to store instructions and data when they are not being used in main memory of the computer (Figure 1–6). A commonly used auxiliary storage device on personal computers is a floppy disk drive, which stores data as magnetic spots on an oxide-coated plastic disk (called a **diskette** or **floppy disk**) about the size of a 45 rpm record. Another auxiliary storage device is called a **hard disk**. A hard disk consists of oxide-coated metal platters which are sealed inside a housing to ensure dust-free operation.

Figure 1–6 A computer normally consists of the input units, the processor unit, the output units, and the auxiliary storage units. Here, the input unit is a keyboard; the output units are the CRT screen and the printer; and the auxiliary storage units are floppy disk drives. Note the diskette lying on the notebook.

COMPUTER SOFTWARE

A computer is directed to perform the input, arithmetic, logical, output, and storage operations by a series of instructions called a **computer program**. A computer program specifies what operations are to be performed and the sequence in which they are to be performed. When directing the operations to be performed, a program must be stored in the main memory unit of the computer. Computer programs are commonly referred to as **computer software**.

There are many instructions which can be used to direct a computer to perform a specific task. For example, there are instructions which allow data to be entered from a keyboard and stored in main computer memory; there are instructions that allow data in main memory to be used in calculations, such as adding a series of numbers to obtain a total; there are instructions which compare two values stored in main memory and direct the computer to perform alternative operations based upon the results of the comparison; and there are instructions which direct the computer to print a report, display information on the CRT screen, draw a color graph on a CRT screen, or store data on a floppy disk. Many computers have more than 100 instructions.

Each computer instruction must be executed in the correct sequence so that the required processing will occur. Computer programs, which contain the instructions the computer will execute, are written by **computer programmers** (Figure 1–7). For a computer to process data, the programmer must determine the instructions necessary to process the data and then write the instructions in the proper sequence. For complex problems, hundreds and even thousands of individual instructions may be required.

When a program is originally written, it is many times entered into main memory by the programmer through the use of the keyboard input device. Once placed in memory, the program can be executed. It can also be stored on an auxiliary storage device, such as a diskette, for use at a later time.

Figure 1–7 A computer programmer writes programs which direct the operations on a computer. Here, the programmer is entering instructions into main computer memory through the keyboard.

Software packages

In general, a person who uses a computer does not write programs to perform the desired processing. Instead, most people, whether they are using a personal computer in their home or a big computer at their company, will use programs written by individuals trained in the science of computer programming. In large corporations, whole staffs of programmers write programs for unique company applications. In addition, for both large companies and other users as well, many thousands of programs which perform tasks usually required for business and personal applications are available for purchase from computer stores and software vendors. Purchased programs are often referred to as **software packages**. They are written to perform many of the tasks required by users of both large and small computers.

Computer software is the key to productive use of computers. Without the proper software, a computer will not perform the tasks desired. With the correct software, a computer can become a very valuable tool.

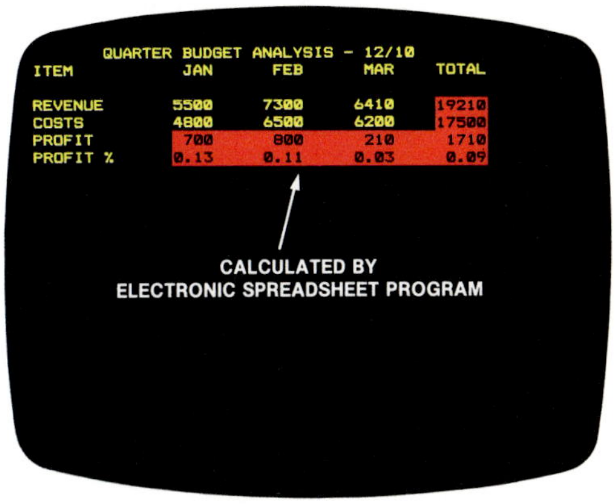

Figure 1-8 The rows and columns of numbers entered into the electronic spreadsheet program can be used in calculations. For the sample application, the user will enter the revenue and costs for January, February, and March. The program will calculate the profit, the profit percentage, and the totals.

A TYPICAL APPLICATION
Input, Process, Output, Storage

In order to illustrate how the input unit, the processor unit, the output unit, the auxiliary storage unit, and the computer software work together to process data, an application utilizing an electronic spreadsheet program will be shown. An **electronic spreadsheet** program allows a user to enter rows and columns of numbers into main memory and perform calculations on the numbers entered. The user can enter various values, and the electronic spreadsheet program will perform calculations as directed by the user.

In the sample application, the user will develop a budget analysis for the first quarter of a year (Figure 1-8). The user is to enter the revenues and the costs for the first three months of the year. The spreadsheet program will calculate the total revenues and total costs, the profit for each month (calculated by subtracting costs from revenues), and the profit percentage (obtained by dividing the profit by the revenues). In addition, the spreadsheet program will calculate the total profit and the total profit percentage.

The diagram in Figure 1-9, together with the diagrams in Figure 1-10 and Figure 1-11 on the next pages, show the steps which occur in order to obtain the spreadsheet output. These steps are explained below.

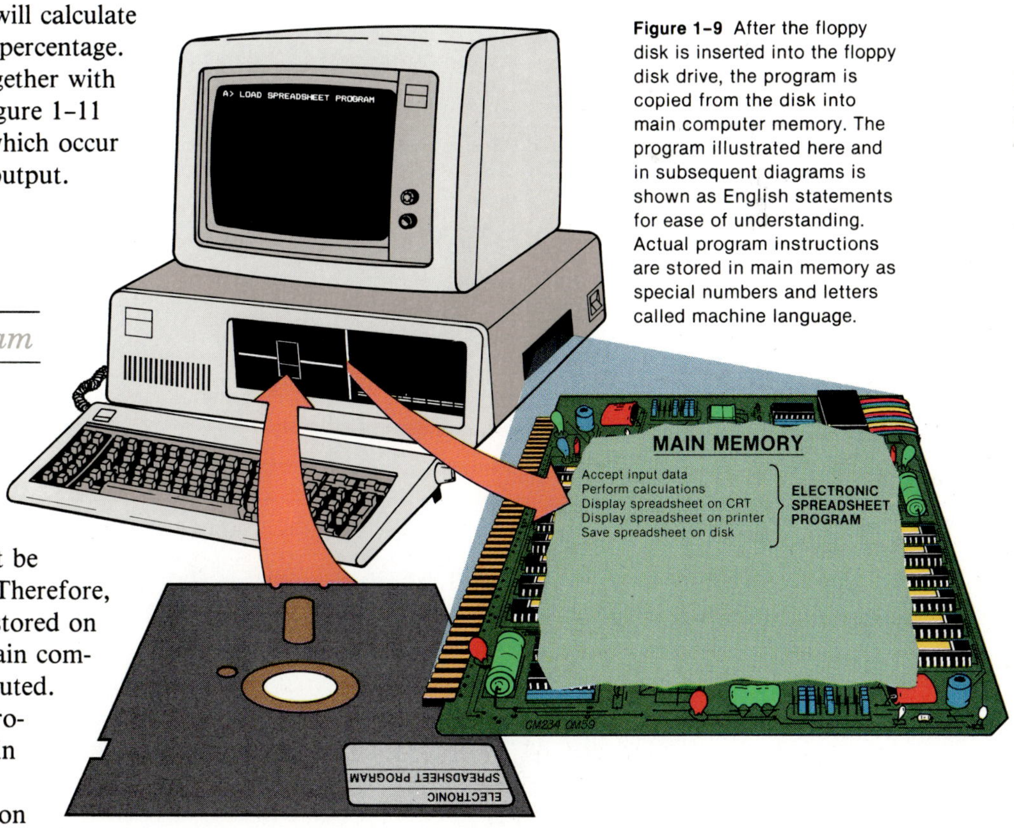

Figure 1-9 After the floppy disk is inserted into the floppy disk drive, the program is copied from the disk into main computer memory. The program illustrated here and in subsequent diagrams is shown as English statements for ease of understanding. Actual program instructions are stored in main memory as special numbers and letters called machine language.

Step one — load the program

Most software packages purchased from a computer store or software vendor are stored on a floppy disk. To be executed, however, a computer program must be stored in main computer memory. Therefore, the spreadsheet program, which is stored on a floppy disk, must be placed in main computer memory before it can be executed. Thus, the first step is to load the program from the floppy disk into main memory.

In Figure 1-9, the floppy disk on which the program is stored is inserted into the floppy disk drive, which is installed in the computer housing. Some personal computers contain the auxiliary storage drives in the housing of the computer system whereas others, such as in Figure 1-6, have the drives as separate components.

Once the floppy disk is inserted into the disk drive, the computer user would issue the command to load the program from the floppy disk into main computer memory. In the diagram in Figure 1-9, main computer memory is illustrated as a printed circuit board. In an actual computer, the components of main memory are attached to a printed circuit board. After the program is loaded into main memory, the user would direct that the computer begin executing the program.

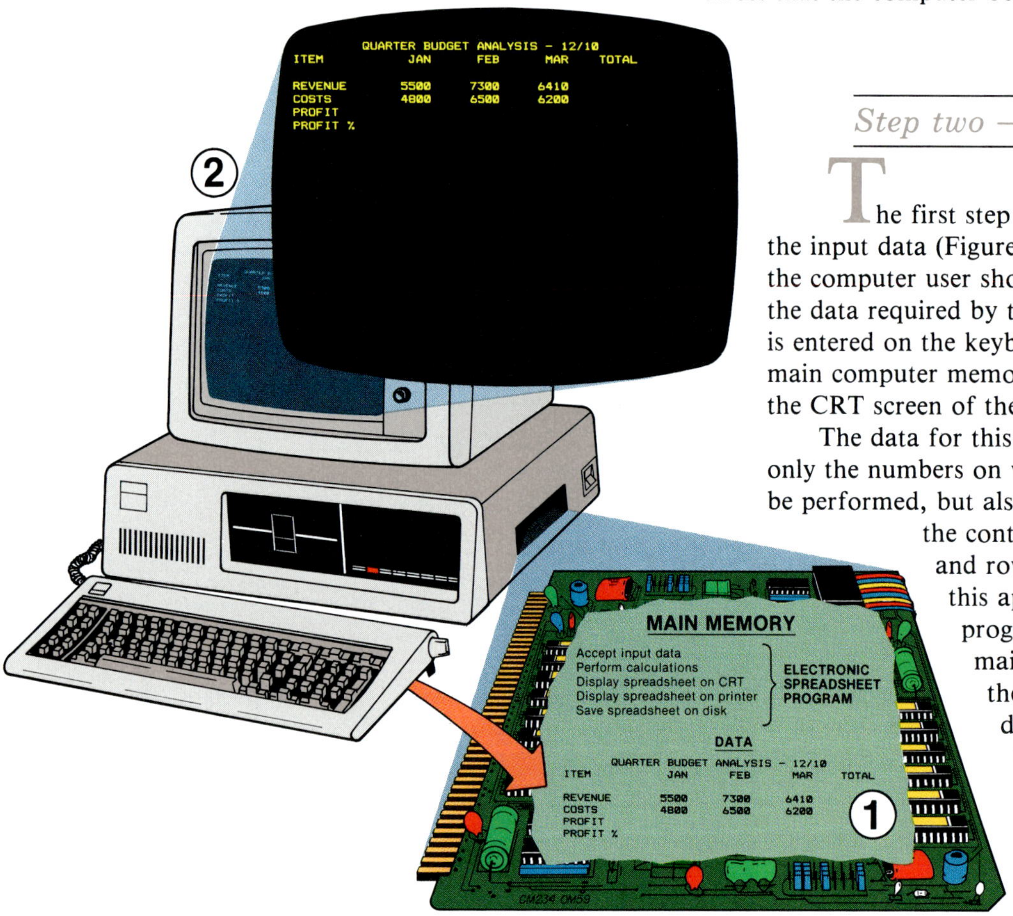

Step two — enter the data

The first step in the program is to accept the input data (Figure 1-10). This means that the computer user should key on the keyboard the data required by the application. As the data is entered on the keyboard, it is: 1) Stored in main computer memory; and 2) Displayed on the CRT screen of the computer display.

The data for this application consists of not only the numbers on which calculations are to be performed, but also some words indicating the content of each of the columns and rows on the CRT screen. In this application thus far, the program has been loaded into main memory by transferring the program from a floppy disk into main memory. Then, the CPU interpreted the program instructions and requested that the operator enter input data. The data is entered from the keyboard.

Step three — perform calculations and display the results

After the user has entered the data, the program will perform the calculations required on the data entered (Figure 1-11). In the sample application, the program is to calculate the profit for each month by subtracting the cost from the revenue, calculate the total revenue for the quarter, the total costs for the quarter, and the total profit for the quarter (1). In addition, the profit percent for each month and the total profit percent are calculated. These operations illustrate the calculating ability of computers.

The calculations take place on data stored in main memory. Whenever any calculations are performed on data, the data must be stored in main computer memory. The results of all calculations remain in main memory. The program can issue instructions to copy the results elsewhere.

In this application, after the calculations have been completed, the program specifies that the spreadsheet, with the results of the calculations, is to be displayed on the CRT screen (2). The program also indicates that the results are to be printed on the printer (3). When this instruction is executed, the spreadsheet is printed on paper so that the results of the processing on the computer can be used by someone other than the computer user.

The spreadsheet is also stored on the hard disk, an auxiliary storage device that is part of the computer shown in this example (4). The data from the spreadsheet is saved on auxiliary storage so that at some later time, after the computer has been turned off or used for another application, the data can be retrieved and utilized again.

Although this application is very much simplified, all of the elements of input, process, output, and storing data on auxiliary storage are used. The use of these elements is usually referred to as the **information processing cycle.**

The spreadsheet application is but one of many thousands which use the information processing cycle. In each case, a program must be stored in main memory to direct the operations of the computer. An understanding of this basic cycle, together with the roles played by each of the components, is important.

Figure 1–11 After the data has been entered, the program specifies that the following processing shall occur: 1) All calculations are performed; 2) The entire spreadsheet, with calculation results, is displayed on the CRT screen; 3) The spreadsheet is printed on the printer; 4) The spreadsheet data and results are stored on auxiliary storage.

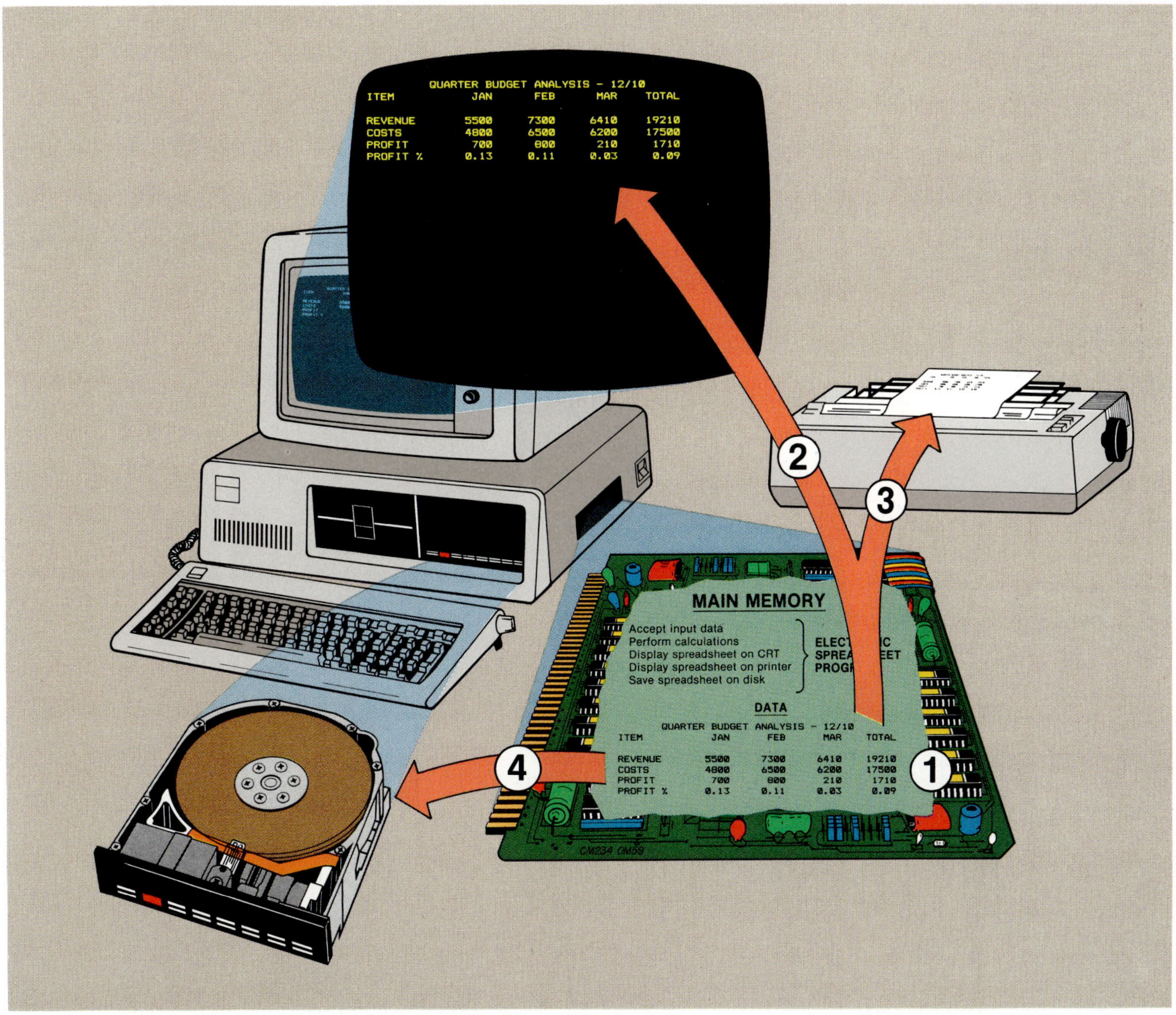

LARGE COMPUTERS

The previous examples have illustrated personal computers that store and manipulate relatively small amounts of data. These machines are normally used by one person at a time. The information processing needs of many companies, however, also require processing large volumes of data and access to the same computer by many different individuals within the company. For example, companies with hundreds of employees must prepare payroll checks for each employee; credit card company personnel from all over the country have need to access the data on the same computer in order to approve millions of purchases each day; and airlines must be prepared to handle thousands of inquiries and bookings for reservations every hour of the day.

For these types of applications, where large volumes of data are required and numerous users need access to the same centralized computer, large computers are used (Figure 1-12). The large centralized computer in most companies is either a **minicomputer** or a **mainframe**. A mainframe has more processing capabilities than a minicomputer. The information processing cycle for large computers is essentially the same as that shown previously for personal computers: data is entered into the computer memory; the data is processed in some manner to produce useful information; and then the information is transferred to an output device. As with personal computers, auxiliary storage devices are used on large computers to store data and programs.

The major differences between personal computers and large computers are

Figure 1-12 A large centralized computer is usually placed in a room designed specifically for the machine. Special air conditioning, humidity control, electrical wiring, and even security measures are required for many installations.

storage capacities and speed. Whereas a typical personal computer may contain computer memory large enough to store 512,000 characters, a large, centralized computer may have memory in excess of 8 million storage positions. Many personal computers have an auxiliary storage device (a hard disk) that can store 10 million characters. Large computers, on the other hand, typically contain auxiliary storage devices capable of storing in excess of 5 billion characters.

A large minicomputer or mainframe executes instructions considerably faster than a personal computer. For example, a typical personal computer can execute 100,000 instructions in one second while a mainframe can execute more than 10 million instructions per second. Because of the larger storage capacities and the faster speeds, minicomputers and mainframes are capable of storing and executing more complex programs at considerably faster rates. In addition, on most large computers many programs can be executing concurrently; and a large number of people can use the computer at the same time.

Large centralized computers are generally under the control of a special department of the company called the Information Systems Department, the Data Processing Department, or sometimes just the Computer Department. The **Information Systems Department** within a company will usually employ people with specialized training in computers and information processing in order to implement applications on the centralized computer. These employees may consist of computer operators to run the computer; programmers to write specialized programs; systems analysts to design the applications which are to be run on the computer; personnel to prepare and enter data into the computer; management to oversee the use of the computer; and other support personnel as well.

A TOUR OF THE INFORMATION SYSTEMS DEPARTMENT

In many companies, the centralized computer is housed in the information systems department. The following pages illustrate a tour of a typical information systems department in order to show the input units, processor unit, output units, and auxiliary storage units used with a large computer, together with some of the specialized personnel associated with running an information systems department.

Input units and data entry

Numerous methods are used to enter data into a large computer for processing. If a person entering data is communicating directly with the computer, a CRT terminal, consisting of a CRT screen and a keyboard, is the most commonly used input device. For example, when a manager enters the production figures for the day (Figure 1–13), the manager is communicating directly with the computer. In this instance, a CRT terminal is usually the most appropriate input device. CRT terminals used for input to the computer can be located in the information systems department or in remote locations.

Figure 1–13 A CRT terminal contains a keyboard and a CRT screen. The person entering data can enter the data via the keyboard and view the response from the computer on the screen.

If a group of data is to be processed at one time as a unit, the data will usually be keyed and stored on disk using a data entry device (Figure 1–14). A **data entry device** is designed to allow fast and accurate keying of data. After all data has been keyed, it is transferred from disk to magnetic tape for entry into the computer. For example, all payroll checks are prepared at one time. Therefore, the data required to prepare the checks, such as the number of hours each employee worked, will be keyed on data entry devices and temporarily stored on disk. The data is then transferred from disk to magnetic tape to be read into computer memory by the payroll program.

When this type of data entry occurs, the keying may take place in a centralized **data entry section** of the information systems department. In some companies, data entry will also take place at a site remote from the information systems department.

Other input devices, such as those which can read printing or understand the human voice, are also used to enter data into a large computers.

Figure 1–14 Data keyed on the data entry device (lower left) is stored temporarily on disk. After keying is complete, the data is transferred from disk to magnetic tape, from which it is entered into the computer (lower right).

Processor unit

The processor unit of a large computer can be housed in a cabinet about the size of a big desk. The processor unit consists of the central processing unit and main computer memory.

Most large computers have multiple programs executing concurrently and many different input/output and auxiliary storage devices being used at one time. To monitor these operations, a computer operator's console is used. The **operator's console** is normally a computer terminal consisting of a keyboard and related CRT screen, both attached to the processor unit (Figure 1–15). By viewing the data displayed on the CRT screen, the operator can monitor and control the activities on the computer.

The computer operator is responsible for a number of different tasks. When the computer is running, messages will periodically be displayed indicating the status of the system. For example, a message may be displayed indicating paper must be placed in a printer. The operator responds to these messages in order to keep the computer running. In many instances, more than one operator is required to run a large computer.

Figure 1–15 The computer operator controls the operation of the computer from the operator's console.

Figure 1–16 A printer produces "hardcopy." Printers used with large computers are high-speed printers.

Output units

The most commonly used output devices for a large computer are a printer (Figure 1–16) and a CRT screen (Figure 1–17). In applications where large volumes of printed output must be produced, high speed printers are used. High speed printers can print from 1,000 lines per minute to over 20,000 lines per minute. The CRT screen is widely used to display both text material and color graphics.

Figure 1–17 Color CRT screens visually emphasize computer output.

Figure 1–18 A large tape library contains thousands of tapes, each with an excess 100 million characters.

Figure 1–19 Removable disk packs are mounted on the disk drives in this picture. Multiple drives such as shown here are commonly found in large computer installations.

Auxiliary storage

The two major forms of auxiliary storage for a large computer are magnetic tape and magnetic disk. With **magnetic tape**, data is stored on one-half inch magnetic tape (similar to audio cassette tape) as electronic impulses. Data can be written from computer memory onto tape and can also be read into computer memory from tape. Reels of magnetic tape are mounted on tape drives for reading and writing by the computer.

When a reel of tape is not in use, it must be stored in a **tape library** (Figure 1–18). In large installations, thousands of reels of tape can contain data which is processed on the computer. These reels must be catalogued and stored so that when they are required, they can be taken to the computer room for use.

Personnel in the tape library have the responsibility of ensuring that the tapes and disks are stored there safely. They must clean tapes and disks so foreign contaminants do not appear on the magnetic surfaces and render the disks or tapes unusable. In addition, installations may have their tape libraries in fireproof rooms and, in many cases, have more than one tape library.

Magnetic disk is the most widely used auxiliary storage on large computers (Figure 1–19). When using magnetic disk, data is recorded on an oxide-coated metal platter as a series of electronic spots. Disk drives can store data on either removable disks or fixed disks. **Removable disks** refer to disk packs which can be removed from the disk drive. In Figure 1–19, the blue containers for the disk packs can be seen sitting on the disk drives. **Fixed disk** drives contain the oxide-coated disks as a part of the drive.

The amount of data that can be stored on magnetic disk depends upon the type of drive being used. The largest fixed disk drives can store 2.5 billion characters. Multiple drives can be attached to a minicomputer or a mainframe. Removable disk packs can generally contain between 100 million and 200 million characters.

Summary — large computer hardware

Large computer hardware, then, consists of the processor unit that houses both the central processing unit and computer memory, and connected to the processor unit the operator console, input devices, output devices, and auxiliary storage devices (Figure 1-20). Under control of a computer program, these units are able to process data at very high speeds with astounding reliability.

Figure 1-20 A large computer consists of input units, the processor unit, output units, and auxiliary storage units.

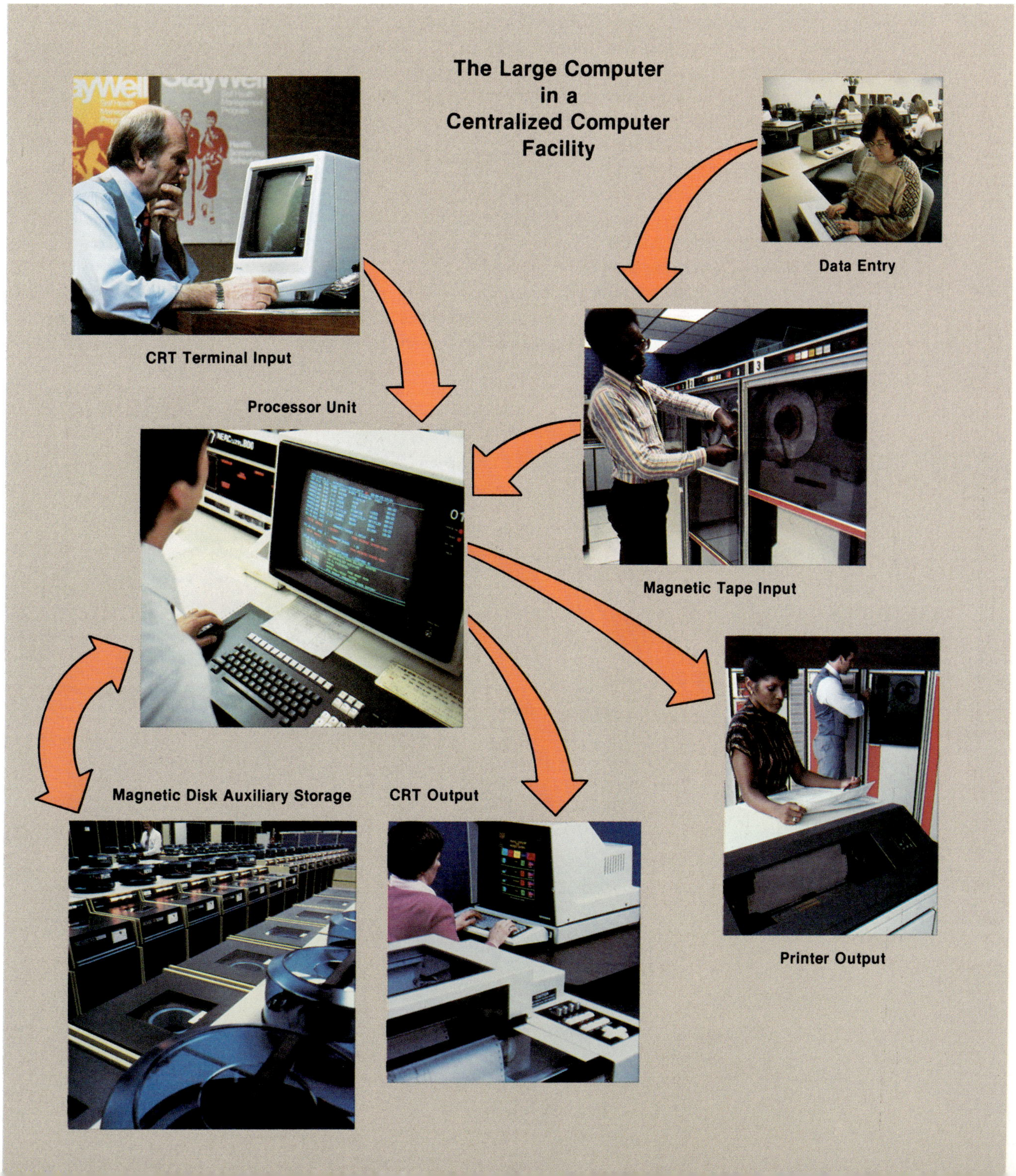

Computer programmers and systems analysts

Two groups of people who work in the information systems department are extremely important to the success of the department. They are systems analysts and computer programmers.

Systems analysts are called upon to review current operations within a company to determine if an operation should be implemented using a computer (Figure 1–21). Current operations may be considered for computer implementation if, among other things, money can be saved or more timely information can be generated to aid in the management of the company. If an operation is to be "computerized," the analyst examines the current operation to identify the data used in the operation, how the data involved in the current operation is processed, and other aspects of the operation which are pertinent to a new system. The analyst then designs the new system by defining the data required for the computer application, developing the manner in which the data will be processed in the new system, and specifying the associated activities and procedures necessary to implement the operation using the computer.

Analysts interact closely with both the people who will be using and benefiting from the new system and the programmers in the information systems department who will be writing the computer programs.

Computer programmers design, write, test, and implement specialized programs which process data on the computer. They follow the specifications from the systems analyst with regard to the processing to be accomplished by a program. The systems analyst will provide direction concerning the data to be processed and the type of processing which is to occur. It is the job of the programmer to develop computer instructions that create the information required by the system.

Figure 1–21 The people responsible for designing and implementing a system for a large-scale computer include, among others (from left to right), the systems analyst, the user, the project manager, and the programmer.

Data control and management

Data is an important asset of any company; therefore, a critical function within the information systems department is the control and management of data. In many companies, the **data base administrator** is responsible for the company's data.

Among other things, the data base administrator must develop procedures to ensure that correct data is entered into the system, that confidential company data is not lost or stolen in some manner, that access to company data is restricted to only those who need the data, and that data is available when needed. This function is very important to most companies where billions of pieces of data are processed on the computer, and the loss or misappropriation of that data could render the company unable to continue operation.

Information systems department management

Management within an information systems department is found at varying levels, depending upon the size and complexity of the department. In general, however, most information systems departments have operations management, systems management, programming management, and a manager of the entire department.

An **operations manager** is responsible for all operational aspects of the information systems department. The **systems manager** oversees the activities in the systems analysis and design area of the department. The **programming manager** is in charge of all programmers within the department.

The information systems department manager manages the entire department. In many cases, the manager is a vice president, with the title, **Vice President of Information Systems**.

Other levels of management such as project managers are also usually required. The exact organizational structure will depend upon the needs of the company.

COMPUTER USE IN THE MODERN BUSINESS WORLD

The hardware and software examined to this point in the chapter have remarkable processing capabilities, but they are of no use whatsoever unless they satisfy the needs of computer users. **Computer users** are those people who either directly use the computer or who benefit from the output of computer processing.

In the modern business world, it is not unusual for the computer to be used by management personnel at all levels to aid in decision making; by office workers in all departments for automating the tasks of preparing documents, filing documents, retrieving data, and communicating information to others throughout the company; and by personnel in the manufacturing and production departments for tasks varying from automated assembly by computerized robots to controlling shipping and warehouse scheduling. Most jobs in modern companies require some knowledge and use of computers.

The needs of the computer user fall into three very broad categories: Information management, management support, and function support. **Information management** refers to the task of managing and controlling the data and information required within an organization for that organization to function. **Management support** consists of those activities carried out within a company to supply management personnel with information on which decisions can be made and action taken. Systems which provide management support are sometimes known as **decision support systems. Function support** refers to the use of the computer by people to perform their jobs faster, more efficiently, and with less cost to the company.

Three ways in which individuals can meet their information management, management support, and function support needs are: 1) Use of personal computers; 2) Use of an information center; 3) Use of a centralized computer. Computers of varying sizes and capabilities, such as minicomputers and mainframes, are used as centralized computers. The paragraphs below discuss these three approaches.

USE OF PERSONAL COMPUTERS

Personal computers are widely used in the business environment by personnel at all levels. Personal computers are often used in conjunction with specialized software packages that have gained almost universal acceptance. These packages include:

1. Word processing software.
2. Electronic spreadsheet software.
3. Computer graphics software.
4. Data base and file management software.
5. Electronic mail software.

A summary of these software packages is illustrated in Figure 1–22, and their use is explained in the following paragraphs.

Word processing software

Word processing software is widely used in the office environment to prepare letters and memos. It allows the user to enter data on a keyboard. As the words and letters are entered, they are displayed on the CRT screen and stored in main memory of the personal computer. If necessary, keying errors may be corrected; words, sentences, paragraphs, or pages may be added or deleted; margins can be established; page lengths can be defined; and many other functions that involve the manipulation of the written word can be performed.

After the text material has been created on the personal computer CRT screen, it can be printed and can also be stored on auxiliary storage for future reference. The personal computer as a word processor is rapidly replacing the typewriter and the dedicated word processor in many offices.

Electronic spreadsheet software

One of the most widely used software packages for management support is the electronic spreadsheet. As seen previously in this chapter, an electronic spreadsheet performs calculations on the numbers entered.

Word Processing is used to write letters, memos, and other documents. As words and letters are keyed by the operator, they are displayed on the CRT screen. The user can easily add, delete, and change any text entered until the text is exactly as desired. When the text is correct, the user can save the text on auxiliary storage and can also print it on a printer. Many printers used with word processors produce letter-quality output.

Figure 1-22 Personal computer software packages

Electronic Spreadsheet Software is a major tool for decision support systems. The user enters as input data the values which are to be used in calculations, and also enters the formulas which are to be used to perform the desired calculations. The program performs calculations on the input data based upon the formulas entered by the user. A most powerful part of electronic spreadsheet software is the ability to ask "what if" questions and have the software perform calculations based upon the new assumptions. In the example below, the user could direct the software to recalculate the profits based upon a percentage increase in sales and a percentage decrease in costs.

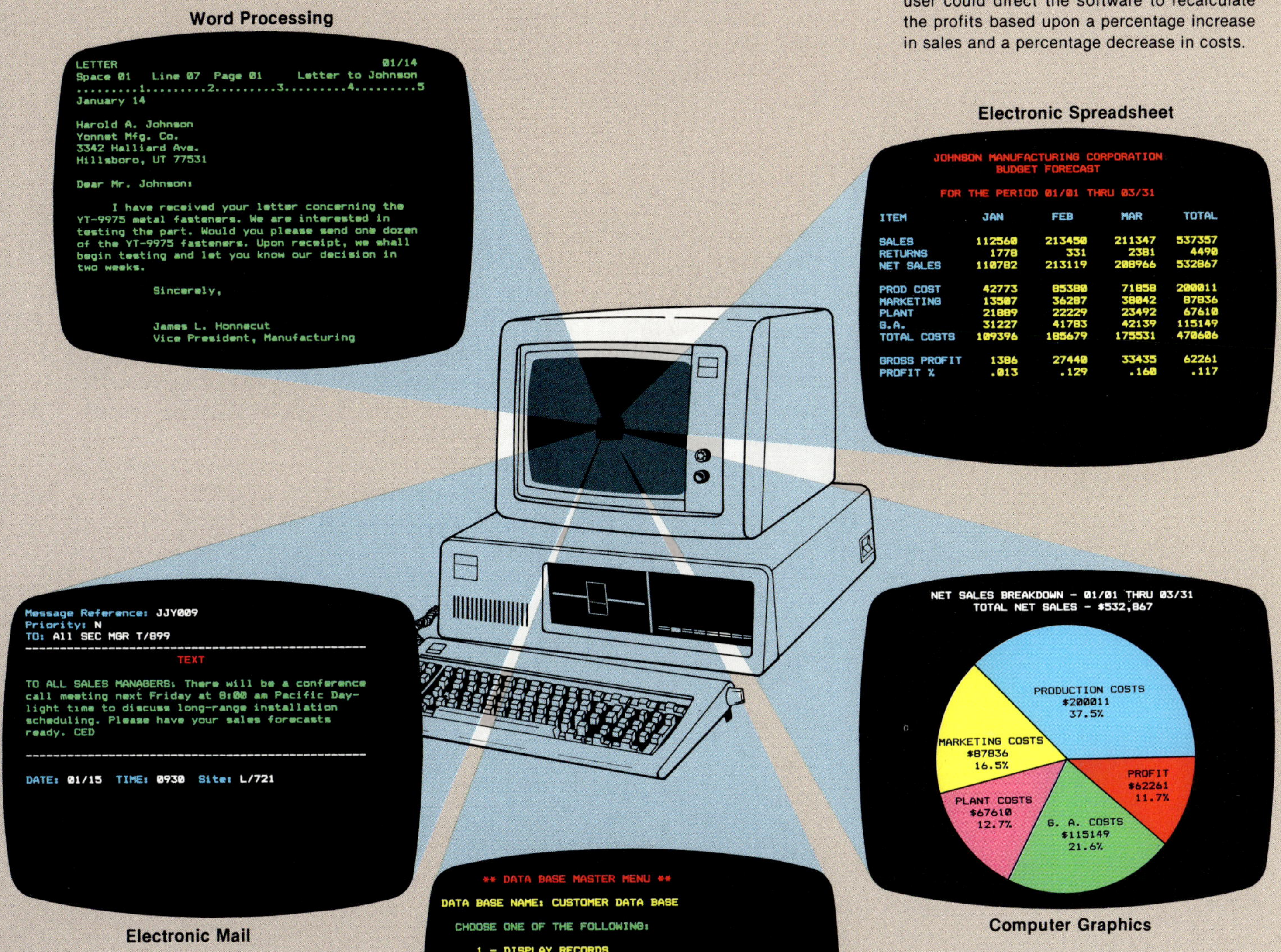

Word Processing
LETTER 01/14
Space 01 Line 07 Page 01 Letter to Johnson
.........1.........2.........3.........4.........5
January 14
Harold A. Johnson
Yonnet Mfg. Co.
3342 Halliard Ave.
Hillsboro, UT 77531
Dear Mr. Johnson:
I have received your letter concerning the YT-9975 metal fasteners. We are interested in testing the part. Would you please send one dozen of the YT-9975 fasteners. Upon receipt, we shall begin testing and let you know our decision in two weeks.
Sincerely,
James L. Honnecut
Vice President, Manufacturing
Electronic Spreadsheet
JOHNSON MANUFACTURING CORPORATION
BUDGET FORECAST
FOR THE PERIOD 01/01 THRU 03/31
ITEM JAN FEB MAR TOTAL
SALES 112560 213450 211347 537357
RETURNS 1778 331 2381 4490
NET SALES 110782 213119 208966 532867
PROD COST 42773 85380 71858 200011
MARKETING 13507 36287 38042 87836
PLANT 21889 22229 23492 67610
G.A. 31227 41783 42139 115149
TOTAL COSTS 109396 185679 175531 470606
GROSS PROFIT 1386 27440 33435 62261
PROFIT % .013 .129 .160 .117
Message Reference: JJY009
Priority: N
TO: All SEC MGR T/899
TEXT
TO ALL SALES MANAGERS: There will be a conference call meeting next Friday at 8:00 am Pacific Daylight time to discuss long-range installation scheduling. Please have your sales forecasts ready. CED
DATE: 01/15 TIME: 0930 Site: L/721
NET SALES BREAKDOWN - 01/01 THRU 03/31
TOTAL NET SALES - $532,867
PRODUCTION COSTS $200011 37.5%
MARKETING COSTS $87836 16.5%
PROFIT $62261 11.7%
PLANT COSTS $67610 12.7%
G. A. COSTS $115149 21.6%
Electronic Mail
Computer Graphics

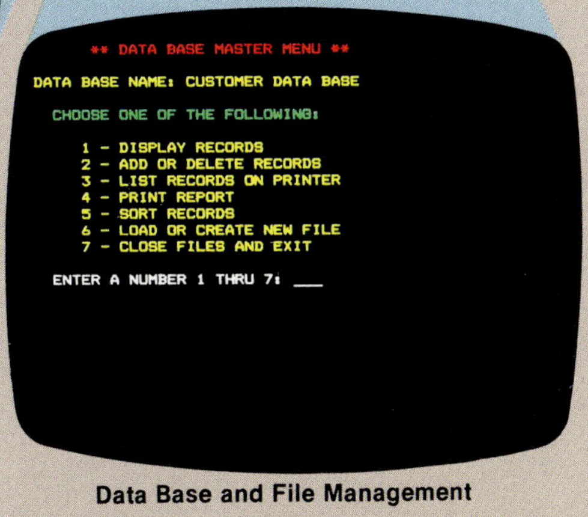

Electronic Mail lets users communicate with each other via their personal computers. Messages can be sent from one personal computer to one or more other personal computers in the personal computer network. The message is stored on auxiliary storage until the receiving user is ready to look at the accumulated "mail." At that time, all messages can be displayed. In the example above, the message from the Vice President of Sales to all sales managers is sent to the personal computer of each sales manager. In this way, the Vice President of Sales does not have to worry that someone will not know of the Friday morning meeting.

Data Base and File Management Software allows the user to access data in any manner required. The screen above illustrates a data base menu. A menu is a list of the activities which can be performed by a program. The user chooses a number corresponding to the function desired. The user can display records from the data base, add or delete records, list and print data on a printer, sort records, and perform other activities as needed.

Computer Graphics Software provides the ability to transform a series of numeric values into a graphic form suitable for easier analysis and more precise presentation. In the example above, the cost values from the electronic spreadsheet have been transformed into a color pie chart. Through the use of color, the various breakdowns for cost are easily seen. These graphs are produced in seconds rather than in the days which were required when a graphic artist had to carefully draw each graph.

Electronic spreadsheet software is particularly useful when "what if" questions are asked by management. For example, the sales and cost figures for a company could be entered into computer memory under the control of the electronic spreadsheet program. After the data has been entered and the profit calculated, a sales manager might ask what would be the profit if sales are increased by 15% and the costs are decreased by 5%. By entering simple commands, the manager can cause the program to recalculate values using the rows and columns of data. Electronic spreadsheets are an invaluable tool for decision support.

Computer graphics software

Studies have shown that information can be communicated to people many times faster in a graphic form than in a written form. Today, there are many software packages which can create **graphic output**. This output includes line charts, pie charts, and bar charts. These charts can be produced in a variety of colors. The charts are generated through the use of computer programs stored in main memory which read and analyze data and then generate the charts based upon the analysis.

Computer graphics software is widely used by management personnel when reviewing information and when communicating information to others within the organization. For example, a production manager who is making a presentation to the president of the company may use color graphics to depict the expenditures of the production department. This presentation would have more impact and lead to better understanding than would a printed column of production figures.

Data base and file management software

A **data base** is a collection of data organized in a manner which allows retrieval and use of that data. A data base consists of one or more files. A **file** is a collection of related data. For example, a file that consists of names and addresses of customers used in a mailing list may be thought of as a data base. Data base software allows the user to organize the data in the manner required for the application, allows retrieval of that data, and also allows the user to easily add, delete, or change data in the data base.

In addition, provision is made in most data base and file management software for the manipulation of the data in the data base, such as arranging the data in ascending or descending sequence by sorting, and displaying all or selected data from the data base by specifying a few simple commands in English-like form.

Data base and file management software allows a personal computer to act very much like a mainframe in terms of its ability to access and manipulate data.

Electronic mail software with networking

Although the stand-alone personal computer is a valuable tool, there is also a need for users of personal computers within a department or a company to communicate with one another through personal computer networks. In a **personal**

computer network, the personal computers are joined together with a cable so that one user can communicate with another user of a personal computer. In addition, data stored on the auxiliary storage of one computer can be accessed and transferred to another personal computer. This ability to electronically communicate and transfer data from one computer to another is called **data communications**.

One application which utilizes data communications is electronic mail. **Electronic mail** software provides users of personal computers with the ability to send messages in the form of letters or memos to others in the network. The message sent will be stored on the auxiliary storage unit of the receiving personal computer. When the user of the receiving personal computer begins using the system, a display will appear on the CRT indicating that a message has been received from someone in the network.

The message can then be displayed and, if necessary, a response sent back to the sender. The use of electronic mail is a step toward what has been called the "paperless office."

Integrated software

Software packages such as the electronic spreadsheet and word processing generally run independently of one another. Therefore, the data entered for the spreadsheet program would have to be re-entered for the word processing program. This inability of programs to communicate with one another and with a common set of data has been overcome through the use of integrated software.

Integrated software refers to software packages that combine functions such as word processing, electronic spreadsheet, and graphics into a single, easy-to-use program. This allows a single set of data to be used for a variety of applications. For example, a sales manager could enter sales and cost figures to calculate profit using the spreadsheet function of the software. The spreadsheet could then be included in a letter to the Vice President of Sales using the word processing function of the software.

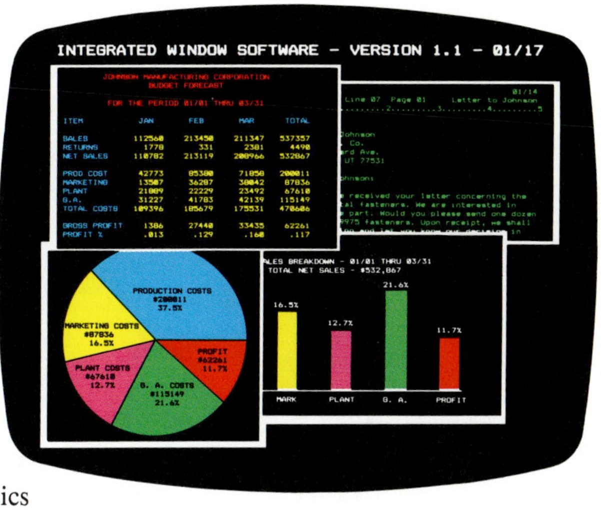

Figure 1–23 Integrated software together with window software allows multiple windows to be displayed on the CRT screen at the same time. In this example, a spreadsheet, two different graphs, and a letter are displayed. The user can move the windows around and can specify that only one window or even just a portion of one window is to fill the entire screen.

A further development in the integration of personal computer software is the use of windows. A **window** is a portion of a CRT screen that is used to display information (Figure 1-23). Window software allows multiple windows to be displayed on the CRT screen at the same time. For example, the sales manager writing the letter to the vice president in the example above could display both the letter and the spreadsheet at the same time on the CRT screen. In this manner, the CRT screen resembles the manager's desk, where both the letter and the spreadsheet can be placed and examined at the same time.

Integrated software is sometimes referred to as the second generation of personal computer software.

Summary — personal computers

Personal computers are an increasingly important tool for companies. The major advantage of a personal computer is immediate access by the user. The computer usually sits on a desk, and the user can access its processing capabilities through the use of software packages such as those explained in the preceding paragraphs. The personal computer is an integral part of the computing facilities in most companies.

Figure 1–24 An information center provides company users with access to sophisticated hardware and software to aid in meeting their information processing needs.

INFORMATION CENTERS

A second major way for users to obtain access to computing power is through the use of an information center. An **information center** is an area within the information systems department that contains a number of CRT terminals, hardcopy generators (usually printers), and perhaps a smaller computer. These devices have direct access to a centralized computer in the information systems department. People within the company go to the information center to use the hardware and software available there (Figure 1–24).

The major reason for an information center is to give employees a simple, effective way to meet their own departmental and individual information processing needs. This is accomplished by providing computing power, training, and access to sophisticated software so users can generate their own reports and develop their own applications. The major difference between an information center and a personal computer sitting on a person's desk is that the information center provides hardware, software support, and training to use sophisticated software with access to the data base stored on a centralized computer.

Thus, the information center provides more sophisticated hardware and software than personal computers. The information center's main goal is to provide extensive computer processing for company users.

Figure 1–25 Users throughout a company can have access to a centralized computer through the use of a CRT which communicates with a computer. Below, a user in the shipping department updates the inventory data base stored on the central computer.

USE OF A CENTRALIZED COMPUTER

When processing large volumes of data or when large data bases must be accessed by many users, a centralized computer is used. Information from a centralized computer is commonly delivered by: Printed reports or as output on a CRT terminal (Figure 1–25).

When a centralized computer is to be used for an application, a formal process will usually be followed to develop the application system. Management and other personnel who will be using the system will be involved with the professional staff of the information systems department in the design and implementation of the system. This process of system design and implementation can be lengthy and difficult.

Once the system is designed, however, it can be used by all personnel who are authorized to use it. In some applications, such as airline reservation systems or large bank accounting systems, a centralized computer will be used because the speed and data access available on a large, powerful computer are required by the application. For example, in a banking application, thousands of accounts must be accessible by hundreds of tellers and other bank employees. A large computer is the only machine with the processing power to satisfy the requirements of this application.

Summary

The determination of the type of computer access to be used depends upon the application. For those uses where software packages are available on personal computers and a small amount of data is required, personal computers can be used. The information center allows the user to develop application programs with access to part or all of a centralized computer data base. For those applications with large amounts of data and complex programming, a system is normally developed by the information systems department for implementation on a large computer.

ELEMENTS OF SUCCESSFUL INFORMATION PROCESSING

Obtaining useful and timely information from computer processing requires more than just the hardware and software described thus far. Successful information processing also requires correct data and well-designed systems and procedures.

The heart of a successful information processing operation is the data which is processed. If the data entered into the computer for processing is incorrect, then all information produced from the data is incorrect. For example, if incorrect sales figures are entered into a computer, then any subsequent sales analysis will produce incorrect results. Therefore, a user of a computer must be aware that proper procedures have to be developed to ensure that correct data enters the system. Control and management of a corporation's data is critical if the information derived from the processing of that data is to be successfully used.

Procedures must also be developed to teach the user how to use the system and to specify how data is to be entered into the system.

In summary, then, not only must computer hardware and computer software be in place for successful information processing, but valid data, complete and correct systems and procedures, and knowledgeable personnel are also required.

Computers Of all Sizes And Shapes

Computers come in all sizes with a myriad of processing capabilities. The following pages illustrate some of the many types and configurations found in the modern world today.

Figure 1–26 Various size computers with many types of input, output, and storage devices are found in large computer centers.

The Home Computer

It is anticipated that within the next few years, the home computer will become as common as the television set. A home computer normally consists of a keyboard, a processor unit, a CRT display screen, and an auxiliary storage device. The auxiliary storage device is usually a floppy disk drive or a cassette tape drive. Additional input units such as joy sticks and graphics pads are also available. The basic keyboard and processor unit for some home computers can be purchased for less than $100.00, although more typically these units cost between $200.00 and $700.00. An entire system, including auxiliary storage and the CRT display screen, will generally cost in the $500.00 to $1,500.00 range.

When first introduced in 1975, the home computer was used primarily by individuals such as programmers or engineers who had previous computer or electronics experience. The earliest home computers were available only in kit form and had to be assembled and tested before they could be used. Most people were merely experimenting with a new electronic gadget.

Today, computers are used in the home by every member of the family to play video games, for educational applications, for household financial planning, for computerized shopping and banking, and for accessing information such as airline schedules, stock market reports, and even reference materials like encyclopedias over data communications networks established on standard telephone lines. The use of the computer in the home is truly influencing the way people play, learn, and work.

Figure 1–27 The home computer is often used for educational purposes. Here, familiarity with a keyboard is taught using a game.

Figure 1-28 Many input devices have been developed for use with home computers. Among the more popular is a graphics pad which can be used to draw pictures on the screen. In this example, the girl touches points on the pad. The pad translates the touch into a color image on the screen.

Figure 1-29 Home computers are often used by hobbyists and those with special interests. In this example, a computer is programmed to specify the notes to be played by the electronic instrument. When the program is executed, the notes specified in the program will be played.

Figure 1-30 Many people play games on home computers. As shown below, joysticks can be used as input devices to the computer.

Figure 1-31 TRS-80 Pocket Computer in a briefcase.

Figure 1-32 The Epson-20 is a portable computer.

Figure 1-33 The Kaypro is a transportable device.

Figure 1-34 The IBM Portable Personal Computer runs the same programs as the full-sized IBM PC.

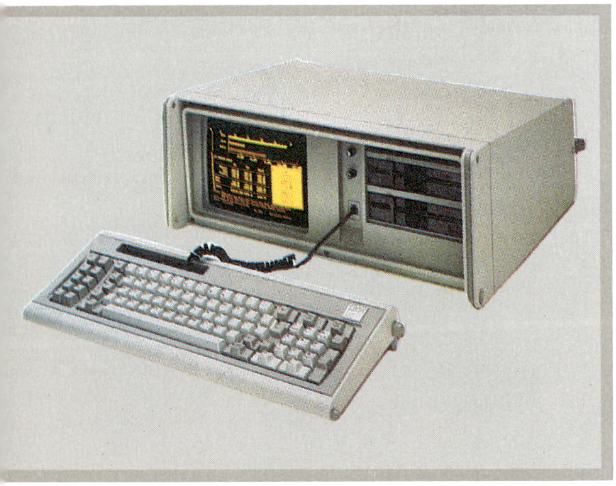

Figure 1-35 The Apple Macintosh, seen here as a desk-top computer, weighs less than 25 pounds and is transportable.

Figure 1-36 Spreadsheets and graphics can be done on this Otrona Attache.

Figure 1–37 This TRS-80 Model 100 computer allows the user to write letters using word processing in any environment.

Portable and Transportable Computers

The first computer system put into operation in 1946 weighed over 20 tons. In 1981, Adam Osborne introduced the Osborne I computer that weighed 23½ pounds and had more calculating ability than the machine of 35 years before. The Osborne I, which was designed to be easily carried as a single unit by an individual, included a keyboard, CRT screen, 64,000 positions of computer memory, and a floppy disk drive. In addition, word processing, electronic spreadsheet, and the BASIC language software were a part of the system for the unheard of price of $1795. The Osborne I, although no longer in production, met with immediate success; and it, together with others which were subsequently introduced, both created and filled a market niche for transportable computers not previously recognized.

Computers which can be carried about allow users to perform common information processing tasks anywhere. These computers fall into three major categories: 1) Hand-held computers, which generally weigh five pounds or less. These machines are used as sophisticated, programmable calculators with storage and varying output capabilities, and typically cost less than $500; 2) Portable computers, which weigh from 5 to 15 pounds. Portable computers generally have a keyboard, up to 512,000 positions of main memory, a display of three to five lines with 20 – 30 characters on each line, the ability to connect to other devices such as printers or auxiliary storage devices, and a cost of under $1500; 3) Transportable computers, which usually fold up into a single case. These computers include up to 512,000 positions of main memory, a built-in floppy disk drive, a CRT screen which may be able to display 25 80-character lines, a keyboard, weigh 15 – 30 pounds, and cost between $1500 – $6000. Both portable and transportable computers have many of the same processing capabilities as microcomputers.

Figure 1–38 Accountants, doctors, attorneys, small manufacturing firms, and many others have found the personal computer ideal for their information processing needs. In addition, big companies are utilizing so-called micro-to-mainframe connections to provide access from personal computers to data bases stored on large, centralized computers.

Personal Computers — The Computers for Small Business

In 1977, the first fully assembled microcomputer appeared on the market. Since that time, the microcomputer, or personal computer, has been improved to the point where today many microcomputers are powerful enough to be used as the only computer in a small business. Personal computers designed for use as small business computers generally cost $3,000.00 to $10,000.00.

A personal computer used for a small business will usually include at least 256,000 positions of main computer memory, a printer, and enough auxiliary storage to store the data required for the various applications. In many cases, this includes a hard disk capable of storing 10 million characters or more. The software packages described in this chapter are useful for small businesses. In addition, most small businesses will acquire software which meets their specific needs. For example, many small businesses have need for software to process their accounting applications, such as accounts payable, accounts receivable, general ledger, and payroll. These software packages are available for microcomputers.

In addition to their accounting and other business application needs, small businesses often use microcomputers for their specific business requirements. For example, an architecture firm might use a microcomputer to aid in designing buildings or in determining the costs of building a structure after the design has been completed. A small law firm may use a microcomputer to bill clients and to prepare certain documents such as wills.

Millions of personal computers have been sold since 1977. Many of them are used by small businesses.

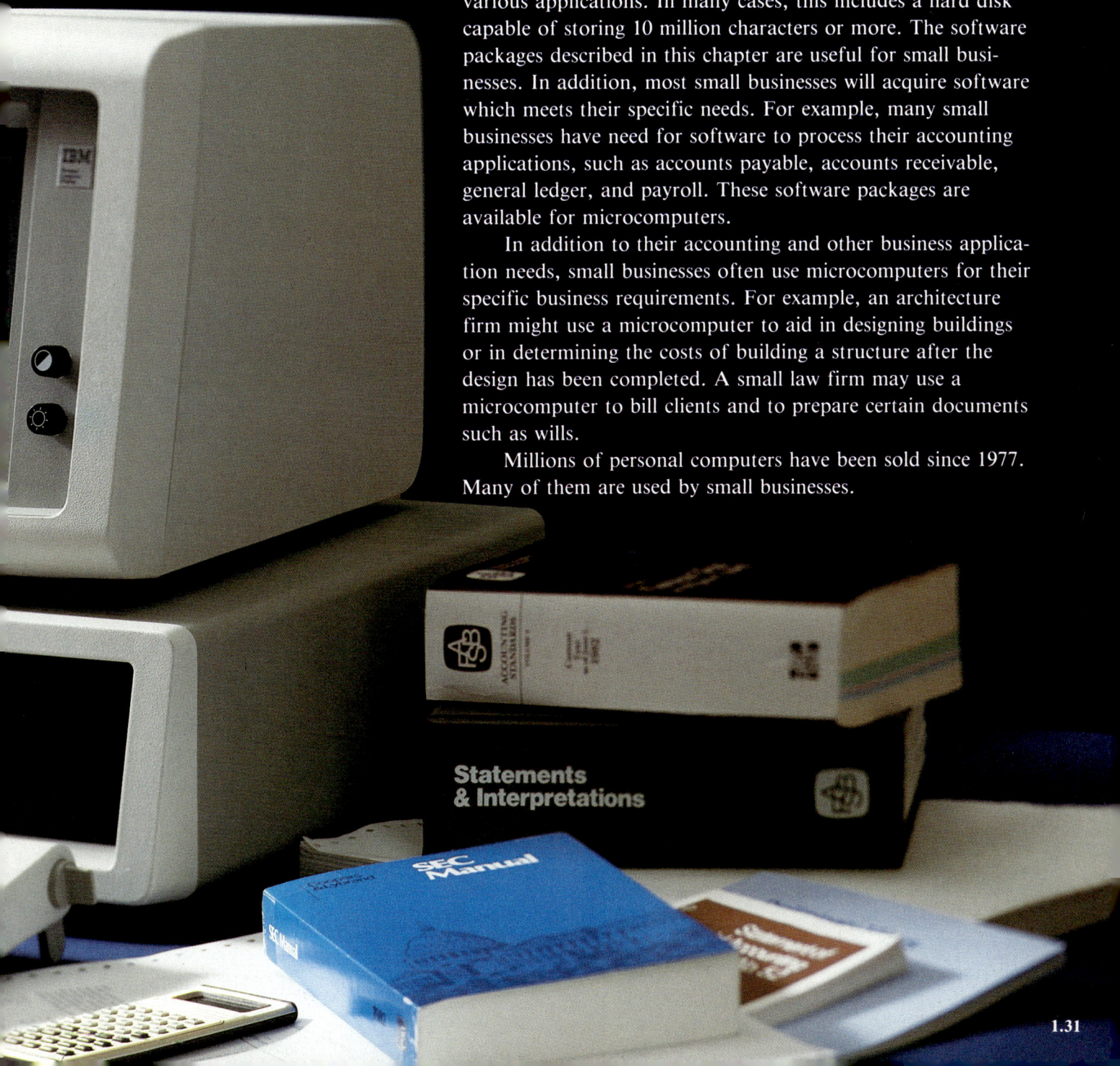

Minicomputers and Mainframes

Prior to 1965, computer manufacturers introduced machines with varying capabilities, but most were large-scale computers dedicated to serving those users who needed considerable computing power. In 1965, a small company in Maynard, Massachusetts called Digital Equipment Corporation (DEC) introduced a small computer which had the characteristics of fast processing speed and limited input/output capability. The first computers produced by DEC were smaller and less expensive than those that had been produced by companies such as IBM, Control Data, and Honeywell. Thus, the term ''mini-computer'' was coined to distinguish these smaller computers from the larger computers known as ''mainframes.'' DEC has since grown to be the second largest computer manufacturer in the world, behind IBM.

Minicomputers differed from mainframes in several significant ways. First, they were smaller and less powerful than mainframes. Second, they were considerably less expensive than mainframes. Third, many early minicomputers lacked extensive and diversified input/output devices, making minicomputers less attractive to business users and better suited to engineering and scientific applications which did not require extensive input/output operations. Fourth, most minicomputers had very little software. They were intended primarily for organizations which were sophisticated enough to write their own software. Finally, many minicomputers offered the ability to connect multiple CRT terminals to the computer, a capability not readily available on many mainframes of that era.

Since their introduction in 1965, minicomputers have evolved to where today they are widely used for all application areas, including business. The differences noted above have largely disappeared.

Figure 1–39 This picture shows a mainframe computer with a CRT operator console, processor unit, and auxiliary storage.

Figure 1-40 The minicomputer above provides computer resources for small companies or departments of large companies.

Input/output devices required for business applications have been developed. Extensive software for both business and scientific applications is now available for use on minicomputers. Minicomputers today perform important roles in all areas where computers are used.

In 1975, two companies, Gould, Inc. and Perkin-Elmer, introduced more powerful computers called superminis. While not as powerful as many mainframes available, these machines executed instructions considerably faster than most minicomputers and were able to have many more positions of main computer memory. They also, of course, cost more money than minicomputers but were generally less expensive than mainframes.

During the 1970's another group of computers were designed primarily for use by businesses which did not need the huge power nor the expense of a mainframe computer. These machines are categorized as small business computers. Most small business computers allow multiple users to use the computer. Depending upon the machine, from three to ten users can use the computer from different CRT terminals at the same time. These systems allow the users to share disk files, printers, software, and other system resources at the same time from diverse areas of a company.

From the previous discussion, it should be evident that for either business or scientific and engineering applications, computers of many sizes and configurations exist. In the pictures on these two pages, Figure 1-39 illustrates a mainframe computer, Figure 1-40 shows a minicomputer, Figure 1-41 contains a multi-user computer, and Figure 1-42 illustrates a single-user business computer.

Figure 1-41 A multi-user business computer allows 3 - 10 users at one time.

Figure 1-42 Single-user computer.

Special Computers For Distinct Tasks

The computers illustrated on the previous pages of this chapter are all called general purpose computers because they can perform any task required simply by changing the application program stored in main memory.

Special purpose computers have also been developed. These computers are designed for specialized applications and can have many different configurations, varying from a single chip to a very large computer system. For example, although they are both called special purpose computers, the small computer on a chip used to control the ignition in an automobile is considerably different from the huge special purpose computer used to monitor and control space shuttle flights.

Special purpose computers consisting of a single microcomputer chip are used for many mundane tasks which just a few years ago either were not done or were done by other means. For example, virtually all automobiles have one or more computers to control such activities as gas consumption. Some automobiles even have voice warning systems controlled by a microcomputer chip. Many home appliances such as refrigerators, televisions, heaters, and microwave ovens contain small computers to monitor or control the appliance. Most cameras today have a computer which controls the shutter speed and the amount of light reaching the film.

Large special purpose computers are also used for many tasks. Virtually all space exploration depends upon computers specifically designed for that purpose. Assembly lines in large plants around the world are controlled by specially designed computers. Much of the recent work in robotics is attributable to the special purpose computers designed in conjunction with the robot machines.

With the increased ability to produce specialized computers at very reasonable prices, it is likely that most tasks which require some type of monitoring and control will be performed by computers in the very near future.

Figure 1-43 This computerized production system automatically performs five separate operations to make single-piece light truck wheels.

Figure 1-44 A special purpose computer generates the graphics which simulate the landing strip.

Figure 1-45 To automate the machining of parts, this parts line is controlled by a special computer.

CHAPTER SUMMARY

1. A computer is an electronic device, operating under the control of instructions stored in its own memory unit, which can accept and store data, perform arithmetic and logical operations on that data without human intervention, and produce output from the processing.
2. A computer can perform input operations, arithmetic operations, logical operations, output operations, and storage operations.
3. Data is the numbers, words, and phrases which are suitable for processing in some manner on a computer.
4. Information is produced by the processing of data on a computer.
5. The production of information by processing data on a computer is called information processing.
6. Processing data on a computer is performed by computer hardware called input units, processor unit, output units, and auxiliary storage units.
7. Input units are used to enter data into a computer.
8. The processor unit is composed of main memory and the central processing unit.
9. Main memory consists of components which electronically store data, including letters of the alphabet, numbers, and special characters. When data is entered into a computer, it is stored in main memory.
10. The central processing unit (CPU) contains the electronic circuits which cause processing to occur.
11. Output units are used to print or display output from computer processing.
12. Auxiliary storage units are used to store instructions and data when they are not being used in main memory of the computer. Floppy disks and hard disks are widely used on personal computers.
13. A computer is directed to perform the input, arithmetic, logical, output, and storage operations by a series of instructions called a computer program. Computer programs are called computer software.
14. Programs which can be purchased from computer stores or software vendors are called software packages.
15. To execute a program, three steps are used: a) Load the program; b) Enter the data; c) Perform calculations and display the results.
16. The information processing cycle consists of entering data, processing the data, placing the data on an output device for use, and storing the data on auxiliary storage for later use.
17. For applications where large volumes of data are required and numerous users need access to the same centralized computer, a large computer is used. This large computer is either a minicomputer or a mainframe.
18. A personal computer can store up to 10 million characters while a large computer can store over 5 billion characters on auxiliary storage. A personal computer can execute 100,000 instructions in one second, and a large computer can execute more than 10 million instructions in a second.
19. A CRT terminal consisting of a keyboard and CRT screen is the most commonly used input device for a large computer when the person entering data is communicating directly with the computer.
20. A data entry device is designed to allow fast and accurate keying of data.
21. The processor unit of a large computer is housed in a desk-sized cabinet. The operator's console is used by the computer operator to monitor and control the activities on the computer.
22. The most commonly used output devices for large computers are high-speed printers and CRT screens.
23. Auxiliary storage devices used on a large computer include magnetic tape and magnetic disk.
24. A tape library is used to store the disk packs and reels of tape when they are not in use.
25. Systems analysts review current operations within a company to determine if an operation should be implemented using a computer. Analysts interact closely with users and with programmers.
26. Computer programmers design, write, test, and implement programs which process data on a computer.
27. A data base administrator is responsible for controlling and managing a company's data.
28. Management within an information systems department includes an operations manager, systems manager, programming manager, and department manager (sometimes called Vice President of Information Systems).
29. Computer users have needs in three major categories: information management; management support, or decision support; and function support.
30. Three ways to meet user needs are: a) Personal computers; b) Information center; c) Centralized computer.
31. When using personal computers, five widely used software packages are: word processing, electronic spreadsheets, computer graphics, data base and file management, and electronic mail.
32. Word processing is used to write letters, memos, and other documents.

33. Electronic spreadsheet software performs calculations on rows and columns of input data based upon formulas entered by users.

34. Computer graphics provides the ability to transform a series of numeric values into a graphic form.

35. Data base and file management software allows the user to access data in any manner required.

36. Electronic mail lets users communicate with other users via their personal computer networks.

37. A data base is a collection of data organized in a manner which allows retrieval and use of that data.

38. A file is a collection of related data.

39. In a personal computer network, personal computers are connected with a cable so one user can communicate with another user of a personal computer.

40. Data communications is electronically communicating and transferring data from one computer to another.

41. Integrated software refers to software packages that combine functions such as word processing, electronic spreadsheets, and graphics into a single, easy-to-use program.

42. A window is a portion of a CRT screen that is used to display information.

43. An information center is an area within the information systems department that contains computer hardware available for company personnel to use.

44. A centralized computer is normally used when large volumes of data must be accessed.

45. Obtaining useful and timely information from computer processing requires computer hardware, computer software, valid data, complete and correct systems and procedures, and knowledgeable personnel.

46. A home computer consists of a keyboard, processor unit, CRT display screen, and an auxiliary storage device. An entire home computer system will generally cost between $500.00 and $1,500.00.

47. Computers which can be carried about by a single individual fall into three categories: a) Hand-held computers; b) Portable computers; c) Transportable computers.

48. Many microcomputers are powerful enough to be used as the only computer in a small business.

49. Minicomputers and superminicomputers address the needs of users who need more processing power than a microcomputer but do not need the power of a mainframe.

50. Special-purpose computers are designed for specialized applications.

KEY TERMS

REVIEW QUESTIONS

1. What is the definition of a computer?
2. Identify the five operations a computer can perform, and explain each of them.
3. What is data? What is information? How is information derived from data?
4. What are the four specific hardware units found on a computer? Describe each of them.
5. What is the difference between main computer memory and auxiliary storage? Why are both necessary?
6. What is computer software? Why is it critical to the operation of a computer?
7. Describe the processing of a typical application on a personal computer.
8. What is the information processing cycle?
9. Identify some of the differences between personal computers and large computers.
10. Who are some of the personnel who work in an information systems department?
11. What is the role of a systems analyst? How does that differ from the job of a computer programmer?
12. What are the three broad categories of computer user needs? Describe and give several examples of each of them.
13. Identify the five universally accepted software packages used with personal computers. Choose two of them, and describe them in detail.
14. Specify the advantages and disadvantages of using an information center and a centralized computer. State applications which are appropriate for an information center and for a centralized computer.
15. Summarize the differences between home computers, portable and transportable computers, and personal computers used as small business computers. What are their similarities?

CONTROVERSIAL ISSUES

1. When Dr. Kemeny made his prediction in 1967 that learning how to use a computer would be as important as learning how to read and write, few people had access to computers. Since that time, millions of computers have been sold. Do you feel that it is necessary for all students to study computers and their uses? If so, at what grade levels: elementary school, high school, or college?
2. The argument is put forth by many people that the computer is taking jobs from people in society. Based on what you have learned about computers in Chapter 1, do you think this is a valid statement, or do you think that computers merely help people do a better job?
3. You learned in this chapter that computers are used for management support through the use of decision support systems. You also learned that correct data is vital in order to be able to use the information derived from processing that data. What are some of the consequences you see if management decisions are based on incorrect data? What obligation does management have to ensure that decisions are based on correct data?

RESEARCH PROJECTS

1. Choose one of the five software packages commonly used with personal computers and prepare a report on different brands of that package. Be sure to include price, capabilities, the type of computer on which the package runs, and the amount of main memory required for the package.
2. Write to a manufacturer of a mainframe computer (IBM, Honeywell, Control Data, etc.) and ask for a brochure describing one of their popular mainframes. Prepare a report for your class based upon what you learned.
3. Prepare a report for your class describing the use of computers at your school. You may choose a single department and focus on that or prepare a general report about computer use.

Chapter Two

Evolution of the Computer Industry

STOCK QUOTATIONS

NEW YORK STOCK EXCHANGE

COMPANY (SYMBOL)	12-MONTH HIGH	12-MONTH LOW	SALES 100s	LAST	LATEST	NET CHANGE
Burroughs (Burrgh)	57-5/8	43-5/8	2700	52	47-1/2	−4-1/2
Commodore Intl.(Comdr)	60-5/8	28	3761	43-3/4	33	−10-3/4
Data General (DataGn)	47-1/2	24	2167	43-5/8	39-3/4	−3-7/8
Digital Equipment (Digital)	132-1/8	64	3302	88-3/8	84-7/8	−3-1/2
Hewlett-Packard (HewPk)	48-1/4	34-1/4	5782	41-1/8	38-3/4	−2-3/8
IBM (IBM)	134-1/4	93-7/8	16260	114-7/8	109-7/8	−5
NCR (NCR)	136-3/4	93-1/4	1267	119	110	−9
Tandy (Tandy)	64-1/2	33	2404	36-3/8	34-1/8	−2-1/4
Texas Instruments (Texinst)	175-1/2	101	2857	131-1/2	127	−4-1/2
Xerox (Xerox)	52-1/8	36-3/4	4009	49-1/2	41-1/4	−8-1/4

OVER-THE-COUNTER EXCHANGE

COMPANY (SYMBOL)	SALES 100s	LAST	LATEST	NET CHANGE
Ashton-Tate (Ashton Tate)	176	10-3/4	9-1/4	−1-1/2
Businessland (Businessland)	226	11-1/8	9-3/4	−1-3/8
Columbia Data Products (Colmbia Data)	78	10-7/8	10-1/2	−3/8
Computer Store (TCSIU)	N/A	N/A	7-3/4	N/A
ComputerCraft Inc. (ComputerCrft)	30	7-1/4	7	−1/4
Computers for Less (CFLI)	N/A	1-1/8	1-1/8	0
Entre Computer Corp. (Entre Comput)	376	17-1/4	15-1/2	−1-3/4
Inacomp (Inacomp Cmp)	125	11-1/2	9	−2-1/2
Kaypro Corp. (Kaypro Corp)	169	5-1/8	6-3/8	+1-1/4
The Math Box (Math Box)	96	10-1/4	12-1/2	+2-1/4
Micro D Inc. (Micro D Inc)	30	8-3/4	7	−1-3/4
P.C. Telemart (PCTM)	N/A	N/A	4-3/4	N/A
Schaak Electronics (Schaak Electr)	65	8	6-3/4	−1-1/4
SofTech Inc. (SofTech Inc.)	644	14-1/4	9-3/4	−4-1/2
Topps & Trowsers (Topps & Trous)	N/A	N/A	N/A	N/A
Valmont Industries (Valmnt Ind)	13	N/A	22-1/4	N/A
Western Micro Technology (WstnMicro)	29	11-1/4	9-3/4	−1-1/2
World of Computers (WOCOU)	N/A	1/8	1	+7/8

OTHER EXCHANGES

COMPANY (SYMBOL)	12-MONTH HIGH	12-MONTH LOW	SALES 100s	LAST	LATEST	NET CHANGE
CPU Computer (CPU Computer)	2-1/8	7/8	1	1-1/4	1-3/8	+1/8

NASDAQ NATIONAL MARKET

COMPANY (SYMBOL)	12-MONTH HIGH	12-MONTH LOW	SALES 100s	LAST	LATEST	NET CHANGE
AGS Computer (AGS Computr)	32-1/4	13-3/4	75	27-5/8	23-3/4	−3-7/8
Altos Computer (Altos Comptr)	25-1/2	7-1/4	420	10-3/4	9-1/2	−1-1/4
Apple Computer (Apple C)	63-1/4	17-1/4	6427	26-1/8	24-3/8	−1-3/4
BPI Systems (BPI Systms)	28-3/4	7-1/4	30	8-3/4	8-1/4	−1/2
Compeq (Compeq Cmpt)	14-7/8	8-1/4	614	9-7/8	9-1/4	−5/8
CompuShop Inc. (CompuShop)	18-1/8	8-1/4	14	9	8-3/4	−1/4
Computer Device (Cmpt Dvice)	16-5/8	1/2	428	15/16	3/4	−3/16
Corvus Systems (Corvus)	22-1/4	6-5/8	244	8-1/8	6-7/8	−1-1/4
Datum Incorp. (Datum Inc)	16-3/4	5	263	8-1/8	6-5/8	−1-1/2
Dysan (Dysan Corptn)	33-1/2	14-1/2	1862	16-1/4	15-1/2	−3/4
Eagle (Eagle Comptr)	24-3/4	6-3/8	143	7-7/8	6-3/8	−1-1/2
Fortune Systems (Fortune Syst)	22-1/2	4-3/4	469	6-3/8	5	−1-3/8
Lotus Corp. (Lotus Develop)	40	30-1/2	808	38-1/4	36-1/4	−2
Onyx + IMI Inc. (Onyx)	19-7/8	6-1/2	633	7-3/4	6-3/4	−1
Seagate Technology (Seagate)	22-1/8	11	2989	13-5/8	11-7/8	−1-3/4
Tandon (Tandon Corp)	35-3/4	13-3/4	5080	15-1/2	14-1/2	−1
TeleVideo Systems (TeleVideo)	40-1/2	9-1/2	1062	13-5/8	10-7/8	−2-3/4
Vector Graphic Inc. (Vector)	11-7/8	1-7/8	108	2-3/8	2-1/8	−1/4
Victor (Victor Tech)	N/A	N/A	N/A	3	N/A	N/A

AMERICAN STOCK EXCHANGE

COMPANY (SYMBOL)	12-MONTH HIGH	12-MONTH LOW	SALES 100s	LAST	LATEST	NET CHANGE
Computer Factory (Cmp Fct)	13-3/4	6-5/8	20	6-3/4	7-1/8	+3/8
Data Products (DataPd)	31-1/2	18-1/4	304	27-3/8	24-1/2	−2-7/8
Verbatim (Vrbtm)	29-1/2	10-5/8	18	14-1/2	12-1/8	−2-3/8
Wang Laboratories (Wang B)	42-1/2	26	5436	30-1/4	28	−2-1/4

ADDITIONAL OTC QUOTES

COMPANY (SYMBOL)	LAST	LATEST	NET CHANGE
Detel Systems Corp. (Detel)	N/A	N/A	N/A
Prodigy Systems (Prodigy Systms)	3-1/2	2-3/4	−3/4
Programs Unlimited (Program Unltd)	3-3/4	3	−3/4
Teleram Communications (Teleram Comm)	2-1/2	2-1/4	−1/4

Objectives

- ☐ Explain the development of computer hardware which has led to modern computing devices
- ☐ Describe the role played by computer software in the history of the computing industry
- ☐ Identify many of the important people who have made contributions in the evolution of the electronic computer industry
- ☐ Describe some of the major companies in the computer industry and the contributions they have made
- ☐ Explain the effect the development of the microprocessor and the microcomputer has had on the computer industry
- ☐ Identify some of the applications where computers are used today

Evolution of the Computer Industry

STOCK QUOTATIONS

NEW YORK STOCK EXCHANGE

COMPANY (SYMBOL)	12-MONTH HIGH	LOW	SALES 100s	LAST	LATEST	NET CHANGE
Burroughs (Burrgh)	57-5/8	43-5/8	2700	52	47-1/2	−4-1/2
Commodore Intl.(Comdr)	60-5/8	28	3761	43-3/4	33	−10-3/4
Data General (DataGn)	47-1/2	24	2167	43-5/8	39-3/4	−3-7/8
Digital Equipment (Digital)	132-1/8	64	3302	88-3/8	84-7/8	−3-1/2
Hewlett-Packard (HewPk)	48-1/4	34-1/4	5782	41-1/8	38-3/4	−2-3/8
IBM (IBM)	134-1/4	93-7/8	16260	114-7/8	109-7/8	−5
NCR (NCR)	136-3/4	93-1/4	1267	119	110	−9
Tandy (Tandy)	64-1/2	33	2404	36-3/8	34-1/8	−2-1/4
Texas Instruments (TexInst)	175-1/2	101	2857	131-1/2	127	−4-1/2
Xerox (Xerox)	52-1/8	36-3/4	4009	49-1/2	41-1/4	−8-1/4

OVER-THE-COUNTER EXCHANGE

COMPANY (SYMBOL)	SALES 100s	LAST	LATEST	NET CHANGE
Ashton-Tate (Ashton Tate)	176	10-3/4	9-1/4	−1-1/2
Businessland (Businessland)	226	11-1/8	9-3/4	−1-3/8
Columbia Data Products (Colmbia Data)	78	10-7/8	10-1/2	−3/8
Computer Store (TCSIU)	N/A	N/A	7-3/4	N/A
ComputerCraft Inc. (ComputerCrft)	30	7-1/4	7	−1/4
Computers for Less (CFLI)	N/A	1-1/8	1-1/8	0
Entre Computer Corp. (Entre Comput)	376	17-1/4	15-1/2	−1-3/4
Inacomp (Inacomp Cmp)	125	11-1/2	9	−2-1/2
Kaypro Corp. (Kaypro Corp)	169	5-1/8	6-3/8	+1-1/4
The Math Box (Math Box)	96	10-1/4	12-1/2	+2-1/4
Micro D Inc. (Micro D Inc)	30	8-3/4	7	−1-3/4
P.C. Telemart (PCTM)	N/A	N/A	4-3/4	N/A
Schaak Electronics (Schaak Electr)	65	8	6-3/4	−1-1/4
SofTech Inc. (SofTech Inc.)	644	14-1/4	9-3/4	−4-1/2
Topps & Trowsers (Topps & Trous)	N/A	N/A	N/A	N/A
Valmont Industries (Valmnt Ind)	13	N/A	22-1/4	N/A
Western Micro Technology (WstnMicro)	29	11-1/4	9-3/4	−1-1/2
World of Computers (WOCOU)	N/A	1/8	1	+7/8

OTHER EXCHANGES

COMPANY (SYMBOL)	12-MONTH HIGH	LOW	SALES 100s	LAST	LATEST	NET CHANGE
CPU Computer (CPU Computer)	2-1/8	7/8	1	1-1/4	1-3/8	+1/8

NASDAQ NATIONAL MARKET

COMPANY (SYMBOL)	12-MONTH HIGH	LOW	SALES 100s	LAST	LATEST	NET CHANGE
AGS Computer (AGS Computr)	32-1/4	13-3/4	75	27-5/8	23-3/4	−3-7/8
Altos Computer (Altos Comptr)	25-1/2	7-1/4	420	10-3/4	9-1/2	−1-1/4
Apple Computer (Apple C)	63-1/4	17-1/4	6427	26-1/8	24-3/8	−1-3/4
BPI Systems (BPI Systms)	28-3/4	7-1/4	30	8-3/4	8-1/4	−1/2
Compaq (Compaq Cmpt)	14-7/8	8-1/4	614	9-7/8	9-1/4	−5/8
CompuShop Inc. (CompuShop)	18-1/8	8-1/4	14	9	8-3/4	−1/4
Computer Device (Cmpt Dvice)	16-5/8	1/2	428	15/16	3/4	−3/16
Corvus Systems (Corvus)	22-1/4	6-5/8	244	8-1/8	6-7/8	−1-1/4
Datum Incorp. (Datum Inc)	16-3/4	5	263	8-1/8	6-5/8	−1-1/2
Dysan (Dysan Corptn)	33-1/2	14-1/2	1862	16-1/4	15-1/2	−3/4
Eagle (Eagle Comptr)	24-3/4	6-3/8	143	7-7/8	6-3/8	−1-1/2
Fortune Systems (Fortune Syst)	22-1/2	4-3/4	469	6-3/8	5	−1-3/8
Lotus Corp. (Lotus Develop)	40	30-1/2	808	38-1/4	36-1/4	−2
Onyx + IMI Inc. (Onyx)	19-7/8	6-1/2	633	7-3/4	6-3/4	−1
Seagate Technology (Seagate)	22-1/8	11	2989	13-5/8	11-7/8	−1-3/4
Tandon (Tandon Corp)	35-3/4	13-3/4	5080	15-1/2	14-1/2	−1
TeleVideo Systems (TeleVideo)	40-1/2	9-1/2	1062	13-5/8	10-7/8	−2-3/4
Vector Graphic Inc. (Vector)	11-7/8	1-7/8	108	2-3/8	2-1/8	−1/4
Victor (Victor Tech)	N/A	N/A	N/A	3	N/A	N/A

AMERICAN STOCK EXCHANGE

COMPANY (SYMBOL)	12-MONTH HIGH	LOW	SALES 100s	LAST	LATEST	NET CHANGE
Computer Factory (Cmp Fct)	13-3/4	6-5/8	20	6-3/4	7-1/8	+3/8
Data Products (DataPd)	31-1/2	18-1/4	304	27-3/8	24-1/2	−2-7/8
Verbatim (Vrbtm)	29-1/2	10-5/8	18	14-1/2	12-1/8	−2-3/8
Wang Laboratories (Wang B)	42-1/2	26	5436	30-1/4	28	−2-1/4

ADDITIONAL OTC QUOTES

COMPANY (SYMBOL)	LAST	LATEST	NET CHANGE
Datel Systems Corp. (Datel)	N/A	N/A	N/A
Prodigy Systems (Prodigy Systms)	3-1/2	2-3/4	−3/4
Programs Unlimited (Program Unltd)	3-3/4	3	−3/4
Teleram Communications (Teleram Comm)	2-1/2	2-1/4	−1/4

Chapter Two

About 40 years ago, no one had such a thing as a computer. Indeed, when Dr. George Stibitz, one of the early leaders in the development of modern computing devices, approached the management of the prestigious Bell Laboratories in 1937 and advised them he had designed a calculator that could perform any general calculations, he was told, "Who wants to spend $50,000.00 just to do calculations?"

Today, the information processing and computational work done by computers in the world could no longer be carried out by hand. It has been estimated that it would take 400 billion people, many times the world population, to tackle this workload.

The computer industry has truly developed into one of the four largest in the world. This phenomenal growth has taken place because of the talents of many people and an industrial environment where the potential of the computer was recognized. Today, more than 10,000 companies with revenues in excess of $75 billion comprise this exciting industry. Many of the companies are publicly held (Figure 2–1).

It is important to understand how the information processing industry developed, for many of the events which have occurred during the past forty years influence what is done today and what may be possible to do tomorrow. This chapter covers the evolution of the information processing industry.

Figure 2–2 Dr. John V. Atanasoff conceived of and designed the first electronic digital computer. For many years his invention was credited to others. In 1974, a federal judge ruled that "Eckert and Mauchly did not themselves invent the electronic digital computer, but instead derived that subject matter from one John V. Atanasoff."

How did it all begin?

Mankind has always responded to a problem with some type of solution. Although some solutions are less acceptable than others, it is usually the search for a solution that leads to advances in man's knowledge and abilities. The birth of the electronic computer is no exception.

In the late 1930's, **Dr. John V. Atanasoff** (Figure 2–2), a mathematics professor at Iowa State College in Ames, Iowa, required a calculating device to perform mathematical operations for 20 masters and doctoral candidates. After examining various mechanical calculating devices then available, Atanasoff concluded that none of the devices was adequate for his needs. Instead, he felt the solution to his problem was in the development of a digital computing device based upon electronics.

Atanasoff, therefore, set about designing his own machine. He faced numerous problems in designing the logic circuitry for the machine. As with many inventors, some ideas were easier to come by than others. In the

Figure 2–3 The Atanasoff-Berry-Computer pictured above was the first electronic digital computer built. It used vacuum tubes as the logic elements within the machine.

winter of 1937–38, frustrated at not being able to complete the design, he drove across the Mississippi River into Illinois and settled in for a drink in a small roadside tavern. For some reason which he could not later identify, the ideas for computer memory and the associated logic which would not come to him in the laboratory came to him as he relaxed in the bar. Thus, some of the basic concepts for the electronic digital computer were formulated that night.

Returning to the laboratory, Atanasoff, together with his assistant Clifford Berry, finished the design and began building the first electronic digital computer. They named the machine the **Atanasoff-Berry-Computer**, or simply the **"ABC"** (Figure 2–3). It is generally agreed that the design of the "ABC" provided the foundation for the next advances in the development of the electronic digital computer.

Mauchly and Eckert begin work

Atanasoff was not the only person who perceived the need for doing calculations faster and with more accuracy. **Dr. John W. Mauchly**, who had learned of the "ABC" in 1940, met several times with Atanasoff and Berry in Iowa during 1941.

Mauchly was shown the computer and was allowed to read much of the manuscript describing the principles of the "ABC," including the detailed design features. The principles of electronic computation described by Atanasoff were to have significant influence on the subsequent development of electronic digital computers by Mauchly and others.

In 1941, Mauchly also became acquainted with **J. Presper Eckert, Jr.**, who was doing graduate work at the University of Pennsylvania. The meeting of these two pioneers in electronic digital computers coincided with a war-time need of the United States.

With the outbreak of World War II, the United States Army had a need for calculating ballistic tables to produce trajectories for artillery and bombing. The Army, at the start of the war, was using "differential analyzers" to calculate the tables. These mechanical devices, together with some manual calculations, could compute a sixty-second trajectory in about 15 minutes. With the tremendous demand for these tables, 15 minutes was not fast enough.

On April 2, 1943, Mauchly and Eckert submitted a memo to the U. S. Army, describing an Electronic Difference Analyzer which would be able to do the calculations in 30 seconds, half the time of the projectile's flight. The really radical aspect of the idea was the proposal to build the machine using 18,000 vacuum tubes and requiring the simultaneous functioning of almost all of these tubes.

Nothing comparable had ever been attempted, and there was considerable pessimism. One mathematician even noted that since "the average life of a vacuum tube is 3,000 hours, a tube failure would occur every 15 minutes. Since it would average more than 15 minutes to find the bad tube, no useful work could ever be done." Despite the pessimism, the army funded Mauchly and Eckert in 1943 to begin the development of the new machine.

ENIAC — the first large-scale electronic digital computer

In 1946, after spending about $400,000.00, Mauchly and Eckert

completed the **ENIAC (Electronic Numerical Integrator and Computer)**, the first large-scale electronic digital computer ever built (Figure 2–4). The ENIAC contained 18,000 vacuum tubes and could multiply two numbers in about 3 milliseconds (3/1000th of a second).

Figure 2–4 The co-inventors of the ENIAC, J. Presper Eckert Jr. (left) and John W. Mauchly, are shown with the machine. The ENIAC weighed 30 tons, contained 18,000 vacuum tubes, and occupied a space 30 by 50 feet.

The ENIAC was programmed by connecting various wires between units of the computer and setting up to 6,000 switches in such a way that the program would be executed. Each time a program was changed, the wiring had to be completely redone.

When it was placed into operation in 1946, the New York Times stated, "It computes a mathematical problem 1,000 times faster than ever before . . . and has not a single moving part." Nine months after it had been in operation, Admiral Lord Mountbatten, President of the British Institute of Radio Engineers said of the ENIAC, "The stage has now been set for the most Wellsian development of all — an electronic brain."

The ENIAC was moved from the Moore School of Electrical Engineering in Pennsylvania to the Aberdeen Proving Grounds of Aberdeen, Maryland. There it was used for not only ballistic tables, but also weather prediction, atomic energy calculations, cosmic ray studies, and random number studies. On October 2, 1955, the machine which led to the era of electronic digital computers was turned off for the last time.

The work of John von Neumann

In 1944, prior to the completion of the ENIAC, the Army asked the Moore School of Electrical Engineering to build a computer more powerful than the ENIAC.

Figure 2–5 Dr. John von Neumann, known to his friends as "Johnnie," became interested in computers after a chance meeting with Herman Goldstine, an early designer on the ENIAC, at the railroad station in Aberdeen, Maryland.

Figure 2–6 This is the first page of the first program written by von Neumann for a modern stored program computer.

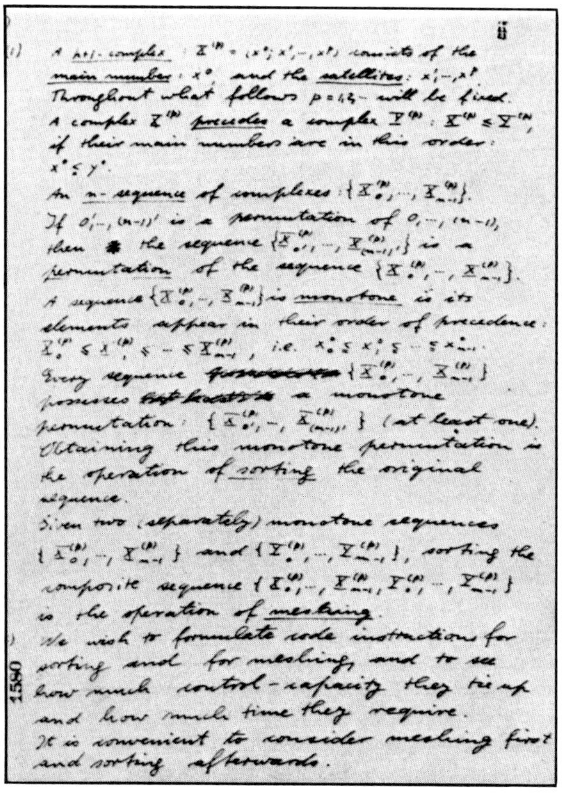

ii

(1) A $p+1$-complex $X^{(p)} = (x^0; x^1, \ldots, x^p)$ consists of the main number x^0 and the satellites $x^1, \ldots, x^p$.
Throughout what follows $p = 1, 2, \ldots$ will be fixed.
A complex $X^{(p)}$ precedes a complex $Y^{(p)}$: $X^{(p)} \leq Y^{(p)}$, if their main numbers are in this order: $x^0 \leq y^0$.
An n-sequence of complexes: $\{X_0^{(p)}, \ldots, X_{n-1}^{(p)}\}$.
If $0', \ldots, (n-1)'$ is a permutation of $0, \ldots, (n-1)$, then the sequence $\{X_{0'}^{(p)}, \ldots, X_{(n-1)'}^{(p)}\}$ is a permutation of the sequence $\{X_0^{(p)}, \ldots, X_{n-1}^{(p)}\}$.
A sequence $\{X_0^{(p)}, \ldots, X_{n-1}^{(p)}\}$ is monotone if its elements appear in their order of precedence: $X_0^{(p)} \leq X_1^{(p)} \leq \ldots \leq X_{n-1}^{(p)}$, i.e. $x_0^0 \leq x_1^0 \leq \ldots \leq x_{n-1}^0$.
Every sequence $\{X_0^{(p)}, \ldots, X_{n-1}^{(p)}\}$ possesses a monotone permutation: $\{X_{0'}^{(p)}, \ldots, X_{(n-1)'}^{(p)}\}$ (at least one).
Obtaining this monotone permutation is the operation of sorting the original sequence.
Given two (separately) monotone sequences $\{X_0^{(p)}, \ldots, X_{n-1}^{(p)}\}$ and $\{Y_0^{(p)}, \ldots, Y_{m-1}^{(p)}\}$, sorting the composite sequence $\{X_0^{(p)}, \ldots, X_{n-1}^{(p)}, Y_0^{(p)}, \ldots, Y_{m-1}^{(p)}\}$ is the operation of meshing.
(2) We wish to formulate code instructions for sorting and for meshing, and to see how much control-capacity they tie up and how much time they require.
It is convenient to consider meshing first and sorting afterwards.

1580

In 1945, a Hungarian-born mathematician, **Dr. John von Neumann**, responded to that request (Figure 2–5). In a report for Contract No. W-670-ORD-4926 between the United States Ordnance Department and the University of Pennsylvania, he described the **EDVAC (Electronic Discrete Variable Automatic Computer)**. In addition to describing a number of new concepts for the computer hardware, this report contained the first written documentation of the **stored program concept** under which virtually all digital computers have since been built.

The stored program concept

Von Neumann proposed placing computer instructions, in the form of numbers, in main computer memory in a manner similar to the way data is stored in computer memory for processing. Thus, whenever a new program was to be executed on the computer, the program would be read into main computer memory rather than thousands of switches and wires being changed as required with the ENIAC.

Although accepted as "modus operandi" today, this concept was a brilliant breakthrough in 1945. The concept is largely credited to von Neumann because of his report. Several historians and colleagues who were present at the time suggested, however, that J. Presper Eckert, Jr. had mentioned the idea a year or two before von Neumann's paper.

Regardless of the originator of the stored program concept, the stage was now set for increased activity in the world of electronic digital computers.

The first stored program computer actually built

In 1946, von Neumann and others conducted classes at the University of Pennsylvania on computer design and the concept of stored program computers. One of the students was **Maurice V. Wilkes** from Cambridge University, England. Upon his return to England, Wilkes and his colleagues at Cambridge began work on the **Electronic Delay Storage Automatic Calculator (EDSAC)**. Completed in May of 1949, it was the first computer which operated using the stored program concept (the EDVAC, developed by von Neumann, was not to work until 1951). Wilkes said later that "the principles of the modern computer were then clear, and the events of the last 25 years have been their logic working out. However, not everyone recognized this was the case, and much energy had to be spent in countering the arguments of those who did not accept the stored program principle or who did not have sufficient faith that electronic technology would prove equal to the demands that would be made on it."

The business of computers begins 1950 — 1955

The work on the ENIAC, the EDVAC, the EDSAC, and other computers which were developed in the late 1940's was largely experimental. The machines were used for scientific or engineering applications. It was evident to some pioneers, however, that electronic digital computers could have uses in more areas than just engineering. One of the first to recognize the potential of computers were the developers of ENIAC, John W. Mauchly and J. Presper Eckert, Jr.

Accordingly, in 1947, not long after the ENIAC had become operational, they formed their own company, the Eckert-Mauchly Computer Corporation. Their intent was to design and build computers for use in government and industry.

Shortly after forming their company, they began the design of the **UNIVersal Automatic Computer,** called the **UNIVAC I.** In need of financial support, Eckert and Mauchly approached several major companies. Remington-Rand purchased their company and their talents. Thus, Remington-Rand was launched into the computer field with a product that was years ahead of its competitors.

Their first major contract called for the delivery of a Univac I to the U. S. Bureau of the Census for use in the 1950 census. The first Univac I was delivered June 14, 1951, marking this as the first computer dedicated to business applications as opposed to scientific, military, or engineering processing. For almost five years following its installation, the Univac I was considered one of the best large-scale computers available.

Figure 2-7 J. Presper Eckert, Jr. is seated at the console of the first UNIVAC I, delivered to the U. S. Bureau of the Census in 1951. This machine was the first commercially available electronic digital computer.

Figure 2-8 This UNIVAC I computer predicted the results of the 1952 presidential election, and was the first exposure the general public had to computers.

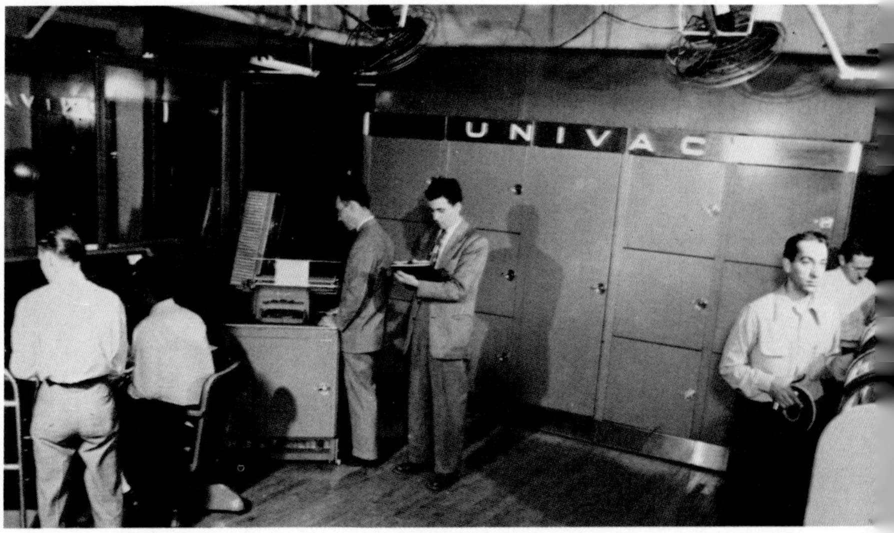

A public becomes aware

The development of electronic digital computers took place in university laboratories, and as a consequence, the public was largely unaware of these

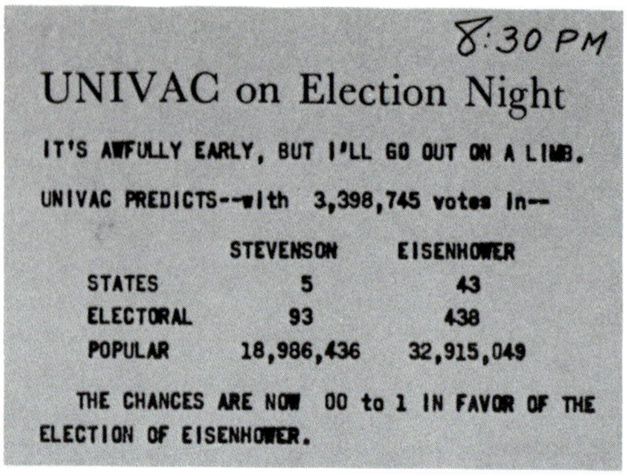
8:30 PM

UNIVAC on Election Night

IT'S AWFULLY EARLY, BUT I'LL GO OUT ON A LIMB.

UNIVAC PREDICTS--with 3,398,745 votes in--

	STEVENSON	EISENHOWER
STATES	5	43
ELECTORAL	93	438
POPULAR	18,986,436	32,915,049

THE CHANCES ARE NOW 00 to 1 IN FAVOR OF THE ELECTION OF EISENHOWER.

Figure 2-9 This is the report issued by the UNIVAC I when it predicted the presidential election.

machines. All that changed on November 4, 1952, when the Univac I computer predicted that Dwight D. Eisenhower would defeat Adlai E. Stevenson in the presidential election after analyzing only 5% of the tallied vote. CBS, fearful that the machine could not possibly be correct with such a small number of votes counted, withheld the information until it could be confirmed by actual votes. In a very short time, the public became aware of "giant brains" which would be able to outthink man and take his jobs. This is, of course, not true, but it was the first impression of the computer which the general public seemed to acquire.

The giant awakens

Although the business world had not yet seen the need for the computer, businesses had, for almost 40 years, been using **punched cards** and **electromechanical machines** to process large volumes of data (Figure 2-10). Over 90 percent of these machines were built and marketed by the International Business Machines Corporation (IBM), under the leadership of Thomas J. Watson, Sr.

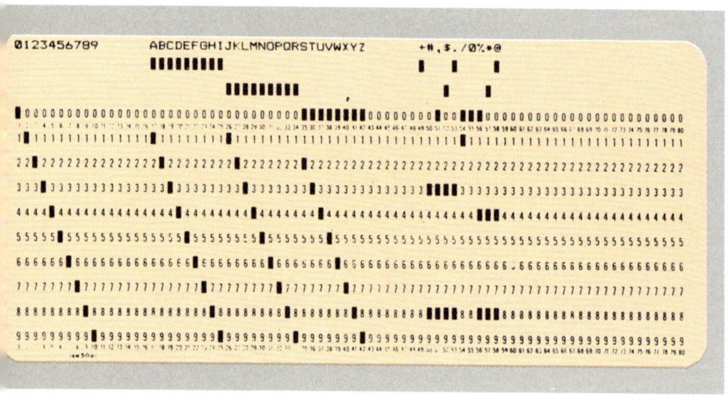

Figure 2-10 The punched card, with a combination of holes in a column on the card representing a number, letter of the alphabet, or special character, was used on IBM accounting machines and became an important input medium for computers for many years.

These machines were widely used in businesses to perform billing operations, process payrolls, and prepare sales reports. By 1950, IBM had a virtual monopoly on all such equipment.

Although the punched card machines produced by IBM were electromechanical, IBM was not unaware of the potential of more sophisticated computing devices. In 1937, IBM committed $500,000 and some of its most creative engineers to Howard H. Aiken of Harvard University to build a new kind of calculating machine. When it was completed in 1944, the Mark I calculator was donated to Harvard by IBM. The Mark I, which was electromechanical, followed a sequence of instructions stored on paper tape.

Watson, Sr., however, did not want his company to devote much of its effort to something which would not prove commercially successful. Therefore, IBM did not enter the computer business with abandoned enthusiasm. In fact, shortly after forming

Figure 2-11 Thomas J. Watson, Sr. (right), a superb salesman and the guiding force behind IBM for forty years, reluctantly allowed IBM to enter the computer industry in the early 1950's. His son, Thomas J. Watson, Jr. (far right), led IBM during the time it became the world leader in computers. He was one of the people at IBM who foresaw early the impact computers would have on business and science.

their company, Mauchly and Eckert approached IBM to discuss the possibility of joining resources to put their new Univac I computer on the market. Their proposal was rejected by a memo from Watson, Sr. stating that "there can be no reasonable interaction possible between Eckert-Mauchly and IBM." Watson felt, as many did, that at most eight to ten of the large "brains" would be sufficient for the entire scientific community, and only a few businesses would be able to use these machines.

One person who did not share these ideas, however, was Thomas J. Watson, Jr., who had become President of IBM. Thus, Watson, Jr. was placed in the unenviable position of advocating a plunge into computers; while his father, the Chairman of the Board for IBM, did not want to rush headlong into a position which could seriously hurt IBM financially.

When, however, the Univac I computer was placed in the U. S. Bureau of the Census in 1951, IBM lost business because some of their punched card machines were displaced by the computer. It is in this period of time that the decision was made by IBM to become an active force in the computer industry. It was a decision which would lead to IBM's becoming one of the four or five largest corporations in the world and a dominant force in the computer industry.

A period of development and competition

During the early 1950's while new hardware developments were taking place in both university laboratories and private industry, IBM and Remington-Rand emerged as the two leading computer companies. The Univac I computer had been installed in such companies as Sylvania and General Electric. IBM, the late entrant in the field, delivered its first computer, the 701 Data Processing System, to the government in late 1952. By the end of 1953, thirteen companies were manufacturing computers. IBM and Remington-Rand led the field with a combined total of nine installations.

In 1953, IBM announced their 650 electronic computer, a medium-sized machine suitable for business applications (Figure 2–12). IBM's position in the punched card business data processing field gave them a tremendous marketing advantage because hundreds of businesses saw the 650 as the next step up from punched card accounting machines. IBM planned to produce only 50 of their 650 computers; instead, over 1,000 of the machines were leased in the ensuing years.

Until 1956, Remington-Rand computers outsold IBM computers; but by the end

Figure 2–12 IBM leased over 1,000 of their 650 computers after the machine was announced in 1953.

of 1956, IBM had delivered 76 machines compared to 46 for Remington-Rand and had firm orders for 193 machines compared to Remington-Rand's 65. IBM had taken the lead in the computer industry — a lead it would never relinquish.

Figure 2–13 With machine language programming (right), the programmer is required to write instructions by means of numbers, letters of the alphabet, and special characters, each of which has a special meaning when interpreted by the computer's electronic circuitry.

Step No.	Inst. Address	Instruction OP	A/I	B		Effective No. of Characters Inst	Data	Total
1	500	,	003			4		4
2	504	1				1		5
3	505	/	199			4		9
4	509	L	079	179		7		16
5	516	L	551	102		7		23
6	523	Y	080	101		7		30
7	530	C	079	179		7		37
8	537	B	546	/		5		42
9	542	5	505			4		46
10	546	.	505			4		50
11	551	4	1				2	52

Figure 2–14 When using symbolic programming languages (below), simple words or abbreviations are substituted for the numbers, letters of the alphabet, and special characters required in machine language. These abbreviations must be translated into machine language before the program can be executed.

PG	LINE	TAG	OPERATION	NUM	OPERAND
02	01	START	SEL		100
	02		RD		WHSE INV
	03		TRA		ERROR
	04		RAD		RECEIPTS
	05		SUB		WITHDRAW
	06		ST		BALANCE
	07		TRP		ROUTINE 1
	08		TR		ROUTINE 2
	09	MOVE REC	RCV	0	OUTPUT BLK
	10		TMT	0	WHSE INV
	11		ADD	01	(+1)
	12		CMP	01	(5)
	13		TRE	01	WRITE
	14		AAM	02	MOVE REC
	15		TR		START

The problem of programming

Although the stored program concept of von Neumann made a tremendous impact on the way computers were programmed, the programming process was nevertheless cumbersome, error-prone, and difficult. Indeed, von Neumann stated, "I am not aware of any other human effort when the result really depends on a sequence of a billion steps . . . and where furthermore it has the characteristic that each step really matters . . . yet precisely this is true of computing machines."

The programmer who wrote a computer program had to write the instructions for the computer in a "language" that the computer hardware "understood" called **machine language** (Figure 2–13). Large amounts of time were required to write the program, and most programs contained errors which could be traced back to the difficulty of writing instructions in the primitive language that had to be used.

The difficulty in using machine language was apparent to some in the early 1950's. In fact, some experimental work on automatic programming had been done in the late 1940's and early 1950's.

Automatic programming, as the term was used then, referred to writing a computer program in a notation other than machine language, thereby simplifying the programming process.

Figure 2–15 Dr. Grace Hopper, a commodore in the U. S. Navy, was one of the first-ever computer programmers, and was instrumental in developing high level languages. Over the years, she has remained a very influential person in the computing industry.

Symbolic programming becomes possible

One of the first steps toward automatic programming was the use of symbolic notation to represent operations to be performed. This somewhat improved the programming process, yet it was still necessary for each single step which had to be performed by the computer to be written as an instruction.

Dr. Grace Hopper (Figure 2–15) was an early leader in the development of automatic programming.

Dr. Hopper established the first automatic programming group associated with a commercial computer when she worked with the Eckert-Mauchly Computer Corporation. A scientific paper she wrote in 1952 entitled "The Education of a Computer" reported on what is considered to be the first programming system handling symbol manipulation.

```
C     LINEAR REGRESSION
      READ (2,2) N,XEST
    2 FORMAT (I5,F1Ø.5)
      XSUM=Ø.Ø
      YSUM=Ø.Ø
      XXSUM=Ø.Ø
      XYSUM=Ø.Ø
      DO 6 I=1,N
      READ (2,4)X,Y
    4 FORMAT (2F1Ø.5)
      XSUM=XSUM+X
      YSUM=YSUM+Y
      XXSUM=XXSUM+X*Y
    6 XYSUM=XYSUM+X*Y
      FN=N
      XMEAN=XSUM/FN
      YMEAN=YSUM/FN
      A=YMEAN
      B=(XYSUM-FN*XMEAN*YMEAN)
      WRITE(3,8)A,B
```

Figure 2–16 The example of a FORTRAN program above shows that the program statements are written in a manner very similar to the notation used by mathematicians. These program statements must be translated into machine language in order to be executed on a computer.

High level programming languages are developed

To further improve automatic programming, a small group of IBM employees headed by **John Backus** began work in 1954 to develop a "high-level" automatic programming language for use by scientists, mathematicians, and engineers. This language was to be far removed from the internal characteristics of the machine. Instead of writing machine language, the programmer would write a statement in a mathematical notation. That statement would then be translated by the computer into the required machine language instructions.

Three years later, in April of 1957, FORTRAN was introduced (Figure 2–16). **FORTRAN (FORmula TRANslation)**, which is still in use today, allows the programmer to write a program in mathematical terms. A **translator**, or **compiler**, then interprets the program and converts it to machine language which the computer can execute.

It has been shown that the use of a high-level programming language such as FORTRAN can significantly reduce programming errors (although not to the extent predicted at the time when the first report on FORTRAN said, "FORTRAN should virtually eliminate coding and debugging . . ."). In addition, FORTRAN proved conclusively that languages could be developed which are not only easier to use than machine language, but that could also produce efficient programs for executing on computers.

New programming languages appear

Other manufacturers began developing automatic programming languages for each new computer they introduced. They were trying to provide an easy method for programming the computer, and at the same time, increase their sales with better languages than their competitors. By 1959, over 200 different programming languages had been developed in universities and by industry.

Flowmatic, FACT, Algol, Commercial Translator, and other programming languages were created in an attempt to make the process of writing instructions for the computer easier, faster, and less error-prone.

Business programming follows suit

Some members of the data processing community recognized all these computer languages as a potential problem. Programs written for one machine could not be executed on a different model machine from the same or different manufacturer. A

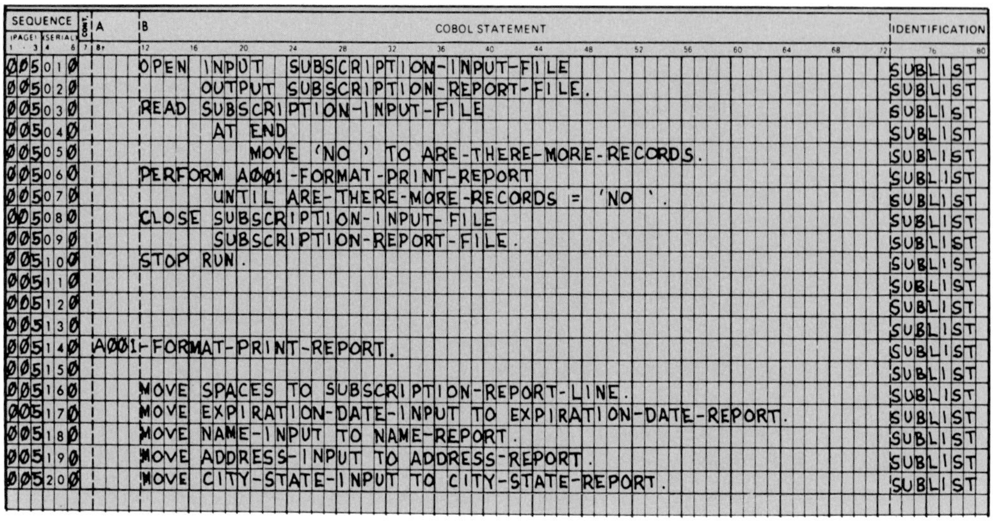

```
SEQUENCE        A   B                                COBOL STATEMENT                                          IDENTIFICATION
005010              OPEN INPUT  SUBSCRIPTION-INPUT-FILE                                                       SUBLIST
005020                   OUTPUT SUBSCRIPTION-REPORT-FILE.                                                     SUBLIST
005030              READ SUBSCRIPTION-INPUT-FILE                                                              SUBLIST
005040                    AT END                                                                              SUBLIST
005050                       MOVE 'NO ' TO ARE-THERE-MORE-RECORDS.                                            SUBLIST
005060              PERFORM A001-FORMAT-PRINT-REPORT                                                          SUBLIST
005070                    UNTIL ARE-THERE-MORE-RECORDS = 'NO '.                                               SUBLIST
005080              CLOSE SUBSCRIPTION-INPUT-FILE                                                             SUBLIST
005090                    SUBSCRIPTION-REPORT-FILE.                                                           SUBLIST
005100              STOP RUN.                                                                                 SUBLIST
005110                                                                                                        SUBLIST
005120                                                                                                        SUBLIST
005130                                                                                                        SUBLIST
005140          A001-FORMAT-PRINT-REPORT.                                                                     SUBLIST
005150                                                                                                        SUBLIST
005160              MOVE SPACES TO SUBSCRIPTION-REPORT-LINE.                                                  SUBLIST
005170              MOVE EXPIRATION-DATE-INPUT TO EXPIRATION-DATE-REPORT.                                     SUBLIST
005180              MOVE NAME-INPUT TO NAME-REPORT.                                                           SUBLIST
005190              MOVE ADDRESS-INPUT TO ADDRESS-REPORT.                                                     SUBLIST
005200              MOVE CITY-STATE-INPUT TO CITY-STATE-REPORT.                                               SUBLIST
```

Figure 2-17 The COBOL program to the right illustrates the English-like phrases which are used in the language. The fact that COBOL programs could be executed on all makes of computers led to COBOL becoming one of the most widely used programming languages in the world.

group of concerned people from the academic world, computer users and manufacturers, met at the University of Pennsylvania in April, 1959, to explore solutions to the problem. Agreeing that a project to develop a single, machine-independent programming language for business applications was desirable, they approached the Department of Defense for sponsorship of the project.

On May 28 - 29, 1959, a meeting sponsored by the Department of Defense was held at the Pentagon. A committee was charged with the task of developing a programming language for business applications that would be machine-independent; that is, programs written in the language would be able to be executed on any computer made by any manufacturer.

This committee developed the programming language **COBOL (COmmon Business Oriented Language)**, which was released in 1960 and is today one of the most widely used programming languages in the world. COBOL introduced several significant advances to the state of the art of programming languages, but perhaps its greatest contribution was that the programs could be written in English-like fashion and could be compiled and executed on computers made by different manufacturers.

With the advent of COBOL, FORTRAN, and other high-level languages, significant steps had been made in the science of programming; significant advances were also being made in computer hardware in the late 1950's.

The second generation is born (1958 — 1964)

In 1947, three scientists at Bell Laboratories, J. Bardeen, H. W. Brattain, and W. Shockley, invented a device called the **transistor**, for which they would later receive the Nobel prize. As most people are aware, the invention of the transistor led to radios that could fit into their pockets. Less well known is that the invention of the transistor led to significant changes and advances in computers.

The computers of the early 1950's used vacuum tubes in their electronic circuitry. There were several significant disadvantages of vacuum tubes; among which were the tremendous heat they generated, the fact that they were not terribly reliable, the space which they required in a computer, and perhaps most importantly, the speed at which they could process data. Even though computers were able to process data at faster rates than ever before, there was still a great deal of room for improvement. The transistor caused much of the improvement.

The first transistorized computer (TRADIC) was built in 1954 by Bell Laboratories, where the transistor was invented. It contained about 800 transistors. By December of 1955, it was reported that the Univac II, a newer model of the Univac I, contained 500 transistors. It soon became evident that transistors could replace vacuum tubes as the basis for the internal circuitry of computers.

Nineteen fifty-eight saw IBM announce the 7090 and 7070 computers. These machines used transistors exclusively. The business-oriented IBM 1401, another completely transistorized computer, was announced in 1959. These machines, together with others announced by various companies, ushered in the **second generation** of computers and signaled the death of vacuum tubes in the controlling circuitry of a computer.

The second generation machines containing transistors were not only faster than their predecessors, they were also smaller and less expensive. Thus, computers could now be afforded by many companies that could not consider the use of a computer for business applications only a few years prior to 1958.

To appreciate the impact of the transistorized computers, it is useful to examine the number of computers which were being used during the middle to late 1950's. In 1955, it is estimated that there were 244 computers in the United States. All of these computers together could perform 250,000 addition instructions in one second. This speed, incidentally, is equal to about one small computer today.

By 1958, there were approximately 2,550 computers in the United States. A few years later, in 1964, it is estimated there were 18,200 computers. This tremendous growth is attributable to the fact that transistorized computers such as the IBM 7090 and the IBM 1401 were less costly and more reliable than previous machines. Companies were finding that the computer could be helpful in performing activities critical to their operations. The computer revolution was well on its way in the early 1960's.

Figure 2-18 The IBM 7010 computer system is typical of "second generation" computers using transistors instead of vacuum tubes. The lower cost of these systems led to increased use of computers in business and industry.

A myriad of machines

By the beginning of 1964, the world of computers consisted of many different machines from a variety of manufacturers. The major manufacturers now included IBM, Sperry-Rand, RCA, General Electric, Burroughs, Honeywell, NCR, and Control Data.

The striking thing about most of the computers produced by these manufacturers was that few of their computers were compatible with one another; that is, the internal designs of the various systems were each unique. Thus, computer instructions written in a symbolic programming language for one computer would not run on a computer from a different manufacturer; or, for that matter, on a different model computer from the same manufacturer. For example, a program written for an IBM 1401 computer would not run on a Burroughs computer; nor would the 1401 program run on an IBM 7090 computer.

One of the primary reasons for the incompatibilities was that computers were viewed by both manufacturers and users as either scientific or business machines. Thus, IBM produced the 7090 series of computers for scientific applications and the 1401 series of computers for business applications. This concept of separate machines for business and scientific processing stemmed from the earliest days of computing. It was an attitude that, in 1964, was about to change forever.

THE THIRD GENERATION OF COMPUTERS (1964 - 1970)

April 7, 1964, may well go down as the most important product announcement date in the history of computers; for on that date, IBM announced the **System/360 computer systems** (Figure 2–19). When announced, the System/360 consisted of a family of six computers, all compatible, with 40 different input/output and auxiliary storage devices, and a variety of main computer memory sizes ranging from 16,000 to over one million memory positions.

The System/360 family of computers was designed for both scientific and business use. It is said that the new computers were called the "360" because they could be used for all types of processing, encircling the full range of both business and scientific applications.

This announcement tended to obsolete many existing computer systems, including those previously offered by IBM. IBM is reported to have expended nearly 5 billion dollars in the development of this new product line.

One IBM executive is purported to have called the System/360 computer system project, "You bet your company," for the success of the newly announced computers was vital to the continued success of IBM.

Figure 2–19 This half-acre room belonging to IBM is where much of the development of the System/360 took place. In the foreground is the console of one of the early models of the System/360. Tape and disk auxiliary storage devices can also be seen, as well as card readers and printers.

Solid logic technology

The System/360 offered a number of new features never before found on computers. For one, it incorporated what IBM called **Solid Logic Technology** (SLT). With this technology, the electronic components which make up the controlling circuitry of the computer are stored on small chips rather than as discrete components such as transistors and diodes on a board.

A study of 10 billion hours of operation of the electronic components using solid logic technology revealed that such components rarely fail. Statistically, a failure would occur after 33 million hours of operation, a far cry from the prediction 19 years before that said computers could not operate because vacuum tubes failed every 15 minutes. The circuitry in solid logic technology substantially improved the computer's internal processing speed; and in addition, the components could be mass produced at a low cost.

The IBM System/360 is considered to be the first of the third generation of computer systems.

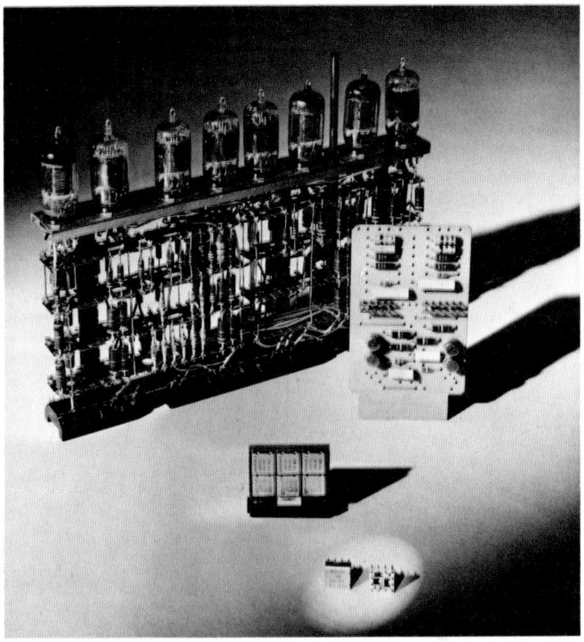

Figure 2–20 The three generations of computer components are shown in the picture above. The first generation needed vacuum tubes, the second generation used discrete components such as transistors and diodes on a board, and the third generation used solid logic technology and integrated circuits.

BATCH PROCESSING AND TIME-SHARING

Most processing on computers in the early 1960's utilized **batch processing**.

When batch processing is used, the data to be processed is gathered together in a group and is processed together as a single job. The next job, with its batched data, is processed when the previous job is completed. At peak processing times, there may be many jobs waiting to be processed.

In 1964, **Dr. John Kemeny** (Figure 2–21), a mathematics professor at Dartmouth College, was anxious to have large numbers of students use a computer for his classes. He realized, however, that batch processing was not suitable, since students would submit their jobs and then wait hours for it to be processed. If the job contained a single error, the student would have to correct the error and then resubmit the job, again waiting hours for the results of the computer processing. Dr. Kemeny knew that students would not stand for this type of delay, and he also knew that it was unfair for students to have to wait in this manner.

Figure 2–21 Dr. John Kemeny developed the Dartmouth Time-Sharing System and also led the development of the BASIC programming language. The influence of Dr. Kemeny on the world of computers is significant because the BASIC language he developed is used on millions of personal computers today. More people know how to program today using the BASIC language than any other programming language.

Enlisting the assistance of Dr. Thomas Kurtz and a group of undergraduate students, Dr. Kemeny developed time-sharing software for implementation on a General Electric 265 computer. With the Dartmouth **time-sharing** system, many typewriter-like terminals were attached to the central computer. These typewriter devices were used for both input and output. The time-sharing software alternately serviced each user on a terminal. Because of the speed at which the computer operated, it seemed to each user as if they had complete control of the computer, even though many users could be using the computer at the same time. With the advent of time-sharing, computer processing became **interactive**, meaning that users could enter their programs and data and get an almost immediate response from the computer.

Dr. Kemeny also implemented a programming language called **BASIC**, which stands for **B**eginner's **A**ll-purpose **S**ymbolic **I**nstruction **C**ode. This language, developed initially so that Dartmouth students could easily write programs on the Dartmouth Time-Sharing System, has been implemented on millions of personal computers in the past few years.

The software industry is born

Another new phase of the computer industry was born during this period of time. One of the distinct needs for computers, of course, is reliable software. Various individuals and companies recognized the need for software, and software and consulting firms were being formed to provide these services. Whereas in 1958, a few individuals who had become consultants were called "bold adventurers," by 1968 consulting and software firms became critical to the success of many large computer installations.

In 1968, Computer Sciences Corporation became the first software company to be listed on the New York Stock Exchange. Fletcher Jones, then President of C.S.C., predicted that at least one $100 million software company would emerge in the next few years.

His prediction was helped considerably in 1969 when IBM announced the "unbundling" of their software. Up to that point, IBM leased their computer hardware and software as a package, at a single price. This stymied the software industry because, effectively, users were receiving IBM software at no cost. Under pressure from the industry, IBM announced in 1969 that some of their software would be separately priced from the computer hardware. This allowed software firms to compete with IBM and opened up the software industry for considerable expansion in the 1970's.

The minicomputer emerges

In 1965 Digital Equipment Corporation (DEC) introduced a small, inexpensive computer called a **minicomputer**. DEC grew from a relatively small company to a major manufacturer and supplier of computers during the late 1960's. Many other enterprising engineers and businessmen saw great opportunities in producing minicomputers as well.

Companies such as Hewlett-Packard, Data General, General Automation, and others began the development of a very important segment of the computer industry, centered around the manufacture of small computers, with processor units at that time costing as little as $5,000.00. These companies expanded their product line during the next decade and remain today a significant factor within the industry.

Are computers really worth it?

Despite the fact that the use of computers was increasing, the late 1960's found people asking whether computer use was economically a good choice for many companies.

A 1968 report by McKinsey and Company stated that of 27 companies they surveyed, two-thirds of them were making only limited use of their computers and were still a long way from covering current money outlays for the computers, much less recovering their initial investments in the machines.

Businesses had begun to take a closer look at the computers which they had unquestionably installed in the 1960's. Many companies did not like what they found.

Industry experts noted a major reason for poor performance was that computer specialists were ordering hardware and developing software without careful analysis by top-level management. It was at this time that management began to involve itself in the increasingly important computer applications within their companies.

Figure 2–22 The error in using computers noted in the article below is typical of the publicity received by computers during the late 1960's and early 1970's. Although the majority of problems encountered could be traced to human error, the "computer" gained a reputation for mistakes and unreliability among the public.

Welfare Recipients Receive $80,000 in Duplicate Checks

DETROIT – A computer in the state's Department of Social Services recently sent out $80,000 in duplicate checks to welfare clients throughout the state.

According to Gerrold Brockmyre, assistant deputy director of the state agency, the duplicate checks resulted when the same batch of supplemental emergency payments was fed into the computer on two separate days. The error was discovered when merchants who were asked to cash two checks grew suspicious.

Many of the 887 twice-paid recipients are cashing the second check under the mistaken impression that they are entitled to the money, but some clients "are sending the extra checks back," said Brockmyre.

"Those who have spent the money have received a rather strong letter suggesting they make an arrangement to repay the money," he added.

Unreliable programs

Another major reason computer systems were not fulfilling their promise for many businesses was the unreliability of computer programs. Programs which had been developed simply did not always process the data accurately and reliably. Newspaper articles such as "Water Bill Issued to Homeowner for $200,000.00" or "Voting System Felled by Programmer's Error" were all too commonly found.

As computers were used for more and more applications, these errors were increasingly affecting the general public. A problem which has not yet been solved — the safeguarding of public and private information and the proper processing of this information — had become apparent during the late 1960's.

Some did not survive

Even though the period from 1965 through 1970 was one of frantic growth, with many new products and services developed, some of the major manufacturers of computers did not survive the battle.

Expenditures in excess of $100 million for the research and development of both the hardware and software necessary to have a computer ready for market were not unusual. In addition, because of the rapidly changing technology, heavy expenditures for research and product improvement were necessary.

This, coupled with the difficulties in competing with IBM, led to the rather startling announcement in 1970 that General Electric was quitting the computer business. That announcement was followed in 1972 with the news that RCA was leaving the computer business. In 1975, Xerox Corporation, which had entered the business in the mid-1960's, also announced that they would no longer manufacture and market computer systems. Although the computer business was extremely promising, it was also found that the competition was great, and the cost to remain in business was high.

Evolutionary growth (1970 — 1974)

By 1970, an estimated 100,000 computers were in operation. The growth of the data processing industry continued, but the period of development from 1970 - 1975 may best be described as "evolutionary" rather than "revolutionary." Behind the scenes, however, in laboratories across the country, discoveries and developments were taking place at a rapid rate. These developments would radically affect the computer industry in the late 1970's.

New product announcements continued from a variety of manufacturers. IBM announced the System/370, which used the same architecture as the System/360 but was faster, cheaper, and offered more main memory and auxiliary storage. Many System/370 computers were ordered with over one million positions in main computer memory and over a billion characters in auxiliary storage.

In 1965, a single electronic "chip," approximately 1/4" square, could contain as many as 1,000 circuit elements. By 1970, using what is called "**large scale integration,**" or **LSI**, the number of elements on a single chip increased to over 15,000. This use of large scale integration on computers designed in the 1970's, including the IBM System/370, is considered the beginning of the **fourth generation of computer systems**.

Smaller machines also gained prominence, with DEC continuing its inroads into the general purpose computer market. IBM announced the System/3 computer system, a relatively small computer targeted for smaller companies than had previously been able to afford computers. The business computer was becoming an indispensible management tool for both large and medium-sized companies.

The industry recognized that one of the least cost-effective areas within data processing operations was the data entry department, where data is placed in a machine-readable form to be processed. Accordingly, the punched card, which had been the primary means for entering data into a batch processing computer system since the inception of the computer, began to be replaced by magnetic tape and disk. In the early 1970's, with the increased use of data entry machines which could place data directly on tape and disk, some experts expected punched cards would no longer be used by 1978. This forecast proved to be inaccurate, as punched cards are still in use, but they are no longer the primary media for data entry.

Computers learn to communicate

During the 1970's, a major change took place relative to the way data was made available to a computer for processing. Up to the early 1970's, with the exception of a few time-sharing systems, computers operated in the batch mode.

With the added sophistication of both hardware and software, the 1970's saw increased use of another mode of processing data — a **transaction-oriented mode.** In this mode, data is entered into the computer system at the time a transaction occurs rather than batching the transactions. For example, when a sales order is received, it would be immediately entered into the system by a person using a computer terminal.

Figure 2-23 Transaction-oriented order entry systems use computer terminals at remote sites to process orders as they are received.

The ability to perform this type of processing depends largely on two capabilities which were developed during this time — the ability to store large amounts of data on auxiliary storage devices and data communications.

Most computers introduced in the early 1970's provided for large amounts of data to be stored on auxiliary storage devices. Software developed during this time provided a number of ways in which this data could be stored and retrieved for usage.

The second major factor was data communications, which allows computers to electronically communicate with each other and also allows a user to access a computer through a terminal located at a remote site. The key to data communications is that the communication between computers or between a user and the computer takes place over telephone lines or other communication methods. Thus, someone in Cleveland can communicate with a computer located in Atlanta. This ability allowed transaction-oriented processing to occur.

Data communications became a reality for many companies in the early 1970's. Today, many experts have difficulty separating the computer business from the communications business because they are so closely allied.

Social issues become a concern

During the early 1970's, leaders in the industry and many of the professional organizations were becoming increasingly concerned with what may be described as the social issues in computing.

With auxiliary storage devices capable of storing billions of characters, **data banks** containing information about thousands of individuals were being developed by credit reporting agencies, the Federal Bureau of Investigation, and other government and private organizations. The primary issue confronting data processing was whether the ability to obtain and store this information together with the ability to communicate this information through data communications lines and remote computer terminals would lead to an invasion of privacy.

Stories were written in newspapers and magazines concerning the so-called invasion

_op-Level Review Headed by Ford

Nixon Wants Privacy Shield for All

By E. Drake Lundell Jr.
Of the CW Staff

WASHINGTON, D.C. – Vice-President ;erald Ford has been tapped to head resident Nixon's top-level review of the ntire issue of personal privacy – particu- ırly in relation to computerized data anks.

The review committee – made up en- relv of administration functionaries – "a personal shield for

posals, that could be acted on immedi- ately.

Nixon, whose administration has been accused of violating personal privacy through wiretapping, concentrated most of his 15-minute radio address on the issue of privacy and problems with com- puter data banks, and specifically told the commission not to go into the issue of wiretapping which is being studied by another administration committee.

"Many things are necessary to lead a " Nixon said, "but none of

zens' right to privacy fails to respect th citizens themselves," he added.

"Data banks affect nearly every man woman and child in the U.S.," Nixon said, noting that computerized data bank "scattered across the country" now con tain the names of over 150 million Ameri cans.

Often the privacy of individuals ha been "seriously damaged – sometimes be yond repair" by the operation of such systems, the President said.

Your Body May Be in MIB Information System Today

By E. Drake Lundell Jr.
CW Washington Bureau

WASHINGTON, D.C. – More than 12 illion Americans "should have an abso- te right to know what secret intelli- nce information about them lurks in electronically controlled data banks the Medical Information Bureau B)," senators were told recently at a ring on proposed amendments to the Credit Reporting Act.

rthermore, John E. Gregg of the yholders Protective Association told Senate committee, "Every A

William Proxmire (D-Wi bring medical inf visions of th

Under th sumer wou denied credi medical repo to have "such licensed physici

In addition, th to be informed o information that that was the reas

Secret White House Data Bank Uncovered

By E. Drake Lundell Jr.
CW Washington Bureau

WASHINGTON, D.C. – A secret da bank on more than 5,000 individu accessible only to the White House m be the "ultimate in governmental d banks," according to Sen. Sam J. Er (D-N.C.).

The secret file was uncovered in a vey of governmental data banks lucted by Ervin's Subcommittee on itutional Rights, but so far White H fficials have not delivered requeste rmation to the committee abou the file

Computer 'Accomplice' In Thefts

By Marvin Smalheiser
CW Correspondent

LOS ANGELES – The ar-old president of a ngeles communications ment firm was arrested las allegedly stealing ne th of Pacif

Study to Probe the Evil Computer

CW Washington Bureau

WASHINGTON, D.C. – With the aid of a grant from

In conducting the program, the investigators are to com- plete

Check Fraud Scheme Uncovered, 7 Charged

NEW YORK – Fraudulent checks s to be in excess of $1 million were app

Figure 2–24 As the influence and effect of computers became better known, newspaper headlines such as the ones shown here were constantly seen. Stories such as these illustrate the great concern for privacy and computer crime shown by the media and general public during the early 1970's.

of privacy acts committed by a number of agencies of the government and private industry (Figure 2–24). People reported losing driver's licenses, being arrested, and in one case, being shot by police because of errors in the data stored in data banks.

The data processing organizations, private citizens, and, increasingly, senators and congressmen were asking what steps could be taken to ensure that "big brother" did not become a reality. There were three questions to be answered: first, was there a right for these data banks to exist; second, what could private citizens do to ensure that the data about themselves was accurate; and third, who could access the data.

After much debate, the **Privacy Act of 1974** was passed by the United States Congress. This act provided that justification would have to be shown by federal agencies whenever a data bank was to be established or accessed. In addition, both governmental agencies and private industry would have to allow access by a citizen to the store of information concerning that citizen whenever it was requested. This freedom of information act, although not without flaws, aided greatly in protecting the rights of citizens and demonstrated that the computing industry did indeed have a conscience.

Computer crime and fraud

Related to the social issues was the increased possibility of computer crime and fraud. With the ability to access large amounts of data, those with the inclination were able to obtain information which in the past was considered proprietary.

One enterprising thief, using a computer terminal, ''tapped into'' the phone lines and determined the method for ordering equipment that the telephone company used from their main computer to their warehouse. On his own terminal, this clever fellow would then enter orders which would be sent to the warehouse. The warehouse would gather the equipment together, not realizing the order was from a thief, not from authorized personnel. The thief would then send his own trucks to pick up the equipment ordered. When he was caught, the thief served his time in prison. Today, he is a consultant to many companies, advising them how to protect their data and not allow thieves access to it.

Computer crime and unauthorized access have continued to be a problem. So-called ''hackers,'' using personal computers and programs designed to dial telephone numbers until they dial the number of a computer, have gained access to many restricted data bases. Larceny through the use of computer terminals or personal computers and data communications equipment has become much more common and remains a concern in today's modern computer society.

Figure 2-25 The National Semiconductor INS 8900 microprocessor chip in the picture below contains thousands of circuits and transistors. Microprocessor chips such as this one are generally made through the process of photolithography.

THE DEVELOPMENT OF MICROELECTRONICS

Undoubtedly, one of the most revolutionary technological developments in the history of mankind has occurred in the field of electronics. Nearly unbelievable advances have taken place in the past 40 years. Shortly following the invention of the transistor in 1947 came a breakthrough where electronic engineers learned to define transistors and related circuitry by ''**photolithography**.'' Using this technique, circuits are drawn according to specifications. These circuits are then photographed and reduced. Through the use of sophisticated methodologies, the circuits are then etched on a thin wafer sliced from a large crystal of germanium or silicon (Figure 2-25).

Figure 2-26 Dr. Ted Hoff of the Intel Corporation is credited with developing the first microprocessor chip, the Intel 4004.

The era of the microprocessor

In 1969, **Dr. Ted Hoff** (Figure 2-26), a young engineer with his Ph.D. from Stanford University, obtained employment with Intel Corporation, an electronics manufacturing firm in northern California. Hoff was given the challenging assignment of designing the microelectronic components for a desk top calculator.

Using then-current design methodologies, a number of chips would be required to perform the various functions of the calculator. Hoff conceived the idea of placing the calculator's arithmetic and logic circuits on a single chip of silicon; resulting effectively, in the creation of the central processing unit of a computer on a single silicon chip.

This central processing unit, developed on a chip smaller than a fingernail and called a **microprocessor**, almost matched the power of the ENIAC with its 18,000 vacuum tubes. Intel's original announcement of this exciting new product proclaimed "a new era of integrated electronics . . . a microprogrammable computer on a chip." This small central processing unit, when combined with other chips to provide for main computer memory and other control functions, formed the basic electronics of a complete computer system — all stored on a printed circuit board less than one foot square.

The development of this microprocessor led to substantial changes in the design and use of computers. Microprocessors began to be used for specialized applications such as controlling machinery or home appliances. Computer terminals, which before had only been able to communicate with a large computer, now became "intelligent," with the ability to process data without the power of a large computer; and most importantly, the microcomputer industry was spawned.

Figure 2–27 Hobbyists who had electronics experience purchased computers and then made modifications to them. Here, the owner of an IMSAI 8080, one of the earliest microcomputers, alters the computer to fit his needs.

The birth of the microcomputer industry (1974 — 1980)

In the July, 1974, issue of a magazine called *Radio-Electronics*, an article appeared describing the technique for constructing a personal computer built around a microprocessor. This article is considered by many to have launched an industry that would revolutionize the way computers were used in our daily lives and in business.

Shortly thereafter, in January, 1975, a small company in Albuquerque, New Mexico, called MITS announced the availability of a $500.00 kit which could be used to build a "microcomputer." The computer was based upon the Intel 8080 microprocessor which had been introduced in 1974. Toggle switches on the front panel of the processor unit were used to load programs into main memory. Audio cassette recorders were adapted as a form of auxiliary storage. Input devices were paper tape readers and teletypewriter units. Television sets were adapted for use as output units to display processing results.

Other companies followed MITS and developed computer kits. People interested in electronics and computers as a hobby ordered thousands of these kits. Computer clubs sprang up in many cities, as people with a common interest shared information about assembling the computers, programming them, and using them. One of the earliest and most active computer clubs was the Homebrew Computer Club based in northern California. It was from this area of the country that the next major excitement took place in the microcomputer industry.

The microcomputer

In 1976, **Steve Jobs** worked for Atari and **Steve Wozniak** worked for Hewlett-

Packard. They both were also members of the Homebrew Computer Club. After Hewlett-Packard rejected a single-board computer they had designed, Jobs and Wozniak showed their computer to members of the Homebrew Computer Club, who were excited about the computer and wanted to buy one. A local computer store ordered fifty of them, but wanted them assembled. Borrowing money, Jobs and Wozniak assembled the first fifty computers in Wozniak's parents' garage. They called the computer Apple I. Then, realizing they had a product that might be marketable, they organized a company called Apple Computer, Inc., modified their computer slightly, and in May, 1977, delivered their first **Apple II** computer.

In July, 1977, at the National Computer Conference in Dallas, Texas, Commodore, Ltd. startled the computing world by announcing a fully assembled microcomputer in a single housing called the **Personal Electronic Transactor (PET).** The machine consisted of a keyboard, processor unit, CRT, and built-in cassette tape recorder for $595.00 (Figure 2–28). The programming language, BASIC, was built into the system. Thus, for less than $600.00, a fully programmable, powerful computer system was now available for home or personal use. Later in 1977, Radio Shack Corporation announced the TRS-80 computer as well. At the end of 1977, then, Apple, Commodore, and Radio Shack had complete computers on the market.

Figure 2–28 The PET computer from Commodore, Ltd. was the first microcomputer completely contained in a single unit. It featured a CRT screen, keyboard, processor unit with 4,000 positions of main memory, and a built-in tape cassette unit. It cost $595.00 when announced in 1977.

Other companies began to develop computers also. Hundreds of thousands of these new computers were sold over the next several years. With these sales came new developments in microcomputer hardware, including color CRT monitors, miniature floppy disk drives, and small printers especially designed for use with microcomputers. Computer retail stores devoted to selling these new devices began to appear. Numerous magazines devoted to the microcomputer industry were published. In short, the microcomputer industry was on its way.

Microcomputer software

The early software for microcomputers centered primarily around games. Through the use of color graphics and specially designed input devices such as joysticks, computers became sophisticated game machines.

More serious software soon began to appear, however. Word processing software offered microcomputer users the ability to write and modify letters, memos, and other text-oriented documents. **Computer-assisted instruction (CAI)** programs, mostly consisting of drill-and-practice applications, became available.

The major piece of software of the time, however, came from a programmer who worked previously on word processing systems for DEC and who had returned to Harvard Business School for an advanced degree. **Dan Bricklin** was given an assignment at Harvard to perform some complex business analysis requiring considerable calculations. The only tools he had were a calculator and a pencil. Bricklin asked what if numbers and values could be manipulated in the same manner as text is in word processing applications.

Armed with his new idea, Bricklin, together with his friend **Bob Frankston,** formed a company called Software Arts. There, they implemented the first electronic spreadsheet program, **VisiCalc**. When VisiCalc was released, it ran only on the

Apple II computer. The Apple II, which up until this time in 1979 had attracted almost no interest from the business community, all of a sudden became an important business tool because of VisiCalc. Business people, particularly accountants and others in the financial world, were quick to recognize that VisiCalc could save them many hours and days of calculations, quickly paying for both the computer and the software.

Most people consider VisiCalc to be the single most important reason that microcomputers gained acceptance in the world of business. Once business people saw that the microcomputer could be used for more than playing games, they quickly moved to place microcomputers in their businesses. During this time, a good percentage of the microcomputers being sold to business were Apple II's.

The growing acceptance of the personal computer

By 1981 it was apparent that the microcomputer, now called by some the personal computer, was to have great impact in the home, school, small businesses, and large corporations. One organization which watched this phenomenon with interest was IBM. In August, 1981, after having analyzed the market and attempting to determine the type of personal computer required particularly for business, IBM announced the IBM Personal Computer. While many people were not overly impressed with the IBM PC when it was announced, IBM quickly proved the doubters wrong, as it garnered the largest share of the personal computer market and a majority of the personal computers found in business. With IBM's announcement, the microcomputer took its place as an important tool for use in solving the information processing needs of both large and small businesses.

Other major manufacturers of minicomputers and mainframes made announcements similar to that of IBM in the ensuing year. DEC, Wang, NCR, Honeywell, and others all announced personal computers. The impact of these new machines was evident in the market. In 1981, it is estimated that 313,000 microcomputers were sold. In 1982, the total number of microcomputers sold jumped to 3,275,000 machines.

Today, many managers and business executives have access to personal computers. They use them for word processing, electronic spreadsheet processing, graphic software, and a myriad of other applications. It is predicted that within a very few years, every manager and office worker will be using a personal computer to aid in improving their productivity.

What is the future?

Personal computers have made computing available to virtually everyone. Continual advances in both microelectronic technology and software developed for personal computers will undoubtedly make significant contributions to the hardware available in the future.

Significant advances will be made in computer software as well. The application programs currently available on personal computers will be enhanced and improved. Applications which are not even considered at this time, such as spreadsheet programs just a few years ago, will appear and be welcomed by the computer-using public.

Large computers will continue to be made bigger and faster. It is recognized that much more powerful hardware is required for such applications as weather forecasting and simulation applications. Reports are issued stating new technologies may increase the speeds of computers a thousand times. These technologies are still in the laboratory but may one day find their way into new computers.

Many throughout the world are working on what is termed the fifth generation of computers. These machines combine hardware and software to produce machines with near human intelligence. According to a report issued by the Institute of New Generation Computer Technology (ICOT) in Japan, ICOT plans to develop ''knowledge information processing based on innovative inference functions and technologies that meet the needs anticipated in the 1990's, including intelligent interaction between man and machine and inference using knowledge bases.''

Exotic, intelligent computers are not the only future developments which will have significant impact. Because of the widespread availability and use of computers, society as a whole will have to learn to cope with computers. This means that people will learn to use computers in their homes and in their businesses (Figure 2–29). Students will almost surely have to access computers. This increased reliance on computers presents a very difficult social problem, however. While many people will be able to afford computers, others will not. Therefore, the question arises concerning whether the computer will increase the distance between the ''haves'' and the ''have nots.'' It is an issue which must be solved.

The computer industry will be fast changing during the years to come. Some companies which have experienced substantial success will become bankrupt while others not yet even formed will become the stars of the future.

Truly, the future world of computers offers hope, challenge, and excitement. As Dr. Grace Hopper recently said, ''We've been through the preliminaries of the computer industry and we now have the Model T. It's a bright beginning for what will be the largest industry in the U. S. because computers will be in everything.''

Figure 2–29 In the future, computers will be found in many homes for such tasks as home security, communications, entertainment, and education.

The Application Of Computers in Modern Society

The computer is used in virtually all areas of business and science. The following pages illustrate a few of the many applications where computers play a vital role in our modern society.

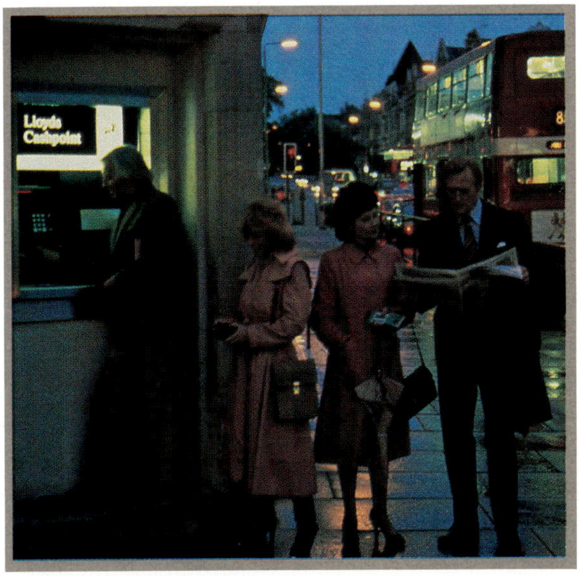

Figure 2–30 Most citizens use automatic bank teller machines as an everyday part of their lives, whereas just a few years ago such a service from banks was impossible.

Figure 2–31 Many high schools now require at least one course in computers as a requirement for graduation. In addition, many high schools and colleges offer classes in computer programming and classes designed to teach students how to use the computer as a tool for problem solving. The personal computer has made computing power available to schools at every level.

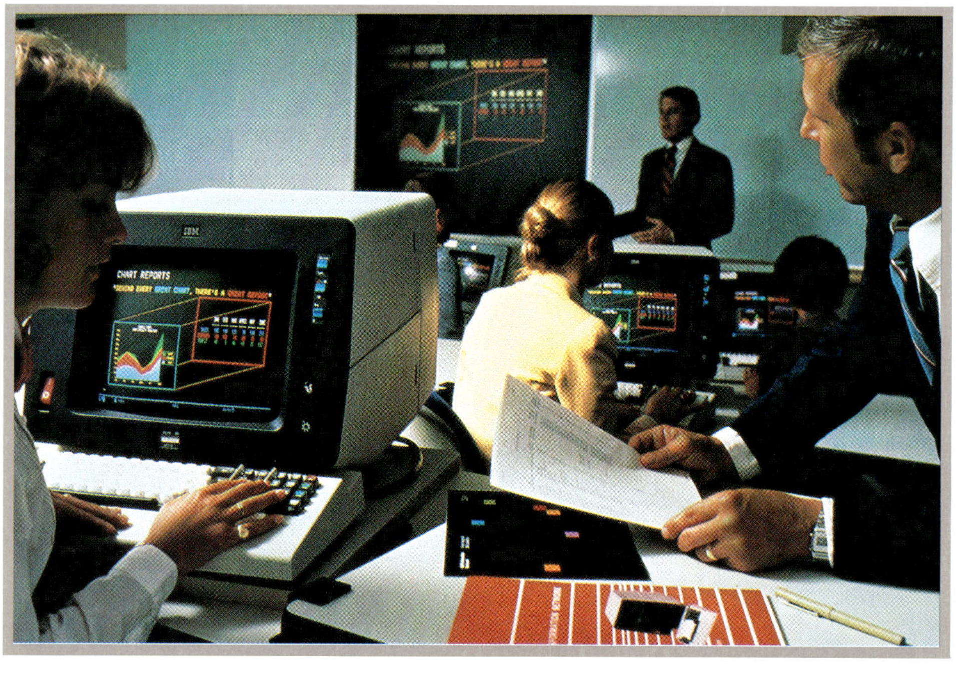

Figure 2–32 It is predicted that within a few years, more than 20 million computers will be in use in business. This has resulted in a tremendous need for the education of individuals already employed. Most large companies have in-house training programs to teach employees how to use computers. Many companies, such as IBM in this picture, also offer classes to their clients.

Figure 2–33 Computers are often used in elementary schools for Computer Assisted Instruction (CAI). When using CAI, problems (for example, arithmetic problems) are displayed on the screen of the terminal. The student is required to respond with an answer. A correct answer will result in a new question. An incorrect answer will result in a message indicating the wrong answer, followed by further instruction. After a session, the computer can display the number of correct and incorrect answers, determine if the student should continue with the next lesson, and store the results for teacher review.

Reading, Writing, and Computer Literacy

For many years the three R's of "reading, 'riting, and 'rithmetic" were considered the foundation of the education needed to function in society. Today, with millions of computers being used in the home and in all occupational areas, an educated person must also be computer literate.

Computer literacy can be defined as the ability to recognize an application in which the use of a computer is appropriate and the ability to use the computer for that application. Computer literacy is necessary in order for a person to function and be successful in our high technology society.

Today, education for computer literacy can begin at a very young age and continue for the rest of a person's life. Learning about computers and how to use them has become a high priority for many people in the world.

Office Automation

An office has been defined as any location within a business or governmental agency where data is acquired, processed, filed, or distributed. Today in this information age, more than 50 million people work in offices. Their job duties involve processing data and storing and distributing information.

Historically, the tools of office workers have been pencils and pens, paper, typewriters, dictating machines, and calculators. Many of these office tools, some of which have been utilized for more than 100 years, are no longer in use because businesses have entered the age of office automation. **Office automation** refers to an integrated collection of electronic devices which are used to increase office productivity. These devices include word processing systems, personal computers, computer terminals attached to large computers, and electronic communication systems, all of which are useful in acquiring, processing, storing, and communicating information.

Most office automation systems provide: 1) Word processing capabilities; 2) Provision for electronically filing data on auxiliary storage devices such as disk; 3) The ability to rapidly retrieve data stored electronically; 4) Provision for electronic communication of data and information through interconnected computers; 5) Administrative and decision support systems through access to electronic spreadsheet and graphics software; 6) Sophisticated telephone systems allowing storage and retrieval of the spoken word.

The computer is an integral part of the modern office environment. Understanding how to use computer systems in the processing, storing, accessing, and communication of information is an important part of the job skills for office employees.

Figure 2-34 Computers are utilized in this modern office to perform such tasks as letter writing, billing, order entry, credit checking, and filing and retrieval of other information.

Figure 2-35 The Cincinnati Milacron robots shown on this automotive assembly line can track the moving car bodies, welding them in the correct places when necessary. Therefore, this assembly line need not be stopped.

A New Age in Manufacturing

Computer-aided design and computer-aided manufacturing systems (CAD/CAM) are widely used in manufacturing industries for both design and manufacturing tasks. Engineers, architects, and other designers use the computer to assist in designing products by generating drawings on a graphic display screen and then manipulating that drawing until a final design is obtained. Changing a design, which once required hundreds of engineering and drafting hours, now can be done in a second.

Computers are also used to control robots. Industrial **robots** are machines, operating under the control of a computer and related software, that are designed to perform repetitive manufacturing and operational tasks required by a company.

The majority of robots today are used to perform such specific tasks as welding, drilling, and material handling. Robots are ideal for performing repetitive tasks, hour after hour, in a hostile environment, with the last operation being performed using the same precision as the first.

In the illustrations on this page, robots are used for a variety of tasks which either can be performed by a robot more precisely and with more consistency than a human being can perform them, or which are performed in an environment which may endanger the health of a person.

In some companies, the use of robots has created social problems because the robots are performing jobs previously done by people. In many industries, unions, employees, and management are still trying to come to agreement concerning the use of robots.

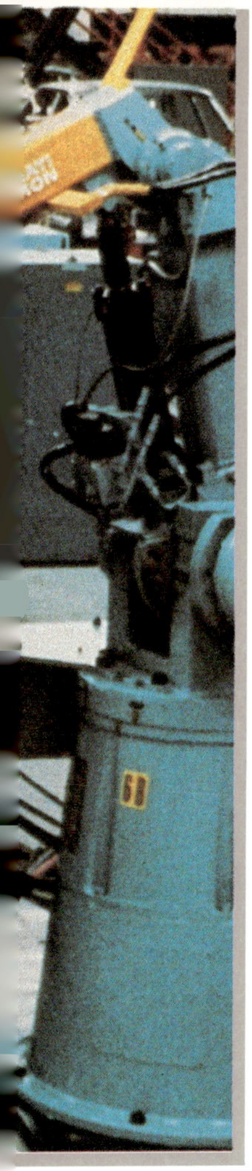

Figure 2–36 The moving robot arm places electronic components on a printed circuit board. Since the board can be moved according to a computer program and the arm can pick up components under computer control, the entire board assembly can take place without human intervention.

Figure 2–37 This robot, called the ARMS-D (Advanced Robot Manufacturing System — Development), made by NEC, is equipped with arms, hands, and optic sensors. It finds its major applications in the precision assembly, adjustment, and inspection of small-sized, solid-state devices.

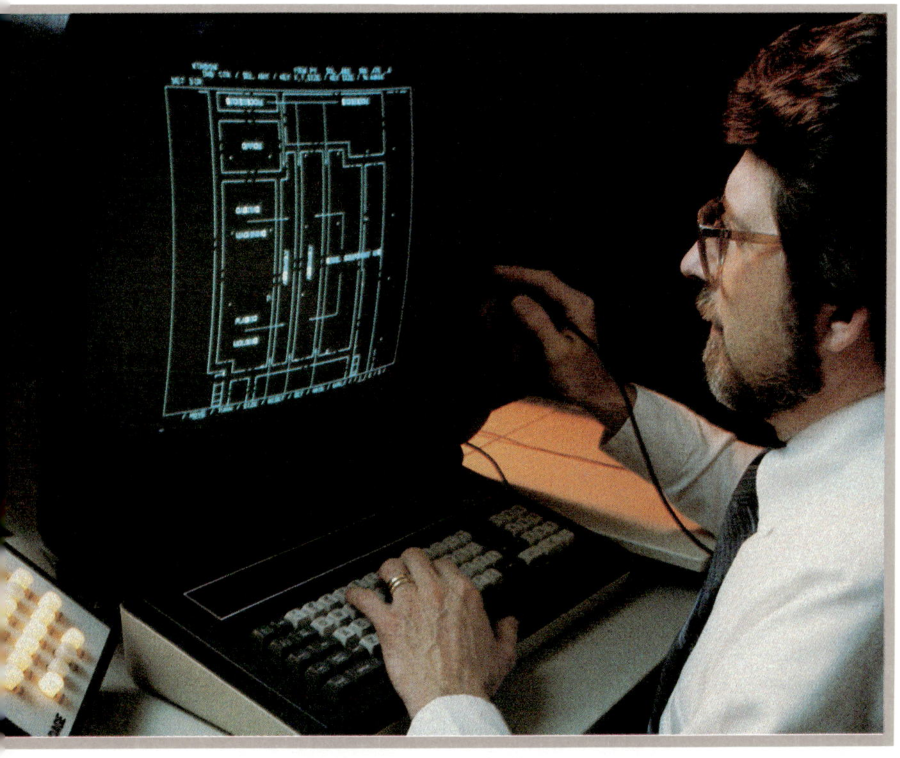

Figure 2–38 Special terminals are used by engineers, architects, and other designers to produce drawings of products they are designing. On the terminal, the user has the options of moving the drawing, turning it, changing its size or perspective, enlarging a portion of it to display more detail, and other options as well. In most cases, hard copy can also be produced.

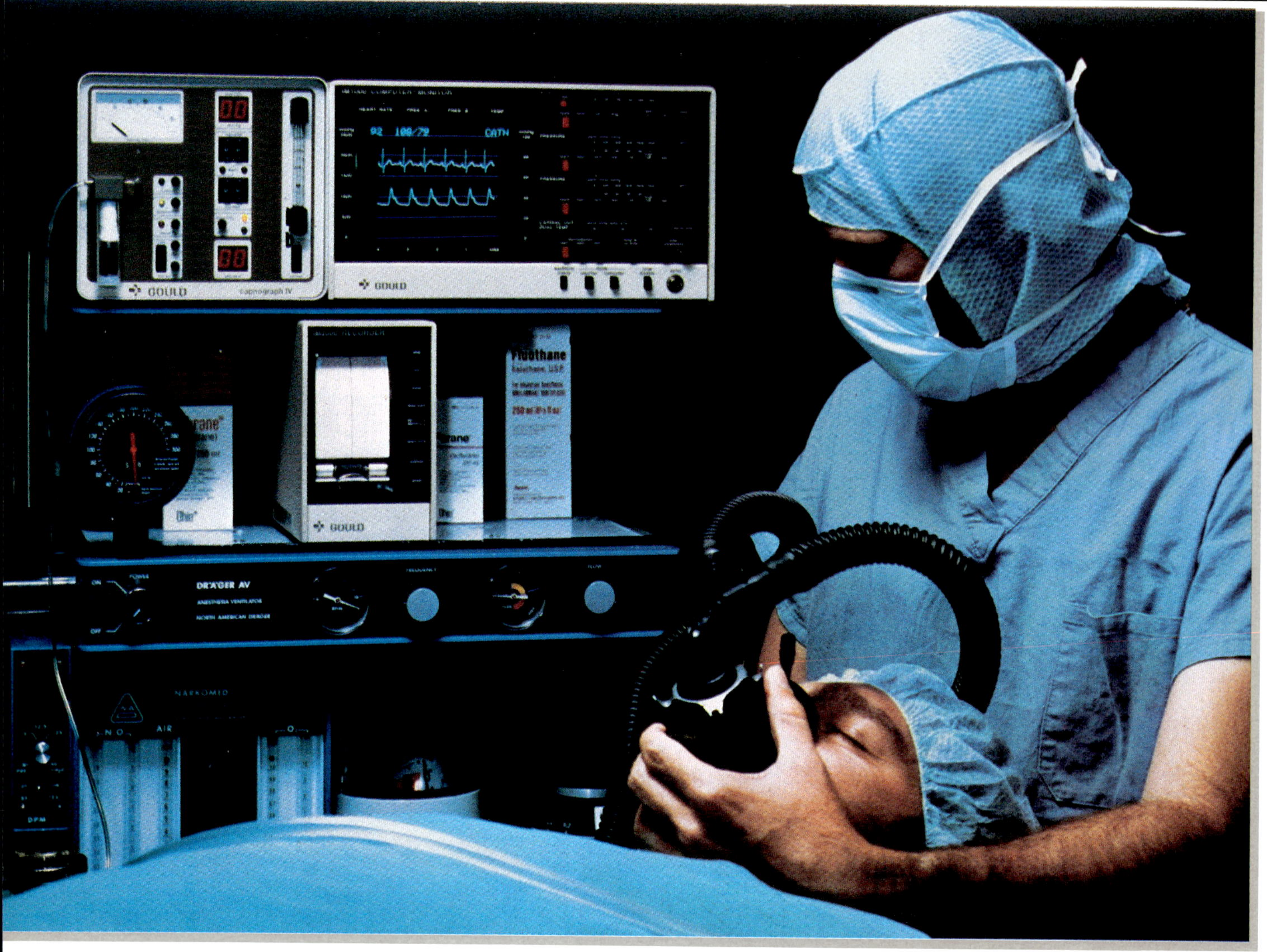

Figure 2–39 The Gould IM1000 computer-monitor shown here provides the anesthesiologist with a continual digital and waveform display of vital signs, including electrocardiogram, heart rate, blood pressure, and temperature. These extensive capabilities illustrate the life-saving uses of computers.

Figure 2–40 Computers are used for many types of scientific experimentation. In this photograph, scientists at Squibb Corporation use the computer to develop a model and then display how molecules interact when new enzyme inhibitors are utilized. Experiments which could take years to produce and analyze can be developed using computer modeling in a shorter period of time with much more precise measurement.

Figure 2–41 The home video terminal illustrated in this picture is used with a videotex home information system. The terminal is linked to computerized data banks providing information ranging from stock market reports and news to theater reviews and advertising. The system can also be used for shopping and banking at home. Videotex will become, in the near future, an important entertainment and information source in the home.

Applications Throughout Society

Computers are used throughout society for a myriad of applications. The uses for computers are expanding at a very rapid rate. Virtually every business, government agency, public agency such as hospitals, and an increasingly greater number of homes all have computers. Indeed, it has been predicted by some experts that by the year 1995, as many as 100 million computers could be in use.

The applications shown on these pages are but a few of the many ways computers are used daily. Computers are, without question, the single-most important technological development of mankind. Their increased use and influence will affect every person in the world.

Figure 2–42 Computer use in law enforcement and fire protection has increased significantly in the past few years. Police officers such as the ones in this picture routinely use computer terminals in their cars to check arrest records, stolen vehicle reports, and to perform other inquiries. The speed of computers and their ability to store large amounts of data allow law enforcement to use them in this manner.

CHAPTER SUMMARY

1. The information processing and computational work done by computers cannot be carried out by hand.
2. Dr. John V. Atanasoff and Clifford Berry designed the first electronic digital computer, called the Atanasoff-Berry-Computer.
3. Dr. John W. Mauchly and J. Presper Eckert, Jr. designed and built the ENIAC, the first large-scale electronic digital computer.
4. ENIAC, put into operation in 1946, was programmed by connecting external wires and setting up to 6,000 switches.
5. Dr. John von Neumann is credited with originating the stored program concept. The first computer to use a stored program was the EDSAC in 1949.
6. UNIVAC I, the first computer to be commercially available, was installed in the Bureau of Census in 1951.
7. The public became aware of computers when the UNIVAC I was used to predict the outcome of the 1952 presidential election with only 5% of the vote counted.
8. IBM, while the leading company in producing and selling electromechanical machines, entered the electronic computer industry when it began to lose business.
9. In the early 1950's, Remington-Rand and IBM emerged as the two leading computer companies. At the end of 1953, 13 companies were manufacturing computers.
10. By the end of 1956, IBM had taken a lead in the computer industry it has yet to relinquish.
11. The first stored program computers were programmed in machine language.
12. Automatic programming referred to writing a program in a notation other than machine language.
13. Symbolic programming languages allowed symbolic notation to represent the operations to be performed by the computer. Dr. Grace Hopper was a leader.
14. In 1957, FORTRAN was announced by IBM. FORTRAN is a high-level programming language which allows the programmer to write a program in mathematical terms. A translator, or compiler, is required to convert a FORTRAN program to machine language.
15. COBOL was released in 1960. It allows programmers to write in an English-like fashion and can be used on machines from different manufacturers.
16. In 1958, transistors became widely used in computers instead of vacuum tubes, ushering in the second generation of computers.
17. By 1958, there were an estimated 2,550 computers installed in the United States. By 1964, over 18,000 had been installed. This growth was largely due to the less costly transistorized computers.
18. The IBM System/360 family of computers, announced in 1964, brought in the third generation of computers. It used solid logic technology, was faster than most previous computers, and could be used for both scientific and business applications.
19. When using batch processing, the data to be processed is gathered together in a group and is processed together as a single job.
20. Dr. John Kemeny developed the Dartmouth Time-Sharing System, on which students could use the BASIC programming language. When using time-sharing, it seems to each user that they have complete control of the computer even though there are many users.
21. Interactive computer processing means that users can enter programs and data and get almost immediate response from the computer.
22. Software companies became an important factor in the late 1960's.
23. The minicomputer, first introduced in 1965, gained importance as numerous companies began producing these machines.
24. The late 1960's found many companies not using their computer systems effectively. One reason was unreliable software.
25. Competition from IBM and the high cost of doing business caused RCA, General Electric, and Xerox to quit the computer business.
26. The fourth generation computers announced in the early 1970's used large scale integration in their electrical circuits.
27. During the 1970's, the transaction-oriented mode of processing data became possible with data

communications, which allows computers to electronically communicate with each other and also allows a user to access a computer from a terminal located at a remote site.

28. Invasion of privacy and computer crime were issues facing the computer industry in the early 1970's. The Privacy Act of 1974 was an attempt to lessen the invasion of privacy for private citizens.

29. Through the use of lithography, very small circuits can be etched on silicon.

30. Dr. Ted Hoff of Intel designed the first microprocessor.

31. The microcomputer was introduced in 1974 as a kit.

32. Steve Jobs and Steve Wozniak designed a small computer they called the Apple I. It was followed by the Apple II, which was the machine they sold.

33. In 1977, Commodore Ltd. announced the PET computer, and Radio Shack announced the TRS-80 Model I computer. These machines had BASIC built into them.

34. Early software for microcomputers included games and CAI.

35. Dan Bricklin and Bob Frankston developed VisiCalc, an electronic spreadsheet program that most people consider the single most important reason microcomputers gained acceptance in the business world.

36. In 1981, IBM announced the Personal Computer.

37. In 1981, an estimated 313,000 microcomputers were sold. In 1982, an estimated 3,275,000 microcomputers were sold.

38. Many managers and business executives have access to a personal computer.

39. The fifth generation of computers will combine hardware and software to produce machines which can produce intelligent interaction between man and machine.

40. Computer literacy can be defined as the ability to recognize an application in which the use of a computer is appropriate, and the ability to use the computer for that application.

41. Computer education can take place at all ages, from very young children to adults.

42. Office automation refers to an integrated collection of electronic devices which are used to increase office productivity.

43. Robots are widely used in manufacturing operations.

44. CAD/CAM systems are speeding up the design process and lead to better products.

45. Computers are used for a myriad of applications throughout society.

KEY TERMS

"ABC" 2.2
Apple II computer 2.21
Dr. John V. Atanasoff 2.1
Atanasoff-Berry-Computer 2.2
Automatic programming 2.8
BASIC (Beginner's All-purpose Symbolic Instruction Code) 2.14
John Backus 2.9
Batch processing 2.13
Dan Bricklin 2.21
COBOL (COmmon Business Oriented Language) 2.10
Compiler 2.9
Computer-assisted instruction (CAI) 2.21
Computer literacy 2.25
Data banks 2.17
EDSAC (Electronic Delay Storage Automatic Calculator) 2.4
EDVAC (Electronic Discrete Variable Automatic Computer) 2.4
ENIAC (Electronic Numerical Integrator and Computer) 2.3
J. Presper Eckert, Jr. 2.2
Electromechanical machines 2.6
FORTRAN (FORmula TRANslation) 2.9
Fourth generation of computers 2.16
Bob Frankston 2.21
Dr. Ted Hoff 2.19
Dr. Grace Hopper 2.8
Interactive 2.14
Steve Jobs 2.20
Dr. John Kemeny 2.14
Large scale integration (LSI) 2.16
Machine language 2.8
Dr. John W. Mauchly 2.2
Microprocessor 2.20
Minicomputer 2.15
Office automation 2.27
Personal Electronic Transactor (PET) 2.21
Photolithography 2.19
Privacy Act of 1974 2.18
Punched cards 2.6
Robots 2.28
Second generation 2.11
Solid logic technology 2.13
System/360 computer system 2.12
Third generation of computers 2.12
Time-sharing 2.14
Transaction-oriented mode 2.17
Transistor 2.10
Translator 2.9
UNIVAC I (UNIVersal Automatic Computer) 2.5
VisiCalc 2.21
Dr. John von Neumann 2.4
Maurice V. Wilkes 2.4
Steve Wozniak 2.20

REVIEW QUESTIONS

1. Explain the significance of the Atanasoff-Berry-Computer.
2. Describe the ENIAC. Who designed the ENIAC, and when did it become operational?
3. Discuss the contributions of Dr. John von Neumann and Dr. Grace Hopper.
4. What are the differences between machine language, a symbolic programming language, and high-level programming languages? Describe the differences between COBOL and FORTRAN.
5. When did second generation computers evolve? Why were they called second generation?
6. Why is the System/360 so important in the history of the computer industry? Explain some of its unique characteristics.
7. What is the difference between batch processing and time-sharing?
8. Why is the emergence of the software industry important?
9. What is meant by unreliable software? What effect did it have in the late 1960's?
10. Discuss the environment which led to some manufacturers leaving the computer industry.
11. What is data communications? What effect does it have on the way data is processed on a computer?
12. What major social problems were faced by the industry in 1970? How were they solved?
13. What did Dr. Ted Hoff invent? What was the effect of his invention?
14. Who are Steve Jobs and Steve Wozniak? Why are they important to the computer industry?
15. What is computer literacy? Where can computer literacy be taught?

CONTROVERSIAL ISSUES

1. Computer literacy is defined in this chapter as, "the ability to recognize an application in which the use of a computer is appropriate, and the ability to use the computer for that application." Some people do not agree with this definition. They say computer literacy is understanding about computers. Others argue that computer literacy is being able to write a program for a computer. What do you think?
2. The Privacy Act of 1974 was intended to regulate what information should be placed in data bases and to allow the private citizen access to information stored about themselves. Some people think this legislation is inadequate and that much more privacy protection is needed. Others think these regulations are adequate. What is your opinion?
3. When Dan Bricklin and Bob Frankston developed VisiCalc, they copyrighted the program to protect their rights. Since the program is purchased on a floppy disk, however, many people merely copy the program onto another floppy disk and use it. Do you think this is ethical? Some software developers place special codes on their floppy disks which do not allow the disks to be copied. Is this the only way they can be really protected? What can be done?

RESEARCH PROJECTS

1. Alvin Toffler in his book, *The Third Wave*, writes about the "electronic cottage," meaning people may return to their homes to do most of their work because of computers. He suggests that "our biggest factories and office towers may, within our lifetimes, stand half empty, reduced to use as ghostly warehouses or converted into living space." Research this book and prepare a report on the electronic cottage.
2. Prepare a report on the 1974 court trial between Sperry Rand and Honeywell where the judge ruled, "Eckert and Mauchly did not themselves invent the electronic digital computer, but instead derived that subject matter from one John V. Atanasoff."
3. Prepare a detailed report on an individual who made a contribution to the history of computing devices.

Chapter Three

Processing Data On a Computer

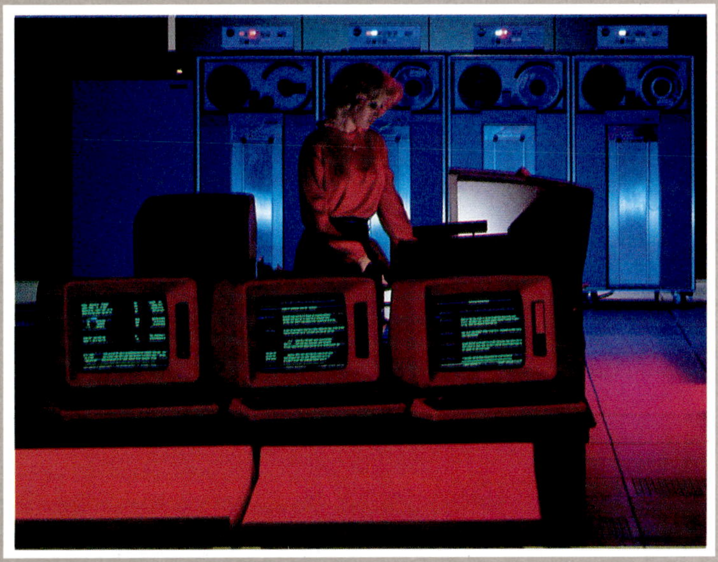

Objectives

- ☐ Explain in detail the information processing cycle, consisting of input, process, output, and storage
- ☐ Specify the role data plays in information processing, the way in which it can be organized, and the important characteristics of data
- ☐ Describe the processing capabilities of a computer, including input operations, arithmetic operations, logical operations, output operations, and storage operations
- ☐ Identify and describe sequential retrieval and random retrieval
- ☐ Identify the need for updating data
- ☐ Describe through the use of examples the three updating operations of adding records, changing records, and deleting records

Processing Data On a Computer

Chapter Three

Computers are applied to the solution of problems in all areas of living. It is important, therefore, to gain an overall understanding of how computers store and process data in those environments where a computer is used to assist in improving the speed and efficiency with which various tasks are done.

To gain this understanding, this chapter will review the information processing cycle on both large and small computers; examine the nature of data, including how it is organized for processing on a computer; and develop a more detailed understanding of the input/output operations, arithmetic operations, logical operations, and storage operations (including updating data). At the conclusion of this chapter, the reader should be able to answer the questions: How does a computer process data, and how is data stored and updated for use on a computer?

Review of the information processing cycle

The **information processing cycle**, as identified in Chapter 1, consists of the following activities: 1) Input; 2) Processing; 3) Output; and 4) Storage. Regardless of the size and type of computer, the information processing cycle is used to produce useful output from a computer.

The activities in the information processing cycle are carried out through the combined use of computer hardware, computer software, and data. The **computer software,** or **programs**, contain instructions which direct the computer hardware to perform those tasks necessary to process the data and produce output.

The diagram in Figure 3-2 on page 3.2 illustrates some of the various hardware units used in conjunction with computer software and data to implement the information processing cycle. **Input units**, it will be recalled, are used to enter data into main computer memory. On microcomputers, the primary input unit is the keyboard. On large computers such as shown in Figure 3-2, a diverse number and type of input devices, such as CRT terminals, tape drives, and disk drives, are used.

The **processor unit** of the computer consists of **main memory** and the **central processing unit**. The function of the input devices is to place data into main memory. The data is read from tape or disk or can be entered directly from a terminal keyboard. In Chapter 1, it was pointed out that data must be stored in main computer memory in order to be processed. It was also noted that the computer program which controls the processing must be stored in main memory.

When the computer program is given control, each instruction in the program is interpreted and executed by the central processing unit. The instructions cause the computer to perform the input, arithmetic, logical, output, and storage operations which can take place on a computer. These operations will be examined in detail later in the chapter.

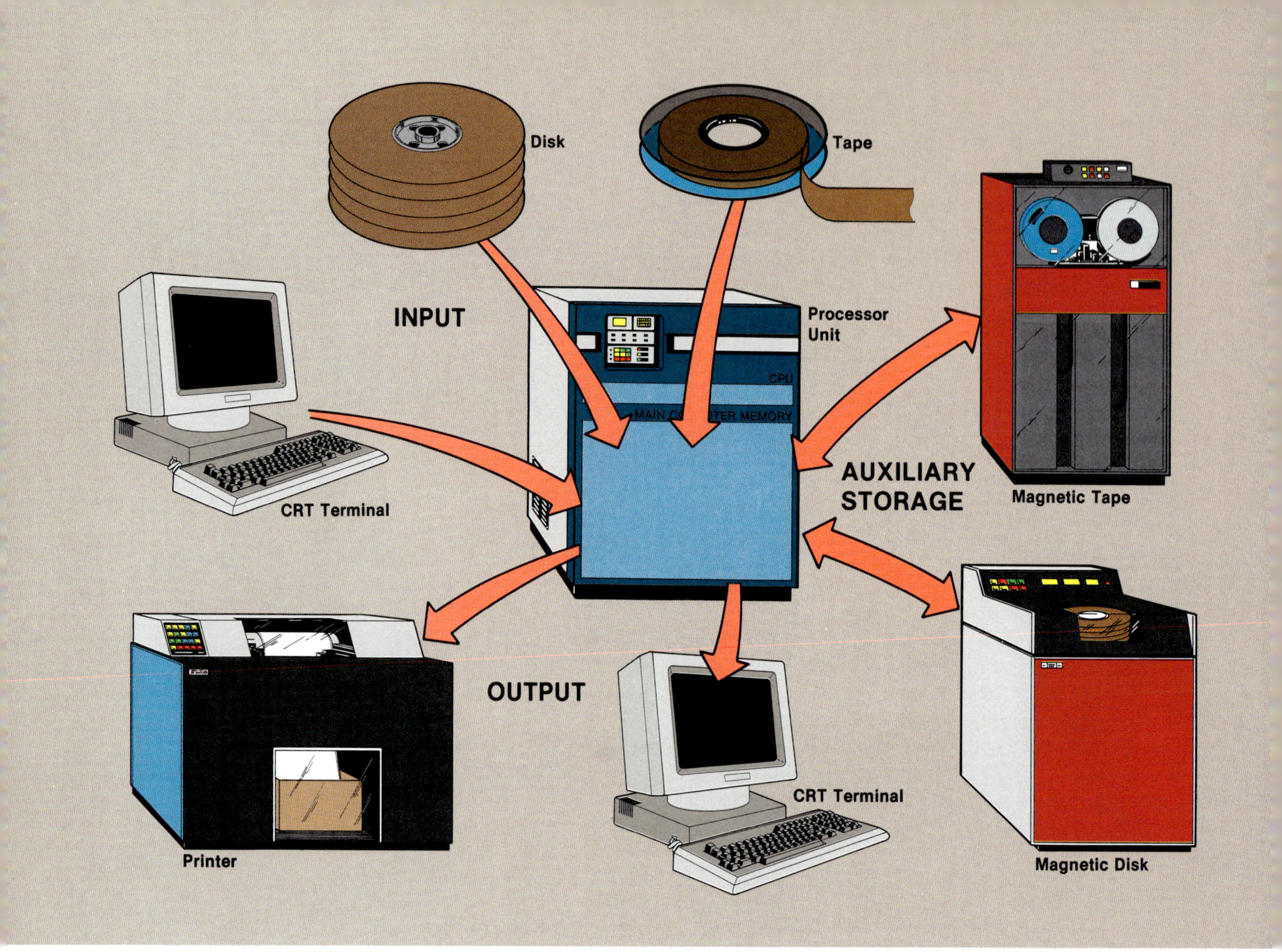

Figure 3–2 A large computer contains input units, the processor unit, output units, and auxiliary storage units. Together, these units implement the information processing cycle — input data into main memory; process the data in main memory under the control of a computer program also stored in memory; after processing, produce output in the appropriate form for use by people; and store the data and program on auxiliary storage for use at a later time.

The primary **output devices** on large computers are printers and CRT screens. The format of a report on a printer or a screen on a CRT terminal is under the control of the program stored in main computer memory. The program will format the data to be printed or displayed and then issue the commands to cause the output.

Auxiliary storage devices commonly used with large computers are magnetic tape and magnetic disk. It should be recalled that auxiliary storage is merely an extension of main computer memory. Ideally, all programs and all data would reside in main memory all the time. They would be immediately accessible at all times. Since, however, the amount of main memory that can be economically available on a computer is limited, programs and data which do not all fit in main memory are stored on auxiliary storage until they are needed, at which time they are loaded into main memory and are used.

It should be noted here that a particular storage medium or device can be used for more than one purpose in the information processing cycle. For example, magnetic tape, as explained in Chapter 1, is used as a storage medium for the input portion of the information processing cycle. Tape can also be used as auxiliary storage. Disk, in a similar manner, is used as an input medium but is also the most important auxiliary storage medium used on a large computer. CRT terminals are also used as both input devices and output devices. Therefore, one must focus on the function being performed in the information processing cycle rather than just the device or storage medium being used.

The information processing cycle is basic to all computers, large or small. It is very important that this cycle be understood, for the remainder of the book depends upon the reader having an understanding and ''feeling'' for the movement of data as it flows through the information processing cycle on a computer.

DATA

Data is found at each step of the information processing cycle — input, process, output, and storage. It is important, therefore, to understand something about data because without data there is no reason for a computer.

Data has been defined as the numbers, words, and phrases which are suitable for processing in some manner on a computer to produce information. For example, in a monthly sales application, the value 01/31, identifying a month and day, is data. In a payroll application, the social security number 332-98-8776 is data. The word RAISE is data. Each of these pieces of data can be referred to as a **data item**, or a **data field**.

Although each data item can be processed in some manner on a computer, most of the time a single data item is not useful or meaningful. A data item is useful only when it is combined with other data items or when a relationship to other data items is established. To illustrate, the month and day 01/31, by itself is not useful. When it is related to monthly sales, however, it becomes very meaningful (Figure 3-3).

In a like manner, the social security number 332-98-8776 becomes a useful piece of information only when it is related to the name of a person and to a paycheck amount (Figure 3-4). Finally, while the word RAISE means little by itself, it takes on significant meaning when it is combined with other data to state, "You have received a RAISE of $100.00."

In summary, then, data items are required for the information processing cycle, but they are not normally very useful until they are combined with other data items or until a relationship is established between data items.

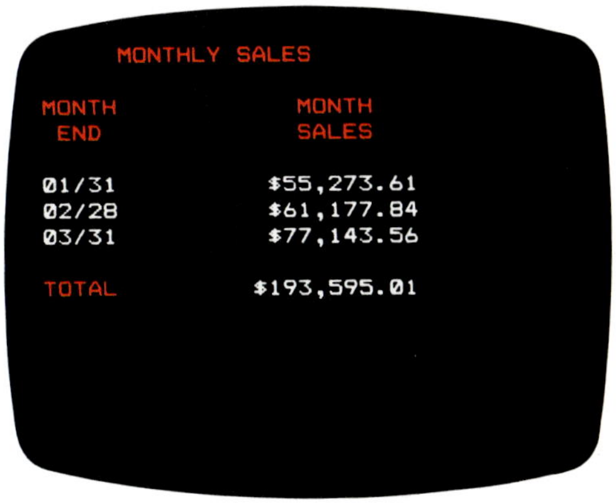

Figure 3-3 The month ending date 01/31, by itself, is not useful. When used on this monthly sales screen, however, it imparts meaning and is useful.

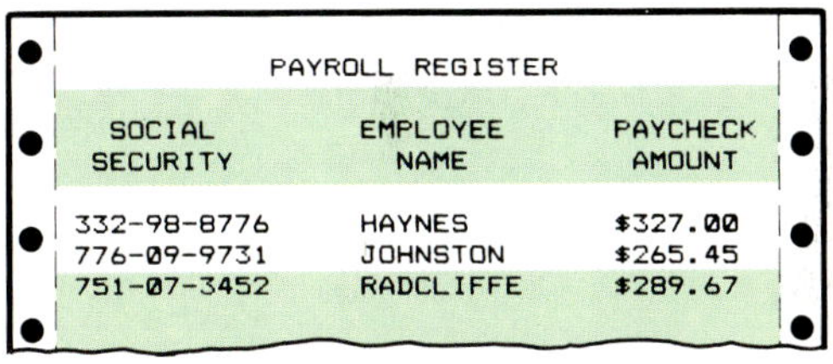

Figure 3-4 The social security number by itself is not a useful data item. When it is combined with the employee name and a paycheck amount, it serves to identify the employee and is very important.

Data organization

When data is processed on a computer using the information processing cycle, it must be organized based upon the application and the data item relationships. Data is often organized as records when processed on a computer.

A **record** is a collection of related data items, or fields. Each record normally corresponds to a specific unit of information. For example, a record which could be used to produce the payroll report in Figure 3-4 is illustrated in Figure 3-5. The fields in the record are the social security number, employee name, and paycheck amount. This is the data used to produce the payroll register report. The first record contains all of the data concerning the employee Haynes. The second record contains all of the data concerning the employee Johnston. Each subsequent record contains all of the data for a given employee. It can be seen how each related data item is grouped together to form a record.

The collection of records shown in Figure 3-5 is called a **file**. A file contains all of the related records for an application. Therefore, the payroll file shown in Figure 3-5 contains all of the records required to produce the payroll register report. Files are stored on some medium, such as magnetic tape or magnetic disk.

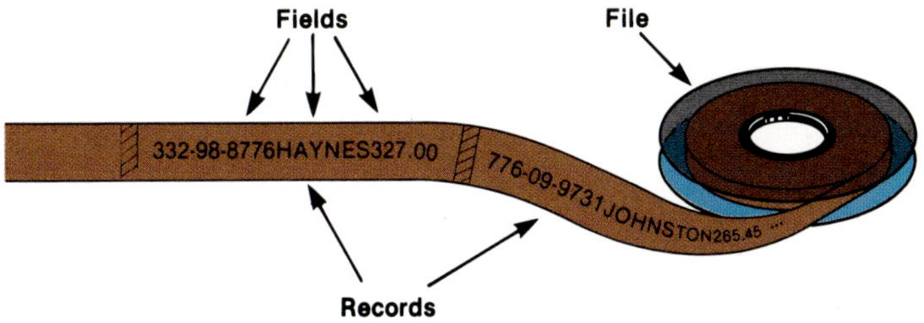

Figure 3-5 This file of payroll records is stored on magnetic tape. Each record contains the social security number field, the employee name field, and the paycheck amount field, which is all of the payroll information for a single employee. The file contains all of the employee records.

Summary of data

Data is the prime ingredient in the information processing cycle. Without data, the computer hardware and computer software have nothing to do. For data to be processed on a computer, data item relationships must be defined based upon the application; and then the data must be organized based upon the data item relationships. Once data is organized, it can be processed on the computer under the control of a computer program.

PROCESSING DATA ON A COMPUTER

Once the data has been defined and the organization of the data has been determined, the data can be placed into main computer memory for processing. The processing operations that can occur within the information processing cycle fall into five major categories: 1) Input operations; 2) Arithmetic operations; 3) Logical operations; 4) Output operations; and 5) Storage operations. Each of these operations is explained in the following paragraphs.

Input operations

Data must be stored in main memory before it can be processed under the control of a computer program. The **input operation** causes data to be stored in main computer memory.

There are many devices that can be used to enter data into main memory, depending upon the size and capabilities of the computer being used. On microcomputers, the primary input device is the keyboard. On larger computers, magnetic tape and magnetic disk are often used. For both large and small computers, specialized devices that can read special bar codes on products, numbers on checks, handwritten characters, and even devices that understand the human voice can be used.

Regardless of the type of input device used, the principle is still the same: the data which is entered from the input device is electronically stored in main computer memory. Once the data is in main computer memory, it can be processed under the control of a computer program.

To illustrate the input operation, the example in Figure 3–6 shows a portion of the input operation required to build a file of employees in a company using a personal computer. The user is to enter the employee's name and the employee's social security number. Part of the processing to be accomplished by the program executing on the computer is to build the employee identification number. The employee identification number consists of the first letter of the employee's last name and the last four digits of the social security number.

The steps involved in entering the data into main computer memory and forming the employee identification number are as follows:

1. A computer program is stored in main memory. The program would normally be loaded into main memory from an auxiliary storage device such as a floppy disk or a hard disk. Under control of the computer program, a message is displayed on the

CRT screen directing the computer user to enter the employee's name. When the computer user types the name on the keyboard of the computer, the name is stored in the Name field in main memory. The location of the Name field in main memory is determined by the computer program.

2. Similarly, the program displays a message requesting that the computer user enter the employee's social security number. As the digits in the social security number are entered, they are stored in a Social Security field in main computer memory that has been defined by the program.

3. After both the name and the social security number have been entered and stored in main computer memory, instructions within the program specify that the first letter of the last name and the last four digits of the social security number are to be moved to the Employee Number field that has been defined by the program. Instructions within the program can cause data to be moved from one location in main memory to another location in main memory.

4. After the employee number has been formed, the program would use it as required to build the file of employees.

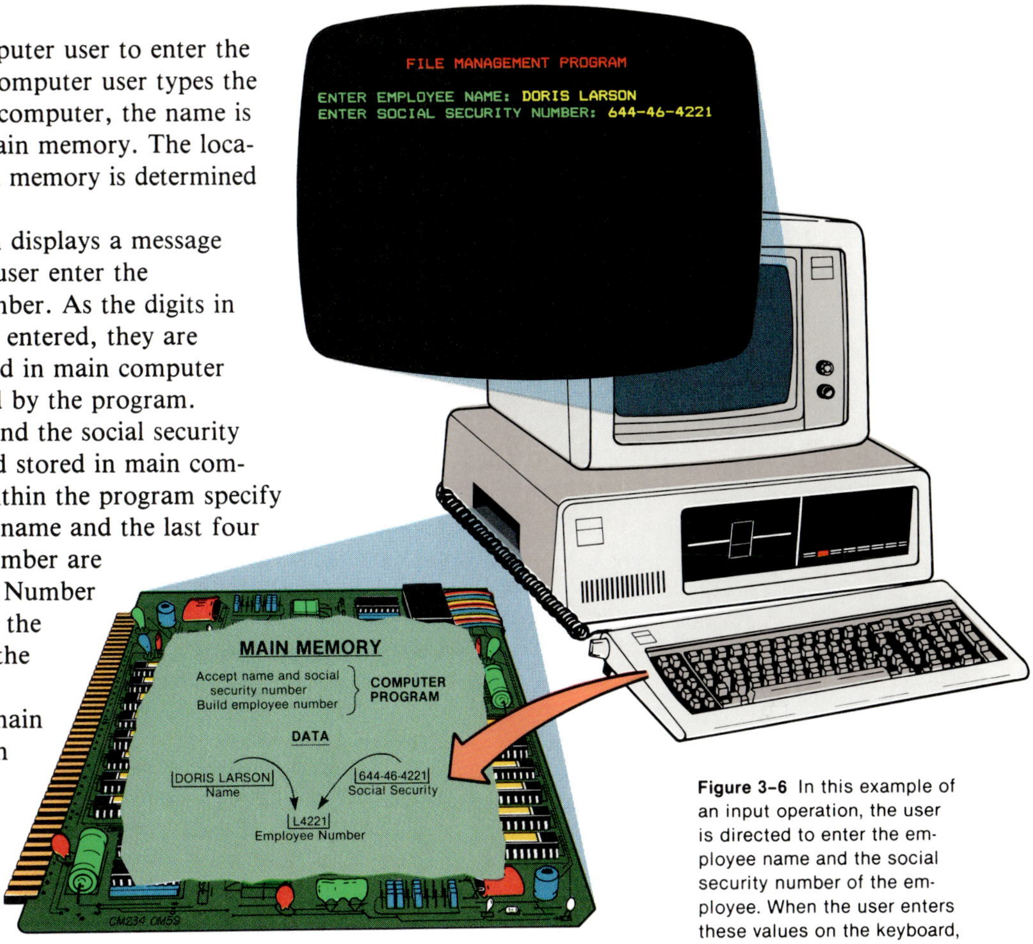

Figure 3-6 In this example of an input operation, the user is directed to enter the employee name and the social security number of the employee. When the user enters these values on the keyboard, they are electronically stored in main computer memory. The program then builds the employee number by moving the first letter of the last name and the last four digits of the social security number to the Employee Number field.

Important facts illustrated by this example are: 1) Processing which occurs on a computer is under the control of a program stored in main computer memory; 2) The data entered from the input device (in this example, a keyboard) is electronically stored in main computer memory. The location, or field, where the input data is stored is determined by the program; 3) Once the data is stored in main computer memory, it can be moved to other locations within main memory under the control of instructions within the program. When data is moved from one location to another in main memory, the data is not destroyed. Rather, it is duplicated. In the example in Figure 3-6, when the first letter of the last name is moved to the Employee Number field, the last name in the Name field is not affected. Similarly, when the last four digits of the social security number are moved to the Employee Number field, the social security number is not affected. Thus, when data is "moved" from one location to another in main memory, it in fact is duplicated.

The input operation is quite important, since data must first be entered into main computer memory before it can be processed.

Arithmetic operations

In many applications of both a business and scientific nature, arithmetic operations such as addition, subtraction, multiplication, and division are performed on data stored in main memory. Thousands and even millions of arithmetic operations

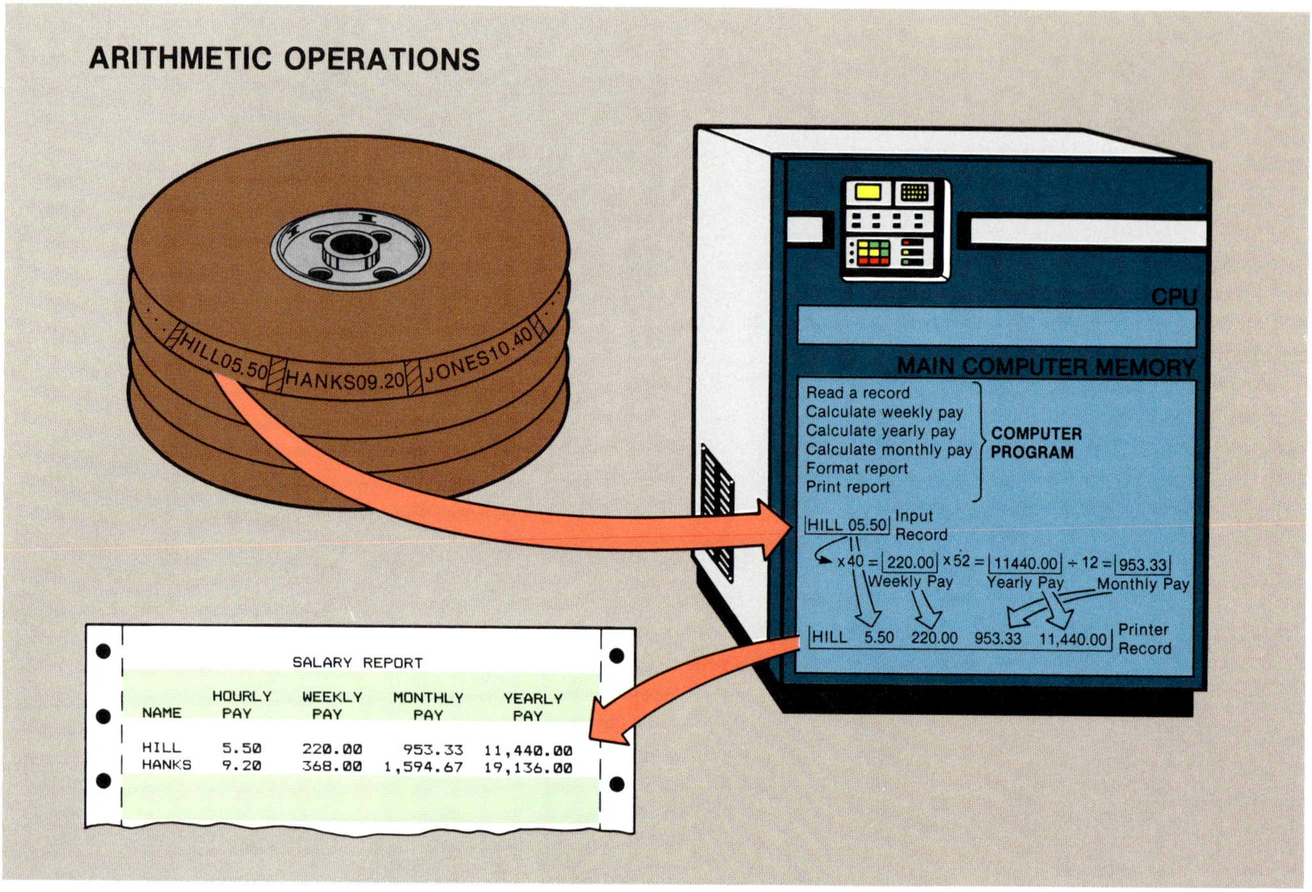

Figure 3-7 In this example, an input record containing an employee name and hourly pay rate is read into main memory. Under program control, the weekly pay, yearly pay, and monthly pay are then calculated and are printed on the salary report. The results of the arithmetic operations are used in subsequent operations and are also printed on the report.

can be performed in one second on many computers. The ability to perform **arithmetic operations** rapidly and accurately is an important characteristic of all computers.

To illustrate the arithmetic capabilities of the computer, an application is developed in Figure 3-7 to determine the weekly, monthly, and yearly pay of an individual based upon the hourly pay of the individual. The operations to be performed in this application must take place under the control of instructions in the computer program. The program must be stored in main computer memory.

After the program is loaded into main memory, the instructions within the program are executed. The first instruction is to read a record from the disk into main memory. The record contains the employee name and the hourly pay rate for that employee. These two data items, the name and the hourly pay, are contained in each record. Each record in the file stored on disk relates to a single employee.

When the record is read into main memory, the instructions in the program direct that the weekly pay, yearly pay, and monthly pay are to be calculated. The weekly pay is determined by multiplying the hourly rate times 40 hours. The yearly rate is obtained by multiplying the weekly rate by 52 weeks. The monthly pay is calculated by dividing the yearly pay by 12. Note that when the yearly and monthly pay are calculated, answers from previous calculations are used. Any numeric data stored in main computer memory, including results of previous calculations, can be used in arithmetic operations.

After the calculations are completed, an instruction in the program specifies that the report is to be formatted and then printed on the printer. Thus, the results of the calculations are moved to the area in memory where the printer record is to be built. The location of this area is defined within the program. After the printer record is built, the program issues the command to print the record on the printer.

In the drawing in Figure 3-7, the first record in the file for the employee HILL has been processed. There are subsequent records in the file for HANKS, JONES, and other employees. The same operations which were performed to calculate the weekly, yearly, and monthly pay for HILL are required for each subsequent employee. The instructions in the program will, therefore, be repeated for each employee record; that is, the instructions Read a Record, Calculate Weekly Pay, Calculate Yearly Pay, Calculate Monthly Pay, Format Report, and Print Report will be repeated for each record so long as there are more records in the file to read. This process of repeating instructions in a program is called **looping** and is very important because it allows a single set of instructions in a program to process many thousands of records.

Important facts illustrated by this example are: 1) The program stored in main computer memory can perform arithmetic operations on numeric data; 2) Answers derived from arithmetic operations can be used in other calculations and can also be used as output from a program; 3) One set of instructions can be repeated any number of times. This process, called looping, allows many records to be processed by one set of program instructions.

Logical operations

The **logical operations** performed on a computer are based upon the ability of a computer, under the control of a program, to compare data stored in main computer memory. All computers have instructions which compare numbers, letters of the alphabet, and special characters. Based upon the results of the comparison, alternative processing can be performed. It is this logical ability of computers that allows them to play games such as chess; to perform medical diagnoses; to make hotel reservations; and to perform any task which is based upon comparing data.

Three types of **comparing operations** are commonly performed by programs directing the processing of a computer. These comparing operations are:

1. Comparing to determine if two values are equal.
2. Comparing to determine if one value is greater than another value.
3. Comparing to determine if one value is less than another value.

Each of these comparing operations is explained in the following paragraphs.

Comparing — equal condition

Comparing to determine if two values stored in main memory are equal is an important capability of a computer. To illustrate this, the example in Figure 3-8 shows a program whose function is to create a grade report. In order to make this report, an input record containing the student's name and grade point average is read. The grade point average is then compared to 4.0. If the grade point average is equal to 4.0, the message "Honor Student" is printed on the report. If the grade point average is not equal to 4.0, the message is not printed on the report.

Figure 3-8 The grade point average in the input record is compared to a constant defined in main memory by the program to determine if the values are equal. If so, a message "Honor Student" is printed on the report, together with the student's name and grade point average. If the values are not equal, the message is not printed.

When comparing two values in main computer memory, the program will specify the processing to be accomplished when the condition tested is true and the processing to be done when the condition tested is not true. In this example, when the condition is true, that is, when the g.p.a. is equal to 4.0, the message is printed on the report together with the student name and the g.p.a. When the condition is not true (the g.p.a. is not equal to 4.0), the message is not printed. Note that when comparing for an equal condition, the program essentially compares for an unequal condition as well.

Important facts illustrated by this example are: 1) A computer program can contain instructions to compare data stored in main computer memory and can perform alternative operations based upon the results of the comparison; 2) Comparing data to determine if one value is equal to another value is a common occurrence in computer processing.

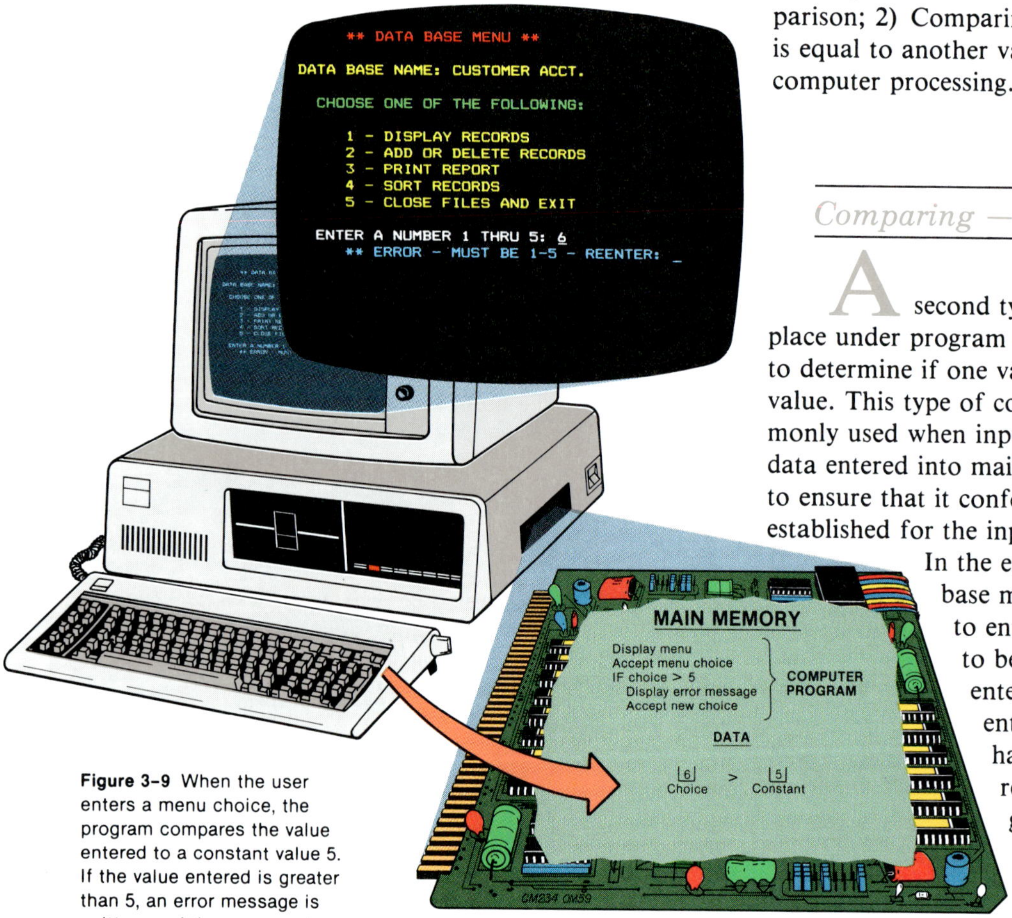

Figure 3-9 When the user enters a menu choice, the program compares the value entered to a constant value 5. If the value entered is greater than 5, an error message is written, and the user must reenter the choice. In this example, the user entered the value 6. Since 6 is greater than 5, the program displayed an error message, and the user was asked to reenter the choice.

Comparing — greater than condition

A second type of comparing that can take place under program control is a comparing operation to determine if one value is greater than another value. This type of comparison operation is commonly used when input data is edited; that is, when data entered into main computer memory is checked to ensure that it conforms to the specifications established for the input data.

In the example in Figure 3-9, a data base menu is displayed, and the user is to enter a choice of which function is to be performed. The user should enter a value 1 - 5. If the value entered is greater than 5, an error has been made, and the user must reenter the menu choice. The program stored in main memory first displays the menu. It then accepts the menu choice from the user. The value entered by the user is then compared to a constant value 5 stored in main memory by the program. If the choice entered by the user is greater than the constant 5, the program displays the message, "** Error — Must be 1 - 5 — Reenter:" and accepts the new user choice. If the value is not greater than 5, the program will continue on and execute the processing specified by the user's choice. In Figure 3-9, the user entered the value 6, so the message to reenter the data was displayed.

In this example, as in the previous one, the comparing operation is performed by the program stored in main computer memory. The alternative processing to be performed is specified by the requirements of the application. It is important to note here that when the program is written by a programmer, the alternative processing to be performed based upon the comparisons must be specified and must always be the same; that is, if a given condition is tested by a comparison of data stored in main memory, the processing to be performed when the condition is true must always be the same. Likewise, the processing to be accomplished when the condition tested is not true must always be the same. If the exact processing which must take place both when the condition is true and when the condition is not true cannot be specified, then the application is not a candidate for implementation on a computer.

Figure 3-10 The value entered by the user is compared to the value 1 to determine if it is less than 1. If so, an error message is displayed on the screen. Here, the user entered the value 0, so the error message was displayed.

Comparing — less than condition

The third type of comparison that is commonly performed on a computer is to determine if one value is less than another value. To illustrate this, the example in Figure 3-9 will be continued in Figure 3-10 to check if the menu choice entered by the user is less than 1. If so, the user has entered an invalid value. The program will display an error message asking the user to reenter the choice and then will accept the new choice. If the value entered by the user is not less than 1, the program will continue with its processing.

As with the previous examples, the exact processing to be accomplished when the condition tested is true and when the condition is not true must be specified. Under program control, the data in main memory is compared and the correct processing is performed.

Output operations

The purpose of entering data into main computer memory and processing it in some manner such as performing arithmetic operations and comparing data is to produce output. **Output** is produced by transferring data stored in main computer memory to a medium or device which can be used by people. Commonly used for output are the printed report and the CRT screen (Figure 3-11).

Figure 3-11 The printed report and the CRT screen are two commonly used ways to present output from a computer.

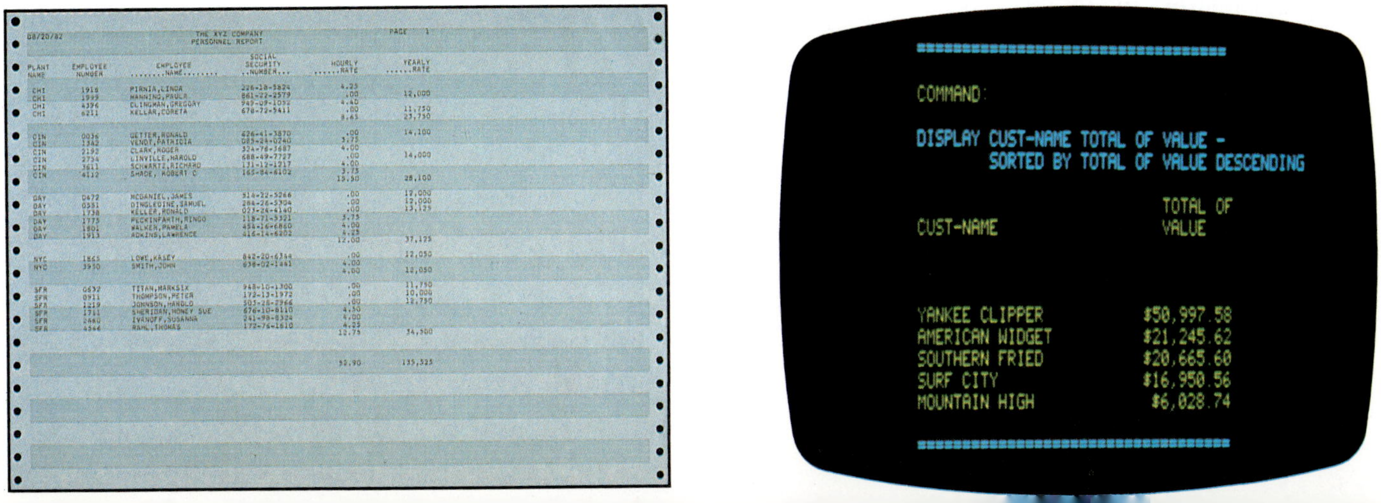

Output produced from computer processing is dependent upon the application. The use of a CRT screen, printed report, or even other types of computer output will depend upon the use to which the output is being put, the logistics of delivering the output to the user, the speed with which output delivery must take place, whether the output is to be permanently kept or is used only at the moment by the user, and other factors as well. Whenever an application is considered for implementation on a computer, the format of the output and the manner in which it will be presented must be defined. If this cannot take place, then the application is not a good candidate for implementation on a computer.

Storage operations

When data is entered into main computer memory as input to a computer program, it, together with any other data generated as a result of processing the input data (for example, results of arithmetic operations) will often be used subsequently in the same or other programs. Therefore, the data must be saved. As has been noted, ideally all data is stored in main computer memory where it can be accessed rapidly by any program needing it. When large numbers of characters must be stored, however, the use of main computer memory becomes too expensive. Therefore, a less expensive means of storing data is used — magnetic storage of data on either magnetic tape or magnetic disk. This storage is called **auxiliary storage**.

A major difference between auxiliary storage and main computer memory is that access to data stored on auxiliary storage is considerably slower than access to data stored in main computer memory. In addition, the data must be organized on auxiliary storage so that it can be stored and retrieved, whereas in main computer memory the data can be retrieved directly from a location in memory.

Data is retrieved in two major ways from auxiliary storage: 1) Sequentially, in the same sequence as the data is stored on auxiliary storage; 2) Randomly, based upon a value in the data itself. Each of these methods will be explained in the following paragraphs.

Sequential storage and retrieval

When data is stored and retrieved sequentially, each record is stored on the tape or disk one after the other, and the data is retrieved in the same sequence as it is stored. For example, in Figure 3–12, the file contains student records stored in sequence by social security number. The data in the file is retrieved one record after another and processed in the same sequence as it is stored in the file. In most cases, when **sequential retrieval** is used, the data is stored in some defined sequence based upon a value in the record (called a **key**), such as the social security number in this example.

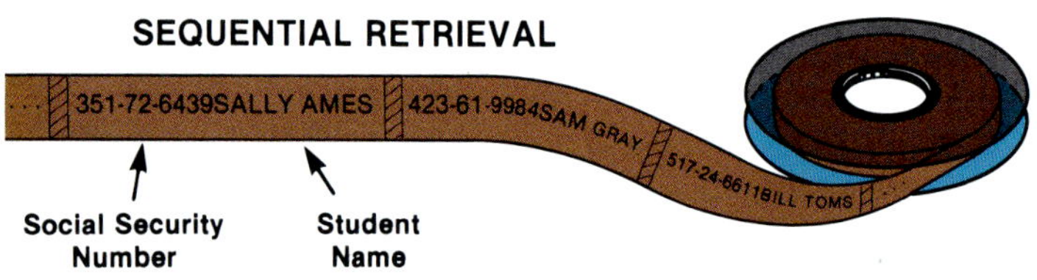

Figure 3–12 The student records in this example are stored sequentially and will be retrieved sequentially. Before reading the third record, the first two records must be read. This is a major disadvantage of sequential retrieval.

Sequential retrieval has a major disadvantage — since records are retrieved one after another in the same sequence as they are stored, the only way to retrieve the third record is to read the two preceding records first. Therefore, in Figure 3–12, if the application required the record for Bill Toms to be retrieved, the program would have to read the record for Sally Ames and the record for Sam Gray before it could retrieve the Bill Toms record. Because of this, sequential retrieval is never used when fast access to a record is required. Instead, sequential retrieval is used when records are processed one after another, such as when creating printed reports.

Random retrieval

Data stored on magnetic disk can be randomly retrieved, which means records can be retrieved regardless of the order in which they are physically stored. When records are stored on tape, they can only be sequentially retrieved. **Random retrieval** can be used when fast access to a record is required.

In most cases, records are randomly retrieved based upon a value within the record itself. To illustrate this, in Figure 3–13 records containing an account number, name of the customer, and the account balance are stored on disk. When a customer with account number 77-8972 wants to know the balance in their account, the application requires that the program be able to immediately retrieve the data. Sequential retrieval, therefore, would not work because all of the records prior to account 77-8972 would have to be read; and there may be thousands of accounts stored on the disk before account number 77-8972. Random retrieval, which allows fast access to any record, is required.

In the example in Figure 3–13, a request is made on the CRT terminal for the balance in account number 77-8972. The program stored in main computer memory will access the record stored on disk based upon the account number. The record associated with the account number will be directly retrieved and brought into main memory. From there the program can display the balance on the CRT screen. This ability to randomly access records based upon a value in the record is very important. In this example, the record is accessed based upon the account number stored in the record.

Another important aspect of the example in Figure 3–13 is that the sequence in which records are stored is not important when randomly retrieving data. The records in this example are not in sequence by account number, yet they can be retrieved based upon the account number. It is also possible that these records could be retrieved

Figure 3–13 The steps in this example are: 1) The operator enters an account number which is stored in main memory under program control; 2) Based upon the account number, called the record key because it identifies the record, the program randomly retrieves a record from the data stored on disk; 3) The record is retrieved and stored in main memory; 4) The program displays on the CRT screen the account balance from the account record. These steps are the basic steps always used when a record is randomly retrieved.

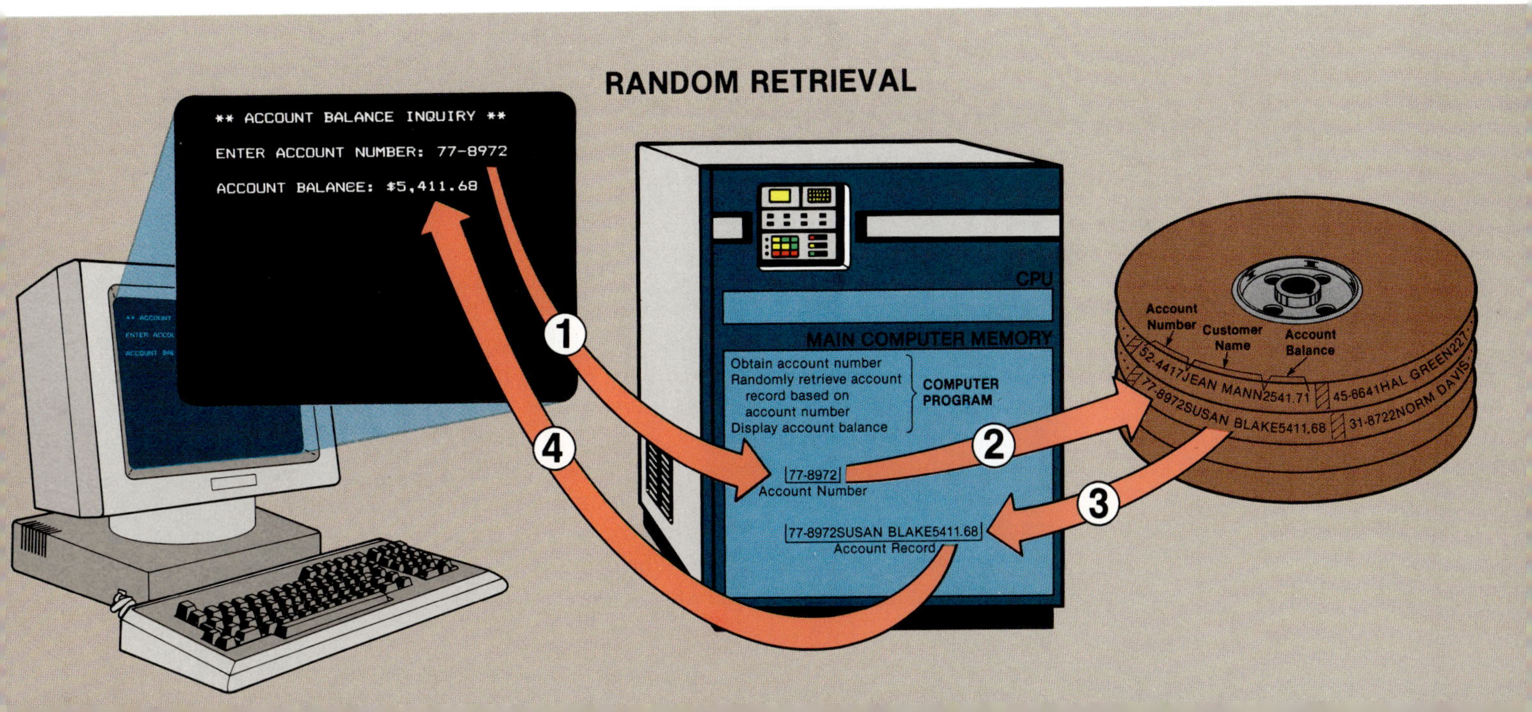

based upon the customer name. For instance, the bank manager could access these records to obtain the account number of Susan Blake. Using random retrieval based upon the name, the program could retrieve the record and display the account number.

Random retrieval is very important in many applications implemented on computers today. Most data stored on auxiliary storage can be randomly retrieved.

Summary

It has been seen that the information processing cycle consists of input, processing, output, and storage. Before it can be processed, data must be placed in main computer memory by the input step. The processing which can occur on data stored in main computer memory consists mainly of arithmetic operations and logical operations. In addition, data can be moved from one location in memory to another location.

The output portion of the information processing cycle produces information which can be used by people. Data is stored on auxiliary storage for subsequent retrieval. Data can be retrieved sequentially when stored on tape or disk and can be retrieved randomly when stored on disk.

DATA MAINTENANCE

Data stored on auxiliary storage must be kept current in order to produce accurate results when it is processed. For example, in Figure 3–13, if the customer made a deposit, the account balance would have to be changed to reflect the balance after the deposit is made. To keep the data current, the records within the files must be updated. **Updating** records within a file consists of adding records to the file, changing records within the file, and deleting records from the file. When updating data, it does not matter if the data is stored as a single file or if it is part of a series of files organized into a data base. The concept of adding records, changing records, and deleting records to keep the data current remains the same. The following paragraphs illustrate adding, changing, and deleting records.

Adding records

Records are added to a file or a data base when additional data is needed to make the file or data base current. For example, in the bank accounting system illustrated in Figure 3–13, if a new customer opened an account, a record must be added to the account file to contain the data for the new customer. The process that would take place to **add records** to the file is shown in Figure 3–14.

1. The terminal operator would enter the new customer data, including the account number, the customer name, and the deposit which will become the account balance. When a record is added to a data base, all the data required for the record must be entered. Thus, the addition would not be correct if the customer name were not included in the data for the new record.

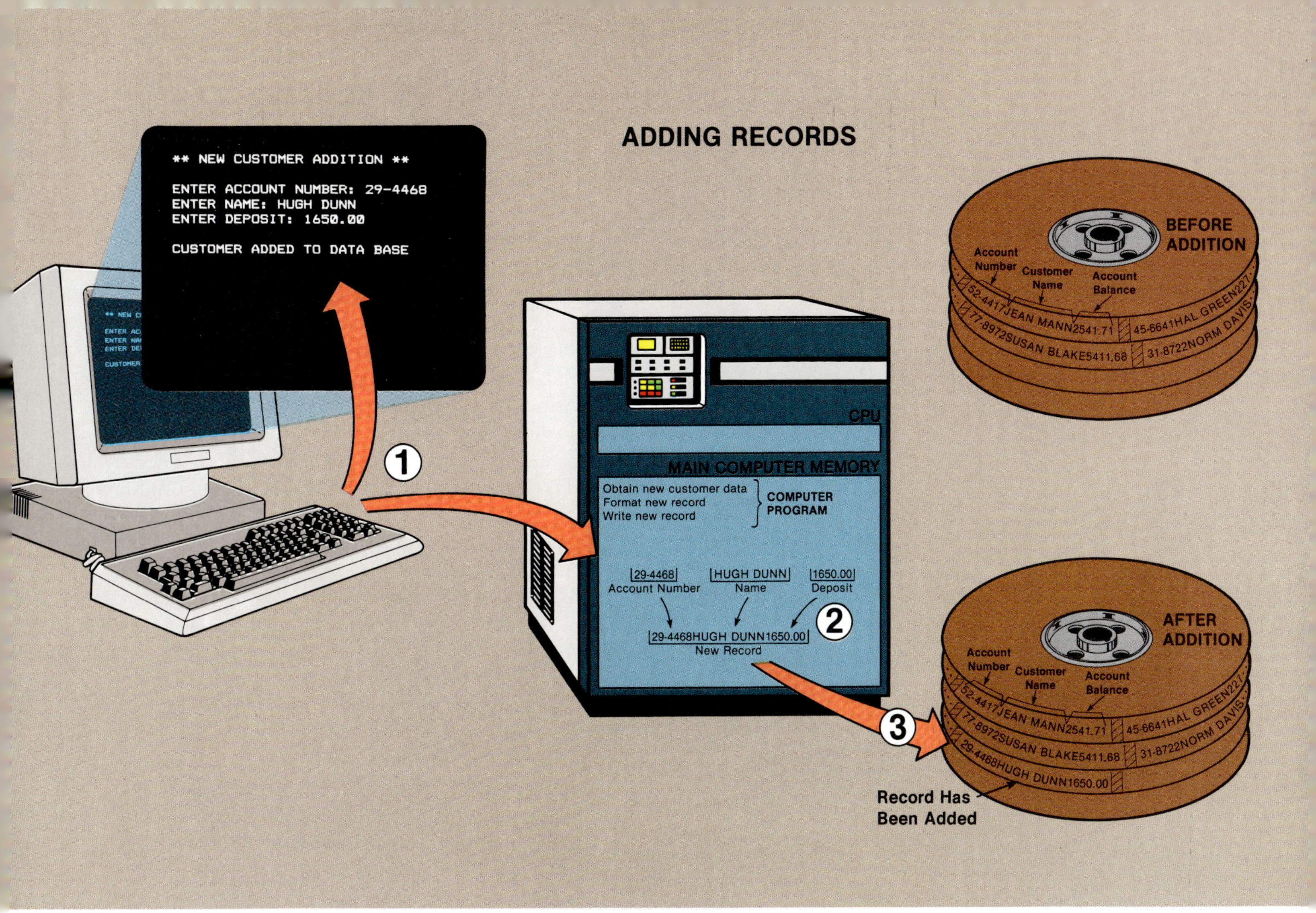

Figure 3–14 In this example of adding records, the terminal operator entered the account number, customer name, and deposit. This data is used to build a record which is then added to the file.

2. Under program control, the data entered by the operator is moved to the new record area in main memory. This area is defined by the program.
3. Once the record is formatted, the program directs that the new record is to be written in the file. The location on the disk where the record is written will be determined by the program. In some cases, a new record will be written between other records in the file. In other cases, such as illustrated in this example, the added record will be written as an additional record at the end of the file.

Whenever data is stored on auxiliary storage for subsequent use, the ability to add records must be present in order to keep the data current.

Changing records

The second task that must be accomplished when updating data is to **change data** that is currently stored in a record. Changes to data stored on auxiliary storage take place for two primary reasons: 1) To correct data that is known to be incorrect; 2) To update data when new data becomes available.

As an example of the first type of change, assume in Figure 3–14 that instead of entering 1650.00 as the initial deposit for the new customer, the terminal operator entered 1560.00. When the customer left the bank, it was not noticed that an error had been made. Later in the day, when the customer returns to question the transaction, the account balance stored in the file must be changed so that it contains the correct amount. Therefore, the terminal operator would enter the value 1650.00 as a change to the account balance in the record. This change was made to replace data known to be incorrect with data known to be correct.

The bank account example can also be used to illustrate the second reason for making a change — to update data when new data becomes available. This type of change is made when a customer deposits or withdraws money. In Figure 3–15, the terminal operator has entered a transaction indicating the customer for account number 52-4417 has withdrawn $500.00. The record for this customer must be changed to reflect the withdrawal. The following steps occur:

1. The terminal operator enters the account number and the amount withdrawn. In the diagram, the operator entered account number 52-4417 and the amount 500.00.
2. Under program control, the record stored on auxiliary storage for account number 52-4417 is randomly retrieved using the account number as the key and is placed in main computer memory.
3. The program then causes the withdrawal amount to be subtracted from the account balance in the record. This operation changes the account balance to reflect the correct balance in the account.
4. After the balance has been changed in memory, the record is written back onto the disk. It is placed in the same location from which it was retrieved. After the change update, then, the account balance has been changed, and the record stored on auxiliary storage contains the correct account balance.

Changing data stored on auxiliary storage to reflect the correct and current data is an important part of the updating process which is required for data.

CHANGING RECORDS

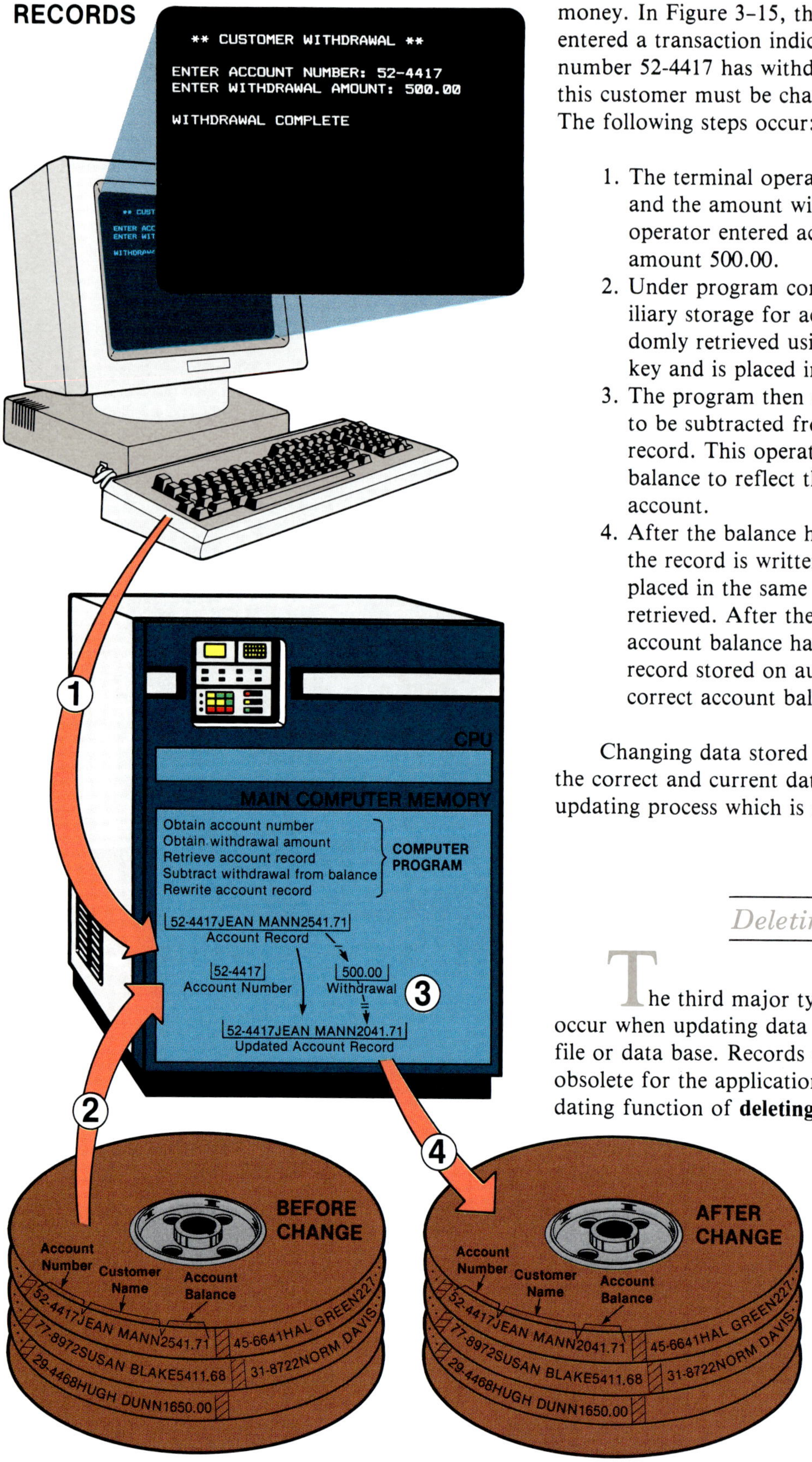

Figure 3–15 When a customer makes a withdrawal, the record for that customer must be changed to reflect the new account balance. In this example, the record for account number 52-4417 is retrieved from the file, and the account balance is decremented by the amount of the withdrawal (500.00). The record is then rewritten back onto the disk in the same position it occupied prior to its retrieval.

Deleting records

The third major type of activity which must occur when updating data is to delete records stored in a file or data base. Records are deleted when they become obsolete for the application. In Figure 3–16, the updating function of **deleting a record** is used to remove a record for a customer who has closed their account. The following steps occur:

1. The terminal operator enters the account number (45-6641) of the record to be deleted.
2. Under program control, the record is retrieved from the disk using the account number as the key. The record is placed in main computer memory.
3. The actual processing that occurs to delete a record from a file varies depending upon whether the record is retrieved sequentially or randomly and depending upon the method used to indicate a record is to be treated as a deleted record. In this example, the record is not removed from the file. Instead, the first three characters of the account number are changed from the actual number to the letters DEL. Thus, the record will not be able to be retrieved based upon the account number because no valid account number begins with the letters DEL. In effect, then, even though the record is still physically stored on the disk, it is effectively deleted because it cannot be retrieved based upon a valid account number.
4. After the letters DEL have been placed in the first three characters of the account number, the record is written back into the file at the same location from which it was retrieved. In the future, this record will not be retrieved.

Deleting records from a file or data base is an important ability when keeping data in the file or data base current.

Summary — data maintenance

The maintenance of data stored on auxiliary storage is critical if information derived from the processing of that data is to be reliable. The major aspect of data maintenance is the updating capability — adding, changing, and deleting data stored on auxiliary storage.

Figure 3-16 In this example, the record for account number 45-6641 is marked as a deleted record by placing the letters DEL in the first three positions of the account number. In this manner, the record cannot be retrieved through the use of the account number as the key, effectively deleting the record from the file even though it is still physically stored on the disk. At some time in the future, the file would be purged of all deleted records by copying the file and omitting all records with the letters DEL in the first three positions of the account number.

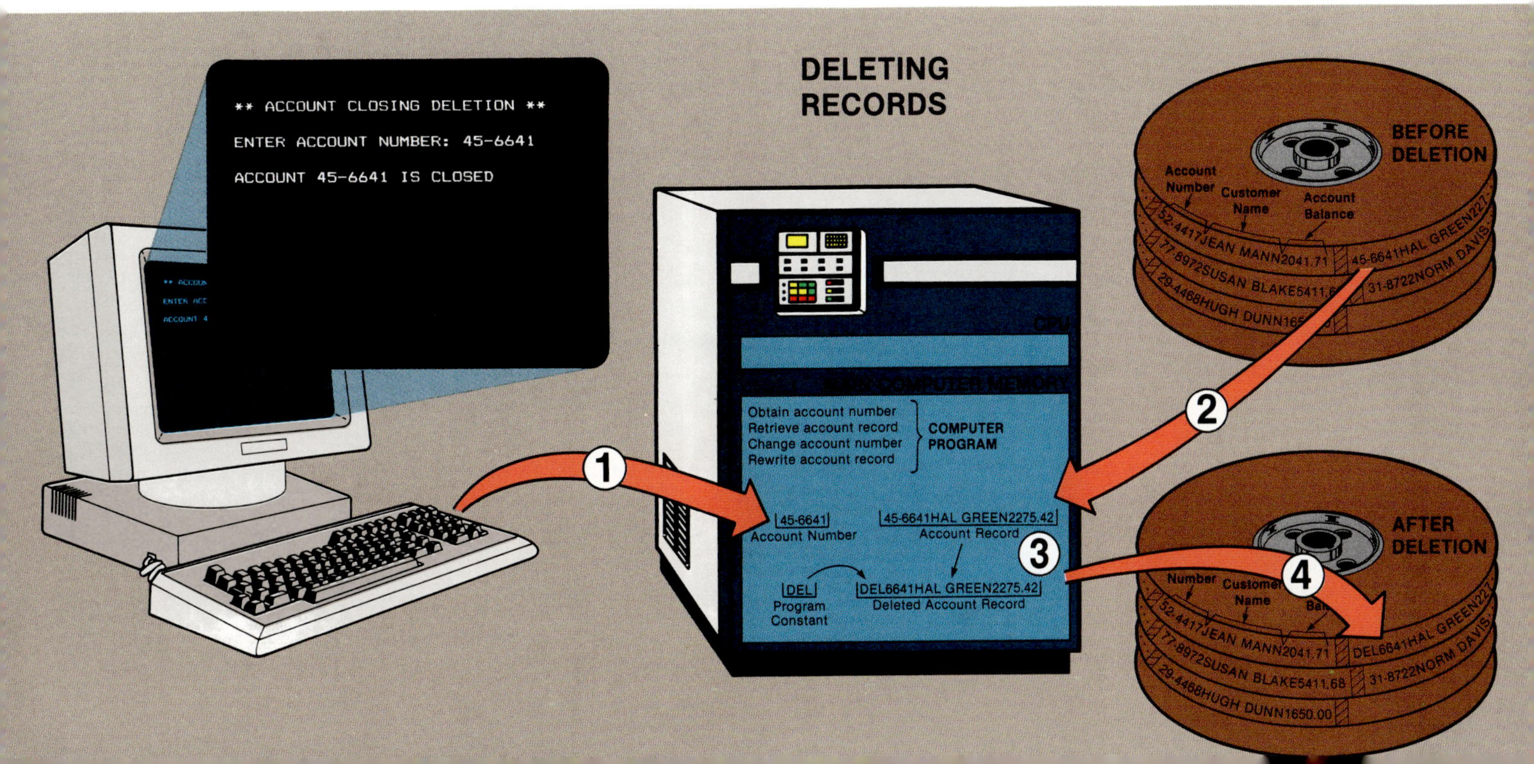

CHAPTER SUMMARY

1. It is important to gain an overall understanding of how computers store and process data.
2. The information processing cycle consists of input, processing, output, and storage.
3. The information processing cycle is used regardless of the size and type of computer.
4. The activities in the information processing cycle are carried out through the combined use of computer hardware, computer software, and data.
5. The computer software, or programs, contain instructions which direct the computer hardware to perform those tasks necessary to process the data and produce output.
6. Input units are used to enter data into main computer memory.
7. On large computers, a diverse number and type of input devices are used.
8. The processor unit consists of main memory and the central processing unit.
9. Data must be stored in main computer memory in order to be processed.
10. The computer program which controls the processing must be stored in main memory.
11. Each instruction in a program is interpreted and executed by the central processing unit.
12. The primary output devices on large computers are printers and CRT screens.
13. Auxiliary storage devices commonly used with large computers are magnetic tape and magnetic disk.
14. Auxiliary storage is merely an extension of main computer memory.
15. A particular storage medium or device can be used for more than one purpose in the information processing cycle. For example, disk can be used for both input and auxiliary storage.
16. Data is defined as the numbers, words, and phrases which are suitable for processing in some manner on a computer to produce information.
17. Individual pieces of data can be referred to as data items or data fields.
18. A data item is useful only when it is combined with other data items or when a relationship to other data items is established.
19. When data is processed on a computer, it must be organized based upon the application and the data item relationships.
20. A record is a collection of related data items, or fields. Each record corresponds to a specific unit of information.
21. A collection of records is called a file. A file contains all of the related records for an application.
22. Files are stored on some medium, such as magnetic tape or magnetic disk.
23. Processing operations fall into five major categories: a) Input operations; b) Arithmetic operations; c) Logical operations; d) Output operations; e) Storage operations.
24. The input operation causes data to be stored in main computer memory. Data which is entered from an input device is electronically stored in main computer memory.
25. Once data is stored in main memory, it can be processed under the control of a computer program, including moving data from one location in memory to another location.
26. When data is moved from one location in memory to another, it is not destroyed; rather, the data is duplicated in the new location.
27. Thousands and even millions of arithmetic operations, including addition, subtraction, multiplication, and division, can be performed in one second on many computers.
28. The results of arithmetic operations can be used in subsequent arithmetic operations, can be moved to other locations in main memory, and can be used for output.
29. The process of repeating instructions in a program is called looping. Looping allows a single set of instructions in a program to process many thousands of records.
30. Logical operations performed on a computer are based upon the ability of a computer, under the control of a program, to compare data stored in main computer memory.
31. Based upon the results of a comparison of numbers, letters of the alphabet, or special characters, alternative processing can be performed.
32. Comparing to determine if two values stored in main memory are equal is an important capability of a computer.
33. A comparing operation can determine if one value is greater than another value.

34. When a program is written, the alternative processing to be performed is specified by the requirements of the application. The alternative processing to be performed when a condition is true must always be the same; likewise, the processing to be performed when the condition is not true must always be the same.

35. A comparison can be used to determine if one value is less than another value.

36. Output is produced by transferring data stored in main computer memory to a medium or device which can be used by people. Commonly used for output are the printed report and the CRT screen.

37. After data is entered into main memory or is generated as a result of processing, it may be subsequently used by the same or different programs. Therefore it must be saved. It is saved on auxiliary storage.

38. Magnetic tape and magnetic disk are the two main mediums for auxiliary storage.

39. Access to data stored on auxiliary storage is considerably slower than access to data stored in main computer memory.

40. Data is retrieved in two major ways from auxiliary storage: a) Sequentially, in the same sequence it is stored on auxiliary storage; b) Randomly, based upon a value in the data itself.

41. When data is stored and retrieved sequentially, each record is stored on tape or disk one after the other, and the data is retrieved in the same sequence as it is stored.

42. When sequential retrieval is used, the data is usually stored and retrieved in some defined sequence based upon a value in the record, called a key.

43. Sequential retrieval is never used when fast access to a record is required because, for example, in order to retrieve the third record in the file, the two preceding records must be retrieved first.

44. Data stored on disk can be randomly retrieved, which means records can be retrieved regardless of the order in which they are physically stored. Random retrieval can be used when fast access to a record is required.

45. The sequence in which records are stored is not important when retrieving records randomly.

46. Most data stored on auxiliary storage can be randomly retrieved.

47. Data stored on auxiliary storage must be kept current in order to produce accurate results when it is processed. To keep the data current, the records within files must be updated, which consists of adding records to a file, changing records within a file, and deleting records from a file.

48. Records are added to a file or data base when additional data is needed to make the file or data base current.

49. Changes to data stored on auxiliary storage take place for two primary reasons: a) To correct data that is known to be incorrect; b) To update data when new data becomes available.

50. When a record is changed, it is normally written back into the file at the same location from which it was retrieved.

51. Records are deleted from a file or data base when they become obsolete for the application.

52. The actual processing that occurs to delete a record from a file varies depending upon whether the record is retrieved randomly or sequentially and depending upon the method used to indicate a record is to be treated as a deleted record.

53. The maintenance of data stored on auxiliary storage is critical if information derived from the processing of that data is to be reliable.

KEY TERMS

REVIEW QUESTIONS

1. What are the four elements of the information processing cycle? What types and sizes of computers can be used to implement the information processing cycle?
2. What is the use of input units? Describe typical input units found on both large and small computers.
3. What is the definition of data? When does an item of data become useful?
4. What is a record? What is a file? What is the relationship of records to files?
5. Name the five major categories of processing operations.
6. What is the input operation on a computer? What happens when the input operation takes place?
7. Describe the processing that takes place when data is moved from one location in main computer memory to another location in main memory.
8. What is looping? Why is it useful?
9. Name three conditions that can be tested when data is compared. What takes place when a condition is true? What takes place when a condition is not true?
10. What are the two major ways that data is retrieved from auxiliary storage?
11. Describe the manner in which data is retrieved sequentially; describe the manner in which data is retrieved randomly.
12. Which access method results in the fastest retrieval of a record? Why?
13. What are the three major tasks performed when files are updated?
14. Why are records added to a file? Why are they deleted from a file?
15. State the two primary reasons changes are made to data stored on auxiliary storage.

CONTROVERSIAL ISSUES

1. In this chapter, it was noted that computers can perform millions of arithmetic operations in a single second. Some people claim that much greater speed is needed for computers so that applications such as weather prediction and space flight simulation can be accurately performed within a reasonable time period. These people think research money should be spent to find ways to develop faster computers. Other people argue that computers process data plenty fast enough and that research money should be spent in other areas, such as developing privacy safeguards for people in society. Take a side in this debate and defend your position.
2. Software is currently available so that it is possible for medical patients to inform a computer of their symptoms by answering a series of questions. The program then compares the answers to symptoms retrieved from auxiliary storage. When equal conditions are found, a diagnosis will be given and, perhaps, medication prescribed. Does this process take away the proper role of a doctor? Is the computer doing the same type of "thinking" that a doctor does when analyzing symptoms? Take a position and defend it.

RESEARCH PROJECTS

1. A banking application was described in this chapter to illustrate random retrieval and updating. Visit a bank or savings and loan in your area. Determine the techniques they use to enter a new customer, make changes in account records when deposits and withdrawals are made, and to close an account. Write a report for your class.
2. Obtain a programming manual for a programming language such as BASIC or COBOL. List and describe all the instructions that are used to compare data and the comparisons which they can make. Include in your report the rules for comparing numeric data to numeric data and alphabetic data to alphabetic data.
3. Obtain a programming manual for a programming language such as BASIC or COBOL. List and describe all the instructions used for arithmetic operations in the programming language. Include all rules for the instructions.

Chapter 4

Interactive and Batch Processing Systems

Objectives

- ☐ Summarize the information processing cycle
- ☐ Identify and describe through diagrams interactive processing, transaction-oriented processing, and batch processing
- ☐ List the attributes of data required for successful computer processing
- ☐ Specify the roles of systems, procedures, and personnel in an information processing system
- ☐ Identify and describe the eight general categories of applications suitable for processing on a computer

Interactive and Batch Processing Systems

Chapter Four

Potential users of computers often ask the question, "Is the computer an appropriate tool for my application?" A computer literate person should be able to answer this question. Answering it, however, requires an understanding of several aspects of information processing not yet discussed in this book, including the manner in which data is entered and processed on a computer; certain attributes of data; systems and procedures; personnel; and the applications which are suitable for computer implementation. This chapter will present these topics so that the question can be answered.

Computer processing review

It is important at this point to place in perspective the topics which have been covered in the previous chapters and the topics which will be covered in this chapter so that the information presented in this chapter will have meaning. To do this, the diagram in Figure 4–2 will be used. In this diagram, the symbols in blue have already been covered, and the symbols in gold will be covered in this chapter.

The diagram illustrates the elements which comprise an information processing system. Data is the heart of an information processing system. As noted before, without data no meaningful processing can occur on a computer. Data is organized into fields, records, files, and data bases for processing on a computer.

Data is input to the information processing cycle, within which five operations can occur: input, arithmetic, logical, output, and storage. These fundamental operations are used on a computer, regardless of the size or type of computer.

The basic operations in the information processing cycle can be used in two primary modes: the interactive mode and the batch mode. These processing modes will be explained in detail in this chapter.

The topics just described comprise the processing that actually takes place on the computer. Other

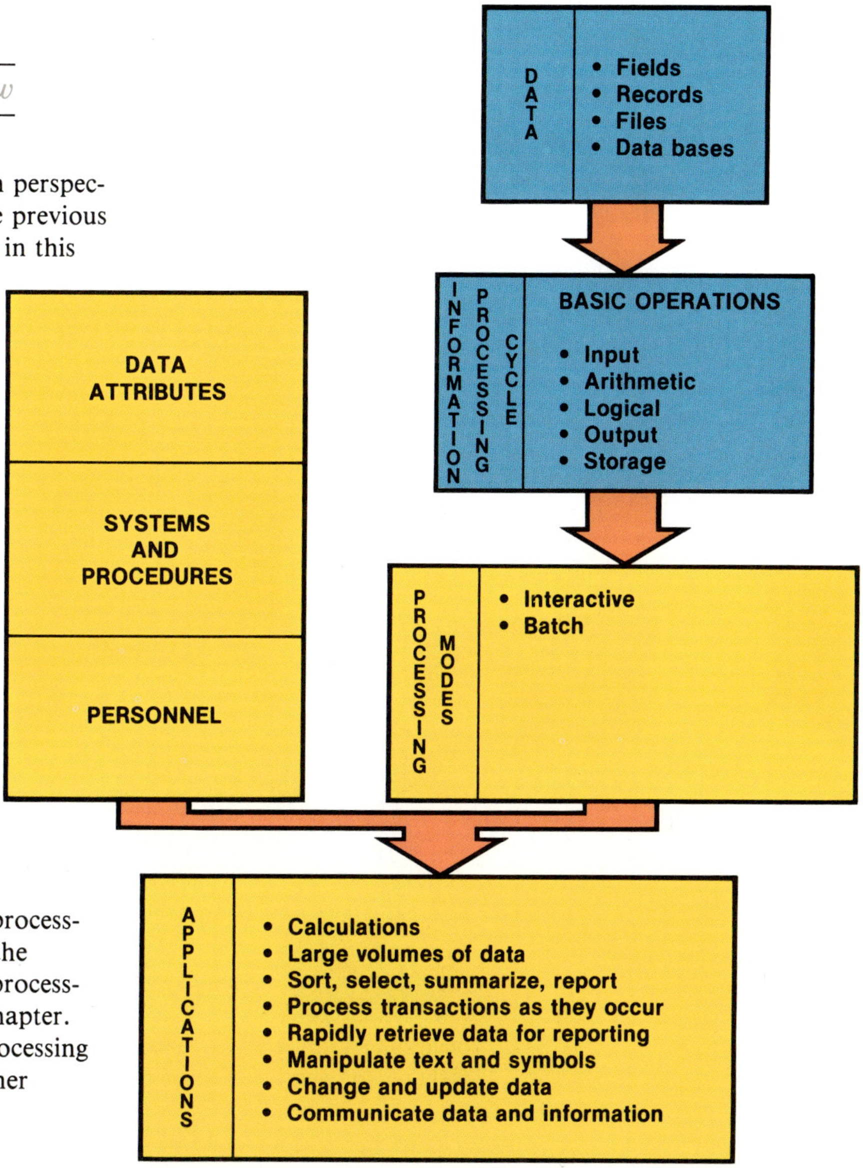

Figure 4–2 An information processing system contains the elements data, the information processing cycle, processing modes, data attributes, systems and procedures, personnel, and applications.

elements are required, however, to ensure successful use of a computer to produce useful information. These elements include an analysis of data attributes, systems and procedures, and personnel.

An analysis of data attributes is required to ensure the reliability of the information generated from processing data. Systems and procedures are required so that people can interface with the computer processing when required. Personnel are required in many areas of computing in order to successfully implement information processing systems. Each of these subjects will be examined in this chapter.

All of the elements just discussed are combined to implement applications in an information processing system. These applications fall into eight general categories, which are specified in the diagram. These categories are discussed in this chapter.

In order to answer the question, "Is the computer an appropriate tool for my application?" each of the parts of the information processing system must be analyzed. The user should first determine which application category or combination of categories are applicable. Then the requirements of that application should be examined. The user must identify the data to be processed and ensure that it can be organized properly for processing on a computer. Then, the processing must be examined to define the operations to be performed on the data. The mode in which the data is to be processed must be determined, based upon the application. The data attributes, systems and procedures, and personnel required to implement the application must be determined so that the implementation will be successful.

By using this type of analysis, the user will be able to answer the question and will be able to successfully implement the application.

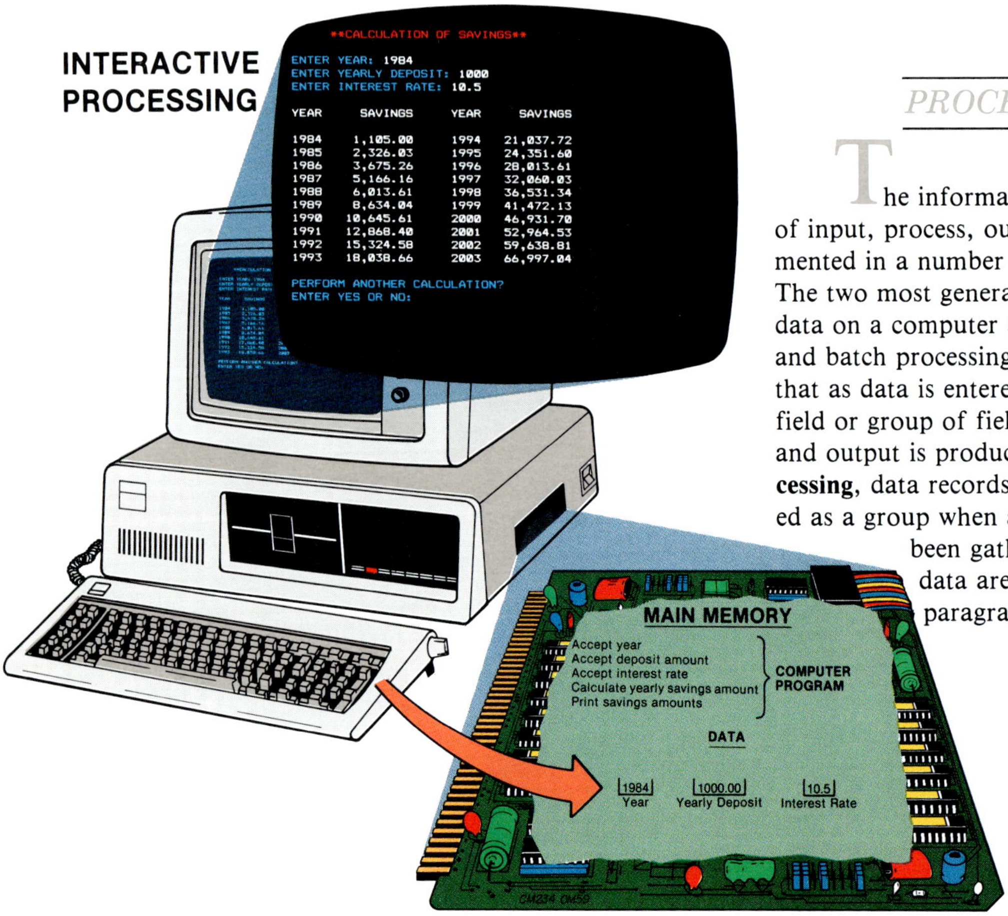

Figure 4-3 In this example of interactive processing, the user enters the beginning year for the calculations, the yearly deposit amount, and the interest rate that will be earned. The program immediately uses this input data to calculate the savings amount for the next twenty years and display these amounts on the CRT screen. Therefore, the requirement for interactive processing of immediate processing and immediate output is fulfilled in this example.

PROCESSING MODES

The information processing cycle, consisting of input, process, output, and storage, can be implemented in a number of different ways on computers. The two most generally used modes for processing data on a computer are called interactive processing and batch processing. **Interactive processing** means that as data is entered into the computer as a single field or group of fields, it is processed immediately and output is produced immediately. With **batch processing**, data records are accumulated and are processed as a group when all of the required records have been gathered. These modes of processing data are explained in the following paragraphs.

Interactive processing

The example in Figure 4-3 illustrates interactive processing. The program accepts a beginning year, a yearly deposit amount, and an interest rate. It then calculates and displays the yearly value of the savings account. This program is interactive because after the user enters the year, deposit amount, and interest rate, the program immediately performs the calculations and produces output for the user.

The example in Figure 4-3 illustrated the use of a personal computer for interactive processing. Large computers, such as minicomputers and mainframes, can also be used for interactive processing. Interactive processing can be performed when access to auxiliary storage is required. For example it will be recalled that in Figure 3-13 in Chapter 3, the bank teller entered a customer's account number, and the program responded with the account balance. In order to obtain the balance, the program randomly accessed a record stored on disk. Interactive processing was used there because as soon as the teller entered the account number, the program retrieved the account record and sent the account balance to the terminal. The key to understanding interactive processing is to realize that as soon as the required input data has been entered, the program performs the processing and generates output.

A special form of interactive processing is called transaction-oriented processing. When **transaction-oriented processing** is used, the computer or terminal operator enters all of the data pertaining to a complete business transaction. After the data is entered, the program performs all of the processing required for that particular transaction.

The example in Figure 4-4 illustrates transaction-oriented processing being used in a car rental agency. When a car is returned, the terminal operator enters all of the data required to prepare the final auto rental agreement. The program immediately

Figure 4-4 In this example, the following takes place: 1) The CRT operator enters the complete transaction data for a person returning a rental car. The data is placed in main memory and is displayed on the CRT screen; 2) The program immediately retrieves the corresponding record from disk and places it in main memory; 3) The calculations take place, including determining the total mileage by subtracting the beginning mileage (11,500) from the ending mileage (12,200), and calculating the mileage cost (140.00) by multiplying the total mileage (700) by the rate per mile (.20); 4) The auto rental agreement is printed; 5) The disk record is rewritten with the new ending mileage.

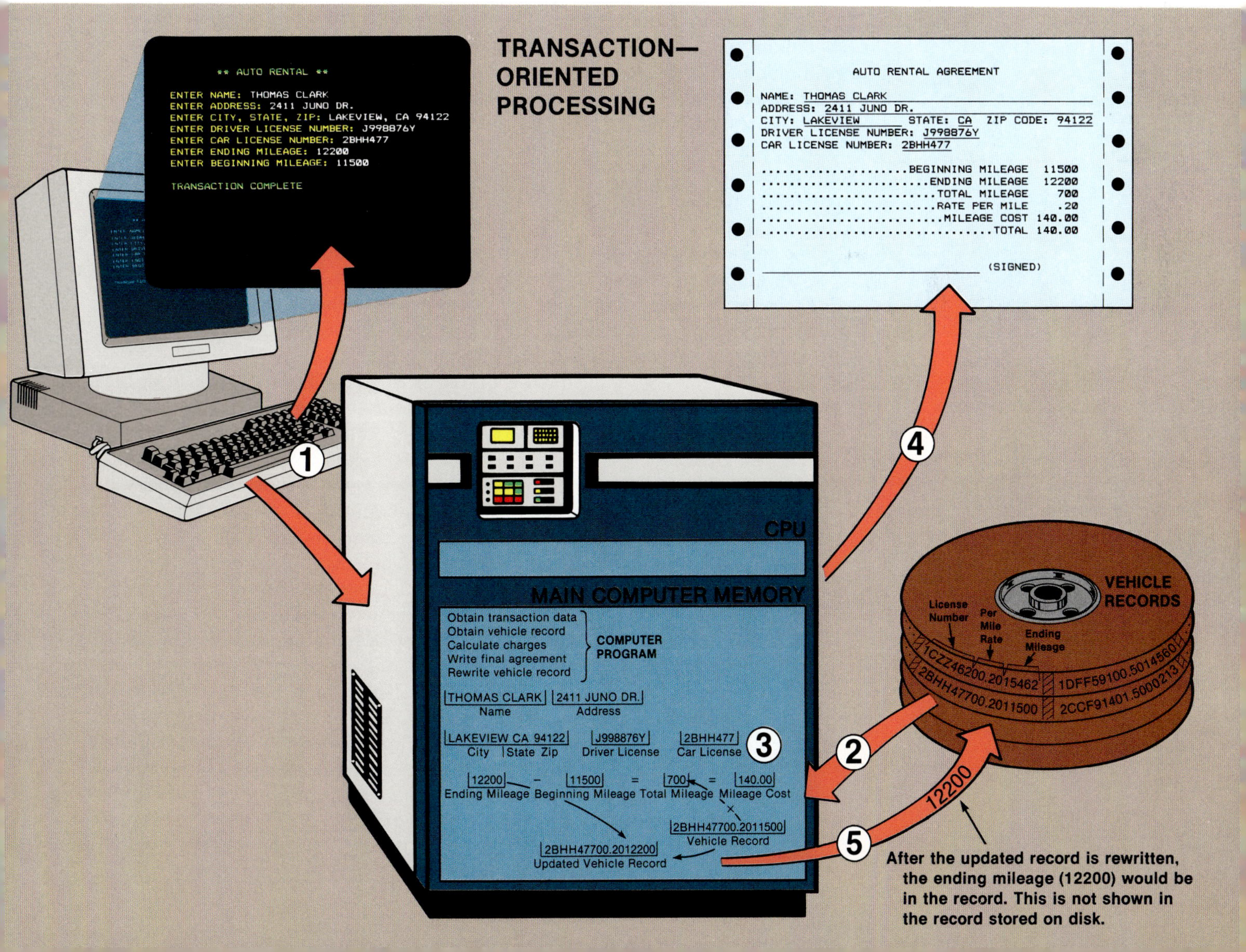

retrieves the auto record from the disk (based upon the auto license number), performs the necessary calculations, and writes the final auto rental agreement on the printer. The operator would then give a copy to the customer. In addition to printing the final rental agreement, the program changed the auto record on disk by placing the ending mileage in the record. After this processing is done, the entire auto rental transaction is completed. Note that the entire transaction was completed immediately after the terminal operator entered the input data.

Batch processing

Batch processing was used almost exclusively when computers were first implemented in business. In many cases, **source documents** containing the data to be processed were brought to a central location where the data was punched in cards or was placed on magnetic tape. The data, in one single group, or batch, was then read into the computer for processing. Thus, many of the early applications implemented on computers, such as payroll or billing operations, were best processed in a batch environment.

Today, batch processing is still the best way to implement some applications, even though interactive processing has become more prominent. For example, banks which process billions of checks each year, utility companies which must send out millions of bills each month, credit card companies which process thousands of charges and payments each month, and even small companies which must pay their employees all find that batch processing is the best way in which to implement their application.

The application illustrated in Figure 4–5 uses batch processing to create an account statement from a credit card purchase.

The following steps take place:

1. The consumer purchases an item from a store and the sales receipt is made. This sales receipt becomes the source document.
2. The sales receipt is transmitted to the data entry section of the information systems department at the bank or company processing the credit card purchase. In this example, it is the First Federal Bank.
3. In the data entry section, the data on the sales receipt is entered, through the use of a CRT terminal, into a disk file. It should be noted that other CRT terminals would be used at the same time to enter other sales receipts for storage in the disk file.
4. When all of the data from all of the sales receipts for a given time or a given date have been entered, the file of data stored on disk is read into main memory a record at a time. This is batch processing, where all records have been batched into one input file and then are processed at the same time.
5. When the input record is read from the batch input file, a record from the account file is randomly retrieved as well. The account file contains a record for each card holder. The record contains the account number (the key of the record), the card holder's name and address, and the account balance. In the example, the customer's name is Hal Dukes. The address is 613 Acorn Drive, Plain, Wyoming 83742. The account balance prior to processing the purchase record is $265.40. When the account record is retrieved, it is updated to reflect the latest status of the account by adding the purchase amount from the input record to the account balance found in the account record.
6. After the account record is updated, it is rewritten in the account file. Thus, the next time Hal Dukes makes a purchase, the new balance (309.39)

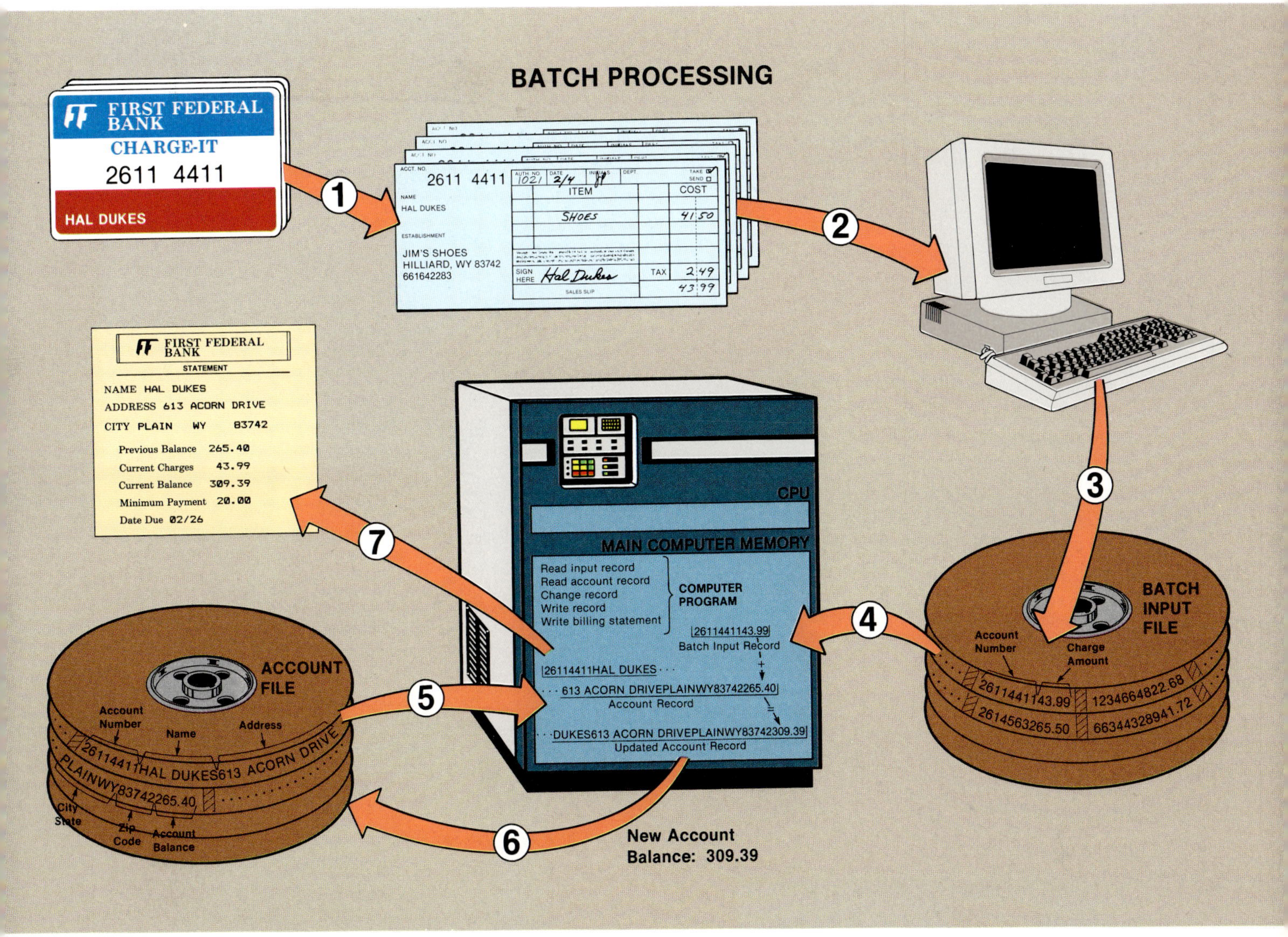

will be in his account record.

7. The information from the batch input record and the account file are used to prepare the account statement which is sent to the customer. The account statement contains the previous balance, the current charges, the current balance, the minimum payment (calculated by the program), and the due date. From this statement, the customer would make a payment.

This example has proceeded through each step which could occur when a purchase is made with a credit card. The important aspect of the example from the perspective of the processing performed on the computer is that the input records are all batched together into a single input file. They are then processed as a group, updating the account file and producing the account statements. In most applications of this type, hundreds and even thousands of records would be processed in one run of the program. It is important to see that batch processing which processes many records and creates many account statements is the appropriate means for processing these records. Processing them individually and creating an account statement individually, such as would be done if interactive processing were used, would not be appropriate for this application.

Figure 4–5 In this batch processing application, after the customer makes a purchase, the sales receipt is used as the source document to prepare an input record. The input records are prepared and processed as a group, or batch. The account record is updated with data obtained from the input record. The account statement is prepared using data from both the input record and the account record.

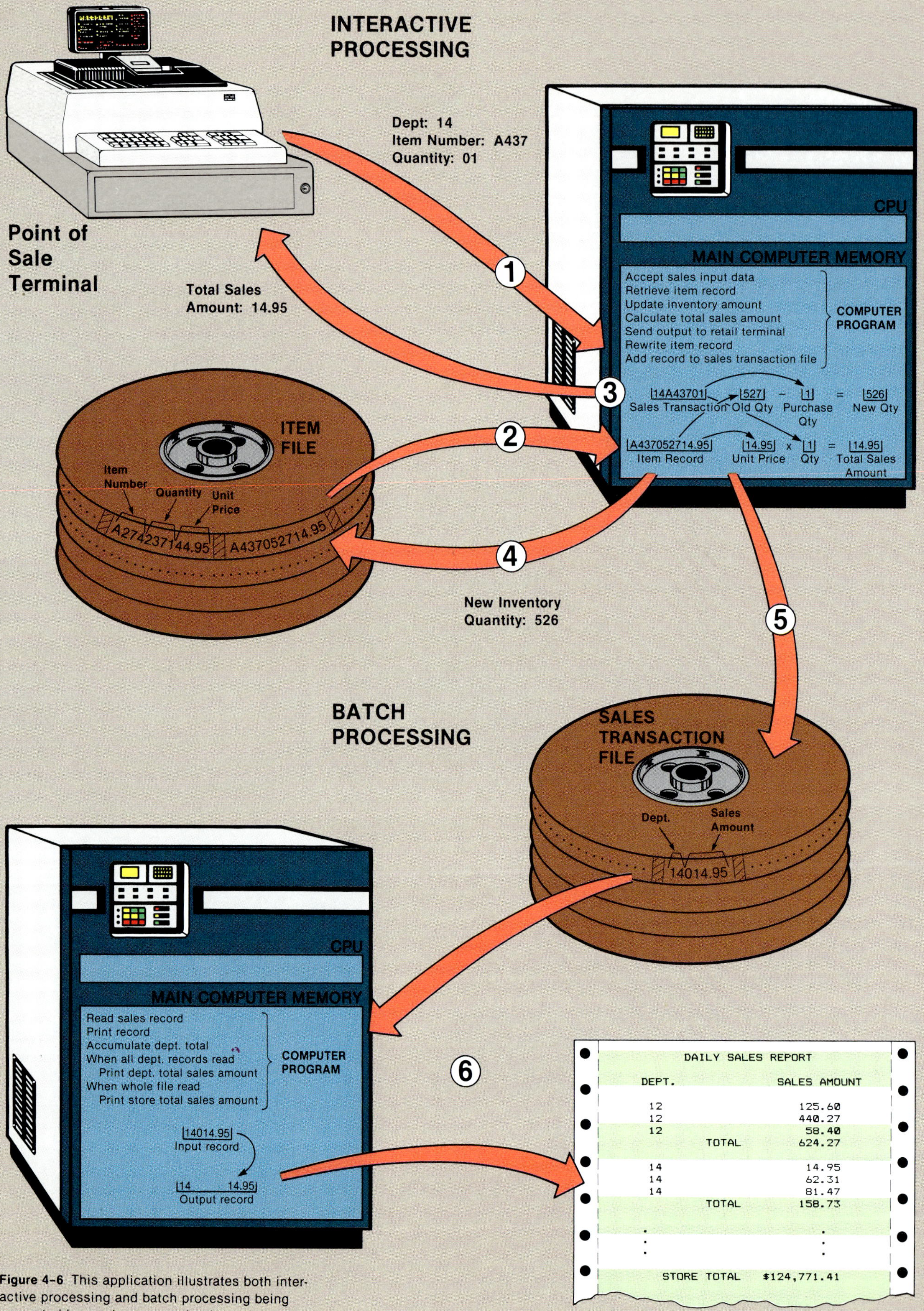
INTERACTIVE PROCESSING
Point of Sale Terminal
Dept: 14
Item Number: A437
Quantity: 01
Total Sales Amount: 14.95
1
2
3
4
5
6
CPU
MAIN COMPUTER MEMORY
Accept sales input data
Retrieve item record
Update inventory amount
Calculate total sales amount
Send output to retail terminal
Rewrite item record
Add record to sales transaction file
COMPUTER PROGRAM
14A43701
Sales Transaction
527
Old Qty
-
1
Purchase Qty
=
526
New Qty
A437052714.95
Item Record
14.95
Unit Price
x
1
Qty
=
14.95
Total Sales Amount
ITEM FILE
Item Number
Quantity
Unit Price
A274237144.95
A437052714.95
New Inventory Quantity: 526
BATCH PROCESSING
SALES TRANSACTION FILE
Dept.
Sales Amount
14014.95
CPU
MAIN COMPUTER MEMORY
Read sales record
Print record
Accumulate dept. total
When all dept. records read
Print dept. total sales amount
When whole file read
Print store total sales amount
COMPUTER PROGRAM
14014.95
Input record
14 14.95
Output record
DAILY SALES REPORT
DEPT. SALES AMOUNT
12 125.60
12 440.27
12 58.40
TOTAL 624.27
14 14.95
14 62.31
14 81.47
TOTAL 158.73
STORE TOTAL $124,771.41

Figure 4–6 This application illustrates both interactive processing and batch processing being generated by a sales transaction in a retail store.

Combined interactive and batch processing

The two major modes of processing data — interactive and batch — can be combined in a single application. This is illustrated in Figure 4-6, where a transaction for a sale in a retail store is shown. The following steps occur:

1. The store clerk enters the details of the sale on a **point of sale terminal** (an input device used for retail sales), which is connected to a large computer. The sales data includes the department number where the sale took place (14), the item number of the item purchased (A437), and the quantity of items purchased (01).
2. As soon as the input data is stored in main memory, the program, which is also stored in main memory, will randomly retrieve a record from the item file. The record retrieved contains the item number (A437), the quantity of the item in inventory (0527), and the unit price for the item (14.95).
3. Next, the program reduces the quantity in the item record (527) by the quantity purchased (1), giving the new inventory quantity (526). It also multiplies the quantity purchased (1) by the unit price (14.95) to determine the total sales amount (14.95). The total sales amount is sent back to the point of sale terminal, where the clerk can complete the transaction with the customer.
4. The item record with the new quantity (526) is written back into the item file.
5. The program also adds a record to the sales transaction file. The sales transaction file contains a record for each sale which is made during the day at the store. These records are accumulated to be used in later processing.
6. After the store is closed and all transactions have been completed, the sales transaction file is input to a program which produces the daily sales report. The report contains the department and sales amount for each sale, the total dollar sales amount for each department of the store, and the total sales in the store for the day.

This application illustrates both interactive processing and batch processing being generated from a single transaction. When the sales clerk enters the sale on the point of sale terminal and the program responds with the total sales amount, interactive processing has occurred because as soon as the data was entered, the program processed the data by performing the calculations and updating the item file, and it produced output.

At the same time, input data for batch processing was developed when the program wrote a record in the sales transaction file. When these transactions were used to produce the daily sales report, batch processing was taking place because all of the transaction records had been batched together to be processed at one time. As with previous examples, it would make little sense to produce the daily sales report until all of the sales transactions for the day had been completed. Thus, in this case, batch processing was the proper way to prepare the report. In the same manner, each sales transaction must be processed as it occurs. Therefore, interactive processing was the correct mode for the sales transaction processing.

Summary

Interactive and batch processing are the two major modes for processing data on a computer. Generally, most processing that is performed on personal computers is interactive processing. On larger computers, the trend is toward more interactive processing, although batch processing is still an important part of the activities found on large computers. In addition, some processing which takes place on computers is difficult to categorize into batch or interactive because there are elements of each involved. Most applications, however, can be easily categorized into one of these two types of processing.

OTHER ELEMENTS OF INFORMATION PROCESSING

In addition to the actual processing which occurs on a computer and which has been described thus far in this chapter, there are other elements of information processing which must be present in order to successfully use computers. These elements include an analysis of certain attributes which data must have, the development of systems and procedures, and the personnel who are involved in information processing.

Attributes of data

As has been noted, without data there is no useful processing that can be performed on a computer. In order to be successfully used, however, data must have certain attributes. These attributes include data integrity, availability, manageability, and security and control. To illustrate these attributes of data, an example of a credit checking bureau will be used. A summary of the application follows:

1. Data for input into the data base of the credit bureau is acquired from numerous sources. The data relates to the credit rating of individuals and includes their income, their history of paying debts, any bankruptcies, any negative personal traits such as alcoholism, and so on.
2. This data is stored on auxiliary storage.
3. Customers of this credit bureau can call the bureau and request the credit rating of an individual. The terminal operator will give the caller a brief history of the person in question (interactive processing), and the system will generate a transaction record which will cause a complete history to be printed that night (batch processing). The report is sent to the customer the next day.

In the following paragraphs, the importance of the data in this application and, through inference, in all applications which are implemented in an information processing system, will be examined.

Data integrity

The first important attribute of data in this application and in any application is its integrity. **Data integrity** determines the confidence a user can have in the processing of that data. The three primary elements of data integrity are:

1. Data accuracy.
2. Reliable data entry.
3. Timeliness.

In order for a user to have complete confidence in the results of data processing, there must be confidence that the data is **accurate** in the sense that the source of the data is reliable and that the data to be entered has been reliably reported. For example, in the credit bureau if someone incorrectly states that an individual did not pay a bill and this information is entered into the data base, there can be serious repercussions. Thus, there must be confidence that the people and organizations providing data to the credit bureau provide accurate data. It is quite important that accurate data be entered into an information processing system.

A second element of data integrity is **reliable data entry**. Data that is entered for processing in computer memory must be entered correctly, which means that the values entered correspond to the values which are supposed to be entered. If, in the credit bureau example, a bank reports that the balance on a credit card account is $200.00, and the balance is incorrectly entered as $20000.00, the information generated from the information processing system would be invalid.

Besides great care on the part of the person entering the data, data editing is the most effective way to ensure reliable data entry. **Data editing** refers to the process of comparing the data entered to predetermined values to ensure that the data entered conforms to the predetermined criteria. For example, when the credit card balance is entered, it may be known that the maximum account balance the bank will allow is $4,000.00 (Figure 4–7). Therefore, the program which accepts the input data from the terminal operator would compare the value entered to the value 4000.00. If the value entered is greater than 4000.00, the program would send an error message to the operator indicating that invalid data had been entered. The operator would then either reenter the correct value or, if the value to be entered was incorrect, determine the accurate value. There are many additional editing tests which can be performed on data to ensure its correctness. These tests will be discussed in subsequent chapters.

The third major element of data integrity is timeliness. **Timeliness** means that data to be processed in an information processing system has not lost its usefulness or accuracy because time has passed. For example, in the credit bureau application, assume that two years ago a salary of $15,000.00 was entered for an individual. Today, that data is not timely because two years have passed, and the individual may be earning either less or more than $15,000.00. Therefore, that data should not be used to produce information from the credit bureau application.

The integrity of data processed on a computer is critical. Before an application is implemented on a computer, all of the criteria for valid data must be defined, and checks for valid data should be placed in the programs.

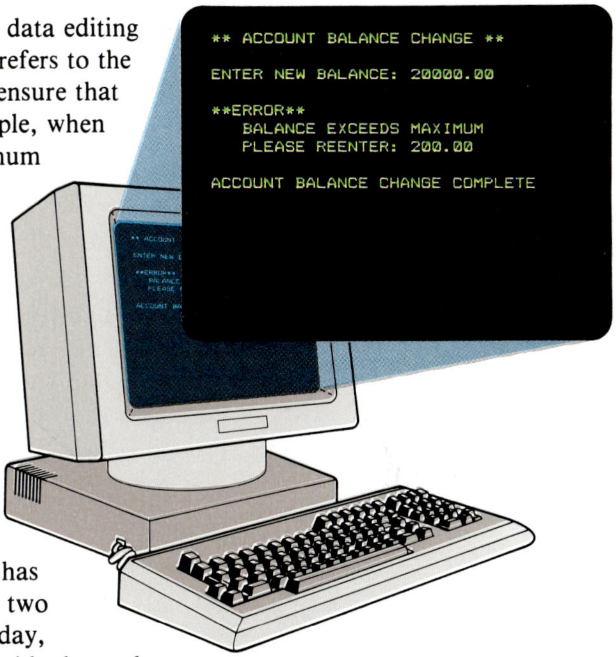
** ACCOUNT BALANCE CHANGE **
ENTER NEW BALANCE: 20000.00
ERROR
BALANCE EXCEEDS MAXIMUM
PLEASE REENTER: 200.00
ACCOUNT BALANCE CHANGE COMPLETE

Figure 4–7 When the data entry person enters a balance of 20000.00, the editing portion of the program obtaining the data determines that the value is not correctly entered. It responds by asking the operator to reenter the data correctly. When a correct value is entered, the program changes the account balance.

Other data attributes

There are other attributes of data which must be present before an application can be implemented using a computer. An obvious attribute is that the data must be available. **Availability** means the data required for the application can be obtained in a manner which ensures the integrity of the data. In the credit bureau application, it would not be possible to implement the system if banks, stores, and other organizations were not willing to provide accurate and timely information about account holders. Therefore, prior to implementing an application on a computer, there must be assurance that the data required is available.

Management of data is critical if an application is to be successfully implemented on a computer. **Data management** refers to techniques and procedures which ensure that the data required for an application will be available in the correct form and at the proper time for processing. It includes techniques that ensure data integrity, procedures which specify how and when data is to be entered into a system, methods for organizing and retrieving data, and methods for making copies of data so that if one file of data is accidentally or even purposely destroyed, recovery can occur and processing can continue.

Concurrent with the requirement for data management is the requirement for **data security and control**. In more and more applications, the security of data used on a computer is a major issue. For example, in the credit bureau application, a person's credit rating and financial transactions are of a confidential nature. Most people do not want this information made widely available. Therefore, the credit bureau must develop systems and procedures that allow only authorized personnel to access the data stored in the data base.

Since data used in information systems is very important, serious consideration must be given to the security and control required for that data.

Summary of data attributes

The attributes of data explained in the previous paragraphs are important when implementing an information processing system. When applications are placed on a computer without adequate attention being given to the use of data, it is likely that the information processing system will not perform in the manner intended.

Development of systems and procedures

People will always be an important part of any processing performed on a computer. They are the major benefactors of the processing, they generally are responsible for entering data into the computer, and they write the programs which process data on a computer. In order for people to successfully interact with computer processing, systems and procedures must be defined and followed.

A **procedure** is a series of logical steps by which all repetitive actions are initiated, carried forward, controlled, and finalized. A **system** is a network of related procedures designed to perform some activity. An information processing system consists of procedures that identify the manner in which the following activities will be performed:

1. Acquiring data and preparing it for input to the computer.
2. Entering the data into the computer, including the format of the data and the manner in which the person entering the data will interact with the computer program.
3. Describing the processing that is to take place on the computer, including the program or programs comprising the system.
4. Obtaining information from the computer processing, including the format of

the output information and the manner in which the information is delivered to the user or the way in which the user can obtain information by interfacing with the computer.

The system includes all procedures necessary to process data and obtain information from the computer. The procedures within a system are described in the system documentation. **Documentation** consists of written words, drawings, and screen messages which tell a person the exact procedures for all activities associated with the system. For the user who interacts with the computer, the documentation explains how to perform every step to obtain the desired results. For example, the documentation for an electronic spreadsheet program could describe how to enter data, what formulas can be entered and how they are entered, how to ask "what if" questions, and so on. Without adequate documentation, a system is essentially worthless.

Systems and procedures, together with the accompanying documentation, are critical for successful use of a computer. Regardless of whether the application is implemented on a home computer or the largest mainframe, procedures must be established within a system to accomplish the processing required, and the procedures must be well documented and easy to use.

Personnel

People are required to make computer processing work. Without knowledgeable personnel, an information processing system will not function. The most important group of people interacting with a computer are the users. **Computer users** are people who use the system or who benefit from the system.

Some computer users, such as executives using an electronic spreadsheet program or secretaries using a word processing program, interface directly with the computer. Others do not interface directly with the computer but receive output, such as printed reports, which they use. Still others, such as students registering for a class, are computer users because their registration procedure is implemented on a computer even though they neither directly interface with a computer nor directly use computer output.

Education and training, particularly for those who interface directly with the computer, is the most important consideration for computer users. The student who registers for college will not be able to register properly until all procedures are understood. Similarly, the executive who uses an integrated software package to produce graphs from electronic spreadsheets must know how to use all the tools available. Training and education can be obtained from minicourses offered by hardware and software companies; from in-house training programs at large companies; from adult and extension classes at high schools and colleges; and from some more progressive software packages that contain their own training courses built into the software. Together with good documentation, good training is mandatory in order for users to receive maximum benefits from the computer.

Summary — data, systems and procedures, and personnel

The data, systems and procedures, and personnel associated with computers are as important as the hardware and software. If any of these areas are ignored, it is unlikely that successful use of the computer will result.

COMPUTER APPLICATIONS

Computers can be used for virtually unlimited applications. It is important, however, to be able to recognize specific applications and situations where computers can be used as an aid to problem solving and as a means for accomplishing tasks more efficiently.

Broadly speaking, applications suitable for processing on a computer fall into eight general categories. Thus, computers should be considered for use when it is necessary or desirable to:

1. Perform numerous and/or complex calculations.
2. Process large volumes of data and produce large volumes of output on a reoccurring basis.
3. Sort, select, summarize, and report on large volumes of data.
4. Process transactions as they occur.
5. Rapidly retrieve data stored in files and/or data bases for the purpose of reporting.
6. Manipulate text and symbols.
7. Change and update data.
8. Communicate data and information.

Many applications fall into more than one of the above categories. The categories are explained below and on the following pages.

Perform numerous and/or complex calculations

Historically, the first computers were designed to be used as tools for scientists, engineers, and mathematicians to assist in performing complex calculations. Today, the computer still serves as an extremely important tool in this area. It is also recognized that business applications can benefit from the computational speed of a computer. The use of electronic spreadsheets illustrates but one of many applications where the computational capabilities of a computer are directly applicable to a business environment.

Whenever an application requires numerous or complex calculations, the use of a computer should be considered.

Processing large volumes of data

For applications which require large volumes of data to be processed on a reoccurring basis and which create large volumes of output, the use of a computer should always be considered. In this context, the term "large volumes of data" is relative; its meaning is dependent upon the user and the type of computer available. A large volume of data for a home computer user might be the names of fifty relatives and friends to whom Christmas cards are sent each year; for a small business or personal computer user, a large volume of data might be the names of 300 customers; and to a large computer user, a large volume of data might mean the names of 300,000 customers who have charge accounts at a department store.

In the world of business, many applications require processing large volumes of data and producing large volumes of output on a reoccuring basis. In most applications of this type, batch processing is used. The example in Figure 4–8 illustrates processing large volumes of data for an electrical utility company. In the example, the following steps occur:

1. Data from the electrical usage source document prepared by meter readers in the field is recorded on a disk for input to the program which prepares the electricity billing statements.
2. Under control of the program in main memory, the data is read a record at a time into main memory.
3. The calculation to determine the electricity usage (300 KW hours) is made by subtracting the beginning meter reading (12391) from the ending meter reading (12691). The billing total ($36.00) is calculated by multiplying the KW hours times the rate per hour (.12).
4. The statement containing the name of the customer, the address, city and zip code, hours, rate, and billing total is printed.

Although this is a very simplified example, it is intended to illustrate the basic steps that occur when processing a large volume of data and producing a large volume of output. In this example, hundreds of thousands of records may be processed during a month. In any related type of application, the same basic steps would occur even though the application may involve more complex calculations or comparing operations.

An important aspect of this application is that the processing is reoccurring. Each month this large volume of data will be read and the statements prepared. The time and money savings realized from computer use increase each time the application is run on the computer.

Any application that involves processing large volumes of data on a reoccurring basis is ideally suited for implementation on a computer.

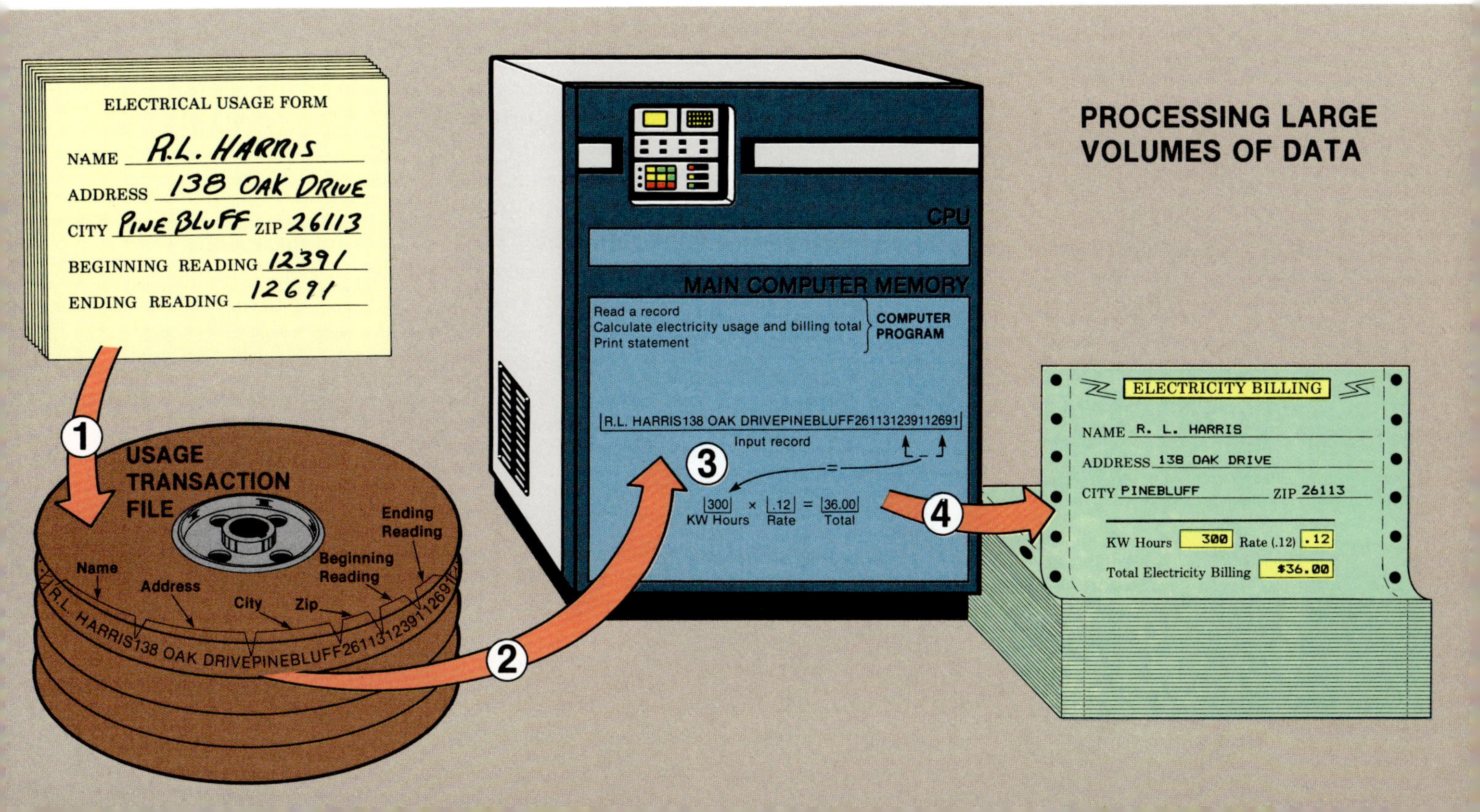

Figure 4–8 In this example, a large volume of data is processed to create the electricity billing statements. Each input record contains the name, address, city, zip code, beginning meter reading, and ending meter reading. The program calculates the usage hours by subtracting the beginning reading from the ending reading. The billing total is then calculated by multiplying the KW hours times the rate per hour. The statement is then printed.

Sorting, selecting, summarizing, and reporting data

When processing large volumes of data, as just illustrated, in many cases the data must be in some sequence in order to be useful. **Sorting** is the process of examining the records in a file and placing them in an ascending or descending sequence based upon the value in a field or fields within the record. Data can be sorted in sequence based upon numeric values in a field and can be sorted in alphabetical sequence based upon alphabetic values found in a field.

In addition to sorting, other common types of processing which take place on large volumes of data are selecting certain data, summarizing data found in files, and reporting the data in a number of different formats.

The example in Figure 4–9 illustrates an application in which various reports are prepared from hospital admittance records. The processing is as follows:

1. As each patient is admitted to the hospital, the admitting clerk enters the name of the patient's doctor, the patient's name, the room number to which the patient is assigned, and the time the patient checked in. This data is stored on the hard disk used for this application.
2. In the evening, after all patients have been admitted for the day, five different reports are prepared from the data entered when the patients were admitted. These reports are:
   a. Report 1 — This report is a record by record listing of the data entered when patients were admitted. It is in time sequence because that is the sequence in which data is entered. The report contains the time in, the patient name, the doctor name, and the room occupied by the patient.
   b. Report 2 — This report is printed in room number sequence. The records have been sorted in ascending sequence by room number; that is, the lowest room number, 102, is the first record printed; the next lowest room number, 112, is the next room number printed; and so on. This report, since it is in room number sequence rather than time sequence as report 1, could be used for an entirely different purpose than report 1 even though they are prepared from exactly the same input data.
   c. Report 3 — Report 3 is a **selective report** listing only those patients who are in rooms 200 - 250. These rooms are the intensive care rooms in the hospital, and the patients in these rooms must be specially identified. Therefore, these rooms have been selected for use on this report.
   d. Report 4 — A listing of the patients for each doctor is on this report. The report is in alphabetical sequence by doctor name and, for each doctor, in ascending sequence by room number. The total number of patients for each doctor is also printed. This report is called a **control break report** because each time the doctor name changes, a control break is said to have occurred. In this report, when a control break occurs, the total number of patients for the doctor is printed. In order for a control break report to be prepared, the records for each doctor must be grouped together. Thus, all records for Dr. Nance must be together, all records for Dr. Ward must be together, and so on. In most cases, sorting is used to place the records together.
   e. Report 5 — This is a **summary report** containing the number of patients for each doctor. The input records have been read, and the number of patients for each doctor were counted. This value is then printed. The total number of patients is the same value which was printed in report 4. The difference here is that this summary report contains only the total number of patients; it does not contain each patient.

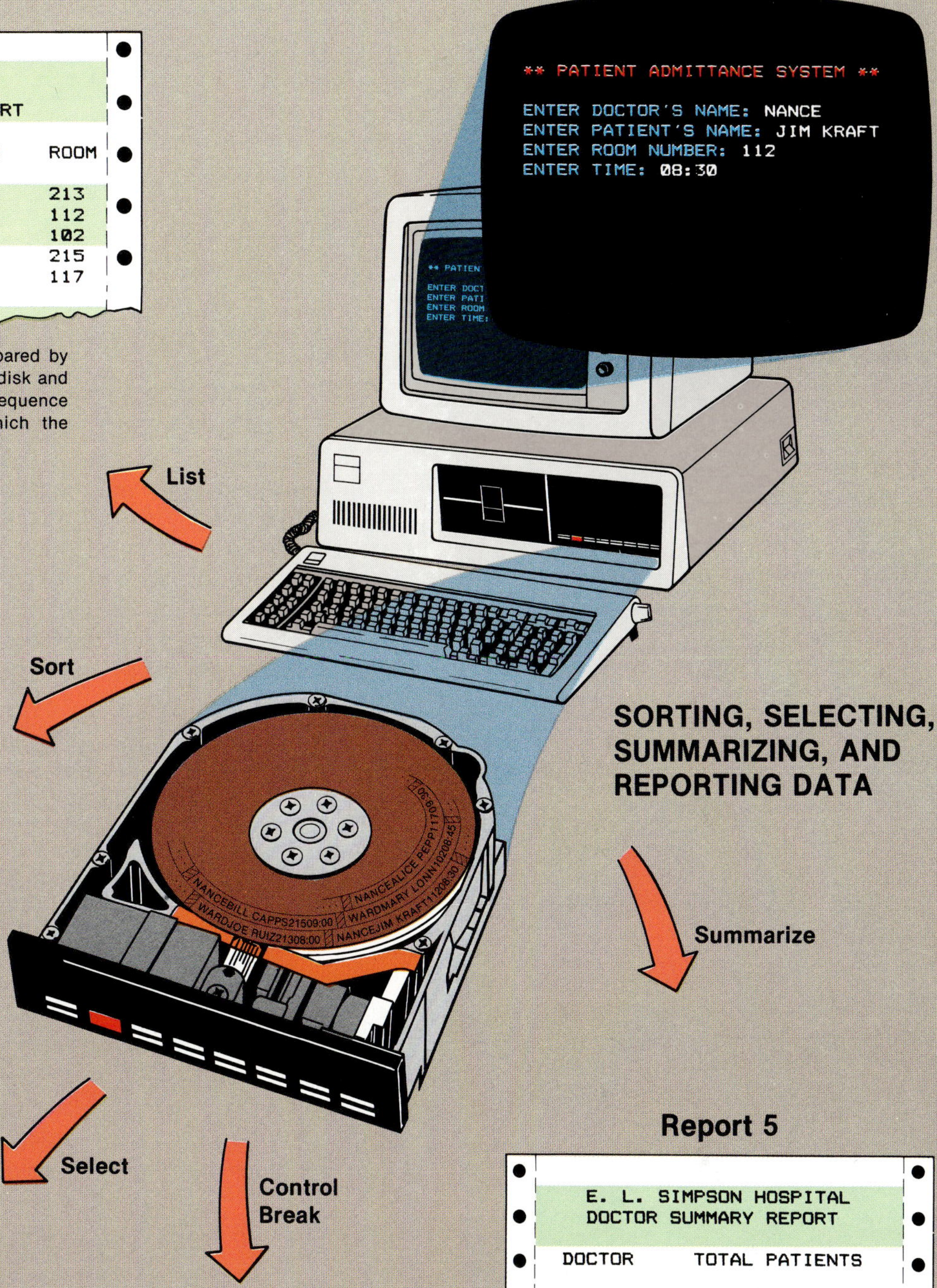

Report 1

E. L. SIMPSON HOSPITAL
PATIENT ADMITTANCE REPORT

TIME IN	PATIENT	DOCTOR	ROOM
8:00	JOE RUIZ	WARD	213
8:30	JIM KRAFT	NANCE	112
8:45	MARY LONN	WARD	102
9:00	BILL CAPPS	NANCE	215
9:30	ALICE PEPP	NANCE	117

Report 1 — Listing: This report is prepared by reading each of the records stored on disk and printing them. They are in time sequence because this is the sequence in which the records were entered.

List

```
** PATIENT ADMITTANCE SYSTEM **

ENTER DOCTOR'S NAME: NANCE
ENTER PATIENT'S NAME: JIM KRAFT
ENTER ROOM NUMBER: 112
ENTER TIME: 08:30
```

Report 2

E. L. SIMPSON HOSPITAL
ROOM ASSIGNMENTS REPORT

ROOM	PATIENT	DOCTOR
102	MARY LONN	WARD
112	JIM KRAFT	NANCE
117	ALICE PEPP	NANCE
213	JOE RUIZ	WARD
215	BILL CAPPS	NANCE

Report 2 — Sorting by Room Number: The records used to create this report are sorted in ascending room number sequence and then they are read and printed. The records are in a different sequence than in report 1 because they have been sorted.

Sort

SORTING, SELECTING, SUMMARIZING, AND REPORTING DATA

Summarize

Report 5

E. L. SIMPSON HOSPITAL
DOCTOR SUMMARY REPORT

DOCTOR	TOTAL PATIENTS
NANCE	3
WARD	2

Report 5 — Summary Report: A summary report contains totals for certain values which can be accumulated. In this report, the number of patients for each doctor is accumulated and then printed. The report does not contain any of the detail data which is used to accumulate the totals. Only the totals are printed.

Select

Control Break

Report 3

E. L. SIMPSON HOSPITAL
INTENSIVE CARE REPORT

ROOM	PATIENT	DOCTOR
213	JOE RUIZ	WARD
215	BILL CAPPS	NANCE

Report 3 — Selecting: Specific records in the input file are selected for printing based upon a predetermined criteria. In this example, all patients in rooms 200 – 250 are printed because these are the intensive care rooms.

Report 4

E. L. SIMPSON HOSPITAL
DOCTOR REPORT

DOCTOR	ROOM	PATIENT
NANCE	112	JIM KRAFT
	117	ALICE PEPP
	215	BILL CAPPS
	TOTAL PATIENTS	3
WARD	102	MARY LONN
	213	JOE RUIZ
	TOTAL PATIENTS	2

Report 4 — Control Break Reporting: A control break occurs when the value in a control field changes. When a control break occurs, unique processing normally will be done. In this report, when the name of the doctor (the control field) changes, a control break has occurred, and the total number of patients for the doctor is printed.

Figure 4–9 Sample reports

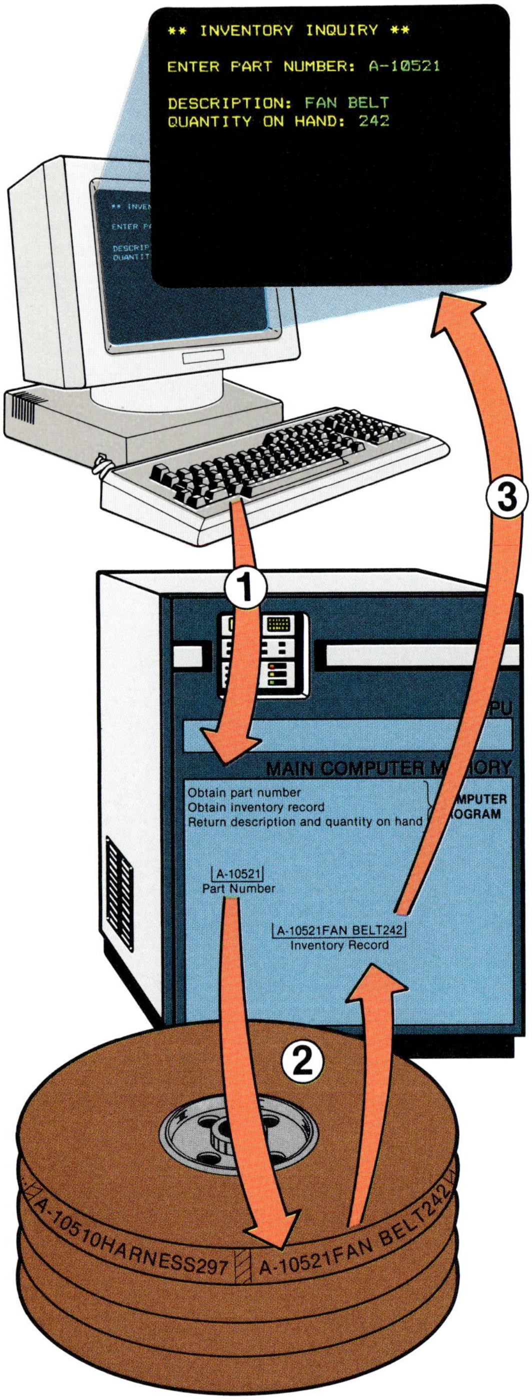

Figure 4–10 The ability to rapidly retrieve data allows this inquiry to determine the quantity on hand for a part. Under program control, the inventory record corresponding to the part number entered by the terminal operator is retrieved from the data base and the description and quantity on hand are sent to the terminal.

The processing illustrated in these five reports is commonly found in applications placed upon computers. Whenever data must be sorted, selected, summarized, and reported, the user should consider using a computer for the application.

Processing transactions as they occur

Previous examples in Figure 4–3, Figure 4–4, and Figure 4–6 have illustrated the use of the computer to process a transaction at the time the transaction occurs. Whether it is calculating savings account earnings, processing a returned car, or completing a sale in a retail store, all of these applications required that the transaction be processed as soon as it occurred. Whenever a need arises to process a transaction when it occurs, the use of a computer should be considered.

Rapid data retrieval

Many applications in both business and science require access to data. In most cases, the access must be rapid because the data is needed for some type of calculation or as information for communication to someone. For those applications which require rapid access and retrieval of data, the computer is the perfect tool.

To illustrate the need for rapid data retrieval and the ability of the computer to provide that function, consider the example in Figure 4–10 where a salesperson on the road must know if there are enough parts in inventory to fill a customer's order. Typically, the salesperson would be in the office of the customer and need to know immediately if the order could be filled. In this example, the salesperson could call the CRT terminal operator in the local office. There, the following processing would occur:

1. The CRT operator would enter the part number (A-10521) on the CRT terminal. The inquiry would be sent to a computer located in the home office of the company.
2. There, the program in the computer would randomly retrieve from the data base the inventory record for the part number entered.
3. The description of the part and the quantity in inventory would be displayed on the CRT terminal, and the operator would then inform the salesperson over the telephone.

In this example, the ability of the computer to rapidly retrieve data stored on auxiliary storage made the application possible. This ability is used in many applications. For example, airlines use this capability to determine if seats are available on a flight, hotels determine if rooms are available, directory service telephone operators use rapid retrieval to provide telephone numbers, and stock brokers use it to determine the latest activity on the stock market.

The processing described here is interactive processing because the data retrieval and return of information occurs immediately. Interactive processing together with rapid data retrieval is a powerful use of computers.

Manipulating text and symbols

A computer has the capability of manipulating text and symbols for display on the CRT screen, for printing on a printer, and for communicating to other computers and terminals. One of the most widely used text manipulating applications found on a computer is word processing. As an example of the ability of word processing programs to manipulate data, the drawings in Figure 4–11 illustrate three CRT screens. On the first screen, a memo has been written to all sales managers concerning a new bonus plan. Before sending it, however, several changes were necessary, including correcting the last sentence which was incorrectly written. On screen 2, additions have been made. The person from whom the memo is sent has been added. The year the bonus takes effect was added, and the words PLEASE NOTIFY were added to the last sentence. When these additions were performed, text was moved from one position to another by the word processing program.

On screen 3, some deletions from the text were made. The mention of the board of directors was deleted, and the date with reference to Hanna Butler was deleted. When deletions were made, the text was changed so that the words were properly spaced. Whenever an application requires text manipulation, computer use should be considered.

The computer is also quite capable of manipulating symbols and drawings, both on CRT screens and for display on a printer. Examples of symbol manipulation include line drawings made for engineers, color graphics for applications ranging from business graphs to games played on home computers, and symbols which are used to control the computer.

Whenever an application calls for text or symbol manipulation, the use of a computer should be considered.

Changing and updating data

When an application requires data to be kept up to date, consideration should be given to using a computer to store and update the data. This use of computers was shown in Chapter 3 and has been illustrated several times in this chapter. For example, in Figure 4–4 on page 4.3, the auto rental agency entered data to prepare the final auto rental agreement. In addition, the record for the auto in the vehicle records file was changed to reflect the new mileage on the car.

In Figure 4–5 on page 4.5, each purchase by a credit card customer caused the customer's record in the account file to be changed to show the new account balance. And, the example in Figure 4–6 on page 4.6 illustrated updating an inventory quantity in an item file each time a retail transaction occurred.

Updating can be done in either an interactive processing mode or a batch processing mode. When updating data in an interactive mode the data must be retrieved randomly because sequential retrieval takes too long.

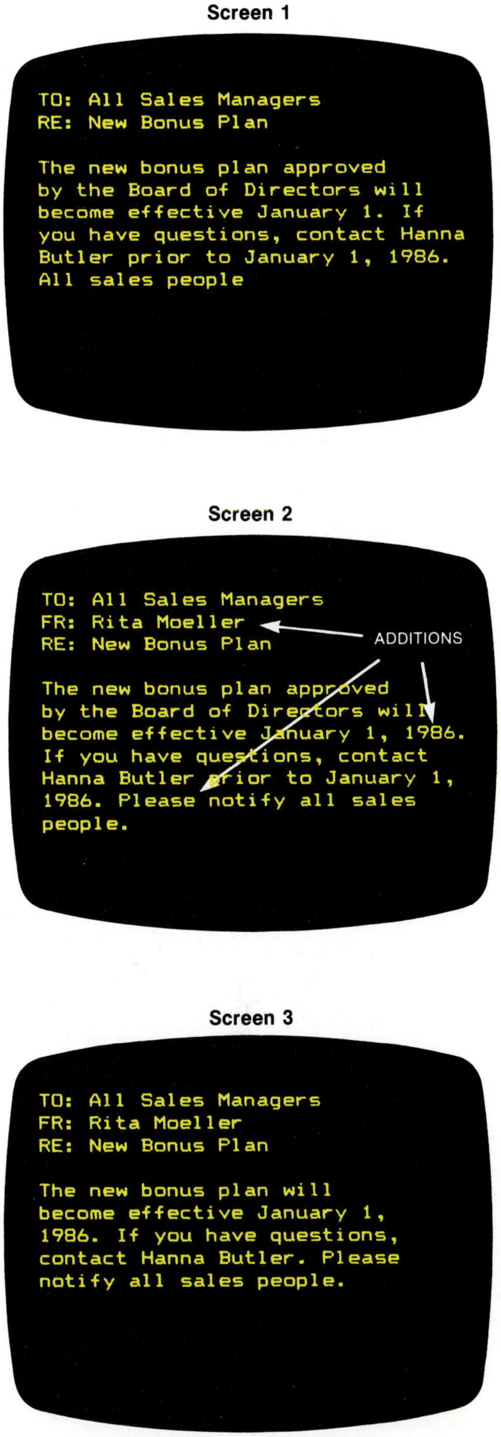
Screen 1
TO: All Sales Managers
RE: New Bonus Plan
The new bonus plan approved
by the Board of Directors will
become effective January 1. If
you have questions, contact Hanna
Butler prior to January 1, 1986.
All sales people
Screen 2
TO: All Sales Managers
FR: Rita Moeller
RE: New Bonus Plan
ADDITIONS
The new bonus plan approved
by the Board of Directors will
become effective January 1, 1986.
If you have questions, contact
Hanna Butler prior to January 1,
1986. Please notify all sales
people.
Screen 3
TO: All Sales Managers
FR: Rita Moeller
RE: New Bonus Plan
The new bonus plan will
become effective January 1,
1986. If you have questions,
contact Hanna Butler. Please
notify all sales people.

Figure 4–11 The three screens shown here illustrate the progressive development of a memo using word processing. In screen 1, the name of the sender was omitted, and the last sentence was incomplete. In screen 2, these errors were corrected, and the year for the effective date was added. Note how words were moved to different lines when the additions were made. In screen 3, deletions were made, resulting in the memo which was actually sent.

In summary, if an application requires data to be kept in a current status, then a computer may be the proper tool to use.

Communicating data and information

As noted previously, computers can communicate over long distances with each other and with terminals. When an application requires data and information to be communicated over a distance, a computer may be the most effective means for doing it. The example in Figure 4–12 shows an application where a law firm has offices in cities throughout the United States. The firm has a need to communicate for two purposes:

1. The first is for communications within the company. To accomplish this task, the personal computers found in the firm can all communicate with one another. In Figure 4–12, an attorney in Washington, D. C. has sent a message concerning an anti-trust ruling which may affect some of the cases within the firm. The message also indicates that the ruling has been stored in the data base maintained by the law firm on its computer in Washington. Therefore, any attorney who needs to read the ruling can obtain it from the computer in Washington.
2. The second purpose of electronic communications within the law firm is to access a large computer operated by a legal services company which contains decisions from cases throughout the United States. In Figure 4–12, an attorney in Los Angeles asked for cases where software copyrights have been an issue. The computer returned citations for three cases which might be useful.

A major function of computers is to electronically communicate. The communication need not take place over large geographical distances. Many applications exist where users of personal computers communicate with one another from office to office or even from desk to desk within an office. In most cases, each of these computers can access a common data base that is maintained either on one of the personal computers or on a larger computer. Communications is an important application of computers.

Summary — computer applications

The eight general categories of applications discussed in this section can be used as a guideline to the types of applications which can be placed on a computer. Many applications fall into more than one category. Each general category shares common characteristics, among which are:

1. They use the information processing cycle (input, process, output, storage).
2. They process data in some manner.
3. They require exact definitions of the processing to be performed, including calculations to be performed, comparisons and alternative processing to occur, and the format of the output to be produced.
4. They require systems and procedures to be designed.
5. They require knowledgeable people to use them.

Whenever a similar application with the characteristics specified above is encountered, it is likely the application could be implemented on a computer.

Figure 4–12 (opposite page) The law firm has personal computers in each office which can communicate with each other over telephone lines. In addition, the personal computers communicate with a large computer operated by a legal services company over both telephone lines (from Chicago and Los Angeles) and satellite (Washington and Dallas).

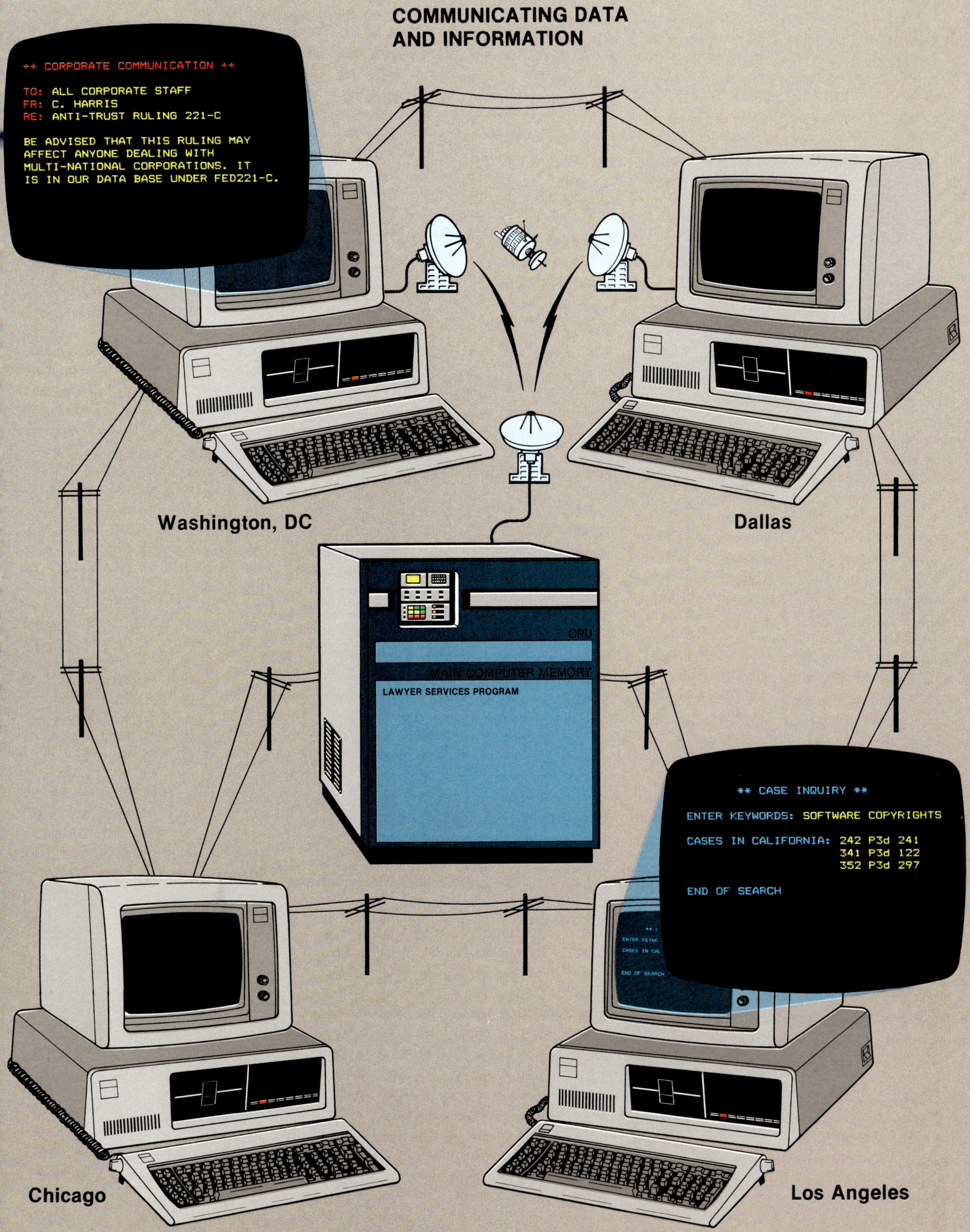
COMMUNICATING DATA AND INFORMATION
++ CORPORATE COMMUNICATION ++
TO: ALL CORPORATE STAFF
FR: C. HARRIS
RE: ANTI-TRUST RULING 221-C
BE ADVISED THAT THIS RULING MAY AFFECT ANYONE DEALING WITH MULTI-NATIONAL CORPORATIONS. IT IS IN OUR DATA BASE UNDER FED221-C.
Washington, DC
Dallas
CPU
MAIN COMPUTER MEMORY
LAWYER SERVICES PROGRAM
** CASE INQUIRY **
ENTER KEYWORDS: SOFTWARE COPYRIGHTS
CASES IN CALIFORNIA: 242 P3d 241
341 P3d 122
352 P3d 297
END OF SEARCH
Chicago
Los Angeles

Processing Large Volumes of Data

One of the eight general categories of applications which are implemented on a computer is processing large volumes of data and producing large volumes of output on a reoccurring basis. Any business organization that is involved in processing large volumes of data should seriously consider the advantages of performing such processing using a computer.

A large volume of data must be entered into the computer for processing. In many companies, the data is entered into the computer for processing in either the batch mode or the interactive mode or a combined batch and interactive mode from numerous locations or departments throughout the company. The personnel in each department enter data which is appropriate for the function performed in the department. Thus, the marketing department would enter data concerning marketing applications, such as sales forecasts, customer information, sales data, and so on. The accounting department would enter data concerning accounting applications, including accounts payable and accounts receivable.

To illustrate this concept, the photograph on the right shows the order entry department for a large electronic distribution company. The order entry department has the responsibility of processing orders received by the company. This distribution company receives hundreds of orders each day. The personnel in the order entry department enter the orders directly into the computer for combined interactive and batch processing. The orders are entered through the many terminals placed on the desks of the order entry clerks.

The use of terminals located in departments throughout a company to enter large amounts of data has proved to be an efficient and cost-effective means for data entry.

Figure 4–13 An order entry department where large volumes of data are processed in a combined interactive and batch mode.

Figure 4-14 Complex scientific equations can rapidly be solved using a computer program designed for the application.

Performing Numerous and Complex Calculations

Whenever there is a need to perform numerous and complex calculations, consideration should be given to the use of a computer. Historically, computers were developed to solve complex mathematical and scientific problems that could take hours, days, and even weeks to solve manually. The rapid calculation capabilities of computers are indispensable in such diverse fields as space exploration, genetic research, and chemical analysis.

Today, in addition to their use for solving scientific, engineering, and mathematical problems, the calculating capabilities of computers are being used each day in the world of business and finance. Computers are often used for modeling business environments in order to perform "what if" simulation exercises. Without the computer, many of the scientific and business developments that are occurring so rapidly would not be possible. We are, indeed, a society that is dependent upon the computer.

Figure 4-15 The computer is a valuable tool for business people who must perform calculations as a part of their job duties.

Figure 4–16 The photograph above illustrates a physical chemist using a computer workstation to interactively set up large scale molecular mechanics calculations for determining the minimum energy conformations of molecules and to display the results of the calculations.

Manipulating Text and Symbols

Although computers have traditionally been thought of as devices which are utilized to ''compute,'' that is, perform calculations rapidly and accurately, the ability of the computer to manipulate text and symbols, under operator control, is a powerful capability that has found use in many applications in all areas of business and science.

Manipulating text material refers to the computer's

ability to manipulate letters of the alphabet and numbers. This capability is necessary in word processing systems. With word processing systems, correspondence such as letters and memos can be stored in main computer memory. Corrections can be made to the data, and letters, words, sentences, and paragraphs can be added, deleted, or changed as required.

The ability of the computer to manipulate symbols allows mathematical models of data to be displayed on the CRT screen. With very high resolution color screens, parts of machines, equipment, or other engineering designs can be displayed, rotated, and changed in a three-dimensional form.

Figure 4–18 The computer's ability to manipulate alphabetic data has led to the development of sophisticated word processing systems.

Figure 4–17 (opposite page) Very high resolution screens from Computervision are used to display geometric models, surface discontinuities, and other design characteristics for better visualization and model validation.

Figure 4–19 Computer generated business graphics allows numeric data to be displayed in a variety of forms and colors.

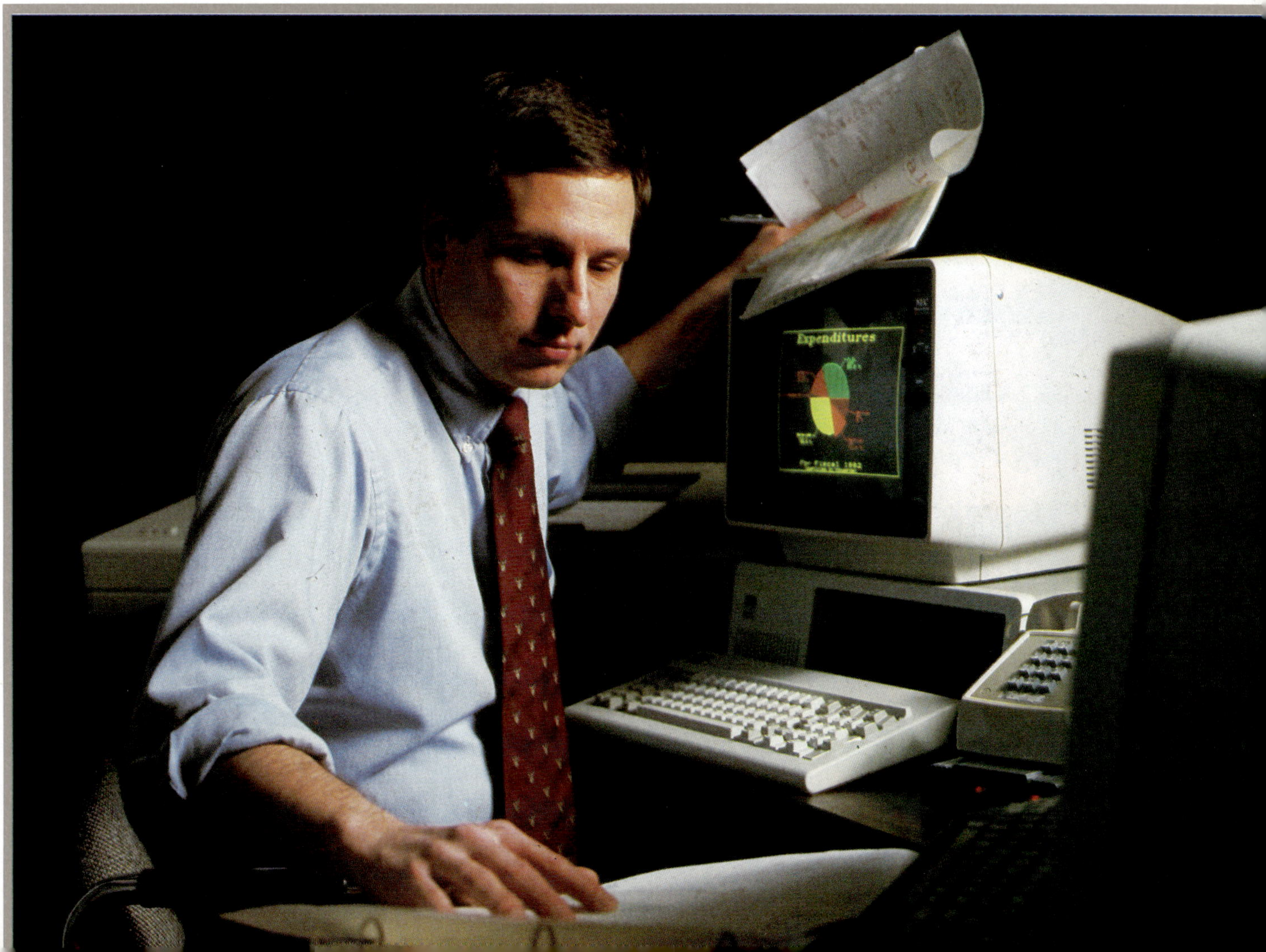

CHAPTER SUMMARY

1. A computer literate person should be able to answer the question, "Is the computer an appropriate tool for my application?"
2. Data is the heart of an information processing system.
3. Data is organized into fields, records, files, and data bases for processing on a computer.
4. Data is input to the information processing cycle, within which five operations can occur: input, arithmetic, logical, output, and storage.
5. The basic operations of the information processing cycle can be used in two primary modes: the interactive mode and the batch mode.
6. Elements required to ensure successful use of a computer to produce useful information include an analysis of data attributes, systems and procedures, and personnel.
7. An analysis of data attributes is required to ensure the reliability of the information generated from processing data.
8. Systems and procedures are required so that people can interface with computer processing when required.
9. Personnel are required in many areas of computing in order to successfully implement information processing systems.
10. Applications implemented on a computer fall into eight general categories.
11. To answer the question, "Is the computer an appropriate tool for my application?" the user should determine the application category or categories; the requirements of the application should be determined; the data to be processed must be identified; the processing must be examined to define the operations to be performed on the data; the mode of processing must be determined; and the data attributes, systems and procedures, and personnel to implement the application must be determined.
12. The two most generally used modes for processing data on a computer are called interactive processing and batch processing.
13. Interactive processing means that as data is entered into the computer as a single field or group of fields, it is processed immediately and output is produced immediately.
14. With batch processing, data records are accumulated and are processed as a group when all of the required records have been gathered.
15. Interactive processing can be used when access to auxiliary storage is required.
16. The key to understanding interactive processing is to realize that as soon as the required input data has been entered, the program performs the processing and returns output to the user.
17. A special form of interactive processing is called transaction-oriented processing. When it is used, the terminal operator enters all of the data pertaining to a complete business transaction; after the data is entered, the program immediately performs all of the processing required for that particular transaction.
18. Batch processing is the best way to implement some applications even though interactive processing has become more prominent.
19. Batch and interactive processing can be combined in a single application.
20. A point of sale terminal is an input device used for retail sales.
21. Generally, most processing performed on personal computers is interactive processing; on large computers, the trend is toward interactive processing although batch processing is still important.
22. Some processing that takes place on computers is difficult to categorize into batch or interactive processing because there are elements of each involved.
23. Data must have the attributes of data integrity, availability, manageability, and security and control.
24. Data integrity determines the confidence a user can have in the processing of that data. The three elements of data integrity are: data accuracy, reliable data entry, and timeliness.
25. Data must be accurate in the sense that the source of the data is reliable, and the data to be entered has been reliably reported.
26. When data is entered into a computer, the values entered must correspond to the values which are supposed to be entered.
27. Besides great care on the part of the person entering the data, data editing is the most effective way to ensure reliable data entry.

28. Data editing refers to the process of comparing data entered to predetermined values to ensure that the data conforms to the predetermined criteria.

29. Timeliness means that data to be processed in an information processing system has not lost its usefulness or accuracy because time has passed.

30. Availability means the data required for an application can be obtained in a manner which ensures the integrity of the data.

31. Data management refers to techniques and procedures which ensure that the data required for an application will be available in the correct form and at the proper time for processing.

32. The security and control of data used in a computer is a major issue.

33. A procedure is a series of logical steps by which all repetitive actions are initiated, carried forward, controlled, and finalized.

34. A system is a network of related procedures designed to perform some activity.

35. The procedures within a system are described in the system documentation. Documentation consists of written words, drawings, and screen messages which tell a person the exact procedures for all activities associated with the system.

36. Computer users are people who use an information processing system or who benefit from the system. Users must be well trained.

37. Applications suitable for processing on a computer fall into eight general categories. Computers should be considered for use when it is necessary to: a) Perform numerous or complex calculations; b) Process large volumes of data on a reoccurring basis; c) Sort, select, summarize, and report on large volumes of data; d) Process transactions as they occur; e) Rapidly retrieve data; f) Manipulate text and symbols; g) Change and update data; h) Communicate data and information.

38. Batch processing is normally used when processing large amounts of data on a reoccurring basis.

39. Sorting is the process of examining records in a file and placing them in an ascending or descending sequence based upon the value in a field or fields within the record.

40. Data can be sorted on numeric values or alphabetic values.

41. A selective report lists only those records which satisfy a certain predetermined criteria.

42. A control break occurs when a change in a control field occurs from one record to the next. A control break report contains unique output when a control break occurs.

43. A summary report contains summaries of data found in each record in a file.

44. One of the most widely used text manipulating applications found on a computer is word processing.

45. Updating can be done in either an interactive processing mode or a batch processing mode. When updating data in an interactive mode, the data must be retrieved randomly.

46. When an application requires data and information to be communicated over a distance, a computer may be the most effective means for doing it. The communication need not take place over large geographical distances.

47. Applications found in the eight general categories all share the following characteristics: a) They use the information processing cycle; b) They process data; c) They require exact definitions of the processing to be performed; d) They require systems and procedures to be designed; e) They require knowledgeable people to use them.

KEY TERMS

Accurate (data) 4.9
Availability (of data) 4.9
Batch processing 4.2
Computer users 4.11
Control break report 4.14
Data editing 4.9
Data integrity 4.8
Data management 4.10
Data security and control 4.10
Documentation 4.11
Education and training 4.11
Interactive processing 4.2
Point of sale terminal 4.7
Procedure 4.10
Reliable data entry 4.9
Selective report 4.14
Sorting 4.14
Source documents 4.4
Summary report 4.14
System 4.10
Timeliness 4.9
Transaction-oriented processing 4.3

REVIEW QUESTIONS

1. What is interactive processing? When is it used?
2. What is batch processing? When is its use appropriate?
3. What mode of processing is normally found on personal computers? On larger computers?
4. What is transaction-oriented processing? Why is transaction-oriented processing used?
5. Why would a computer user use batch processing rather than transaction-oriented processing?
6. Is it possible to have batch processing and interactive processing in the same application? Why wouldn't just one processing mode be used?
7. What is data integrity? What are the three elements of data integrity?
8. What are the two most effective ways to ensure reliable data entry? Describe data editing when entering an account balance.
9. Define the following terms and give examples of each: Data availability; Data management; Data security and control.
10. What is a procedure? What is a system? What activities in an information processing system must procedures identify?
11. Who are computer users? Give examples. What is the most important consideration for computer users, and how can it be obtained?
12. List the eight general categories for computer applications and, through the use of diagrams, illustrate an example of each category.
13. List the common characteristics shared by each category of application found on a computer.

CONTROVERSIAL ISSUES

1. In the past few years, some authorities have advocated that all applications placed on a computer should use the interactive processing mode. These people state that such features as the inherent delays when processing data in a batch mode make batch obsolete. Other experts dispute this, saying that for some applications, batch is the best means for processing data. Take a position on this disagreement and defend your position.
2. Much of the software offered for sale in computer stores today is sold with a small, thin booklet which contains the documentation for the program and system. In many cases, the procedures to implement the software are not clearly presented. Those who sell this software argue that these booklets are adequate because the software used on personal computers is not very complicated. Others present the position that this inadequate documentation of personal computer software threatens the very industry itself because users will not be able to successfully use the software. Which do you think is right and why? If you were to purchase software for a personal computer, would documentation be important to you? Why?

RESEARCH PROJECTS

1. Choose one of the categories of applications specified on page 4.12 of this chapter. Then visit a computer installation and find an application that fits the category you chose. Prepare a report describing the application, including the processing mode used, the manner in which data is entered into the computer, the processing that is performed in the application, the way in which the output is presented, and the requirements for storing and retrieving data on auxiliary storage.
2. Visit a computer installation and obtain a systems and procedures manual for an application which has been implemented on a computer. Prepare a report on the manual, including what is presented in the manual and how it is presented. Give your opinion concerning whether the manual is easy to use and understand.

Chapter Five

Input to the Computer

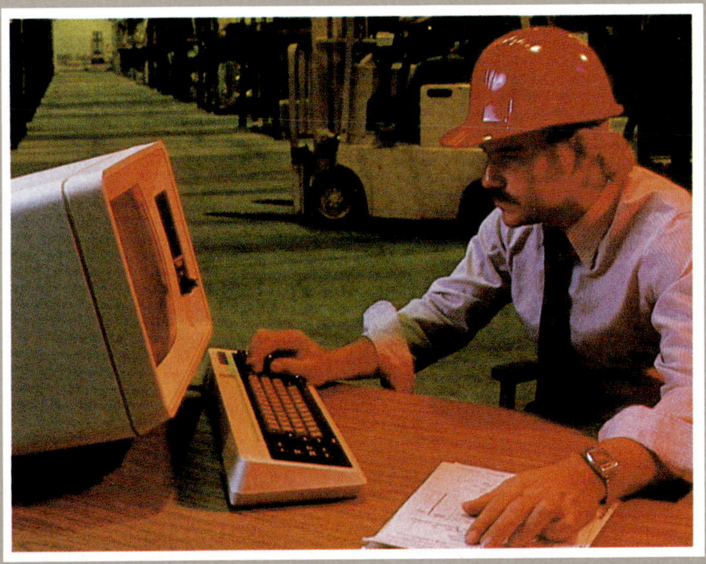

Objectives

- ☐ Describe on-line and off-line data entry and the uses for each
- ☐ Indicate the features of data entry for interactive processing and batch processing
- ☐ Identify the three classes of terminals and how each is used
- ☐ Specify the features found on keyboards and screens for display terminals
- ☐ Describe devices used for off-line data entry in a batch processing mode
- ☐ Illustrate the uses of optical character reading devices
- ☐ List and identify the systems and procedures issues associated with the data entry function
- ☐ Describe point of sale terminals and graphical input devices and their uses

Input to the Computer

Chapter Five

In the information processing cycle, the input step must occur before any data can be processed and any information produced. Without valid input data, a computer is not capable of producing any useful information. When computers were first utilized for business applications, there was not much of a decision to be made concerning the type of input to be used. Nearly all computers used punched cards as input to batch processing systems.

The data was recorded on cards using a device called a **keypunch**. A keypunch is a machine that contains a keyboard and a punching mechanism. As the keys are depressed, holes representing numbers, letters of the alphabet, or special characters were punched in the card. The cards were then grouped together (batched), and read into main computer memory by a card reader, which could interpret the holes in the card and store the correct data in main computer memory.

Today, punched cards are seldom used as input to a computer. In addition, the decision concerning the type of input to use for an application and the device or devices to be used for the input operation is considerably more complex. This chapter will examine the input operations used on a computer and explore the many and varied devices available for entering data into main computer memory for processing.

USES OF DATA

As noted previously, data must be entered and stored in main computer memory prior to any processing taking place on that data. While the basic reason for entering data into a computer is to make the data available for processing by a program also stored in main computer memory, there are three uses to which the data is put once it is entered into main memory. These uses of the data directly influence the type of data entry and the devices used for entering data into main memory. The three uses of data are:

1. Control the computer — One use of the data entered into a computer is to direct the computer to perform certain activities. For example, if a user wanted to use an electronic spreadsheet program, a command would have to be issued to load the program into main computer memory from auxiliary storage, and a command would have to be issued to begin the execution of the program (Figure 5–2).

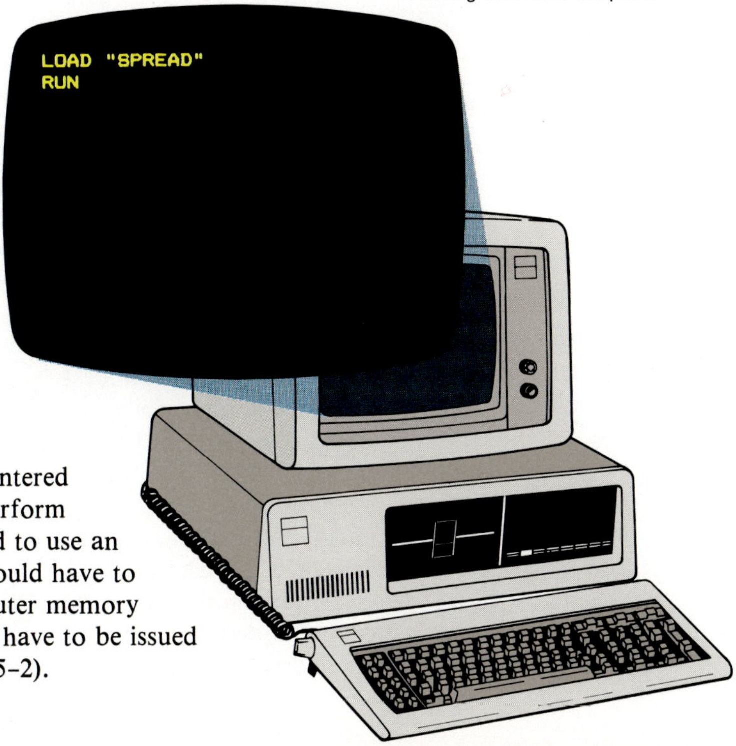

Figure 5–2 In this example, the computer user has entered a command to load the program called "SPREAD" and then issued the command RUN, which will cause the program to be executed. Entering commands to direct the computer to perform an activity is one reason for entering data on a computer.

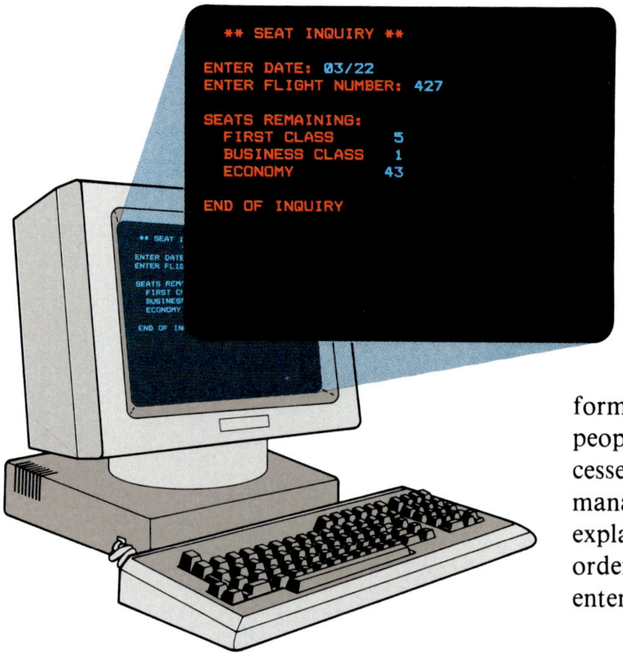

Figure 5–3 An inquiry allows a computer user to request information from a computer. Here, a program which allows a seat inquiry is used to determine the number of seats remaining on an airline flight. The user enters the date and flight number, and the program responds with the number of seats in each class on the flight. Generally, only a small amount of data must be entered to request information via an inquiry. The data entered is not used to generate information; rather it is used to identify what information is desired.

2. Request information from the computer — A user must enter data into a computer when requesting information. The most usual type of request for information is an inquiry. An **inquiry** is an entry into a computer to request information. In most inquiries, a user enters a minimum amount of data, usually only one or two data items, to inform the program of the data requested (Figure 5–3).
3. Serve as the source from which information is produced — This is the use for most data that is entered into a computer. When data is the source from which information is produced, a computer program performs operations on it to produce information that is useful for people. For example, data entered from sales orders can be processed by a computer progam to produce sales reports useful to management. The remainder of this chapter will be devoted to explaining this third use, the manner in which data is entered in order to produce information, and the devices which are used to enter the data.

DATA ENTRY TO PRODUCE INFORMATION

As noted in Chapter 4, applications process data to produce information in either the interactive mode or the batch processing mode. The methods used to enter data for interactive and batch processing differ somewhat. Each of them is explained in the following paragraphs.

Enter data for processing in the interactive processing mode

Data entered for processing in the interactive processing mode will generate immediate output. In virtually every case where interactive data entry takes place, the person entering the data is communicating directly with the computer which will process the data. Therefore, data entry for interactive processing is said to be **on-line,** meaning that the device from which the data is being entered is connected directly to the computer.

The output generated from data entry for interactive processing is not always received at the location where the data was entered. In Figure 5–4, for example, the data is entered from a terminal located in the order entry department. The data entered concerns a purchase by a customer. After the data is entered, a picking slip is generated and is printed on a printer in the warehouse. The worker in the warehouse would then retrieve the item purchased (in this case, a lawn mower) so that when the shipping van arrived, the lawn mower would be ready for shipping. The terminal operator in the order entry department never sees the output generated, yet this is interactive processing because the data entered is processed immediately and output is generated immediately.

The person entering the order in the order entry department may enter hundreds of such orders each day. When large amounts of data are entered by a terminal operator whose only job is to enter the data, the data entry function is said to be

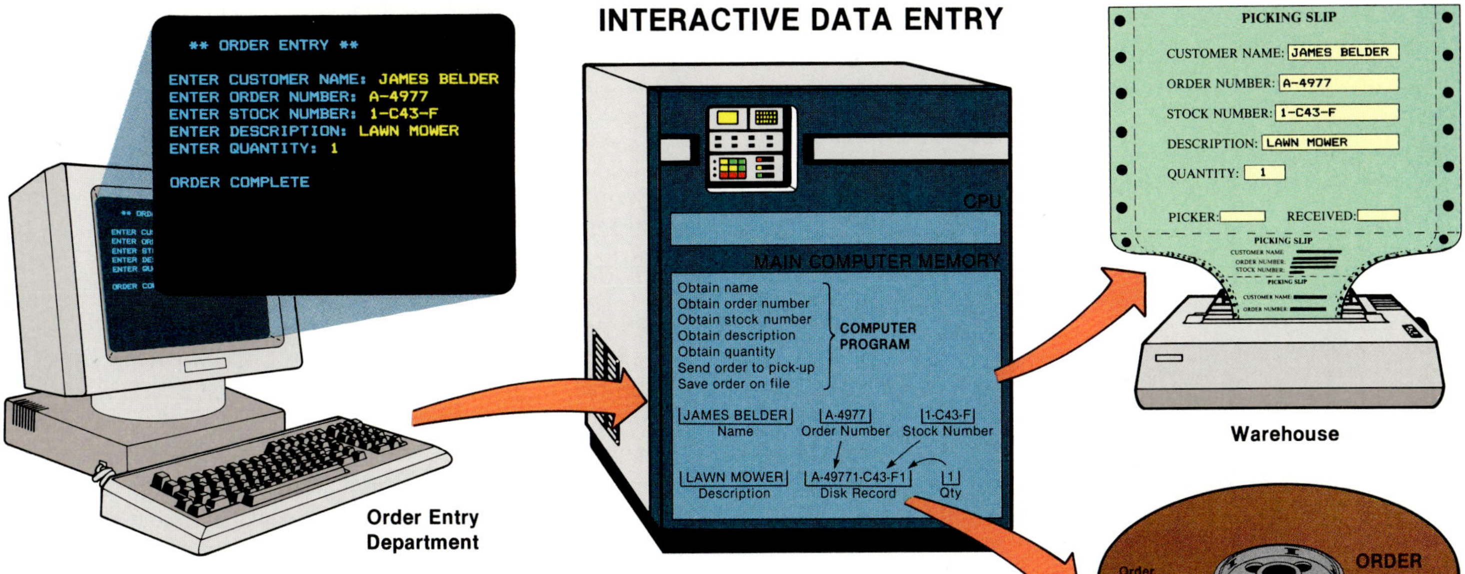

production data entry. Many types of devices are used to enter data for interactive processing, although the vast majority of data is entered using a keyboard attached to a terminal.

Enter data for processing in the batch processing mode

When data is entered for processing in the batch processing mode, the data is stored on a storage medium (usually either tape or disk) for processing at a later time in the batch processing mode. Data entered for batch processing can be entered in either an on-line or an off-line manner. As noted previously, on-line data entry means that the device from which the data is being entered is connected directly to the computer which will process the data (Figure 5–5).

Off-line data entry, on the other hand, means that the device from which the data is being entered is not connected to the computer which will process the data (Figure 5-6). Instead, the data is entered using a special computer or other device devoted to the data entry function. This computer or special device accepts the input data and stores the data on disk or tape. At a later time, the disk or tape can be transported to the site where the data will be entered for processing in a batch mode to produce information.

When off-line data entry is used, source documents must be accumulated prior to entering the data. **Source documents** are documents which contain the data to be

Figure 5–4 In this example of data entry for interactive processing, the data is entered by a terminal operator in the order entry department. The output generated from the processing, however, is printed in the warehouse. In addition, a disk record for the order is created and stored.

Figure 5–5 When on-line data entry is used for data that will be processed in a batch mode, the data is entered directly into the computer. The data is then stored, usually on disk, for processing at a later time by the same computer.

OFF-LINE DATA ENTRY

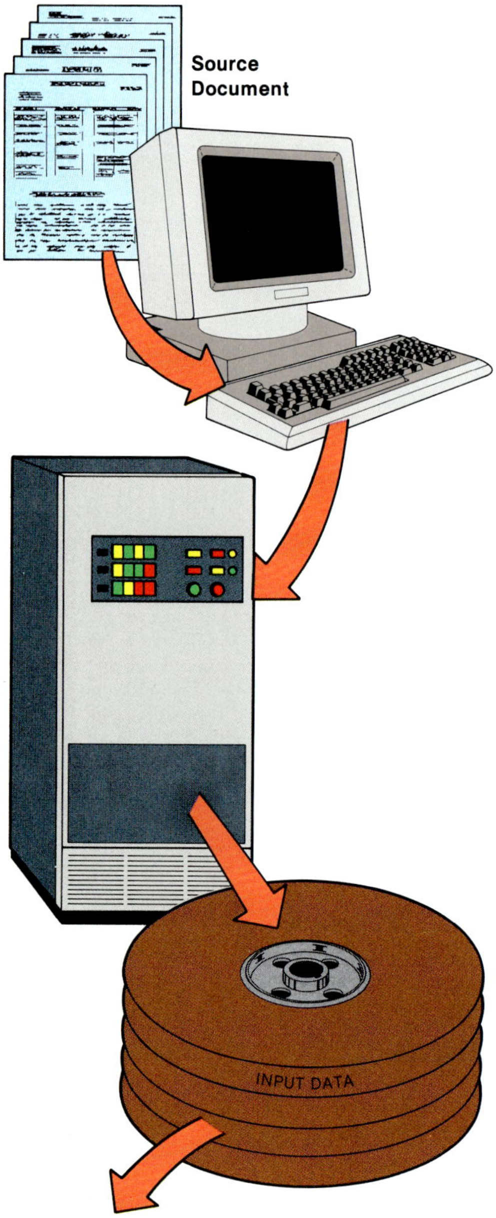

Figure 5-6 When off-line data entry is used, the data from source documents is entered via a terminal or other input device normally connected to a smaller computer, such as a minicomputer. As it is entered, the data is stored on disk. After all data has been entered, the disk can be transported to the main computer room where the data will be processed; or the data can be copied from disk to tape for transporting to the computer room for processing on magnetic tape drives.

entered by the data entry operator. For example, in a payroll application, timecards for hourly employees would be the source documents from which the hours worked would be entered by the data entry operators.

In many applications, batch processing is used to establish controls that ensure data is entered and processed accurately. In a credit card payment application, for example, all payments received would be added manually prior to data entry of the payments. When the payments are processed on the computer, the total amount of the payments would be compared to the total determined from the manual addition performed prior to data entry. If the totals are the same, then it is evidence that the data was entered accurately. If the totals are not the same, however, then further checking must be performed to determine if the data was entered incorrectly. **Batch controls** such as just described are an important reason why batch processing is used.

The devices used to enter data for batch processing vary considerably. Keying devices with a keyboard are very often found. So also are specialized devices which are used for specific types of applications. All of these devices will be examined in detail later in this chapter. Regardless of the type of device used, however, they are all production devices which are designed to enter data rapidly, accurately, and economically for later processing. It must be kept in mind throughout the remainder of this chapter that the devices and techniques for data entry that are discussed all relate to the task of entering data which will be the source of information produced from computer processing.

Types of data entered to produce information

The types of data entered either for interactive processing or batch processing within an organization depend entirely upon the applications implemented on the computer. In most organizations, accounting functions are implemented using the computer. In those applications, the data entered for processing will relate to the accounting functions within the organization. Such data as orders received, expenditures made, money received, money owed, payments made, and so on will be relevant for the accounting applications.

Other applications require data entry related to their needs. For example, the payroll application requires such data as time worked, changes to tax status, changes to pay rate, and so on, in order to produce the payroll information required. Sales applications require data such as who purchased the item, how many items were purchased, the date they were purchased, the credit terms, and so on.

In each case, the source of the data will depend upon the application and the mode of processing. In most batch processing systems, the data is entered from source documents. In many interactive processing systems, the source of data can be the telephone or even personal contact with the person supplying the data. Each case, however, can vary and it is difficult to generalize about the source of data.

In every case, however, the goal of data entry is to enter the data reliably and efficiently, regardless of the source of the data and the mode in which the data will be processed.

Summary — data entry to produce information

Entering data to produce information can take place on-line or off-line. On-line data entry is always used for interactive processing and is often used for batch processing as well. Off-line data entry can be used for batch processing. Source documents from which the data is obtained must be gathered prior to the data being entered when using off-line data entry. In either case, when the purpose of entering data is to produce information, a large amount of data may have to be entered. The methods, devices, and systems and procedures used for this data entry function will be examined in the remainder of this chapter.

DEVICES USED FOR DATA ENTRY

The hardware devices used for data entry fall into two broad categories: terminals and devices specifically designed for the data entry function. The following sections describe these two categories and the devices found in each of them.

Terminals

A terminal used for data entry usually consists of: 1) A keyboard for entering data; 2) A CRT screen to display the data entered and to also display messages which may be sent from the computer with which the terminal is communicating; 3) Some type of communications channel, such as a cable or telephone line, which connects the terminal and the computer, allowing the data entered by the terminal operator to be transmitted to the central computer. When terminals are used for data entry purposes, particularly when data is processed in an interactive mode, they can be spread throughout the company (Figure 5–7). Entering data from various locations throughout an organization is called **distributed data entry**. Distributed data entry allows data to be entered by personnel who are located in the department for which the data is being entered. For example, personnel in the accounting department can enter accounting data, personnel in the marketing department can enter marketing data, and so on.

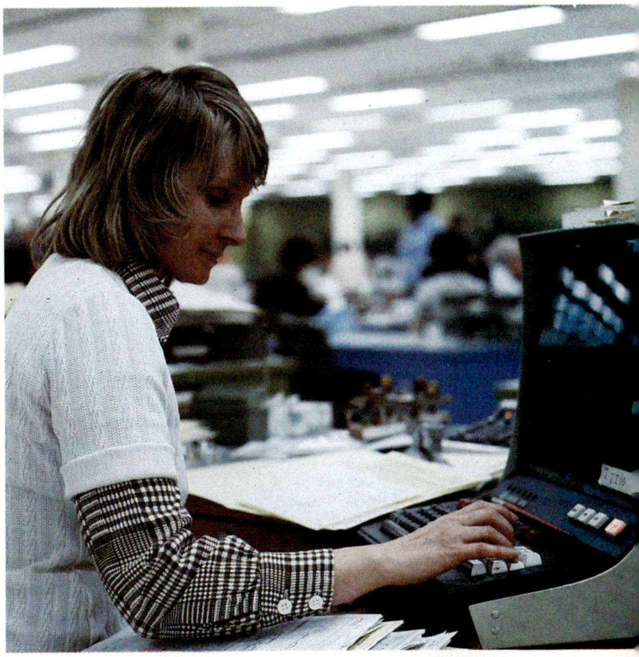

Figure 5–7 Terminals can be placed in various departments within an organization so that data entry takes place from the department for which the data is being entered. Here, a data entry operator is entering data from a large department within a company.

Types of display terminals

Although all terminals perform essentially the same functions and consist of a keyboard and CRT screen, display terminals can be obtained in a variety of models and with varying capabilities. Display terminals fall into three basic categories: 1) Limited function terminals (sometimes called "dumb" terminals); 2) Smart terminals; 3) Intelligent terminals (sometimes called programmable terminals). The features of each type of terminal are explained in the following paragraphs.

Limited function terminals

The first computer terminals utilized in an on-line data entry environment were considered **limited function terminals**. These terminals were sometimes called **dumb terminals** because they did nothing more than pass the data keyed by the operator over some type of communication line to the computer. In addition, certain messages could be sent from the computer to the terminal for display on the CRT screen. In many cases, these messages concerned errors which were made when the data was entered. No other processing occurred when these terminals were used.

With limited function terminals, data is entered a line at a time, and corrections to errors are made by backspacing and rekeying the data. The keyboard consists of typewriter-like keys containing the letters of the alphabet, numbers, and a few special characters. Terminals of this type cost between $500.00 and $1,000.00. Limited function terminals used for data entry have largely been replaced by more sophisticated units which contain some processing capabilities within the terminal.

Figure 5–8 This TEC smart terminal can read magnetic stripe cards. Note the card in the slot in the upper right corner of the keyboard. Through the use of the card, the device can control access to both use of the terminal and to data which can be accessed from the terminal.

Smart terminals

As the microprocessor was developed, it was recognized that microprocessors could be incorporated into a terminal. With a microprocessor and memory, the terminal becomes capable of performing limited processing. So-called **smart terminals** are terminals that have some processing capabilities built into them.

A commonly found capability in smart terminals is text editing. **Text editing** allows the operator to add, delete, or change characters, words, and lines after the data has been entered on the terminal. Smart terminals often provide text editing capabilities through the use of special function keys that operate in conjunction with the microprocessor within the terminal. As might be expected, smart terminals are more expensive than limited function terminals. Smart terminals cost between $600.00 and $5,000.00, depending upon the capabilities of the terminal.

The terminal in Figure 5-8 is a TEC smart terminal with a special capability. It contains a magnetic stripe card-reading device to aid in terminal security. The upper right corner of the keyboard contains a slot into which a special card with a magnetic stripe can be inserted. This magnetic stripe can be encoded with data such as a user identification code and a security code. Based upon the data on the card, the terminal can permit: 1) No use of the terminal; 2) Access to only certain data files by the person using the terminal. The ability to read the encoding data on the card is based upon the processing power of the microprocessor built into the smart terminal. Other special functions and abilities can be found in other smart terminals. Indeed, smart terminals can be tailor-made for specific application environments.

Smart terminals are commonly used as data entry terminals. They provide the ability to edit data entered by the terminal operator according to predefined criteria, and can also perform application-dependent special functions.

Intelligent terminals

Intelligent terminals are display terminals that have substantial processing capabilities built into the terminal. Intelligent terminals are also known as **programmable terminals** because they can be programmed by the user to perform many basic tasks performed by all computers, including both arithmetic and logic operations.

A common task performed by intelligent terminals when they are used for data entry is extensive data editing. A form of data editing for which an intelligent terminal can be programmed is checking the reasonableness of the data entered. For example, when entering payroll data for processing in a batch environment, the terminal could be programmed to assure that the hours worked entered by the terminal operator did not exceed 80 (or some other value determined to be reasonable). If the value entered violated the editing criteria, the operator would be notified that the value entered was in error. Generally, a corrected value would be entered. As noted in Chapter 4, the requirement for reliable data entry is critical when successfully implementing information processing systems. Intelligent terminals enable data editing to be performed at the terminal prior to allowing the data to be transmitted to the computer which will process the data.

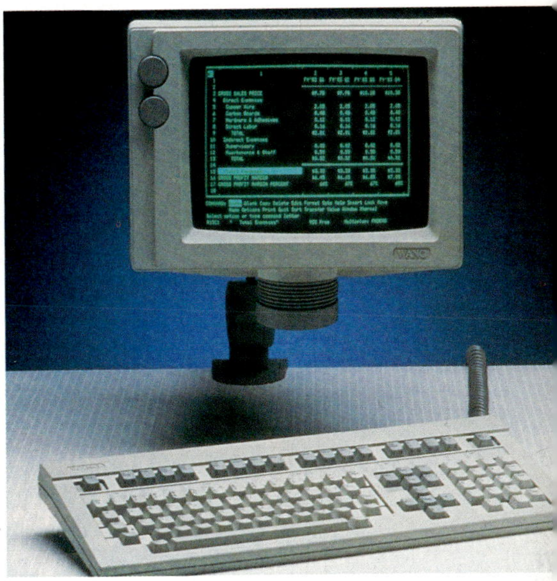

Figure 5–9 This Wang Personal Computer can perform all of the functions of a personal computer. It can also serve as an intelligent terminal when it is attached, through data communications channels, to a larger computer.

Intelligent terminals often contain not only the CRT and keyboard associated with other terminals, but also are supported with disk drives and printers, so they can perform limited processing tasks when not communicating directly with the central computer. In some instances, when the terminal operator enters data, the data will be edited and some type of report will be produced. In addition, the valid data which is entered will be stored on the disk associated with the terminal. After the data has been entered and stored on disk, it will be transmitted over communication lines to the central computer. This operation is sometimes called **uploading,** because the data is loaded up to the main computer. Uploading occurs most often when the data entered is to be processed in a batch processing mode.

Personal computers are frequently used as intelligent terminals (Figure 5–9). As an increasingly greater amount of processing power is incorporated into intelligent terminals, more processing can occur at the site of the terminal prior to sending the data to the large centralized computer. This concept allows the large minicomputer or mainframe at the central site to perform the main processing and serve multiple users faster rather than use its resources to perform tasks that can logically be performed by the intelligent terminal.

When the computer performing the processing on the data is the personal computer itself, such as when a personal computer is used in a small business for accounting activities, then the data entry normally takes place using the keyboard of the personal computer. If the data is processed in an interactive mode, the data is processed on the computer as soon as it is entered. If the data is to be processed in the batch mode, the data is stored on disk until it has all been entered. After all the data has been entered, it is processed as a group.

The CRT screen display

Most terminals used today for data entry contain a CRT screen display. The screen is used to display the data entered on the terminal and messages from the main computer or from the smart and intelligent terminals concerning the data entered or the processing that is occurring.

The most widely used CRT display screens are equivalent in size to a twelve- or fifteen-inch television screen. These screens can typically display both upper and lower case letters of the alphabet and a variety of special characters.

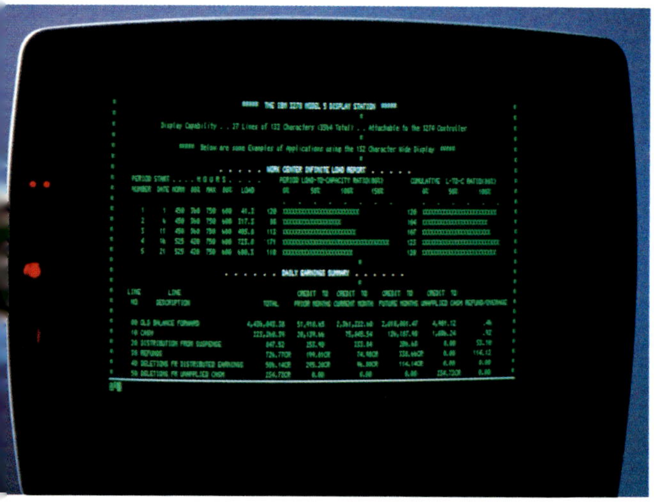

Figure 5-10 The IBM 3278 Model 5 terminal can display 132 characters per line and 27 lines, for a total of 3,564 characters that can be displayed on the screen at one time.

The maximum number of characters per line on the screen and the number of lines which can be displayed on the screen vary greatly among terminals. Some screens used with home computers display as few as 40 characters per horizontal line, with a maximum of thirteen horizontal lines being displayed at one time. For business and data entry applications, it is necessary to have a screen which can display a larger number of characters and lines.

Although there is no standard number of characters displayed on a screen, screens developed by many manufacturers display 80 characters on a line with a maximum of 25 lines displayed at one time. This provides for 2,000 characters on the screen at once.

Some terminals can display up to 132 characters on a single horizontal line. For example, the screen for the IBM 3278 terminal can display 132 characters per line (Figure 5-10). The more characters that are displayed on a line, the smaller the size of the character that is displayed on the screen; therefore, an important consideration when selecting a terminal is the number of characters displayed on the screen at one time and the readability, or character resolution, of the characters displayed.

Most of the early CRT screens displayed data in the form of white characters on a black background. Research has indicated, however, that other color combinations are easier on the eyes when terminals are utilized for long periods of time. Today, many terminals can be found that display either green or amber characters on a black background (Figure 5-11).

Figure 5-11 The screen on the left displays green characters on a black background. The screen on the right displays amber characters on a black background. These two color combinations have been found to be the easiest on the eyes, and therefore, the least fatiguing, of many color combinations that have been tried on CRT screens.

Additional display features

There are a number of additional features that are available on some smart and intelligent terminals which are often useful for computer users and data entry operators. These features include: 1) Reverse video; 2) Underlining; 3) Bold; 4) Blinking; 5) Double size; 6) Scrolling; and 7) Paging.

Reverse video refers to the process of reversing the normal display on the CRT screen. For example, on terminals with reverse video capabilities, it is possible to display a dark background with light characters or a light background with dark characters. Thus, if the normal screen had green characters on a black background, reverse video allows black characters on a green background. This feature permits single characters, whole words or lines, and even the entire screen to be reversed. Through the use of the reverse video feature, certain areas on the screen can be highlighted.

Reverse video is often used to format a screen for data entry. Many businesses use printed forms for conducting daily activities. Most employees are familiar with completing business forms such as purchase orders and sales invoices. Using the reverse video feature of smart and intelligent terminals, forms can be displayed on the screen (Figure 5–12). Displays of this type allow the data entry operator to fill in the forms by entering the data in particular segments of the display. Properly designed display screens can result in increased speed and accuracy for the data entry function, and many times require very little training for the operator to become productive.

The **underlining** feature allows characters, words, lines, or paragraphs to be underlined. This feature allows emphasis to be placed on certain entries on the screen, as well as allowing such items as book titles to be properly underlined. The ability to designate some characters or words as **bold** means that they are displayed at a greater brightness level. The **blinking** feature allows characters or words on a screen to blink, thus drawing attention to the blinking characters. The **double size** feature means that certain characters or words are displayed at twice the size of normal characters and words. The screen in Figure 5–13 illustrates the use of underlining and double size characters in order to highlight data displayed on the screen.

Figure 5–12 A reverse video screen is used in this picture to direct the data entry operator when entering data. After data is entered for a particular field, such as the order number field, the operator can tabulate to the next field, assembly number, and enter that data.

Scrolling allows lines displayed on the screen to be moved up or down by one line as a new line is added and an existing one removed. On some terminals, the line which is scrolled off the screen is lost. On most terminals today, however, the line remains in the memory of the terminal even though it is not displayed on the screen. When the screen is scrolled in the direction opposite the one that took the line off the screen, the line will reappear on the screen. Scrolling is mandatory for word processing applications, and virtually all smart and intelligent terminals allow scrolling in both the up and down directions with no lines being lost when scrolling occurs.

When **paging** is used, an entirely new "page," or screenful, of data can be displayed and changed under terminal control. This feature allows two or more pages of data to be stored and displayed at the option of the terminal operator. While scrolling is often found today on terminals, paging is less often provided.

Various terminals can have other special features, such as split screens and special tabulation capabilities. It is likely that if an application requires special features of some type, they are available on a terminal.

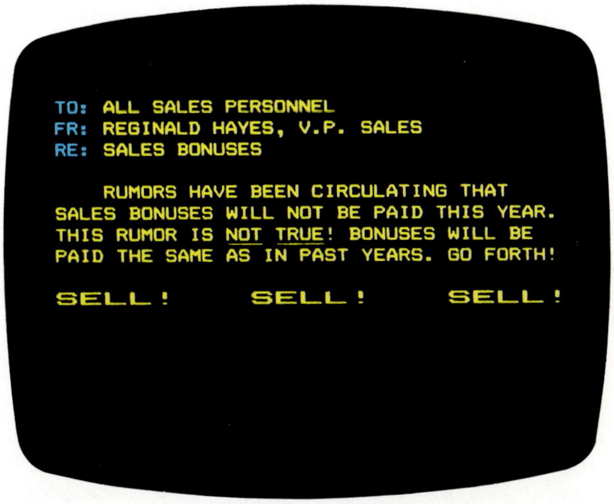

Figure 5–13 The memo shown on the screen above uses both underlining and double size characters to place emphasis on portions of the message. Underlining is used to stress that a rumor is not true, while double size characters are used to encourage all sales personnel to sell.

Color display screens

Many terminals are now available with color display screens. Color display screens are most likely to be found on either smart or intelligent terminals. Color CRT's were once viewed as instruments used almost exclusively by the scientific

community for use in geological research, simulations, and similar types of applications. But, with the reduced cost of color CRT's and the availability of supporting hardware and software, the entry of data using color display screens is becoming increasingly important.

The basic colors provided with color CRT screens include white, yellow, red, blue, green, and black. Some terminals provide additional colors such as cyan, magenta, and brown, and allow for controlling the intensity and shade of the color, resulting in numerous color combinations.

Color is used to enhance alphanumeric displays (Figure 5–14). With respect to the data entry function, messages directing the operator to enter data are often displayed in one color and the actual entry by the operator in another color. Special messages to the operator can be displayed in other colors. Initial research indicates that the use of color displays is less fatiguing for the operator, easier on the eyes, and provides a more enjoyable work environment, resulting in increased productivity with fewer errors.

Figure 5–14 The colors on this screen are used to identify for the terminal operator various messages and actions which can be taken as data is entered.

The terminal keyboard

The most common type of input device used with alphanumeric display terminals for rapidly entering data into the computer is the keyboard. The keyboard used with display terminals is very similar to that used on the familiar office tool, the typewriter. It contains numbers, letters of the alphabet, and some special characters.

On terminals which are designed for rapid data entry, most keyboards are equipped with a special numeric keypad on the righthand side of the keyboard. The numeric keys are arranged in an adding machine or calculator key format. This arrangement of the keys allows skilled operators to rapidly enter numeric data (Figure 5–15).

Special purpose keys for controlling where data entered is displayed on the screen are also available on most alphanumeric display terminals. This type of control is usually obtained through the use of arrow keys. The arrow keys can move the cursor around the screen. A **cursor** is a symbol, such as a reverse video square character or an underline character, which indicates where on the screen the next character entered will be displayed. Depressing the up cursor control key (↑) will cause the cursor to move upward on the screen. The down arrow (↓) causes the cursor to move down, while the left (←) and right (→) arrow keys cause the cursor to move left and right on the screen. Through the use of these keys, the terminal operator can determine where on the screen data will be displayed when it is entered.

Figure 5–15 The keyboard in this picture contains a numeric keypad on the right of the keyboard. The keys are arranged in the same order as an adding machine or a calculator. Arrangement in this order allows those skilled in entering numbers to input numeric data at a much faster rate than if the number keys across the top of the keyboard were used.

Quite often, display terminals have

special keys which can be used to alter the text displayed on the screen. For example, terminals can have keys which allow characters to be inserted or deleted in the text on the screen. Other keys may enable entire lines to be inserted or deleted on the screen. Terminals can also have a key which will erase a character, word, field, or even the complete screen.

Many terminal keyboards have special **function keys** that can be programmed to accomplish certain tasks. For example, a function key might be programmed for use as a help key when the terminal is used for word processing. Whenever the key is depressed, messages will appear which give instructions for a particular function of the word processor. Another key could be programmed to cause all data displayed on the CRT screen to be printed on a printer whenever the key is depressed. Function keys are very convenient and useful when rapid data entry is important. The keyboard on the TEC terminal in Figure 5-16 contains a numeric keypad and eighteen special function keys.

When selecting a display terminal for an application, the requirements of the application must be considered. In some cases, a dumb terminal will be adequate. In others, however, an intelligent terminal with a sophisticated keyboard containing multiple function keys and other features will be necessary.

Figure 5-16 This terminal contains a sophisticated keyboard with a numeric keypad, numerous screen control keys, and eighteen programmable function keys.

Terminal ergonomics

It is anticipated that over 50 million office workers, managers, and executive personnel will interact with personal computers and computer terminals in the near future. Therefore, the manner in which individuals interact with computer terminals has become an important area of research.

Ergonomics is defined as the study of the characteristics that need to be considered in designing and arranging things that are used in order that people and the things will interact most efficiently. Ergonomics as related to terminals is concerned with such factors as the physical design of the keyboard, screens, and related hardware, and the manner in which people interact with these hardware devices.

The first computer terminals contained the keyboard and CRT screen as a single unit. The screen frequently displayed white characters on a black background. Early studies of these terminals and the people who used them found significant dissatisfaction with the terminals. Indeed, one study indicated that 90% of the personnel who used terminals of these early designs complained of health problems, including eye fatigue, blurred vision, itching and burning eyes, and back problems. As more and more workers began using CRT terminals, user interface with these terminals became an important consideration. As a result of many studies concerning this problem, a number of design recommendations for CRT terminals were made. These recommendations included:

1. Computer keyboards should be detached from the screen so that they are movable and can be positioned on a desk for the convenience and comfort of the user.

2. The visual display unit should be movable, and the angle at which the user views the contents of the screen should be adjustable by the user.
3. Amber or green text on a black background is preferable to black characters on a white background or white characters on a black background.
4. The CRT screen should be of high quality to eliminate any flicker of the image and characters on the screen. The characters displayed on the screen should be solid, if possible.
5. The images on the screen should be in sharp focus over the entire screen area.
6. The screen should have an anti-glare coating. Screen glare has been a common complaint of many CRT users, and it is known that glare can be harmful to eyes.
7. On those screens where multiple elements of information will be displayed, color should be used to easily distinguish the different elements, thus cutting down on the strain of looking for and identifying information displayed on the screen.

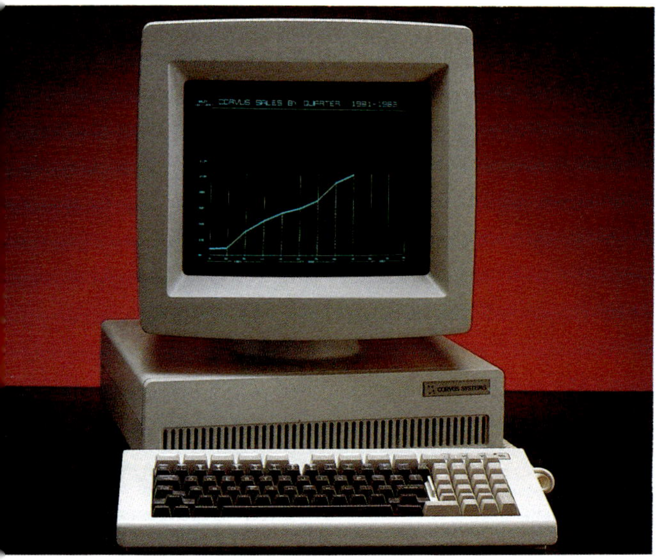

Figure 5-17 This terminal contains many of the design characteristics found most beneficial for people using the terminal, including a detached keyboard and an adjustable screen.

The terminal illustrated in Figure 5-17 incorporates some of the above recommendations. The keyboard is detachable, the visual display unit is adjustable, and the screen has an anti-glare coating.

As more and more workers use a CRT terminal for their daily chores, the importance of an ergonomically-sound terminal increases. Manufacturers in the past few years have become aware of this fact, and as a result, terminals today are considerably more user-oriented than were the early CRT terminals.

OTHER TERMINALS

Terminals other than CRT terminals are also used for certain applications, although not in as great a number as CRT terminals. Two particular types of terminals find use for data entry purposes — keyboard/printer terminals and integrated workstations. These terminals are examined in the following paragraphs.

Keyboard/printer terminals

The first widely used general purpose interactive terminals were typewriter-like devices that consisted of a keyboard and a low-speed printing device housed in a single unit. These units, called **teleprinters**, allowed data to be entered into the computer via a keyboard. The keyboard output and any output transmitted from the computer to the terminal was in the form of hard copy printed output.

Since the introduction of CRT display terminals, teleprinters are not used much as data entry devices when large volumes of data must be entered rapidly. **Portable teleprinters**, however, have proven to be a popular data entry device.

Portable teleprinters typically appeal to business people who travel a great deal and need a small, lightweight terminal that combines in a single unit both input and output capabilities. Teleprinter terminals are housed in a compact carrying case. They contain a standard size keyboard and a built-in printing unit that can print from approximately 30 characters per second up to 200 characters per second. These units contain the necessary electronic circuitry to allow data entered on the keyboard to be transmitted over standard telephone lines into a centralized computer; or data transmitted from the central computer can be received over telephone lines and can be printed (Figure 5-18).

Typical applications where teleprinters are used include data entry, inquiry processing, and word processing. As an example of data entry using a teleprinter, a sales representative could enter sales made for the day, perhaps in a city many hundreds of miles from the centralized computer. The data can be transmitted over telephone lines to the computer for either immediate processing in an interactive mode or for later processing in a batch processing mode. Teleprinters, with the ability to send data and receive data over data communications lines, provide an alternative means for communicating with a computer. They can be used in place of or in conjunction with CRT terminals.

Figure 5-18 The operator using the teleprinter in this picture is entering data and transmitting it to a central computer over telephone lines. The data being entered will be printed on the printer which is a part of the unit.

Integrated workstations

The activities of entering data into a computer, retrieving data from a computer, and communicating with others through the written and spoken word are recognized as activities that are common to executives, managers, and a large number of workers throughout an organization. To accomplish these tasks conveniently and efficiently, **integrated workstations** (sometimes called **executive workstations**) have been developed by a number of manufacturers. These units provide both telephone and computer terminal capabilities within a single unit by allowing both voice and data communications (Figure 5-19).

The purpose of the integrated workstation is to provide at a single, convenient location, easy access to a number of functions that assist employees in performing their jobs better. Numerous studies have shown that executives spend a substantial part of their time communicating both orally and by the written word; therefore, combining both telephone and computer capability into a single workstation appears to be a logical step in the evolution of automating office tasks performed by executives and clerical workers alike.

The capabilities of these terminals allow such functions as telephone communications, electronic mail, word processing, data entry, data storage and retrieval, and inquiries to all be processed using a single unit. Integrated workstations offer capabilities not available on other kinds of terminals. Their use in offices throughout a company has increased significantly in the recent past.

Figure 5-19 The integrated workstation in the picture below contains not only a keyboard and CRT screen, but also a telephone and the built-in electronics that allow it to communicate in voice-to-voice communications and data communications. Multipurpose units such as this are gaining more and more use because they provide all the communication functions required in any work environment.

EXAMPLE — ON-LINE DATA ENTRY

To illustrate the use of terminals for on-line data entry, an example of entering orders will be examined. **Order entry** is the process which is followed when an order is received from a customer. An order entry application proceeds in the following manner:

1. When the order is received from the customer either through the mail or over the telephone, the data concerning the customer and the order are entered into the computer by the data entry operator.
2. When the order is entered, the order entry program performs a credit check to ensure the order can be shipped to the customer by retrieving credit data from a credit file stored on disk. In addition, the order is stored in the open order disk file so that a record of the order is retained.
3. When the order is entered, the order entry program which is controlling the data entry operation determines if the item ordered is in inventory by randomly retrieving a record from an inventory file or data base. If the item ordered is in the inventory, a picking slip is printed in the warehouse. A picking slip alerts the warehouse personnel that an order has been received and specifies who the customer is and what items are to be shipped. Then, or at a later time, the warehouse personnel retrieve the item and package it for shipping. When the item is shipped, they will enter into the computer the fact that the item has been shipped. When this occurs, the record for the order will be removed from the open order file and will be placed in the shipped file.
4. If the item ordered is not in the warehouse inventory, the order record will be placed in the backorder file. A **backorder** is an order for which the item ordered is not in inventory. The order will be held until the item is available, at which time the order will be filled. In addition to placing the order in the backorder file, the customer will be notified that the item is not available.

Figure 5-20 The order entry menu specifies the operations that can be accomplished by order entry processing. Option 1 allows orders to be entered. Option 2 allows the operator to confirm orders and to perform inquiries into the open order file to inspect the open orders. Order maintenance, which allows changes to open orders, is chosen by option 3. Backorders can be changed by selecting option 4; and the order entry program can be terminated by choosing option 5.

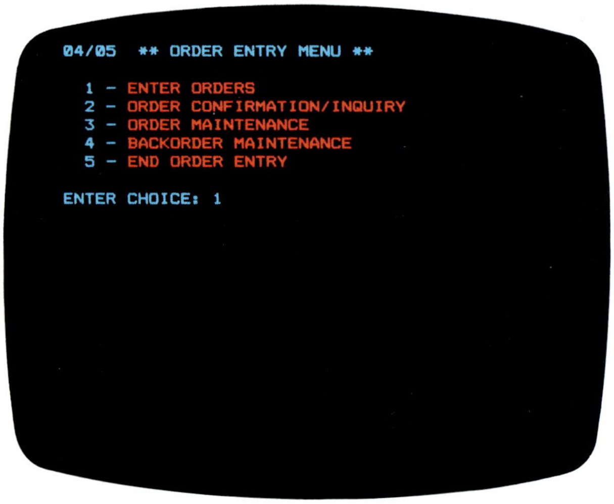

The entry of the order into the computer is a major part of order entry processing. The following paragraphs explain the phases in a data entry procedure which could be followed by a person entering orders using an on-line entry system.

Phase 1 — order entry menu

The data entry process for the sample order entry system requires three different screen displays. The first screen displays the order entry menu from which the data entry operator can choose the function to be performed (Figure 5-20). In this example, the function to be performed is entering orders. Therefore, the data entry operator enters the value 1 to choose the option "enter orders."

Phase 2 — enter orders

In step 1 of Figure 5-21, when the data entry operator chooses option 1 on the

Step 1

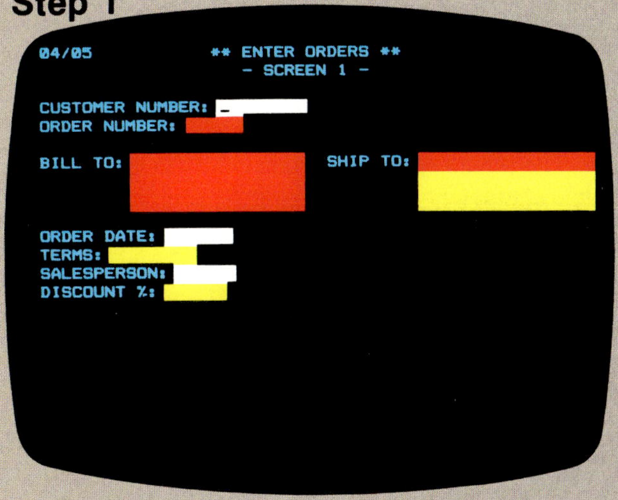

Step 1: Each field is identified by color. The blue fields are titles and prompts. The red fields will contain data that cannot be changed. The white fields must be entered by the operator. The yellow fields are default fields.

Step 2

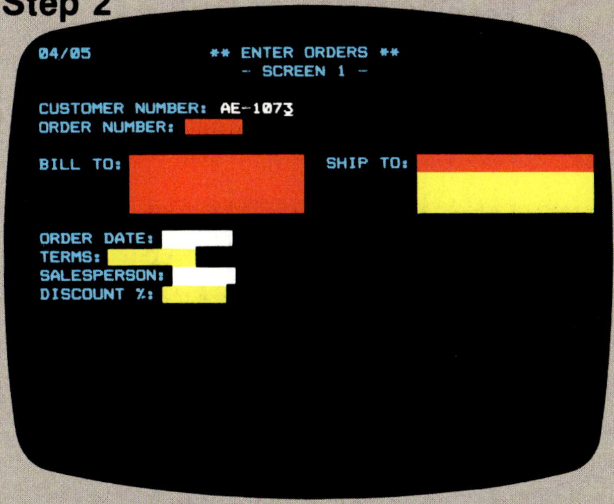

Step 2: In this step, the data entry operator has entered the customer number. The customer number is displayed in white letters because the operator had to enter the data. The operator would then depress the return key to continue.

Step 3

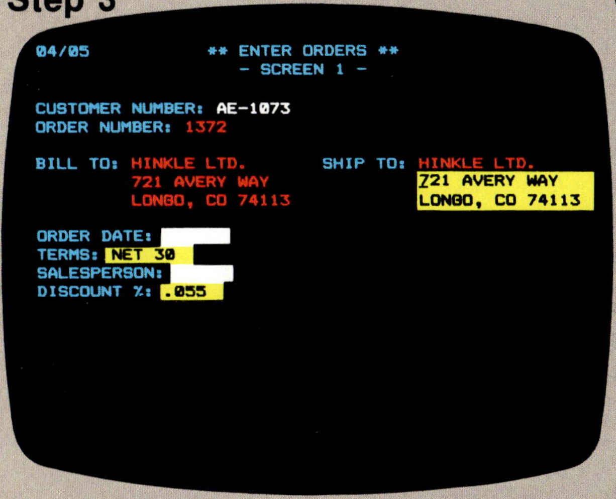

Step 3: Data retrieved from a customer file based upon the customer number is displayed on the screen. The cursor is placed on the ship to address. The operator can enter data here if it is different from the default values.

Step 4

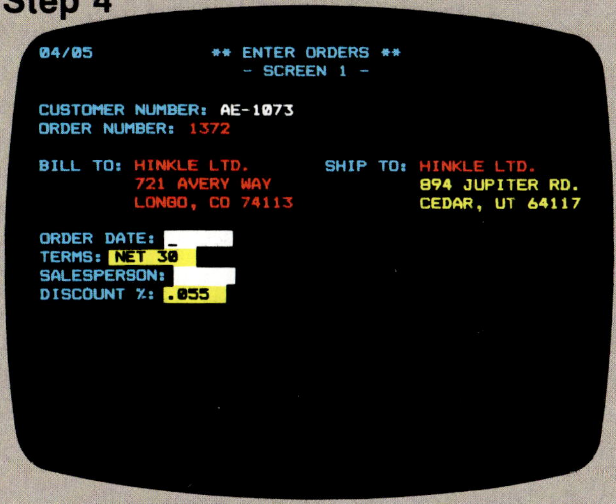

Step 4: The order date must be entered by the operator. Therefore, it is displayed in white. The default values in the ship to field have been changed to yellow characters because they have now been entered.

Step 5

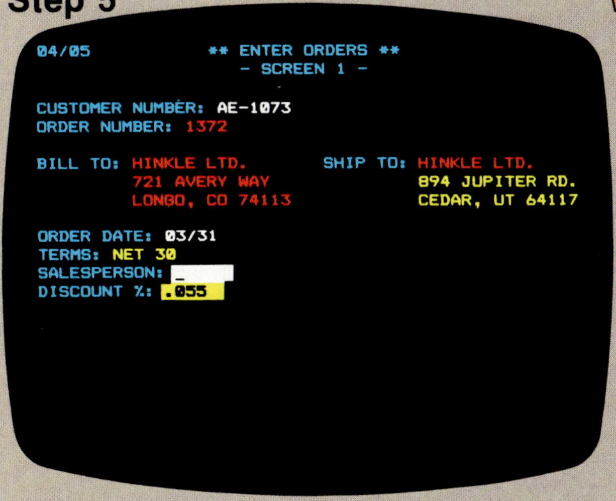

Step 5: The sales person must be entered by the data entry operator. The default value in the terms field specified net 30. The operator accepted the default value by depressing the enter or return key instead of entering new data.

Step 6

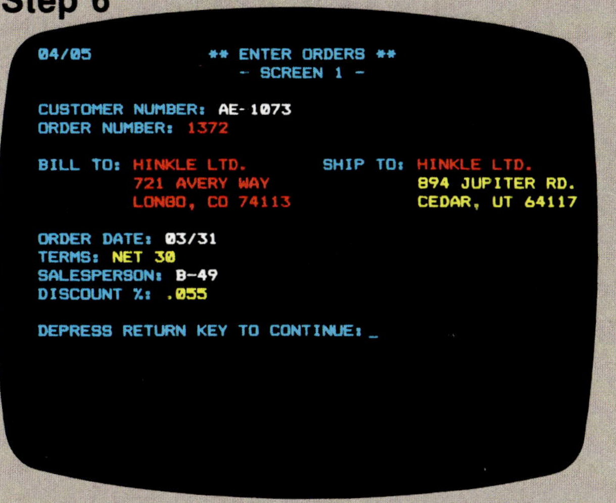

Step 6: After the data entry operation for the first screen has been completed, all data is displayed as color characters on a black screen. The reverse video is not necessary because no data remains to be entered.

Figure 5-21 The six steps involved in entering data for the first screen in an order entry application are illustrated in this diagram.

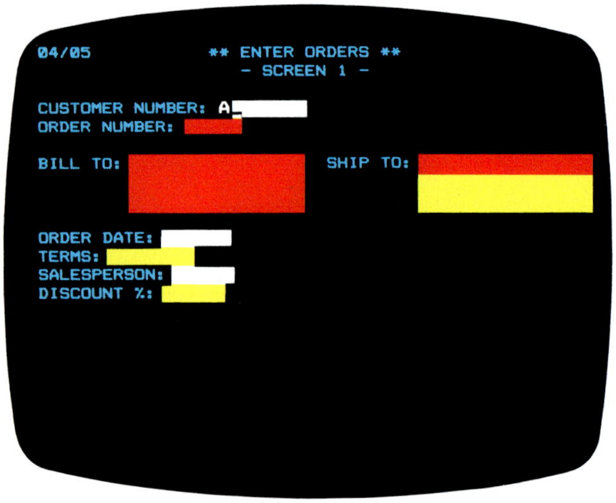

Figure 5-22 When a value is entered and placed in a reverse video field, the normal technique is to display the character in the color of the reverse video field and to remove the reverse video field for the character. Here, the letter A has been entered into a white field. Therefore, the letter is displayed in white on a black background.

main menu, the first screen of the two screens required to enter orders is displayed. The screen contains certain colors in certain areas. All of the blue characters are headings and prompts which identify the fields to be processed on the displayed screen. Each of the areas where data will be displayed or entered is shown in reverse video. The white areas indicate fields which must be entered by the data entry operator. The red areas indicate areas which will contain fixed data based upon the entries of the operator. These fixed areas cannot be changed by the data entry operator. The yellow areas indicate default values which will be displayed but which can be changed by the operator if needed.

In step 2, the operator entered the data for the first field — the customer number. In the example, the operator entered the value AE-1073. This is the customer number for the customer ordering items. Note that instead of reverse video when the data is entered, the actual characters entered are displayed in the same color as the reverse video; that is, the customer number is displayed in white because the reverse video was in white. The process of entering the data is shown in Figure 5-22, where the first character (A) has been entered. The character is white but the rest of the input area on the screen where data has not been entered retains the reverse video. This technique is commonly used on terminals where reverse video is used to identify input fields.

After the customer number is entered, the terminal operator would depress the return or enter key on the keyboard. The screen illustrated in step 3 in Figure 5-21 would then be displayed. The order number is generated by the computer program with which the operator is communicating. It is displayed in red because the terminal operator cannot reference or change the order number. The bill to data is also displayed in red because it will not be changed. The bill to data, which is the name of the company and the address to which the bill for the items will be sent, was obtained from a customer file based upon the customer number that was entered.

The ship to data identifies the place to which the items will be sent. The company name is displayed in red because it will not be changed. The ship to address, however, is displayed reversed on a yellow background because the data is default data. **Default data** is data which is assumed to be correct but which can be changed. It is used in data entry so that data which is normally not changed does not always have to be entered by the operator. In this case, the address shown is the same as the bill to address because most of the time, items ordered by Hinkle Ltd. are shipped to the same address. If the address to which the items are to be shipped is the default address, the operator would merely depress the enter or return key and continue to the next field. In this example, however, the ship to address is to be changed. Therefore, the operator would key in the new ship to address. After it is keyed, it is displayed in yellow characters to indicate that the default data has been entered (step 4).

The cursor is next placed at the order date field by the controlling program (step 4). The operator enters the order date (03/31). The order date field is white because the operator must always enter the order date.

In step 5, the operator has accepted the default terms (net 30) which the program displayed by depressing the return or enter key. The salesperson data must be entered by the operator because it is in white. The default value for the discount percent is also accepted by the operator. Therefore, the screen of data for the order entry operation appears as shown in step 6 after the operator has completed the data entry for screen 1.

When the operator depresses the return or enter key, the second screen required for the order entry operation is displayed (Figure 5-23). On this screen, the operator must enter the item number of the item purchased and the order quantity. The item description and unit price are displayed by the order entry program. The single default value on this screen is the subject to tax field. Here, the operator can change the Y (signifying yes to the question, Is this purchase subject to tax?) to N. In this example, the default value was accepted. The return key can be depressed when all of the data is entered in order to return to the main menu (Figure 5-20) and enter another order.

It should be noted that this example is a composite of many different actual order entry systems. However, it illustrates many of the features that are found in a data entry operation which could occur on terminals.

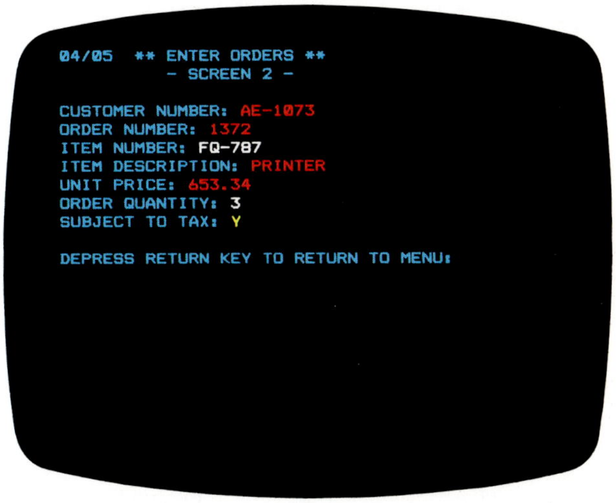

Figure 5-23 On the second order entry screen, the operator must enter the item number of the item sold and the order quantity. If the item is not subject to tax, the value in the default field must be changed.

Summary — display terminals

Display terminals are very important data entry devices. A large percentage of the on-line data entry operations that occur for both interactive processing and batch processing take place using display terminals. A wide variety of terminals with many varying capabilities are available. An understanding of the data entry function in information processing requires an understanding of display terminals.

Off-line data entry devices for batch processing

Interactive processing requires that the data entry function take place on-line; that is, the data entry device must be directly connected to the computer so that the data entered can be processed immediately.

Data entry for batch processing can also take place on-line. The terminal from which the data is entered is connected directly to the computer. The entered data is stored on disk for processing as a group at a later time. The trend today is toward on-line entry for batch processing.

Historically, however, and in many installations today, data entry for batch processing takes place off-line. Devices designed especially for the entry of data to be processed in a batch mode are used.

The first device used for off-line data entry was the keypunch. A keypunch contained a keyboard and a punching mechanism which could punch holes in a card. When the operator depressed a key on the keyboard, the holes which represented the character were punched in the card. Punched cards, while at one time the overwhelming medium for storing data to be batch processed, are seldom used any more.

In the early 1960's, devices were developed which allowed operators to key data on a keyboard and store the data on magnetic tape. These devices became quite popular because tape provided a more compact form of storage, and a single reel of tape could store the same amount of data as many thousands of punched cards. In addition, the tape was reusable whereas the punched cards were not. The development of these key to tape devices signaled the beginning of the end for punched cards.

In the 1970's, IBM developed a data entry device that allowed data to be stored on a diskette, or floppy disk. Using this device, the data in the records to be processed in a batch mode is keyed and the data is stored on the floppy disk. After all of the data is keyed, the floppy disk is transported to a diskette reader which reads the data into the main computer for processing. In some installations today, the key to diskette device is still used for data entry (Figure 5–24).

The diskette has emerged as a primary medium for storing data to be processed on a personal computer. In most cases, when data is to be batch processed on a personal computer, the data will first be keyed and stored on a diskette.

Key-to-disk shared processor systems

As computer terminals and minicomputers came down in price in the 1970's, data entry systems consisting of a number of terminals connected to a minicomputer were developed. When using systems of this type, data to be processed in the batch mode is entered simultaneously by a number of operators (Figure 5–25). The data is temporarily stored on disk. When all of the data has been entered, the data stored on the disk is transferred to tape. The tape is then transported to the computer which will actually process the data, and the data is read for processing. These devices are called key-to-disk shared processor systems.

Key-to-disk shared processor systems have the following characteristics: 1) A number of keying stations are included with the system. These can range from 2 up to 64 stations; 2) The keying stations are under control of some type of processor, normally a dedicated minicomputer; 3) The data keyed on the various keying stations is temporarily stored on disk. When the keying job is complete, the data is transferred to tape for input to the main computer.

Key-to-disk shared processor systems have several significant advantages over other forms of data entry. First, they can greatly improve operator productivity. With each keying station under the control of the dedicated minicomputer, the operator need not be concerned with the many tasks involved in machine set up for each new job. Instead, when source documents are received, keying can begin immediately since the required set up is performed by the attached minicomputer.

In addition, because of the processing capability of the controlling minicomputer, a great deal of data editing is possible. Data editing, it will be recalled, refers to the process of comparing the data entered to predetermined values to ensure that the data conforms to the predetermined criteria. Data editing is performed to ensure as much as possible that the

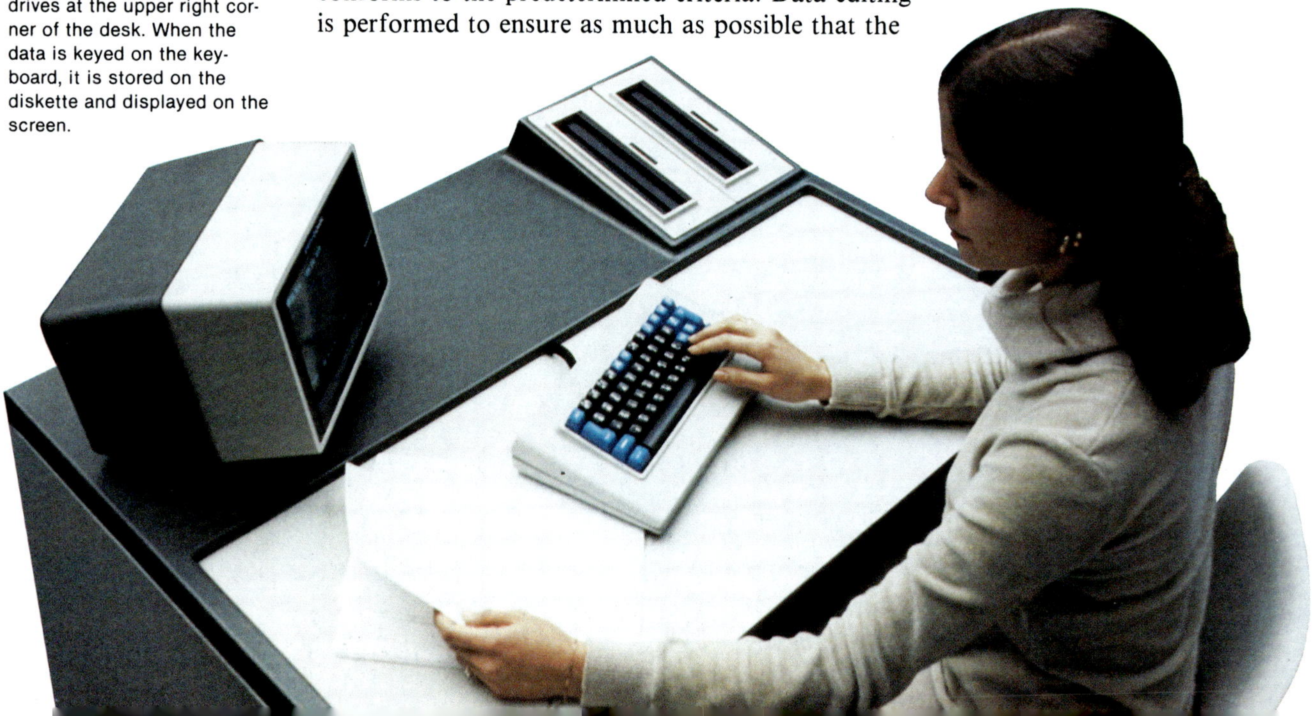

Figure 5–24 The key-to-diskette machine shown in this picture is used for data entry. An 8" floppy disk is placed in one of the two drives at the upper right corner of the desk. When the data is keyed on the keyboard, it is stored on the diskette and displayed on the screen.

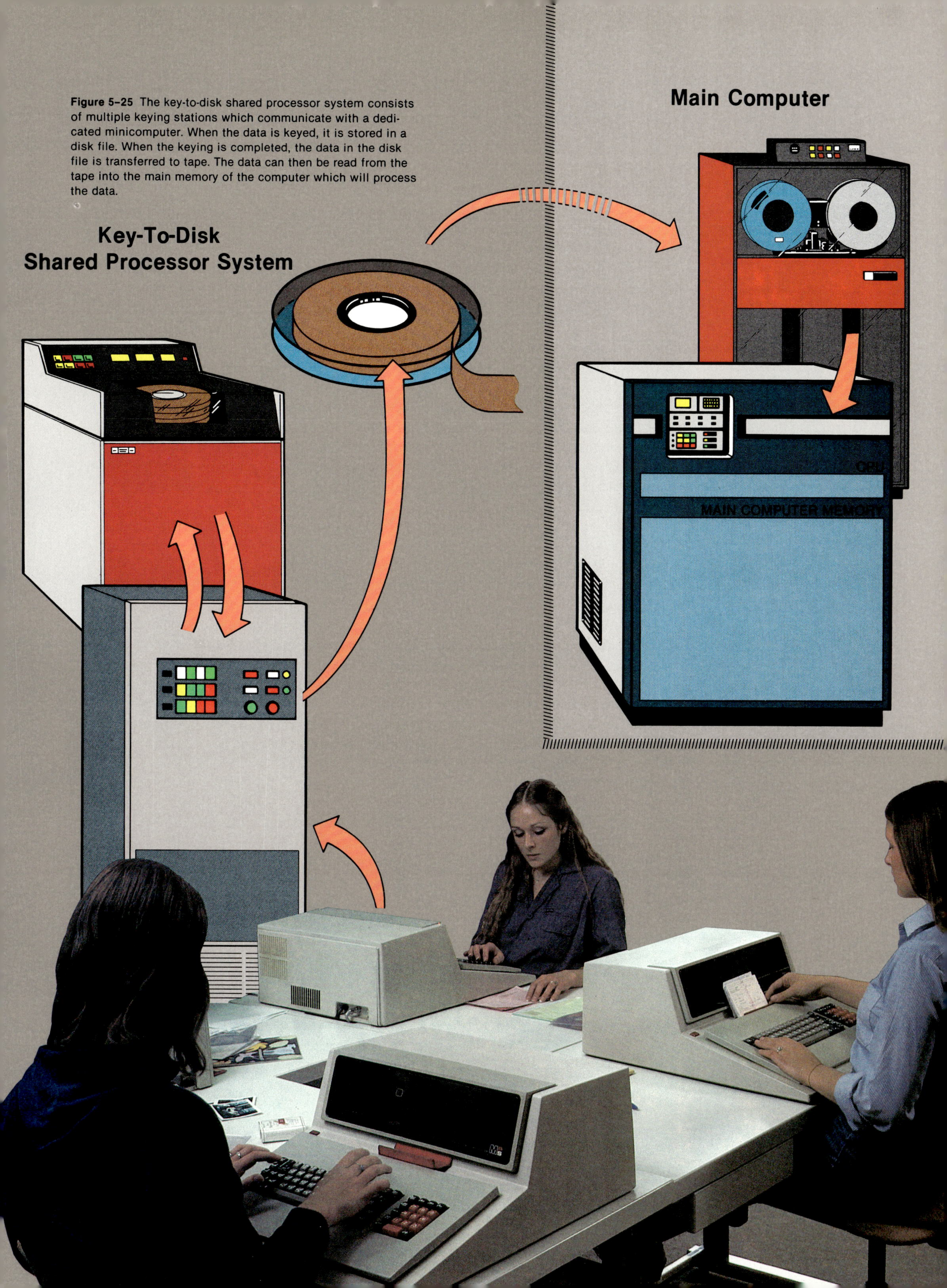

Figure 5–25 The key-to-disk shared processor system consists of multiple keying stations which communicate with a dedicated minicomputer. When the data is keyed, it is stored in a disk file. When the keying is completed, the data in the disk file is transferred to tape. The data can then be read from the tape into the main memory of the computer which will process the data.

values entered correspond to the values which are supposed to be entered. When a key-to-disk shared processor system is used, editing can be performed at the point where the data is initially keyed, relieving the main computer of the task when the data is read into main memory for processing. This ability can save both time and money while producing accurate input data.

Another significant advantage of key-to-disk shared processor systems over stand-alone data entry devices is that commonly used data fields can be stored on disk and can be retrieved automatically by the system to build a record. For example, the data entry operator could key a customer number on the keyboard of the keystation. Based upon the customer number, the minicomputer could retrieve the associated customer name and address that had been stored on the disk. The customer name and address could then be incorporated into the input record. Note that this capability is quite similar to that found in on-line data entry when the input terminal is communicating directly with the main computer (see Figure 5–21 on page 5.15), except that this processing is occurring off-line using a dedicated minicomputer. This capability, of course, cuts down considerably on the number of keystrokes required to enter the data into an input record, resulting in increased speed and reliability in the data entry function.

To assure the accuracy of the data entered by the operator, key verification can be used. **Key verification** is the process in which data is first keyed into the system and then is rekeyed and compared. For example, to begin the operation one operator would key in the required data based upon values found in a source document. During this keying operation, the data keyed is stored on disk. The source documents are then given to a verifying operator who rekeys the same data. The data the verifying operator keys is compared on a character by character basis with the data that has been stored on the disk. If an unequal condition occurs, the verifying operator is notified, and a check can be undertaken to determine whether the original operator or the verifying operator made an error. If the error was made by the original data entry operator, the data on the disk can be corrected. With fields such as the name and address being stored on the disk and being retrieved on the basis of the customer number, verification time is greatly reduced since only the customer number would have to be verified.

Most key-to-disk shared processor systems contain a supervisory console which can be used to enter control programs for jobs to be keyed. It can also be used to obtain operating statistics on each job and each operator. These statistics typically contain the operator identification, a job identification, the operator start and stop time, the number of keystrokes per minute or hour, the number of records keyed, the number of errors, and similar data. The statistics are stored on the disk associated with the system. They can be quite valuable in controlling and analyzing each operator's productivity.

A major disadvantage of key-to-disk processor systems is that they are quite expensive. Therefore, they are normally used only in installations where the volume of input is quite high, and there is a necessity of preparing the data for batch processing. As on-line data entry for batch processing increases, the use of off-line data entry devices such as key-to-disk shared processor systems will most likely decrease.

Special-purpose input devices

A number of input devices exist which are used for particular computer input applications rather than as general input devices for either on-line or off-line data entry. These devices are explained in the following paragraphs.

Figure 5-26 The hand-held optical character reading device in this picture is used to read computer-prepared characters from insurance forms. The data is normally stored on tape or disk for later transmission to a large computer for processing, although in some applications such as retail stores the hand-held wand can be used to enter data that will be processed in an interactive processing mode.

Optical character readers

Optical character reader (OCR) devices read typewritten, computer-printed, and in some cases hand-printed characters from ordinary documents. The machines range from automatically fed machines which can read 2,000 documents per minute to hand-held wands (Figure 5-26).

OCR devices scan the shape of a character on a document, compare the character scanned with a predefined shape, and convert the character read into a corresponding bit pattern for storing in main computer memory. In 1966, the Business Equipment Manufacturing Association (BEMA) proposed that a set of characters with specific shapes be adopted as an OCR standard. These characters were adopted as the United States standard by the American National Standards Institute (ANSI). This standard, called OCR-A, is illustrated in Figure 5-27. In addition to being able to be read by a machine, the characters can be easily read by human beings. OCR-B is a set of standard characters which is widely used in Europe and Japan.

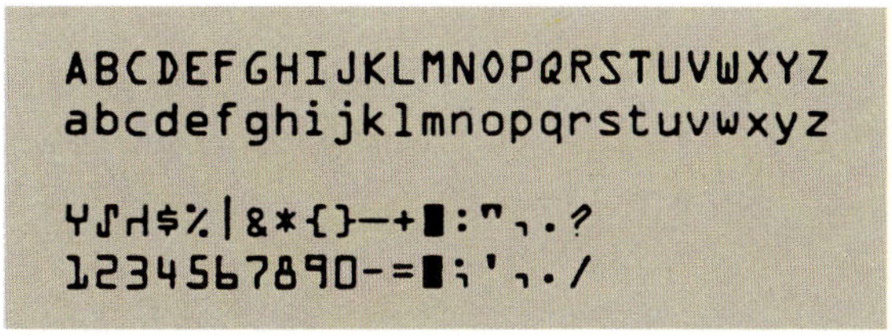

Figure 5-27 The full OCR-A standard character set is shown in this diagram. Characters such as the B and 8, the S and 5, and numeric zero and the letter O are significantly different so an optical character reading device can easily distinguish between them.

Some optical character readers are capable of reading hand-printed characters. The ability of a machine to read and interpret hand-printed characters is a challenging task even in this era of high technology. The characters must be carefully printed according to a strict set of rules regarding the shapes of the characters. The example in Figure 5-28 illustrates the suggested shape of hand-printed

Figure 5-28 These hand-printed characters can be read by some types of OCR devices. The characters must be carefully printed to conform to predetermined rules. The two small dots in each square identify where certain portions of each numeric digit must be placed.

characters which can be read using an OCR device.

The most widespread application for OCR devices is the reading of turn-around documents prepared by computer line printers. A **turn-around document** is one which is prepared by computer output and is sent to a consumer or an organization. The document is then returned, and the data on the document is read by an OCR device. For example, many utility bills, department store bills, insurance premiums, and so on request that the consumer return the statement with the payment check (Figure 5–29). The statement is printed with characters that can be read by OCR devices. When it is returned, it is read in order to give proper credit for the payment received.

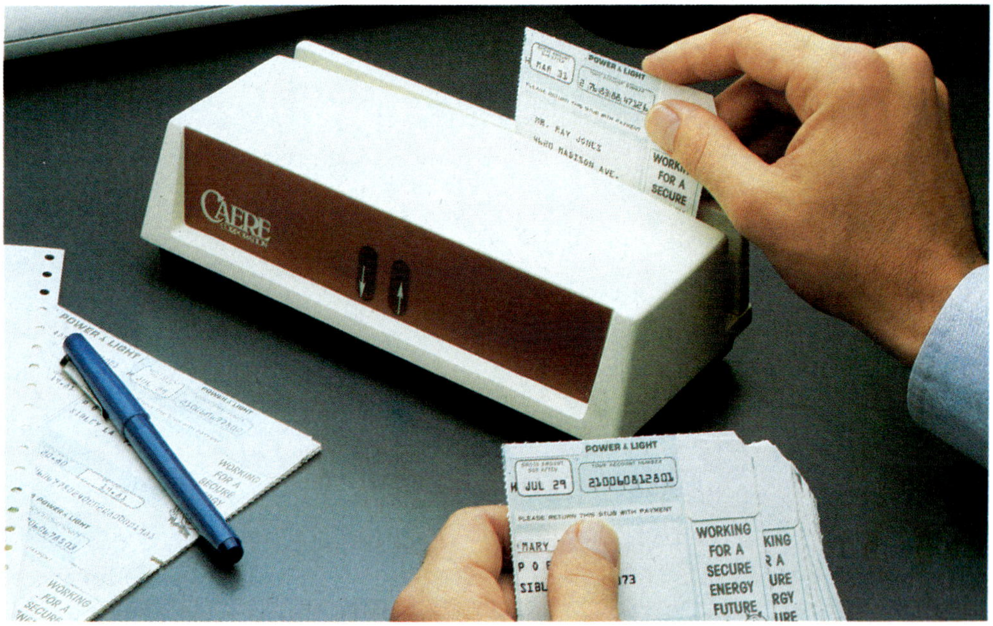

Figure 5–29 In this picture, payment receipts accompanying utility payments are read by the OCR device. The utility payment receipt illustrated here is a turn-around document because it was printed on a computer when the bill was prepared and was sent to the consumer. It was returned (turned around) when the consumer sent it back with the payment.

Some OCR devices, such as shown in Figure 5–29, are desk-top units. In the future, these units will be incorporated into the automated office. They will be able to communicate with various computers and facsimile devices. Newer machines also offer the capability of reading up to eight different fonts, providing flexibility for different applications.

Mark readers

A **mark reader** device can read carefully placed pencil marks on specially designed documents. The pencil marks on the form are single vertical marks which indicate a response to a question or to fill in data specified on the document. The marks on the form can be read and then interpreted by a computer program. Mark readers are frequently used in test scoring applications. The devices which read marked documents are sometimes called **Optical Mark Readers (OMR)**.

Magnetic ink character recognition

Another type of machine-readable data is called **magnetic ink character**

NATIONAL BANK

1-987
210

No._____

New York, N.Y. *Jan 11* 19 *84*

PAY TO THE ORDER OF *Tom Doe* $ *56 70⁄*

Fifty six and 70⁄100 ——————— DOLLARS

John Smith

⑆0 2 ⑆0⑈098 7⑈: 2 200 84 26 70⑉ ⑈04 2⑉ 0000000 56 70⑉

```
CHECK          ABA        ACCOUNT         PROCESS      AMOUNT
ROUTING      TRANSIT      NUMBER          CONTROL
SYMBOL        NUMBER
```

recognition, or **MICR.** MICR is used almost exclusively in the banking industry because in the 1950's, the industry settled on MICR as the method used to encode and read the billions of checks that are written by individuals and companies each year.

When MICR is used, special characters are encoded on the check that identify such items as the bank number and the account number. When the check is to be processed, the amount of the check is also encoded on the check by an operator at the bank. The characters are encoded at the bottom of the check in special MICR characters and ink (Figure 5–30). The ink in the encoded characters can be magnetized during processing. The electronic signals generated from the magnetized characters can be interpreted by MICR readers, allowing the checks to be sorted and processed to prepare bank statements for banking customers.

MICR devices can process from 600 to approximately 1,600 checks per minute (Figure 5–31). In addition to banks, MICR finds usage in utility companies, credit card companies, and other industries which must process large volumes of data.

Data collection devices

Obtaining and entering data for processing on a computer is not confined to offices used especially for that purpose or to people specifically trained in data entry operations. **Data collection devices** have been designed and are used for obtaining data at the site where the transaction or event being reported upon takes place. For example, in Figure 5–32 an individual is taking inventory of printed circuit boards. Rather than write down the number of items and then enter them for processing at a later time, the individual is using a portable data collection device to record in the memory of the device. After the inventory is taken, the data can be transmitted to a computer for processing.

In many cases, data collection equipment is found in a hostile

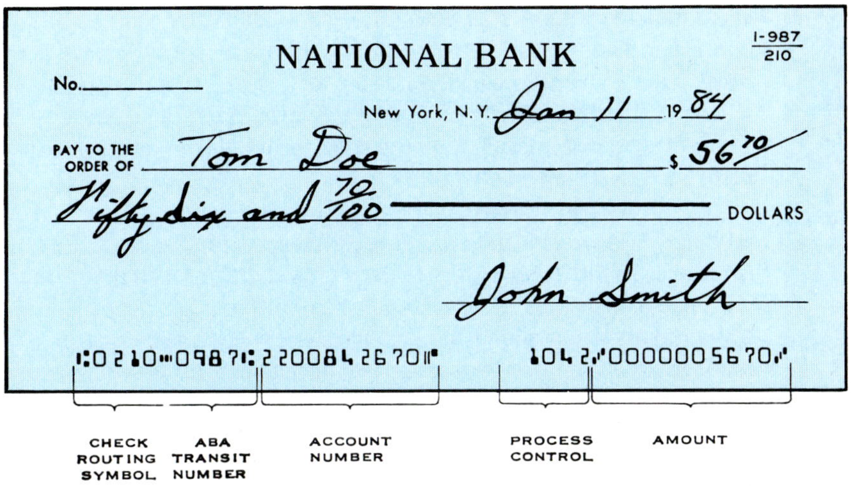

Figure 5–30 (above left) The characters at the bottom of the check can be read by MICR devices. Each group of characters is meaningful for banking applications. All banks in the United States and many in other countries of the world use these types of characters for encoding checks.

Figure 5–31 (above) This MICR reader sorter can read and sort 1,000 documents per minute. After the documents are read, they are placed in the vertical stackers. This reader sorter can be used to store data for later processing in a batch mode or can be attached to a minicomputer, allowing the records to be processed as they are read.

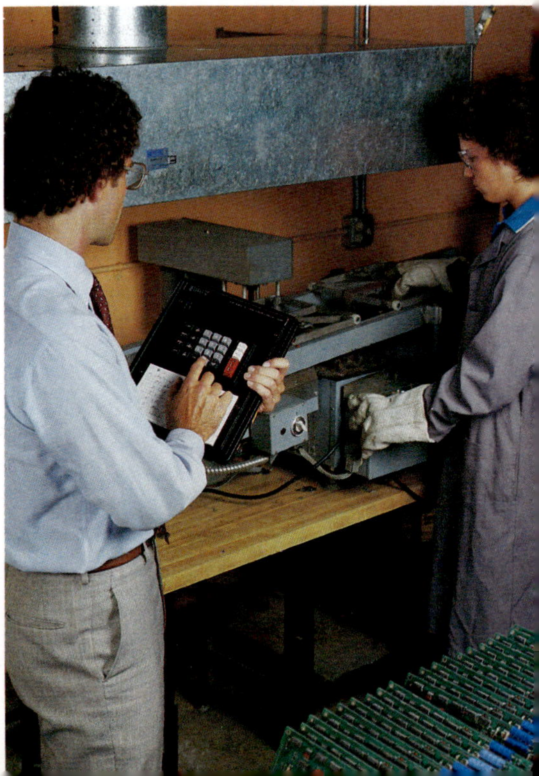

Figure 5–32 The device illustrated here contains memory. When the operator keys the data, it is stored in the memory. Later, the data can be transmitted from the memory of the device to a computer for processing.

Figure 5-33 The input station in this picture is used in a data collection system. The data is being entered under adverse conditions by a worker still operating the forklift. The operator is reporting the removal of an item from inventory as the transaction occurs. Typical of data collection environments, the primary job of the operator is to run a forklift, not to enter data. Therefore, data collection terminals must be simple and quick to operate, so that entering data does not interfere with the main job of the person using the terminal.

environment, where heat, humidity, and cleanliness cannot be controlled (Figure 5-33). In addition, data collection devices are often used by people whose primary task is not to enter the data. Entering the data is only a small portion of their job duties. Therefore, the terminals must be easy to operate in any environment in which they are found.

Utilization of data collection devices has two important advantages over alternative methods of input preparation. First, it reduces the number of times data must be transcribed and the number of locations at which such procedures must take place. Thus, errors are avoided, and many clerical costs are either reduced or eliminated. A second advantage is that as soon as an event occurs, the data about the event is recorded and is available for processing.

Data collection devices range from portable devices that can be carried throughout a store or factory (such as in Figure 5-32) to sophisticated terminal systems with multiple input stations that feed directly into a minicomputer or a large central computer. With the use of microprocessors leading to more sophistication, these devices continue to increase in importance for the data entry function.

Summary — special-purpose input devices

Special purpose input devices are designed to accomplish the data entry function for specific types of applications or in specific environments. While not as widely found as the display terminals discussed previously, they nevertheless play an important role in computer data entry.

SYSTEMS AND PROCEDURES

With the many options available for data entry, it is critical that systems and procedures be developed for the data entry function. The following systems and procedures issues must be addressed in order that data entry be successfully implemented for an application:

1. Origination of data — Data entered for processing on a computer is generated from many sources throughout a company. It is important to identify which people and operations will generate the data so that appropriate procedures can be written to specify what data is to be gathered, how the data is to be gathered, and who is to gather the data.
2. The location of the data entry function — Data is generally entered either from the centralized data entry section of the information systems department or from various locations throughout an organization. In a **centralized data entry** operation, the data is keyed by trained operators from source documents. It can be entered on key-to-disk shared processor systems or it may be entered on-line through the use of display terminals. When data is entered in the centralized data entry section of the information systems department,

it is usually processed in a batch processing mode. Entering data from various locations in an organization is called distributed data entry. Quite often the data entry takes place at the site where the data is generated. An example of distributed data entry is when a travel agent enters an airplane reservation at the travel agency even though the airline computer is many miles away. Much of the time, data entered using distributed data entry is processed in an interactive processing mode, although this is not required. The documentation of the procedures must identify where data is to be entered so that appropriate hardware, software, and personnel instructions are generated.

3. Timing requirements for acquiring the data — In some applications, the time of day or the day of the week when the data becomes available is important to the application. For example, if all timecards for employees must be received by Monday at 4 p.m. in order for employees to be paid Friday afternoon, timing is important and must be specifically identified in the documentation for the data entry.
4. Timing requirements for entering the data — The amount of time that can elapse between the time the event being reported upon takes place and the time the data about that event must be entered should be specified. In some applications, an event can occur and the data need not be entered until hours or even days later. For example, in the payroll application mentioned above, timecards are retrieved Monday at 4 p.m. These timecards recorded the workers' times for the previous week. The data may not be entered until Tuesday. Therefore, more than a week might elapse between when the event occurred and when the data about the event was entered. In most cases where entry time is not a critical factor, the data is recorded on source documents and is given to data entry personnel in either a centralized or distributed location to enter. In other applications, however, the data must be entered as the event or transaction is occurring at the location where the event is occurring. This process is sometimes called **source data collection**. For example, when a retail sale is made using a point of sale terminal, the data must be entered at the moment the sale is made so the sale is recorded and can be completed with the customer. Therefore, it is quite important that the documentation for the system established for data entry specify the timing requirements for entering data.
5. Flow of the input data — The documentation must specify the flow of the data from the point it is originated to the point it is entered for processing on the computer. Any handling which is required, any recording on source documents, and any changes in format from source to data entry must be documented.
6. Transaction volume — The amount of data which must be entered for a given time period and a given location must be estimated. The volume must always be considered with respect to the location where the data will be entered.
7. The manner of entering the data — Based upon many of the factors specified in items 1-6, the procedures must specify how the data is to be entered. These procedures must identify the machines and methods for entering the data. For example, it could be specified that data is to be entered from source documents using off-line key-to-disk shared processor systems in a centralized environment.
8. Editing and error handling — The documentation must specify the editing which will occur on the entered data and the steps to take if the data entered is not valid according to the editing prescribed. Although different applications will have particular criteria for validating input data, there are a number of distinct categories of tests that are performed on input data prior to allowing the data to become part of the processing in a computer.

Some of these tests are:

a. Tests to ensure numeric or alphabetic data is included in a field (Figure 5-34) — For example, a zip code must always be numeric. Therefore, the program performing the editing can check the values in the zip code field to ensure they are numeric. If they are not numeric, the data entered is incorrect. If the zip code entered is numeric, there is no assurance the proper zip code has been entered, but there is assurance the data has been entered in the proper format.

Figure 5-34 In the example above, a non-numeric zip code is entered first. The operator is informed that the zip code is not numeric and is requested to reenter the zip code. When a numeric zip code is entered, the data is accepted.

b. Tests to ensure the reasonableness of data in a field — A reasonableness check is performed to ensure that the data entered is within normal or accepted boundaries. For example, it may be determined that no employee within a company is authorized to work more than 80 hours per week. Therefore, if the value entered in the hours worked field is greater than 80, the value in the field would be indicated as an error.

c. Tests for data consistency — In some cases, data entered cannot, by itself, be found to be invalid. If, however, the data is examined in the context of other data which is entered for the same record or group of fields, then discrepancies can be found. For example, in an airline reservation system, round trip tickets are often purchased (Figure 5-35). If the terminal operator enters the date on which the passenger is leaving, the editing program has little help in determining whether the date entered is valid. Similarly, if the return date is entered by itself, there is no way to know whether the date is valid. If, however, the return date is examined in light of the departure date, then errors may be found. For example, if the return date is earlier than the departure date, then it is likely an error has been made when entering the dates.

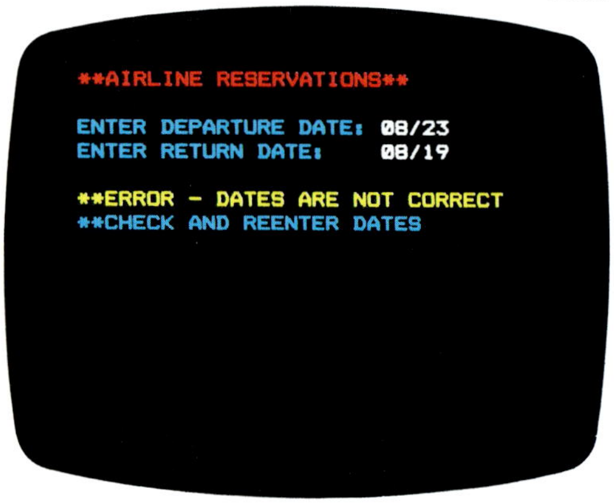

Figure 5-35 On the CRT terminal above, the operator has entered the departure date as 08/23 and the return date as 08/19. Clearly, this is invalid data, but without testing the data for consistency, the error would not have been found.

d. Checking for transcription and transposition errors — When the data entry operator enters data, there is always a possibility that an error will be made when entering the data. These errors are generally classed as either transcription errors or transposition errors. A **transcription error** occurs when an error is made in copying the values from a source document. For example, if the operator keys the customer number 7165 when the proper number is 7765 a transcription error has been made. A **transposition error** happens when two numbers are switched. Such an error has occurred when the number 7765 is entered as 7756. The most common means to detect these types of errors is called a **check digit**. Through the use of an arithmetic formula, an additional digit is calculated for the number in question. For example, the four digits in the number 7765 would be utilized in a calculation to derive a single digit which is appended to the original number. Thus, the number 7765 could be extended as 77658. The number 8 is the check digit which is appended to the end of the original number. When the entire number is subsequently entered back into the computer, the same four numbers used to calculate the check digit (7765) are used in the same formula to again calculate a check digit. If the new check digit matches the one on the number entered into memory, then the number is assumed valid. If, however, the new check digit in the example were not 8, as would happen if the number entered were 71658 or 77568, then the operator would be notified of an error.

9. Data controls and security -- The controls and security which will be applied to the data must be defined. This includes what the controls and security measures are, how they are to be implemented, and what action is to be taken

if the security of the data is compromised in some manner.

10. Personnel requirements — The personnel requirements for both gathering the input data and entering the data must be specified. This includes defining who will gather the data, who will enter the data, and how many people will be required to enter the data for the application. A primary obligation is to educate the personnel with respect to gathering and entering the data. The personnel must be trained how to use the hardware and software, how to ensure reliable data entry, what steps to perform when entering the data, and how to interpret any output received from the computer when interactive processing is used.

The systems and procedures developed for the data entry function are quite critical since accurate data must be reliably entered into a computer to ensure data integrity. In addition, since users can be interacting directly with the computer during the data entry function, procedures and documentation must be quite clear.

Summary — data entry methods and techniques

To summarize, the devices being used to enter data can either be connected to the computer which will process the data (on-line) or not be connected (off-line). When off-line data entry is used, the data can be processed only in the batch processing mode. When on-line data entry is used, either batch or interactive processing is possible.

Within the batch processing modes for both on-line and off-line data entry, the location of the devices being used for data entry can be either distributed throughout the company or can be centralized, or both approaches can be used. When the data entry devices are centralized, data is entered from source documents. When distributed locations are used, both source documents and source data collection can be the source of input data.

Other Input Devices

Input devices have been designed and built to perform specific tasks for particular industries or functions within industries. The following pages illustrate a few of these devices.

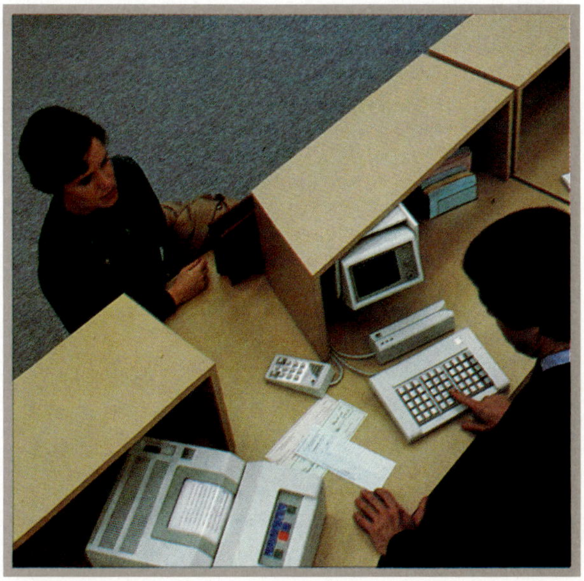

Figure 5-36 These IBM terminals are designed specifically for use by bank tellers.

Figure 5-37 The NCR 2160 lodging system includes a specially designed terminal with keys that not only contain letters of the alphabet and numbers, but also keys labeled room change, bar, valet, laundry, and others which identify various charges that can be made in a hotel. The terminal can be used to verify a credit card purchase and can communicate with computers at other locations to make future reservations.

Figure 5-38 This hand-held terminal uses an optical reading device to read bar codes. The data read from the bar code is stored in the memory of the terminal. After data has been read, the terminal can be connected to a computer, and the data is transmitted from the memory of the terminal to the computer memory for processing.

Terminals in All Environments

Terminals are found in virtually every environment that can generate data for processing on a computer. While many terminals are standard **video display terminals (VDT),** another term for CRT terminals, others are designed to perform specific jobs within the environment. They contain display screens, keyboards, optical character readers, and other features uniquely designed for use in a particular industry.

The terminals found on these two pages are used in retail grocery stores and hotels. The terminals at the checkout stand in the grocery store and in the hotel are called point of sale terminals. **Point of sale terminals** allow data to be entered at the time and place the transaction with a customer occurs. Point of sale terminals serve as input to either minicomputers located in the retail establishment or to larger computers located elsewhere. The data entered is used to maintain sales records, update inventory, perform automatic calculations such as sales tax, verify credit, and other activities critical to running the business. Point of sale terminals are designed to be easy to operate, requiring little technical knowledge.

Computer manufacturers have responded to the unique application needs of particular industries with input terminals designed for that industry. It is expected that this specialization of input terminals will continue into the future.

Figure 5-39 Most modern grocery stores use optical scanning devices such as the one shown here. A laser beam is emitted from the star-like opening in the device. The beam is able to read a bar code, which is a series of vertical bars that represents numbers and letters of the alphabet (see inset). Most retail products today have the **Universal Product Code (UPC)**, a special set of bar code characters which have been universally accepted by retailers, imprinted on their label. The UPC uniquely identifies the manufacturer and the product from the manufacturer. The data read from the UPC printed on the merchandise label is transmitted to a minicomputer in the store. The price and description is retrieved from auxiliary storage on the minicomputer and is displayed on the terminal display. A cash receipt tape is also printed and is given to the customer.

Figure 5-41 The Hipad Digitizer shown here is used with the Apple II personal computer to read a line drawing of a modem into computer memory and to display the drawing on the CRT screen.

Figure 5-40 An aerospace engineer is using a digitizer to read the lines on a printed wiring board layout into a computer for processing. The device in the engineer's hand, called a **cursor** (not the same as the cursor which appears on a CRT screen to mark the location for the next entry of a character), can translate the coordinates read from the lines on the drawing to coordinates which the software in the computer can duplicate, resulting in the drawing's being stored in computer memory.

Figure 5-42 The operator on the Adage 4250 Color Work Station is using a light pen to change the graphic image on the screen. When the light pen is placed at a point on the screen and the sensing device within the pen is activated, it is able to sense light on the screen and transmit the location of that light to computer memory, where the program being executed can perform the desired tasks. Tasks which can be accomplished include drawing lines from one point to another, erasing lines appearing on the screen, and moving lines from one location to another.

Graphical Input Devices

Graphics output is an important way in which computer output is presented to the user. In many applications, graphics output is generated from data which is based on graphics input. In these applications, it is important to be able to translate graphic input data into a form that can be processed on a computer. Graphical input devices are used for this purpose.

Three major devices which are used for graphics input are light pens, digitizers, and graphics tablets. A **light pen** is used directly on the display screen to create or modify graphics (Figure 5–42). A **digitizer** converts points, lines, and curves from a sketch, drawing, or photograph to digital impulses and transmits them to a computer (Figure 5-40 and Figure 5-41). Digitizers are used extensively by engineers, cartologists, and medical specialists. A **graphics tablet** works in a manner similar to a digitizer, but it also contains unique characters and commands which can be called out by the person using the tablet (Figure 5–43).

With the increased use of graphics display output, the need for graphical input devices has increased as well.

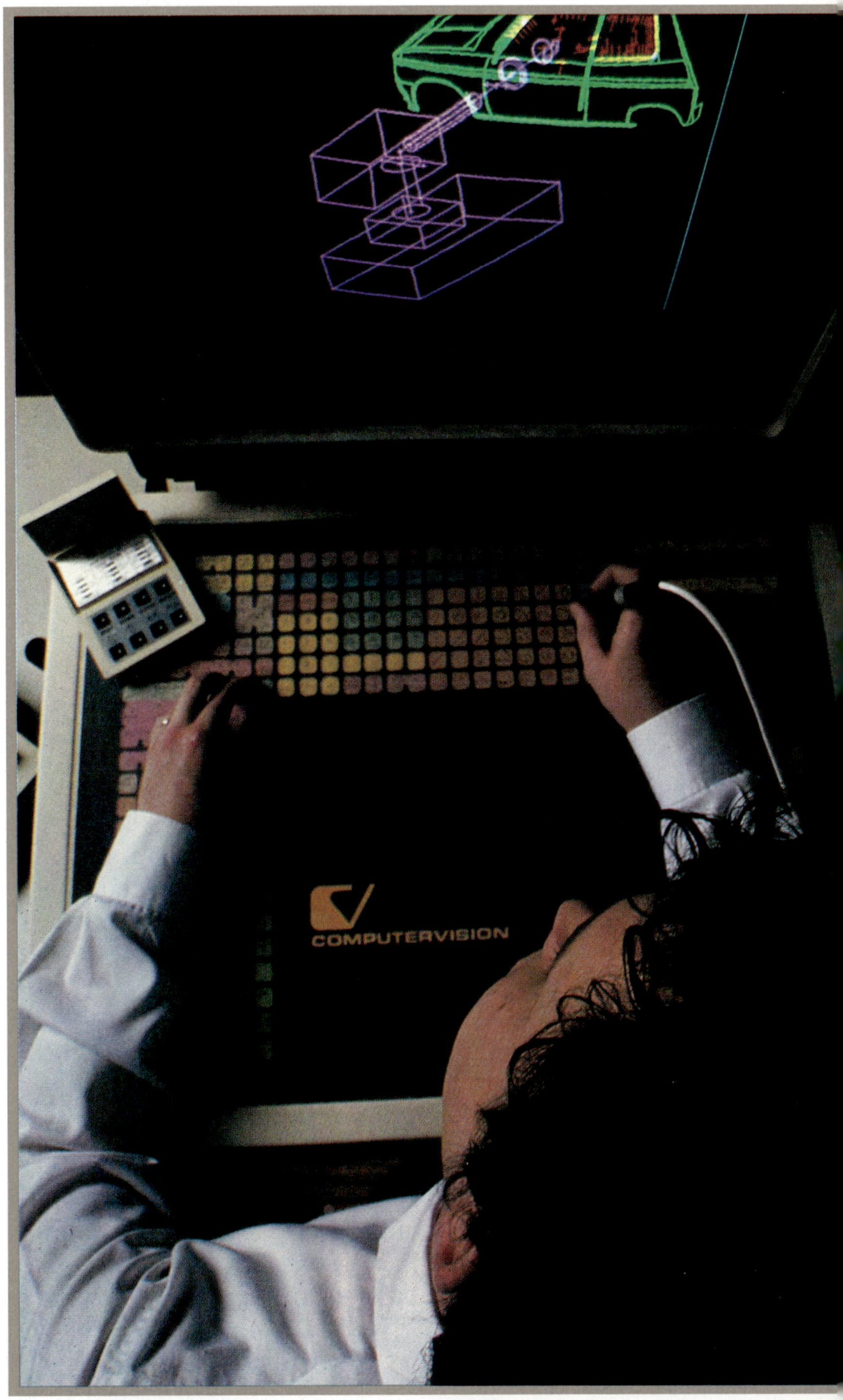

Figure 5–43 The graphics tablet in this picture is used by an automotive design engineer at Peugeot for the development and definition of a car body. A typical car involves over 5,000 elements that must be considered during initial styling. Through the use of **computer-aided design (CAD)**, as implemented using the tablet and graphics screen, significant time can be saved. For example, 35 percent less time is required to create electrical schematics. On the tablet shown are various commands that the engineer can issue to change or modify the graphics on the screen. For example, with one touch of the **stylus** being held by the engineer, the car body shown could be rotated 45°, 60°, or 90°. Another command could move the drawing so the view was from the top of the car body instead of from the side as illustrated. Graphical input devices play an important role in computer-aided design.

CHAPTER SUMMARY

1. There are three uses to which data is put once it is entered into main memory: a) Control the computer; b) Request information from the computer; c) Serve as the source from which information is produced.
2. An inquiry is an entry to request information. In most inquiries, a user enters a minimum of data.
3. When data is the source from which information is produced, a computer program performs operations on the data to produce information that is useful to people.
4. On-line data entry means that the device from which the data is being entered is connected directly to the computer which will process the data. On-line data entry is required for interactive processing.
5. When large amounts of data are entered by a terminal operator whose only job is to enter the data, the data entry function is said to be production data entry.
6. Data entered for batch processing can be entered in either an on-line or an off-line manner.
7. Off-line data entry means the device from which the data is being entered is not connected to the computer which will process the data.
8. When off-line data entry is used, source documents must be accumulated prior to entering the data. Source documents are documents which contain the data to be entered by the data entry operator.
9. Devices used for batch input are all production devices designed to enter data rapidly and accurately.
10. Hardware devices used for data entry fall into two broad categories: terminals and devices specially designed for the data entry function.
11. A terminal used for data entry consists of: a) Keyboard; b) CRT screen; c) Communications channel.
12. Limited function terminals (sometimes called dumb terminals) pass the data keyed by an operator over a communications line to the computer. They cost between $500.00 and $1,000.00.
13. Smart terminals have processing capabilities. They can edit text. They cost $600.00 - $1,500.
14. Intelligent terminals have substantial processing capabilities. They can be programmed and are commonly used for extensive data editing. These terminals are often supported by disk drives and printers.
15. The most widely used CRT screens are equivalent in size to twelve or fifteen inch television screens. The maximum number of characters that can be displayed on a line varies from 40 to 132.
16. Reverse video refers to the process of reversing the normal display on the CRT screen.
17. The underlining feature of terminals allows characters, words, lines, or paragraphs to be underlined.
18. Displaying characters in bold means they are displayed at a greater brightness level than other characters.
19. Scrolling allows lines displayed on the screen to be moved up or down by one line.
20. When paging is used, an entirely new page or screenful of data can be displayed.
21. Many terminals are now available with color screens.
22. The most common input device used with terminals is the keyboard. Keyboards contain letters and numbers; they can also contain special function keys and special purpose keys to control the CRT screen.
23. A cursor is a symbol which indicates where on the screen the next character entered will be displayed.
24. Ergonomics is defined as the study of the characteristics that need to be considered in designing and arranging things that are used in order that people and the things will interact most efficiently.
25. Ergonomics for terminals includes: a) Detachable keyboard; b) Movable display unit; c) Amber or green text on black background; d) High quality CRT screen; e) Sharp focus on screen; f) Anti-glare coating; g) Color.
26. A teleprinter allows data to be entered on a keyboard and be printed on the attached printer.
27. Data entered on teleprinters can be transmitted over data communication lines to a central computer.
28. Integrated workstations have both telephone and computer terminal capabilities.
29. Order entry is the process followed when an order is received from a customer.
30. A backorder is an order for which the item ordered is not in inventory.
31. Some data entry devices used off-line can store data entered from a keyboard on a floppy disk.
32. Key-to-disk shared processor systems have the following characteristics: a) Many keying stations; b) Keying stations are controlled by some processor, such as a minicomputer; c) The data is temporarily stored on disk.
33. When using key-to-disk shared processor systems, often used data can be stored on disk and retrieved automatically for building a record.
34. Key verification is the process of keying data into the system and then rekeying and comparing it.
35. Most key-to-disk shared processor systems contain a supervisory console which can be used to enter control

programs for the jobs to be keyed and to obtain operating statistics for each job and operator.

36. Optical character reader (OCR) devices, some of which can be hand-held, can read typewritten, computer-printed, and hand-printed characters from ordinary documents.

37. A turn-around document is one which is prepared by computer, sent to a consumer or organization, and then is returned for processing on the computer. Many turn-around documents use OCR devices.

38. A mark reader can read carefully placed pencil marks on specially designed documents.

39. Magnetic ink character readers (MICR) are used in the banking industry to read characters printed on checks.

40. Data collection devices are used to obtain data at the site where the transaction or event being reported upon takes place. Data collection devices can be found in a hostile environment.

41. In a centralized data entry operation, data is keyed from source documents by data entry personnel working in the centralized data entry section of the information systems department.

42. Entering data from various locations in an organization is called distributed data entry.

43. Source data collection occurs when data is entered at the time and place the event is occurring.

44. Typical editing that can occur on data entered into a computer are: a) Tests to ensure alphabetic or numeric data is in a field; b) Tests to ensure the reasonableness of data; c) Tests for data consistency; d) Checking for transcription and transposition errors.

45. A transcription error occurs when an error is made in copying values from a source document.

46. A transposition error happens when two numbers are switched.

47. A check digit, derived from an arithmetic formula, is used to determine if an input error has occurred.

48. Point of sale terminals allow data to be entered at the time and place the transaction occurs.

49. An optical scanning device contains a laser beam which can read a bar code.

50. The Universal Product Code (UPC) is a special set of bar codes that are used for retail products.

51. A light pen is used directly on a display screen to create a graphic image.

52. A digitizer converts points, lines, and curves from a sketch, drawing, or photograph to digital impulses and transmits them to a computer.

53. A graphics tablet works like a digitizer but also contains unique characters and commands.

54. A cursor used with a digitizer can translate the coordinates read from lines on a drawing to coordinates which the software in the computer can duplicate, resulting in the drawing's being stored in computer memory.

55. Computer-aided design (CAD) allows engineers to design electronic and mechanical devices on the computer.

KEY TERMS

Backorder 5.14
Batch controls 5.4
Blinking 5.9
Bold 5.9
Centralized data entry 5.24
Check digit 5.26
Computer-aided design (CAD) 5.31
Cursor (CRT screen) 5.10
Cursor (digitizers) 5.30
Data collection devices 5.23
Default data 5.16
Digitizer 5.31
Distributed data entry 5.5
Double size 5.9
Dumb terminals 5.6
Ergonomics 5.11
Executive workstations 5.13
Function keys 5.11
Graphics tablet 5.31
Inquiry 5.2
Integrated workstations 5.13
Intelligent terminals 5.7
Key-to-disk shared processor systems 5.18
Key verification 5.20
Keypunch 5.1
Light pen 5.31
Limited function terminals 5.6
Magnetic ink character recognition (MICR) 5.22
Mark reader 5.22
Off-line data entry 5.3
On-line 5.2
Optical character reader (OCR) 5.21
Optical mark readers (OMR) 5.22
Order entry 5.14
Paging 5.9
Point of sale terminals 5.29
Portable teleprinters 5.12
Production data entry 5.3
Programmable terminals 5.7
Reverse video 5.8
Scrolling 5.9
Smart terminals 5.6
Source data collection 5.25
Source documents 5.3
Stylus 5.31
Teleprinters 5.12
Text editing 5.6
Transcription error 5.26
Transposition error 5.26
Turn-around document 5.22
Underlining 529
Universal product code (UPC) 5.29
Uploading 5.7
Video display terminals (VDT) 5.29

REVIEW QUESTIONS

1. What are the three uses of data when it is entered into a computer? Give an example of each.
2. What is on-line data entry? What is off-line data entry? When is each of them used?
3. What are the two broad categories of devices used for data entry?
4. Name the three types of display terminals. Describe each type.
5. Identify five display features which are often useful for computer users and data entry operators.
6. What is terminal ergonomics? List and describe six ergonomic features a terminal should have.
7. Describe the basic steps in an order entry system.
8. Draw a step-by-step diagram of screen displays which would occur when data is entered in an order entry system.
9. List three characteristics of key-to-disk shared processor systems.
10. Describe two different optical character reader devices. Identify two different types of characters read by OCR devices.
11. What is MICR? For what is it used?
12. Identify three different applications where data collection devices would be appropriate.
13. What is centralized data entry? What is distributed data entry? Name the advantages and disadvantages of each.
14. Identify and illustrate the difference between a transcription error and a transposition error.
15. What is a point of sale terminal? To what use can data entered on point of sale terminals be put?
16. Describe three different types of graphical input devices. Name an application where each type could be used.

CONTROVERSIAL ISSUES

1. The use of video display terminals (VDT) has increased significantly during the past ten years. With the increased use has come claims that sitting in front of a cathode ray tube and using the terminals is harmful to a person's health. It has been claimed that pregnant women have had miscarriages, and back ailments are common when video display terminals are used. Some unions have questioned the advisability of sitting in front of a terminal for eight hours. Several state legislatures have proposed laws which would require up to 15-minute breaks for each hour using a terminal. Terminal manufacturers have argued that all this is nonsense and ergonomically designed terminals present no danger to health. Research the arguments, and take a position on this controversy.
2. Key-to-disk shared processor units that are used for data entry have the capability of monitoring an operator's performance by counting the number of keystrokes and the number of errors made by the operator. While data entry supervisors claim this information is critical when managing a data entry installation, some unions and employees have claimed the monitoring is an invasion of privacy. Present a case for or against monitoring.

RESEARCH PROJECTS

1. The data entry function has changed significantly during the history of business data processing. Research the history of the data entry function, and prepare an oral or written report. Include in your report the hardware devices used, the manner in which data was entered, the location from which data was entered, and the different procedures which have been used for data entry over the years.
2. Visit a retail or grocery store in your area, and prepare a report on the point of sale terminals in use. Be sure to identify the type of terminal used, the manner in which data is entered, the computer to which the terminal is connected, and any problems or difficulties employees have had using the terminals.
3. Bring a turn-around document which you have received in the mail to class, and explain it to the class.

Chapter Six

Obtaining Output From the Computer

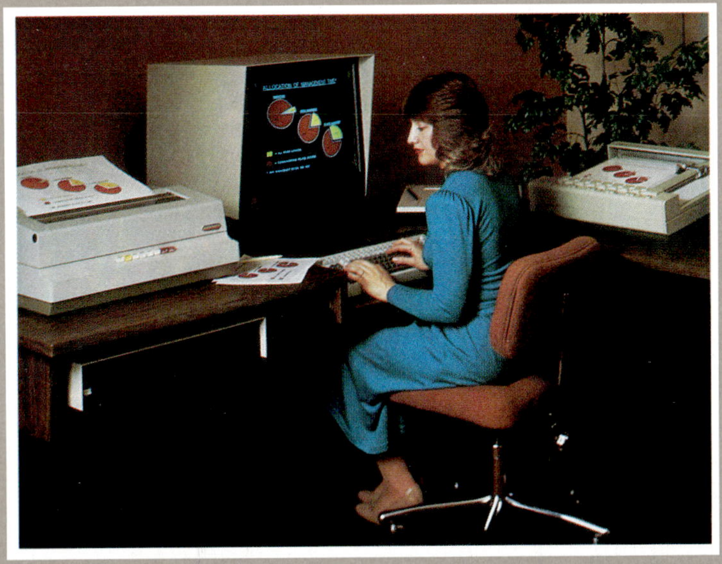

Objectives

- ☐ Describe the classifications of printers
- ☐ Identify the types of printers available for home and personal computers
- ☐ Describe in detail the various attributes of dot matrix printers
- ☐ Identify the quality obtainable from various types of printers
- ☐ Describe printers used for large computers
- ☐ List the various systems and procedures associated with printed output
- ☐ Describe displayed output, and in particular the CRT monitor
- ☐ List the capabilities of graphics display devices
- ☐ Specify other types of output devices used with computers

Obtaining Output From the Computer

Chapter Six

The primary use of a computer is to produce useful information. For many years, this information was presented in the form of a printed report. Today, however, there are a wide variety of ways to present computer output which serve the diverse needs of computer users. In a modern computer environment, printed reports or graphic output may be produced on printers. Computer terminals may be used to display alphanumeric data or graphics output such as charts and graphs. High resolution drawings can be generated on color CRT's. Plotters are used to produce complex diagrams. Microfilm devices can store information in a very compact form. Even vocal response generated from data stored in main computer memory may be used to convey information to users.

The selection of the type of output to be generated from a computer and the manner in which the information is made available to the user depends upon the needs of the user and the hardware and software currently available. The purpose of this chapter is to explain the types of output that can be generated from computers and to describe the characteristics of the devices that can be utilized with various size computers to produce the output.

PRINTERS

Printed reports are a widely used form of computer output (Figure 6–2). Therefore, it is important to be aware of the types of printers that are available, and the characteristics of each type.

In the past, when computers were used primarily in a batch processing environment, printers were usually large devices designed to produce output as rapidly as possible from large volumes of input. With the introduction of the personal computer, however, and the increased use of interactive and transaction-oriented processing, a variety of printers is necessary to meet the needs of computer users. For example, the user of a personal computer selling for less than $1,000.00 does not need, nor want, a printer capable of printing 2,000 lines per minute. On the other hand, users of mainframe computers, such as utility companies which send printed bills to hundreds of thousands of customers each

Figure 6–2 The printed report allows the user to not only read the material but also to transport the report to others who can read the information. In addition, comments can be written on reports, and the pages of a report can be separated to give to different people. Printed reports will remain an important means for communicating output from a computer.

month, can effectively utilize printers which are capable of printing thousands of lines per minute. These different needs have resulted in the development of printers with varying capabilities for use with computers. The following paragraphs discuss the attributes of these printers.

Classification of printers

Although there are a number of ways printers can be classified, all computer printers fall into two broad categories. These categories are: 1) Impact printers; 2) Nonimpact printers.

Computer printers may be further classified by the method used to form a character (a series of dots or a solid character); by speed (low speed, high speed, very high speed); and, of course, by cost. All of the above factors are important considerations in choosing a printer for a computer.

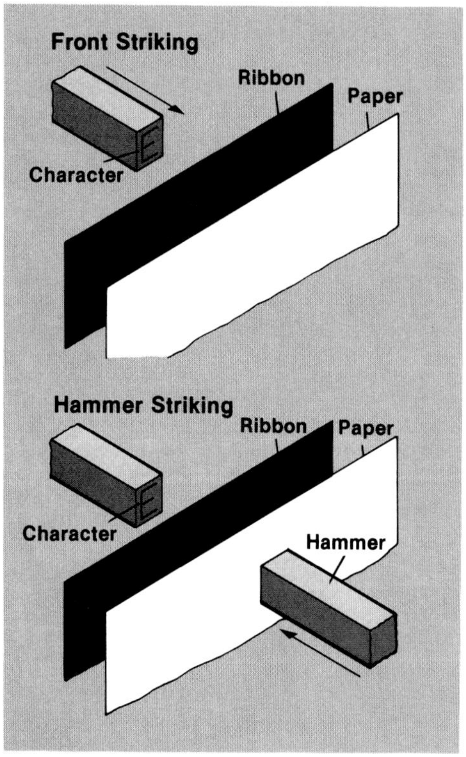

Figure 6–3 Impact printers operate in one of two ways: front striking or hammer striking. With front striking, the character strikes the ribbon first and then the paper, leaving an impression. On hammer striking printers, hammers strike the paper which strikes the ribbon and then the character.

Impact printing

Impact printing devices transfer the image onto paper by some type of printing mechanism striking the paper, ribbon, and character together. One of two techniques is often used (Figure 6–3). The first technique is **front striking,** where a printing mechanism containing a solid character or a series of pins which can form a character strikes a ribbon against the paper to form an image. The second technique utilizes a **hammer striking** device in which the ribbon and paper are struck against the character by the hammer to form the image on the paper.

There are numerous types of print mechanisms to accomplish impact printing. The quality and speed of the printed output is directly related to the method used.

Nonimpact printing

A number of technologies are used to accomplish nonimpact printing. As the name implies, **nonimpact printing** means that printing occurs without having characters striking against a sheet of paper. Ink jet printers are a form of nonimpact printing. With ink jet printers, small drops of ink are used to form a character on a page. Other nonimpact printers use specially coated or sensitized papers that respond to thermal or electrostatic stimuli to form an image. Still others use laser beams to cause printing.

Each method used for placing an image on paper has its advantages and disadvantages. Impact printing is relatively noisy because the paper is struck when printing occurs. On the other hand, since the paper is struck, interleaved carbon paper can be used to create multiple copies of pages in a report. Nonimpact printers cannot create carbon copies. They are, however, very quiet, and some nonimpact printers are very fast.

Printer speed classification

Printer speed is an important consideration when selecting a computer printer. Printers may be broadly classified by the speed at which characters are printed on the page. The rate of printing for low speed printers is expressed in the number of characters that can be printed in one second. **Low speed printers** can print from 15 characters per second to 600 characters per second. Most low speed printers are **serial printers,** meaning that the characters are printed one at a time.

The rate of printing for high speed and very high speed printers is stated in terms of the number of lines per minute that can be printed. Printers that can print from 300 to 3,000 lines per minute are classified as **high speed printers.** These printers are also called **line printers.**

Very high speed printers can print in excess of 3,000 lines per minute. Some very high speed printers can print in excess of 20,000 lines per minute. These printers are sometimes called **page printers.**

A number of factors influence the speed at which printers operate. A printer can operate at varying speeds depending upon the number of characters that are printed on a line, and with certain impact printers, the density of the characters printed.

Low speed printers are normally used with home, personal, and small business computers. High speed printers are used with large computers where thousands of lines of output must be produced each month. Very high speed printers are used only with large mainframes for applications such as utility company billing.

PRINTERS FOR HOME AND PERSONAL COMPUTERS

When selecting a printer for use with a home computer, a personal computer, or for a small business computer, a number of factors must be considered. These factors include:

1) The quality of print.
2) The number of characters which can be printed on each line.
3) The speed of printing.
4) The ability of the printer to print graphics.
5) The availability of color printing.
6) The type of paper feed mechanism.
7) Cost.

These factors should be kept in mind in the discussion of printers in the following paragraphs.

Thermal printers

The least expensive printers available for home and personal computers are called **thermal** or **electro-sensitive printers.** Printers of this type require the use of special sensitized paper to form images on the page. These printers can typically print from 30 to 120 characters per second. The print quality is relatively poor. Such

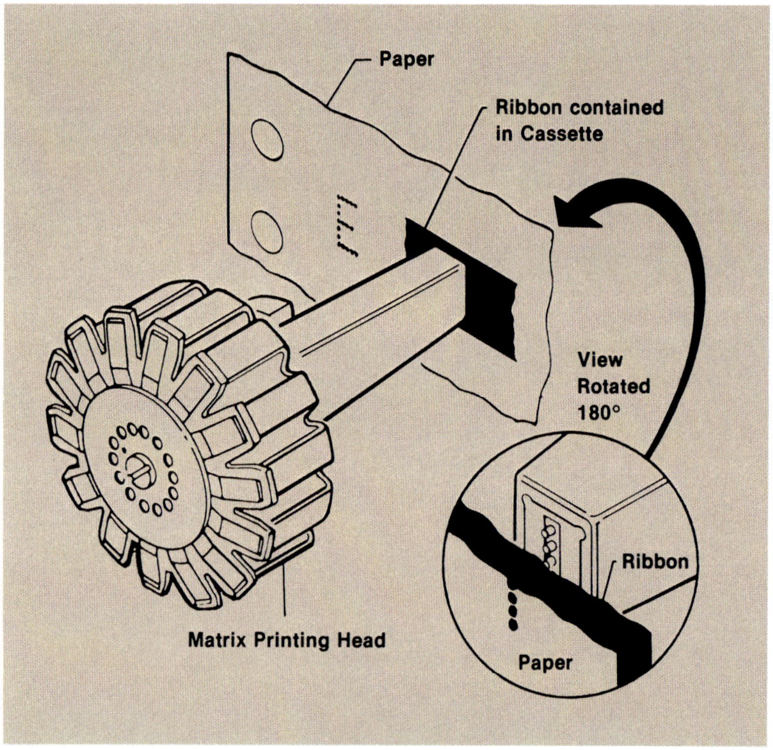

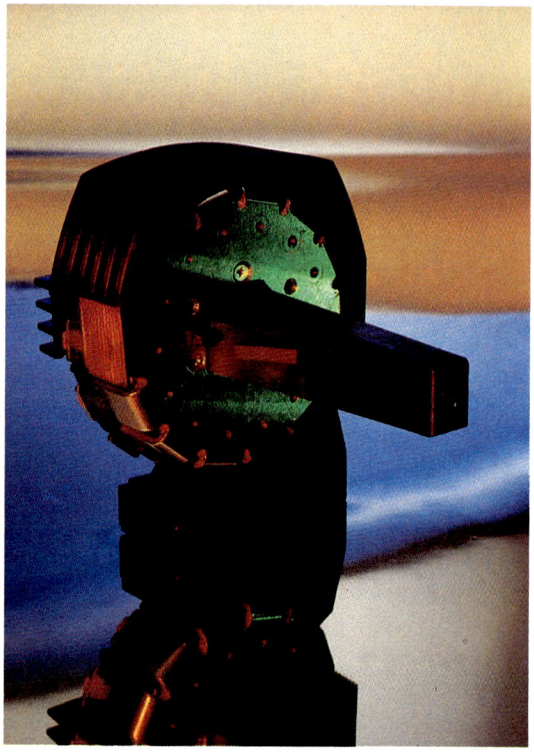

Figure 6–4 The print head for a dot matrix printer consists of a series of wires which, when activated by the electronics within the printer, strike the ribbon which strikes the paper, creating a dot on the paper. Characters consist of a series of closely printed dots.

printers can be obtained for less than $200.00. Their use is normally restricted to low speed printing where print quality is not important.

Dot matrix printers

The **dot matrix printer** is used with more home and personal computers than any other type of printer. It is quite versatile and relatively inexpensive. These printers are impact printers that use a **movable print head** consisting of a series of small vertical tubes containing wires that when pressed against a ribbon and paper causes small dots to print. The combination of small dots printed closely to one another forms the character (Figure 6–4).

To print a character using a dot matrix printer, the character stored in main computer memory is sent to the printer's electronic circuitry. A dot pattern representing a particular character is generated by the printer. It then activates the vertical wires in the print head, causing the selected wires to press against the ribbon and paper. The print head moves horizontally across the page, printing the required series of dots to form the character. Characters are printed one at a time.

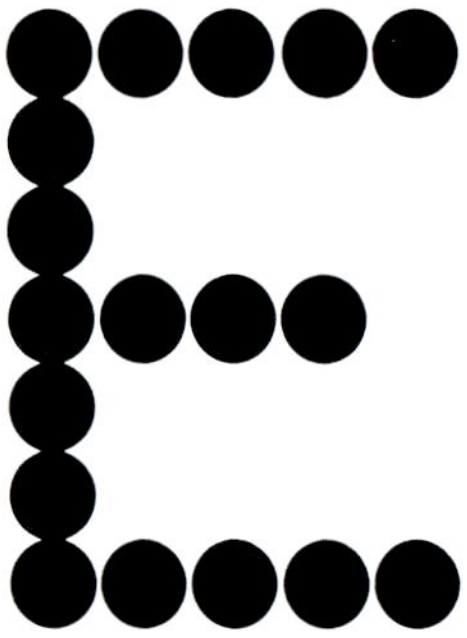

Figure 6–5 The letter E is formed as a dot matrix character using seven vertical dots and five horizontal dots. This letter was printed by a printer using a 7 × 9 matrix. The two remaining vertical dots which are not shown on this capital letter are used as descenders, which are portions of lower-case characters such as a "p" or a "g" that go below the bottom of a capital letter. Only five horizontal dots are used in order to give the character the proper perspective.

Dot matrix printers can contain a varying number of wires, depending upon the manufacturer and the printer model. A print head consisting of nine vertical tubes and related wires is often used. Characters are formed by printing dots in a 7 × 9 matrix. The number 7 indicates the number of times the print head moves horizontally to form the character. The number 9 indicates the number of wires, arranged vertically, that are used to cause printing. With a 7 × 9 matrix, the characters will be no taller than nine dots, nor wider than seven dots. Figure 6–5 illustrates the formation of the letter of the alphabet E using a dot matrix printer.

Some printers print **bidirectionally**; that is, the head prints while moving from left to right, and then prints while moving from right to left. Printing bidirectionally almost doubles the number of characters that can be printed in a given period of time.

Dot matrix printers print at varying speeds. Generally, the higher the speed, the greater the cost. Typical costs range from less than $300.00 for units that print at 50 characters per second to $700.00 for units that print at 160 characters per second. Some dot matrix printers are available (at a higher cost) that print at even greater speeds.

The Epson FX-80 printer shown in Figure 6–6 is a well-known dot matrix printer.

Figure 6–6 The Epson FX-80 printer is a dot matrix printer that can print 160 characters per second.

Dot matrix printers — Print quality

The term "**letter quality**" is frequently used as a guide to the quality of the printed character produced on a printer. A letter quality printed character is a fully formed, solid character that is easy to read. A character produced by a dot matrix printer is normally not considered to be letter quality because it is made up of a series of dots. The quality of a dot matrix character ranges from poor to very good, or near letter quality. The quality of print produced is mostly dependent upon the number of dots used to form the character. A 5×7 dot matrix print head produces lower quality printed output than does a 7×9 dot matrix print head because with the 7×9 matrix, the dots are closer together.

Several methods are used to improve the quality of dot matrix printers. One method is to print a line twice. Using this technique a line is printed, and then the paper or print head is shifted very slightly and the line is printed again. This has the effect of filling in spaces between the dots, giving the appearance of solid characters (Figure 6–7). The disadvantage, of course, is that the printing takes twice as long since each character is printed twice.

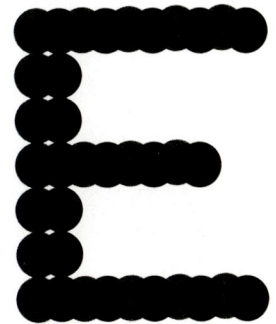

Figure 6–7 The letter E in this example is formed by overprinting; that is, the character is printed twice. When it is printed the second time, the print head is offset just slightly so that the gaps between the dots are filled in. Thus, while the character is still printed using dots, the dots touch.

Newer print head design for dot matrix printers makes use of as many as 18 wires for forming characters. These print heads consist of two vertical rows of nine tubes and wires positioned very closely together and slightly offset. Because of the greater number of dots being used to form a character, higher quality characters result.

Many dot matrix printers also allow the characters to be printed in two or more sizes and densities. Typical sizes include: 1) Condensed print; 2) Standard print; 3) Enlarged print. In addition, each of the three print sizes can be printed with increased density, or darkness. The chart in Figure 6–8 illustrates examples of some of the various types of output that can be produced from a dot matrix printer.

CONDENSED PRINT - NORMAL CHARACTERS
CONDENSED PRINT - EMPHASIZED CHARACTERS

STANDARD PRINT - NORMAL CHARACTERS
STANDARD PRINT - EMPHASIZED CHARACTERS

ENLARGED PRINT - NORMAL CHARACTERS
ENLARGED PRINT - EMPHASIZED CHARACTERS

Figure 6–8 Three type sizes are shown in this example — condensed, standard, and enlarged. All three are printed using normal characters and emphasized characters. These characters were printed on an Epson FX-80. They are representative of the types of printing that can be done using a dot matrix printer.

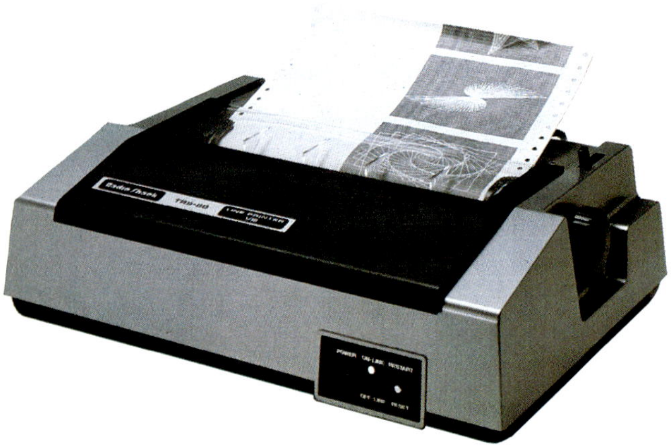

Figure 6-9 The Radio Shack printer in this picture is capable of graphics printing. The ability to draw graphics depends on the printer and the software which directs the printer.

Dot matrix printers — graphics mode

Some dot matrix printers have the ability to print graphics. When a printer has graphics capabilities, software can specify that one or more dots should be printed by the print head. The software can then direct that the print head move, and another set of dots be printed. These dots are printed in a combination specified by the software. The dots do not have to be in the form of letters of the alphabet or numbers. In addition, printers with graphics capability have the ability to space in smaller increments than with normal printing. This causes the printing of the dots closer together than when numbers or letters of the alphabet are printed in standard mode.

The result of this graphics capability is the ability of dot matrix printers to produce pictures and graphs (Figure 6-9). When special software packages are used, dot matrix printers can print in many different type styles and sizes (Figure 6-10). The flexibility of the dot matrix printer has resulted in very widespread use of this type of printer for personal computer users.

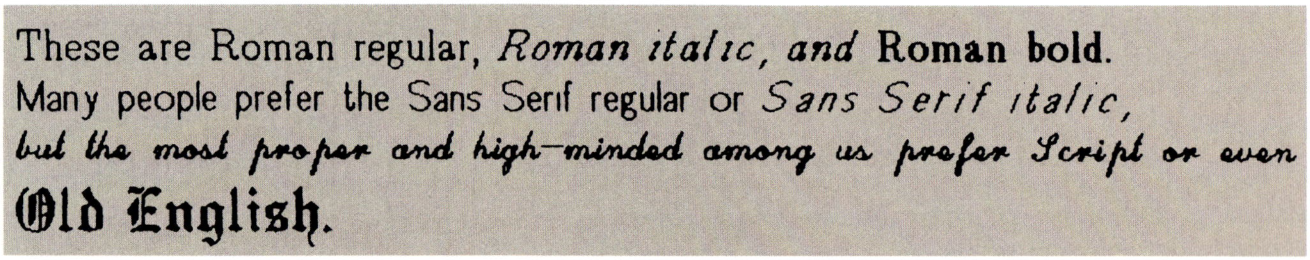
These are Roman regular, Roman italic, and Roman bold.
Many people prefer the Sans Serif regular or Sans Serif italic,
but the most proper and high-minded among us prefer Script or even
Old English.

Figure 6-10 The styles of letters shown in this example illustrate the abilities of dot matrix printers that can print graphics. The formation of the letters is dependent upon the software directing the printer. Software packages are available which can print up to twenty different styles.

Dot matrix printers — color

Dot matrix printers that can print in multiple colors are available. These printers use ribbons that contain the colors red, green, and blue. By repeated printing and repositioning of the paper, print head, and ribbon, color output is obtained. Such printers can be useful in printing graphs and charts, but the quality of the output is not comparable to color produced by other types of printers. These units cost $2,000.00 or more.

Additional printer features

Additional features which should be considered when evaluating printers include: 1) The maximum number of characters which can be printed on a line; 2) The size of paper that can be used; 3) The type of paper feed mechanism.

Although some thermal printers print 40 characters or less across a horizontal line, most dot matrix printers, in a standard print mode, print either 80 or 132 characters on a line. For printers that print 80 characters per line, the standard paper size is 8½ × 11 inches. Printers that print 132 characters per line use 11" × 14" paper.

Many printers utilize only continuous form paper. **Continuous form paper** has each page connected for continuous flow through the printer (Figure 6–11).

Two types of feed mechanisms are found on dot matrix printers. They are called tractor feed and friction feed. **Tractor feed mechanisms** transport continuous form paper through the printer by using sprockets which fit into holes on each side of the paper. Tractor feed provides for an even flow of paper through the printer.

Figure 6–11 Continuous form paper has each sheet connected with the next sheet, separated by perforations. When the paper runs through the printer, a tractor feed mechanism can pull the paper by using the holes on each side of the form. After a report has been printed, the continuous form can be "burst," meaning that the pages are separated along the perforations.

Most printers equipped with tractor feed units do not allow single sheets of paper to be inserted into the machine one at a time. Where it is necessary or desirable to feed single sheets of paper into the printer, **friction feed mechanisms** are used. As the name implies, paper is moved through friction feed printers by pressure on the paper and the carriage. As the carriage rotates, the paper is transported through the printer.

The selection of a tractor feed or friction feed printer is dependent upon the needs of the user. Where it is desirable to load single sheets of paper into the printer one at a time, a printer with friction feed should be obtained.

Letter quality printers

Some dot matrix printers produce near letter quality characters, and the trend is toward even better character quality with dot matrix printers. When, however, high quality output is required, such as in word processing applications or other types of correspondence, solid type printers are usually used. These solid type printers are sometimes called "letter quality" printers.

The letter quality printer most often used with personal computers is the daisy wheel printer (Figure 6–12). The **daisy wheel printer** uses impact technology. It consists of a type element that contains raised characters which strike the paper through an inked ribbon.

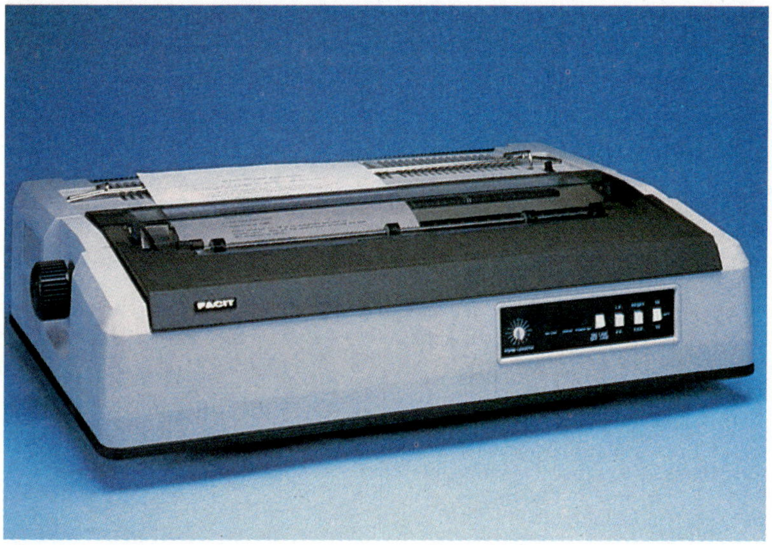

Figure 6–12 A daisy wheel printer such as shown here can fit on a desk top. Some daisy wheel printers allow either continuous form feed or single sheet form feed.

The daisy wheel element somewhat resembles the structure of a flower, with many long, thin petals (Figure 6–13, page 6.8). Each petal has a character on the tip. When printing occurs, the print unit (daisy wheel) rotates so that the character to be printed is in printing position. A hammer then fires and forces the selected character against the ribbon and paper, causing the character to be printed. Because of the

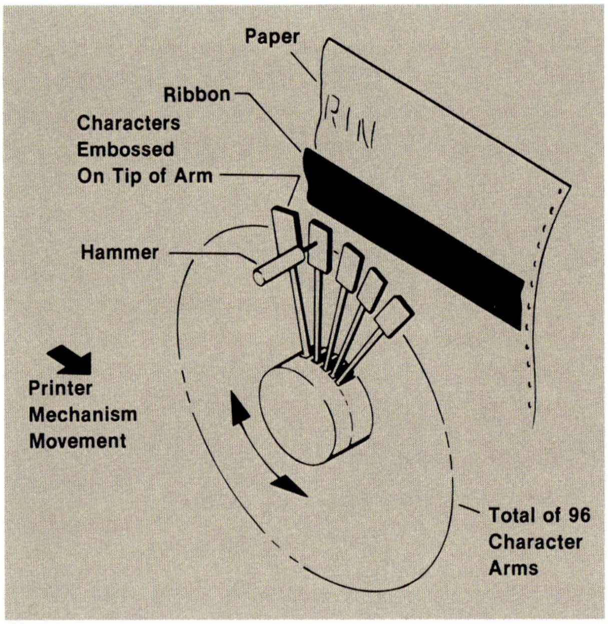

Figure 6–13 The daisy wheel element itself consists of a number of arms, each with a character on the end. When the printer is running, the wheel spins until the desired character is lined up with the hammer, at which time the character is struck against the ribbon and paper. Since daisy wheel printers are impact printers, they are fairly noisy when they are printing.

time required to rotate the daisy wheel, the daisy wheel printer is normally slower than a dot matrix printer; however, the print quality is higher. Printing speeds vary from 20 to 60 characters per second.

An additional advantage of the daisy wheel printer is that the daisy wheel is removable. Daisy wheels can be obtained with a variety of typefaces, such as script, gothic, and roman faces. Therefore, whenever the user wishes to change typefaces, or type fonts as they are sometimes known, one daisy wheel can be removed and the desired wheel put on the printer. The cost of daisy wheel printers ranges from approximately $600.00 to over $5,000.00

Figure 6–14 The Hewlett-Packard Thinkjet® printer is an ink jet printer which sells for less than $500.00. It brings ink jet technology within the same price range as dot matrix technology.

Ink jet printers

An increasingly popular type of nonimpact printer is called an **ink jet printer**. To form a character, an ink jet printer uses nozzles that spray liquid ink drops onto the page. Ink jet printers produce relatively high quality output, and print between 150 and 270 characters per second. They are very quiet because the paper is not struck as it is when dot matrix or daisy wheel printers are used. A disadvantage is that they cannot produce multiple copies. Some of these printers sell for less than $500.00. The ink jet printer in Figure 6–14 is designed for use with personal computers.

Specially designed ink jet printers can produce output in a variety of colors. By overlaying the basic ink colors of yellow, cyan, and magenta, color ink jet printers can produce more than 100 different color combinations with relatively high quality color graphic output on paper (Figure 6-15).

Figure 6-15 The color produced from ink jet printers is reasonably high quality. The printing is not fast, however. A typical page may take more than one minute to be printed when the entire page is in color.

Laser printers

One of the newest printers for use with personal computers is the laser printer. The **laser printer** is a nonimpact printer that converts data from the personal computer into a beam of laser light that encodes an organic photoconductor with the data, forming the images to be printed. The photoconductor then attracts particles of toner. When the toner is brought into contact with the paper, an image is produced on the paper. The toner is fused onto the paper by heat and pressure.

An advantage of the laser printer is that numbers and alphabetic data can be printed in varying sizes and type styles. The output produced is of very high quality, with the images resembling professional printing rather than typewritten characters on a page.

Laser printers for personal computers print in the range of eight pages per minute. These units can produce both text and graphics. They cost in the $3,000.00 range.

Summary — personal computer printers

In summary, a variety of printers can be used with home or personal computers. Inexpensive thermal printers are available for less than $200.00, but they require special paper and produce rather poor quality output.

The dot matrix printer is very popular with personal computer users. These units range in cost from approximately $300.00 to over $2,000.00, depending upon speed and related features. They are capable of producing characters in various sizes, densities, and type styles. Dot matrix printer speeds range from approximately 50 characters per second to 160 characters per second, although even faster units are available. The quality of print varies from fair to near letter quality. Most dot matrix printers use continuous form paper, although friction feed units are available as well. The number of standard size characters that can be printed on one line is either 80 or 132.

For letter quality output, solid type printers are usually recommended. The most popular solid type printer is the daisy wheel printer. Daisy wheel printers are relatively slow, printing from 20 to 60 characters per second. Their cost runs from approximately $500.00 to over $2,000.00.

Ink jet printers produce relatively high quality output, are relatively fast, and are quiet because they are nonimpact printers. Color can be produced by some ink jet printers as well.

A variety of printers with numerous features are available to the user of personal computers; therefore, it is important to understand the characteristics, advantages, and disadvantages of each type of printer.

Selecting a printer for the personal computer

The process of selecting a printer for use with a personal computer involves an evaluation of a number of factors. The following questions should be answered prior to selecting a printer:

1. What print quality is necessary?
2. How many characters must be printed across the page on one line, and what size paper is going to be used?
3. What printing speed is required?
4. Are different size print or different print styles required or desirable?
5. Are graphics necessary or desirable?
6. Is color necessary or desirable?
7. Is continuous form paper satisfactory, or must single sheets be used?
8. How much money can be spent for the printer?

The selection of a printer must be based upon a careful review of the requirements of the user and of the applications which are to be processed using the printer.

Figure 6–16 The chain, or train, printer contains all of the characters on a chain which rotates at a constant high rate of speed. It also has hammers at each print position. The paper and ribbon are placed between the hammers and the chain. As the chain rotates, the hammer "fires" when the proper character is in the proper print position. The chain printer produces good print quality at up to 3,000 lines per minute.

PRINTERS FOR LARGE COMPUTERS

Minicomputers and mainframes are frequently used to process and print large volumes of data. As the demand for printing information from a computer increases, the use of high speed printers is required. High speed printers operate in the range of 300 to 3,000 lines per minute. Although some dot matrix printers operate in the low end of this speed range, the three types of printers usually designated as line printers are chain printers, band printers, and some laser printers.

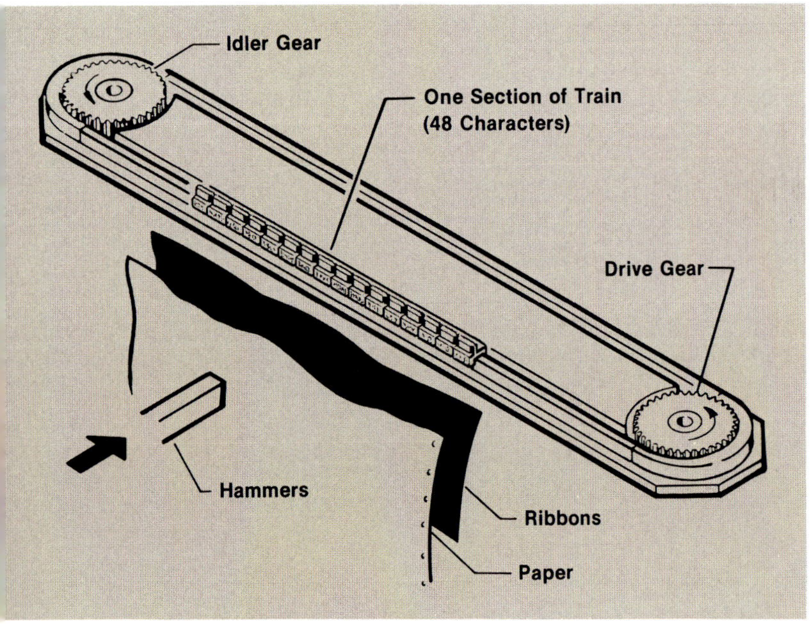

Chain printers

For many years, the most widely used printer has been the **chain printer** (sometimes called a **train printer**). The chain printer contains numbers, letters of the alphabet, and selected special characters on a rotating chain (Figure 6–16). The chain consists of a series of type slugs which contain the character set. The character set on the type slugs is repeated two or more times on the chain mechanism. The chain rotates at a very high rate of speed. Each possible print position has a hammer that can fire against the back of the paper, forcing the paper and ribbon against the type slug. As the chain rotates, the hammer fires when the type slug with the character to be printed is in the proper position.

The chain printer has proven to be very reliable and produces good print quality up to 3,000 lines

per minute. The cost ranges from $10,000.00 to over $100,000.00. The printers in the large computer installation in Figure 6–17 are chain printers.

Figure 6–17 These high speed chain printers are used in a large computer installation to produce many thousands of lines of printed output per hour.

Band printers

Band printers are also used when high speed printing is required. These printers utilize a horizontal, rotating band containing characters. The characters are struck by hammers situated behind the paper and a ribbon to create a line of print on the paper (Figure 6–18).

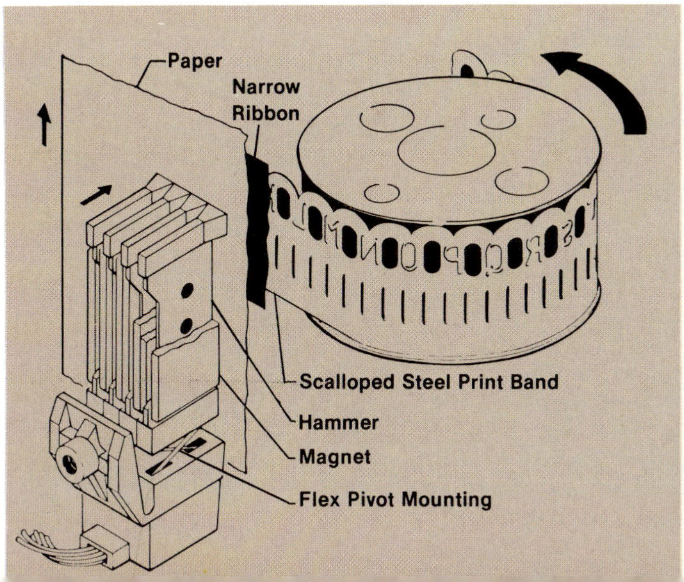

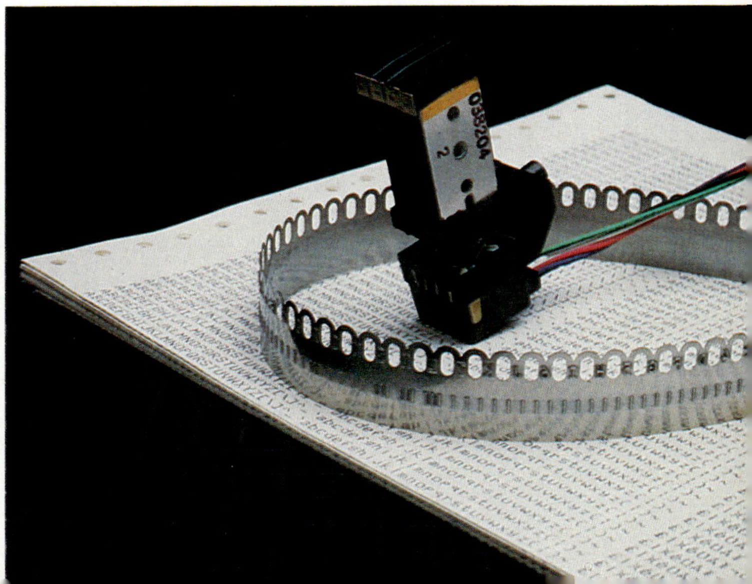

Figure 6–18 A band printer uses a type band which contains solid characters used to form images on the paper. The print hammers (shown inside the picture of the band) strike the paper and ribbon, forcing them into the band.

Interchangeable type bands can be used on band printers. The different type bands contain many different styles of fonts. A band printer can produce numerous carbon copies (5 to 6), has good print quality, high reliability, and depending on the manufacturer and model of the printer, can print in the range of 300 to 2,000 lines per minute. Their costs range from approximately $5,000.00 to $25,000.00.

Laser printers

L**aser printers** are now available in the high speed range. For example, a recent Datapoint laser printer prints 1,300 lines per minute. The unit was designed for office applications and can produce very high quality output in a variety of type styles.

Very high speed printers

During the first 25 years of computer use for business applications, most high speed printers were impact printers which operated at speeds of from 600 to 1,000 lines per minute. Even at 3,000 lines per minute, however, computers were able to process data much faster than printers were able to print it. Some printers were operated off-line, where data was stored on magnetic tape, and the tape was transported to a tape drive connected to the printer. The printer then printed the data stored on the tape, and the computer was not burdened by the relatively slow speeds of the printers.

Even so, printers were operating for many hours in large retail, credit card, or utility companies that were sending monthly statements to hundreds of thousands or even millions of customers each month. With the increased amount of computer usage relative to producing printed material, the high speed printers were just not adequate to provide the printing capacity required. Therefore, research was conducted by industry to develop printers with very high speed capabilities. Today, for the production of a very large number of print lines per month, nonimpact printers that can print 20,000 lines per minute are available for use (Figure 6–19).

Figure 6–19 This 9800 series laser printer from DatagraphiX operates at speeds up to 21,000 lines per minute. The printer in this picture is off-line. The source of the data to be printed is the tape which is mounted on the associated tape drive.

Using a process similar to that used for copying machines, Xerox, IBM, DatagraphiX, and other companies have developed these very high speed devices. The printers use a laser beam to project a data image on the surface of a rotating drum. A toner is applied to the pattern created on the drum. Paper is then pressed against the drum, transferring the image to the paper. The image on the paper is then fused on the paper by heat.

Very high speed printers can create print in different type styles, can generate graphics, and can even have a forms overlay feature that allows entire forms to be printed (Figure 6–20). The printers cost between $150,000.00 and $300,000.00. Obviously, such printers can be justified only by companies with very large printing needs.

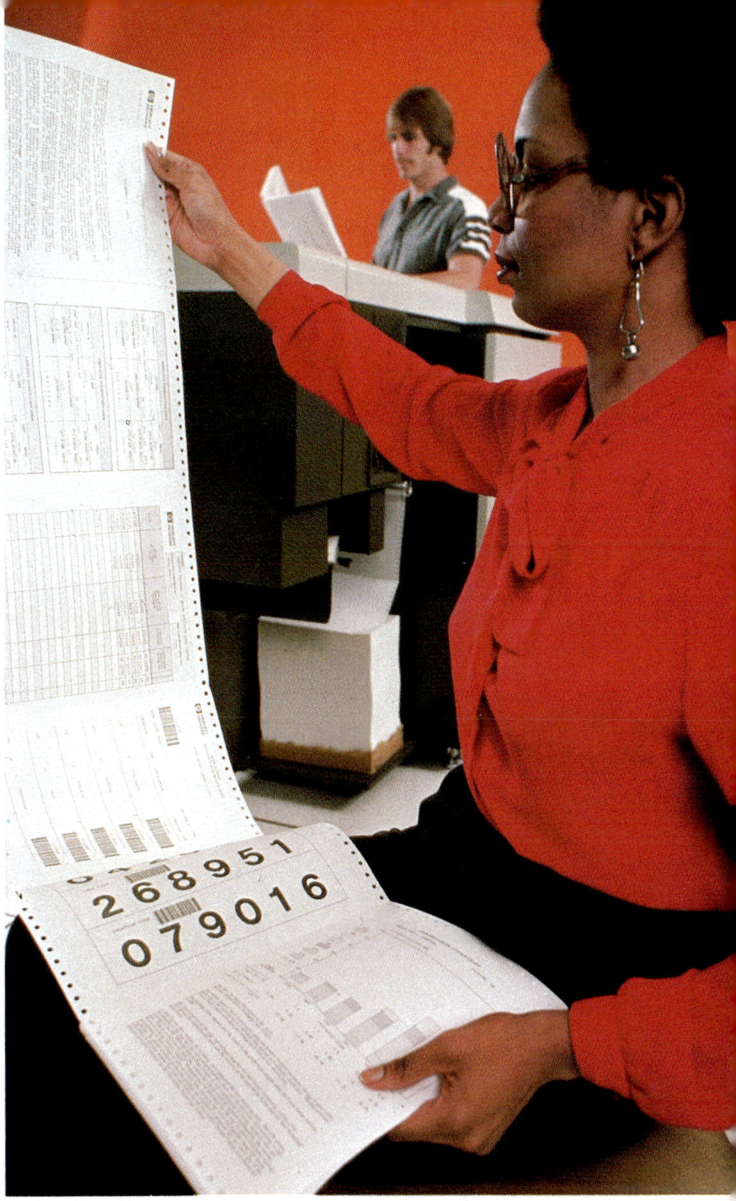

Figure 6–20 The output illustrated in this picture was produced by a Hewlett-Packard laser printer. Note that the listing contains preprinted forms, bar codes, different size type, different type styles, and even a bar graph. The printer which produced this output prints at a speed of forty-five pages per minute.

Systems and procedures — printer output

When output information is produced in the form of a printed report or printed document, certain systems and procedures must be established in order for the output to be produced properly and to be used well. The systems and procedures address the following issues:

1. The volume of printed output to be produced — From the previous material in this chapter, it is evident that the choice of printer to be used is, to a great extent, dependent upon the volume of output to be produced. In addition, the volume of information identifies the amount of time that will be required to produce the output and the amount of materials (including paper) needed. It is necessary to identify the volume of output to be printed early in the system design process.
2. The people who will use the printed output — Many important factors, including the design of the output and even the selection of the type of printer to be used, depend upon who will use the printed output. When personal computers are used in the home, the user will normally be the person who owns the computer. In that case, the computer owner is the user and can determine all of the factors for the printed output. When the output is to be used by others, however, their identity is important. Within a business organization, two classes of printed reports are produced: internal reports and external reports. An **internal report** is one that is used within the business organization, usually by individuals in the daily performance of their jobs. For example, a daily sales report that is distributed to sales management personnel is an internal report because it is used only by personnel within the organization. An **external report** is one which is used outside the organization. For example, payroll checks that are printed and distributed to employees each week are external reports.

   The major consideration for internal reports is that they be clear and easy to use so the people can perform their jobs. Often, dot matrix printers produce good enough quality. For external reports, on the other hand, the quality of the printed output may be very important. Letter quality printers are often required for external reports.

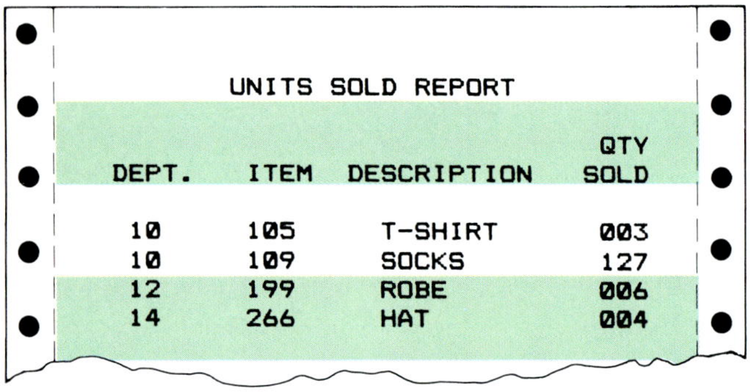

UNITS SOLD REPORT

DEPT.	ITEM	DESCRIPTION	QTY SOLD
10	105	T-SHIRT	003
10	109	SOCKS	127
12	199	ROBE	006
14	266	HAT	004

Figure 6–21 The data for this detail report is obtained from each input record that is read. A line is printed for each record. If a detail report is produced through the selection process (see Chapter 4), then a line may not be printed on the report for each input record, but the report is still considered a detail report.

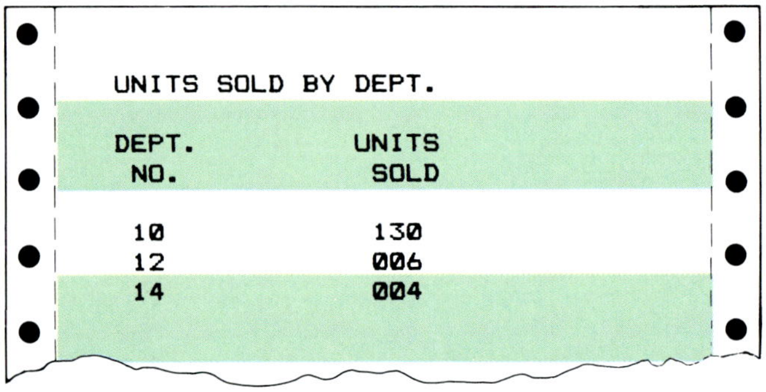

UNITS SOLD BY DEPT.

DEPT. NO.	UNITS SOLD
10	130
12	006
14	004

Figure 6–22 This summary report contains the sales for each department. The report can be prepared from the same data which prepared the report in Figure 6–21.

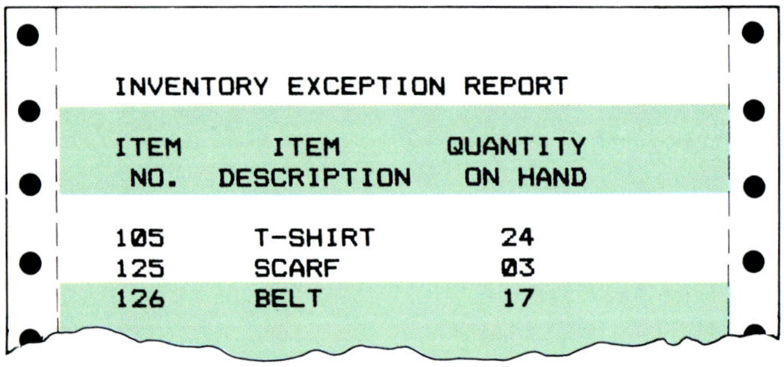

INVENTORY EXCEPTION REPORT

ITEM NO.	ITEM DESCRIPTION	QUANTITY ON HAND
105	T-SHIRT	24
125	SCARF	03
126	BELT	17

Figure 6–23 This exception report contains those items with a quantity on hand less than 25. The three items on the report could have been selected from thousands of detail records. Exception reports provide a cost-effective way to present information.

Another consideration is the number of copies which are required. If multiple copies of a report must be distributed, then it is likely an impact printer will have to be used instead of a nonimpact printer. The quality of the copies must also be examined. While the first two or three carbon copies produced from an impact printer are usually quite legible, fourth, fifth, or sixth copies are often difficult to read.

3. The use of the printed output — How the printed output will be used plays an important role in the design of the report. Generally, three types of reports are found — detail reports, summary reports, and exception reports. A **detail report** is one where each line on the report usually corresponds to one input record that has been read. Detail reports contain a great deal of information and can be quite lengthy. They are usually required by individuals within an organization who need access to the day-to-day data that reflects the operating status of the organization. For example, people within the sales department should have access to the number of units sold within a retail store. The units sold report in Figure 6–21 contains a line for each item, which corresponds to each input record.

   A **summary report** summarizes data. It contains totals for certain values found in the input records. For example, the summary report illustrated in Figure 6–22 contains a summary of the units sold for each department. The information on the summary report consists of totals from the information contained in the detail report in Figure 6–21. Summary reports are most useful for individuals at high levels of management who do not require a detailed knowledge of each fact. Indeed, it has been found that when high-level management is presented with detail reports, the reports are not used because there is more information than the executive has time to review. When, on the other hand, summary reports are prepared, the executive can review the information. Thus, in some instances, the type of report produced will determine whether the executive will use the information for decision making.

An **exception report** contains information which is deemed to be "exceptional," meaning that attention should be brought to the information. Exception reports are produced when there is a need to know specific information in order to make decisions or take specific action. For example, the report in Figure 6–23 contains those items in an inventory with a quantity on hand of less than 25. When the quantity on hand reaches this level, the purchasing department has to reorder the item. The advantage of exception reports is that they save a great deal of time and money. In a large department store, for example, there may be over 100,000 inventory items. A detail report containing all of those items could be over 2,000 pages in length. To search through the report to determine those items which must be reordered would be a difficult and time-consuming task. With the exception report, however, the items to be reordered, which might number 100 - 200, could be extracted and placed on a 2 - 4 page report that could be prepared in just several minutes.

4. Outside requirements — The format of the printed report, the data on the report, and even the quality of the printing on the report may be dictated by requirements not inherent in the application. Company policy, legal requirements, or government regulations may dictate the type of output to be produced. For example, the W-2 form in Figure 6–24 must be used when preparing employees' year-end earnings reports. Government regulations apply in this application. The example in Figure 6–24 also illustrates the use of a preprinted form. A **preprinted form** contains fixed information which is printed on the form prior to its being used on the computer printer. Although these forms are expensive, they may be required for certain external reports. Some high-speed nonimpact printers have the capability of duplicating the preprinted information on plain paper.

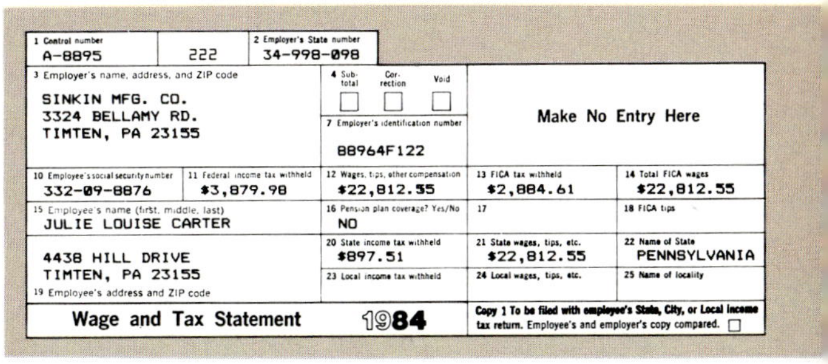

Figure 6–24 This W-2 form is a preprinted form for external output. The format of the data on this form must conform to the standards established by the Internal Revenue Service.

5. Timing requirements — Whenever reports are produced for people who depend on the information in the reports to perform their jobs, timing is important. For example, if the people in the purchasing department depend upon the report in Figure 6–23 to determine what items must be ordered, then that report should normally be on their desks by 8 a.m. In addition, if certain reports must be used by management in order to make decisions, those reports must be prepared and delivered on a timely basis. The two major timing elements are: a) When is the report required; b) How long does it take to prepare the report. From this information, the scheduling of the report can take place.
6. Control and security — Information which is printed on reports can, in some applications, be sensitive data that should not be available to all people. Thus, report security and control is a consideration when developing the systems and procedures for printed reports. For example, a report containing the profit and loss statement for a company should be closely monitored so the information does not become available to people who should not see it. In some companies, this is accomplished by setting up procedures which carefully account for the reports. Further steps for report security include allowing only one approved operator to run the computer when these reports are generated; destroying any carbons which are used for the reports; and in some high security applications such as defense work, having a single machine which processes only one highly sensitive application.
7. Personnel requirements — The personnel who use printed reports must be trained to interpret and understand the information on the reports. In addition, when the formats of the reports are designed, the people who will be using the reports should always be consulted to obtain their views regarding how information should be presented on the reports.

As with all phases of information processing, the systems and procedures established for printed reports can lead to their successful use. Properly established systems and procedures are imperative.

DISPLAYED OUTPUT

Printers provide an important form of output. The CRT display monitor is also a very important output device. In interactive processing systems, responses obtained from inquiries are displayed on CRT display monitors; in word processing applications, the output to be produced is usually displayed on a CRT display monitor as the operator keys the data, and the operator can review and change the data on the screen prior to producing a printed copy of the document; and through the use of personal computer or large computer software, the CRT monitor can be used to display electronic spreadsheets, electronic mail, and graphs of various types. Indeed, virtually any and all output produced from computer processing can be and is displayed on CRT monitors.

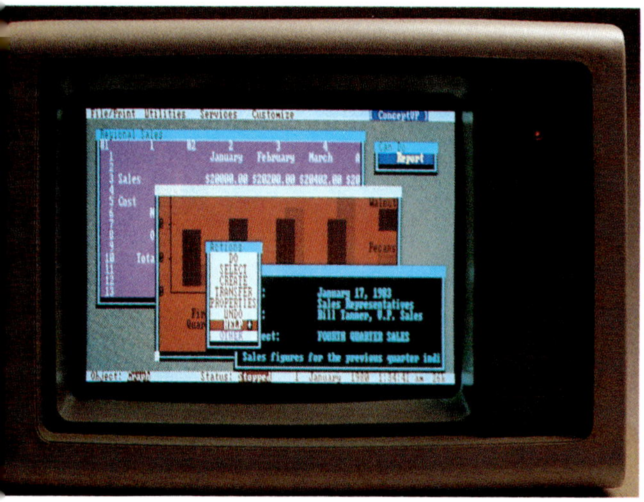

Figure 6–25 The monitor in this picture uses color to distinguish the windows and highlight information. The use of color has been found to increase screen legibility, leading to increased productivity on the part of individuals using color monitors.

As discussed in Chapter 5, most display terminals can display both upper and lower case letters of the alphabet, numbers, and some special characters. Although the maximum number of characters which can appear on a screen varies, 25 lines of 80 characters each are commonly found.

The monitor itself may be **monochrome** (meaning only one color plus a black background is used), or it may be able to display characters, graphs, and backgrounds in a variety of colors (Figure 6–25). Display monitors with the ability to display color are increasingly being used in all areas of business and science, because it has been found through numerous studies that color enables the user to more easily read and understand the information displayed on the screen.

In addition to the characteristics just mentioned, display monitors with very high resolution graphics capabilities, up to more than one million different color capabilities, and other abilities as well are currently available. The following sections examine some of the attributes and capabilities of display monitors.

Displaying data on a CRT monitor

Most display monitors used with personal computers and most display terminals utilize a Cathode Ray Tube (CRT). The vast majority of CRT monitors used in connection with computers are **raster-scan CRT monitors**. To produce an image using a raster-scan CRT monitor, the following steps occur (Figure 6–26):

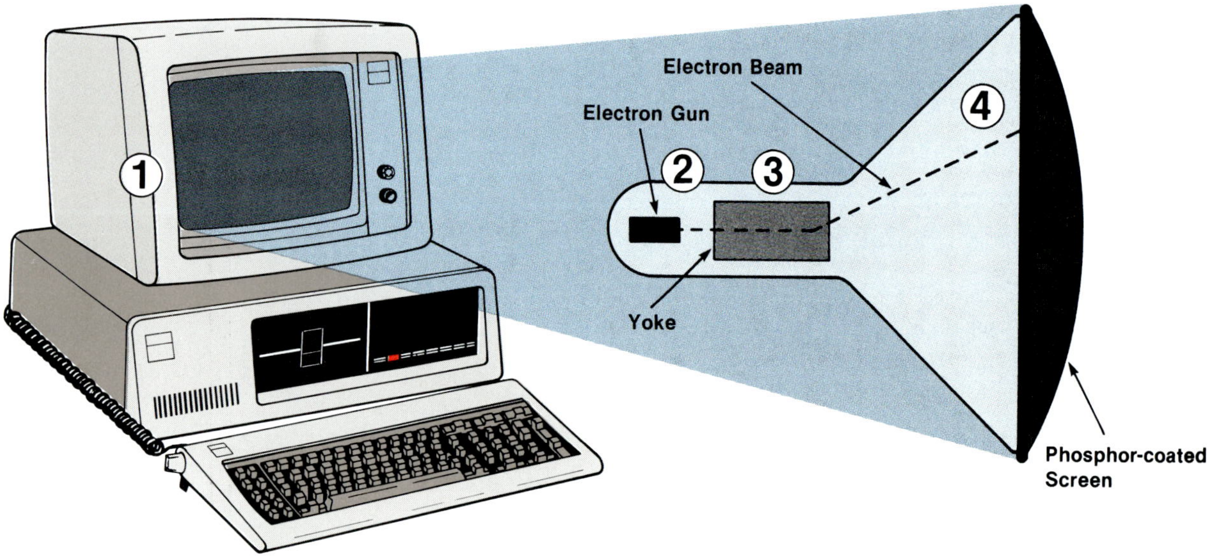

Figure 6–26 The CRT monitor shown in this drawing depicts the steps which occur when an image is formed on the screen. First, electronic data corresponding to the desired information to be displayed is sent to the monitor. The electron gun then generates an electron beam. The beam is directed across the screen by the yoke. As the electron beam strikes the phosphor-coated screen, the selected pixels which are required to form the character are lit.

1. The image to be displayed on the screen is sent electronically from the computer to the cathode ray tube.
2. Based upon the electronic data received from the computer, an electron gun generates an electron beam.
3. The yoke, which generates an electromagnetic field, directs the beam to the **phosphor-coated screen.**
4. The electronic beam causes the desired phosphors to emit a light. It is the phosphor-emitted light which causes an image on the CRT screen.

On most raster-scan CRT monitors, the phosphors which emit the light causing the image on the screen do not stay lit very long. They must be **refreshed** by having the electron beam light them again. This occurs by the beam scanning the entire screen anywhere from 30 to 60 or more times per second (hence the term raster-scan). If the screen is not scanned enough times per second, the phosphors will begin to lose their light. When this occurs, it appears that the characters on the screen are flickering. To eliminate flicker, a scan rate of 60 times per second is normal when the screen is used for alphanumeric display.

The brightness of the image on the screen depends upon the intensity of the electron beam striking the phosphor, which in turn depends upon the voltage applied to the beam. As the beam scans each phosphor dot on the screen, the intensity is varied precisely to turn each dot on or off.

When CRT monitors are used with computers, the monitor screens are divided into addressable locations. The manner of indicating the number of addressable locations varies with the type of monitor. With a display monitor that is used primarily for characters and alphanumeric displays, the number of locations on the screen is usually identified by specifying the number of lines and the number of characters per line that can be displayed (sometimes called the character display addressing scheme). Many character display monitors display 25 lines with 80 characters on each line.

Display monitors which are used for graphics are called **dot-addressable displays**, or sometimes **bit-mapped displays**. With these monitors, the number of addressable locations on the screen corresponds to the number of dots that can be illuminated on the screen. Each addressable dot that can be illuminated is called a **picture element**, or **pixel** (Figure 6–27). The matrix of pixels on a graphics device can vary from 200 rows and 320 pixels per row, to more than 1,000 rows and 1,000 pixels per row.

With dot-addressable displays, the resolution of the characters on the CRT screen depends to a great extent upon the number of pixels on the CRT screen. The greater the number of pixels, in general the better the screen resolution. The number of pixels on a screen is determined through a combination of the software in the computer, the connection between the computer and the CRT screen, and the CRT screen itself. Some CRT's and computers operate in two or more resolution modes. For example, the IBM Personal Computer, when operating in the graphics mode, can use either medium resolution or high resolution. In medium resolution, the screen contains 64,000 individual pixels, arranged in 200 rows with each row containing 320 pixels. When high resolution is used, each of the 200 rows on the CRT screen contains 640 pixels, for a total of 128,000 distinct points that can either be lit or not.

Higher resolution graphics requires a great deal of storage, and it is more difficult electronically to maintain a steady image on the screen. In the past few years, however, there have been great improvements in picture resolutions. In addition, costs have been reduced so that high resolution graphics are now widely used.

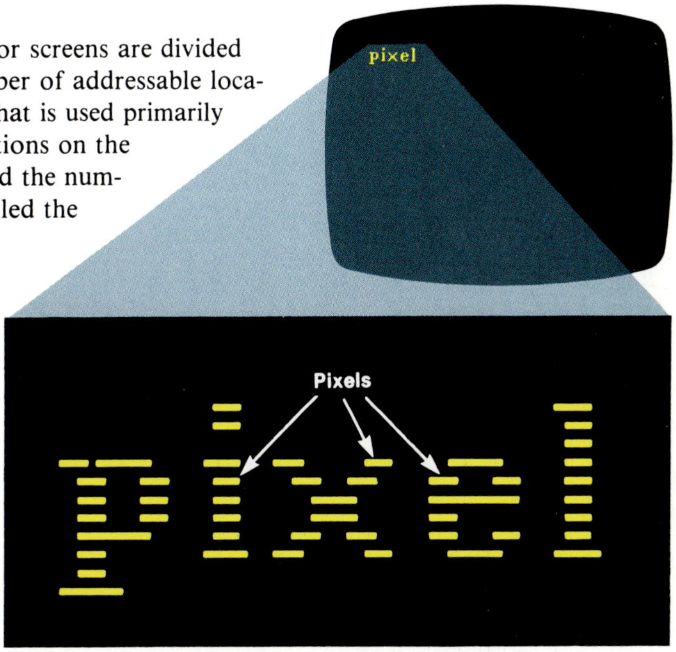

Figure 6–27 The word pixel shown in this drawing is made up of pixels as they would be displayed on a dot-addressable, or bit-mapped, CRT screen. Each pixel is a small rectangular spot of light which appears on the screen at the point where it is activated by a scanning electronic beam. These pixels must be refreshed about 60 times per second in order to remain a solid character without screen flicker.

Types of CRT monitors

Three basic types of CRT monitors are used with personal computers and display terminals. These three are: 1) Standard black and white or color television sets; 2) Monochrome video monitors; 3) Color video monitors.

A standard television set, either black or white or color, may be used as a display unit. Televisions, however, have low resolution due to the relatively few phosphor dots found on the screen and have relatively poor quality. Usually, no more than 40 characters can be legibly displayed on a single line, and the graphics sometimes appear blurry. Television sets should be used only by the casual user who requires the display of limited text material. Television sets are sometimes used with home computers for playing video games.

Monochrome video monitors specially designed for use with personal computers or for use as computer terminals usually display white, green, or amber characters on a black background. The characters are displayed without flicker and with very good character resolution. Some of these monitors have limited graphics capabilities, but they are generally not designed for graphic uses. Most monochrome monitors use the character display addressing scheme. They find their major uses in applications where the personal computer or terminal is to be used for alphanumeric applications such as word processing.

The third type of monitor which is available for use with personal computers, minicomputers, or large computers is a color monitor. Color monitors are dot-addressable displays. Two types of color monitors can be obtained: a) Composite video monitors; b) RGB monitors. Both monitors produce color images, and both monitors can be used for color graphics.

In order to understand the difference, it is necessary to understand how color is produced on a CRT monitor. It will be recalled that when a monochrome CRT monitor is used, a single electron beam strikes the phosphorous screen, causing the chosen phosphor dot to light. With a monochrome monitor, if the characters are green on a black background, then the phosphors emit a green light when activated. Similarly, if the characters are amber on black, the phosphors emit an amber light.

In order to cause color to appear on a CRT monitor, three phosphor dots are required for each pixel. These dots are red, blue, and green. The electron beam must turn on the desired color phosphors within the pixel in order to generate an image. In the simplest configuration, eight colors can be generated — no color (black), red only, blue only, green only, red and blue, red and green, blue and green, and red, blue, and green (white). By varying the intensity of the electron beam striking the phosphors, many more colors can be generated. Some very high resolution terminals provide more than 16 million gradations of color.

A **composite video monitor** uses a single electron signal to turn on the color

Figure 6–28 The graphic on the left was produced using a composite video monitor, and the graphic on the right was produced using an RGB monitor. The graphic from the RGB monitor has brighter colors, is better defined, and has a much sharper image. When very good graphics are required, RGB monitors are normally used.

phosphors within the pixel. An **RGB monitor**, on the other hand, uses three signals, one for each color, to turn on the required phosphors. The resulting difference is that the RGB monitor produces a much clearer display with much better color and character resolution (Figure 6–28).

Composite video monitors for personal computers sell for approximately $300.00 to $500.00. RGB monitors cost in excess of $500.00, and some cost more than $2,000.00. As has been noted previously, however, in most cases the more the monitor costs, the better the display.

Computer graphics

One of the chief benefits of the use of a computer is the ability to input data, process data, and produce output in seconds rather than days or weeks. One problem presented by this ability to generate information rapidly, however, is that managers and executives may be overwhelmed by the amount of information which is available to aid them in decision making, and therefore, may not be able to effectively use the information.

Computer graphics is often used to assist business executives in analyzing data and to assist individuals in preparing data for analysis and presentation to others. Computer graphics allows information to be displayed in the form of charts, graphs, or pictures so that the information can easily and quickly be understood (Figure 6–29). Facts contained on a report many pages in length and data relationships that are difficult to see on a printed report can often be summarized in a single chart or graph. A single graphic display can effectively represent pages and pages of printed data.

In the past, graphics were not widely used in the business world because each time data had to be revised, a graphic artist would have to redraw the chart or graph. Today, relatively inexpensive graphic software makes it possible to redraw a chart, graph, or picture within seconds rather than hours or days as was previously required. This software is available for both personal computers and larger computers. Computer graphics is now an important tool which should be used and understood by anyone working in the modern business world.

Types of charts and graphs

Most graphic software packages can generate charts and graphs from numeric data entered by the user, from data stored in files or data bases, and from data generated in electronic spreadsheets. The three most popular types of charts and graphs are: 1) Pie charts; 2) Bar charts; 3) Line charts.

A **pie chart** is normally used to depict data that may be expressed as a percentage of a whole (Figure 6–30). Pie charts allow easy visual comparisons that show the relative size of each component within a whole,

SALES BY CATEGORY	
HIGH SCHOOLS	2,500
COLLEGES	6,200
VO-TECHS	1,200
PRIVATE SCHOOLS	890

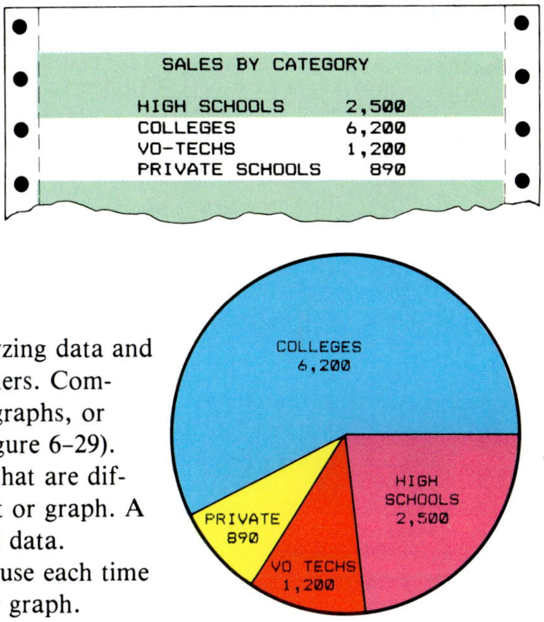

Figure 6–29 In this example, a small report listing contains sales of magazines by school category. While the report is legible, the relationship of how many magazines were sold in each category is difficult to see. With the pie chart below, however, it is easily seen that colleges accounted for more than half of the sales, and that private schools represented a small percent of the sales. Both ways of presenting this information used exactly the same data, but the graph brings much more meaning to the data.

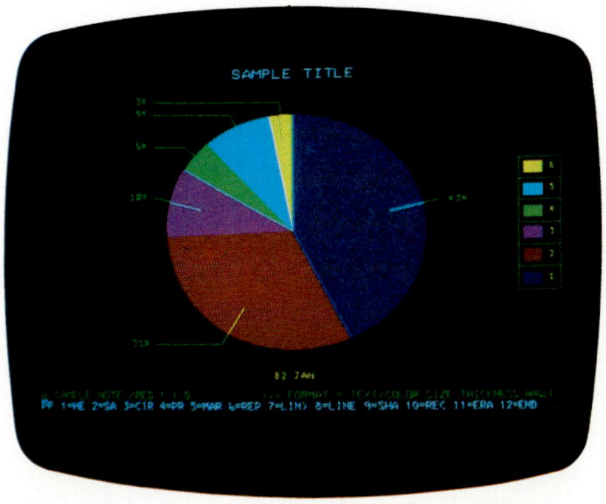

Figure 6–30 Pie charts are used to show the relationship of a part to a whole. The color helps distinguish the parts of the pie chart.

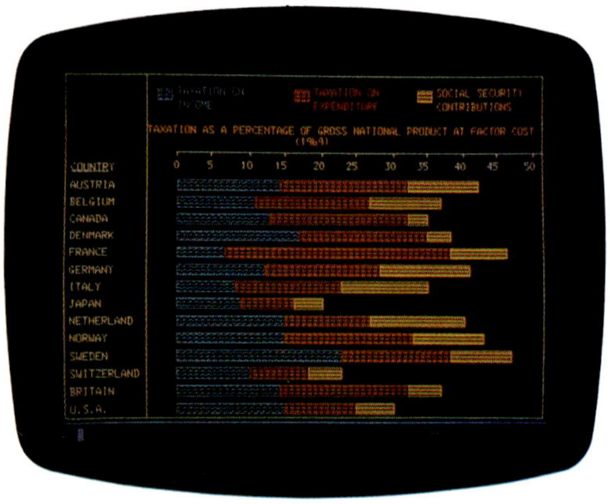

Figure 6–31 A bar chart (right) can have vertical or horizontal bars. The horizontal bars in this picture depict taxation as a percentage of the gross national product for different countries. The length of the bars represents the total taxation. The colors within the bars represent the different parts of the whole taxation amount.

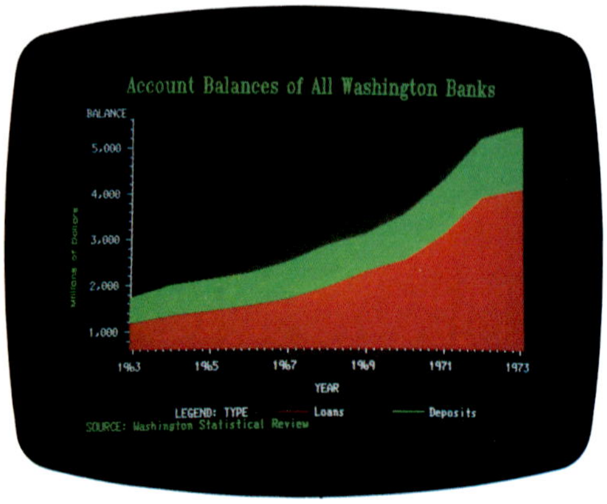

Figure 6–32 The line chart in the picture on the far right is used to show account balances over a period of time. The total amount is the top of the green shading. The total consists of the loans (red shading) and the deposits (green shading). As with many line charts, this one is used to show changes over a period of time.

where the whole represents 100 percent. Most graphics software allows each component to be displayed in a different color, allows text material to be placed on the screen in various colors, and allows shading. Some graphics software even allows certain segments of the chart to be slightly offset from the chart for emphasis.

Bar charts are among the most versatile and popular types of display charts used for comparing data (Figure 6–31). Bar charts represent data by vertical or horizontal bars. They are quite useful for comparing data in which sizes or quantities vary, and the amount of variance needs to be readily apparent. Graphic software can display bars of different colors, vertical or horizontal bars, and text material where required.

Line charts may also be generated through the use of graphic software. These charts represent data relationships by a continuous line across the chart (Figure 6–32). Line charts are particularly useful when showing a change in a value or quantity over a period of time.

From the examples of the various types of graphs and charts, it can be seen that computer graphics offers a powerful tool for the business worker who must present data in a meaningful manner, or for the business executive who must review, analyze, and make decisions based upon data relationships.

Very high resolution graphics

Devices are currently available which offer very high resolution graphics. These devices may have a matrix of 1024 × 1024 pixels on the screen, leading to extremely high resolution almost equivalent to the quality of a picture (Figure 6–33). The ability of the computer to produce very high resolution graphics on CRT screens has led to a revolution in the design and engineering world. Today, computers are used by architects, engineers, and many others who design products. These machines are transforming the way products are designed and manufactured.

Figure 6–33 The picture on the left shows a drawing which utilizes very high resolution graphics on a CRT screen. The picture on the right uses very high resolution graphics as well, but it could be used for actual simulation exercises. For example, this picture could be shown to driving students to ask them what action should be taken when a car is encountered in the location shown. Through the use of the computer, this picture could quickly be changed to show the car entering the intersection, and the students could again be queried.

Computers and computer graphics are being used to design products ranging from automobiles and airplanes to buildings and electronic circuits. The application of the computer to the design process is called **CAD (computer-assisted design)**. The use of the computer in the manufacturing process is called **CAM (computer-assisted manufacturing)**. Frequently these abbreviations are combined as **CAD/CAM**.

One of the first applications of CAD was to automate the drafting process, which is the process of creating drawings of products (Figure 6–34). Today, technology allows three-dimensional objects to be displayed in a wide variety of colors (Figure 6–35). The objects may then be turned, rotated, or displayed in a variety of sizes or angles. Furthermore, using mathematical modeling, the engineer can subject the object to mechanical stresses, heat, motion, and pressure, and observe the results on the graphic terminal display (Figure 6–36).

The use of very high resolution graphics has added a new dimension to the capabilities of computers.

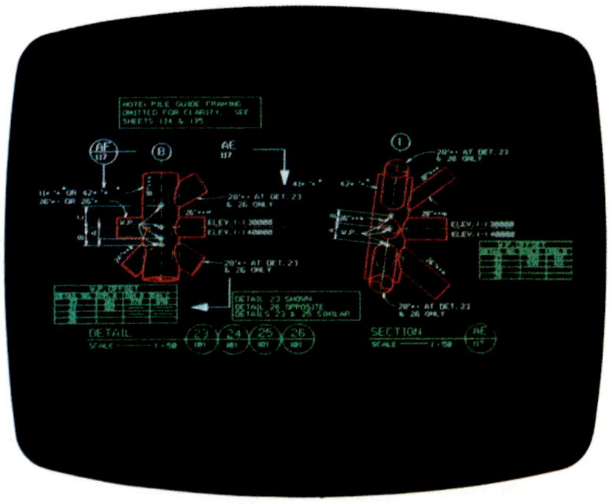

Figure 6–34 Drafting was one of the first uses of very high resolution graphics. Here a drafting design is shown on the screen. The designer can easily make changes to the design without having to completely redraw the entire drawing.

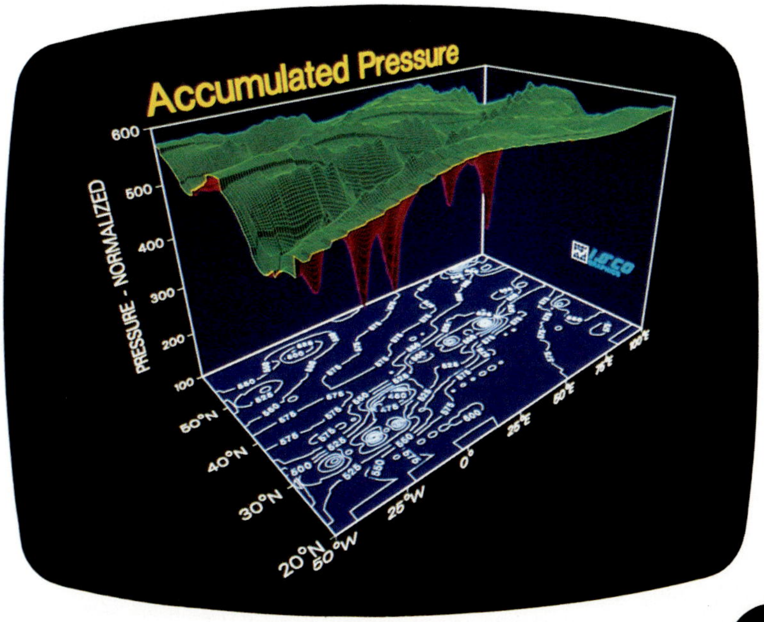

Figure 6–35 The use of color and the three-dimensional effect with these very high resolution graphics allows intricate and complicated drawings to be placed on CRT screens. As in the other pictures, changes can be made to this drawing relatively easily.

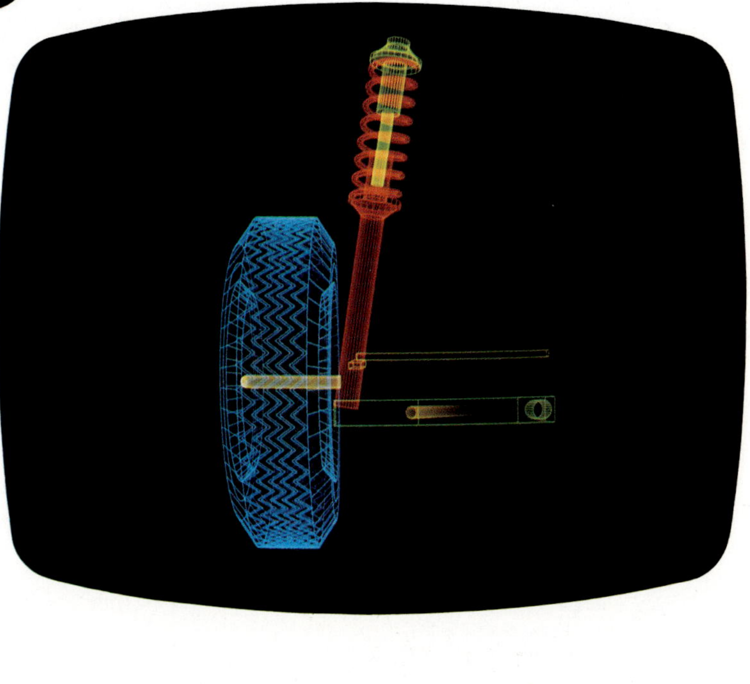

Figure 6–36 In this picture, the shock absorber and wheel are drawn by a computer program. The program can then simulate the wheel and tire moving on different surfaces and watch the effect the movement will have on the shock absorber and tire. Modeling and simulation capabilities using computers and very high resolution graphics have led to better designs being developed faster and less expensively.

Figure 6–37 This IBM 581 plasma display screen contains 737,000 grid intersection points which can be used to create an image on a screen 10.7 × 13.4 inches. As a result, the screen can display 69 lines with up to 160 characters on each line. Since every element on the display surface can be addressed, the screen can be used to display any combination of character fonts, line drawings, charts, sketches, letters, photographs, or even still frames from videotape.

Plasma displays

The plasma screen, which is different from a CRT monitor, uses a relatively new display technology. The **plasma screen** consists of a grid of conductors sealed between two flat plates of glass. The space between the glass is filled with neon/argon gas, which when excited at an intersection in the grid, creates an image.

A plasma screen produces a bright, high-resolution image with no flicker (Figure 6–37). The screens themselves are relatively flat, so that they can conveniently be installed on desks or walls, taking up very little space.

Each intersection of the grid of wires in a plasma screen is addressable. Therefore, characters in a variety of type styles, line drawings, charts, or even pictures can be displayed. Pictures displayed approach the appearance of a photograph. Plasma screens are now being used on terminals found in banks and retail stores.

Flat panel displays

With the development of truly portable computers that can be conveniently carried by hand or in a briefcase came a need for an output display that was equally as portable. Although several technologies have been developed, **liquid crystal displays (LCD)** are used as the output display for a number of portable computers (Figure 6–38). LCD displays are used in watches, calculators, and other electronic devices as well.

In this type of display, a liquid crystal material is deposited between two sheets of polarizing material. When a current is passed between crossing wires, the liquid crystals are aligned so that light cannot shine through, producing an image on the screen. LCD displays vary in the number of characters which can be shown. The NEC portable computer in Figure 6–38 uses an LCD display that can display 48 horizontal characters on eight separate lines. The Apple IIc computer uses an LCD that displays 25 lines of 80 characters each. Flat panel displays will become more widely used as portable computers become more important.

Figure 6–38 The liquid crystal display used with this NEC portable computer can display numbers, letters of the alphabet, special characters, and even has limited graphics capabilities.

OTHER OUTPUT DEVICES

Although printers and display devices comprise the large majority of output devices used with computers, other devices are available for particular uses and applications. These devices include plotters, computer output microfilm devices, and voice output devices. Each of these is examined in the following paragraphs.

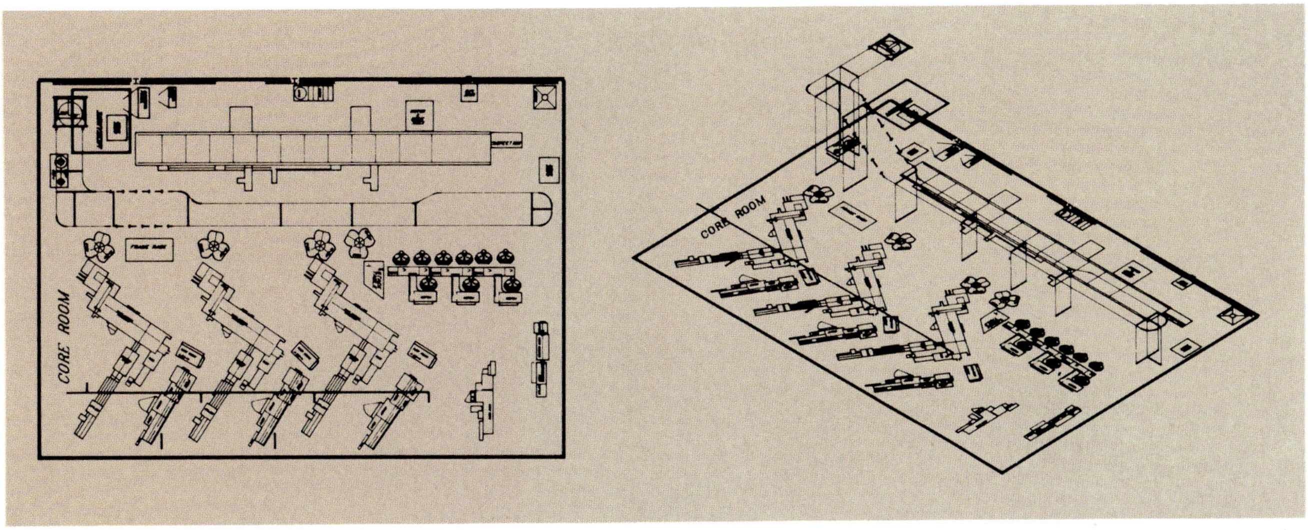

Figure 6–39 The two drawings here were created by a plotter. Note that both a top view and a three-dimensional view were created from the same set of data. The software in the computer developed these views. The printing on the two drawings is done from the proper perspective as well.

Figure 6–40 This Radio Shack flatbed plotter can be used in conjunction with TRS-80 personal computers. It costs less than $1,000.00.

Plotters

Although some dot matrix printers are capable of creating line drawings, when hard copy drawings of good quality are required, computer plotters are normally used as the output device.

A **computer plotter** is an output device that can create drawings, charts, diagrams, and similar types of graphic output (Figure 6–39). In addition, the plotter may print numbers or letters of the alphabet to identify selected portions of the output. The cost of plotters has dropped significantly in the past few years. Today, plotters for personal computers may be obtained for less than $1,000.00 (Figure 6–40).

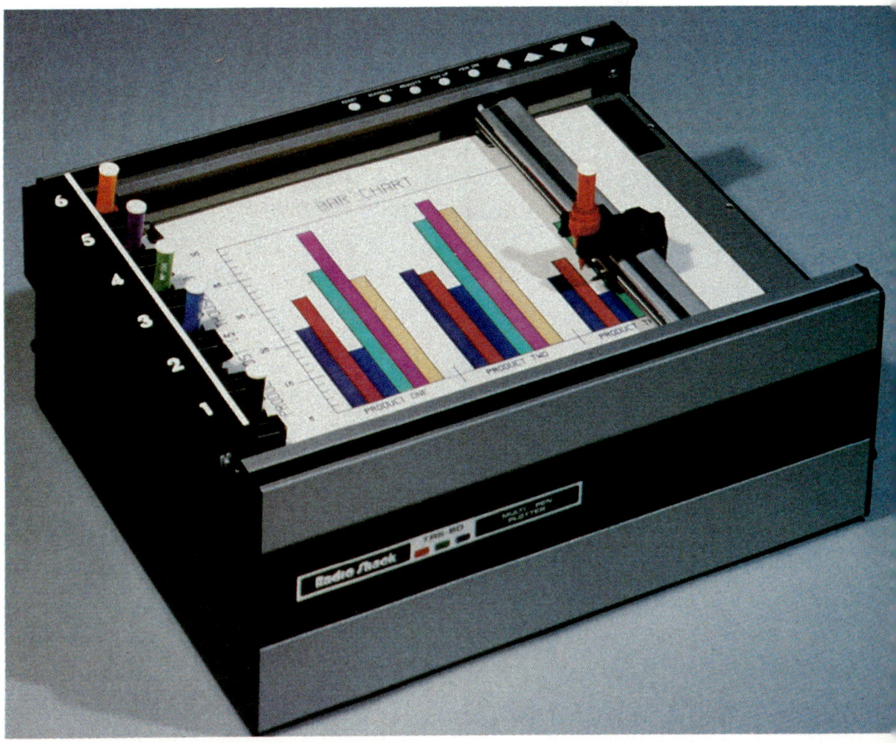

There are several types of plotters. These are: 1) Pen plotters; 2) Electrostatic plotters. As the name implies, **pen plotters** create images on a sheet of paper by the movement of one or more pens over the surface of the paper or by the movement of the paper under the tip of the pens.

Two distinct types of pen plotters are found: 1) Flatbed plotters; 2) Drum plotters. When a **flatbed plotter** is used to plot or draw, under software control the pen or pens are instructed to move to the down position so the pen contacts the flat surface of the paper. Further instructions then direct the movement of the pens to create the image. Most flatbed plotters are available with from one to six pens of varying colors. These color pens create color output. The plotter illustrated in Figure 6–40 is a flatbed plotter that can create color drawings.

A **drum plotter** uses a rotating drum or

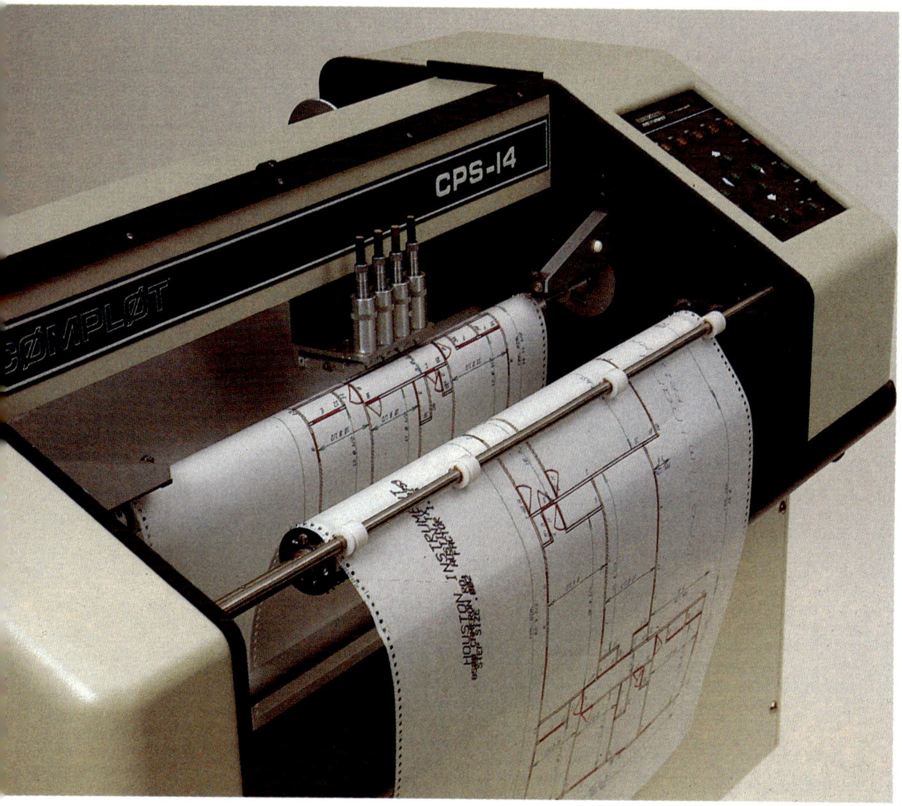

Figure 6–41 This drum plotter utilizes four pens of different colors to create diagrams. As the paper moves forward and back, the pens move left and right and, under software control, draw where instructed.

cylinder over which drawing pens are mounted. The pens can move to the left and the right as the drum rotates, creating an image (Figure 6–41). An advantage of the drum plotter is that the length of the plot is virtually unlimited, since roll paper can be used. The width of the plot is limited by the width of the drum.

An **electrostatic plotter** produces drawings through the use of a row of styli across the width of the paper. As the paper rotates on a drum, an electrostatic charge is created on the paper. The paper then passes through a developer and the drawing emerges. The electrostatic printer image is made up of a series of very small dots, resulting in a relatively high quality output. In addition, the speed of plotting is faster than with pen plotters.

Factors affecting the cost of a plotter are based upon the resolution of the drawing and the speed at which the plotting may occur. The resolution of the drawing is determined by the smallest movement a pen can make on the paper. Typical plotter movements may vary from .001 to .0005 inch. Plotting speeds of three feet per second are possible. Costs range from under $1,000.00 to over $100,000.00 for very high speed plotters with extremely fine resolution.

Computer output microfilm

Computer output microfilm (COM) is an output technique that records output from a computer as microscopic images on roll or sheet film. The images stored on COM are the same as the images which would be printed on paper. The COM recording process reduces characters 24, 42, or 48 times smaller than would be produced from a printer. The information is then recorded on sheet film called **microfiche** or 16mm, 35mm, or 105mm roll film.

The data to be recorded on the microfilm can come directly from the computer (on-line) or from magnetic tape which is produced by the computer (off-line). The data is read into a recorder where, in most systems, it is displayed internally on a CRT. As the data is displayed on the CRT, a camera takes a picture of it and places it on the film. The film is then processed, either in the recorder unit or separately (Figure 6–42). After it is processed, it can be retrieved and viewed by the user.

Microfilm has several advantages over printed reports or other storage media for certain applications. Some of these advantages are: 1) Data can be recorded on the film at up to 30,000 lines per minute — faster than all except very high speed printers; 2) Costs for recording the data are less. It is estimated that the cost for printing a 3-part 1,000 page report is approximately $28.00, whereas the cost to produce the same report on microfilm is estimated to be approximately $3.11; 3) Less space is required to store microfilm than printed materials. A microfiche that weighs an ounce can store the equivalent of 10 pounds of paper; 4) Microfiche provides a less expensive way to store

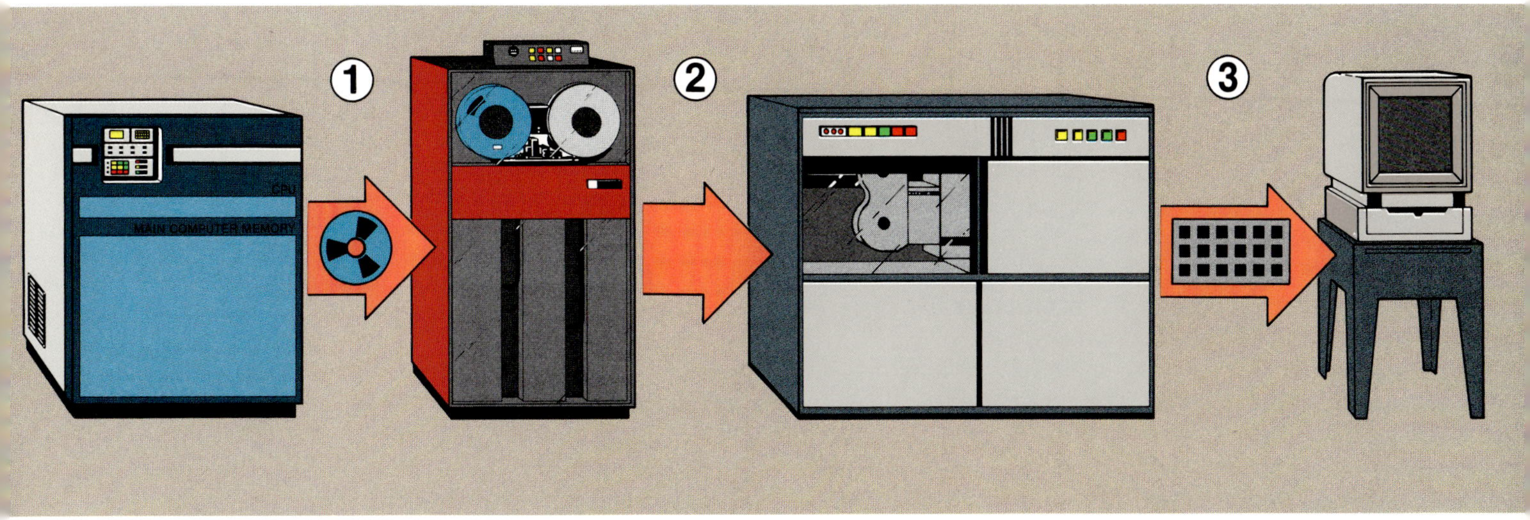

Figure 6–42 In this drawing, the data to be stored on microfilm is first stored on magnetic tape. The data on the tape is then read into the microfilm recorder, which places the image on the film. After data is stored on the film, it can be viewed on a variety of film viewing devices.

data than other media provide. For example, it is estimated that the cost per million characters (megabyte) on a disk is $20.00, while the cost per megabyte on microfilm is $.65.

To access data stored on microfilm, a variety of readers are available which utilize indexing techniques to provide a ready reference to data. Some microfilm readers can perform automatic data lookup, called **computer-assisted retrieval**, under control of an attached minicomputer. With powerful indexing software and hardware now available, a user can usually locate any piece of data within a 200,000,000 character data base in less than 10 seconds at a far lower cost per inquiry than using an on-line inquiry system consisting of a CRT, hard disk, and computer.

For certain applications, COM is a viable way to store and retrieve data.

Voice output

One other important means for generating output from a computer is voice output. **Voice output** consists of spoken words which are conveyed to the computer user from the computer. Thus, instead of reading words on a printed report or CRT monitor, the user hears the words over earphones, the telephone, or other devices from which sound can be generated.

The data which causes voice output is generally created in one of two ways. First, a person can talk into a device which will encode the words in a digital pattern. For example, the words, ''The number is,'' can be spoken into a microphone, and the computer software can assign a digital pattern to the words. The digital data is then stored on a disk. At a later time, the data can be retrieved from the disk and translated back from digital data into voice, so that the person listening will actually hear the words.

A second type of voice generation is new but holds great promise. It is called a **voice synthesizer**, which can transform words stored in main computer memory into human speech. The words are analyzed by a program which examines the letters stored in memory and generates phonemes for the letter combinations. These phonemes are then combined into sounds. The software can apply rules of intonation and stress to make the speech sound as though a person were speaking. The speech is then projected over speakers attached to the computer.

Voice output today is used primarily by the telephone company for number information and other types of communication with the telephone user. The data to be spoken is stored on disk for later transmission. In the future, however, voice technology will be used for many different applications.

CHAPTER SUMMARY

1. All computer printers fall into two broad categories: a) Impact printers; b) Nonimpact printers.
2. Computer printers may be classified by the method used to form a character, by speed, and by cost.
3. Impact printing devices transfer the image onto paper by some type of printing mechanism striking the paper, ribbon, and character together.
4. Impact printers can be front striking or hammer striking.
5. A nonimpact printer creates an image without having characters strike against a sheet of paper.
6. Impact printing is noisy but multiple copies can be made.
7. Nonimpact printers are quiet and some print very fast.
8. The printing rate of low speed printers is expressed as the number of characters that can be printed in one second; the printing rate for high speed printers is stated as the number of lines per minute.
9. Low speed printers, sometimes called serial printers, print from 15 to 600 characters per minute.
10. High speed printers, sometimes called line printers, print from 300 to 3,000 lines per minute.
11. Very high speed printers, sometimes called page printers, print in excess of 3,000 lines per minute. Some can print in excess of 20,000 lines per minute.
12. Factors to be considered in printing are quality of print, number of characters to be printed on each line, the speed of printing, the ability to print graphics, color printing, type of paper feed mechanism, and cost.
13. The least expensive printers for personal computers are thermal or electro-sensitive printers.
14. The dot matrix printer is used with more personal computers than any other type of printer.
15. Dot matrix printers print by having small wires contained in a movable print head striking paper and ribbon.
16. Some dot matrix printers print bidirectionally, meaning the print head prints while moving in either direction.
17. Dot matrix printers usually print from 50 to 160 characters per second.
18. A letter quality printed character is a fully formed character that is easy to read.
19. The quality of a dot matrix printer ranges from poor to near letter quality.
20. Most dot matrix printers can print condensed print, standard print, and enlarged print.
21. Some dot matrix printers can print graphics, and some can print in color as well.
22. Continuous form paper means each page is connected for continuous flow through the printer.
23. Tractor feed mechanisms transport continuous form paper by using holes on the side of the paper.
24. Friction feed mechanisms move paper through a printer by pressure between the paper and the carriage.
25. The most widely used letter quality printer with personal computers is the daisy wheel printer.
26. Speeds of a daisy wheel printer vary from 20 to 60 characters per second.
27. An ink jet printer uses a nozzle to spray liquid ink drops onto the page. Some ink jet printers print color.
28. To select a personal computer printer, the following questions should be asked: a) What print quality is necessary? b) How many characters must print on a page? c) What printing speed is required? d) Are different size print or different print styles required? e) Are graphics necessary? f) Is color necessary? g) Is continuous form or single sheet paper to be used? h) How much money can be spent for the printer?
29. Chain printers print up to 3,000 lines per minute.
30. Band printers have interchangeable bands with many different styles of fonts.
31. Very high speed printers are used when 20,000 lines per minute or more must be printed.
32. The choice of a printer is to a great extent dependent upon the volume of output to be produced.
33. An internal report is one which is used within an organization by people performing their jobs.
34. An external report is used outside the organization.
35. The major consideration for internal reports is that they be clear and easy to use. For external reports, the quality of the printed output may be very important.
36. A detail report is one where each line on the report usually corresponds to one input record.
37. A summary report contains summarized data, consisting of totals from detail input data.
38. An exception report contains unique information that will cause someone to take action or make a decision.
39. Company policy, legal requirements, or government regulations may dictate the type of output to be printed.
40. A preprinted form contains fixed information which is printed on the form prior to use on the computer.
41. CRT monitors are either monochrome (display one color only), or they can display color.

42. A raster-scan CRT monitor projects an electron beam onto a phosphor-coated screen to form an image.
43. Phosphors on a CRT screen must be refreshed sixty times per second to eliminate flicker.
44. Dot-addressable or bit-mapped displays allow each dot (pixel) on the screen to be addressed.
45. The resolution of a bit-mapped display monitor depends upon how many pixels are on the screen. The more pixels, the higher the resolution. More pixels also require more computer memory.
46. There are three types of CRT monitors: a) Standard televisions; b) Monochrome video monitors; c) Color video monitors. The two types of color monitors are: a) Composite video monitors; b) RGB monitors.
47. Monochrome monitors usually display green, white, or amber characters on a black background.
48. To display color on a color monitor, three separate dots (red, blue, green) are turned on by an electron beam. A composite video monitor uses a single beam to do this, while an RGB monitor uses three beams.
49. Computer graphics are used to present information so it can be quickly and easily understood.
50. A pie chart is normally used to depict data that can be expressed as a percentage of a whole.
51. A bar chart, quite popular and versatile, is best used for comparing sizes or quantities.
52. Line charts are particularly useful when showing changes over a period of time.
53. Very high resolution graphics devices may have a 1024 $\times$ 1024 matrix of pixels.
54. The application of the computer to the product design process is called computer-assisted design (CAD).
55. The use of the computer in the manufacturing process is called computer-assisted manufacturing (CAM).
56. Products can be drawn and manipulated on the screen to determine the results of stress, heat, and motion.
57. A plasma display can produce all kinds and sizes of type styles, charts, and drawings.
58. Liquid crystal displays use a polarizing material and liquid crystal to form images.
59. A computer plotter is an output device that can create drawings, diagrams, and similar types of output.
60. Computer output microfilm (COM) is an output technique that records output from a computer as microscopic images on roll or sheet film.
61. COM offers the advantages of faster recording speed, less cost for recording the data, less space required for storing the data, and less cost for storing the data.
62. Voice output consists of spoken words which are conveyed to the computer user from the computer.
63. A voice synthesizer can transform words stored in main memory into human speech.

KEY TERMS

REVIEW QUESTIONS

1. What are the two major categories of printers? What are the differences between the two?
2. What are the factors to be considered when examining printers for use with personal computers?
3. How does a dot matrix printer produce an image? What effect on the quality of print does this method have? What techniques are used on dot matrix printers to improve the print quality?
4. What does the term "letter quality" mean? What types of printers print with letter quality?
5. Describe some of the print capabilities with respect to graphics and character size and style found on many dot matrix printers.
6. How does an ink jet printer produce images? What are some advantages of ink jet printers.
7. What are the three major types of high speed printers? List the characteristics such as speed and manner of printing for each one.
8. List seven major issues with respect to systems and procedures for printed output. Pick one of them and describe both the problems and potential solutions.
9. List the steps involved in displaying an image on a raster-scan CRT monitor. What differences are there when the monitor is monochrome and when the monitor is color?
10. What types of CRT monitors are used with computers? List the features of each.
11. What are the advantages of displaying information in a graphic form? What are the disadvantages? What are the three most commonly used types of charts?
12. For what are plotters used? Describe some of the different types of plotters and the manner in which they produce drawings.

CONTROVERSIAL ISSUES

1. Authorities in business management have pointed out that much of the paperwork generated within a business organization is not used. Further, they have noted that executives do not have time to examine the reams and reams of paper in order to gain the information they need to make decisions. These authorities have argued that very high speed printers which produce more than 20,000 lines of print per minute contribute to the paperwork explosion and, therefore, contribute to rather than help solve the problem. Others argue that in their right place, these printers are invaluable. Take a side in this dispute and prepare an argument.
2. "Automation — The Curse of Modern Society" was the title of a speech given recently at a meeting of union leaders. In the speech, it was stated that the ability of the computer to produce output that controls machines, to develop drawings that are equal to or better than those prepared by skilled graphic artists, and to control the manufacturing process directly threatens the skilled worker. Others have said that the computer performing these jobs frees people to do more creative work. What do you think?

RESEARCH PROJECTS

1. The speed, quality, and prices of printers are constantly changing as new innovations appear. Examine a current issue of a personal computer magazine and clip out four advertisements for printers. Write the printer manufacturers and obtain detailed information about the printers. Then, make a presentation to your class concerning what you found.
2. Visit an installation in your area which uses plotters. Bring back and share with your class the drawings which are produced on the plotters.
3. Very high resolution graphics are used for a myraid of applications. Research magazines, books, or local installations to find a unique use of high resolution graphics. Prepare a report for your class.

Chapter Seven

User Interface with Information Systems

Objectives

- ☐ Describe the importance of the user interface with information systems, and identify the elements comprising user interface
- ☐ Identify the hardware components of user interface, and list their advantages and disadvantages
- ☐ Trace the evolution of user interface software
- ☐ Define the term menu, and illustrate various forms of menus
- ☐ Describe the user interface when using a mouse and icons on a desktop screen
- ☐ Illustrate the use of a natural language to retrieve data from a data base
- ☐ Define the importance of the user in user interface. List the elements of concern for users and the problems which can occur

User Interface with Information Systems

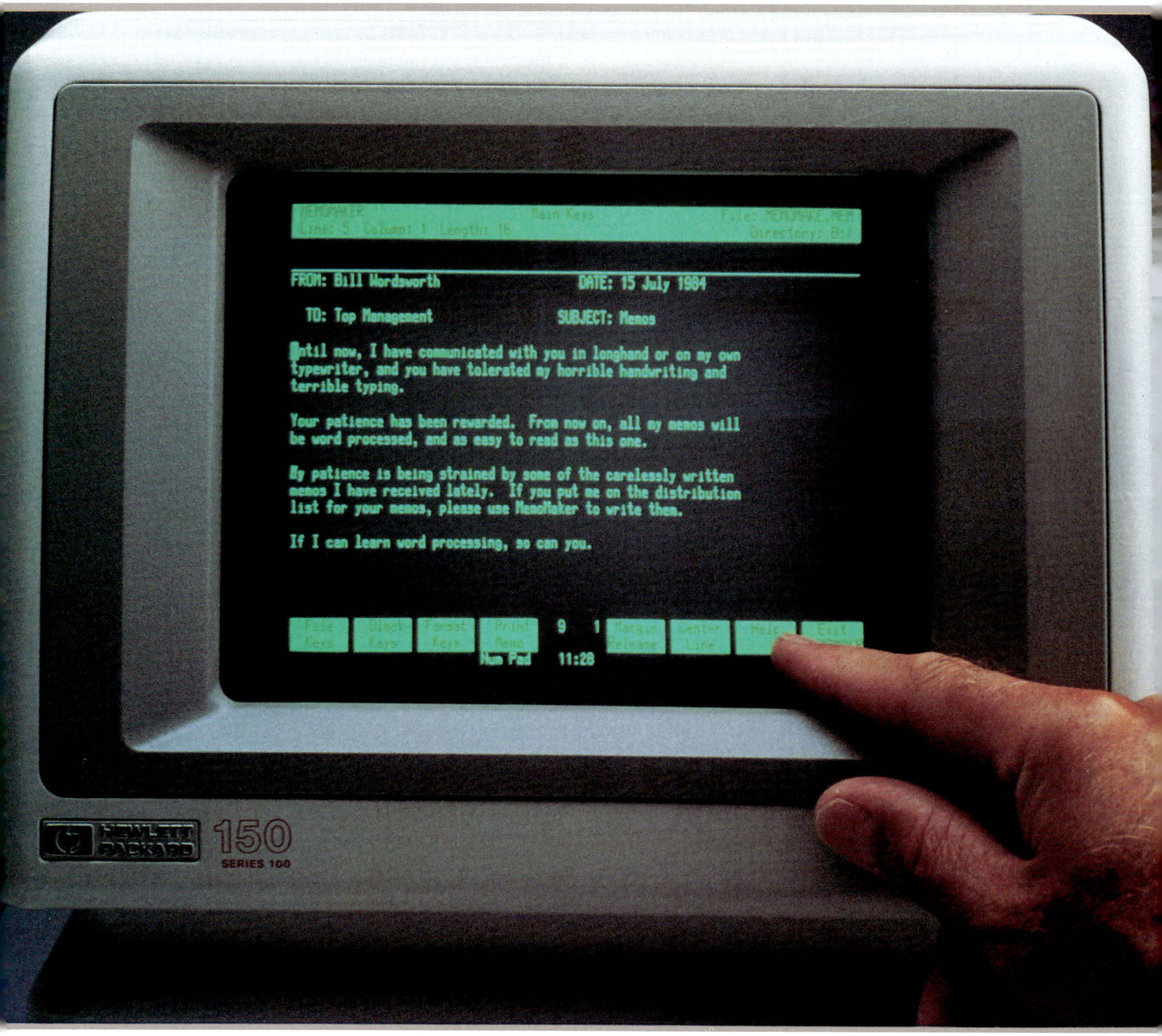

Chapter Seven

In recent years, with the increased availability of personal computers and computer terminals attached to minicomputers and mainframes, the use of the computer has changed dramatically. Computers and information systems today are designed to directly serve people by placing computing power on their desks. Those individuals who directly use computers to help in the performance of their jobs are called **end users**.

End users are not all alike. Although they may be professionals in their own fields, many have a limited knowledge of computers. Others may have had many years of experience using computers. Some end users interact with computers daily, others periodically, and still others, very infrequently.

With this varying range of computer experience on the part of end users, information systems must allow users who are not computer specialists to interact with and use the computer in a timely fashion when required.

When end users interact with computers, they must enter data. It will be recalled from Chapter 5 that there are three uses of the data entered into a computer. The three uses are: a) Control the computer; b) Request information from the computer; c) Serve as the source from which information is produced. The data entry devices and techniques discussed in Chapter 5 were concerned with the third use of data. The information presented in this chapter pertains to the first two uses of data entered into main computer memory.

In some instances, a user of a personal computer will enter data to be processed and create information. In many cases, however, when a single end user utilizes a personal computer or computer terminal, that user is not entering data for processing on the computer. Rather, the intent is to command the computer to perform certain tasks so that requested information is obtained. It is the purpose of this chapter to review the hardware devices and software techniques that allow users to interact with personal computers, minicomputers, and mainframes.

What is a user interface?

A **user interface** is the combination of hardware and software that allows a user to communicate with and control the functional aspects of an information system. Through the user interface, a user is able to control the computer, request information from the computer, and respond to messages presented by the computer.

Thus, a user interface provides the means for dialogue between the computer program and the end user. It is important to note that a user interface consists of both computer hardware and computer software. Inherent in this combination of hardware and software are the systems and procedures which must be followed by users in order to implement a user interface.

The most commonly found hardware associated with a user interface is the CRT terminal. The device for displaying messages and providing information is most often a CRT monitor. The hardware devices for controlling the computer include the keyboard. Other pointing devices are used as well. The software associated with an interface are the programs which engage in the dialogue with the user. These programs determine the messages which will be given to the user, the manner in which the user can respond, and the actions which will occur based upon the responses of the user. The goal of most software written today is to be **user friendly**, meaning that the software can be easily used by individuals with limited training. It is the hardware and software working together which form a user interface.

What does a user interface do?

As noted, a user interface with a computer allows the user to communicate with and control the functional aspects of an information system. In order to do this, the interface software and hardware display messages to the user and allow the user to react to the messages by entering data in the form of commands or other responses.

When a user interfaces with a computer, one or more of the following activities occur:

1. The user submits a command to perform an activity or request information.
2. A message reports on the software's reaction to the input entered by the user.
3. A message reports on an error made by the user, and the user enters input to correct the error.
4. A message is displayed to request the user to choose among alternatives, and the user responds to the request.
5. A message is displayed that requests missing information.
6. A message reports that processing is progressing.
7. A message reports that processing is complete.

All of these activities must be performed in a manner which allows noncomputer professionals to interact with the computer in a nonthreatening easy-to-use way. The following pages explore the various types and styles of user interfaces.

USER INTERFACES WITH COMPUTERS

The following items must be considered when implementing a user interface:

1. A device on which messages, responses, and information can be displayed.
2. A device from which the user can enter data and commands.
3. Software which controls the messages displayed and the actions that occur.
4. The user.
5. Systems and procedures pertaining to the manner in which the user is to use the interface.

While it is somewhat difficult to talk about each of these items without reference to others, the following paragraphs separate them for purposes of explanation. Where required, reference and a minimum of explanation of components not yet covered will be included.

CRT display monitor

The CRT display monitor, which has been described in detail in previous chapters, is the overwhelming choice as the hardware device used to display messages to users. Both monochrome and color CRT display monitors are used. Important features of display monitors as related to the user interface are the monitor cursor, the capability of reverse video, graphics capabilities, color, and monitor ergonomics. These are discussed in the following paragraphs.

A **cursor** on a CRT screen is a symbol which indicates where on the screen the next character entered will be displayed. It can also be used as a marker on a screen to identify choices which a user can make. Cursors generally are one of three shapes, depending upon the computer and the CRT screen. These shapes are shown in Figure 7-2. In addition, most cursors blink when they are displayed on the screen so the operator has little difficulty finding the location of the cursor.

An important function when the end user interacts with the computer is moving the cursor to different positions on the screen. This activity is required because by its position on the screen, the cursor identifies what data on the screen is to be processed. While a number of different devices can be used to position the cursor on the screen, the cursor is positioned in one of two ways: absolute movement or relative movement. **Absolute cursor movement** means the user can indicate the specific location on the screen where the cursor should be placed (Figure 7-3). **Relative cursor movement** means the user must locate the current cursor position and then specify the movement required to move from the current location to the desired location (Figure 7-4). This movement is specified using devices which can control the cursor, such as specifically

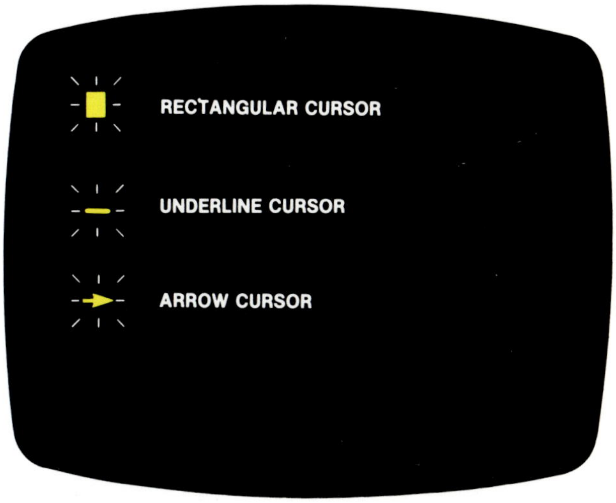

Figure 7-2 Three types of cursors are shown in this diagram — a rectangular cursor, an underline cursor, and an arrow cursor. In most cases, when these characters are used as cursors, they blink on the screen to make them easily identifiable.

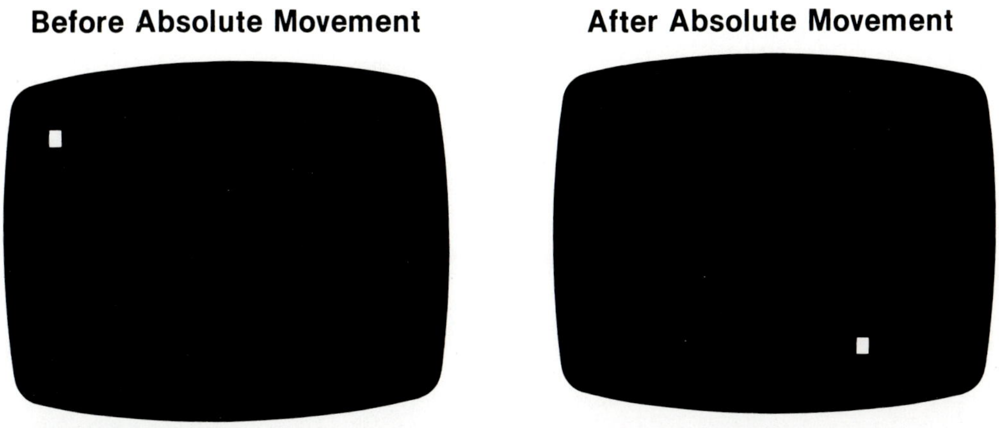

Figure 7-3 In this example, the placement of the cursor on the screen was moved from the upper left corner to the lower right corner. The user merely indicated where the new location of the cursor should be and it appeared there. For absolute cursor movement to occur, a device such as a light pen which can point directly to the new location for the cursor must be used.

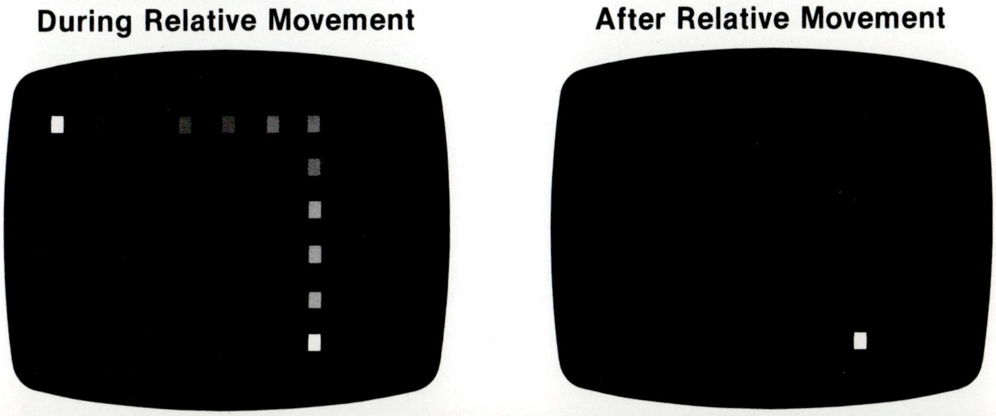

Figure 7-4 When a cursor is moved using relative movement, the cursor must be moved from where it is currently to where the user desires it to be. In this example, cursor control keys on a keyboard could be used to indicate that the cursor is to move to the right and down so that it appears where the user wishes.

designated keys on a keyboard. Absolute cursor movement is generally faster but requires input control devices which can cause the movement. Relative cursor movement is found more often.

Reverse video can be used when the user has an option from which to choose displayed on the screen. It will be recalled that reverse video is the process of reversing the normal display on a CRT screen. Thus, if the normal display is white characters on a black background, reverse video is black characters on a white background. Reverse video is used to identify choices which users can make from a list of possibilities. For example, in Figure 7-5, the user has five choices. By using a pointer device to move the reverse video from one choice to the next, the user can select which choice is to be implemented.

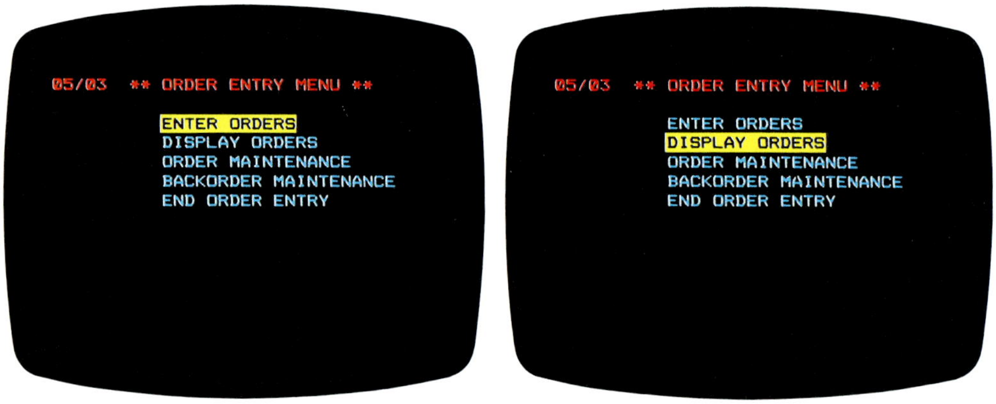

Figure 7–5 The reverse video in this example is used to identify choices which the user can make from the menu. Any one of many different pointing devices can be used to move the reverse video down or up the menu. When the desired choice is highlighted in reverse video, the user would perform an action such as pushing a button or depressing the return key in order to make the choice.

Graphics and icons — pictorial representations

Graphics screens using bit-mapped displays are becoming more widely used to provide a graphics interface to the user. A very popular graphics screen is found on the Apple Macintosh™ computer. These screens use icons to communicate with the user (Figure 7-6). An **icon** is a pictorial representation of a function to be performed

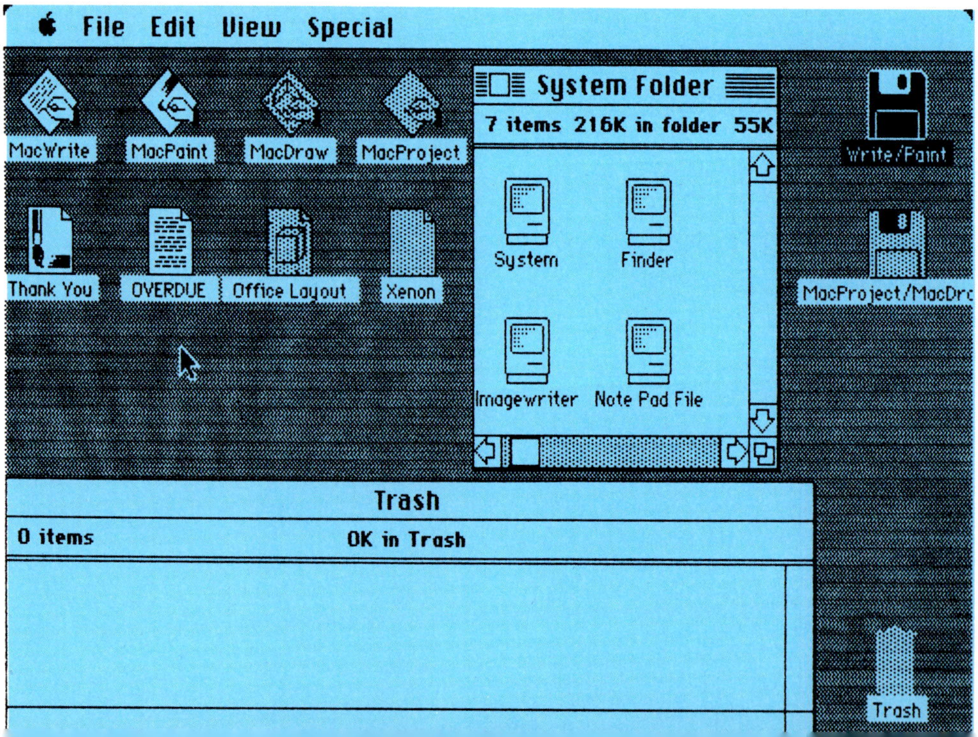

Figure 7–6 This screen illustrates the use of icons to depict data and functions that can be performed on the computer. For example, the icon of a hand writing words is for the word processor (MacWrite), the icon of a hand painting a picture is for the graphics program (MacPaint), and the trash can represents the task of deleting files or other data from the system. Through the use of icons, the user can quickly and easily see the functions to be performed and make a choice.

on the computer. For example, in Figure 7-6, the word processing program (MacWrite) is represented by a hand writing words, a graphics program is represented by the icon of a hand drawing a picture, and documents generated from the word processor are represented as pages with the corner turned back. A picture representing functions to be performed on a computer is helpful because people not familiar with computer jargon can still use the machine.

Color and ergonomics

As has been seen in previous chapters, color is also used to identify user options and to provide clarity. Color can be used with any of the techniques just discussed to enhance the legibility of information displayed on the screen.

A part of the user interface with respect to CRT monitors is the monitor ergonomics. Ergonomics, it will be recalled, deals with the interaction of people with their working environment. As noted in Chapter 5, CRT monitors must be designed to maximize the usability of the monitor and minimize user fatigue. The ergonomic elements examined in Chapter 5 for data entry display terminals apply equally when discussing user interface.

DATA AND COMMAND ENTRY DEVICES

The second item required for successful user interface is a device which can be used to enter data and to cause the cursor to move about the screen in order to position it to display information or make a choice for processing to be accomplished. The following sections describe some of the devices used for these functions.

Keyboards

A device quite often used to enter data into a computer to issue a command or to initiate an inquiry to obtain information is the keyboard. As seen in Chapter 5, the keyboard used with CRT display terminals contains a typewriter-like set of keys for the letters of the alphabet, numbers, and some special characters. Many keyboards used with terminals also contain a ten-key calculator-like numeric pad from which numeric data can be rapidly entered. These keys are used primarily to enter data.

Keyboards also contain keys which can be used to position the cursor on the screen. On most keyboards, these keys take the form of arrow keys which will move the cursor in the same direction as the arrow points. In Figure 7-7, for example, the cursor control keys have an up arrow, a down arrow, a left arrow, and a right arrow. When any of these keys is depressed, the cursor is moved one space in the direction specified by the arrow. In addition, many keyboards contain other cursor control keys such as the HOME key, which when depressed sends the

Figure 7-7 The keys with the up (↑), down (↓), left (←), and right (→) arrows are used to control the cursor movement. When one of the keys is depressed, the cursor is moved one position in the direction indicated by the key. While sufficient for many applications, the use of these keys is sometimes unsatisfactory when the cursor must be moved large distances on the screen numerous times.

cursor to the upper leftmost position on the screen. Other keys, such as a page down key which will send the cursor to the bottom of the screen when depressed, are found on some keyboards. In general, the keyboard, while very good for entering data, is less than ideal for moving the cursor around on the screen. Thus, many personal computers and terminals are found with both keyboards and a pointing device. A **pointing device** is used to move the cursor around on the screen. With these systems, the keyboards are used to enter data, and the pointing devices are used to move the cursor around the screen and to make selections based upon the options on the screen.

While a keyboard has significant advantages, such as wide availability and a potential for considerable data entry speed, there are several disadvantages which are particularly applicable to its use as an input device when used by the end user. First, considerable training is required to be proficient at using a keyboard. Many potential end users of computers may not have these keyboarding skills, making the keyboard an inappropriate device for them to use. Second, some studies have indicated that many high level executives view keying operations as being a clerical activity and have not, therefore, made effective use of the computing power that is available to them. Since it has further been shown that these attitudes are difficult to change, alternate input devices are required for these people.

The mouse

A device called a mouse, which was initially designed by Xerox, has become quite popular for use with personal computers and some computer terminals. A **mouse** is a small, lightweight device that can easily fit in the palm of one's hand and be moved across a flat surface (Figure 7-8). It can be used to control the movement of the cursor on a CRT screen. The mouse is attached to the computer by a cable. On the bottom of the mouse are one or more wheels or balls. As the mouse is moved across the flat surface, the movement of the wheels can be electronically sensed. Hence, the direction of the movement of the cursor on the screen can be made to correspond to the movement of the mouse (Figure 7-9). When the mouse is moved left on the surface of the table or desk, the cursor moves left on the screen. When the mouse is moved

Figure 7-8 (right) The mouse can be held in the palm of one's hand. The key on the top of the mouse can be depressed to perform various functions, depending upon the software being used. Other versions of the mouse device have two or three keys, and some models have the keys on the front edge of the mouse instead of on the top.

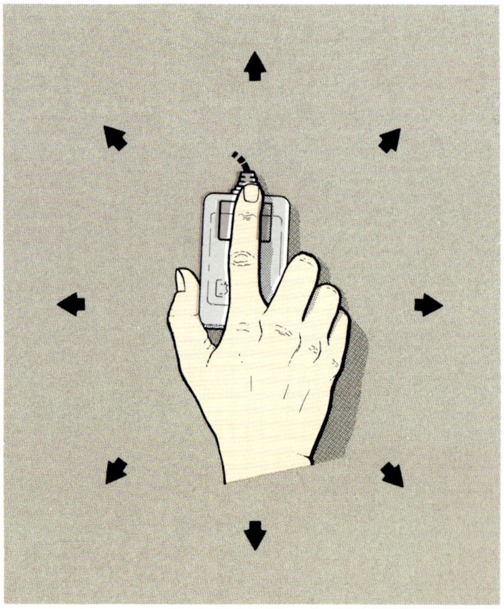

Figure 7-9 (far right) This drawing illustrates the use of a mouse. The index finger, which rests on the top of the mouse, acts as a pointer to guide the movement of the mouse and the related movement of the cursor on the screen. Moving the cursor from the bottom of the screen to the top of the screen is easily accomplished by an upward movement of the mouse.

right, the cursor is moved right, and so on. On the top of the mouse are one or more buttons that, when depressed, allow the user to select menu choices (Figure 7–10), or perform other functions.

The use of the mouse is not limited to selecting items from a list. In word processing applications, the mouse can be used to position the cursor to point to characters or words that should be deleted from the text or to areas within the text where characters or words should be added. The mouse, when used in conjunction with a keyboard, can control the deletion or addition of characters, words, and paragraphs and can perform many other word processing functions as well.

Some software systems used in conjunction with the mouse allow drawings to be created on the screen by recreating the movement of the mouse on the flat surface. Systems also allow icons such as those shown in Figure 7–6 to be moved about on the screen. The mouse and related software provided with many computers are truly important tools for providing a convenient form of user interface for large numbers of people.

The mouse has both advantages and disadvantages. A primary advantage is that it is easy to use. Proponents of the mouse as a pointing device say that with a little practice, a person can use a mouse to point to locations on the screen just as easily as one can use a finger. In addition, with the buttons available on the mouse, the user can make menu choices, choose letters or words in a word processing application for addition or deletion, move data as well as the cursor from one point on the screen to another point, and perform many other actions which have to do with moving and rearranging data and information displayed on the CRT screen.

There are two major disadvantages of the mouse. First, its use requires empty desk space where it can be moved about (Figure 7–11). While this is not a problem in many cases, in other cases a mouse may not be used because of lack of space. The second disadvantage is that the user must remove a hand from the keyboard and place it on the mouse whenever the cursor is to be moved or a command is to be given. Some keyboarding experts have noted that taking hands from the keyboard will slow the effective data entry speed considerably. Thus, some people have said the mouse is not an effective tool in those environments where keying must be performed rapidly, such as in word processing applications. Others, however, say that the use of a mouse is far superior to using the cursor control keys on a keyboard. The issue is yet to be resolved.

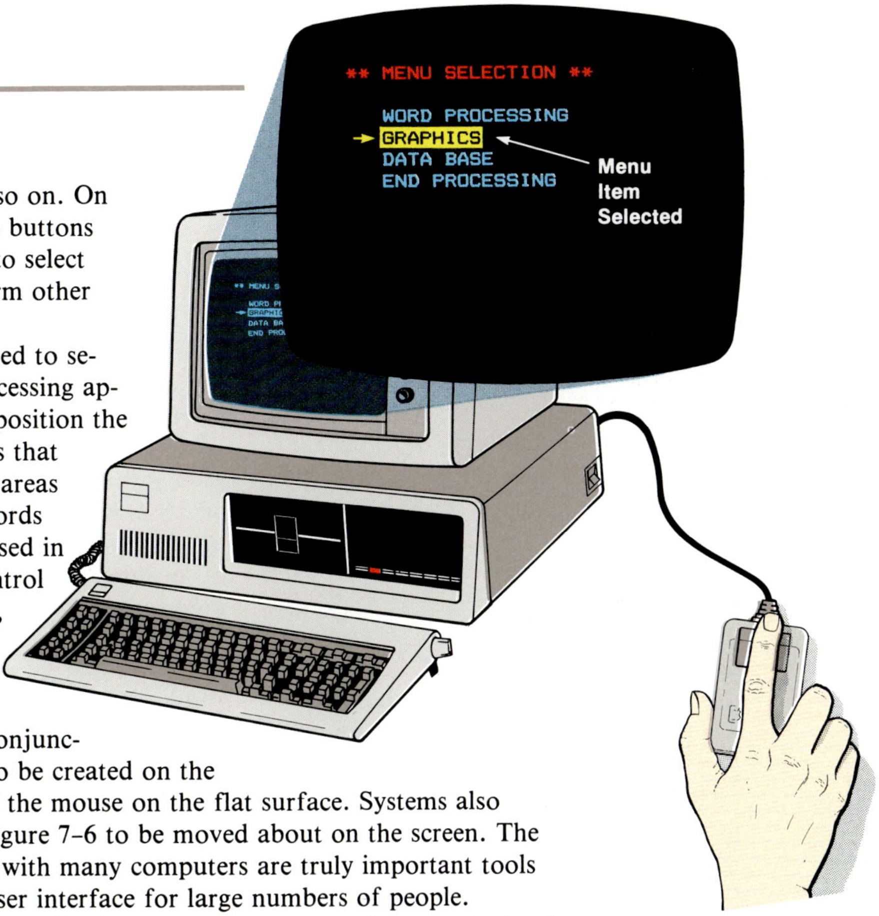

Figure 7–10 The mouse, which in this diagram is connected to a personal computer, can be used to move the cursor and the reverse screen images up and down as the mouse is moved up and down. When the cursor and reverse image rest on the choice of the user, the key on the mouse can be depressed, and the program implementing the choice will be executed. In this example, the user chose graphics. When the key is depressed, the graphics program will begin execution.

Figure 7–11 The user in this picture is using a mouse. Note the desk space to the right of the computer required for moving the mouse. While in most instances this is not a problem, in some environments the need for open space on a desk will restrict the use of a mouse.

Figure 7–12 The touch screen in this picture illustrates graphics on the screen. The user can touch the screen to choose certain actions. The software associated with the device will determine where the user touched the screen and, based upon the location of the touch, perform the processing requested by the user.

Touch screens

Some personal computer and computer terminal monitors allow users to merely touch areas of the monitor screen to enter data. These devices are called **touch screens**. Touch screens allow the business professional to interface with a computer at the touch of a finger rather than with a keyboard which requires typing or a mouse which must be moved about on a flat surface. To utilize a touch screen, the user merely touches words, numbers, or locations identified on the screen and data is entered (Figure 7–12).

A number of different electronic techniques are used to allow a touch on the screen to be changed into electronic impulses that can be interpreted by the computer software. One of the most common utilizes beams of infrared light which are projected across the surface of the computer's screen. When the beams of infrared light are interrupted by a finger or other utensil touching the screen, an electronic signal is generated and interpreted. This signal identifies the location on the screen where the touch occurred. When it is determined what area of the screen was touched, the software of the system can then perform the required function.

Touch screens are not used to enter large amounts of data. They are quite appropriate, however, for applications where the end user must issue a command to the software to perform a particular task or where the user must choose from a list of operations to be performed.

There are both advantages and disadvantages to touch screens. A significant advantage is that they are very ''natural'' to use; that is, people are used to pointing to things. With touch screens, they can point to indicate their desires with respect to the processing to be performed on the computer.

Touch screens are usually fast for the user to use. Moving a mouse or keying special keys on a keyboard are not required. Instead, as quick as it takes to point a finger, the request from the user is being processed. Touch screens also allow absolute cursor movement; that is, the user can point a finger at the location where the cursor is to appear and it will. This can be considerably faster than repeatedly depressing arrow keys to move the cursor from one location on the screen to another.

Two major complaints are lodged against touch screens. First, the resolution of the touching area on a touch screen is not really precise. Thus, while a user can point to a box or fairly large area on the screen and the electronics can determine the location of the touch, the ability to point to a single character in a word processing application, for example, and indicate that the character should be deleted is not available on most touch screens. Therefore, in most cases, a touch screen must be used in conjunction with a keyboard.

A second complaint is lodged with respect to the ergonomics of a touch screen which requires the user to touch a vertical screen. After a period of reaching for the screen, the user's arm may become fatigued. Some manufacturers now make their touch screens tiltable so that the user can make the screen surface more horizontal.

Touch screen technology is still being developed. It is likely that touch screens will play an important role is making the human to computer interface easy and efficient for large numbers of people.

Voice input

One of the more exciting developments in computer user interface is the use of voice input. As the name implies, **voice input** allows the user to enter data and issue commands to the computer with spoken words (Figure 7-13).

In order to use voice input, most systems require the user to "train" the system by speaking, a number of times, the words which will be used. As the words are spoken, they are digitized by the system; that is, they are broken down into digital components that the computer can recognize. After each word is spoken several times, the system has developed a digital pattern for the word which can be stored on auxiliary storage. When a user later speaks a word to the system to request that a particular action occur, the system compares the word entered to words which were previously entered and which it can "understand." When a match is found, the software will perform the activity associated with the word. For example, in voice controlled word processing systems, spoken words can be used to control such functions as single and double spacing, type styles, and centering text.

For the executive, software is available that allows the user to give a voice command such as "Display monthly sales." The software will interpret this command and, based upon the predefined action that is to occur when these words are entered, will retrieve the information from auxiliary storage and display it on the CRT screen.

Figure 7-13 This executive has just used his voice input system to request that sales data be presented in a bar graph. The data displayed on the screen was generated as a result of the voice input request. The Texas Instrument system illustrated here is a leader in personal computer voice input usage.

At the current time, the number of words which can be entered and stored (called the system's **vocabulary**) is limited to several hundred words. These words are, of course, selectable by the user. In the future, however, it is anticipated that much larger vocabularies will be able to be used.

A technology that is still in its early research but which holds great promise is **voice recognition** regardless of the speaker and regardless of the words which are spoken, that is, a system which understands human speech. While some systems have been developed which are capable of understanding a few words, the technology is not yet available to allow this to happen. Considerable amounts of money, however, are being invested in research for unrestricted voice recognition and input. It is expected that someday a primary way for users to interface with computers will be to speak to them.

The major advantage of voice input is that the user need not key, move, or touch anything in order to enter data into the computer. Currently, the major disadvantage is that the user must train the system, and the vocabulary of the voice input devices is limited. As noted, however, voice input will be a significant factor in the years to come.

Summary — data entry and pointing devices

The devices illustrated in the previous sections play an important role in the user interface. While each has its advantages and disadvantages, each has areas where it is the superior means for entering data and commands.

USER INTERFACE — SOFTWARE

The third item of user interface is the software which accepts user input, displays messages and information on the CRT screen, and carries out the actions requested by the user. In most instances, the software determines the quality of the user interface. That is, given an appropriate display device and an appropriate input and pointing device, the software determines how effectively these devices can be used by the end user.

It is important, therefore, to examine the way in which user interface software has evolved, where the user interface software technology is today, and to examine what might be available in the future. The following sections explore user interface software.

Early user interface software

When computers were first used for business processing, users did not interact with the computer. Programmers and computer operators were the only people allowed to control the processing on the computer. While some programmers were also users (for example, scientists who wrote programs so they could use the results in their own work), there was little need to worry about the interface with users. All that was required was a means for technicians such as operators and programmers, who were familiar with the computer and its operations, to communicate with the software.

In addition, during the early years of computer usage, computers were extraordinarily expensive. For example, to add 8,000 positions of memory to a computer might cost as much as $100,000.00. Therefore, the software had to be designed to be efficient on the computer. The ease of its use was normally secondary to the fact that it must use very little memory and operate fairly quickly.

As a result of these factors, when terminals were connected to mainframe computers and users began to have access to the computers, the first software with which they interfaced was designed very much like the software with which the professional programmers and operators were communicating. The software frequently required the computer operators, and hence the end users, to have a detailed knowledge of a special control language that directed the computer to perform the tasks desired. This control language normally consisted of special characters, words, and cryptic abbreviations which made the language difficult to learn and even more difficult to retain. Thus, users who used a computer occasionally often had to retrain themselves each time they wanted to have access to the machine.

/LOGON,"JACOB",12/15/67
/T.1
/EXEC.TXT.EDT
/END

Figure 7-14 The entries illustrated here are representative of the types of entries which were required when users first began to have access to mainframe computers. The user needed to know not only what data to enter but also the exact format and punctuation to use. Many users were not successful with this type of user interface.

The example in Figure 7-14 illustrates a typical procedure and the language which a user had to use in order to communicate with a mainframe computer. Generally, users first had to "log on" the computer by identifying themselves so the software could determine if the person should have access to the computer. While this is still common today, the mechanics for doing it today differ considerably from those used in earlier years. Note that the user had to begin the message with a single slash (/) followed by the word LOGON. This entry was followed immediately by a comma, open quotation marks, a name, and closed quotation marks. A comma was entered next and then the date. This format had to be followed exactly. A missing comma, quotation mark, slash, or even any one of these in the wrong position would cause the software to issue an error message. Thus, the user needed to know not only the data which must be entered, but also the exact format and syntax, or rules, which must be followed.

In the example in Figure 7-14, if the user entered the first line correctly, the second line had to be entered. The almost unintelligible entry /T.1 means that terminal one was being used by the user. Again, the entries had to be made in the exact format or the system would not allow the user to continue.

The next entry designated the program which was to be executed, and the last entry informed the software that the user had entered all of the commands that were to be entered. When the /END command was entered, the software would begin performing the processing requested by the user.

The entries illustrated in this example were not difficult to learn or use by computer specialists such as computer operators or the computer programmers, but such commands were not easy for the end user to master and use effectively. Therefore, there was considerable room for improvement in the software which was developed for user interface. After a short period of time, both users and computer professionals recognized that the software which communicated with users would have to be more user oriented. Steps began to be taken to improve the software.

Prompts

Users and computer specialists alike realized that in order for a control language to be effectively used by noncomputer personnel, there was a need to tell the user what data to enter and in what format the data should be entered. Thus, one of the first steps in improving user interface software was displaying prompts on the CRT screen. A **prompt** is a message displayed to the user which provides information or instructions to the user regarding some entry to be made or action to be taken.

The example in Figure 7-15 illustrates the use of prompts. On the first line, the prompt ENTER LAST NAME: appears on the screen. This message to the user states that the last name is to be entered. Note that the user is now directed what to enter, as opposed to the example in Figure 7-14 where no message is given at all.

After the user enters the last name, a second prompt is displayed. This prompt, ENTER DATE (MM/DD/YY), indicates to the user not only what is to be entered but also the exact format in which the date is to be entered. The entry MM/DD/YY is intended to convey that the date should be entered as a two-digit month number, followed by a slash (/), a two-digit day number followed by a slash, and a two-digit year number. For example, the entry 04/29/86 is a valid entry.

It is important that prompts be clear and easy to understand for all users. If prompts are not clear to the user, they may be more harmful than helpful in aiding the user to enter valid data.

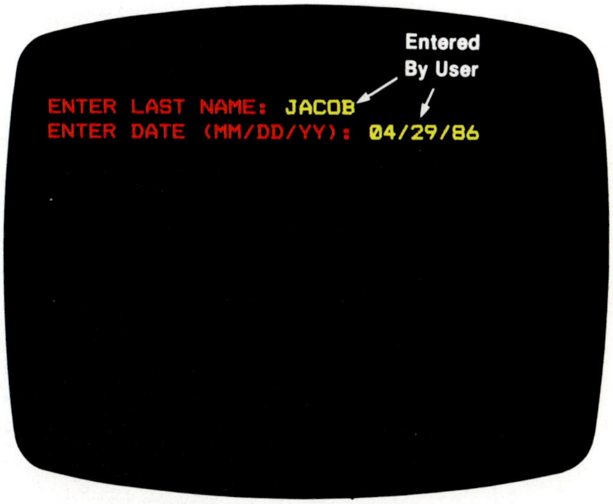

Figure 7-15 Prompts are used to aid the user when entering data. The prompts tell the user what data to enter and also, on the second line, specify the format of the data to be entered. Prompts were the beginning of user interface which gave as much consideration to the user as it did to the computer.

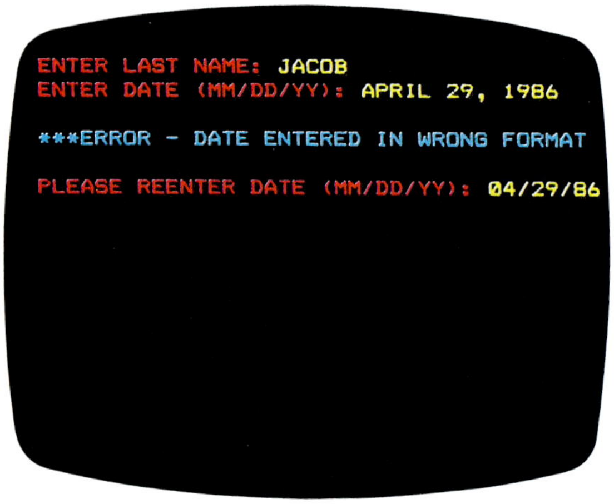

ENTER LAST NAME: JACOB
ENTER DATE (MM/DD/YY): APRIL 29, 1986
***ERROR - DATE ENTERED IN WRONG FORMAT
PLEASE REENTER DATE (MM/DD/YY): 04/29/86

Figure 7-16 The software used in this example checks the date entered by the user to ensure that it conforms to the format requested.

Data editing

As with data entered in a production environment, it is essential that the user issuing commands or requesting information enter data in the correct format so that the entry will be interpreted and processed correctly by the software. To help ensure that valid entries are made by the user, the software which communicates with the user must edit the data entered to ensure that it is in the proper format and that the values entered are acceptable.

When data is entered incorrectly by the user, a message should be displayed so that the user is aware of the error and can reenter the data in the correct format. The example in Figure 7-16 illustrates what might occur when the data is not entered in the correct format. Note that an error message is displayed, and the user is requested to reenter the date.

Prompts, together with data editing, were a great stride forward in making the user interface with the computer more acceptable to the user. Today, prompts are still of great value in assisting end users to effectively communicate with computers.

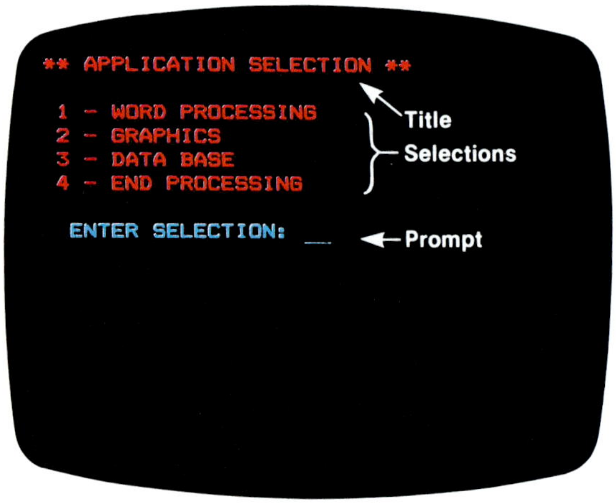

Figure 7-17 A menu consists of the title, the selections which can be made, and a prompt which directs the user to enter a selection.

The use of menus

While prompts aided in the user interface with computers, it began to be recognized by system designers and others associated with computers that the real goal was to develop a user-computer dialogue so that the user and the computer could "talk" back and forth. A critical part of this was to allow the data entered by the user to be entered in as easy a manner as possible.

Together with that realization was the recognition that much of the data entry required of users when issuing commands or requesting information was involved with choosing alternatives. For example, the user might have to choose which software program to execute, which document to use when using word processing, or which function to be performed in an electronic spreadsheet application. To allow the user to make an easy entry to choose from various alternatives, menus were developed.

A **menu** is a display on a CRT screen that allows a user to make a selection from multiple alternatives. A menu generally consists of three parts (Figure 7-17): 1) A title; 2) The selections; 3) A prompt. The title identifies the menu and orients the user to the choices which can be made. The selections consist of two parts — words which describe the selection and a means for identifying the selection. The prompt asks the user to enter a selection.

The screens in Figure 7-18 illustrate a variety of ways which are used by menus to identify selections and allow the user to choose a selection. In example 1, each of the selections is identified by a number. The user may enter the numbers 1, 2, 3, or 4 to select the functions to be performed. If a 1 is entered, the word processing program will be retrieved from auxiliary storage and brought into main memory for execution, allowing the user to utilize the word processing software. If a 2 is entered, the graphics program will be brought into main memory and executed; and if the number 3 is entered, the data base program will be brought into main memory from auxiliary storage and executed. Menus should always contain an entry to allow the user to exit from the menu being displayed. This may be accomplished in example 1 by selecting the entry 4.

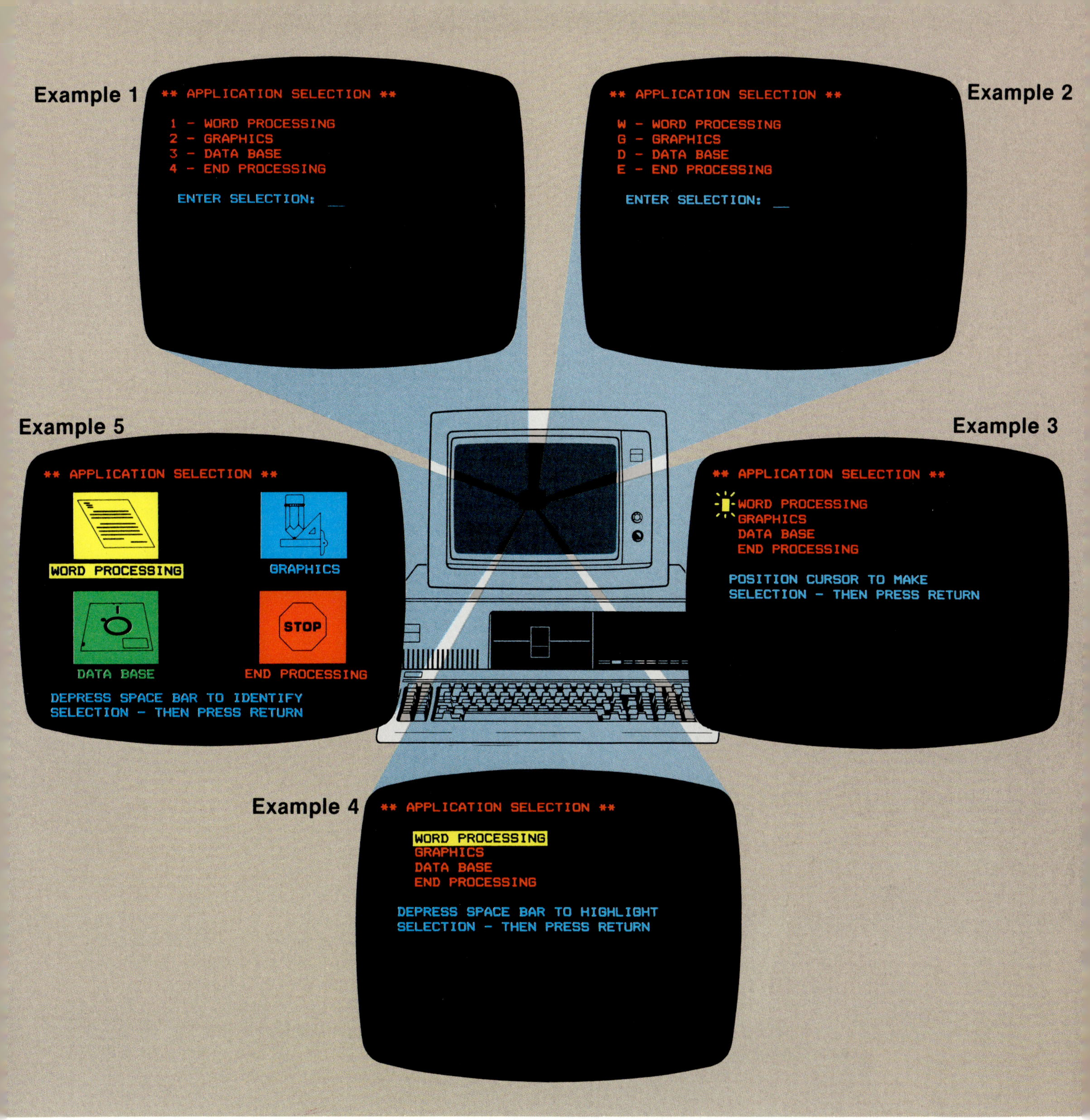

Figure 7–18 In this example, five different types of menus and menu selection methods are illustrated.

In example 2 in Figure 7–18, letters of the alphabet are used to identify the various functions. A selection is made by entering the letter of the alphabet specified adjacent to the function description. Thus, W is entered to select word processing, G is entered to select graphics, D will select data base, and E will end the processing using the current menu. On some menus, selections are identified by the letters of the alphabet A, B, C, etc. Where there are a large number of selections, however, sequential numbering of the selections is considered easier to use.

The third example in Figure 7–18 illustrates a menu where the selection is made by positioning the cursor adjacent to the desired selection. Once the cursor is positioned next to the selection, the return key is pressed in order to make the choice.

The fourth example illustrates the use of reverse video to highlight each of the selections. The directions specify that the space bar should be depressed to highlight each selection. Thus, when the space bar is depressed, the reverse video would move from word processing to graphics. When the space bar is depressed again, the reverse video would highlight data base. Usually, when this type of menu selection is used, **wraparound** occurs, meaning that if the space bar is depressed when reverse video is highlighting end processing, the reverse video would move to word processing. When the desired function is highlighted, the user would depress the return key to select the function.

In example 5, the same principle is used to highlight the choices with reverse video, but the choices are also identified by graphic drawings. When the space bar is depressed, each of the words under the graphics would be highlighted by reverse video. When the return key is depressed, the function highlighted would be chosen.

From these examples, it is clear that a variety of methods are used with respect to menus to identify the selections and to choose which selection is desired. In each case, however, the menu is used to choose from a set of alternative selections. Menus are very widely used today on both personal computers and terminals which communicate with larger computers.

Figure 7–19 A submenu is commonly used when further selections must be made within an application. In this example, the main menu allows the user to pick which applications software will be used. When word processing is chosen, a submenu is displayed to present further choices to the user. Numerous submenus can be used within an application.

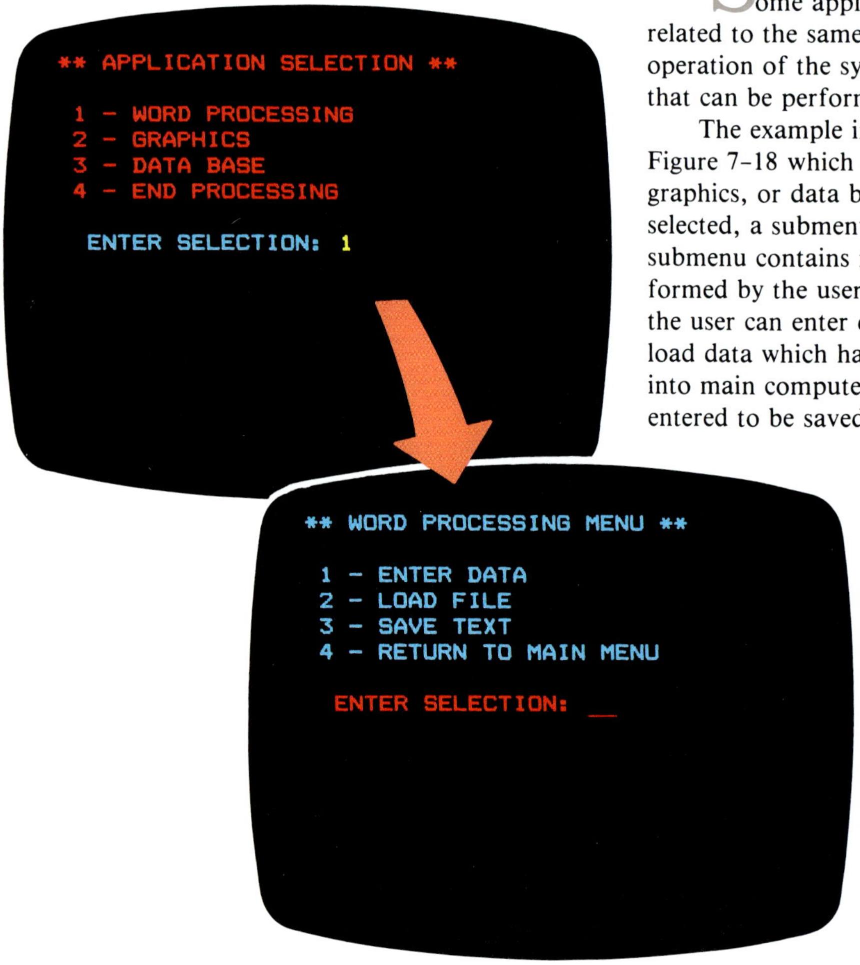

Submenus

Some applications require the use of several menus related to the same application area to guide the end user in the operation of the system. Menus which further define operations that can be performed are called **submenus**.

The example in Figure 7–19 illustrates the main menu from Figure 7–18 which allows the user to select word processing, graphics, or data base. When the word processing function is selected, a submenu also shown in Figure 7–19 will appear. This submenu contains more detailed functions which can be performed by the user. In the example, if number one is selected, the user can enter data. If number two is selected, the user can load data which has previously been stored on auxiliary storage into main computer memory. Selection 3 will allow the data entered to be saved, while selection 4 returns to the main menu.

Depending upon the selection from the submenu in Figure 7–19, additional menus could be displayed. For example, if the user selected option number 1 from the submenu shown in Figure 7–19, a third menu could appear which would display selections relative to margin settings, page length, and similar information.

Summary — menus

Menus are used with many sizes and types of computers. There are, of course, both advantages and disadvantages to menus. Some of the advantages are:

1. The necessity for users to remember the names and formats of special commands is eliminated. The user merely chooses from a list of options.
2. The end user can become productive with a minimum of training. Instead of learning a lot of computer-oriented jargon in order to use the computer, the user needs merely to understand the application and the results of choosing a particular option from the menu.
3. The operator remains oriented within the application. Since the options which are available are presented by the menu, the user will not become lost in the application and be unable to determine what steps can be taken.
4. The computer becomes usable for a larger number of users because less training is required, and more people can understand the use of menus as opposed to computer-oriented command languages.

Menus also have some disadvantages, among which are:

1. There are no standard ways for presenting options and having the user choose the desired selection. Therefore, several of the different forms of menu selection illustrated in Figure 7–18 may be used in the same application. This usage tends to confuse users and certainly slows down production, since the user cannot react instinctively but rather must examine each menu to determine how to enter the selection.
2. For experienced users, the use of a menu might be slow and restrictive. For example, the menus illustrated in Figure 7–19 on page 7.14 are good for the novice or infrequent computer user because they take the user step-by-step through the possible operations that can be performed. The experienced user, on the other hand, knows what processing is desired. Therefore, that user may often prefer to enter a few quick commands and immediately begin work instead of having to view and respond to two or more menus.

In summary, menus are often used when selections must be made. Notwithstanding their disadvantages, they have proven to be quite useful tools with respect to user interface.

Graphics, desk-top screens, and pull-down menus

In recent years, particularly since the increased use of personal computers, computer manufacturers and software developers have studied the end user interface issues very closely. In addition to determining that menus are useful tools, they also discovered that graphics can play an important role in aiding the user to effectively interact with a computer. They also found that users feel most comfortable with a computer when the use of the computer resembles tasks that they are used to performing.

As a result of this research, recently announced computers and computer software have shared some common user interface features. First, bit-mapped CRT screens are being used to display graphics for users. For example, icons, such as those illustrated in Figure 7–6, are used to represent various tasks which can be performed. Second, software developers, together with hardware manufacturers, have developed software that allows the CRT screen to resemble a user's desk. Thus, the user can move the icons about on the screen through the use of devices such as the mouse. Third, innovative designs have been developed for menus in an attempt to make them even easier to use and understand.

To illustrate these innovative moves in user interface, the screens in Figure 7–20 will be used. These screens were developed on an Apple Macintosh™ computer. The following takes place:

Screen 1: This screen contains icons which indicate the application programs that can be selected and other functions that can be performed. A screen displayed in this manner is sometimes referred to as a **desktop screen** because a number of tasks are "sitting on the desk," and the user merely chooses which one to implement. Notice that these icons on the screen are basically a menu, since they offer the user a choice of functions to be performed. They are similar in use to example 5 of the menus in Figure 7–18. The arrow on the screen is the cursor, or pointer. The user points the arrow at the particular function to be performed through the use of a mouse. In this example, the word processing program called MacWrite™ is to be executed. Therefore, the arrow is pointed at the icon which represents MacWrite. After the arrow has been pointed, the user would push the button on the mouse (sometimes called "clicking" the mouse). This action selects MacWrite as the program to be executed. The user then moves the arrow to the word FILE at the top of the screen and clicks the mouse again (this step is not shown). The MacWrite screen shown in screen 2 then appears.

Screen 2: This screen is displayed when MacWrite is chosen. Note that the words across the top of the screen have changed, a rule has been displayed across the top of the screen, and different icons are also displayed. The words at the top specify certain functions which can be performed when the MacWrite program is executing. The rule is used to identify the character positions on the screen. The icons also specify certain activities that can be performed by MacWrite, including setting margins, setting the form spacing, and indicating whether the copy will be left justified, right justified, or centered. At this point, the user would normally choose those attributes which are desired for the document to be created. The attributes can be specified through the use of pull-down menus, such as shown in Screen 3.

Screen 3: In this screen, a menu has been "pulled down" for use. To display a **pull down menu**, the user moves the arrow to the desired menu name and clicks the mouse. Here, the user placed the arrow on the word FONT, the menu name for the menu which identifies types of print which can be used for the data to be entered. When the button on the mouse is depressed, the menu specifying all of the different fonts that can be used is displayed. Note that nine different fonts can be chosen. To choose a font, the check mark is moved down the list by moving the mouse and keeping the button depressed. When the check is next to the desired font, the button is

Figure 7–20 The screens in this example illustrate the step-by-step procedures which could be followed to use a word processing program that is controlled by a mouse, icons, and pull-down menus.

Screen 1

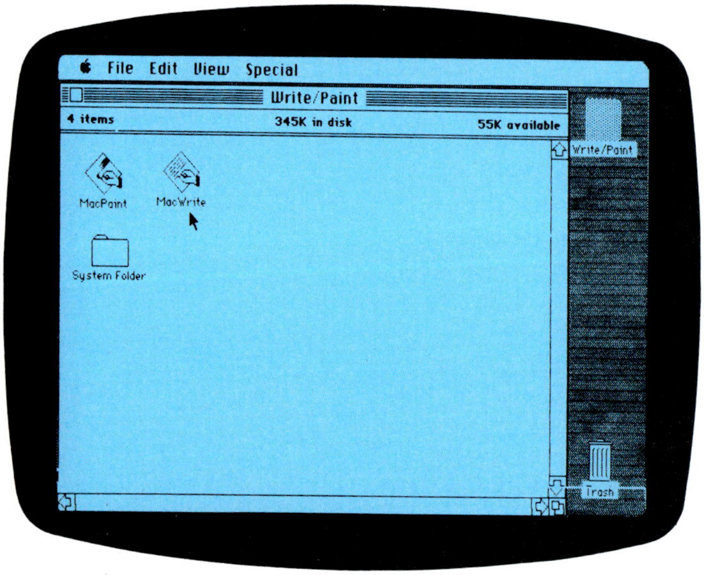

Screen 2

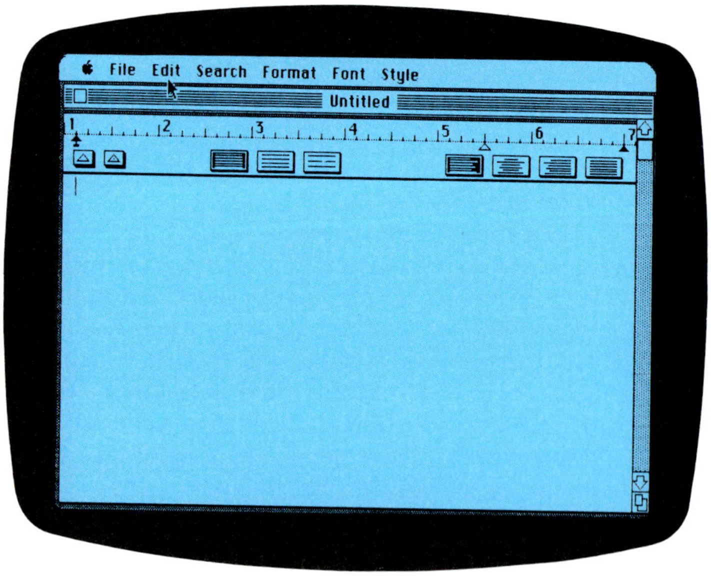

Screen 3

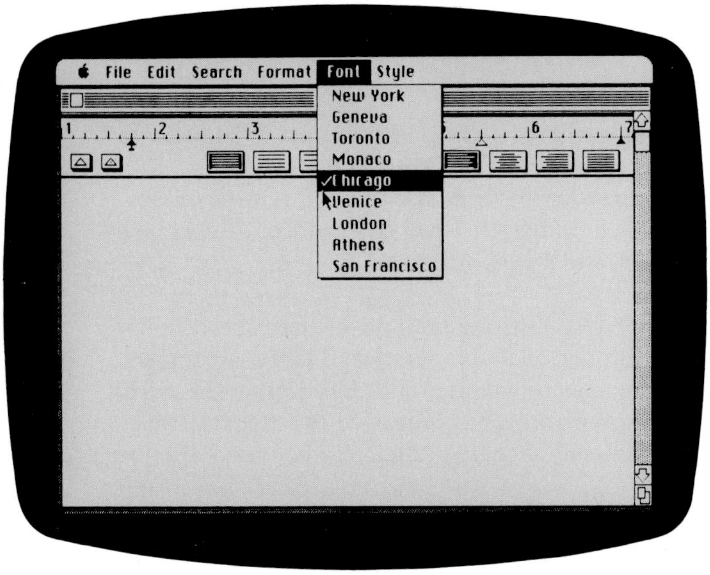

Screen 4

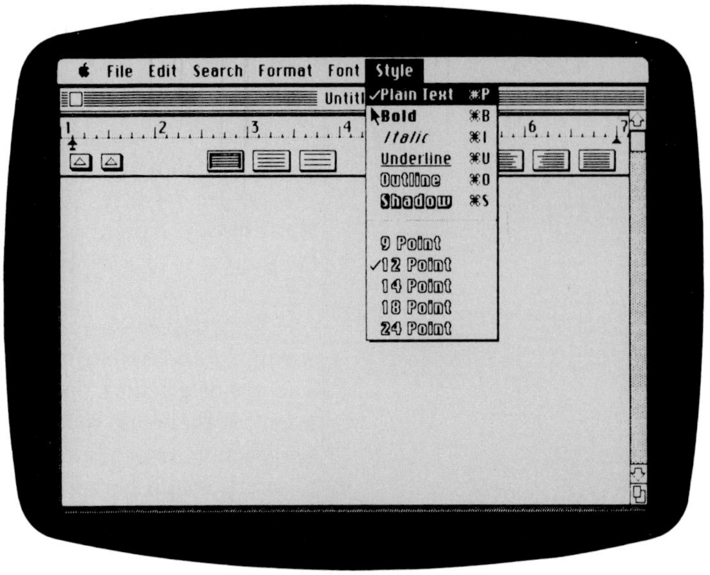

Screen 5

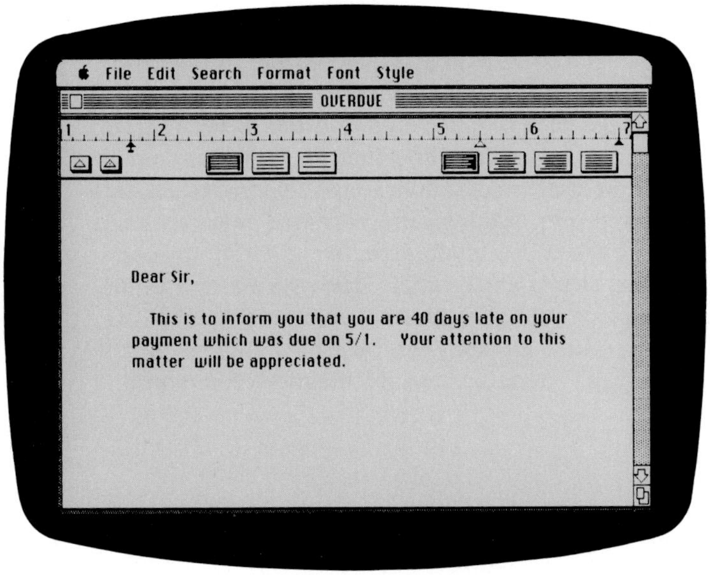

Screen 6

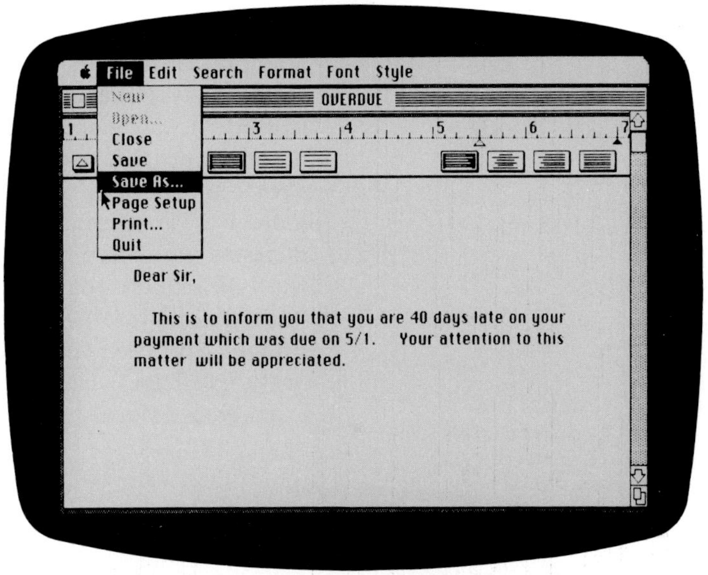

released. In this example, the user chose the Chicago font. When the mouse button is released, the pull down menu disappears from the screen.

Screen 4: The style menu has been pulled down using the same technique explained for screen 3. The choices made by the user were plain text in a 12-point size.

Screen 5: In this screen, the user has entered text. The text was entered through the use of a keyboard. Thus, the Macintosh uses the mouse to point to icons and menu choices and a keyboard to enter data.

Screen 6: After the text has been entered, the user wishes to save it so that it can be referenced at a later time. To do this, the pointer is moved to the word FILE at the top of the screen, and the file menu is pulled down. One of the options on the file menu is "Save As." This means that the user will name the document which is to be stored on auxiliary storage.

Screen 7

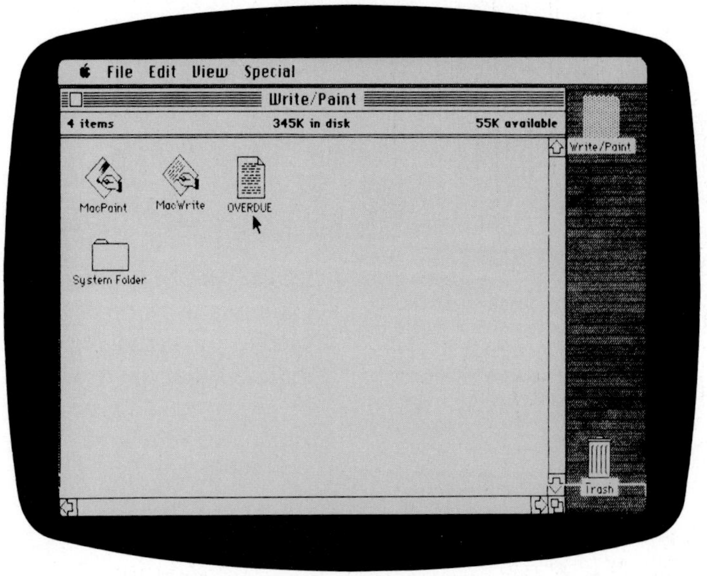

When that option is chosen, the user will enter the name which will be used (this step is not shown). The text will then be saved on auxiliary storage.

Screen 7: After the text is saved, the user leaves MacWrite and returns to the main screen. Note that an item not shown on Screen 1 has been added. The name of the item is OVERDUE, and it is the text which was saved in Screen 6.

This step-by-step example is intended to illustrate the type of user interface which is gaining widespread acceptance on both personal computers and larger computers. The use of graphics, pointing devices such as the mouse, and desk-top screens which resemble the work space typically used by workers has improved the user interface significantly over the terse, cryptic command languages required when users first began to interact with computers.

USER INTERFACE — QUERY LANGUAGES

While prompts and menus provide considerable aid to the end user when interacting with a computer, they do not perform all the functions which are required by users. It will be recalled that users have need to enter data in order to perform an **inquiry**, which is a request to the computer to produce information. When an inquiry is performed, the software with which the user is communicating requires certain data in order to return the information desired. For example, if a personnel manager were interested in the names of people who worked in a given department within the company, the request would require the manager to enter certain data, such as the department number. In order to enter this type of data for inquiry purposes, a number of methods have been developed for users. These methods can be grouped under the title **Query Languages**. The following paragraphs describe some of the more commonly found types of query languages.

** QUERY LANGUAGE **
ENTER COMMAND:
SELECT NAME
FROM EMP
WHERE DEPT = 01

Figure 7-21 The command query language shown in this example requires the user to enter the exact words in the exact sequence in order to select data for use. Here, as a result of the entries shown on the screen, the names of all employees who work in department 1 will be made available.

Command query languages

The most basic type of query language uses preselected keywords which direct the software to perform a certain function. This type of query language is sometimes called a **command query language**. If the personnel manager discussed above were using a query language of this type, the entries shown in Figure 7-21 might be used.

The keyword SELECT indicates to the query language that a particular field from a file or data base is to be selected for use. The word NAME is the name of the field which will be selected. FROM is a keyword which specifies the file or data base from which the information is to be extracted. In this example, the file is EMP. The WHERE keyword is used to further identify the data which is to be extracted. Here, the clause DEPT = 01 indicates that the department field must contain the value 01 in order for the data to be displayed. As a result of the statement in Figure 7-21, then, the names of those employees who work in department 1 will be selected for use.

While command query languages allow access to data bases and can extract data for use, they suffer from some of the same problems exhibited by the command languages first available to users some years back. The number of functions that can be performed are limited. The commands to invoke the functions must be specified in exactly the right sequence, with the correct spelling and punctuation. For these reasons, the use of command query languages requires formal training. These languages are not easily used by the occasional computer user.

Natural language

A number of different types of query languages have been developed to allow easy user inquiry into data bases. Without question, the most desirable form of user interface with the computer would be voice input in natural language, so the user could communicate with the computer as one would with another human being. Although this is not technically possible at this time, software is available that allows a form of **natural language communication** with the computer for the purpose of accessing and retrieving data stored in a data base. As a user, one merely keys on a keyboard a question or retrieval request in normal English, phrased any way the user desires. The software system will then analyze the words, obtain the requested information, and display it to the user.

One natural language that is widely used is called Intellect™. Intellect is produced by the Artificial Intelligence Corporation. Intellect allows users to enter requests using virtually any phrase desired. The Intellect software interprets what the user entered and formulates a request based upon what it has determined the user wants. For example, in Figure 7–22, the user entered a sequence requesting the number of employees in the company. Intellect interpreted the request and returned an answer.

In the example in Figure 7–23, the user asked a question concerning administrators. The software interpreted the question to mean how many employees have the job administrator. Note that the interpretation could also be how many employees with the name Administrator work for the company. This is unlikely, however, and Intellect always interprets requests for the most likely meaning. The third example, in Figure 7–24 on page 7.20, illustrates a request that generated more than just a very simple answer. Based upon the interpretation of the request, Intellect generated an entire report concerning actual sales versus forecast sales.

In addition to Intellect, a number of other software packages that allow natural language queries are available. In each case, the software requires no codes, structure, syntax, punctuation, definitions, or keywords. To retrieve information, the user needs merely to enter a question from the keyboard. If the software does not understand the question, it will tell the user. Otherwise, it will return the information requested.

Natural languages are still being improved, and a great deal of research time and money is being spent on developing software that can understand virtually any

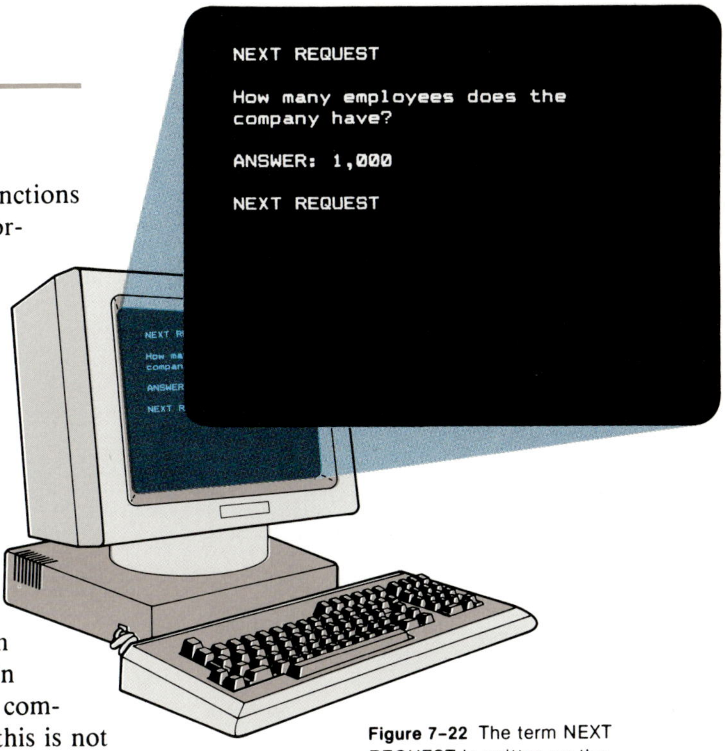

NEXT REQUEST
How many employees does the company have?
ANSWER: 1,000
NEXT REQUEST

Figure 7–22 The term NEXT REQUEST is written on the screen by the Intellect software. The user then asks the question concerning how many employees does the company have. The software interprets the question, accesses the data base to determine the answer, and then responds with the answer.

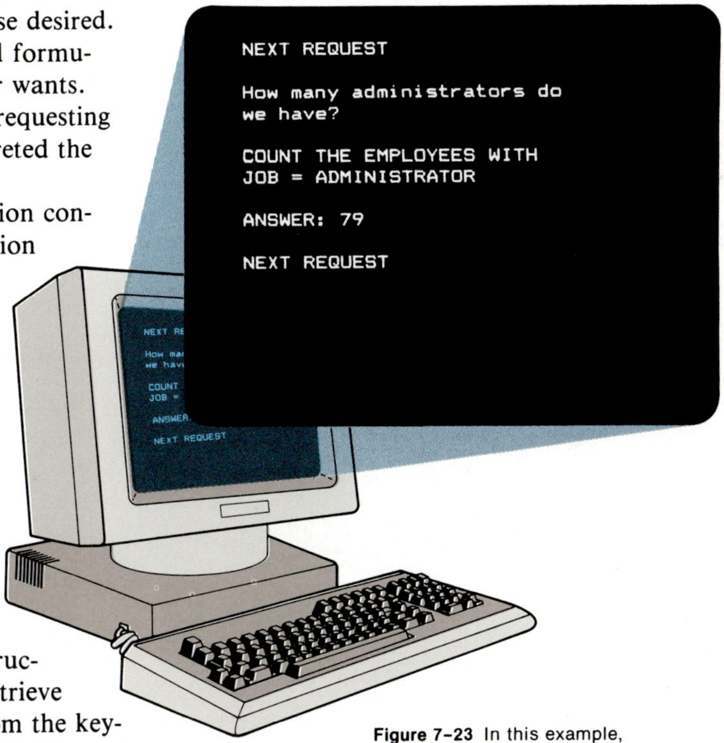

NEXT REQUEST
How many administrators do we have?
COUNT THE EMPLOYEES WITH JOB = ADMINISTRATOR
ANSWER: 79
NEXT REQUEST

Figure 7–23 In this example, the Intellect software interprets the question from the user and then informs the user of its interpretation.

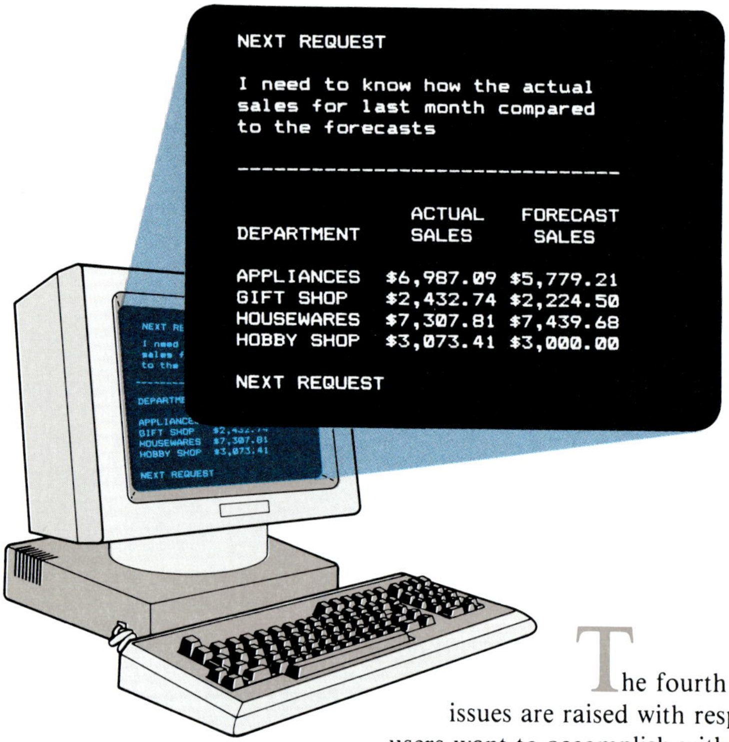

NEXT REQUEST
I need to know how the actual sales for last month compared to the forecasts
DEPARTMENT
ACTUAL SALES
FORECAST SALES
APPLIANCES $6,987.09 $5,779.21
GIFT SHOP $2,432.74 $2,224.50
HOUSEWARES $7,307.81 $7,439.68
HOBBY SHOP $3,073.41 $3,000.00
NEXT REQUEST

Figure 7-24 The response returned from this natural language inquiry consists of a report containing multiple lines and columns.

question a person may ask. Using principles of artificial intelligence, this software will one day allow any user to key any question and receive an answer.

Summary — user interface — software

The software that is used to implement the user interface has matured significantly, moving from short, unintelligible commands to graphic pictures and natural language queries. It is a vital ingredient in the items comprising user interface.

THE USER

The fourth item required for user interface is the user. Five major issues are raised with respect to users: 1) Who are the users? 2) What task do the users want to accomplish with the computer? 3) What data and information do users require to accomplish their task? 4) What information do they generate? 5) What methods do they employ to accomplish their task?

The most important of the questions is Who are the users? A good user interface must consider the people who are going to be using the computer. In particular, the developer of the interface must determine the experience level of the people. Individuals who have had years of experience using computers require a different interface than people who have minimum experience and use a computer only occasionally. For example, a menu is quite appropriate for inexperienced personnel, but experienced personnel will normally prefer a command language capability. Some well designed systems allow both, depending upon the preference of the user.

The tasks which users expect to accomplish with a computer are normally dependent upon the jobs of the users. The jobs also dictate to a great extent the data and information the users require to perform their task, the information they generate, and the methods they use to accomplish their tasks. A user interface must match the "domain" of the user; that is, the use of the computer must be natural to the user. If a user must change significantly the manner in which a job is done, then it is likely the user interface is not well designed.

Each of these issues must be addressed when designing a good user interface and the accompanying systems and procedures.

SYSTEMS AND PROCEDURES

The fifth item of user interface is the systems and procedures which are developed that allow the user to interact with and use a computer. The following factors are relevant with respect to systems and procedures for user interfaces:

1. System responses to the user — When the user interface software is designed

by systems analysts and programmers, the system responses returned to the user are critical. **System responses** are those messages and other actions taken by the computer when a user enters data into the computer. One element of system response is the type of feedback the user receives. In any well designed system, the user always receives feedback when any user action is taken. Feedback can be shown in two ways. First, a message can be displayed which tells the user something is happening. For example, when a large program is being loaded into main computer memory from auxiliary storage, a message "Program Loading" would appear on the screen. A second type of feedback occurs when the screen changes based upon an entry by the user. For example, in Figure 7-19 on page 7.14, when the user chose selection 1 from the main menu, a submenu was immediately displayed on the screen. This action told the user that the data had been accepted by the computer and was being operated upon. Without feedback, the user does not know whether the input was accepted or not. This can lead to confusion and frustration on the part of the user.

A second issue with respect to user response is response time. **Response time** is the time that elapses between the instant a user enters data and the instant the computer responds to the entry. Ideally, response time should never be greater than two seconds. With a response time greater than two seconds, the user begins to wonder if the input entered was received by the computer. In some cases, the activity requested by the user will require more than two seconds for the computer to accomplish. In those cases, a message should be returned to the user, stating that the input has been received and an answer will be returned as soon as the processing is completed.

2. Screen design — The design of the messages and pictures that appear on the screen can have a significant impact on the usability of the system. The most important rule is to keep the screen uncluttered and simple. Each message and each action which a user must take should be clearly seen and understood.

Another important characteristic of a well designed user interface is that all messages, menus, prompts, and so on are used in a consistent manner. Therefore, once the user knows how to respond to one menu in the system, the user knows how to respond to all menus in the system. This consistency is found in all well designed user interfaces.

3. Operator responses — Operator input can vary from complex command languages to pointing an arrow on a screen and pushing a button. In most applications, the simpler the entry required from the user, the better the user interface. Users are often not typists skilled in keyboard usage. Therefore, if the user does not have to enter a large number of characters, the data entry will be faster and less error prone.

4. Error recovery — Since it is inevitable that users will make errors, it should be as easy for a user to recover from an error as it is to make the error in the first place. Whenever the user makes an error, three activities must take place: The user is alerted that an error has been made, the error must be identified, and then the user must be able to recover from the error. In general, error recovery can take place in three ways: The user can reenter the data which caused the error, or the user can "backup" to a previous operation, or the user can exit from the operation where the error was made. All three options are available to a user in a well designed system.

5. Control and security — When terminals and even some personal computers are used by multiple users, authorization may be required to use the terminal or computer. In addition, on both large and small computers there is the possibility that certain data stored on the machines should not be available to all users. Therefore, many systems will require users to "sign-on" to the computer by entering their computer identification and, often, a password. A **password** is a value, such as a word or number, which is associated with the user. Unless the user enters the password, the computer will not allow the user access to the machine.

The systems and procedures associated with user interface play an important role in providing users with a smooth and successful dialogue with computers.

CHAPTER SUMMARY

1. Individuals who directly use computers to help in the performance of their jobs are called end users.
2. When a single end user utilizes a personal computer or computer terminal, the intent usually is to command the computer to perform certain tasks so that requested information is obtained.
3. A user interface is the combination of hardware and software that allows a user to communicate with and control the functional aspects of an information system.
4. The most commonly found hardware associated with user interface is the CRT terminal.
5. When a user interfaces with a computer, one or more of the following activities occur: The user submits a command; a message reports on the software's reaction to the user's input; a message reports on an error made by a user and the user corrects the error; a message is displayed to choose among alternatives and the user responds; a message requests missing information; a message reports processing is progressing or is complete.
6. The following items are required for user interface: A device to display messages, responses, and information; a device from which the user can enter data; software; the user; systems and procedures.
7. The CRT display monitor is the overwhelming choice as the hardware device used to display messages.
8. A cursor on a CRT screen is a symbol which indicates where the next character entered will be displayed.
9. An important function is moving the cursor to different positions on the screen.
10. Absolute cursor movement means the user can indicate the specific location on the screen where the cursor should be placed. Relative cursor movement means the user must locate the current cursor position and then specify the movement required to move from the current location to the desired location.
11. Reverse video can be used to identify choices which users can make from a list of possibilities.
12. An icon is a pictorial representation of a function to be performed on the computer.
13. The device used very often to enter data into a computer to issue a command or to initiate an inquiry to obtain information is the keyboard.
14. Keyboards contain keys, which usually take the form of arrow keys, that can be used to position the cursor on the screen. The cursor moves in the same direction the arrow points when the key is depressed.
15. A pointing device is used to move the cursor around the screen.
16. Disadvantages of a keyboard include the need for training and the fact that some executives will not use a keyboard.
17. A mouse is a small, lightweight device that can easily fit into the palm of one's hand and be moved across a flat surface. It can be used to control the movement of the cursor on the CRT screen.
18. A mouse usually has one or more buttons on it so the user can select menu choices, control the cursor, and perform other functions.
19. Two disadvantages of a mouse are: It requires empty desk space, and a hand must be removed from the keyboard in order to use the mouse.
20. Touch screens allow a user to enter data by merely touching words, numbers, or locations identified on the screen.
21. One of the most common techniques used to implement a touch screen is the use of infrared light and sensors.
22. Touch screens are not used to enter large amounts of data, but they are appropriate to issue a command or make a selection from a list.
23. Advantages of touch screens are they are natural to use, they are fast to use, and they allow absolute cursor movement. Disadvantages of touch screens include their ergonomics and low resolution of the touch area.
24. Voice input allows the user to enter data and issue commands to the computer with spoken words.
25. Most voice input systems require the user to train the system by speaking the words to be used a number of times.
26. The number of words that can be understood by a voice input system is called its vocabulary.
27. Voice recognition is a technology that understands human speech.
28. The major advantage of voice input is the user need not key, move, or touch anything in order to enter data.
29. In most instances, software determines the quality of the user interface.
30. In earlier years, only programmers and operators communicated with computers. In addition, computers were very expensive. Therefore, software was designed to be efficient on the computer.
31. The first software that was designed to interface with users was designed very much like the software that

communicated with programmers and operators. Users required a detailed knowledge of a control language to use the software.

32. A prompt is a message displayed to the user which provides information or instructions to the user regarding some entry to be made or action to be taken.

33. The software that communicates with the user must edit the data entered to ensure it contains no errors.

34. A menu is a display on a CRT screen that allows a user to make a selection from multiple alternatives.

35. A menu has three parts: a) Title; b) Selections; c) A prompt.

36. The selection on a menu can be made in a variety of ways, including entering a number, entering a letter, and moving the cursor or reverse image to the choice.

37. Menus which further define operations that can be performed are called submenus.

38. Advantages of menus are: a) The user need not remember names and formats of commands; b) A minimum of training is required to use a menu; c) The operator remains oriented; d) The computer becomes more usable.

39. Disadvantages of menus are: a) No standards; b) For experienced users, the use of a menu might be slow and restrictive.

40. Graphics can play an important role in aiding the user to effectively interact with a computer.

41. Software is available that allows the CRT screen to resemble a user's desk. This produces a desktop screen.

42. A pull-down menu is one which can be pulled down on the screen through the use of a mouse and the cursor.

43. When an inquiry, which is a request to the computer to produce information, is performed, the software with which the user is communicating requires certain data to return the information required.

44. Query languages are the languages used to obtain information from data bases.

45. With command query languages, the functions that can be performed are limited, and the commands to invoke the functions must be specified in the right sequence, with the correct spelling and punctuation.

46. A natural language allows a user to communicate with the computer in the same way one would with another person. A user keys a question in any format. The software interprets the question and returns the answer.

47. Natural language software requires no code, structure, syntax, punctuation, definitions, or keywords.

48. Five major issues are raised with respect to users: a) Who are the users? b) What tasks do the users want to accomplish? c) What data and information do users require? d) What information do they generate? e) What methods do they employ? The most important question is Who are the users?

49. The developer of the interface must consider the experience level of the user.

50. In any well designed system, the user always receives feedback when any user action is taken.

51. Response time is the time that elapses between the instant a user enters data and the instant the computer responds to the entry. Response time should never be greater than two seconds. If an activity is to take longer than two seconds, the user should be informed that the activity is in progress.

52. Users will make errors. Therefore, it should be just as easy to recover from an error as it is to make an error.

53. Error recovery can take place in three ways: Reenter the data, backup to a prior point, or exit.

54. A password is a value, such as a word or number, which is associated with a user. Unless the user enters the correct password, the computer will not allow the user access to the machine.

KEY TERMS

Absolute cursor movement 7.3
Command query language 7.18
Cursor 7.3
Desktop screen 7.16
End users 7.1
Icon 7.4
Inquiry 7.18
Menu 7.12
Mouse 7.6
Natural language communication 7.19
Password 7.21
Pointing device 7.6
Prompt 7.11
Pull-down menu 7.16
Query languages 7.18
Relative cursor movement 7.3
Response time 7.21
Submenus 7.14
System responses 7.21
Touch screens 7.8
User friendly 7.2
User interface 7.1
Vocabulary (voice input) 7.9
Voice input 7.9
Voice recognition 7.9
Wraparound (menus) 7.14

REVIEW QUESTIONS

1. What is a user interface? What is its importance?
2. What are the activities that occur when a user interfaces with a computer?
3. Name the five items required for user interface. Briefly describe each item.
4. What is the importance of a cursor on the CRT display screen? How is it moved about on the screen?
5. What is an icon? Why is an icon used?
6. Describe the differences between a keyboard and a pointing device.
7. Describe a mouse and list its advantages and disadvantages.
8. Write a short narrative describing the evolution of user interface software.
9. What is a prompt? What are the attributes of a good prompt?
10. Draw five different types of menus. List the advantages and disadvantages of each.
11. Why would a user interface designer use menus as part of the user interface? Why wouldn't a designer use menus?
12. What is a pull-down menu? What hardware and software is required to implement a pull-down menu?
13. What is a natural query language? Write a request using a natural query language to display the last names of the people in your class.
14. List and describe the five major issues with respect to users.
15. List two important features of a well designed screen with respect to user interface.
16. What is response time? How can response time affect the use of a computer system?
17. What is a password? Why is it used?

CONTROVERSIAL ISSUES

1. Manufacturers of computer hardware and computer software which use the mouse as an input device and icons on the screen claim that the majority of people who use computers will prefer this methodology. They claim this on the basis that most people are not familiar with computers and the easier computers are to use, the more people who will use them. Some of their competitors, on the other hand, claim that these devices are useful when people just begin to use a computer but that users quickly tire of the "cuteness" and prefer a device on which more productive work can be done. Which argument do you think is correct? Could they both be correct?
2. Proponents of touch screen technology claim that the touch screen is the answer to user interface problems because all a user must do is touch the screen to input data. Opponents claim it is much too limited as an input device and while somewhat interesting, is not a real competitor to the keyboard. Take a position on this dispute.
3. Attack or defend the following statement: "Allowing novice users to use a computer is inviting disaster. Since they know little about computers, they will destroy data bases and cause chaos in computer installations."

RESEARCH PROJECTS

1. A branch of computer science called artificial intelligence is largely responsible for creating natural query languages. Scientists are making rapid strides toward computers eventually being able to communicate with people. Find an article in a computer magazine concerning artificial intelligence and prepare a report.
2. Visit a local computer store that sells a computer that uses a mouse and icons. Use the machine for a period of time and report back to your class concerning the good points and bad points of the machine.
3. Visit a local bank or retail store that has terminals communicating with a large computer. Ask a person at the establishment to show you how they interface with the computer. Pay particular attention to the screen formats, the data which the user must enter, and the response times. Prepare a report on your experiences for your class.

Chapter Eight

Processor Unit and Data Representation

Objectives

- ☐ Define a bit and describe how a series of bits in a byte is used to represent data
- ☐ Recognize data stored using the ASCII code, and describe the use of the ASCII code
- ☐ Demonstrate an understanding of the sizes of computer memory by identifying the typical sizes of memory found on small and large computers
- ☐ Illustrate data entered from a keyboard being stored in addressable main computer memory
- ☐ Identify data stored using EBCDIC
- ☐ Identify the components of the CPU and describe their use
- ☐ Illustrate through the use of a drawing a typical instruction being executed on a computer

Processor Unit and Data Representation

Chapter Eight

The information processing cycle of input, processing, output, and storage requires that data be read into main computer memory prior to being processed. Once the data has been stored in main computer memory, the computer, under control of a computer program, can process the data and create output information.

Main computer memory is contained in the processor unit of the computer. The central processing unit is found in the processor unit as well. The electronic circuitry of the **central processing unit (CPU)** controls reading data into main computer memory, controls the arithmetic and logic operations that must take place on the data stored in main computer memory, and directs the output produced as a result of the processing to the appropriate device.

The **processor unit**, containing both main computer memory and the CPU, as well as related circuitry, may be housed on a single board in personal computers (Figure 8–1). Large mainframe computers, on the other hand, may require a number of printed circuit boards to house the CPU, main memory, and the related electronic circuits. Regardless of the size of the computer, however, the processor unit performs essentially the same functions — stores instructions and the data to be processed, and under control of the computer program, processes the data and produces output.

It is the purpose of this chapter to examine the way in which data is stored in main computer memory, to explain the concept of addressable storage, and to assist in developing an understanding of the sequence of operations which occurs when instructions are executed on a computer.

How data is stored

Computers store data electronically. Through various methods and electronic components, the circuitry of a computer can sense the presence or absence of electronic impulses. It is the ability of the computer's electronic circuitry to sense these impulses that allows data to be stored in main computer memory.

The basic unit for storing data in main computer memory is the **bit (binary digit)**. A bit can represent one of only two values. These values are zero (0) and one (1). Within computer memory, a bit that contains the value zero can be represented by an open circle, and a bit which contains the value 1 can be represented by a closed circle (Figure 8–2). A bit which contains the value zero is said to be "off," and a bit which contains the value one is said to be "on."

Figure 8–2 A bit (binary digit) can assume one of two values in main computer memory — "on" or "off." This is symbolically represented by a darkened circle indicating the bit is "on," and an open circle indicating the bit is "off."

The determination of whether a bit is "off" or "on" is made by the electronics in the computer hardware. Some computers make this determination by the polarity of magnetized material, while others determine the status of a bit by whether or not electricity is flowing along a circuit. Regardless of the electronic means used to detect whether a bit is "on" or "off," however, it is the ability of the electronic circuitry

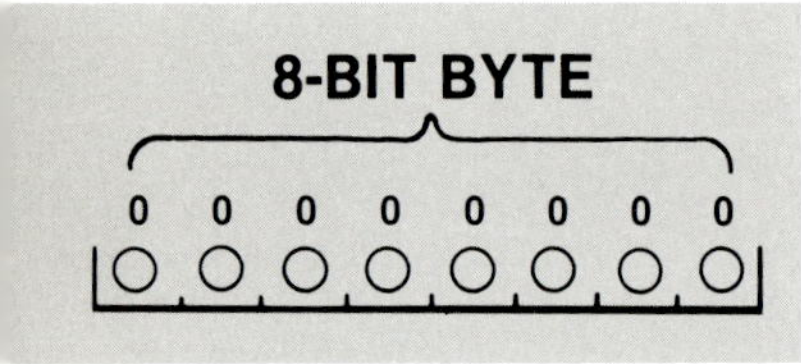

Figure 8–3 The 8-bit byte is used by many computers for storing data in main computer memory. A combination of bits being "on" and bits being "off" within the byte represents numbers, letters of the alphabet, and special characters.

to detect the status of a bit which is the basis for storing data in main computer memory.

A single bit which can only be "off" or "on" cannot be used to represent the decimal digits 0 – 9, nor can a single bit represent the letters of the alphabet or special characters. For a computer memory to be useful, however, it must be able to store numbers, letters of the alphabet, and special characters. To accomplish such a task, computer designers utilize a series of bits. Codes are assigned to the various combinations which can be obtained from the series of bits being "on" or "off." The various combinations represent letters of the alphabet, numbers, and special characters.

Many computers use a combination of eight bits as a unit for storing data. These eight bits are called a **byte** (Figure 8–3). Thus, a byte is a location in main computer memory consisting of eight adjacent bits. A combination of bits "on" and bits "off" is used to represent and store numbers, letters of the alphabet, and special characters.

Figure 8–4 When the key for the letter A on the keyboard is depressed, an electronic signal is sent to the computer. The computer electronics convert the signal into a combination of bits being "on" and "off." The combination represents the letter A.

ASCII code

One of the most widely used coding systems to represent data in main computer memory is the **American Standard Code for Information Interchange**, called the **ASCII code**. The example in Figure 8–4 illustrates the letter of the alphabet A stored in an 8-bit byte in main computer memory using the ASCII code.

As the character is entered from the keyboard, the electronic circuitry of the computer interprets the character and stores it in main memory as a series of bits being "on" and "off." In the example, since the letter A was entered from the keyboard, the specific combination of bits that are "on" and "off" represents the letter A to the circuitry of the computer. When the data in the byte is displayed, printed or otherwise processed, the computer circuitry will interpret the bits as the alphabetic character A.

The ASCII code uses the rightmost seven bits of the 8-bit byte to represent numbers, letters of the alphabet, and special characters. This provides for the representation of a maximum of 128 individual characters. With the ASCII code, the leftmost bit is not used to represent characters.

Representing numeric values using the ASCII code

When the ASCII coding system is used, each digit in a numeric value is stored in a single byte. For example, the numeric value 4263 would require four bytes of memory when stored using the ASCII code.

To provide a mathematically logical method for representing numbers in memory, each of the bits of the byte, beginning with the rightmost bit, has a "place value" associated with it. The **place values** are based upon the binary number system (for a detailed explanation of the binary number system, see Appendix B). These values (from right to left) are: 1, 2, 4, 8, 16, 32, 64, and 128 (Figure 8-5).

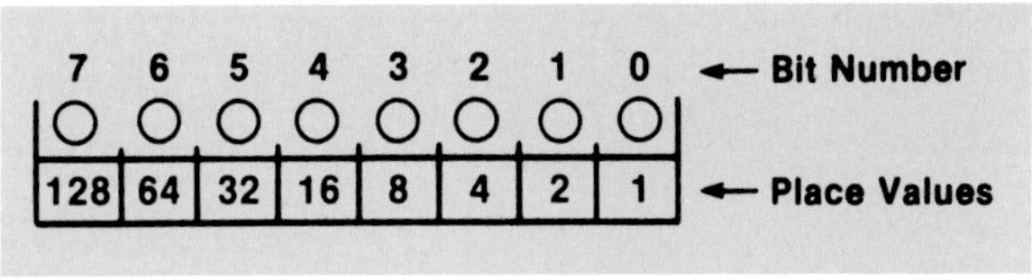

Figure 8-5 Each bit of the byte is assigned a place value based upon the binary number system. The rightmost bit is assigned the value 1, the next bit to the left 2, the next bit to the left 4, and so on. To reference the bits, moving from right to left each is given a consecutive number, beginning with zero. Some bit representations begin numbering the rightmost bit as 1 and move to the left.

For reference purposes, the bits of the byte are numbered 0 – 7, beginning with the rightmost bit. Thus, the rightmost bit is referenced as bit 0, and the leftmost bit is referenced as bit 7.

When representing decimal numeric values using the ASCII code, bits 0 – 3 are used to represent the numbers 0 – 9 by turning "on" the proper combination of bits to represent the numeric value to be stored. Bits 4 and 5 are always "on" and bits 6 and 7 are always "off" when a number is stored in a byte.

In Figure 8-6, each of the numbers 0 – 9 is shown as represented by the ASCII code. The value zero is represented by the bits 4 and 5 being "on" and the rightmost four bits of the byte (bits 0 – 3) all being "off." The value 1 is represented in the byte by bits 4 and 5 being "on," and bit 0 (which has a place value of 1) being "on." The other bits are "off." The digit two is represented by bits 4 and 5 being "on" and bit 1 (with a place value 2) "on." The remainder of the bits are "off." The digit three is represented by bits 4 and 5 being "on" and both bit 0 and bit 1 (with a combined place value of 3) being "on." The remainder of the decimal digits are similarly represented.

It is the proper combination of bits 0 – 3 being "on," together with bits 4 and 5 being "on," that represents decimal digits in main computer memory when data is stored using the ASCII code. It should again be noted that each decimal digit requires a single byte when using ASCII. Therefore, numbers such as 18, 24, or 86 require two bytes of memory — one for each digit.

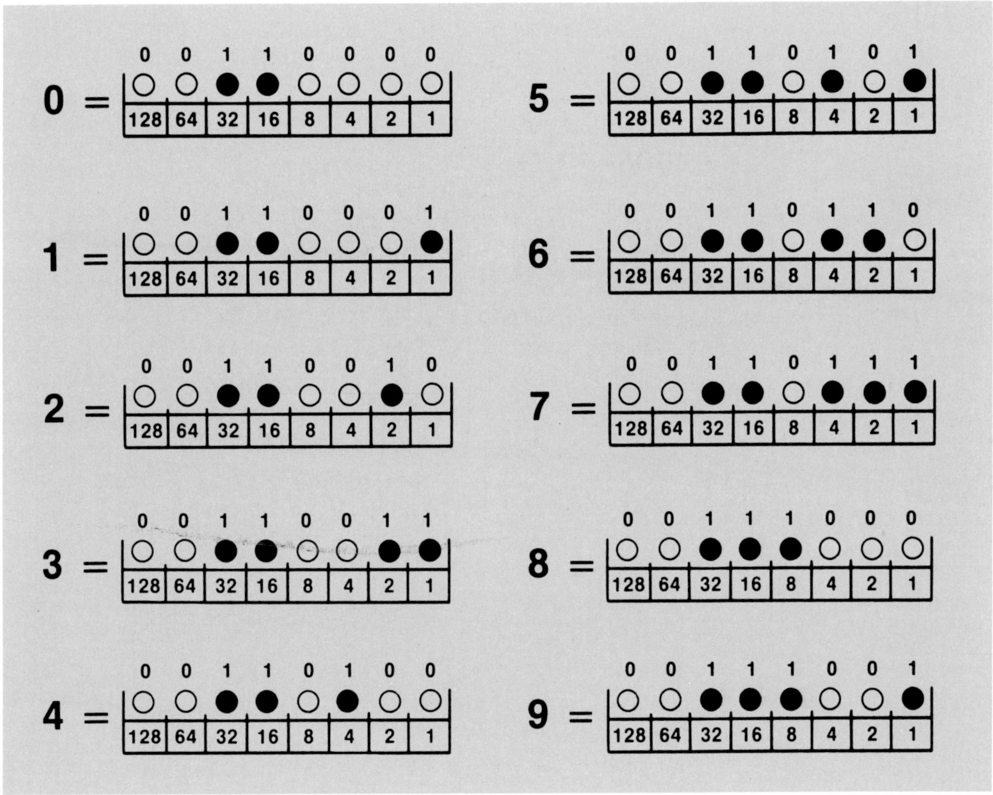

Figure 8-6 Numbers are represented using the ASCII code by turning "on" bits 5 and 6, and turning "on" the appropriate rightmost four bits to represent the desired digit. The appropriate bits are turned "on" when a numeric value is accepted into memory from an input or auxiliary storage device.

Representing alphabetic and special characters in the ASCII code

Each letter of the alphabet is represented in the ASCII code by a unique combination of bits being "on" or "off." The chart in Figure 8-7 illustrates the representation of the letters of the alphabet A - Z and some special characters.

From the chart it can be seen that the letter of the alphabet A is represented by the notation 01000001 in the byte. The 0's represent the bits that are "off," and 1's represent the bits that are "on." The letter B is represented by the notation 01000010, meaning that bits 0, 2, 3, 4, 5, and 7 are "off" and bits 1 and 6 are "on." Other letters of the alphabet and special characters are represented by unique combinations of bits as well. Note that there is even a code that represents a blank space.

Figure 8-7 Letters of the alphabet and special characters are represented in memory using the ASCII code by a unique combination of bits being "on" or "off."

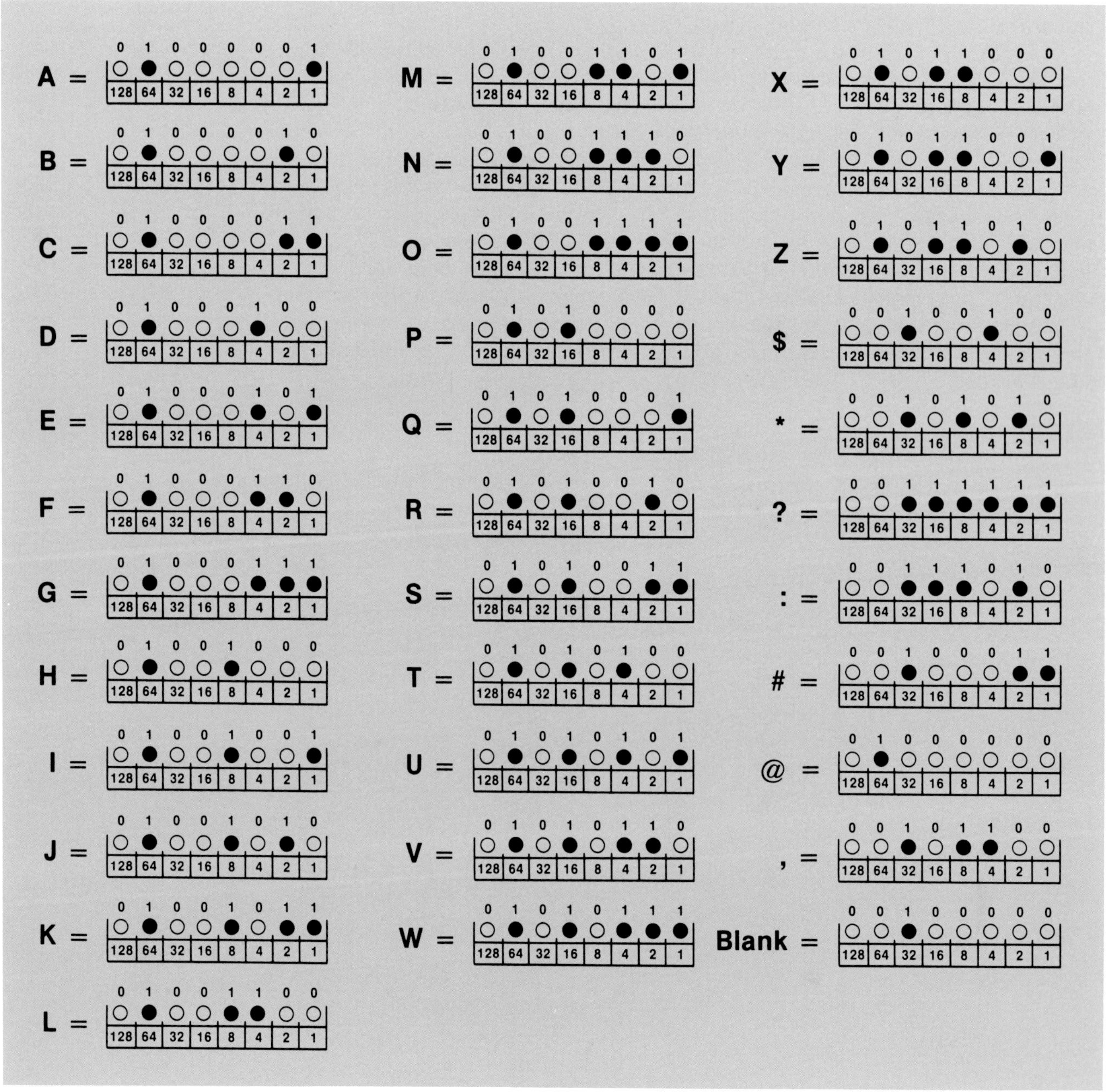

Special codes

There are a number of codes that are used by the computer to control special functions. These codes are a unique combination of bits within a byte which indicate that a certain function is to be executed. For example, there is a code that can control the size of the typestyle that is being printed on the printer, and there is a code that will cause a bell to ring or a buzzer to sound if that hardware is a part of the computer. Although the user is normally not required to have a detailed understanding of how data is stored in main computer memory, a basic knowledge is often helpful in understanding how computers are used and function.

The ASCII code in decimal form

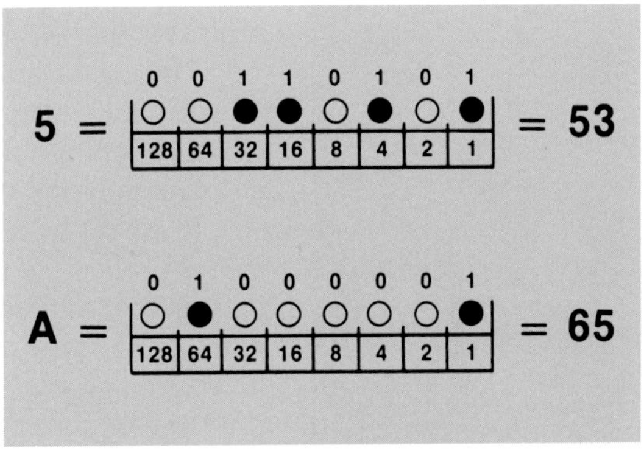

Figure 8-8 These examples illustrate the method used to determine the decimal representations for the digit 5 and the letter A stored in the ASCII code. Decimal codes are frequently used in reference manuals in place of binary representations.

The binary notation for the ASCII representation of numbers, letters of the alphabet, and special characters is difficult to remember and work with. For example, it is difficult for most people to remember that the binary representation for the digit 1 is 00110001, or that the representation for the alphabetic letter A is 01000001.

To facilitate the communication of the ASCII codes and for ease of reference, many technical manuals contain charts which specify not only the binary representation for the various characters in ASCII but a decimal representation as well. The decimal representation converts the binary representation of the bits in a byte to a decimal number. For example, the value 5 stored in a byte is again illustrated in Figure 8-8. The binary representation for the digit 5 is 00110101. To convert this binary notation to a decimal code, all that is necessary is to add the place values for the bits that are "on." For the number 5, then, these are the bits with the values of 32, 16, 4, and 1. The decimal code would be 32 + 16 + 4 + 1, which equals 53. Thus, the ASCII code for the digit 5 using a decimal representation would be the value 53.

In a similar manner, the letters of the alphabet can also be represented by a decimal value. For example, the binary representation for the letter A when using the ASCII code is 0100001 (Figure 8-8). By adding the place values for the bits that are "on," it can be determined that the decimal value for the letter A is 65. The chart in Figure 8-9 illustrates the ASCII characters, the ASCII codes in a binary form, and the decimal values for the numbers 0 - 9, the letters A - Z, and some of the special characters.

Figure 8-9 These charts illustrate the representation in both binary and decimal of ASCII characters.

ASCII								
ASCII Character	Binary	Decimal	ASCII Character	Binary	Decimal	ASCII Character	Binary	Decimal
0	0011 0000	48	C	0100 0011	67	O	0100 1111	79
1	0011 0001	49	D	0100 0100	68	P	0101 0000	80
2	0011 0010	50	E	0100 0101	69	Q	0101 0001	81
3	0011 0011	51	F	0100 0110	70	R	0101 0010	82
4	0011 0100	52	G	0100 0111	71	S	0101 0011	83
5	0011 0101	53	H	0100 1000	72	T	0101 0100	84
6	0011 0110	54	I	0100 1001	73	U	0101 0101	85
7	0011 0111	55	J	0100 1010	74	V	0101 0110	86
8	0011 1000	56	K	0100 1011	75	W	0101 0111	87
9	0011 1001	57	L	0100 1100	76	X	0101 1000	88
A	0100 0001	65	M	0100 1101	77	Y	0101 1001	89
B	0100 0010	66	N	0100 1110	78	Z	0101 1010	90

Size of main computer memory

Main computer memory does not contain just a single byte of memory, but is composed of many bytes. Therefore, an important consideration with respect to a computer is the number of bytes in main computer memory.

The size of main computer memory is normally expressed in terms of the number of 1,024 byte units of memory found within the processor unit. The letter of the alphabet K (standing for Kilo, which means thousand) is used to represent the value 1,024. For example, the size of memory for a personal computer could be expressed as 64K, meaning the computer contains sixty-four 1,024 byte units of memory, for an actual memory size of 65,536 bytes.

The size of memory found on most home and personal computers varies from as little as 4K of memory up to more than 512K of memory. Large mainframe computers typically contain over one million bytes of storage (called one megabyte — mega meaning million), with some machines containing as much as 64 megabytes.

It should be remembered that both data and software are stored in main computer memory when the software is executed. Therefore, the size of main computer memory is an important consideration because if computer memory is not large enough to store both the software and the data to be processed, then the software cannot be executed on the computer. Thus, the size of main computer memory may determine what software can be run on the computer (Figure 8–10).

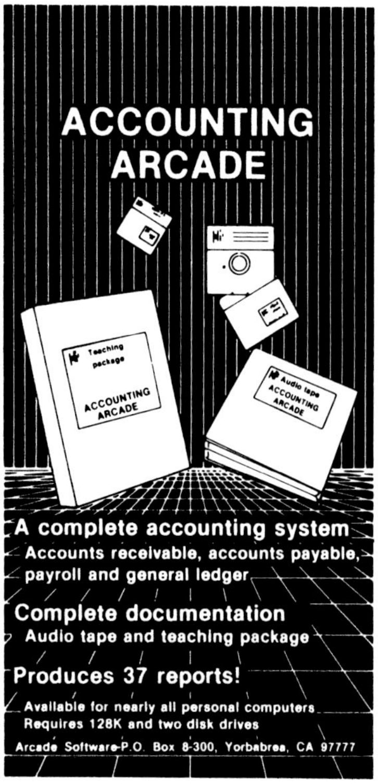

Figure 8–10 This advertisement taken from a popular computer magazine indicates that the software being advertised requires 128K of memory. Therefore, a computer with less main computer memory will not be able to execute this software.

Computers with limited memory (under 64K) may run only the simplest programs and have limited use in the business world. For example, an electronic spreadsheet program may require 96,000 bytes of memory. Obviously, such a program could not be run on a computer with 4K, 32K, or even 64K of main computer memory. A minimum requirement would be a computer with 128K of memory. For most software packages, the size of the computer memory required for the software is specified. For programs written by programmers within a company, the amount of memory needed must be estimated by a senior programmer/analyst prior to beginning the project to ensure that the software will be able to be executed on available hardware.

The cost of main computer memory has dropped substantially in the past few years, and new technology is rapidly providing larger and faster memory capacities for even the smallest of computers. It is predicted that within a few years, computers with more than a billion bytes of main computer memory will be available.

Addressable memory

When data is entered into main computer memory from a keyboard, floppy disk, or other type of input or auxiliary storage device, each character is interpreted by the electronic circuitry and is stored in a byte with the proper bits turned "on" or "off." When the data is being read into main computer memory, the computer program, which is also in main memory, must indicate to the electronic circuitry in the CPU where the data being entered is to be stored. After the data is stored in memory, the program must be able to indicate where data to be processed is stored and where the results of processing are to be stored in main memory. To accomplish this, each byte in main computer memory has a unique address associated with it.

A **memory address** is a number that identifies each byte of main computer memory. These addresses are assigned to each byte when the processor unit is designed by the engineers. When a computer instruction is executed which causes a character to be read into main computer memory, the instruction must specify where in memory the character is to be placed by specifying the address. In the example in Figure 8–11, a code is entered from the keyboard. The computer instruction which causes the character to be read from the keyboard specifies that the character is to be stored in the byte referenced by address 6000. Address 6000 references a single byte of memory which can store one digit, a letter of the alphabet, or a special character. Computers with 64K of memory have 65,536 unique addressable locations where a digit, letter, or special character can be stored.

The ability to store data at unique addresses within main computer memory allows use of the data in subsequent operations. When required, the data at any given address can be referenced and processed as required in arithmetic, logical, output, or any other type of operation.

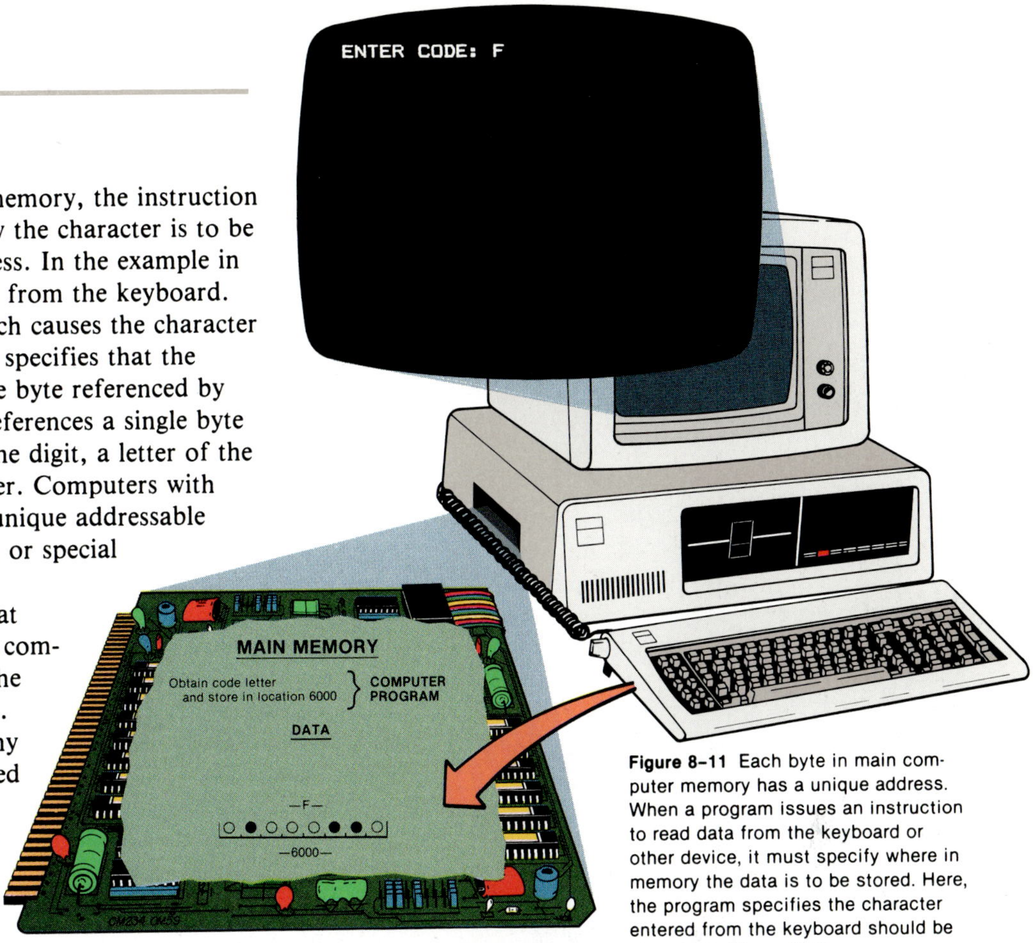

Figure 8–11 Each byte in main computer memory has a unique address. When a program issues an instruction to read data from the keyboard or other device, it must specify where in memory the data is to be stored. Here, the program specifies the character entered from the keyboard should be stored at address 6000.

Storing fields

A group of numbers or letters entered into memory as a unit of data (called a **field**) are recorded in main computer memory in adjacent, addressable locations. For example, in Figure 8–12, the account number 62R is entered into memory locations 15001, 15002, and 15003. Once in memory, this data can be processed as a field because it is known where the account number is stored.

When a field is processed, computer instructions must specify not only the location of the field in memory, but also the number of characters in the field. Typically, computer instructions will specify the address of the first byte of the field and the length of the field. In this way, the electronic circuitry of the computer can reference the correct data. For example, to reference the account number in memory, a computer instruction must indicate that the account number is stored beginning at memory location 15001 and is three bytes in length.

In summary, as input data is read into main computer memory, each character is stored at an addressable

Figure 8–12 When a field of data consisting of more than one character is entered, the program must specify the beginning address where the data is to be stored and the number of characters that will be entered and stored. In this example, three characters are entered, and they are stored beginning at address 15001.

memory location. Thereafter, each character and field stored in memory can be referenced by specifying the location of the data and the number of characters to be processed.

Manipulating data in main computer memory

Once data has been recorded in main computer memory, it can be referenced and processed as required by the application. For example, data recorded in memory can be moved to other locations. The data can also be used in arithmetic operations, be compared to other data also stored in memory, or otherwise be processed to prepare output information. This is possible because computer instructions can direct the electronic circuitry to process data located at specific addresses.

In Figure 8-13, a segment of the operations required to produce a printed report from data contained in a disk file is shown. Under control of the computer program, the data from the record on the disk is read into main computer memory beginning at memory address 26001. The fields stored in memory are then moved to the area in memory, beginning with location 45671, from which the report record will be printed. The computer instructions that cause the fields to be moved from one location to another in memory would reference the address of the data in the disk record area and the address of the printed report area of memory. After all the data has been moved to the report area, a line is printed on the report.

The ability to store data in main computer memory at specific addresses and then reference the data by these addresses forms the basis of the internal operations of a computer.

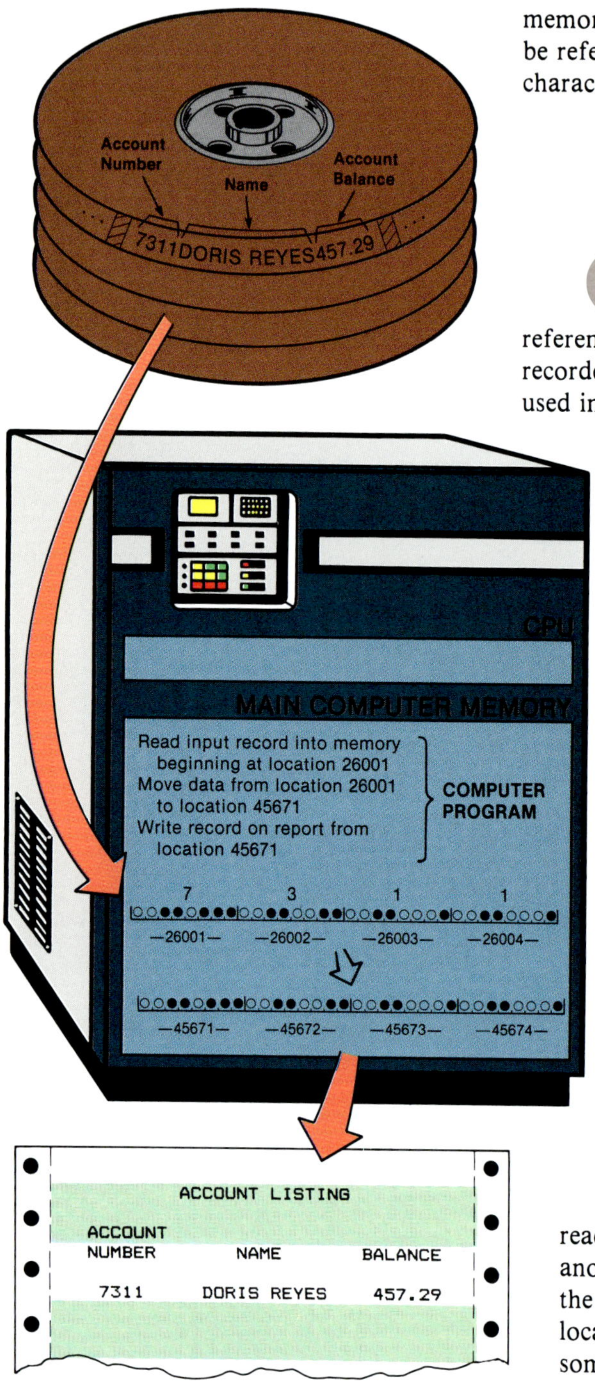

Figure 8-13 In this example, only the account number is shown. In reality, the entire record would be stored in adjacent locations. After the account number is stored at locations 26001 - 26004, it is moved to locations 45671 - 45674. Note the account number is still stored at locations 26001 - 26004 as well. Thus, data is essentially duplicated in main computer memory when it is moved from one location to another.

Use of main computer memory

When a number, letter of the alphabet, or special character is read into main computer memory or is moved from one location to another, the assigned bit pattern for the character is stored in memory at the address specified by the program. Once data has been stored at a location in main computer memory, it will remain at that location until some other data is explicitly placed into the same location.

This fact has two important consequences. First, once data is placed in a location in memory, it will remain there until changed. This allows the program to reference the data for any processing which might be required.

Second, since the data which is moved to or read into a particular location in memory replaces data which was stored there, a single set of instructions in a computer program which references particular locations in main computer memory can be used to process many different records which are stored in the same memory locations when they are processed. This ability enables a programmer to write one sequence of instructions which can process hundreds, thousands, or even millions of records.

The example in Figure 8-14 illustrates the processing that could occur as a series of area codes is entered into computer memory from a terminal keyboard. The first

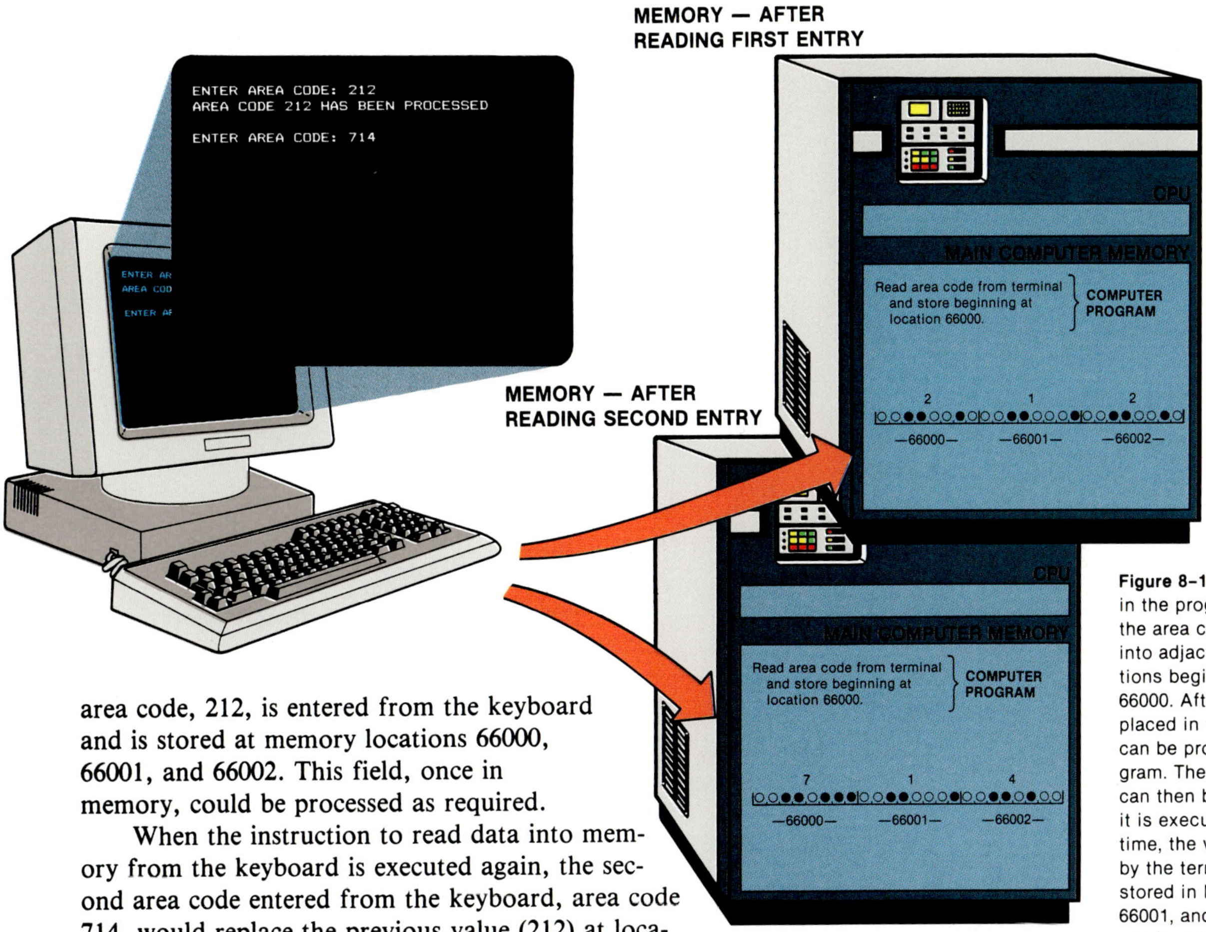

Figure 8–14 The instruction in the program specifies that the area code is to be read into adjacent memory locations beginning with location 66000. After the data is placed in these locations, it can be processed by the program. The same instruction can then be repeated. When it is executed the second time, the value 714 entered by the terminal operator is stored in locations 66000, 66001, and 66002, where it can be processed by the same instructions which processed area code 212.

area code, 212, is entered from the keyboard and is stored at memory locations 66000, 66001, and 66002. This field, once in memory, could be processed as required.

When the instruction to read data into memory from the keyboard is executed again, the second area code entered from the keyboard, area code 714, would replace the previous value (212) at locations 66000, 66001, and 66002 in memory. Area code 714 could then be processed by the same instructions which processed area code 212.

The process of reading data into memory replacing previous data at the same location or moving data from one location to another, replacing the data at the second location, is called **destructive read in.**

On most computers today, data is retained in main memory as long as the system has power. If power is turned off, the contents of memory will be lost.

EXTENDED BINARY CODED DECIMAL INTERCHANGE CODE (EBCDIC)

While the ASCII code is widely used on personal computers and many minicomputers, it is not the only coding format used on computers. One of the most commonly used coding schemes for mainframes is called the **Extended Binary Coded Decimal Interchange Code (EBCDIC).** With EBCDIC, each eight-bit byte is divided into two portions — the zone portion and the digit portion (Figure 8–15). The bits in both the **zone portion of the byte** and the **digit portion of the byte** are assigned numeric values based upon the binary number system, forming the basis for a logical representation of data in storage.

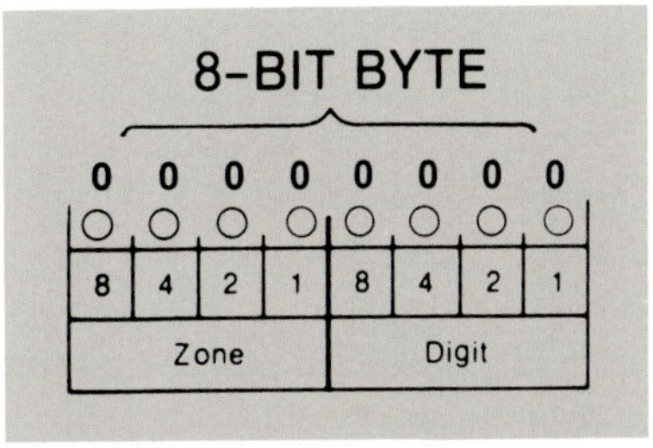

Figure 8–15 Each bit in the zone portion of the byte and each bit in the digit portion of the byte is assigned a value based upon the binary number system. It is a particular combination of these bits being "on" or "off" that represents data using the EBCDIC code. There are 256 possible combinations in the EBCDIC code because all eight bits of the byte are used.

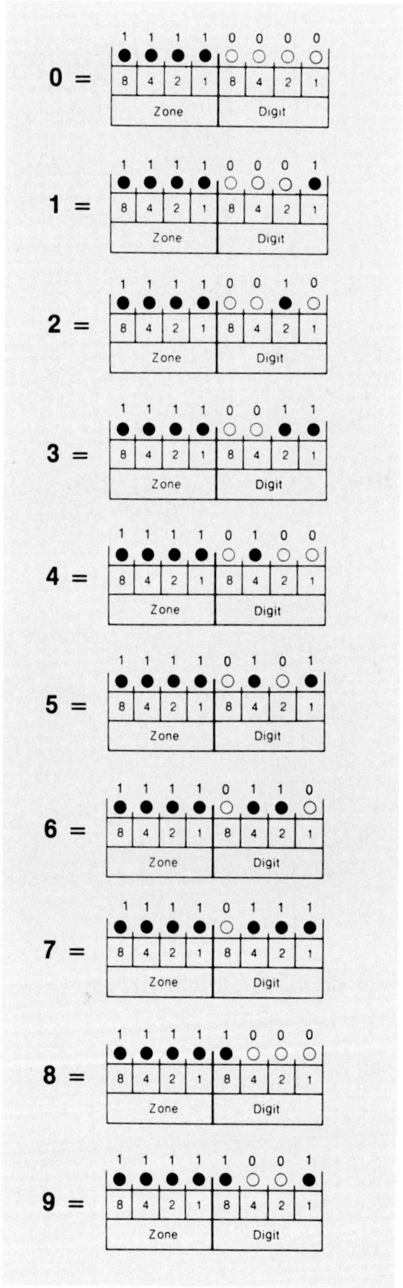

Figure 8–16 Numbers are represented in EBCDIC by all of the zone bits being "on" and digit bits being "on" that represent the particular number

Representing numeric values using EBCDIC

Numeric values are represented in EBCDIC with all the zone bits "on," and the proper combination of bits in the digit portion of the byte "on" to represent the particular numeric value.

In Figure 8–16, the value zero is represented by all of the bits in the zone portion of the byte being "on," and all of the bits in the digit portion of the byte being "off." The value one is represented by the bits in the zone portion of the byte being "on" and the bit with the place value of 1 in the digit portion of the byte being "on."

The digit portion of the byte to represent the value 2 has the bit with the place value 2 "on." The digit portion of the byte representing the value 3 has the bit with the place value 2 and the bit with the place value 1 "on." The numbers 4–9 are represented in a similar manner.

It is the proper combination of bits "on" in the digit portion of the byte, together with all of the bits in the zone portion of the byte being "on," which represents numeric values in main computer memory using the EBCDIC coding format. Each decimal digit is stored in a single byte when using EBCDIC. Therefore, as with the ASCII coding scheme, numbers such as 10, 11, or 12 require two bytes of memory — one for each digit.

Representing alphabetic data using EBCDIC

Alphabetic data is represented using EBCDIC with a combination of bits "on" and "off" in both the zone and digit portions of the byte (Figure 8–17). The letters A through I have the bits corresponding to the 8 and 4 values "on" in the zone portion of the byte. The digit portion of the byte has the bit corresponding to 1 "on" for an A, the bit corresponding to 2 "on" for a B, and so on.

The letters J through R have the bits corresponding to the 8, 4, and 1 values "on" in the zone portion of the byte. In the digit portion of the byte, the value 1 bit is "on" for a J, the value 2 bit is "on" for the K, and so on. The letters S through Z contain bits 8, 4, and 2 "on" in the zone portion of the byte. The digit portion of the byte has the bit corresponding to the value 2 "on" for the letter S, and so on.

Thus, each of the letters of the alphabet is represented in storage by a particular combination of bits being "on" or "off" in the zone and digit portions of a byte.

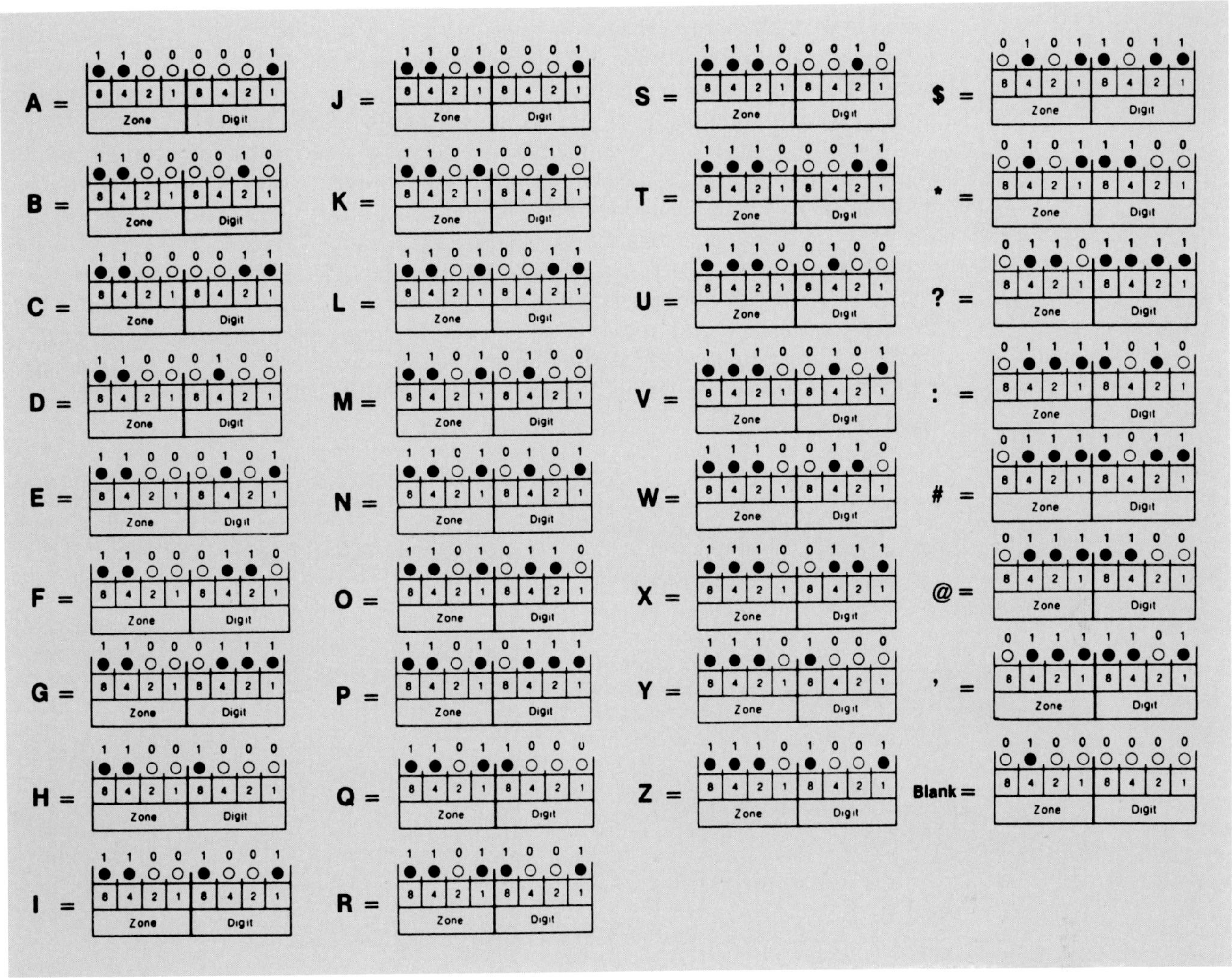

Figure 8-17 The letters of the alphabet and the special characters each have a unique bit configuration when using EBCDIC. EBCDIC gained prominence when introduced together with the IBM System/360 computers in 1964.

REPRESENTING NUMERIC VALUES IN BINARY

The previous pages in this chapter have illustrated storing and manipulating characters stored in single addressable locations in main computer memory using either the ASCII or the EBCDIC code. Each character occupied one byte of memory.

It should be noted as well that many computers store numbers using a variety of different methods all based upon the binary number system. One method uses two adjacent bytes to form a "sixteen-bit word." Using this methodology for storing numbers, the first fifteen bits of the byte are assigned binary place values. The left-most bit is effectively used to indicate the sign of the number (Figure 8–18).

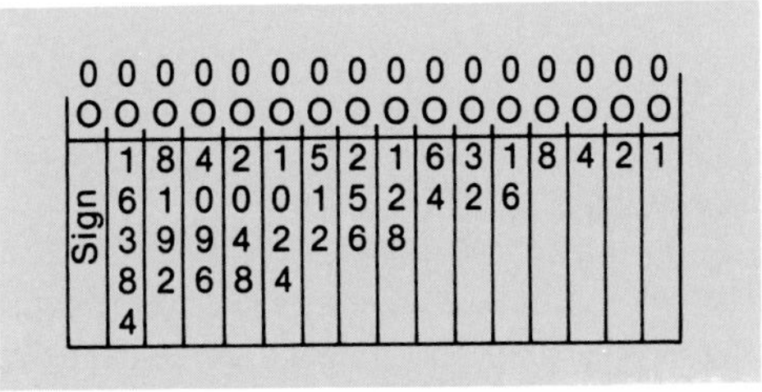

Figure 8–18 A sixteen bit word is illustrated in this drawing. Each bit corresponds to the values shown. The high-order (left-most) bit is effectively used as the sign of the number, so that both positive and negative numbers can be stored in the word.

Numbers read into memory are stored in the 16-bits as a binary value by turning "on" the proper combination of bits to represent the number read from the input device. For example, in Figure 8-19, the number 2053 is entered from a keyboard and stored in a 16-bit word in main computer memory. The binary number corresponding to the decimal number 2053 is 0000100000000101. A number stored in this representation is often referred to as an **integer** because the number is a whole number, and the binary representation of the number is the exact value of the number.

The maximum size number that can be stored in a 16-bit word (where the 16th bit is used for the sign) is 32,767. To represent larger numbers, and numbers that contain decimal values, other techniques are used, including scientific notation in which numbers are represented as a number and an exponent.

Although the ASCII code, the EBCDIC code, and the 16-bit binary word are widely used for representing data in memory, there are numerous other methods. The method used will depend upon the type of computer and on the type of data being processed. A detailed understanding of the internal representation of data in memory requires a review of the technical reference manual supplied with each particular computer.

Figure 8-19 The value stored in the word in main computer memory is 2053. This value is computed by adding together the values represented by the bits which are "on." Thus, the value in the word is 2048 + 4 + 1 = 2053

TYPES OF MEMORY

As has been noted, electronic components are used to store data in computer memory. The actual materials and devices used for memory have changed throughout the years. The first major device used for storing data was the vacuum tube. Subsequent to the vacuum tube, magnetic core memory was used. **Magnetic core memory** consisted of small, ring-shaped pieces of metal that could be magnetized, or polarized, in one of two directions. The polarity indicated whether the core was "on" or "off." Core memory was used successfully for many years.

Today, **semiconductor memory** is used in virtually all computers (Figure 8-20). Semiconductor memory is manufactured from silicon or other semiconductor metal which is placed on a chip in layers. **Transistors** are etched into the semiconductor material. Each transistor acts as a bit. The transistors either block electrical current or allow the current to pass, thus representing the bit being "off" or being "on."

When core memory was used as main computer memory, the time required to access data stored in the memory was measured in **microseconds** (millionths of a second). Access to data stored in semiconductor memory, on the other hand, is measured in **nanoseconds** (billionths of a second). In addition, the cost of semiconductor memory is just a fraction of the cost for core memory. Indeed, today one can buy 64K of semiconductor memory for about $75.00, whereas just a few years ago 64K of core memory could cost as much as $15,000.00.

Several different types of semiconductor memory are found in most computers. These types are RAM, ROM, PROM, and EPROM. **RAM** stands for Random Access Memory. **Random access memory** is used for main computer memory. It is the type of memory that has been discussed thus far in this chapter. Data and programs can be stored in RAM from input devices or auxiliary storage devices. Data stored in RAM can be changed using instructions within a computer program. Data stored in RAM can be displayed on a CRT screen or printed on a printer. In short, data can be placed into the memory and can be extracted from the memory.

ROM stands for **Read Only Memory**. With ROM, data is recorded in the memory when the memory is manufactured. The data or programs which are stored in ROM can be read and used, but the data or programs stored in ROM cannot be altered. ROM is used to store data and programs which will not be altered, such as BASIC interpreters used with personal computers. In addition, many of the special purpose computers used in automobiles, appliances, and so on use small amounts of ROM to store instructions which must be executed from time to time.

Figure 8-20 This photograph illustrates 32 transistors on an NCR semiconductor chip that is used for computer memory. The transistors are enlarged 600 times their actual size.

PROM means **Programmable Read Only Memory**. PROM acts the same as ROM when it is part of the computer; that is, it can be read, but its contents cannot be altered. With PROM, however, the data or programs are not stored in the memory when it is manufactured. Instead, the user of the PROM can store data in the memory prior to assemblying it with the computer. A variation of PROM is **EPROM**, which is **Erasable Programmable Read Only Memory**. In addition to being used in the same way as PROM, EPROM allows the user to erase the data stored in the memory and to store new data or programs in the memory. EPROM is erased through the use of special ultraviolet devices which destroy the bit settings within the memory.

One or more of these types of memory are found on every computer. Virtually all general purpose computers use RAM, and most have some amount of ROM, PROM, or EPROM which is used to store permanent data and/or programs.

Summary — computer memory

The types of memory found on a computer and the way in which data is stored in that memory can vary from machine to machine. Some machines use ASCII, while others use EBCDIC. Some store numbers in a binary form. Some machines use both ASCII or EBCDIC and a binary form for storing data. Regardless of the manner of representing data, however, the principles remain the same. Bits which can be considered either "on" or "off" are combined in some manner to represent the data.

THE CENTRAL PROCESSING UNIT (CPU)

A computer program is composed of many individual computer instructions. In a complex program, there may be thousands of individual instructions. Each of these instructions is stored in main computer memory. They specify the operations which will occur within the computer when the program is executed. Computer instructions are executed one at a time; however, hundreds of thousands, and even millions, of instructions can be executed on large computers in one second. When an instruction is executed, the electronic circuitry of the central processing unit (CPU) interprets the instruction and causes processing to occur.

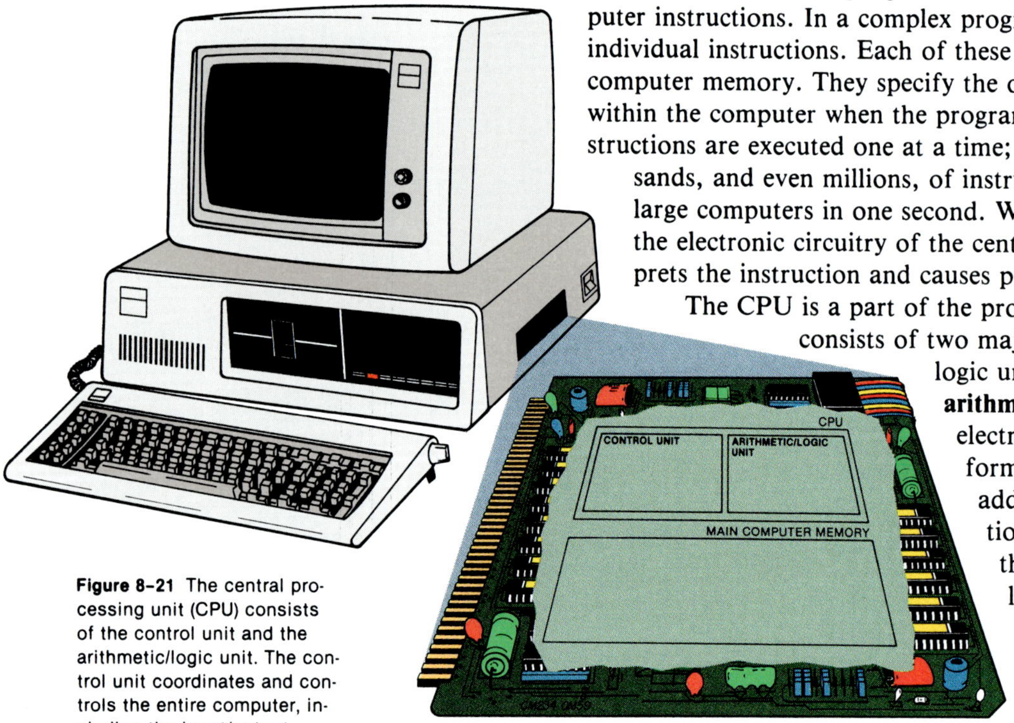

Figure 8–21 The central processing unit (CPU) consists of the control unit and the arithmetic/logic unit. The control unit coordinates and controls the entire computer, including the input/output operations to main computer memory. The arithmetic/logic unit performs arithmetic and logic operations on data.

The CPU is a part of the processor unit (Figure 8-21). It consists of two major components: the arithmetic/logic unit and the control unit. The **arithmetic/logic unit** contains the electronic circuitry necessary to perform arithmetic operations such as addition, subtraction, multiplication, and division. It also contains the circuitry required to perform logical operations such as comparing one number to another and indicating the results of that comparison.

The **control unit** of the CPU directs and coordinates the activities of the entire computer. Its tasks include controlling the input/output units, controlling the operations of the arithmetic/logic unit in the CPU, and transferring data to and from main computer memory.

Computer instructions

The program which will be executed on the computer must be stored in main computer memory. The program instructions which the CPU interprets and executes must be in the form of machine language instructions. A **machine language instruction** is one which the electronic circuits in the CPU can interpret and execute. A knowledge of the basic characteristics of machine language instructions is useful in understanding how a computer operates.

In general, a machine language instruction is composed of: 1) An operation code; 2) Values indicating the number of characters to be processed by the instruction: 3) The addresses in main computer memory of the data to be used in the execution of the instruction (Figure 8–22).

The **operation code** is a unique value which is typically stored as the first byte in the instruction. This unique value indicates to the computer electronics what operation is to occur. For example, the letter of the alphabet ''A'' stored as the operation code might indicate that an addition operation is to occur. The letter ''D'' might mean that division is to take place.

The number of characters to be processed must be included in the machine language instruction so that the electronic circuitry of the processor unit will reference the proper number of digits in the field to be processed. For example, if a four digit field were to be added to another four digit field, the number of characters specified in the instruction for each field would be four.

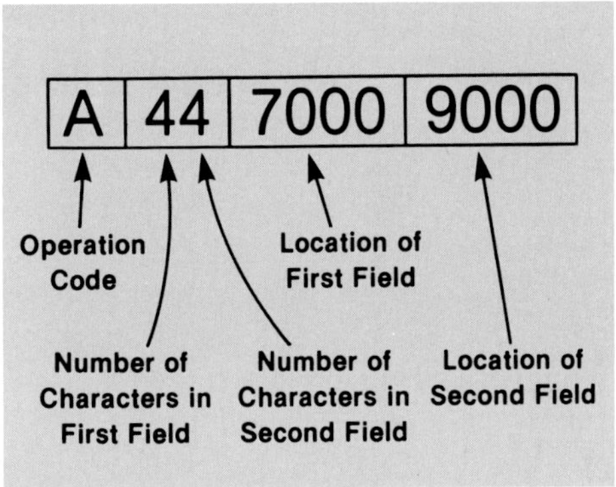

Figure 8-22 A machine language instruction consists of an operation code, the lengths of the fields to be processed, and the main computer memory addresses of the fields.

The main memory addresses of the fields involved in the operation must be specified in the instruction to enable the circuitry to identify where in memory the data to be processed is located.

Although the formats of computer instructions vary a great deal among different computers, the basic elements of operation code, number of characters to be processed, and the addresses of the data to be processed will almost always be present.

Executing instructions on a computer

Executing an instruction on a computer requires the control unit of the CPU to fetch, or obtain, the instruction from main computer memory and place the instruction in an instruction register. An **instruction register** is nothing more than an area of memory within the control unit of the CPU which can store a single instruction at a time. The control unit will also fetch any data required for the execution of the instruction and place the data in special registers which can be referenced by the arithmetic/logic unit of the CPU.

The arithmetic/logic unit of the CPU is then given control. It will perform the actual execution of the instruction and store the answer in another register. The control unit will then place the answer into main computer memory.

The illustration in Figure 8–23 on page 8.16 shows the steps involved in executing a computer instruction on a typical computer. The computer instructions are stored in main computer memory. The control unit keeps track of the next instruction to be executed. When an instruction is to be executed, the following steps occur: 1) The instruction is fetched from main computer memory and is placed in an instruction register. In Figure 8–23, the instruction A44 7000 9000 indicates that two fields, each four digits in length, are to be added together; 2) After the control unit has analyzed the instruction, it causes the data stored at the two addresses specified in the instruction to

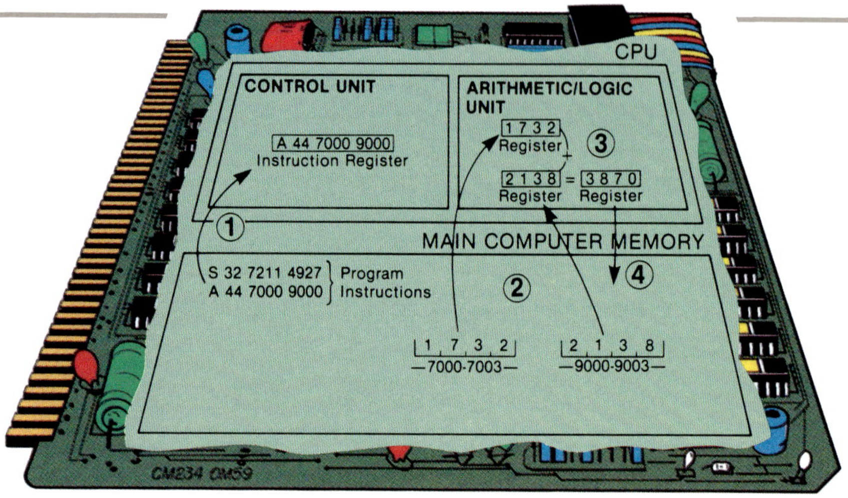

Figure 8–23 The control unit and the arithmetic/logic unit of the central processing unit actually execute computer program instructions. Here, an add instruction is executed. The answer from the add instruction would normally be stored in the address for the first field. This is not shown in the diagram.

be fetched and placed in registers available to the arithmetic/logic unit in the CPU; 3) The arithmetic/logic unit executes the actual instruction. In the example in Figure 8–23, the two numbers obtained from main computer memory are added. The sum is stored in a different register; 4) The control unit would then move the answer from the register back to main computer memory.

Although this process appears to be cumbersome and time-consuming, large computers can perform millions of these operations in one second. This basic sequence of fetch the instruction, fetch the data, execute the instruction, and store the results is fundamental to most computers.

8-BIT, 16-BIT, AND 32-BIT COMPUTERS

Computers are sometimes referred to as being either 8-bit, 16-bit, or 32-bit machines. This terminology refers to the internal design of the particular computer. The internal design is based upon the microprocessor chip used within the computer that acts as the central processing unit, and the electronic circuitry associated with the microprocessor. In general, the CPU in an 8-bit computer can process eight bits at a time, while the CPU in a 16-bit computer can process sixteen bits at a time, and a 32-bit computer can process thirty-two bits at a time.

As has been explained, computers store and process data as a series of electronic bits. These bits are transmitted internally within the circuitry of the computer along a series of lines capable of transmitting electrical impulses. The bits must be transferred from memory to the CPU, from the CPU to memory, from memory to output devices, and from input devices to memory. The lines along which the bits are transmitted are called **busses**. An 8-bit computer utilizes an 8-bit bus, or eight lines, to transmit bits from one location to another, from memory to the CPU, or from the CPU to memory (Figure 8–24). Thus, 8 bits can be moved from memory to the CPU or from the CPU to memory at the same time. In addition, an 8-bit computer often uses an 8-bit bus to transmit data from an input device to memory or from memory to an output device. On 16-bit machines, the bits can be moved from place to place 16 bits at a time using a 16-bit data bus, and on 32-bit machines, the bits are moved 32 bits at a time using a 32-bit data bus.

Generally, the larger the number of bits that are handled at one time, the faster the computer can process data. For example, assume a number in memory occupies four 8-bit bytes. An 8-bit machine would require four steps to transfer the data from memory to the CPU because on the 8-bit data bus, the data in each 8-bit byte would be transferred in individual steps. With a 16-bit machine, there are 16 lines in the data bus. Therefore, only two separate transfers would be necessary. On a 32-bit machine, the entire four bytes could be transferred at one time. The fewer number of transfer steps required, the faster the processing of the data occurs.

The amount of memory which can be addressed by the CPU is also a factor of the bit size of the CPU and computer. The larger the machine, the more positions of main computer memory the machine can address. For example, the maximum amount of memory addressable by most 8-bit computers is 64K RAM. Some 16-bit computers, on the other hand, can address in excess of 512K bytes, and 32-bit machines can typically address in excess of 16 million bytes.

In summary, the determination of whether an 8-bit computer is satisfactory, or whether a 16-bit or 32-bit machine is needed, must be based upon the use of the computer. Eight-bit computers can contain only up to 64K of memory, but may be useful and fast enough for many routine business applications, such as word processing, electronic spreadsheets, or accounting applications. Sixteen-bit computers are widely used today when more complex software requires more than 64K of memory. Thirty-two bit computers are considered very powerful and are useful where complex and time-consuming calculations must be performed — in scientific applications or in applications where there may be several users utilizing the processor unit at one time through computer terminals. A few personal computers, many large minicomputers, and most mainframes are thirty-two bit computers.

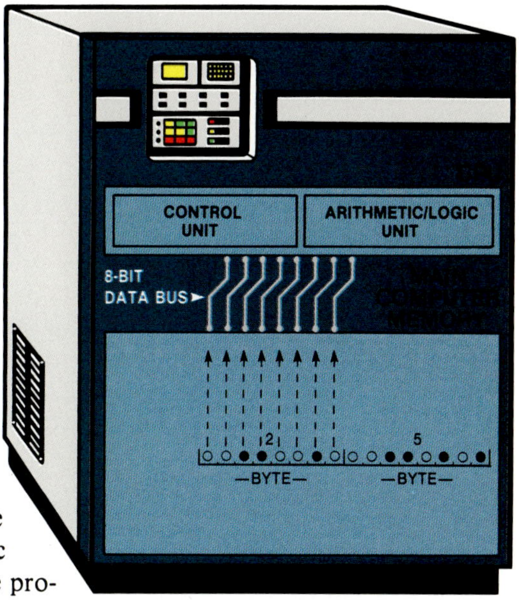

Figure 8–24 In this example, an 8-bit bus connects main computer memory with the CPU. When data is transferred from memory to the CPU or from the CPU to memory, eight bits at a time can be transferred. Thus, if the value 2 is stored using the ASCII representation, the single character can be transferred from memory to the CPU. if the number 25 had to be transferred to the CPU, two steps would be required.

Summary

This chapter has examined the various means used to store and process data on a computer from the standpoint of the internal electronics of the machine. While a detailed understanding of this material is not a prerequisite for computer literacy, and while a further examination of this material would require a reference to a particular computer, the computer literate person should understand the principles involved in storing and processing data electronically on a computer.

Main Computer Memory

The cost of main computer memory today allows personal computers with more than 700K RAM to sit on one's desk. The following pages illustrate manufacturing semiconductor memory.

Figure 8–25 This picture shows an acid bath used when making semiconductor memory.

1

Making Semiconductor Memory

Semiconductor memory is used in most computers today for main computer memory. Its use has coincided with the unbelievable technological growth which has occurred in the electronics field.

The trend toward miniaturization began soon after the development of the transistor. By the mid-1960's, as many as 1,000 different circuit elements could be stored on a small chip. By the mid-1970's, this number had grown to over 15,000 circuit elements. Today, over one million

2

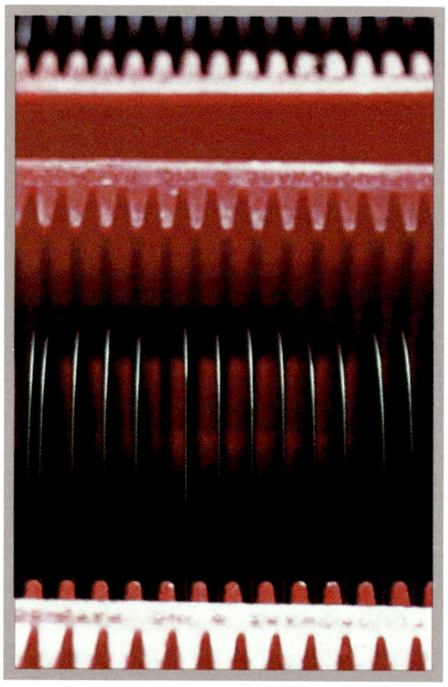

3

Figure 8–26 The production of a memory chip includes a number of technically sophisticated steps. Some of these steps are summarized by the following: **1)** The circuits which are produced are etched on silicon wafers. The first step to make a wafer is to develop very pure silicon crystals; **2)** These crystals are then heated to a temperature of 1420° C., where they become liquified. While the liquid is turning in the crucible on the heating machine, a small "seed" is dipped into the liquid and then is pulled out. Each time the seed is dipped, a little more of the crystal grows on it. Eventually, an ingot about four inches in diameter and about thirty inches in length is grown; **3)** The ingot, after being smoothed, is taken to a diamond saw where it is cut into "wafers." The wafers vary in thickness from 1/91" to 1/50". The wafers are then polished to a very smooth surface on one side. They are now ready for a circuit to be etched on them; **4)** Circuits which are placed on the wafers must be designed by engineers. While some circuits take a month or two to design, others have taken over two years to design. Using light pens and sophisticated terminals, the designers design each of the circuits which will be etched on the chip. Most chips will have 4 - 6 layers on them in order to completely perform the function for which they were designed. After the circuits are designed, a photomask such as shown in the picture is developed. The

4

5

circuit elements can be stored on a chip less than ¼" square; and by the year 2000, 100 billion elements may be stored on a small chip.

One of the reasons for this phenomenal growth is the sophisticated production capabilities developed to build the circuits on these small chips. Whereas twenty years ago circuits were almost completely hand built, today machines such as electron microscopes, diamond saws, heating chambers controlled to ½° C, and other devices allow the chips to be mass-produced cheaply and reliably.

As shown by the pictures on these pages, the manufacturing process requires sophisticated machines to keep the tolerances required by these amazing devices.

10

photomask can be up to 500 times larger than the actual circuit. The engineer can closely scrutinize the mask to be sure it is absolutely correct. The mask is then photographically or electronically reduced to the size of the circuit on the chip; **5)** The wafer of silicon must be placed in ovens at specific temperatures to form oxide and layers of other minerals on it. It is these layers which are "etched" to form the circuits; **6)** After the layers are on the wafer, the photomask for the circuit is carefully placed on the wafer. The registration for the different layers must be within one micrometer, so high-powered microscopes such as shown in the picture are used to ensure proper registration. After ensuring the mask is on properly, the layers on the wafer are exposed to ultraviolet light and then are "washed" in an acid. The portions of the layers not exposed to the ultraviolet light are washed away, leaving a circuit; **7)** The process of oxidizing, masking, exposing to ultraviolet light, and washing continues until all levels are on the wafer and the chip is complete. Each chip is then cut apart from the wafer by a diamond saw, as shown; **8)** The result of this process is a chip, such as this 100 megabit memory chip; **9)** Each chip is then placed in a package containing wires which connect the chip to the "outside world"; **10)** The final circuit is contained in a hard plastic covering with a number of pins to be used for connecting the device to other devices.

8

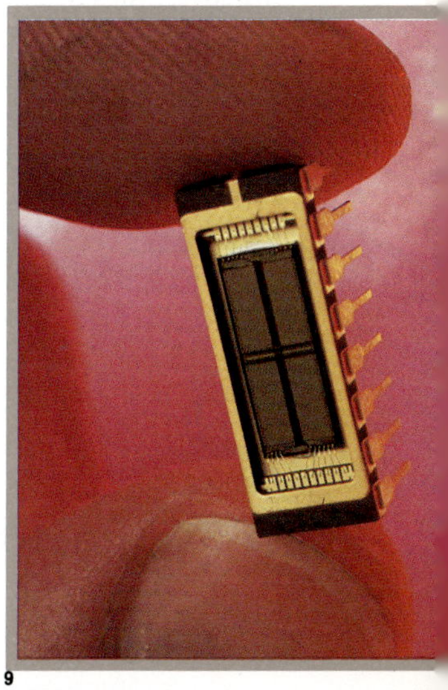

9

6

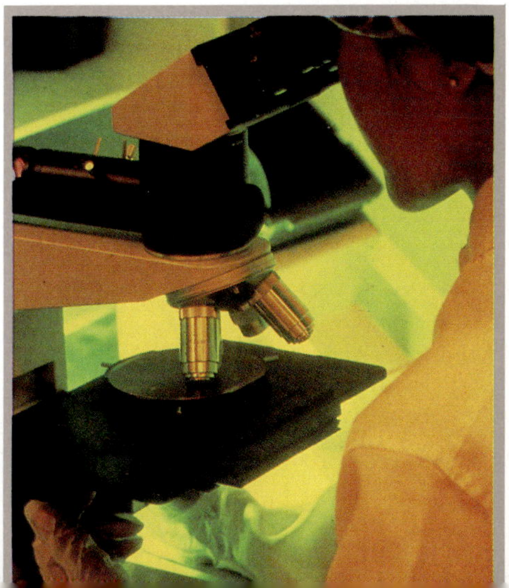

7

CHAPTER SUMMARY

1. Main computer memory and the central processing unit (CPU) are contained in the processor unit.
2. It is the ability of the computer's electronic circuitry to sense the presence or absence of electronic impulses that allows data to be stored in main computer memory.
3. The basic unit for storing data in main computer memory is the bit (binary digit).
4. A bit can represent one of only two values — zero and one. A bit that contains the value zero is said to be "off," while a bit which contains the value one is said to be "on."
5. The determination of whether a bit is "off" or "on" is made by the electronics by either determining the polarity of magnetized material or by measuring whether electricity is flowing along a circuit.
6. To represent characters and numbers in main computer memory, codes are assigned to the various combinations which can be obtained from a series of bits being "on" and "off."
7. Many computers use eight bits, called a byte, for storing data. A byte is a location in main memory consisting of eight adjacent bits.
8. One of the most widely used coding systems to represent data in main memory is the American Standard Code for Information Interchange, called the ASCII code.
9. When a letter is entered into main memory from a keyboard, the electronic circuitry interprets the character and stores the character in memory as a series of bits being "on" and "off."
10. The ASCII code uses the rightmost seven bits of the 8-bit byte to represent numbers, letters of the alphabet, and special characters. The leftmost bit of the eight bits is not used.
11. When the ASCII code is used, each digit in a numeric value is stored in a single byte.
12. The place values in a byte using the ASCII code are based on the binary number system.
13. To facilitate the communication of the ASCII codes and for ease of reference, many technical manuals contain charts which specify not only the binary representation for the characters but also the decimal representation as well. The decimal representation converts the binary representation of the bits in the byte to a decimal number.
14. The size of main computer memory is normally expressed in terms of the number of 1,024 byte units of memory found in the processor unit. The letter K is used to represent 1,024.
15. The size of memory on personal computers varies from 4K to 512K or more. Large mainframes contain up to 64 million positions (64 megabytes).
16. The size of main computer memory may determine what software can run on a computer.
17. A memory address is a number that identifies each byte in main computer memory.
18. When a computer instruction is executed which causes a character to be read into main computer memory, the instruction must specify where in memory the character is to be placed by specifying the address.
19. The ability to store data at unique addresses within main computer memory allows use of the data in subsequent operations.
20. A group of numbers or letters entered as a field are stored in adjacent, addressable locations in memory.
21. When a field is processed, computer instructions must specify not only the address of the data but also the number of characters to be processed.
22. The ability to store data in main computer memory at specific addresses and then reference the data by these addresses forms the basis of the internal operations of a computer.
23. Once data is stored at a location in memory, it will remain there until some other data is explicitly placed into the same location.
24. A single set of instructions which references particular locations in main computer memory can be used to process many different records which would be stored in the same locations as they are processed.
25. On most computers, data is retained in memory as long as the computer has electrical power.
26. The process of reading data into memory replacing previous data at the same location or moving data from one location to another, replacing the data at the second location, is called destructive read in.
27. A coding scheme for mainframes is the Extended Binary Coded Decimal Interchange Code (EBCDIC).
28. When EBCDIC is used, each 8-bit byte is divided into two portions — the zone portion and the digit portion.
29. Numeric values are represented in EBCDIC with all the zone bits "on" and the proper combinations of bits in the digit portion "on" to represent the particular numeric value.
30. Many computers store numbers using a variety of different methods, all based upon the binary number

system. One method uses two adjacent bytes to form a sixteen-bit word.

31. A numeric value stored as a binary number is often referred to as an integer value because the number is a whole number, and the binary representation of the number is an exact value of the number.

32. Magnetic core memory consisted of small, ring-shaped pieces of metal that could be magnetized, or polarized, in one of two directions.

33. Semiconductor memory, which is used in virtually all computers, consists of transistors etched into a semiconductor material such as silicon.

34. A microsecond is a millionth of a second. A nanosecond is a billionth of a second. Access to data stored in semiconductor memory is measured in nanoseconds.

35. RAM stands for Random Access Memory. Data can be written into and read from RAM.

36. ROM stands for Read Only Memory. Data or programs are stored in ROM when the memory is manufactured, and they cannot be altered.

37. PROM means Programmable Read Only Memory. PROM acts the same as ROM except data can be stored into the memory by the user prior to being assembled into the computer.

38. EPROM, which is Erasable Programmable Read Only Memory, can be erased and reprogrammed through the use of special ultraviolet devices.

39. The CPU consists of two major components: the arithmetic/logic unit and the control unit. The arithmetic/logic unit performs arithmetic and logic operations. The control unit directs and coordinates all of the activities on the computer.

40. A machine language instruction is one which the electronics in the CPU can interpret and execute.

41. A machine language instruction generally consists of three parts: a) Operation code; b) Number of characters to be processed; c) Main memory addresses of the data to be processed.

42. The operation code is a unique value, often stored in the first byte of the instruction, which indicates what operation is to occur when the instruction is executed.

43. The main memory addresses of the fields involved in the operation must be specified in the instruction to enable the circuitry in the CPU to identify where in main memory the data to be processed is located.

44. An instruction register is an area of memory within the control unit of the CPU which can store a single instruction at a time.

45. The terminology 8-bit, 16-bit, or 32-bit computer refers to the internal design of the microprocessor chip and associated electronic circuitry in a computer.

46. A bus is the line on which bits are transmitted between memory and the CPU, between input devices and memory, and between memory and output devices.

47. An 8-bit bus can transmit eight bits at one time.

48. Sixteen-bit computers can process 16 bits at one time, and 32-bit computers can process 32 bits at one time.

49. Generally, the more bits that can be processed at one time, the faster the computer can process data.

KEY TERMS

ASCII code 8.2
American Standard Code for Information Interchange 8.2
Arithmetic/logic unit 8.14
Binary digit 8.1
Bit 8.1
Busses 8.16
Byte 8.2
Central processing unit (CPU) 8.1
Control unit 8.14
Destructive read in 8.9
Digit portion of the byte 8.9
EBCDIC 8.9
EPROM 8.13
Erasable programmable read only memory 8.13
Extended Binary Coded Decimal Interchange Code 8.9
Field 8.7
Instruction register 8.15
Integer 8.12
Machine language instruction 8.15
Magnetic core memory 8.12
Main computer memory 8.1
Memory address 8.6
Microseconds 8.13
Nanoseconds 8.13
Operation code 8.15
PROM 8.13
Processor unit 8.1
Programmable read only memory 8.13
RAM 8.13
ROM 8.13
Random access memory 8.13
Read only memory 8.13
Semiconductor memory 8.12
Transistors 8.13
Zone portion of the byte 8.9

REVIEW QUESTIONS

1. What is the basic unit for storing data in memory? How does it store data?
2. Define the term byte. For what is a byte used?
3. What is the ASCII code? Draw representations in ASCII for the number 7 and the letters A, Q, and Y.
4. Illustrate by means of a string of zeroes and ones the value RT9 using the ASCII code.
5. Designate the decimal values of the ASCII letters B, G, and L. Designate the decimal values of the special characters $, *, and #.
6. What does the letter K stand for when referencing main computer memory? What is the significance of the amount of main memory a computer has?
7. Describe how a group of characters entered into the computer as a field are stored in main computer memory. Illustrate through the use of a diagram the letters HELP as they would be stored using the ASCII code beginning at main computer memory address 45663.
8. What makes it possible for one set of instructions to process thousands of records?
9. What is EBCDIC? What is the difference between EBCDIC and ASCII?
10. Illustrate the integer value 4562 stored in a sixteen-bit word using a binary representation.
11. Define each of the following terms: RAM; ROM; PROM; EPROM.
12. What are the components of a machine language instruction? Describe the steps which occur in main memory and the CPU when two numbers are added together.
13. Identify the differences between an 8-bit, 16-bit, and 32-bit computer. What is an advantage of a 32-bit computer?

CONTROVERSIAL ISSUES

1. A recent announcement in the trade magazines heralded a new personal computer software package which could perform graphics, word processing, and electronic spreadsheet applications in an integrated manner. Included in the announcement was the information that the software required 640K in order to run. Old-timers in the computer business remember when 8K was enough memory for most computer programs. They claim that the people writing programs today waste memory, causing the user to purchase much more memory than should be required. The programmers today claim that modern, user friendly software is just much more complex than software used to be. What do you think? Is it ridiculous to require a personal computer to have 640K in order to run a program?
2. The American National Standards Institute (ANSI) approved the ASCII code as a standard way in which to represent data in memory. IBM developed EBCDIC for their line of mainframe computers and use it today. Some people claim EBCDIC is a more effective means for data representation because it uses all eight bits in a byte, while ASCII uses only seven. Others say it is more important to have standards. Take a position on this dispute.

RESEARCH PROJECTS

1. Many different types of devices and schemes have been proposed and used for main computer memory. Research the history of main computer memory and prepare a report. Remember to include such factors as the way in which the data was stored, the speed of the memory, any limiting factors with respect to the memory, the amount of memory which could be used, and the cost of the memory.
2. The semiconductor industry is a very competitive industry. It develops both the microprocessors and the memory chips used in most computers today. Not only is the industry competitive in the United States, but significant competition is also found from the Japanese. Prepare a report on the industry as it is found in the United States today, and include an analysis of its competitive stance with respect to the Japanese.

Chapter Nine

Auxiliary Storage

Objectives

- ☐ Identify the primary devices used for personal computer auxiliary storage
- ☐ Describe the manner in which data is stored on diskettes and fixed, hard drives
- ☐ List the speeds and storage capacities of commonly used personal computer auxiliary storage devices
- ☐ Describe the attributes of diskettes and fixed, hard disks which affect the speeds and storage capacities found
- ☐ Identify the types of disk storage used with large computers
- ☐ Define the role of tape storage with respect to both personal computers and large computers
- ☐ Determine the appropriate auxiliary storage device for both personal computers and large computers, given the needs of the application

Auxiliary Storage

Chapter Nine

The ability to store and access data is required when using computers of all types. Main memory is used to temporarily store data while the data is being processed, and **auxiliary storage** is used to store data when it is not being processed on the computer. The data stored on auxiliary storage can be accessed at a later time.

When using a home or personal computer, the amount of data to be stored may be relatively small. For example, the names, addresses, and telephone numbers of several hundred friends or customers of a small business might require 20,000 bytes of auxiliary storage (200 records × 100 characters per record). Large companies, on the other hand, may have need for auxiliary storage devices that can store billions of characters.

The user of modern computers has several categories of auxiliary storage devices from which to choose. For the personal computer user, there are diskettes, hard disk, and cassette tape. For the large computer user, magnetic tape, removable disk, and fixed disk are used. Within each category of auxiliary storage, devices are available in different configurations. The configurations are based upon storage capacity, the speed at which data can be accessed, and, of course, cost.

It is the purpose of this chapter to review the various types of auxiliary storage devices and media that are available, and discuss the characteristics, advantages, and disadvantages of each type.

Diskettes

In the early 1970's IBM introduced a new medium for storing data. This medium consisted of a circular piece of thin plastic material, approximately eight inches in diameter, that was coated with an oxide material similar to that used on magnetic tape. The circular piece of plastic, called a disk, was enclosed in a square protective jacket with a cut out so that the magnetic surface was exposed (Figure 9-2). When inserted in the appropriate hardware device, the disk was rotated inside the protective jacket, allowing keyed data or data from main computer memory to be stored on the rotating disk. Once data was stored on the disk, it could be read from the disk into main computer memory. This new medium for input and auxiliary storage was called a **diskette**, or **floppy disk**. These terms are used interchangeably.

One of the first uses for the diskette was data entry. The early diskettes, which could store approximately 250,000 characters, gained acceptance in installations

Figure 9-2 A floppy disk, or diskette, consists of the disk enclosed within a protective jacket usually made of a vinyl material. The liner of the diskette is essentially friction-free so that the disk can turn freely, but the liner does contact the disk and keep it clean. The magnetic surface of the diskette, which is exposed through the window in the jacket, allows data to be stored. The large hole (hub) in the diskette is used to mount the diskette in the disk drive. The small hole is used to indicate to the disk drive where to store data.

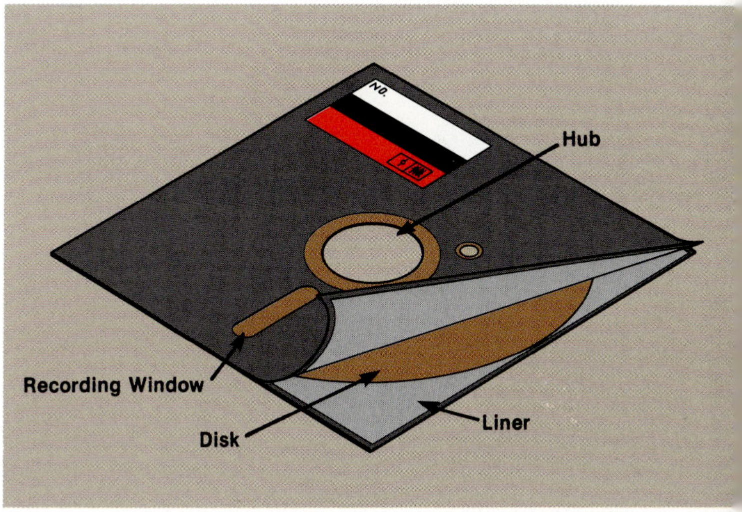

that had previously used punched cards. In addition, small business computers and word processing systems began using the diskette as the principle means of auxiliary storage.

When personal computers were developed, the computer manufacturers adopted the diskette, together with cassette tape, as the primary medium for auxiliary storage because it was convenient, reliable, and relatively low cost. Today, the diskette, or floppy disk, is used as a principle auxiliary storage medium with many home, personal, and small business computers (Figure 9-3).

Storing data on a diskette

Diskettes are now available in a number of different sizes. Although the original 8-inch diskette is still used, most personal computers use a diskette 5 1/4 inches in diameter. Even smaller sized diskettes (approximately 3 1/2 inches in diameter) are also available.

Regardless of the size of the diskette, however, the method of storing data is essentially the same. Data is stored on a diskette in tracks. A **track** is a very narrow recording band forming a full circle around the diskette (Figure 9-4). The width of this recording band depends on the number of tracks on the diskette. Each recording band is separated by a very narrow blank gap. Tracks are established by the disk drive using the diskette. The tracks are not visible when looking at the diskette.

Figure 9-3 (above) In this picture, a floppy disk is being inserted into the disk drive located in the side of the Apple IIc computer.

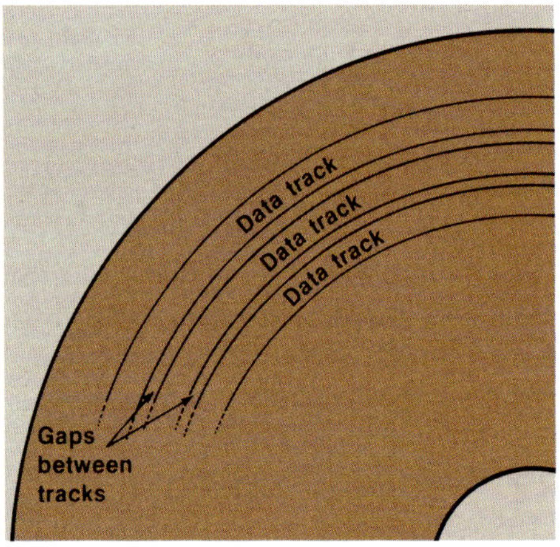

Figure 9-4 (right) Each track on a diskette is a narrow, circular concentric band around the diskette. Each data track is separated by a small gap.

The number of tracks that a diskette drive (also called a floppy disk drive) writes on a diskette varies from manufacturer to manufacturer. The two most commonly found configurations are 40 tracks and 80 tracks. When 40 tracks are recorded on a diskette, the tracks are numbered from 0 to 39 (Figure 9-5).

To read data stored on a diskette or to store data on a diskette, the diskette is inserted in a disk drive. The large center hole fits over a hub mechanism which positions the diskette in the unit. The disk within the protective covering is rotated at approximately 300 revolutions per minute. To read or write data, a read/write head in the disk drive rests on the surface of the rotating disk, sensing or generating electronic impulses representing bits to be read or recorded. Characters are stored on a diskette as bytes in the same manner as they are stored in main computer memory (see Chapter 8). To read data from the different tracks, the read/write head moves from track to track.

Figure 9-5 (below) On a diskette containing 40 tracks, the outside track is called track 0, and the inside track is called track 39. The distance between track 0 and track 39 on a 5 1/4 inch diskette is less than one inch.

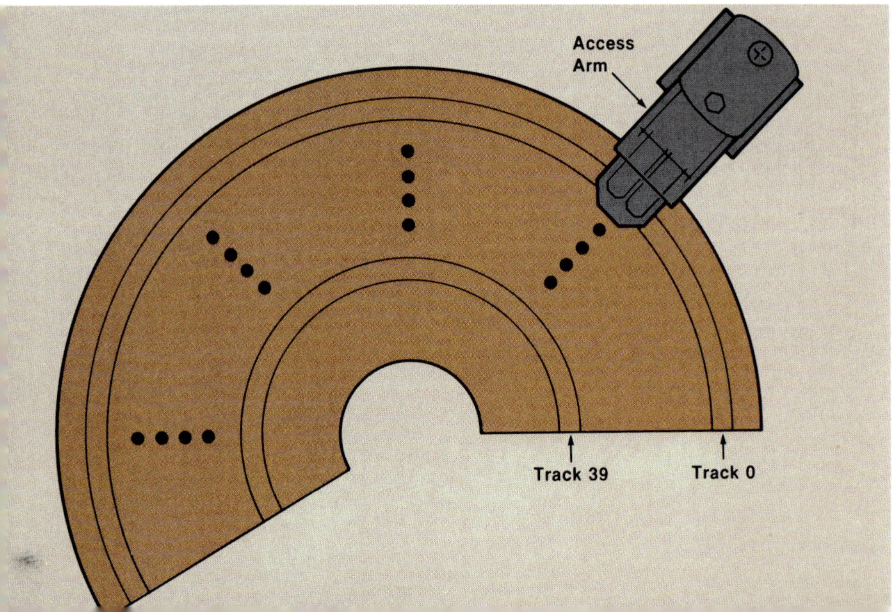

Storage capacity of diskettes

Diskette drives and the related diskettes can provide storage capacities that vary from approximately 80,000 characters per diskette to approximately three million characters per diskette (Figure 9–6). The number of characters that can be stored on a diskette by a disk drive is dependent upon three basic factors: 1) The number of sides of the diskette used; 2) The recording density of the bits on a track; 3) The number of tracks on the diskette. The actual number of characters that are stored on the diskette is dependent upon these factors plus the formatting of the disk which is performed by software. Each of these elements is discussed in the following paragraphs.

Figure 9–6 The storage capacity of a diskette depends upon the type of drive being used and the size of the diskette. Diskette drives with many different capabilities are available.

Single and double sided diskettes

The first diskettes and drives were designed so that data could be recorded on only one side of the diskette. The drives were called **single-sided drives**. Similarly, diskettes on which data can be recorded on one side only are called single-sided diskettes.

To increase storage capacity, diskettes were manufactured so that data could be recorded on both sides of the diskette. Initially, to record on the second side of the diskette, it was necessary to turn the diskette over and insert it back into the drive because the drive could only read and write one side of the diskette at a time. Today, diskette drives are available that have read/write heads to record and read data on both sides of the diskette when it is inserted into the drive (Figure 9–7). Diskettes and drives that can read and write data on both sides of the diskette are called **double-sided**. The use of double-sided drives and diskettes approximately doubles the number of characters that can be stored on the diskette.

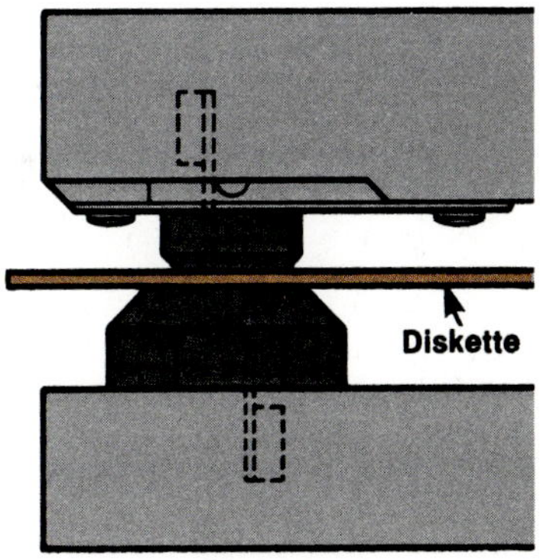

Figure 9–7 When a double-sided diskette is used, two heads are used — one for the top side and one for the bottom side. As the diskette spins, data stored on the diskette comes under the heads. The heads move back and forth (left to right and right to left in this drawing) in order to reference the tracks on the diskette.

Recording density

Another important factor when evaluating floppy disk drives is the recording density provided by the drive. The **recording density** is stated in technical literature as the number of bits that can be recorded on a diskette in a one-inch circumference of the innermost track on the diskette. This measurement is referred to as **bits per inch (bpi).**

For the user, the diskettes and drives are identified as being either **single density (SD)** or **double density (DD)**. These terms refer to the bits per inch that can be recorded. The bits per inch which identify single and double density varies from manufacturer to manufacturer. As an example, however, one manufacturer specifies that single density drives can store 2,768 bits per inch on the innermost track. Double density drives, according to this manufacturer, can store 5,876 bits per inch. As might be expected, double density drives and the related diskettes are more expensive than single density drives and diskettes.

With improved technology, it is anticipated that recording densities in excess of 10,000 bits per inch will be possible.

TYPE OF DISK DRIVE (5¼")	BITS PER INCH	TRACKS PER INCH	TRACKS/SIDE	TRACKS/DISK
Single Sided, Single Density	2,768 bpi	48	40	40
Single Sided Double Density	5,876 bpi	48	40	40
Double Sided Double Density	5,876 bpi	48	40	80
Double Sided Double Density Double Track	5,876 bpi	96	80	160

Figure 9–8 This chart illustrates some of the recording characteristics of diskette drives.

Number of tracks on a diskette

The third factor that influences the potential number of characters that can be stored on a diskette by a drive is the number of tracks where data can be recorded on the diskette. The number of tracks is dependent upon the drive being used. Many drives record 40 tracks on the surface of the diskette. Other drives, however, can record 80 tracks on the diskette. These drives are sometimes called **double track drives**. The diskette used is dependent upon the recording capabilities of the drive.

Although 40 tracks are actually available for recording data on the diskette, a common measure of the number of tracks a drive can record is **tracks per inch.** This measurement describes the number of tracks which would be recorded if the recording surface of the diskette was one inch wide. For example, most drives which record 40 tracks per diskette record the tracks at a density of 48 tracks per inch. Thus, the recording surface of the diskette is less than one inch wide. Track densities for double track drives that store 80 tracks on the diskette are 96 tracks per inch.

The chart in Figure 9-8 illustrates a few of the characteristics of diskette drives. While not exhaustive, this chart gives some indication of the recording capabilities of diskette drives.

Hard and soft sectors

Each track on a diskette is divided into sectors. Sectors are the basic unit for diskette storage. When data is read from a diskette, a minimum of one full sector is read. When data is stored on a diskette, one full sector is written at one time.

Disk drives and the associate diskettes are classified as either hard-sectored or soft-sectored, depending upon how the drive keeps track of where the sectors are located on the diskette. A **hard-sectored diskette** has a hole in front of each sector, normally near the center of the diskette (Figure 9-9). These holes provide timing information to the drive. Hard-sectored diskettes will always contain the same number and size of sectors because the sectors are defined by the sector holes. Therefore, the exact storage capacity of a hard-sectored diskette can always be determined. For example, a hard-sectored diskette that contains 16 sectors with 256 bytes per sector will always be used to store a maximum of 4096 bytes per track (16 × 256). When the diskette is two-sided and contains 40 tracks per side, the total storage capacity of the diskette is 327,680 bytes (4096 × 40 × 2).

Soft-sectored diskettes, on the other hand, have a single index hole in the diskette which indicates the beginning of the track (Figure 9–10). The number of sectors per track and the number of characters that can be stored in each sector is defined by a control program used with the computer. The process of defining the number and size of sectors on a soft-sectored diskette is called **formatting the diskette.**

A diskette is formatted based upon the capabilities of the disk drive and the specifications in the software which does the formatting. For example, using a drive with double density, two-sided capabilities (Figure 9–11), a diskette could be formatted by one program as 40 tracks, 16 sectors per track, and 256 bytes per sector, for a total storage capacity of 327,680 characters (40 × 16 × 256 × 2). Using the same disk drive, the same diskette could be formatted by another program with 40 tracks, 9 sectors per track, and 512 bytes per sector, for a total of 368,640 characters stored on the diskette (Figure 9–12).

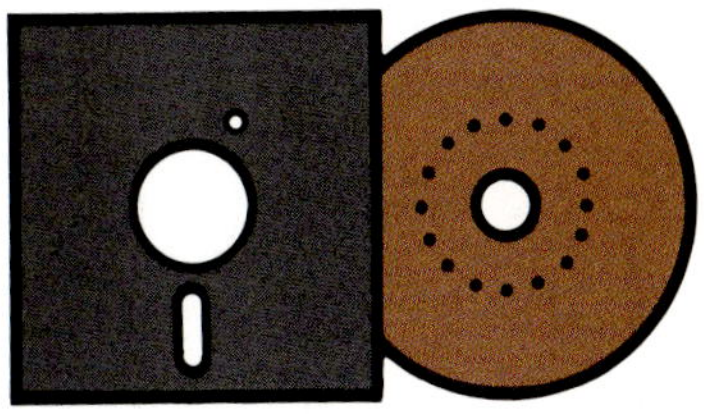

Figure 9–9 The disk within the protective jacket of a hard sectored diskette contains sixteen holes, evenly spaced around a circle on the disk. The holes indicate to the disk drive exactly where a sector begins on the disk itself.

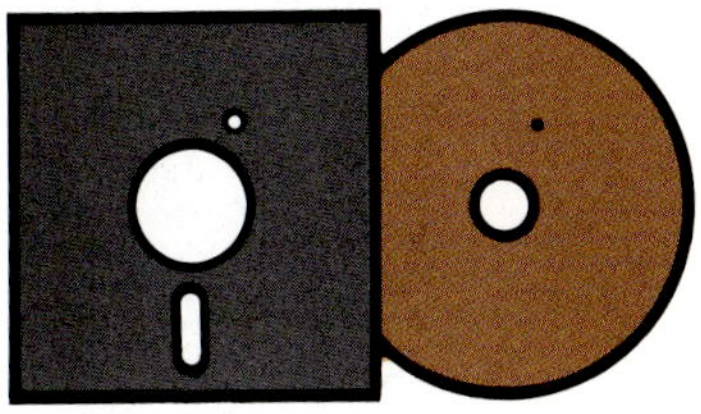

Figure 9–10 (above) On a soft sectored diskette, only a single hole is contained in the disk. The drive can use the hole to find the beginning of a track. The number of sectors on a track and the number of bytes in each sector is determined by the software which formats the diskette.

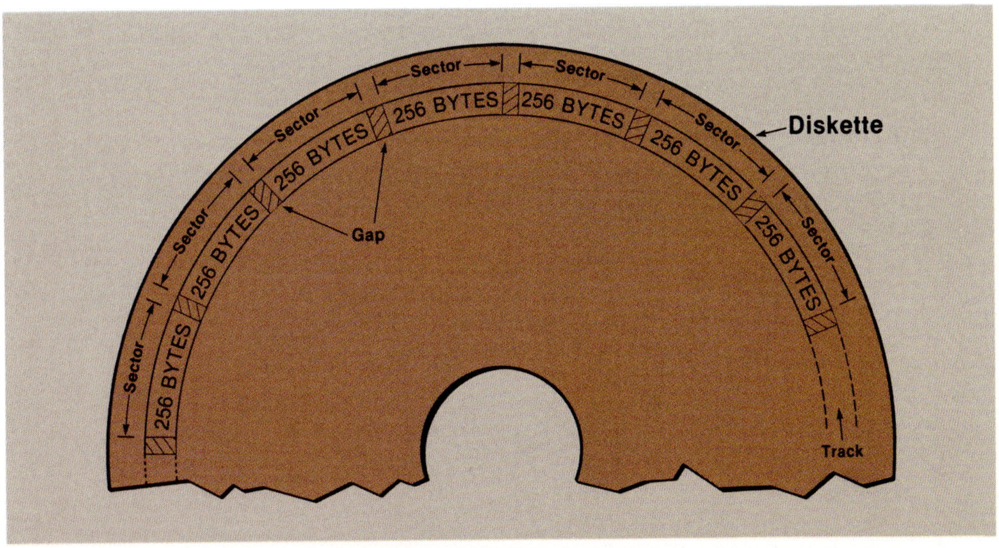

Figure 9–11 (left) In this drawing, a soft sectored diskette is formatted with sixteen sectors per track and 256 bytes per sector. A gap appears between each sector. This is required so the disk drive can determine where a sector starts and stops on the track.

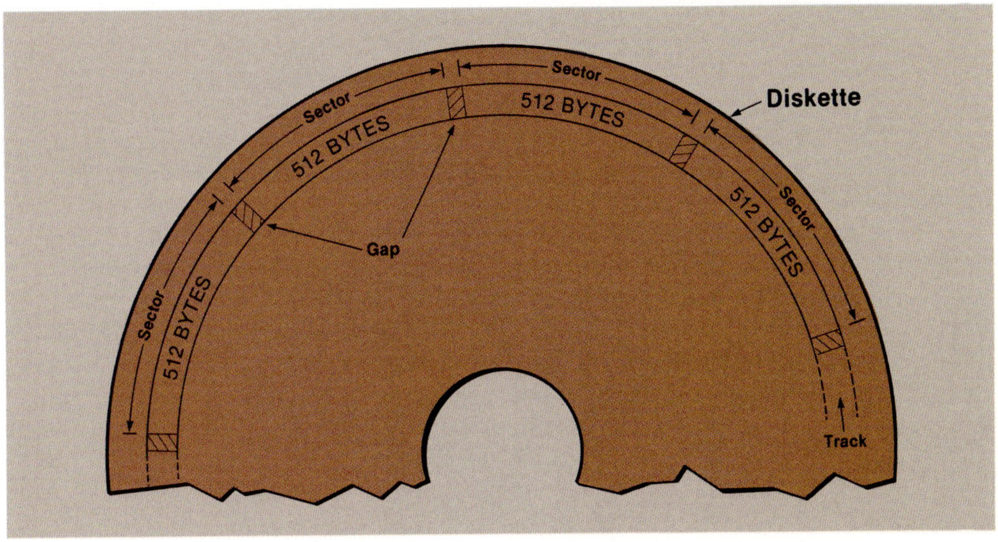

Figure 9–12 In this drawing, the soft sectored disk is formatted with 9 sectors per track, and each sector contains 512 bytes. Since there are fewer sectors per track, there are fewer gaps per track than when the diskette is formatted as shown in Figure 9–11, leading to more efficient use of the storage space available on the diskette.

The determination of the exact number of characters that will be stored on a diskette, then, is dependent upon whether one or two sides of the diskette are used for recording, the number of tracks that are written on the diskette when it is formatted, the recording density, and the number and size of the sectors as defined when the diskette is formatted by software. The table in Figure 9–13 illustrates a few of the many combinations which can be found with diskette drives and the associated diskettes.

TYPE OF DISK DRIVE (5¼")	TRACKS PER SIDE	SECTORS PER TRACK	BYTES PER SECTOR	TOTAL CHARACTERS
Single Sided Single Density	40	16	128	81,920
Single Sided Double Density	40	16	256	163,840
Double Sided Double Density	40	16	256	327,680
Double Sided Double Density	40	9	512	368,640
Double Sided Double Density Double Track	80	16	256	655,360

Figure 9–13 This table shows a few of the many configurations that are available when formatting a diskette, depending upon the drives and software being used. The formula to determine the number of characters that can be stored on a diskette is bytes per sector × sectors per track × tracks per side × number of sides.

Access time

Data stored in sectors on a floppy disk must be retrieved and placed into main computer memory in order to be processed. The time required to access and retrieve the data (called the **access time**) can be important in some applications.

The access time for a floppy disk drive is dependent upon four factors: 1) The time it takes to position the read/write head over the proper track; 2) The time it takes for the sector containing the data to rotate under the read/write head (called **latency**); 3) The time required for the read/write head to be placed in contact with the disk (called the **settling time**); 4) The time required to transfer the data from the disk to main computer memory (called the **data transfer rate**). The access time for floppy disk varies from about 175 milliseconds (one millisecond equals 1/1000 of a second) to approximately 300 milliseconds. What this means to the user is that, on the average, data stored in a single sector on a diskette can be retrieved in approximately 1/5 to 1/3 of a second.

The microfloppy

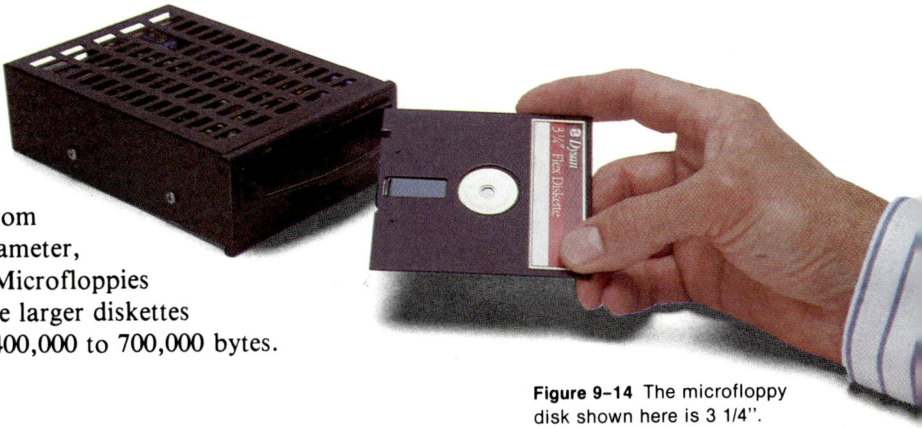

A number of manufacturers have introduced diskettes smaller than 5 1/4 inches. These diskettes, which vary in size from 3 1/4 inches to approximately 4 inches in diameter, are called **microfloppy disks** (Figure 9-14). Microfloppies share many of the same characteristics of the larger diskettes and have storage capacities in the range of 400,000 to 700,000 bytes.

Figure 9-14 The microfloppy disk shown here is 3 1/4". The maker of this disk, Dysan, calls it a "flex diskette."

Hard disks for personal computers

To provide large auxiliary storage capabilities for home and personal computers, hard disks are used. **Hard disks** consist of one or more rigid metal platters coated with a metal oxide material that allows data to be magnetically recorded on the surface of the platters (Figure 9-15). The oxide material used is very similar to that used on floppy disks.

A variety of hard disk drives have been developed. Some hard disk auxiliary storage units contain disks which are removable. Other auxiliary storage units contain disks that are fixed, that is, permanently mounted in the storage unit.

A type of hard, fixed disk drive called a **Winchester disk** is often used with personal computers. The term Winchester originated from a code name in the early 1970's for a new type of disk drive developed by IBM. These disks had the following characteristics: 1) The metal disks, the read/write heads, and the mechanism for moving the heads across the surface of the disk were enclosed in a sealed case with air continuously filtered and circulated through the enclosure to prevent contamination (Figure 9-16); 2) The disks rotated at a very high rate of speed, typically 3,600 revolutions

Figure 9-15 A fixed, hard disk consists of one or more disk platters such as being held by the technician in this picture. Each side of the platter is coated with a metal oxide substance that allows data to be magnetically stored. These platters range in diameter from 3 1/2 inches to 14 inches, depending upon the drive. The technician is wearing clean room garments which are designed to keep contamination to a minimum.

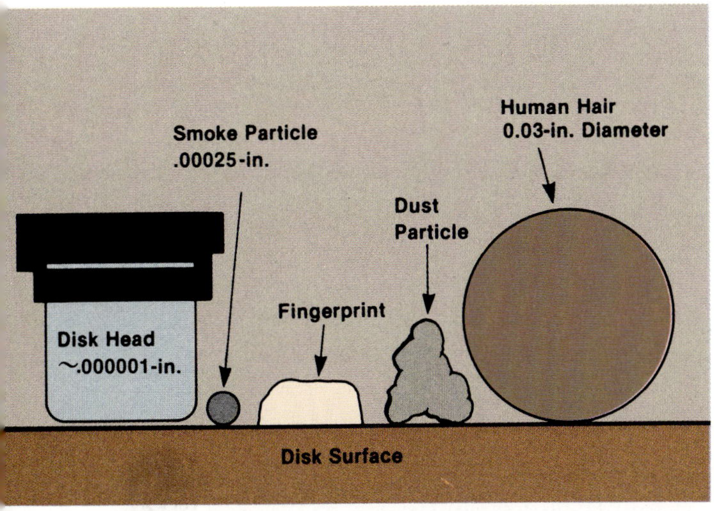

Figure 9-16 This drawing illustrates the head clearance between a flying disk head and the disk surface (1 millionth of an inch). With these tolerances, contamination such as a smoke particle, fingerprint, dust particle, or human hair could render the drive unusable. Therefore, sealed Winchester disk drives are designed to minimize contamination.

per minute; 3) The disks provided relatively high storage capacities and fast access time.

The original Winchester disks were 14 inches in diameter. Subsequent to their introduction, smaller diameter disks were developed. The first were 8 inches in diameter, followed by 5 1/4 inch disks, and even more recently, 3 1/2 inch Winchester disks have become available. For home and personal computers where large storage capacities are needed, the 5 1/4 inch or 3 1/2 inch Winchester disks are most often used.

Characteristics of hard, fixed disks

Storage of data on hard, fixed disks (sometimes called **rigid disks**) is similar to that on floppy disks in that data is recorded on a series of tracks. The tracks can be divided into sectors when the disk is formatted.

Figure 9–17 This picture of a fixed, hard disk drive illustrates the access arm and the read/write heads which are over the surface of the disk. The heads shown here are called Whitney heads (the triangular design). These heads are extremely stable and can read and write tracks very close together on the surface of the disk.

Each disk drive contains a spindle on which one or more disk platters are mounted. The spindle will rotate the disk platters at a high rate of speed, commonly 3,600 revolutions per minute. In order to write data on the surface of the spinning disk platter or to read data stored on the disk platters, the disk drives are designed with **access arms**, or **actuators** (Figure 9–17). The access arms or actuators contain one or more **read/write heads** per disk surface on which data can be recorded (Figure 9–18). These read/write heads "float" on a cushion of air and do not actually touch the surface of the disk. The distance between the head and the surface varies from approximately one millionth of an inch to 1/2 millionth of an inch.

When reading data from the disk, the read head senses the magnetic spots that are recorded serially on the disk along the various tracks and transfers the data to main computer memory. When writing, the data is transferred from main computer memory and is stored as magnetic spots on the tracks on the recording surface of one or more of the disks. As the disk rotates at a high rate of speed, the read/write heads move in and out over the surface of the disk (called **flying heads**) and record or read data.

Figure 9–18 The read/write heads on the end of the access arms in this picture are used to read and write data on each of the surfaces of the disk. The top surface is not used for storing data.

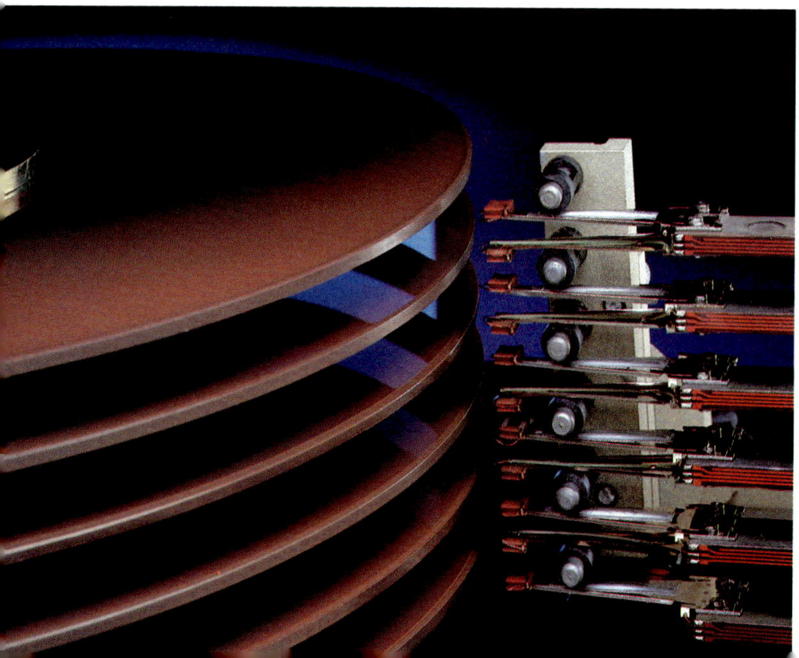

Besides the size of the disk platter itself, several other variations are found on hard disk drives. First, the number of platters permanently mounted on the spindle in the drive can vary. The number of platters for 5 1/4 inch drives varies between one and four platters. On many of the drives, each surface of a platter can be used to store data. Thus, if one platter is used in the drive, two surfaces are available for data. If two platters are used, four sets of read/write heads are used to record and read data from the four surfaces, and so on. Naturally, the more platters, the more data that can be stored on the drive.

In addition, a number of different techniques are used when writing data on the disk. Because of these different techniques, a wide variety of recording densities are found on fixed disk drives. For example, manufacturers list 6,270 bpi, 6,006 bpi, 7,900 bpi, 9,036 bpi, and 9,300 bpi as the recording densities for different models of Winchester disk drives. The number of tracks per inch varies as well, ranging in these same models as 172 tpi, 500 tpi, 256 tpi, 360 tpi, and 345 tpi.

Because of the widespread variations in hardware configurations, it is difficult to generalize about the storage capacities of fixed, hard disks except to say that 5 1/4 inch drives range in storage capabilities from just over 5 million characters to approximately 140 million characters. Drives of the 3 1/2 inch size store in the range of just over 5 million characters to about 40 million characters.

To illustrate a "typical" drive found on a personal computer, however, one drive widely used contains two nonremovable 5 1/4 inch disks. Since each surface can be used for recording data, there are four read/write heads. A single disk surface contains 306 tracks (recorded at a density of 345 tracks/inch). Therefore, a total of 1,224 tracks (306 × 4) are available.

When the disk is formatted (hard, fixed disks are formatted in the same manner as soft-sectored floppy disks), 17 sectors per track are established, with 512 bytes per sector. As a result of this configuration, 10,653,696 bytes can be stored on the disk.

In addition to a larger storage capacity than floppy disks, hard disks provide a faster access time as well. The typical access time is approximately 25 milliseconds, which is much faster than floppy disk drives.

Figure 9-19 The computer user here is inserting a disk cartridge used in conjunction with an IBM Personal Computer.

Disk cartridge

Another form of auxiliary storage available for use with personal computers is the **disk cartridge** (Figure 9-19). One type of disk cartridge contains one or more hard disks housed in a cartridge that can be inserted and removed from a disk drive (Figure 9-20). Cartridge sizes include 5 1/4 inches and 3.9 inches. Cartridges can typically store from 6 to 12 megabytes. Unlike fixed, hard disk, the cartridges can be removed, providing greater flexibility in meeting auxiliary storage requirements.

Disk cartridges are used with personal computers for three primary purposes: 1) As standard auxiliary storage for storing active files; 2) To back up floppy disks and hard disks; that is, make copies of existing files in case the original files are accidentally destroyed; 3) For archival purposes; that is, to maintain records of data which must be retained for reference purposes or for governmental purposes.

Figure 9-20 This picture shows a cutaway disk cartridge being inserted into the disk drive. In this example, a single disk platter is contained in the cartridge.

Half-height disk drives

When building a floppy or hard disk drive into a personal computer, space is at a premium. Therefore, in order to gain more space, disk engineers have designed floppy disk and hard disk drives which are one half the height of the full-size drives. Thus, whereas the height of a full-size 5 1/4 inch floppy disk drive from one manufacturer is 3.25 inches, the height of the **half-height drives** from this manufacturer is 1.63 inches. Similarly, the height of a full-size 5 1/4" Winchester disk drive is 3.38 inches, and the half-height drive is 1.63 inches.

In order to manufacture these drives, newly designed motors and other hardware and electronics had to be developed. Interestingly, as a result of the design efforts, the storage capacities of the half-height drives is almost equal to, and in a few cases exceeds, that of the full-size drives. It is projected that the use of half-height drives will become as widespread as the use of full-size drives.

Figure 9–21 The tape cartridge being inserted in this Rexon high-speed streaming cartridge-tape drive is used to back up 20 megabyte hard disk drives. The tape moves in the cartridge at a rate of 90 inches per second when being read or written upon.

Disk backup on tape cartridges

It is important that **backup copies** of all files and programs stored on auxiliary storage be made in case the original copies are accidentally destroyed or become unusable for some reason.

When files or programs are stored on diskettes, the normal method of backup is to make a copy of the diskette; that is, the data on one diskette is copied to another diskette.

When using hard, fixed disks, however, the user is faced with a more serious problem because of the amount of data which can be stored on a single fixed disk. For example, to back up a hard, fixed disk containing 10 million characters, approximately 30 diskettes that could each store 360,000 characters would be required.

The device most often used to back up fixed, hard disks on personal computers is the **streaming cartridge-tape drive** (Figure 9–21). A streaming tape cartridge can contain approximately 450 feet of 1/4 inch tape. This tape cartridge can store 45 million characters. When data is stored on the tape cartridges using streaming cartridge-tape drives, the tape moves continously; it does not start and stop (hence the term streaming). The device stores data very efficiently, yielding the large amount of data which can be stored on the tape. Using a streaming cartridge-tape drive, an entire hard disk containing 20 million bytes can be backed up in approximately four minutes.

Figure 9–22 The tape cassette reader shown here with a home computer can be used for auxiliary storage when slow sequential processing of the data is acceptable.

Cassette tape

The first personal computers utilized **cassette tape**, such as found in audio

tape recorders, for auxiliary storage (Figure 9–22). These units stored both data and programs sequentially on the tape and were very slow and error-prone. Cassette tape recorders are still available for inexpensive auxiliary storage on home computers, although most users prefer floppy disk.

Figure 9–23 The first magnetic disk unit developed by IBM was called the RAMAC. The unit was extremely large and relatively slow by today's standards, but it was the first direct access storage device available to the industry.

AUXILIARY STORAGE FOR LARGE COMPUTERS

Magnetic disk devices are often called **direct access storage devices (DASD)** because of the ability to randomly store and retrieve data stored on disk. On large computers, including both minicomputers and mainframes, disk drives with very large storage capacities capable of very rapid access to data stored on the disk are required. Although rapid access, high capacity disk drives encompass a number of different technologies, they can be divided into two broad categories: 1) Removable disks; 2) Fixed disks. There are many different models of both removable and fixed disks.

Removable disks

Magnetic disk units have been developed over the years using a number of different approaches. One of the first rigid disk units, called RAMAC (RAndoM ACcess), was developed by IBM more than 30 years ago. It consisted of 50 metal platters, each approximately 24 inches in outside diameter (Figure 9–23). The disk drive could store five million characters.

In the early 1960's IBM introduced removable disk packs, which consisted of a number of platters (typically from 5 to 11) attached to a common disk hub. The platters were 14 inches in diameter, and taken as a unit, formed the **removable disk pack**. The packs could be mounted and removed by the computer operator (Figure 9–24).

Disk packs are still used today. Although the amount of data that can be stored on a disk pack varies, one manufacturer provides disk drives that utilize disk packs containing 11 metal platters with 20 recording surfaces. Storage capacity is 200 million characters. With 10 disk drives attached to the computer, two billion characters can be stored on the auxiliary storage of the computer (Figure 9–25).

Figure 9–24 (above) In this picture, the computer operator is mounting a removable disk pack into the disk drive. The ability to remove the disk packs from the drive and replace them with others gives almost unlimited storage. The amount of data that can be processed at one time, however, depends on the number of disk drives that are connected to the processor unit.

Figure 9–25 (left) This installation contains many disk drives which read and write data on removable disk packs.

Figure 9–26 Disk cartridges of varying sizes can be used on minicomputers and small business computers for removable disk storage.

Disk cartridges

Disk cartridges are sometimes used for auxiliary storage on small business computers and minicomputers. Disk cartridges, which can be mounted on and removed from the disk drive, contain one or two rigid disks housed within a container (Figure 9-26). Storage capabilities range from approximately two million to twenty million characters, with an access time of approximately seventy-five milliseconds.

Fixed disks

As the need for larger auxiliary storage capacities evolved, significantly increased recording densities were required. The mechanical precision necessary for the increased densities could not be engineered into the removable disk packs and the associated drives. In addition, the increased densities required a contaminant-free environment for the disk surfaces and disk drive heads.

The next step in the development of disk storage technology, then, was the design of **fixed disks**. With fixed disks, the disks, spindle, and the access mechanism with read and write heads are sealed in an enclosure and permanently mounted in a disk drive. The disks cannot be removed by the computer operator (Figure 9-27).

As an example of this type of device, the IBM 3380 direct access storage unit uses fixed disk technology. It contains two fixed disk spindles in a unit. Using thin film recording technology, the two spindles in the unit can store 2.52 billion bytes of data (2.52 **gigabytes**). Four such units provide a storage capacity of over 10 billion bytes of data. Data can be written onto the disk or read from the disk at approximately three million bytes per second.

Figure 9–27 Row after row of fixed disk drives illustrate the direct access storage requirements of some installations.

Physical organization of data on disk

Data is physically organized in one of two ways on disks used with large computers, depending on the manufacturer and the model disk drive being used. One means is the sector method and the other is the cylinder method.

As with the floppy disks and Winchester disks used with personal computers, the **sector method** for physically organizing data on disks divides each track on the disk surface into individual storage areas called sectors (Figure 9-28). Each sector can contain a specified number of bytes. Data is referenced by indicating the sector where the number is stored.

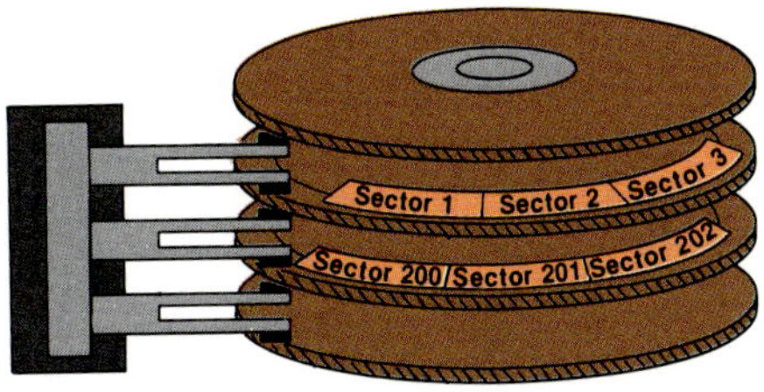

Figure 9-28 The sector method of disk addressing divides each track into a number of sectors. In order to locate data, the particular sector number where the data is stored is specified.

The **cylinder method** uses a cylinder as the basic reference point. On one recording surface of a disk platter, an access arm can reference one track of data. A fixed or removable disk pack can contain up to 20 different tracks, one for each recording surface, that can be referenced by the recording heads on the access arm at each discrete location where the access arm can be positioned. These 20 tracks which can be referenced at one position of the access arm are called a **cylinder**. On each track, the data stored can be divided into one or more physical records. Therefore, in order to physically reference a record stored using the cylinder method, a computer program must specify the cylinder number, the recording surface number, and the record number (Figure 9-29).

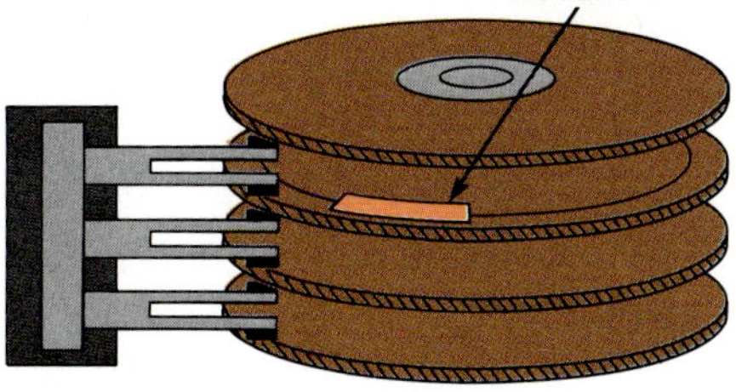

Figure 9-29 With the cylinder concept, the location of a record is determined by the cylinder number, the recording surface number, and the record number. Here, the record is stored on cylinder 10, recording surface 2, and is the first record on that cylinder and surface. Special data stored on each track specifies the beginning of the track so that the first record, second record, third record, and so on, can be identified.

Whether data is stored using the cylinder method or the sector method is determined by the manufacturer of the drive. Many of the latest disk storage units use the sector method. Some manufacturers call this **fixed block architecture.**

MAGNETIC TAPE

Another type of auxiliary storage used with large computer systems is magnetic tape. **Magnetic tape** was first used for storing data in the early 1950's on one of the first Univac computers. The tape was made of flexible metal and was stored on reels. The metal was plated with a thin film of iron, which allowed data to be stored as a series of small magnetized spots. Although the tape provided a compact form of storage, it was extremely heavy and not universally accepted. IBM, in fact, contended at the time that tape was unreliable, untested, and risky; partly, it is said, because their allegations had some elements of truth and partly because the use of magnetic tape threatened the continued use of the 100,000 tons of punched cards IBM sold each year.

Although these early reels of metal tape were capable of storing large amounts of data, it was not until scientists developed a very thin, flexible material called mylar that tape processing gained wide acceptance. This plastic mylar was coated with an iron-oxide which could be magnetized to store data. The oxide-coated mylar tape

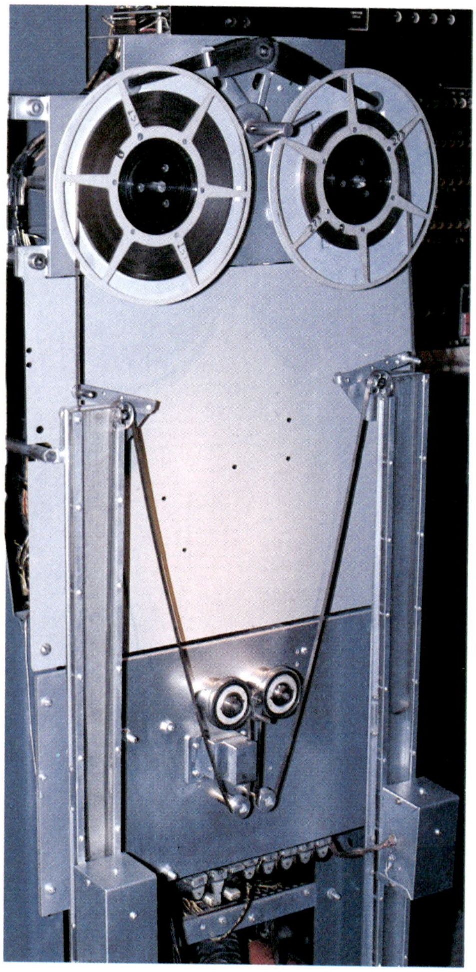

Figure 9-30 One of the first magnetic tape drives developed by IBM is pictured here. This was the first drive to place slack tape in vacuum columns, allowing the tape to be rapidly started and stopped without breaking.

proved to be successful and was soon universally accepted in the computer industry. Many tape drives were developed to read and write data on the tape (Figure 9-30). In the 1950's and early 1960's, magnetic tape was the primary means for storing large amounts of data.

Storing data on magnetic tape

Data is recorded on magnetic tape in the form of magnetic spots that can be read and transferred to main computer memory. The magnetic spots on the tape are organized into a series of horizontal rows called channels. The presence or absence of magnetic spots representing bits in each of the channels is used to represent a given character on the tape.

Several different coding structures are used with magnetic tape, including both ASCII and EBCDIC. The coding structure for **EBCDIC** divides 1/2" tape into nine horizontal channels. A combination of bits in a vertical column which consists of the nine horizontal channels is used to represent characters on the tape (Figure 9-31).

Tape density, which is the number of characters or bytes which can be stored on an inch of tape, varies depending upon the tape drives being used. Common densities are 800 bytes per inch (bpi) and 1,600 bpi, with some devices capable of reading and writing at a density of 6,250 bpi. This high density is advantageous because a large amount of data can be stored on a reel of tape.

Figure 9-31 One of the most common coding structures found on magnetic tape is EBCDIC stored in nine channels on the tape. Eight channels are used to store the bits representing a character. The ninth channel (marked "P" in the drawing) is a parity channel. It is used to ensure the bits are written correctly to form a character by being either "on" or "off" as required to ensure an odd number of "on" bits for each character. For example, for the letter A it is "off" because an A is represented by 3 bits. The parity bit is "on" for the letter C because a C is represented by 4 bits, and the parity bit must be on to ensure an odd number of bits. If an even number of bits are read, then the tape drive indicates an error condition.

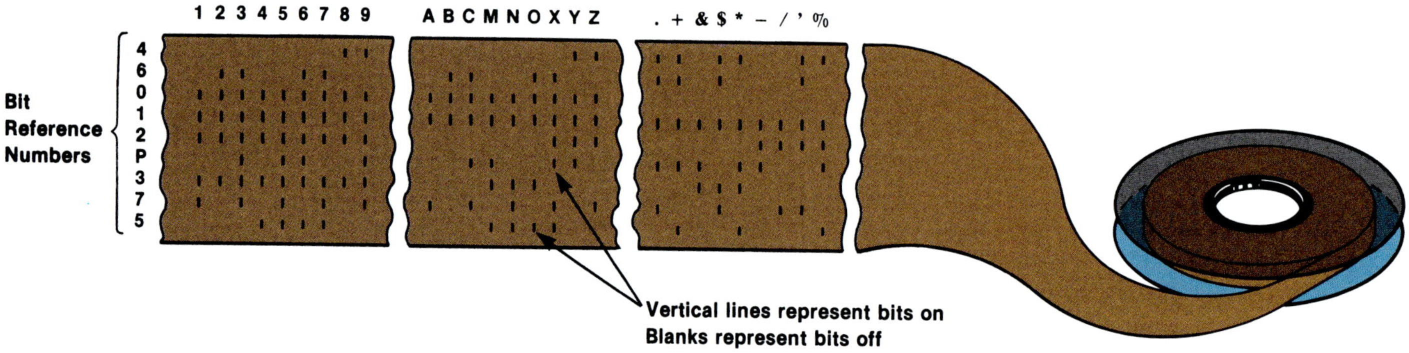

On the reel-to-reel tape drives used with large computers, the tape is transported over read/write heads from a file reel to a take-up reel (Figure 9–32). Depending on the density of the data stored on the tape and the speed at which the tape is moved over the read/write heads, data can be transferred from the tape to main computer memory at rates varying from 15,000 to 1,250,000 characters per second.

Figure 9–32 A series of tape drives is used to store large amounts of data in installations.

Format of records stored on tape

When records are stored on tape, they are stored sequentially. **Sequential organization** means that records are stored one after the other on the tape. Tape records are also read sequentially, one record after another.

Records stored by tape drives used with large computers are separated by an **interblock gap** (Figure 9–33). This gap is used to allow for the starting and stopping of the tape during reading and writing operations. Note that this organization differs from the streaming cartridge-tape drives described earlier in the chapter which do not start and stop as the data is recorded on the tape. Because of the density of the data stored on the tape, the interblock gap may be longer than the portion of tape used to store the record. Thus, much of the tape recording space is wasted.

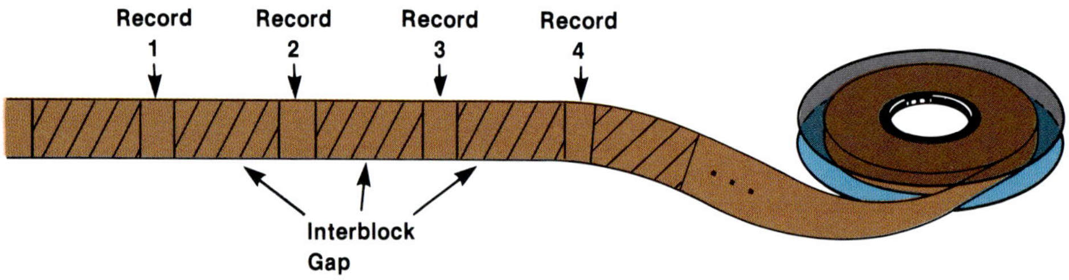

Figure 9–33 Records stored on tape are stored sequentially, and are separated by an interblock gap, which allows for the starting and stopping of the tape drive. The interblock gap is typically .6 inches wide.

To overcome this inefficiency for storing data, **blocked records** are normally used. Blocking refers to placing two or more individual records, called **logical records**, into a block to form a **physical record** (Figure 9–34). Using blocking offers two significant advantages: 1) The tape is used more efficiently, allowing more data to be stored on a reel of tape; 2) Since an entire physical record is read into memory each time data is read from the tape, reading data takes place faster because two or more logical records are read each time data is transferred from the tape to main computer memory.

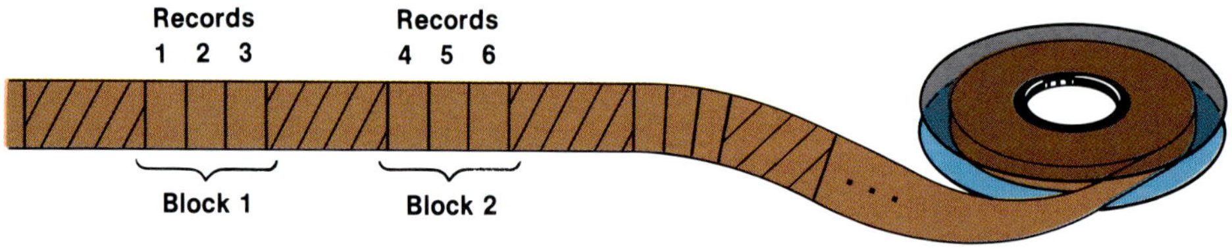

Figure 9–34 Three logical records are stored in a block in this diagram. An entire block of records is brought into main computer memory each time the tape file is read. Therefore, the primary restriction on the number of records stored in a single block is the amount of main computer memory that can be used to store the block of records.

Use of magnetic tape

Since the majority of applications require random access to data stored on auxiliary storage, and since tape allows only sequential retrieval, tape is not widely used today as a primary medium for auxiliary storage. It is used, however, for backup purposes; that is, to store copies of files stored on disk. If, for any reason, the data in the disk files is destroyed, the data in the tape backup file can be used to restore the disk file.

OTHER FORMS OF AUXILIARY STORAGE

While the so-called magnetic media of disk and tape comprise the vast majority of auxiliary storage devices and media, several other means for storing data are used for certain applications. These include bubble memory and optical storage.

Bubble memory

Bubble memory is composed of small magnetic domains (bubbles) formed on a thin single-crystal film of synthetic garnet (Figure 9–35). These magnetic bubbles, which are actually magnetically charged cylinders only a few thousandths of a centimeter in size, can be moved across the garnet film by electrical charges. The presence or absence of a bubble can be used to indicate whether a bit is "on" or "off."

Since data stored in bubble memory is retained when power to the memory is turned off, it can be used for auxiliary storage. Since it is small, lightweight, and does not use very much power, bubble memory is finding a great deal of use as auxiliary storage in portable computers. It is expected that as more portable computers are developed, bubble memory will become more widely used.

Figure 9–35 The magnetic bubble lattice device shown above is .00007 square inches. This section can hold 350 bubbles — or bits of information — a density of 5 million bits per square inch.

Optical disk systems

Optical disk systems are a relatively new means for storing large amounts of data. They utilize a laser reading and writing optical disk device to store data on a disk 12 inches in diameter. The disk is quite similar to video disks. Once the data is written on the disk by the laser beam, the data cannot be erased or changed. Thus, these disks are referred to as write-once, read-often disks.

Large amounts of data can be stored on an optical disk. For example, one manufacturer's drive can store one billion bytes on a single 12-inch disk. The bits are written at a density of 15,000 bits per inch, and there are 15,000 tracks per inch contrasted to 96 tracks per inch on double track floppy disk drives. Thus it can be seen how large amounts of data can be stored on the optical disk.

Optical disk is currently used for storing archival data and data which will remain constant and does not need to be changed.

CHAPTER SUMMARY

1. Auxiliary storage is used to store data that is not being processed on the computer.
2. A diskette, or floppy disk, consists of a plastic disk enclosed within a square protective jacket. The surface of the disk is exposed so data can be stored on it.
3. The diskette, or floppy disk, is used as a primary auxiliary storage medium with many home, personal, and small business computers.
4. Most personal computers use a diskette 5 1/4 inches in diameter. Even smaller diskettes (approximately 3 1/2 inches in diameter) are also available.
5. Data is stored on a diskette in tracks. A track is a very narrow recording band forming a full circle around the diskette.
6. The number of tracks most often found are 40 tracks or 80 tracks per diskette.
7. To read or write data on a diskette, the diskette is placed on the diskette drive. The disk within the protective covering rotates at about 300 revolutions per minute. The read/write head rests on the disk and senses or generates electronic impulses representing bits.
8. Diskette storage capacities range from 80,000 characters to about 3 million characters.
9. The factors dictating diskette storage capacity are: a) The number of sides of the diskette used; b) The recording density of the bits; c) The number of tracks on the diskette. The actual number of characters stored is dependent upon these factors plus the formatting of the disk performed by software.
10. Single-sided drives record data on only one side of a diskette. Double-sided drives record data on both sides of the diskette.
11. The recording density is stated as the number of bits that can be recorded on a diskette in a one inch circumference of the innermost track on a diskette. The measurement is referred to as bits per inch (bpi).
12. Single density diskette drives store about 2,768 bits per inch; double density drives record about 5,876 bpi.
13. Drives which record 80 tracks per inch on a diskette are called double track drives.
14. Each track on a diskette is divided into sectors. Sectors are the basic unit for diskette storage. A minimum of one full sector of data is read from a diskette, and a minimum of one sector is written on a diskette.
15. A hard-sectored diskette contains holes in the diskette indicating where a sector begins. A hard sectored diskette always contains the same size sectors.
16. Soft-sectored diskettes contain one hole indicating where a track begins. The number of sectors and the number of characters in each sector is determined by the software which formats the diskette.
17. The time required to access and retrieve data stored on a diskette is called the access time.
18. Access time is dependent upon four factors: a) The time it takes to position the read/write head on the correct track; b) The time it takes for the data to rotate under the read/write head (latency); c) The time required for the head to be placed in contact with the disk (settling time); d) The time required to transfer the data from the disk to main computer memory (data transfer rate).
19. The access time for floppy disk drives varies from 175 milliseconds to about 300 milliseconds.
20. A microfloppy disk is approximately 3 1/2 inches in diameter and can store from 400,000 to more than 700,000 bytes.
21. A hard disk consists of one or more rigid metal platters coated with a metal oxide material.
22. A Winchester disk has the following characteristics: a) The metal disks, read/write heads, and access arm are enclosed in a sealed case with continuously filtered air; b) The disks rotate at a high rate of speed (typically 3,600 revolutions per minute); c) The disks provide high storage capabilities and fast access times.
23. On personal computers, most hard disks are 3 1/2" or 5 1/4" in diameter.
24. To read and write data on a hard disk, an access arm moves read/write heads in and out, with the heads very close to the surface of the disk. The heads generate or sense electronic impulses, representing bits.
25. The number of platters in a hard disk can vary from one to four. On many disks, both sides of the platters can be used for storing data.
26. Storage capacities for 5 1/4 inch hard disks vary from about 5 million characters to over 140 million characters. Storage for 3 1/2 inch drives varies from about 5 million to about 40 million characters.
27. The typical access time for a hard disk is about 25 milliseconds.
28. Disk cartridges containing hard disks can be inserted into drives used with personal computers.

29. Half-height floppy disk and hard disk drives are one-half the height of full-size drives (1.63 inches compared to about 3.25 inches).

30. Backup copies of a disk are used to restore data on the disk if the data is destroyed for some reason.

31. The normal method for diskette backup is to copy to another diskette. For hard disk, the disk is often copied to a streaming cartridge-tape drive, which writes on 1/4 inch tape that moves continuously when being used.

32. Cassette tape can be used for low-cost, low-speed auxiliary storage on home computers.

33. Disk drives used with large computers can be divided into removable disks and fixed disks.

34. Removable disk packs, which contain between 5 and 11 disk platters, can be mounted and removed from disk drives. A typical removable disk pack can contain up to 200 million characters.

35. With fixed disks, the disks, spindle, and access mechanism with read and write heads are sealed in an enclosure and permanently mounted in the disk drive.

36. The IBM 3380 fixed disk drive can store approximately 2.52 billion bytes (2.52 gigabytes).

37. Data can be read or written using the IBM 3380 disk drive at about 3 million bytes per second.

38. The sector method (identifying the sector number) or the cylinder method (identifying the cylinder, recording surface, and record number) can be used to physically organize and address data stored on disk.

39. The tracks which can be referenced at one position of the access arm are called a cylinder.

40. The sector method is sometimes referred to as fixed block architecture.

41. Data is recorded on magnetic tape as a series of magnetic spots along a horizontal channel. Each spot represents a bit in a coding scheme. EBCDIC on nine track tape is commonly used on large computers.

42. Tape density is the number of characters or bytes which can be stored on one inch of tape. Common densities are 800 bytes per inch, 1,600 bytes per inch, and 6,520 bytes per inch.

43. Data can be transmitted from tape to memory or vice versa at rates varying from 15,000 to 1,250,000 characters per second.

44. Sequential organization means records are stored one after the other on the tape.

45. An interblock gap separates records stored on tape.

46. Blocked records mean two or more logical records are stored in a physical record on the tape.

47. Magnetic tape is used primarily for backup purposes in large computer installations.

48. Bubble memory is composed of small magnetic domains (bubbles) formed on a thin single-crystal film of synthetic garnet. These bubbles can be moved across the garnet in order to represent bits "on" and bits "off."

49. Optical disk systems, known as "write-once, read-often disks," can store very large amounts of data using a laser beam recording and reading method.

KEY TERMS

Access arms 9.8
Access time 9.6
Actuators 9.8
Auxiliary storage 9.1
Backup copies 9.10
Bits per inch (bpi) 9.3
Blocked records 9.16
Bubble memory 9.17
Cassette tape 9.10
Cylinder 9.13
Cylinder method 9.13
Data transfer rate 9.6
Direct access storage devices (DASD) 9.11
Disk cartridge 9.9, 9.12
Diskette 9.1
Double density (DD) 9.3
Double-sided (drives) 9.3
Double track drives 9.4
EBCDIC 9.14
Fixed block architecture 9.13
Fixed disks 9.12
Floppy disk 9.1
Flying heads 9.8
Formatting the diskette 9.5
Gigabytes 9.12
Half-height drives 9.9
Hard disks 9.7
Hard-sectored diskette 9.4
Interblock gap 9.16
Latency 9.6
Logical records 9.16
Magnetic tape 9.13
Microfloppy disks 9.7
Optical disk systems 9.17
Physical record 9.16
Read/write heads 9.8
Recording density 9.3
Removable disk pack 9.11
Rigid disks 9.8
Sector method 9.13
Sequential organization 9.16
Settling time 9.6
Single density (SD) 9.3
Single-sided drives 9.3
Soft-sectored diskettes 9.5
Streaming cartridge-tape drive 9.10
Tape density 9.14
Track 9.2
Tracks per inch 9.4
Winchester disk 9.7

REVIEW QUESTIONS

1. Differentiate between the uses of main computer memory and auxiliary storage.
2. Draw a diagram of a diskette and label the main parts of the diskette.
3. What is a track on a disk or a diskette? What relationship does a track have to the amount of data that can be stored on a disk or diskette?
4. What are the factors influencing the storage capacity of a diskette? Briefly describe each of them and note how these factors influence the storage capacity.
5. What are the differences between a single-sided and a double-sided diskette? What are the differences between a single density and a double density diskette?
6. Describe the differences between a hard-sectored diskette and a soft-sectored diskette.
7. Identify the factors which influence the access time of a diskette drive. What are the ranges for the access time of a diskette drive?
8. Describe the characteristics of a Winchester disk drive. What sizes are used with personal computers?
9. What is disk backup? How are diskettes normally backed up? How are fixed, hard disks backed up?
10. Describe the differences between removable disks and fixed disks with respect to large computers.
11. Contrast the storage capacities and speeds of a typical fixed disk used with a large computer to the capacities and speeds of hard, fixed disks typically used with personal computers.
12. Describe the sector method of disk organization. Describe the cylinder method of disk organization.
13. How is data stored on magnetic tape? What are typical tape densities and tape data transmission speeds?
14. Describe some advantages and disadvantages of bubble memory and optical disk systems as auxiliary storage.

CONTROVERSIAL ISSUES

1. A recent study of a large number of personal computer owners and users found that less than ten percent of the users regularly back up files and data bases they use. The consensus of these users was that new auxiliary storage devices, particularly the Winchester hard disk drives, are so reliable and error-free that backup is a waste of time and valuable auxiliary storage. Experts who examined this report wrote that these users were inviting disaster because even a few failures are enough to justify extensive file and data base backup. Who is right — the users or the experts? Take a position on this dispute and defend your position.
2. The cost of semiconductor memory has decreased significantly in recent years. In addition, research is being done constantly to find new ways for storing data. As a result, some experts feel magnetic memory such as tape and disk will be obsolete in only a few years. Others say this will never happen. What is your opinion?
3. "Tape Drives Make Good Boat Anchors" was the facetious title of a speech given recently by an expert who feels magnetic tape has no use as auxiliary storage. Defend or attack this position.

RESEARCH PROJECTS

1. The storage capacities of fixed, hard disks vary considerably. Obtain the names of five different manufacturers of fixed, hard disk drives used with personal computers. Write each of the manufacturers to obtain literature concerning their drives and prepare a report on the storage capacities of the drives.
2. In some cases, the storage and access speeds of magnetic storage devices have reached the maximum because of physical laws of motion. For example, removable disk packs can store an approximate maximum of 300 megabytes. Thus, research is being done to find bigger and faster auxiliary storage. Consult your library and find articles describing a new type of auxiliary storage being developed. Write a paper describing what you find.
3. Develop a price list for personal computer auxiliary storage devices that includes storage capacities.

Chapter Ten

File Organization And Data Base

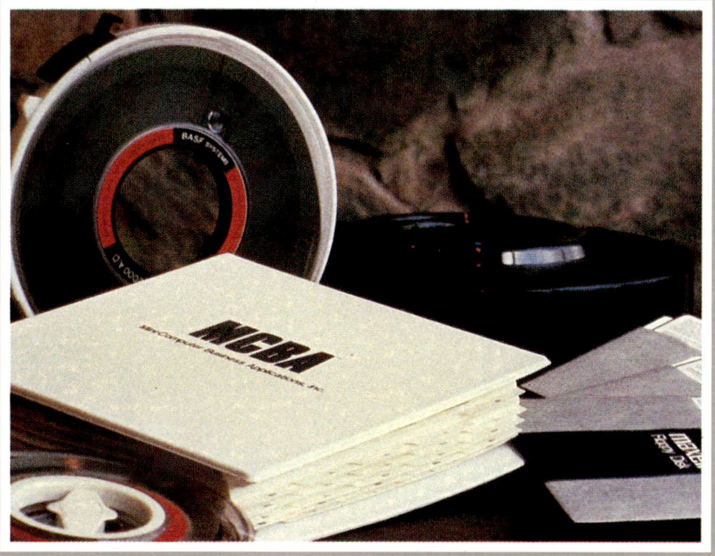

Objectives

- ☐ Identify the difference between sequential file retrieval and random file retrieval
- ☐ Describe sequential files, indexed files, and relative (or direct) files
- ☐ Define the role of a data base management system (DBMS)
- ☐ Describe a hierarchical data base system
- ☐ Describe a network data base system
- ☐ Describe a relational data base system
- ☐ Define the methods for loading data into a data base and retrieving data from a data base
- ☐ Describe the attributes of distributed data bases

File Organization And Data Base

Chapter Ten

The information in Chapter Nine illustrated the devices that are used for auxiliary storage. Equally important, however, is the manner in which the data is organized, stored, and retrieved from auxiliary storage. The purpose of this chapter is to examine file organization and to explain the use of data bases on both large and small computers.

It is now recognized in most organizations that the data and information accepted and processed within the organization is a valuable resource, and this resource must be carefully organized, managed, and controlled. Some experts have even stated that the most important asset of a company, other than its people, is the information it has accumulated. This chapter will also examine the handling of this information so that maximum use of it is made within a company.

Figure 10–2 This payroll file stored on tape contains payroll records. Each payroll record contains a social security field, a name field, and a paycheck amount field.

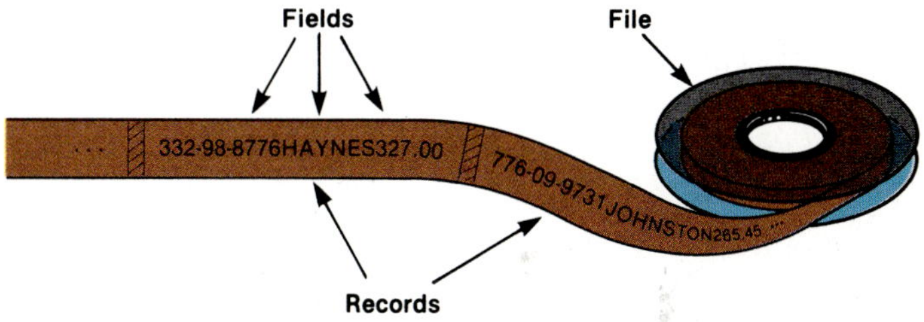

REVIEW OF FILE PROCESSING CONCEPTS

As noted in Chapter Three, data must be both stored on auxiliary storage and must be accessed, or retrieved, from auxiliary storage. The **physical organization** of data stored on auxiliary storage consists of fields, records, and files (Figure 10–2). A **field** is a single data item or element. A **record** is a collection of related data items or fields. A **file** is a collection of records.

When data is retrieved from auxiliary storage, it can be retrieved either sequentially or randomly. When **sequential retrieval** is used, data is retrieved one record after another based upon the sequence in which the data is stored on auxiliary storage. For example, data stored on tape is retrieved in the same sequence in which it is stored (Figure 10–3). **Random retrieval** means records are retrieved from auxiliary storage regardless of the order in which they are stored. For example, the first record in a file can be retrieved first, followed by the 50th record, and then the third record. For random retrieval, data must be stored on disk.

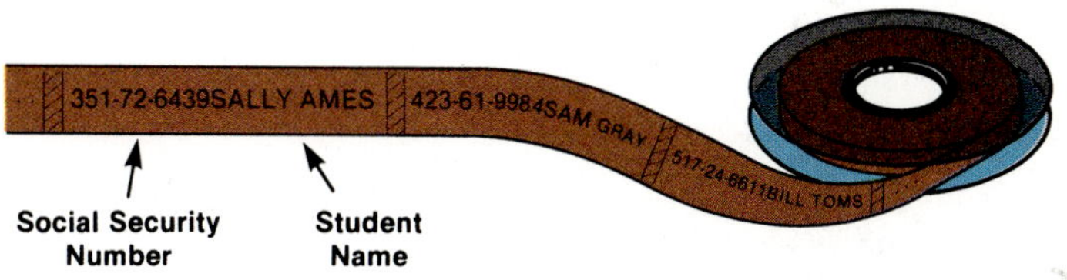

Figure 10–3 The student records in this file are stored sequentially and will be retrieved sequentially.

Files and data management systems

Files stored on auxiliary storage are built and maintained by application programs. These programs create the files, add data to the files, delete data from the files, and change data currently stored in the files. The actual physical process of reading

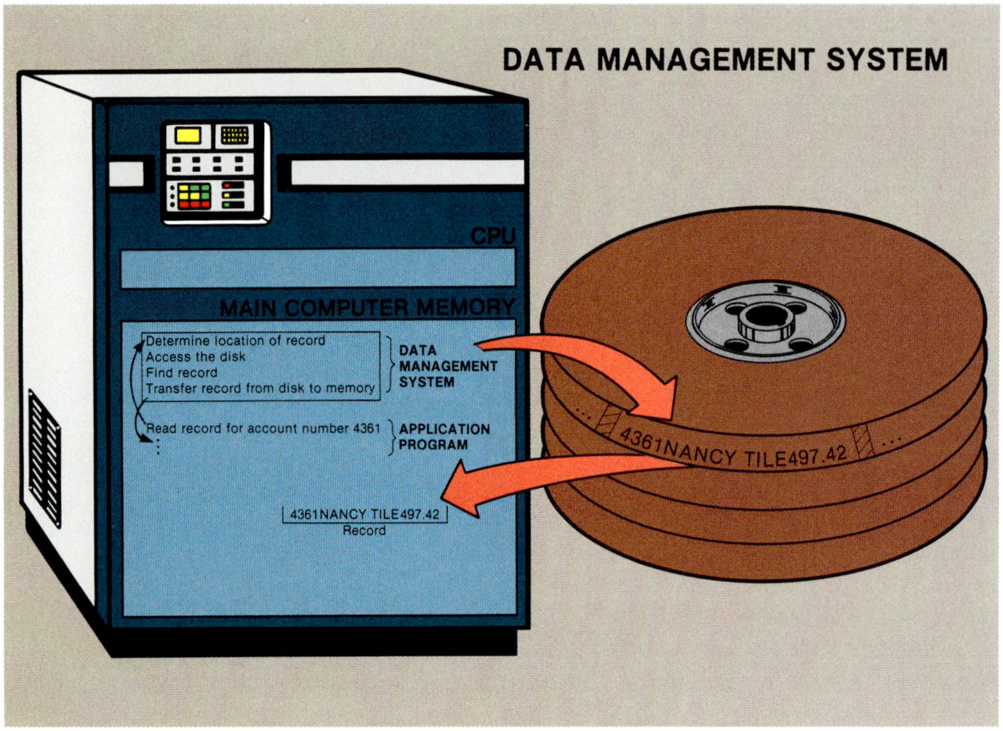

Figure 10–4 A data management system interfaces between an application program and the actual retrieval of data stored on auxiliary storage. A data management system exists for each type of file organization and access method.

data from a file stored on disk or tape or writing a record into a file, however, is not performed by the application program. Instead, a group of programs collectively called a **data management system** or a **file management system** are used (Figure 10–4). These programs contain the instructions which cause the actual transfer of data from main computer memory to auxiliary storage or from auxiliary storage to main computer memory.

The data management systems actually determine the type of physical organization and the type of access which will be available. There are three major categories of data management systems: 1) Sequential; 2) Indexed; 3) Direct or relative. Each of these is discussed in the following sections.

Sequential file organization

As noted, **sequential file organization** means records are stored one after the other, normally in a prescribed sequence based upon a value in each record, such as the social security number in Figure 10–3 on page 10.1, called a **key**. Records which are stored using sequential file organization are also retrieved sequentially.

Sequential file organization must be used when records are stored on tape and can also be used when records are stored on disk. The most likely use of sequential files in the modern computer center is as backup files, where data from a disk is copied onto a tape or another disk so that if the original data becomes unusable, the original file can be restored from the backup file.

Data stored and processed sequentially, however, can be useful in certain batch operations where reports are prepared. Whenever data is stored sequentially, it must be maintained. Data maintenance, it will be recalled from Chapter Three, requires data stored in a file to be updated by adding records, changing records, and deleting records. Each time a sequential file is updated, the file is rewritten; that is, a new,

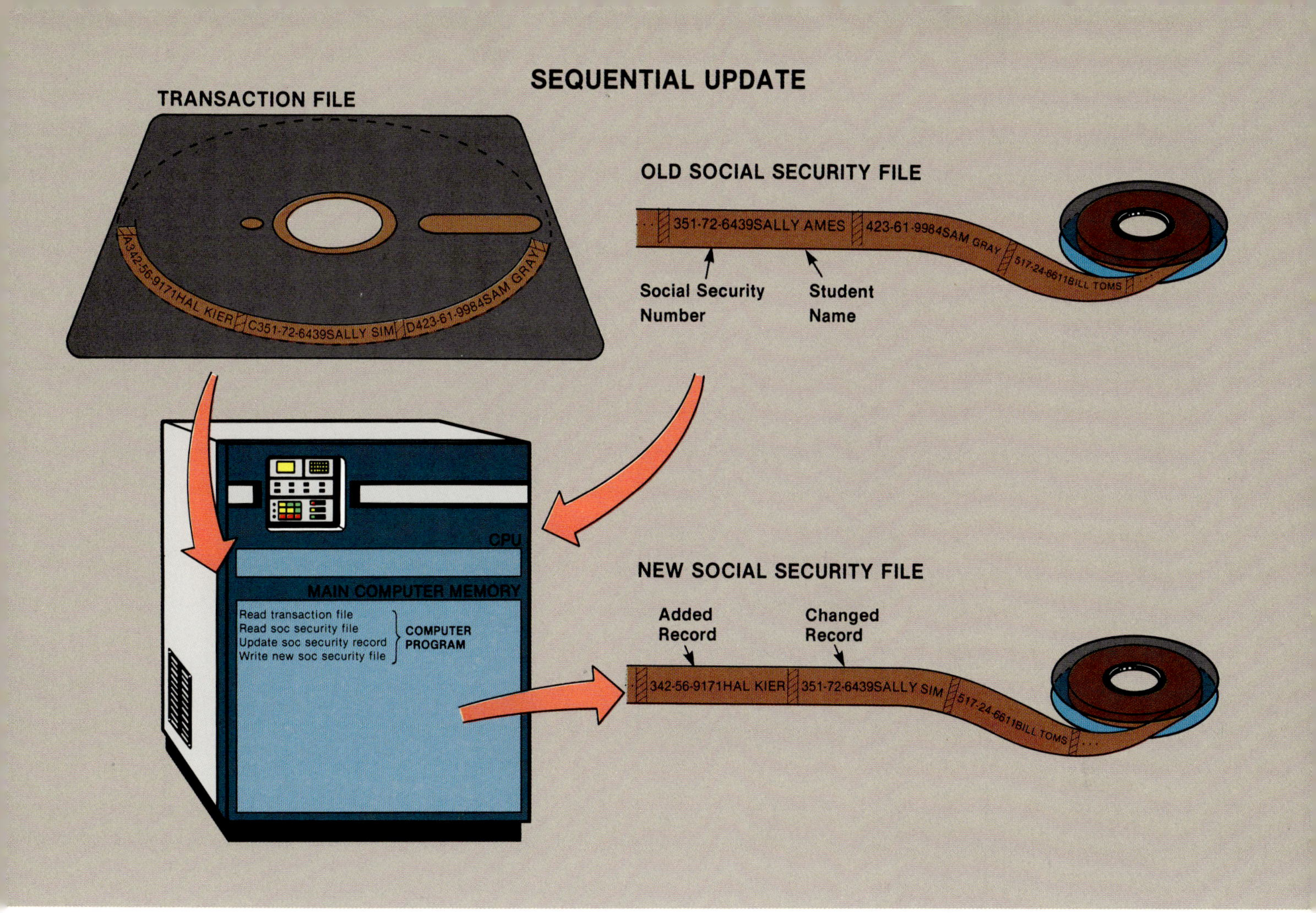

updated file is created. The process to update a sequential file is illustrated in Figure 10–5.

Figure 10–5 When a sequential file is updated, a file containing the updated data is created. Records which are added are placed in the proper sequence by key. Records which are deleted are not written in the new file. Both the transaction file and the file to be updated must be sorted in the same sequence on the same key field in order for the update to take place.

In the example in Figure 10–5, the old social security file contains data that is to be updated. The records which indicate the updating to take place are contained in the transaction file. Thus, a record from the transaction file and a record from the old social security file are read into main computer memory. Based upon the code in the transaction file, the record from the old social security file is updated. The letter A in the first position of the transaction file record indicates add a record. The letter C indicates change the name in the old record with the same social security number. The letter D indicates the record with the corresponding social security number should be deleted from the file. From Figure 10–5, it can be seen that the processing indicated by the transaction file records took place (record 342-56-9171 was added, the name for record 351-72-6439 was changed, and the record for 423-61-9984 was deleted). Since a new file is created when sequential file updating occurs, a record is deleted by not writing the record in the new file.

Sequential files are extensively used for disk backup and can be used for files which are processed sequentially.

Indexed file organization

A second method used to organize data in a file is called the **indexed file organization**. Records are stored in an indexed file in an ascending or descending sequence based upon the key of the record. In this respect, the storage of the records in an indexed file resembles the storage of records in a sequential file.

An indexed file, however, also contains an index. An **index** consists of entries

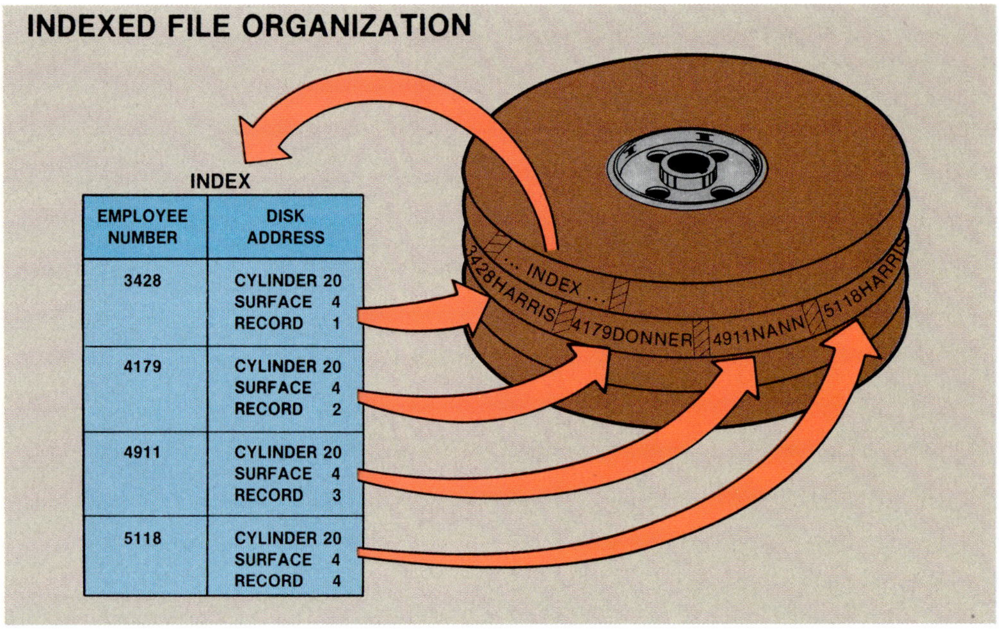

INDEXED FILE ORGANIZATION
INDEX
EMPLOYEE NUMBER
DISK ADDRESS
3428
CYLINDER 20 SURFACE 4 RECORD 1
4179
CYLINDER 20 SURFACE 4 RECORD 2
4911
CYLINDER 20 SURFACE 4 RECORD 3
5118
CYLINDER 20 SURFACE 4 RECORD 4
... INDEX ...
3428HARRIS
4179DONNER
4911NANN
5118HARRI

Figure 10-6 The index in an indexed file contains the record key value and the disk address of the corresponding record. In this example, the index contains the employee number, which is the key for the employee file, and the disk address for the corresponding employee record.

containing the key to the data records stored in the file and also the disk address of the record in the file (Figure 10-6). This index is usually stored on the same disk as the file when the file is created. It is retrieved from the disk and placed in main computer memory by the data management system when the file is to be processed. Using the index, records can be randomly accessed in an indexed file.

For example, records containing an employee number and employee name can be stored in a file in ascending sequence by the key, employee number (Figure 10-6). The index contains the employee number in ascending sequence and also the physical address where the records are stored on the disk. In the example, the address is specified as cylinder, surface, and record number. This physical address could also be specified as a sector number if the records were physically addressed by sector on the device being used.

Records can be accessed in an indexed file both sequentially and randomly. Sequential retrieval can occur in one of two ways. First, sequential retrieval can begin with the first record in the file and continue through the file. This is the same method used with a sequentially organized file. A second manner of sequential retrieval is to begin the retrieval with a given record. For example, in Figure 10-6 sequential retrieval could begin with employee 4911. After the beginning record for the sequential retrieval is located using the index, each subsequent record in the file would be read in the same manner as if retrieval had begun with the first record in the file.

Random access can also be used with indexed files. To randomly access a record in an indexed file, the index is searched until the key of the record to be retrieved is found. The address of the record found in the index is then used to access the record directly from the file without reading any other records. For example, if an inquiry was received from the personnel office asking the name of employee number 5118, the index could be searched until key 5118 was found (Figure 10-7, page 10.5). The corresponding disk address (cylinder 20, surface 4, record 4) would then be used to read the record directly from the disk into main computer memory.

Updating indexed files is performed randomly. When a record is to be changed, the key to the record is located in the index, the record is retrieved from the file, and the change takes place under program control. When a record is deleted, it is not physically removed from the disk. Instead, an entry is made in the index to treat the record as if it were not present in the file. Thus, whenever a reference to the deleted record takes place, the associated data management software indicates that the record is deleted even though it is still physically a part of the file. Records are added in a random fashion. They are not stored in a sequential manner. The indexes are updated in a way, however, that allows the records to be sequentially retrieved even though they are not stored sequentially on the disk.

The data management systems associated with indexed files perform the tasks of establishing the indexes when records are stored in the file, retrieving the records either sequentially or randomly when requested by a program, adding records and modifying the index accordingly when records are added, and other tasks as well. The data management systems (also sometimes known as **logical input/output systems**) play an important role in programming because they allow an applications programmer to write a program that accesses data stored on auxiliary storage without the programmer's worrying about all of the detailed physical requirements associated with accessing a record.

Direct or relative file organization

A **direct file** (sometimes called a **relative file**) contains records which are stored in relative locations within a file. The program which stores and accesses records in a direct file must specify either the exact physical address of a record in the file (for example, cylinder, surface and track number, or track and sector number), or the relative location within the file beginning with the first record in the file.

The location into which a record will be stored and from which the record can be retrieved is based upon a key value found in the record. For example, a file could be established in which there are nine predefined locations where records can be stored (these locations are sometimes called **buckets**). If the key in the record is a one digit value (1 – 9), then the value in the key would specify the relative location within the file where the record was stored. For example, the record with the key 3 would be placed in relative location 3; the record with the key 6 would be placed in relative location 6, and so on.

Most uses of relative files are not so simple. For instance, it may be found that the maximum number of records to be stored in a direct file is 100, but the key for the record is a four digit number. In this case, the key of the record could not be used to specify the relative or actual location of the record because the key would specify up to a maximum of 9,999 records. In cases such as these, an arithmetic formula must be used to calculate the relative location or actual location in the file where the record is stored. The process of using a formula and performing the calculation to determine the location of a record is called **hashing**.

One hashing method that can be used is the division/remainder method. Using this method, a prime number close to but not greater than the number of records to be stored in the file is chosen. A **prime number** is a number divisible by only itself and one. For example, the number 97 is the closest prime number to 100 without being greater than 100. The key of the record is then divided by the prime number chosen, and the remainder from the division operation is the relative location where the record is stored. For example, if the record key is 3428, the

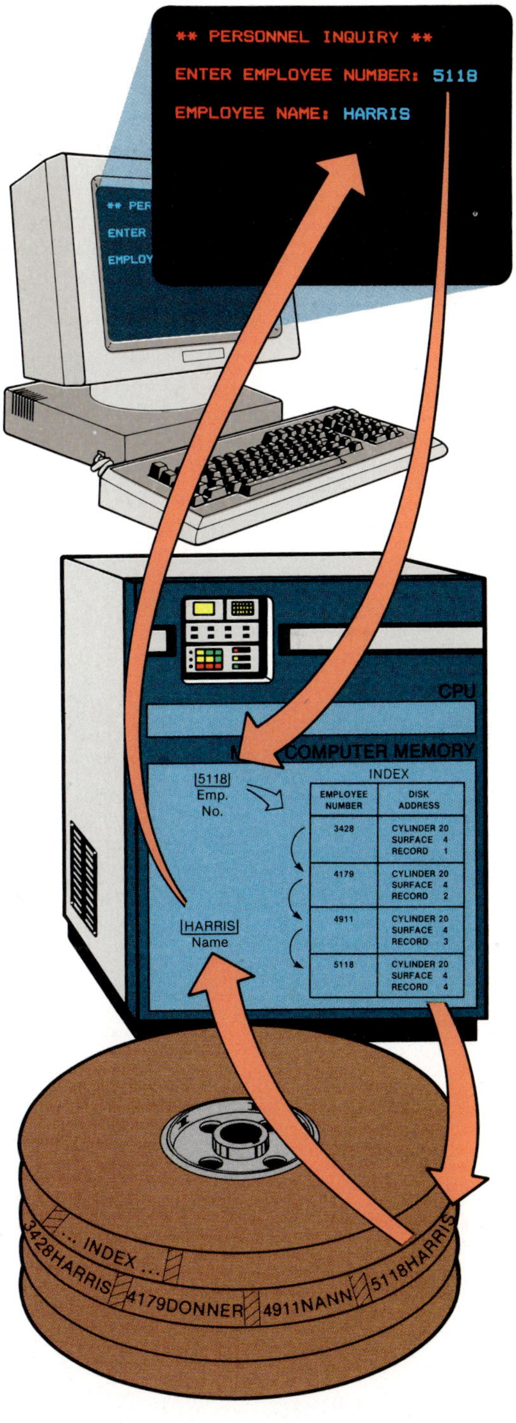

Figure 10–7 In this example of random retrieval using an indexed file, the inquiry has requested the employee name of employee number 5118. When the employee number is placed in main computer memory, the data management software would search the file index until employee number 5118 is found. The corresponding disk address in the index is then used to retrieve the record stored at that address. In this case, the employee name in the record is Harris. This name is then sent back to the terminal making the inquiry.

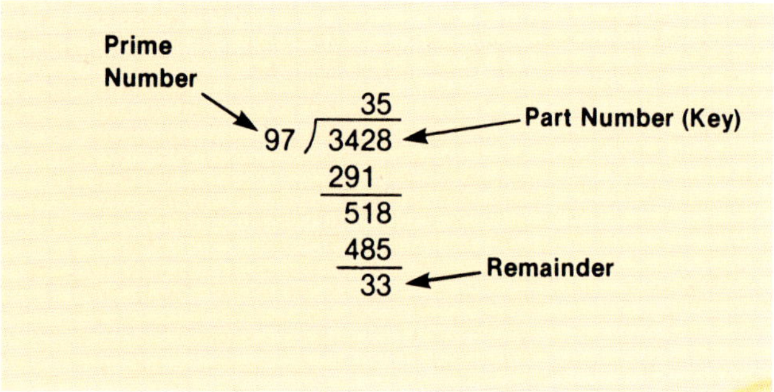

Figure 10–8 When the value 3428 is divided by the prime number 97, the remainder is 33. This remainder is used as the bucket where the record with a key 3428 is stored in the direct file.

relative location where the record will be stored in the file is location 33 (Figure 10–8).

Once a record is stored in its relative or physical location within a direct file, it can be retrieved either sequentially or randomly. Sequential retrieval can occur by indicating that the record from the first relative location is to be retrieved, followed by the record from the second relative location, and so on. All of the records in the file are retrieved based upon their relative location in the file. This does not guarantee that the records will be retrieved in key sequence. For example, the relative location for key 1233 is 69 (1233 ÷ 97 = 12, remainder 69) (Figure 10–9).

The more common access method for direct files, however, is random retrieval. In order to randomly retrieve a record from a direct file, the program must first obtain the key of the record to be retrieved. The program then performs the same hashing process as was performed when the record was initially stored in the file in order to determine the location of the record. Thus, to retrieve the record with the key 3428, the key value would be divided by the prime number 97. The remainder, 33, specifies the location of the record in the file. The program would then direct the data management software to retrieve relative record 33 from the file.

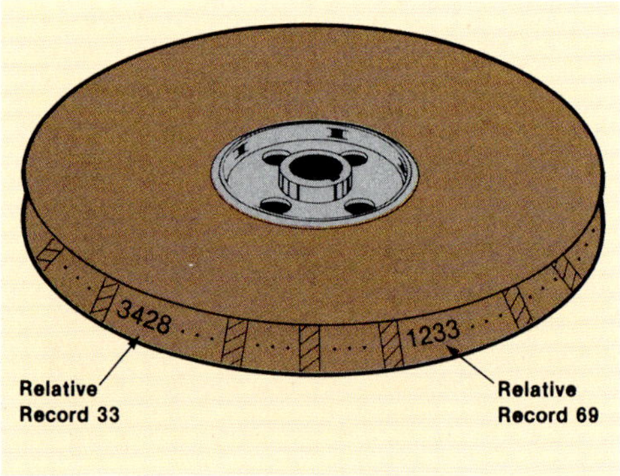

Figure 10–9 Even though the key value 3428 is greater than the key value 1233, the record with key 1233 is stored at relative location 69. If records are sequentially retrieved in relative location sequence, it is likely the records will not be in record key sequence.

The random retrieval of a record stored in a direct file, therefore, involves merely a few arithmetic instructions and a single read from the disk. This method allows the fastest access to data stored on disk of any file organization method.

Direct files present one problem not encountered with sequential or indexed files. In all three file organization methods, the key in the record must be unique so that it can uniquely identify the record. For example, the employee number, when acting as the key in an employee file, must be unique. When a hashing technique is used to calculate a disk address, however, there is a possibility that two different keys could identify the same location on disk. For example, the employee number 3331 generates the same relative location (33) as employee number 3428. When the location generated from the different keys is the same, a **collision** has occurred. The record addresses generated from two different keys are called **synonyms**. A collision is resolved by several different methods. A method often used is to add 1 to the location generated from the hashing process. For example, if a record with the key 3428 is already stored in the file when a record with the key 3331 is to be stored, then the value 1 is added to location 33, and a check is made to determine if a record is stored in location 34. If not, the record with the key 3331 is stored in location 34. If so, location 35 is examined. This process may continue for ten times, each time looking for an empty bucket. When an empty bucket is found, the record is written in the location.

Summary — files

Files are organized as either sequential, indexed, or direct files. Sequentially organized files can only be accessed sequentially. Indexed files can be accessed either sequentially or randomly. Direct files are normally accessed randomly, although they can be accessed sequentially.

DATA BASES

Data is an important resource for an organization. Ideally, data is accessible to any authorized person in an organization for whatever application and in whatever format desired. Files, however, do not allow this type of access. Files are designed to be used for just one application and the set of programs associated with that application. They generally have little or no relation to other data used and required within an organization because they are initiated and developed independently. Files are often unrelated to user's requests for information, particularly when these requests change in unpredictable ways.

When files are designed for a specific application and when an organization has many applications, the files will often contain **redundant data**, which means the same data is stored in more than one file. For example, an employee's name and address might be contained in both a personnel file and a payroll file. In addition to requiring more auxiliary storage space, redundant data presents updating problems, since updating data in one file will not update the same data in another file. As a result, data in one file may not correspond to data in another file even though it is supposed to.

Since files are designed for application-specific programs, a change in the format of data can affect many applications and many programs. If a field has to be added to a file, then the associated programs must be changed. Therefore, the programs are data dependent.

To overcome the problems of data unrelated to user's needs, data redundancy, and program dependency on data, data bases have been developed. A **data base** is a collection of data organized in a manner which allows retrieval and use of that data by anyone needing it. A data base is organized and designed to allow a large number of users to draw information from it for many different purposes in many different formats.

A data base can be analyzed from two viewpoints — the physical storage of the data and the logical, or conceptual, view of the data. Files are used to physically store data in a data base. Most data bases use either direct files or indexed files, or a combination of the two, to physically store data on disk.

The **logical**, or **conceptual, view** of a data base is concerned with how data is logically organized and how the data can be retrieved for information purposes. The three conceptual views of a data base are a hierarchy data base, a network data base, and a relational data base. Each of these is discussed in the following sections.

Hierarchy data base

For the illustrations of the three types of data bases on the next several pages, assume the following application. A company that owns computer stores has a store in Chicago and a store in Dallas. Each store has an inventory of parts and computer components which it sells. These parts and components are purchased from various vendors. Each part has a unique description. Orders are received for various parts the store sells. The set of data which could be used for this application (and for the two applications which follow) is illustrated in Figure 10–10. The owners of the company

STORE

STORE NAME	CITY
STORE 1	CHICAGO
STORE 2	DALLAS

VENDOR

VENDOR NUMBER	VENDOR NAME
3428	SPINETICS
4911	ELECTRO INC.
5726	MAGNO-TEK

INVENTORY

STORE NAME	PART NUMBER	QUANTITY
STORE 1	PT-1	50
STORE 1	PT-3	20
STORE 2	PT-2	100
STORE 2	PT-1	30

PART

PART NUMBER	DESCRIPTION
PT-1	PRINTER
PT-2	DISKETTE
PT-3	DISK DRIVE
PT-4	CRT MONITOR

ORDERS

STORE NAME	PART NUMBER	VENDOR NUMBER	ORDER NUMBER	QUANTITY
STORE 1	PT-3	3428	0052	10
STORE 2	PT-2	3428	0098	7
STORE 2	PT-3	3428	0098	15
STORE 2	PT-4	5726	0099	1

Figure 10–10 Five different groups of data are shown here — Store, Vendor, Inventory, Part, and Orders. This data is used in the explanations of hierarchy, network, and relational data bases.

want the data shown in Figure 10–10 to be organized into a data base so that various questions based upon the data can be answered, such as What are the outstanding orders for Store 1? or How many PT–1 devices does the store in Chicago have in stock?

The first conceptual view to be considered is the hierarchy data base. A **hierarchy data base**, shown in Figure 10–11, consists of elements which act in a **parent-child relationship**. In the computer store example, the parent element Store is linked to, or points to, child elements (Inventory and Orders). In order to obtain information from the order element, the search must first go through the store parent element. For example, to answer the question, What orders are outstanding in the Chicago store? the data base management system which controls the data base would first go to the Store element (the parent element). The parent element then points to one or more Orders child elements which contain the information requested.

Several points should be made about hierarchy data bases. First, data stored on lower levels of the hierarchy can only be accessed through the parent element. Thus, to gain information about the inventory in a store, the inventory element must be accessed through the store parent element. Second, the relationships within the hierarchy data base are established when the data base is created; that is, the person who designs the data base must indicate that an inventory record is a child element of the store element when the data base is created. Subsequently, all accesses to the data base must be made through the links established when the data base is created. Third, an element within a hierarchy data base can have only one parent element. Therefore, in Figure 10–11, the inventory element can have only one parent element, in this case the store element.

Figure 10–11 The hierarchy data base shown here contains the parent element, Store; and two child elements, Inventory and Orders. In order to retrieve data from either of the child elements, control must pass through the parent element. For example, to obtain the number of parts ordered on a given order such as order 0052, the inquiry must specify that the order was for store 1.

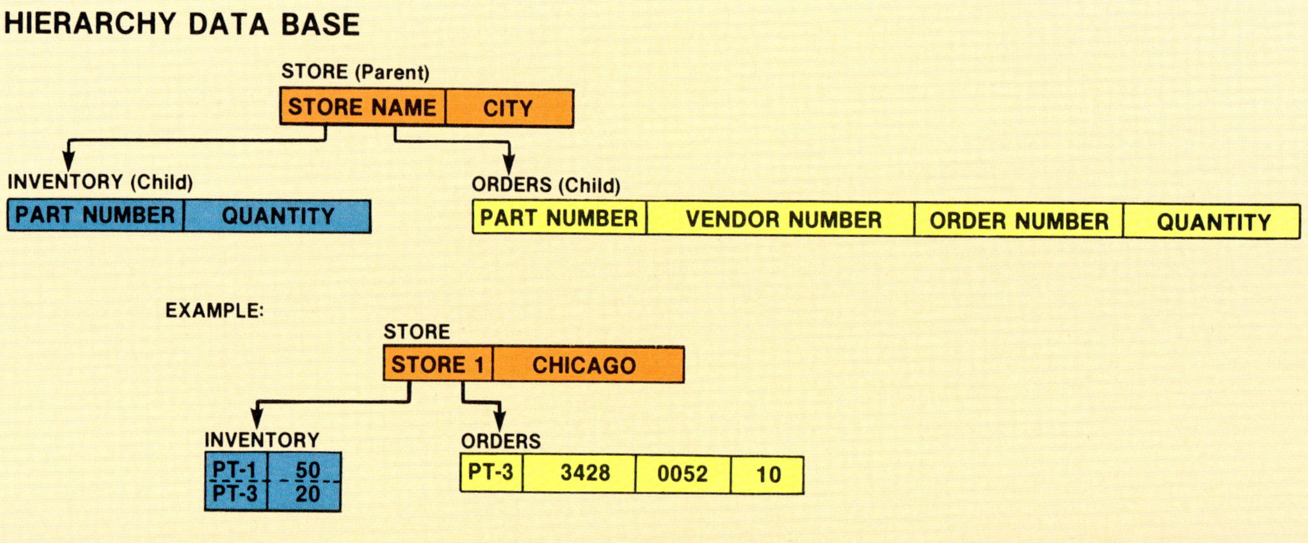

The hierarchy data base is the oldest of the conceptual data bases, and it has been recognized that better designs are available. Hierarchy data bases, particularly IMS from IBM, have been used successfully for a number of years and will continue to be used in the future, but newer conceptual data bases are more important.

Network data base

A **network data base** acts in much the same manner as a hierarchy data base except that an element can have more than one parent. In network data base nomenclature, a parent is called an **owner** and the child is called a **member**. A form of network data base which has received wide usage is the CODASYL (Conference on Data Systems Languages) data base. A CODASYL data base consists of conceptual files and owner-coupled sets.

A **conceptual file** contains record keys and the fields in the records of the file. For example, in the application for the computer stores just presented, five conceptual files are found — the Store conceptual file, the Vendor conceptual file, the Inventory conceptual file, the Part conceptual file, and the Orders conceptual file. In the Store conceptual file, the store name is the key; in the Vendor conceptual file, the vendor number is the key, and so on. It is quite important at this point to understand that the conceptual files being described here do not necessarily reflect the actual physical files which are stored on disk. Conceptual files present the view of the data as the user or as the data base administrator sees it, not as it is physically stored on disk. It will be recalled that most data bases use direct files, indexed files, or a combination of the two to physically store the data.

An **owner-coupled set** in a CODASYL data base (Figure 10–12) is a set made up of owner records and member records from the conceptual files. Each of these owner-coupled sets must be specified when the CODASYL data base is created. For example, in Figure 10–12 three owner-coupled sets are defined — one with Store as owner and Inventory as member; one with Store as owner and Orders as member; and one with Part as owner and Inventory as member. To retrieve data, the user must specify the owner and the member to be retrieved. For example, to display the inventory of the Chicago store, the owner (Store) and the member (Inventory) must be specified. Note that this arrangement is quite similar to a hierarchy data base in that the relationships of data must be defined at the time the data base is created and that certain paths (i.e., owner-member) must be followed. The difference is that a member can have more than one owner (such as both Store and Part being owners of Inventory).

Figure 10–12 This network data base has three owner-coupled sets illustrated. In each set, the owner-member relationship is a so-called 1:n relationship, meaning that for each owner there can be one or more members. For example, for each store, there can be one or more inventory records; for each store there can be one or more orders; and for each part, there can be one or more stores with that part in inventory.

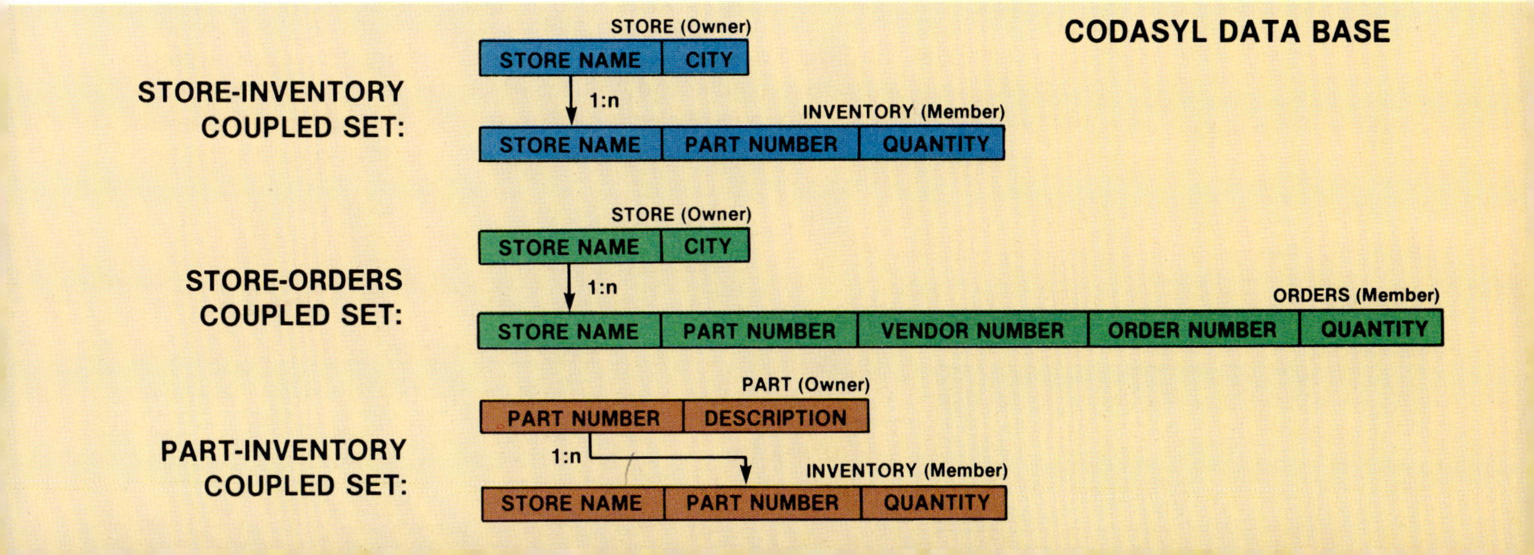

All of the owner-coupled sets and relationships established for a given network data base are called the **data base schema**. Since a data base can contain hundreds of owner-coupled sets, it is often the case that not everyone using the data base should have access to all of the owner-coupled sets. Therefore, user **subschemas** that specify only those relationships available to a given user can be defined. For example, if a user is writing a program to list the inventory in the stores, the program need not have access to the Store-Order or Part-Inventory sets. Instead, a subschema would be defined allowing the program access to the Store-Inventory owner-coupled set only.

While a network or CODASYL data base is more flexible than a hierarchy data base, it still has the limitation that the data base schema must be defined at the time the data base is created, and retrieval of data is based solely on the schema. Network data bases, however, have been successfully implemented and marketed by a number of software vendors.

Relational data bases

A **relational data base** is the newest conceptual view of data and offers many advantages. The most important advantage is that the relationships between data can be determined dynamically at the time the user requests information from the data base.

To begin, a **relation** is defined as a conceptual file where each conceptual record is unique and each conceptual record has the same number and type of fields. A conceptual file containing records is also called a **table** and each record within the file is sometimes called a **tuple**.

The data illustrated in Figure 10–10 is in fact organized as relations. The five relations are the Store relation, the Part relation, the Vendor relation, the Inventory relation, and the Orders relation. Each record within the relation must be unique. When a request for information from the relational data base is made, one or more of the three relational operations is performed: Selection, Projection, or Join. Each of these operations creates a new relation based upon the request for information.

A **selection relational operation** selects certain records from a given relation. For example, in Figure 10–13, when the request is, "Find and list parts in inventory with a quantity greater than 40," the selection operation is applied to the Inventory relation to create a new relation containing those records with a quantity greater than 40. Once the new relation is created, the report or listing can be prepared from the data in the new relation.

A **projection relational operation** selects specified columns from a given relation which will produce a new conceptual file. The projection operation then removes any duplicate records, creating a new relation (recall that in a relation, each conceptual record is unique). To illustrate the projection operation, suppose the request for information is, "Display the part number and vendor number for any part that has been ordered in a quantity greater than five on a single order." First, the projection operation finds all records in the Orders relation with a quantity greater than five. In the

Figure 10–13 When the selection relational operation is performed, certain records from a single relation are placed in a new relation, based upon the criteria specified for building a new relation. Here, the criteria is that the records selected must have an inventory quantity greater than 40. The selected relation which is created contains only records with a quantity greater than 40.

REQUEST: Find and list parts in inventory with a quantity greater than 40

INVENTORY

STORE NAME	PART NUMBER	QUANTITY
STORE 1	PT-1	50
STORE 1	PT-3	20
STORE 2	PT-2	100
STORE 2	PT-1	30

SELECT OPERATION →

SELECTED RELATION

STORE NAME	PART NUMBER	QUANTITY
STORE 1	PT-1	50
STORE 2	PT-2	100

REQUEST: Display the part number and vendor number for any part that has been ordered in a quantity greater than five on a single order.

ORDERS

STORE NAME	PART NUMBER	VENDOR NUMBER	ORDER NUMBER	QUANTITY
STORE 1	PT-3	3428	0052	10
STORE 2	PT-2	3428	0098	7
STORE 2	PT-3	3428	0098	15
STORE 2	PT-4	5726	0099	1

PROJECTION OPERATION Step 1

CONCEPTUAL FILE

PART NUMBER	VENDOR NUMBER
PT-3	3428
PT-2	3428
PT-3	3428

PROJECTION OPERATION Step 2

PROJECTED RELATION

PART NUMBER	VENDOR NUMBER
PT-3	3428
PT-2	3428

example of the two-step process shown in Figure 10–14, there are three records. Then the projection operation eliminates any duplicates. After the second step, a relation has been created that includes only those part numbers and vendor numbers for parts that have a quantity of more than five on order.

A **natural join relational operation** is used to join two different relations. The process is controlled through the use of common fields found in each of the relations. For example, the Part relation and the Inventory relation have a common field — the part number. Therefore, a natural join relational operation can be performed on the two relations based upon the part number field. Suppose, for example, a request is made to "Display all parts in inventory and include the part description." The data in the Inventory relation must be joined with data from the Part relation to satisfy this request. This process is shown in Figure 10–15. Note that the essential process is to replace each occurrence of the part number in the Inventory relation with the Part record containing the same part number.

Requests for information from a relational data base can be considerably more complex than those just illustrated. The same relational operations are performed on the data, however. The strength of relational data bases is that the operations are performed at the time the request is made without predetermined schemas such as are required with hierarchy and network data bases. Thus, a relational data base is much more user-oriented because the user can ask virtually any question and the relational data base management system will perform the necessary relational operations to create the relation that contains the data requested. Virtually all modern data base management systems support relational data bases. They are the best way known to make data available to users when they need it and in the form they need it.

Figure 10–14 The projection relational operation selects specified columns from one relation. Here, as a result of the natural language request, the projection operation first creates a conceptual file containing all part numbers and vendor numbers for all orders where the order is for more than five of the parts, and then creates a relation by eliminating duplicate part numbers.

Figure 10–15 The natural join relational operation creates a joined relation from two separate relations. The joined relation is based upon the common fields found in each of the separate relations. In this example, the common field is the part number. In the joined relation, the part number and part description from the Part relation has replaced the part number from the Inventory relation.

DATA BASE MANAGEMENT SYSTEMS

A **data base management system**, which is a series of programs written by

REQUEST: Display all parts in inventory and include the part description.

PART

PART NUMBER	DESCRIPTION
PT-1	PRINTER
PT-2	DISKETTE
PT-3	DISK DRIVE
PT-4	CRT MONITOR

INVENTORY

STORE NAME	PART NUMBER	QUANTITY
STORE 1	PT-1	50
STORE 1	PT-3	20
STORE 2	PT-2	100
STORE 2	PT-1	30

JOIN OPERATION

JOINED RELATION

STORE NAME	PART NUMBER	DESCRIPTION	QUANTITY
STORE 1	PT-1	PRINTER	50
STORE 1	PT-3	DISK DRIVE	20
STORE 2	PT-2	DISKETTES	100
STORE 2	PT-1	PRINTER	30

computer manufacturers or software vendors, provides the essential services to implement and maintain a data base. A data base management system usually provides the following features: 1) Establishment of data relationships within the data base; 2) The facilities to implement the data base and load it with data; 3) The facilities to maintain and update the data base; 4) The facilities which allow the user to interface with and use the data in the data base; 5) Data security and control. Each of these is examined in the following paragraphs.

A given data base management system generally supports and implements one of the three types of data bases. Systems are available to implement data bases on the largest mainframe computers and on personal computers as well. The DBMS contains commands which allow an individual to specify the schema, subschema, or other features of the data base that might be required, depending upon the type of data base being implemented. Prior to placing data in the data base, the structure of the data base must be established.

The data base management system also provides for loading data into the data base. When a large data base is loaded, the data will normally be prepared in a production environment. All of the various keys, relationships, and other mechanics necessary to provide access to the data will be established by the DBMS.

As has been noted, data is unusable if it is not kept up-to-date. Therefore, the data base management system provides facilities to update the data stored in the data base. In many instances, it is the responsibility of the data base administrator to oversee updating within the data base to ensure that only those authorized to do so have access to the data base for updating purposes.

The facilities to access a data base for information purposes are extremely important. Generally, data base management systems provide access both for programs which are written in the installation (called **internal access**) and access for users to enter inquiries on terminals or personal computers (**external access**). As seen in the discussion of the three types of data bases, the manner in which the data is accessed and the information which can be obtained from an inquiry are critical in the use of a data base.

Control and security of data in a data base are crucial. The data base management system must provide security measures such as passwords so that unauthorized users do not have access to the data base. In addition, certain users should not be allowed to access certain data within the data base. This control is contained within the DBMS as well.

SYSTEMS AND PROCEDURES

Data cannot be organized, loaded, and stored on auxiliary storage using either files or a data base for use by personnel within an organization without an extensive set of systems and procedures. Among other things, the systems and procedures must address the following issues: 1) Who has access to what data; 2) What are the backup procedures, including what data is backed up and how often it is backed up; 3) What controls must be placed on the data so only authorized personnel have access to the data; 4) When and how is data to be updated; 4) If data is downloaded to personal computers, what controls will be placed on that data; 6) In a distributed data base environment, where data is placed on multiple computers in different geographic locations and the computers are linked by data communications, how is access and updating of this data to be controlled.

Addressing these issues is vital if data is to be successfully used within an organization.

CHAPTER SUMMARY

1. The physical organization of data stored on auxiliary storage consists of fields, records, and files.
2. Sequential retrieval means records are retrieved in the sequence in which they are stored. Random retrieval means records are retrieved without regard to the sequence in which they are stored.
3. A data management system or file management system is a set of programs that contains instructions to cause the actual transfer of data from main computer memory to auxiliary storage or vice versa.
4. Sequential file organization means records are stored one after the other, normally in a prescribed sequence.
5. Records are stored in an indexed file in ascending or descending sequence based upon the key of the record.
6. An index consists of entries containing the key to the records and the disk addresses of the records.
7. Random access and sequential access can be used with indexed files.
8. A direct or relative file contains records stored in relative locations that can be accessed randomly.
9. The process of using a formula and performing calculations to determine record location is called hashing.
10. A data base is a collection of data organized in a manner which allows retrieval and use of that data by anyone needing it and authorized to use it.
11. The logical, or conceptual, view is concerned with how the data is organized and how it can be retrieved.
12. A hierarchy data base consists of elements that act in a parent-child relationship.
13. Data stored on lower levels of a hierarchy data base can only be accessed through the parent element. The relationships within a hierarchy data base are established when the data base is created. An element within a hierarchy data base can have only one parent element.
14. In a network data base, a parent is called an owner and a child is called a member. A conceptual file contains record keys and the fields in the records of the file.
15. An owner-coupled set is a set made up of owner records and member records in conceptual files.
16. A data base schema is all the owner-coupled sets for a given network data base. A user subschema is the user's view of the data that specifies what data the user can access.
17. A relation is a conceptual file where each conceptual record is unique and each record has the same number and type of fields. A conceptual file is also called a table. A record is also called a tuple.
18. A selection relational operation selects certain records from a relation. A projection relational operation selects specified columns to create a new relation. A natural join relational operation is used to join two different relations based upon common fields in the records.
19. A data base management system is a series of programs that provides data base facilities.

KEY TERMS

Buckets 10.5
Collision 10.6
Conceptual file 10.9
Conceptual (view of data) 10.7
Data base 10.7
Data base management system 10.11
Data base schema 10.10
Data management system 10.2
Direct file 10.5
External access 10.12
Field 10.1
File 10.1
File management system 10.2
Hashing 10.5
Hierarchy data base 10.8
Index 10.3
Indexed file organization 10.3
Internal access 10.12
Key 10.2
Logical input/output systems 10.5
Logical (view of data) 10.7
Member 10.9
Natural join relational operation 10.11
Network data base 10.9
Owner 10.9
Owner-coupled set 10.9
Parent-child relationship 10.8
Physical organization 10.1
Prime number 10.5
Projection relational operation 10.10
Random retrieval 10.1
Record 10.1
Redundant data 10.7
Relation 10.10
Relational data base 10.10
Relative file 10.5
Selection relational operation 10.10
Sequential file organization 10.2
Sequential retrieval 10.1
Subschemas 10.10
Synonyms 10.6
Table 10.10
Tuple 10.10

REVIEW QUESTIONS

1. What is a field? What is a record? What is a file?
2. Identify the functions performed by a data management system.
3. Describe sequential file organization. How are sequentially organized files retrieved?
4. What is an indexed file? How can records be retrieved both sequentially and randomly from an indexed file?
5. How is the location where a record is stored in a direct file determined?
6. What are a collision and a synonym? How are these problems solved?
7. What problems that exist for files are overcome by a data base?
8. Define a data base. What is the difference between a conceptual view of a data base and the physical view of the data base?
9. What are the three main conceptual views of a data base? Briefly describe each of them.
10. Describe the parent-child relationship between data in a hierarchy data base. Given an example.
11. What are an owner and a member in a network data base? How do they work together in an owner-coupled set?
12. What function is performed by a data base schema? By a data base subschema?
13. Define the following terms as they relate to relational data bases: Relation; Conceptual file; Conceptual record; Table; Tuple.
14. How is the resulting relation of a selection relational operation derived? Of a projection relational operation? Of a natural join operation? Give an example of each.
15. List the five features normally provided by a data base management system and describe each of them.
16. Describe six issues which must be addressed by the systems and procedures associated with data bases.

CONTROVERSIAL ISSUES

1. "Although the goal of placing a company's data in a data base for access by authorized personnel is quite admirable, the truth of the matter is that it is impossible to do," said one noted authority recently. Others on the panel discussing data bases disagreed, noting many companies successfully place their corporate data in a data base. Is placing all of a company's data into one data base for access by everyone possible? Is it a good idea?
2. Criminologists have said that the risk of computer crime increases when a data base is used in a company as opposed to when application-related files are used. They theorize that since all of the data is accessible in one place, the ability to manipulate the data for illegal purposes increases. They are rebutted by data base management systems developers, who maintain that data bases are just as secure as files. What do you think?
3. A data base expert on large data bases recently wrote that the public is being deceived by vendors who claim data bases for personal computers are true data bases. She maintained they are nothing but file processors. Is she correct? Research the question and then take a position on this issue.

RESEARCH PROJECTS

1. Consult recent journals and magazines to find articles on relational data bases. Prepare a report on the performance characteristics of relational data bases, particularly with respect to the time required to perform a complex join operation on large data bases.
2. Many data bases are offered for use on personal computers. Prepare a report on various data bases available for use on various computers, paying particular attention to the type of data base, the manner in which the data is loaded into the data base, and the manner in which data is retrieved from the data base.
3. Select a data base management system for either large computers or personal computers and prepare an in-depth report on the DBMS.

Chapter Eleven

Data Communications

Objectives

- ☐ Describe the basic components of a data communications system
- ☐ Specify the hardware and software required for a personal computer in order for the personal computer to be a part of a data communications system
- ☐ Identify the role of modems and communications control units
- ☐ Describe the various line configurations and the manner in which communication takes place on each configuration
- ☐ Demonstrate an understanding of network organization by drawing schematics of the three major types of networks
- ☐ Define a local area network, and identify the components of a local area network
- ☐ Specify the type of transmission media used for local area networks, the various means for transmitting along the media, and the two major types of network access

Data Communications

Chapter Eleven

Many authorities think the use of the computer as a communication device will have even greater importance than the use of the computer as a computing device. Some even believe that the computer used as an inexpensive communication device will have as much impact on society as did the development of the printing press almost 500 years ago. It is now possible for a computer to communicate with other computers anywhere in the world. This capability allows users to access large volumes of information instantly.

Computers which communicate are used in both business and personal applications. In business applications, banks, retail stores, airlines, hotels, and many others use computers for communication purposes. In personal computer use, it is possible to access numerous data bases to obtain the latest weather reports, stock market information, news stories, medical diagnosis information, or even theater and movie reviews. It is predicted that within a very few years, it will be possible to access from a home computer the information contained in the world's greatest libraries.

The task of communicating data from one computer to another is accomplished by connecting one computer to another through communication channels such as standard telephone lines. Communicating data over communication channels using computers is called **data communications**. It is the purpose of this chapter to provide an overview of the field of data communications and explain some of the technical aspects of data communications as related to the use of the computer in the home and in the business world.

The early history of data communications

Communication means the exchange of information. In 1876, when Alexander Graham Bell uttered the words, "Mr. Watson, come here, I want you," into a telephone, the world of communications began a dramatic change. The feasibility of transmitting both data and voice over communication lines led to the development of an amazingly complex network of communication systems which allows millions of individuals and companies to be in contact with locations throughout the world.

The ability to remotely communicate with a calculating machine was first demonstrated by Dr. George Stibitz in 1940 at Dartmouth College in Hanover, New Hampshire, when he used standard telegraph lines to communicate with a calculator in New York City. One of the first attempts to combine information processing and communications occurred in 1954 when IBM introduced a punched card "transceiver." This device transmitted data stored in punched cards to computers at remote locations.

As computer technology developed in the 1950's, it became evident that computers and communication facilities could be effectively combined in many application areas. One of the first large-scale commercial applications of the use of computers and data communications was the Sabre airline reservation system. Developed jointly by

American Airlines and IBM, the system used approximately 2,000 terminals placed throughout the United States. These terminals were all connected to a central computer by telephone lines. The system became operational in 1962 after six years of development. It was one of the first on-line computerized reservation systems.

Data communication systems require special communication equipment and sophisticated programs. The technology of the early 1960's had not yet developed to the point where widespread data communications was economically feasible except for the very large user. The seed had been planted, however, and others began to look at the concept of processing data from remote locations.

DATA COMMUNICATIONS TODAY

Today, computers of all sizes, including personal computers, are able to communicate with each other and with remote terminals. While a myraid of computer and terminal configurations are possible, an examination of all systems reveals three basic combinations: 1) Small computer or terminal to a large host computer; 2) Large computers to large computers; 3) Small computers to small computers in special local area networks. The following sections examine each of these combinations.

Small computer or terminal to large host computer

Personal computers can be used as intelligent terminals in a data communications network to communicate with a large host computer. Other types of terminals can also be used in this manner. One application where the personal computer or terminal is often used is to access the numerous data bases that are now available on large computers. The data bases include such information as the latest news stories, stock market quotations, and even shopping services.

The basic components of a data communications system which allows access to a large computer and its data base are illustrated in Figure 11–2. These components include: 1) A personal computer or computer terminal located at a site remote from the large host computer with which it communicates; 2) A device called a modem which converts digital data (data in the form of bits) generated by the personal computer or computer terminal to an analog signal (audio tone) which can be sent over communication channels; 3) The communication channel over which the data is sent. Standard telephone lines are often used, but other communication channels such as microwave and satellite are available; 4) A modem at the other end of the communication channel to convert the analog data back to a digital form; 5) The large host computer with which communication takes place.

When the user of a personal computer wishes to obtain data from one of the data bases on the large computer (such as obtaining an airline schedule and making a reservation), the user enters several commands which establish the link with the large computer. Each time the user enters a command or data to be transmitted, it is electronically sent to the modem as a series of bits. The modem may be housed within the personal computer or may be located in close proximity to the computer. The modem converts the data from digital form to analog form. The data, in analog form, is then sent from the modem down the communication line.

When the data arrives at its destination, it must again be sent through a modem. The modem converts the data from analog form back to digital form. The data is then sent to main computer memory of the host computer where it can be processed. When data is sent from the large host computer to the personal computer or terminal, essentially the same steps occur in reverse order.

Each component just illustrated can have many forms and configurations. The following paragraphs discuss details of each of the components. The overall system illustrated in Figure 11-2 should be kept in mind during this discussion.

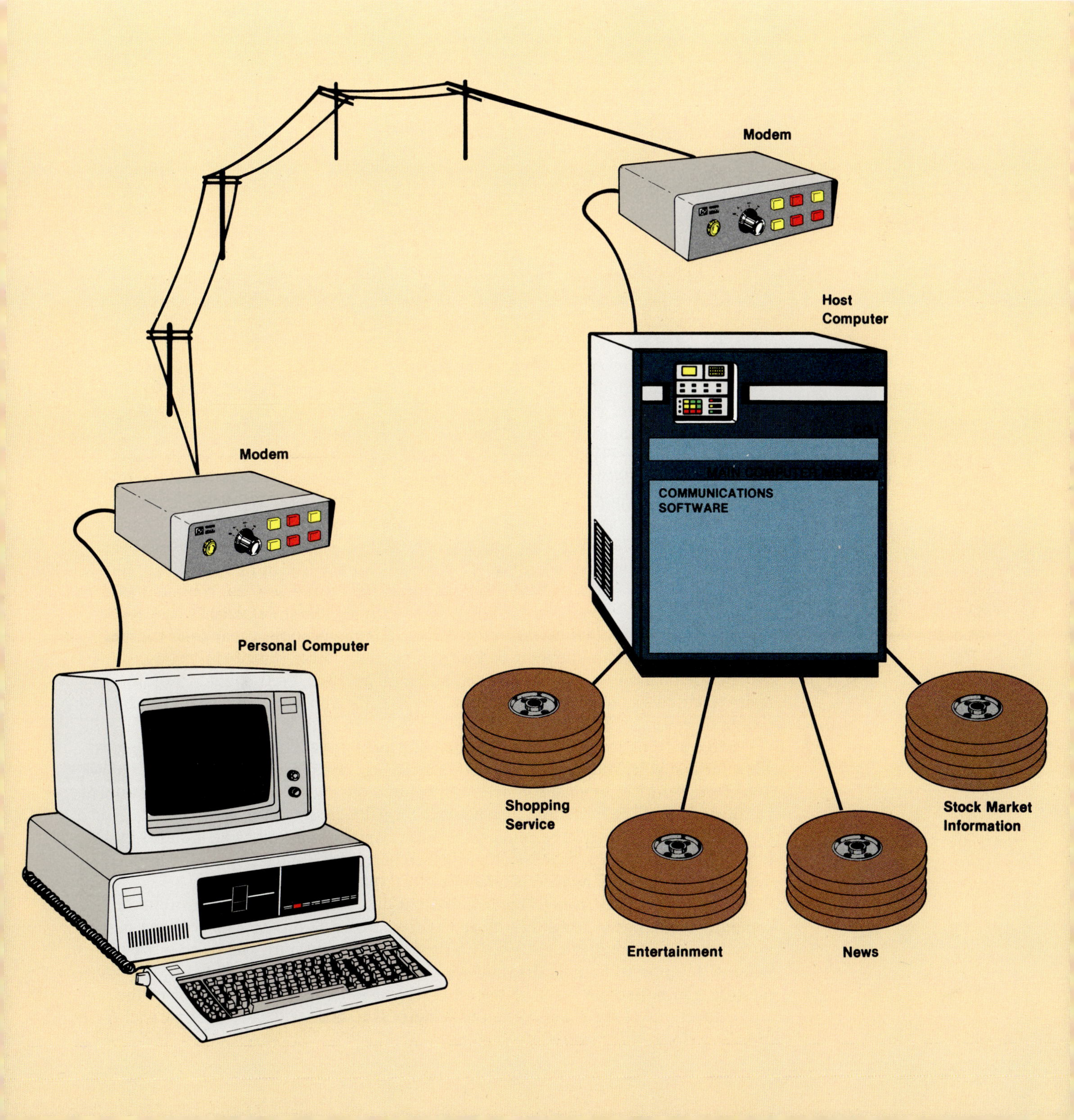

Figure 11-2 The basic components of a data communications network using a personal computer to communicate with a large host computer are shown in this diagram.

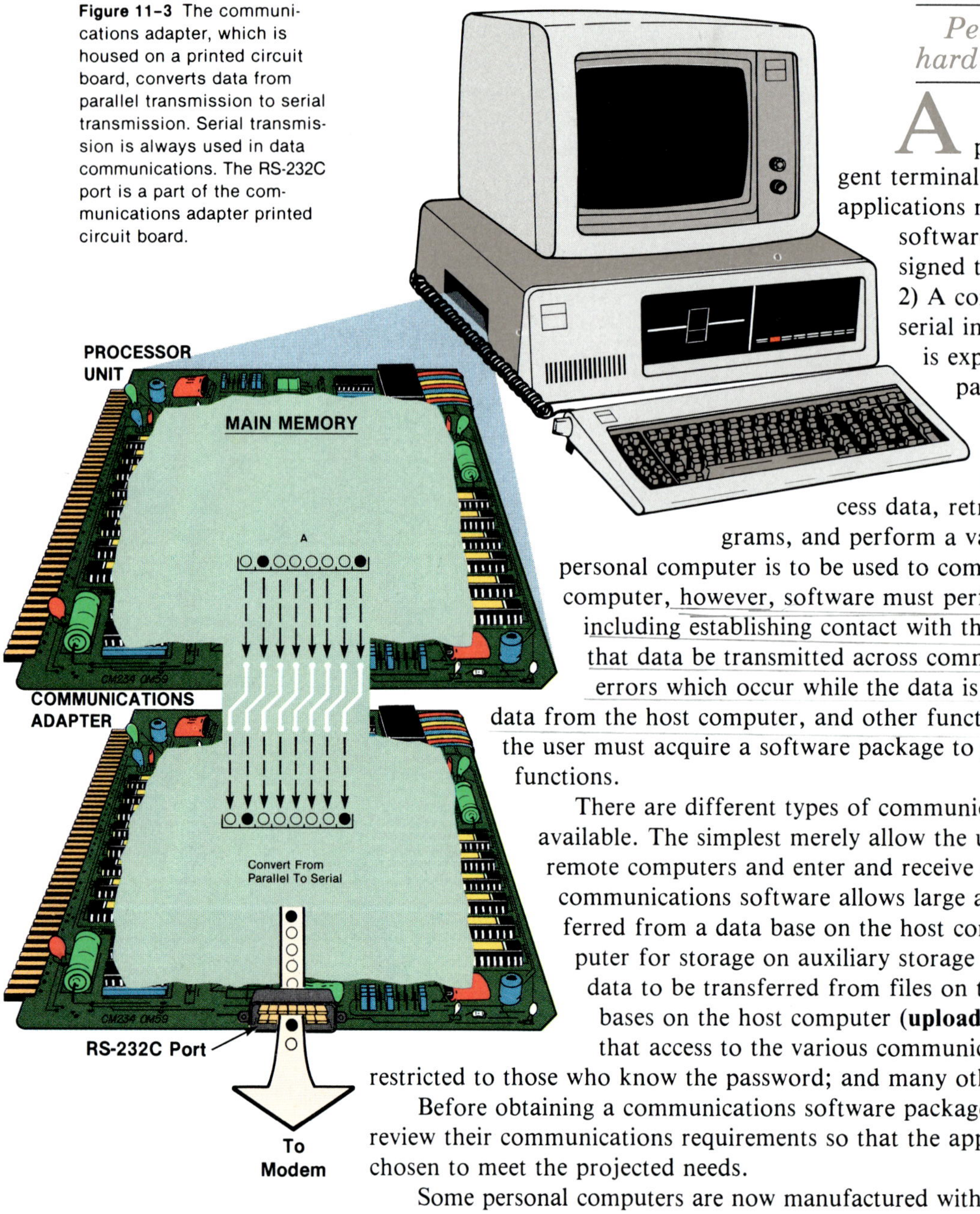

Figure 11–3 The communications adapter, which is housed on a printed circuit board, converts data from parallel transmission to serial transmission. Serial transmission is always used in data communications. The RS-232C port is a part of the communications adapter printed circuit board.

Personal computer hardware and software

A personal computer or intelligent terminal used for data communication applications requires certain hardware and software, including: 1) Software designed to allow data communications; 2) A communications adapter with a serial interface. Each of these items is explained in the following paragraphs.

The standard software available with personal computers allows the user to process data, retrieve, store, and execute programs, and perform a variety of other tasks. When a personal computer is to be used to communicate with a large host computer, however, software must perform additional functions, including establishing contact with the host computer, directing that data be transmitted across communication lines, handling errors which occur while the data is being transmitted, accepting data from the host computer, and other functions as well. Therefore, the user must acquire a software package to perform the communications functions.

There are different types of communications software packages available. The simplest merely allow the user to establish contact with remote computers and enter and receive data. More sophisticated communications software allows large amounts of data to be transferred from a data base on the host computer to the personal computer for storage on auxiliary storage (called **downloading**); allows data to be transferred from files on the personal computer to data bases on the host computer (**uploading**); establishes passwords so that access to the various communications capabilities can be restricted to those who know the password; and many other functions.

Before obtaining a communications software package, users should carefully review their communications requirements so that the appropriate software can be chosen to meet the projected needs.

Some personal computers are now manufactured with all the hardware required to allow the computer to communicate with a large host computer. Most, however, are not. Therefore, before a personal computer can be used for data communications, additional hardware must often be added. This hardware usually consists of a circuit board called a **communications adapter.** The communications adapter can normally be installed by fitting the board into an available slot on the computer (an internal electronic connector in the computer provided by the manufacturer for expansion purposes).

It will be recalled from Chapter Eight that data is moved internally within the computer along busses which can move either 8, 16, or 32 bits at a time. When bits are moved in groups, such as eight bits at a time on a bus, they are said to be moved in **parallel**. In order to transfer data down a communication channel, however, the bits must be transmitted one bit after the other (called **serial transmission**). One of the major functions of the communications adapter is to change data from a parallel form to a serial form for transmission (Figure 11–3).

To allow the serial stream of bits to be communicated to other components, a **serial interface**, or **port**, is needed. Data is transmitted in and out of the computer through the serial interface. A serial interface consists of a standard plug and socket with predefined connections. One of the most widely used types of serial interfaces is called the **RS-232C** (RS stands for recommended standard; 232 is a number to reference this agreed upon industry standard; C indicates a third revision of the standard). The RS-232C interface, which is a part of the communications adapter, acts as a pathway through which the computer transfers serial data to and from modems.

The communications adapter also performs other functions, including such tasks as adding and deleting required control bits, interfacing with the software to control the speed of transmission, error checking, and similar tasks.

Figure 11-4 This external direct connect modem is an example of modems which can be used with personal computers. It transmits data at a rate of 1,200 bits per second.

Figure 11-5 The circuit board shown here is an internal modem which can be installed in a personal computer.

Modems for the personal computer

The second component in the data communications system which allows a personal computer to communicate with a large host computer is a **modem**. As previously explained, the purpose of the modem is to change digital data consisting of bits into an analog signal that can be transmitted over telephone lines; and on the receiving end, change the analog signal transmitted over the telephone line into digital data that can be stored in main computer memory of the host computer.

A variety of modems are available for personal computers, including: 1) External, direct-connect modems; 2) Internal modems; 3) Acoustic couplers.

External, direct connect modems are attached to a personal computer by a cable. These modems are contained in a relatively small housing which can be placed adjacent to the computer (Figure 11-4). A cord from the modem plugs directly into a standard telephone jack to allow communication over telephone lines.

An **internal modem** consists of a printed circuit board, with the related electronics, that is installed internally in the personal computer (Figure 11-5). An advantage of the internal modem is that no computer-to-modem cable is required, and there is no extra electronic unit connected externally to the computer. In addition, they often cost less than external units. A disadvantage is that internal modems are machine dependent and are designed to fit a specific computer, while external modems can be used with any computer equipped with an RS-232 interface.

An **acoustic coupler** (Figure 11-6) is a modem that is

Figure 11-6 The acoustic coupler in this picture allows a portable computer user to communicate with another computer over telephone lines. Note the telephone headset is placed in the molded rubber cups on the acoustic coupler.

Figure 11–7 This acoustic coupler is used in a bus station with a regular pay telephone. Acoustic couplers provide flexibility because they can be used with any telephone anywhere.

connected to a personal computer or terminal by a cable. A standard telephone headset is placed into molded rubber cups on the acoustic coupler. The acoustic coupler converts the digital signals generated by the terminal or personal computer into a series of audible tones which are picked up by the mouthpiece in the headset in the same manner as if one were speaking into the telephone. The analog signals are then transmitted over the communication channel. An acoustic coupler provides portability because it can be used with any telephone headset in any setting (Figure 11–7). It is generally less reliable than an internal or external modem, however, because even small outside sounds can be picked up by the acoustic coupler as sounds which are to be transmitted.

A factor which must be considered when selecting a modem is the maximum speed at which the modem can send and receive data. The speed most often found when personal computers are transmitting and receiving is 300 bits per second, which is the equivalent of about 30 characters per second. Data transmitted at 30 characters per second appears on a CRT screen at a comfortable reading speed. For the average user who is entering data from the keyboard and receiving relatively small amounts of data, a transmission rate of 300 bits per second is adequate. When large amounts of data are transferred from one computer to another, such as when downloading or uploading data or software, higher speed modems which transmit 1,200 bits per second should be considered.

Modems are available with a number of different capabilities in addition to different speeds. The most basic modems require the user to perform most of the work necessary to establish contact with a host computer. For example, when using an acoustic coupler, the user must dial the required number to establish contact, wait for a response, and then insert the telephone headset into the acoustic coupler. To receive data, the user must know when the data is to be sent and make the necessary telephone connection to the acoustic coupler.

More sophisticated modems, called **intelligent** or **smart modems**, contain a microprocessor that controls many functions, allowing easier and more flexible use of data communications. For example, when used in conjunction with the communications software, smart modems allow frequently used telephone numbers that access host computers to be dialed automatically, either at the request of the user or on a timed interval basis. Similarly, a personal computer can be set, through the use of a smart modem, to automatically answer an incoming call and accept data, in much the same way a telephone answering machine would answer and accept incoming calls.

Modems are required whenever data is transmitted over lines requiring an analog signal. Some data communication channels are capable of directly transmitting a digital signal. These channels do not require a modem.

Transmitting data over communication channels

The third component of a data communication system allowing a personal computer or terminal to communicate with a host computer is the **communication**

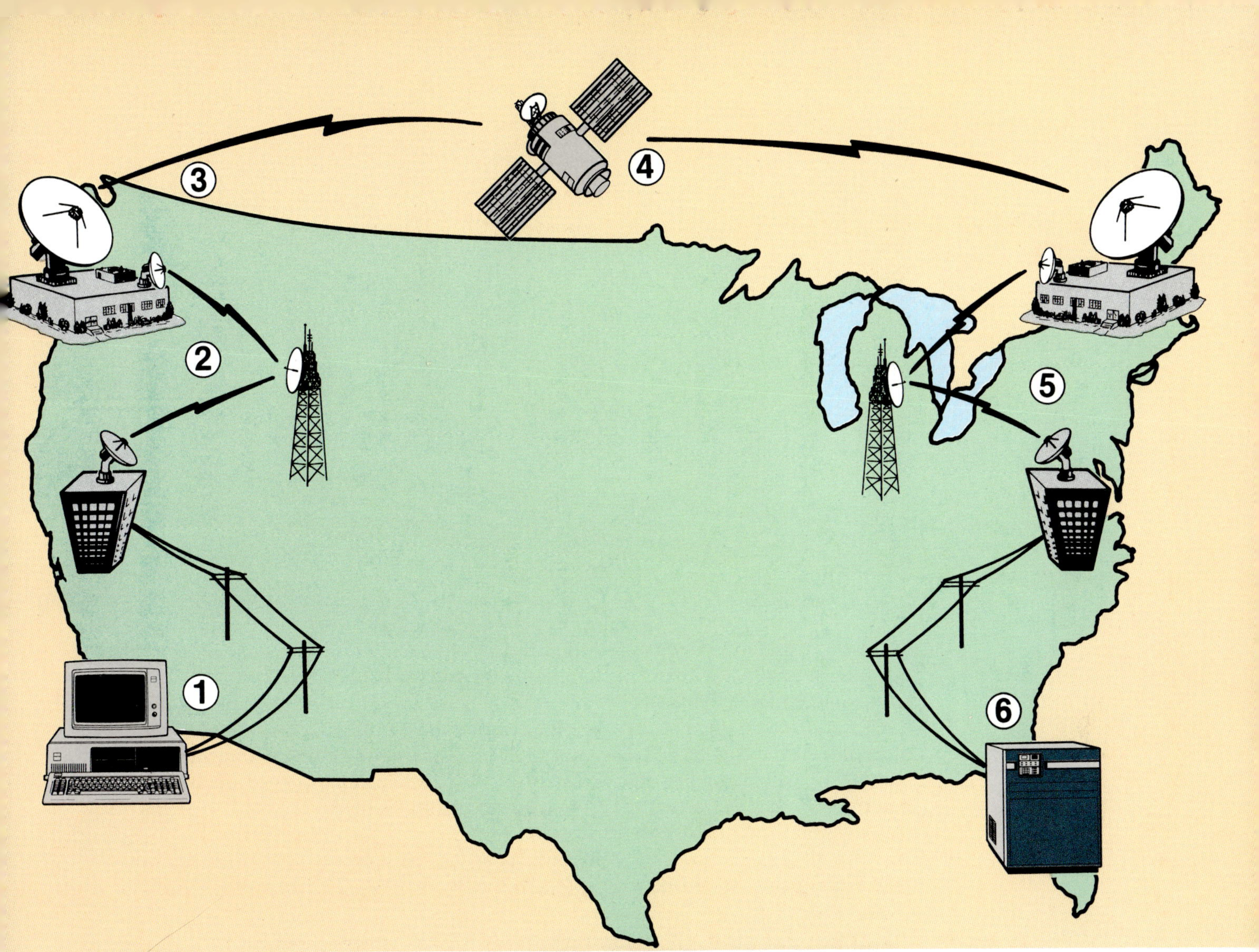

channel over which the data is sent. When data is transmitted over long distances, it is likely that a number of different types of communication channels will be called into use.

The diagram in Figure 11-8 illustrates some of the various communication channels which could be used to transmit data from a personal computer on the west coast of the United States to a host computer on the east coast of the United States. The steps that could occur are: 1) An entry is made on the personal computer. The data is sent over telephone lines from the computer to a microwave station; 2) Microwave stations transmit data through open space much like radio or television signals. Microwave stations are characterized by antennas positioned on tops of buildings, towers, or mountains (Figure 11-9). Data is transmitted on a line of sight path to other microwave stations approximately 30 miles away. In the drawing, the data is transmitted from the last microwave station to an earth station;

Figure 11-8 This diagram illustrates the use of telephone wires, microwave transmission, and satellite transmission to allow a personal computer to communicate with a large host computer.

Figure 11-9 The round antenna on this tower is used for microwave transmission.

Figure 11-10 Earth stations which communicate with communication satellites must have large antennas and must be able to communicate with other ground stations as well, as indicated by the microwave tower in the left of the picture.

3) An earth station is a communication facility that contains a very large antenna that can transmit data to a communication satellite (Figure 11-10). Satellites positioned approximately 22,000 miles above the earth (Figure 11-11) can relay signals from one earth station to another; 4) The satellite relays the data to an earth station on the other side of the country; 5) The data received at the earth station is transmitted to a microwave station; 6) The data is finally sent by the telephone lines to the host computer. When data is transmitted from the host computer to the personal computer, the transmission would take place in a similar fashion.

Not all data transmission is as complex as the example just illustrated, but the potential for this type of network exists to satisfy the needs of data communication users.

Figure 11-11 Communication satellites such as this one being launched from the space shuttle enable data communications around the world.

When personal computers communicate with a large host computer, data is sent over the communication lines using **asynchronous transmission**. When asynchronous transmission is used, one character at a time is transmitted or received. Each character, which consists of a series of bits, is identified by a start bit and a stop bit. Thus, the character "A" transmitted in asynchronous mode would be preceded by a start bit and would be followed by a stop bit (Figure 11–12). The next character sent down the line is also preceded by a start bit and followed by a stop bit. Because of the need to generate and interpret both a start and stop bit, and because each character is separated by an idle time gap, asynchronous transmission is relatively slow. It is used, however, for modems which transmit either 300 bits per second or 1,200 bits per second.

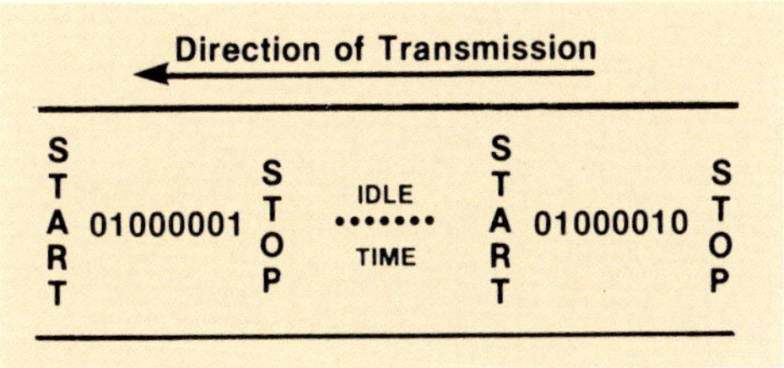

Figure 11–12 In this drawing, asynchronous transmission is used to transmit the letters A and B in the ASCII code. The start bit notifies the modem that a character is being sent. The bits for the character follow the start bit. After all bits for the character have been transmitted, the stop bit indicates the end of the character. A start bit can immediately follow the stop bit, or there can be idle time following the stop bit, depending upon the terminal sending the data.

For applications where faster transmission is required, such as when data stored on a disk is transmitted from one large computer to another over a data communication channel, synchronous transmission is used (Figure 11–13). **Synchronous transmission** allows characters to be sent down the line as a group without start-stop bits. Each character is identified by the bits comprising the character. The beginning and end of the character is determined by a timing mechanism within a modem. Once transmission is begun, the timing mechanism samples the communication channel at specified intervals to obtain a bit. When it has sampled the required number of bits, the character is sent to the receiving computer. Synchronous transmission is normally used when more than 2,000 bits per second are to be transmitted. Data can be sent at speeds of 19,200 bits per second and higher using synchronous transmission.

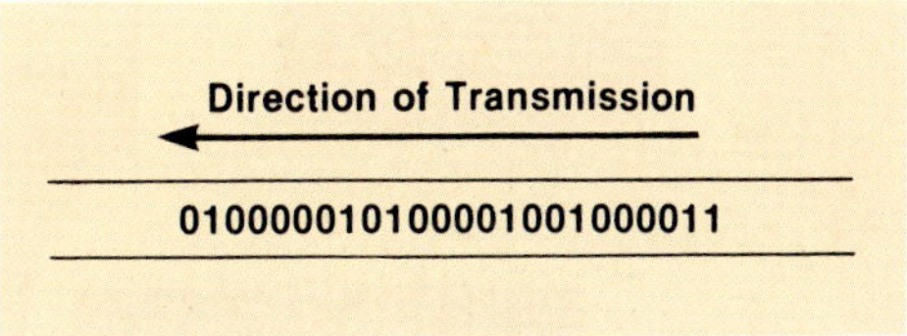

Figure 11–13 Synchronous transmission allows data to be sent as a group over a data communication channel. At specified time intervals, the line is sampled by the modem and the bit is detected. The accumulated bits are then sent to the host computer. Since the data is sent without start-stop bits and without idle time between each character, much faster speeds are achieved with synchronous transmission than with asynchronous transmission. The biggest disadvantage with synchronous transmission is that on occasion because of line interference, the modem and the line get out of synchronization. When this occurs, much of the data which is sent is lost and must be retransmitted.

There are three basic ways in which communication channels are used for transmitting data: 1) Simplex; 2) Half-duplex; 3) Duplex. A **simplex channel** allows data to be transmitted in one direction only. For example, if a simplex channel were used, a personal computer could only send; it could never receive (Figure 11–14). In a modern data communications environment, simplex channels are rarely used because even if data is only sent from a personal computer, there is usually an acknowledgement made to the sending device.

Figure 11–14 A simplex channel allows data to be transmitted in one direction only. Although the arrow illustrates a personal computer to host computer direction, the one-way communication could take place from the host computer to the personal computer.

On a **half-duplex channel**, data can be sent in either direction, but in only one direction at a time (Figure 11–15). Half-duplex channels are often used when a personal computer is communicating with a large host computer because the typical sequence is for the personal computer user to send data to the host computer and then for the host computer to respond to the data sent by the personal computer user. The data entered by the personal computer user goes in one direction on the line and the data from the host computer goes in the opposite direction, but there is no need for data to be going both ways at the same time. When half-duplex lines are used, the

Figure 11–15 A half-duplex line allows data to be sent in both directions, but it cannot be sent in both directions at the same time.

transmission flow in one direction must be stopped each time the direction of transmission is reversed. The time to accomplish this is called "turnaround time" and is typically 50 to 250 milliseconds (thousandths of a second).

Data can be transmitted in both directions at the same time on **full duplex** communication channels (Figure 11–16). A major advantage of full duplex communication channels is that turnaround time is not required. Therefore if there are high-speed communications occurring between two computers, they do not have to wait for turnaround. Although the time may seem insignificant, if five messages were sent from computer A to computer B, and five messages were sent back from computer B to computer A, a total of nine turnarounds will be required if half-duplex lines were used. This could amount to almost 2½ seconds. When 9,600 bits are sent in one

Figure 11–16 A full-duplex line allows data to be sent in both directions at the same time. A major advantage of full-duplex lines is that no turnaround time is required to reverse directions of transmission.

second, the time lost for turnaround could have been used to send 24,000 bits, or 3,000 characters on a full-duplex line. Full-duplex communication channels are most often used when high-speed transmission is taking place between two computers.

Figure 11-17 A large computer is usually required as a host computer in a data communications network. In many cases, specialized hardware is required to handle the processing needs.

Large host computer

The fifth component of the data communications system allowing a personal computer to communicate with a large computer is the large host computer itself. When communication occurs over telephone lines or other medium where an analog signal is used, a modem is required at the receiving end as well as at the sending end. Therefore, the communication channel will hook into a modem at the host computer site.

When a large computer is used for data communications, in most cases a **communications control unit** interfaces between the modem and the computer. This unit assembles the bits received from the modem into characters for transmission to main computer memory of the host computer. It can also perform error recovery when a signal is lost or when noise distorts the signal on the line, interpret and process control information, and interface with many lines and modems and control each one so the computer need not perform these functions.

The most sophisticated communications control units, sometimes called **front-end processors**, can be programmed by the user. These units, which are actually minicomputers designed especially for the task of front-end processor, can be programmed to edit input records for valid data, control the network and allow only authorized users to have access to the computer, and a number of similar activities.

The advantage of a front-end processor is that the tasks accomplished by the front-end processor do not have to be performed by the host computer. This allows the computer to concentrate on processing application programs and producing useful output. It has been found with large data communication networks that up to 30 percent of the processing time for a computer can be spent monitoring the communication channels and performing the same functions that can be performed by the front-end processor. Thus, in large data communication networks, the use of a programmable front-end processor can significantly increase the amount of processing that can be accomplished by the host computer.

The large computer which serves as the host in a data communication network can vary considerably in terms of size and capabilities. In large networks, with many lines and terminals requiring large amounts of applications processing, mainframe computers are normally used (Figure 11-17). These machines require large main computer memory (typically several megabytes), sophisticated systems and applications software, and a multitude of communications equipment.

LARGE COMPUTERS TO LARGE COMPUTERS

In addition to personal computers or terminals communicating with large host computers, large computers can communicate with other large computers. This may be required so that data can be exchanged between the computers. For example, in a retail store operation with many branch stores, each store may have a computer with an inventory data base. During the day, the inventory for the store is updated interactively as sales are made. At the end of the day, the inventory in a given store must be sent to a main computer at the home office so that the corporate inventory data base is up to date. In most cases, this data will be sent from the computer in the store to the computer in the home office using data communications.

A number of factors must be considered when large computers communicate with large computers. Many of these factors are also applicable to data communication systems where small computers or terminals communicate with a large host computer. These factors include: 1) Sizes of computers; 2) Communication channels; 3) Line configurations; 4) Networks; 5) Value added networks. Each of these factors is discussed in the following paragraphs.

Sizes of computers

As noted previously, virtually every size computer can participate in data communications. Personal computers, when communicating with larger machines, act essentially like intelligent terminals. Larger computers, such as minicomputers, can communicate directly with other computers and can also be part of networks of computers. Large mainframes act as host computers in communication networks and can also communicate directly with other large computers. While all sizes of computers can communicate with one another, the size does dictate the type of processing that can be accomplished by the computer in data communication systems.

Figure 11–18 A few of the many types of coaxial cable available to transmit data are shown in this picture.

Communication channels

Three types of communication channels — telephone lines, microwave signals, and satellite signals — were discussed in the application where a personal computer communicated with a large host computer. These channels are used when large computers communicate with each other as well. In addition, two other types of communication channels can be used for both small computer to large computer and large computer to large computer communications. These are coaxial cables and fiber optics.

A **coaxial cable**, which consists of a multitude of wires within a cable enclosure (Figure 11–18), is a high quality communication line that can be laid under the ground or under the ocean. Data can be transmitted at a much higher bits per second rate on coaxial cable than on telephone lines.

Fiber optics (Figure 11–19) is a technology that may serve to eventually replace conventional wire and cable in thousands of communication systems. The

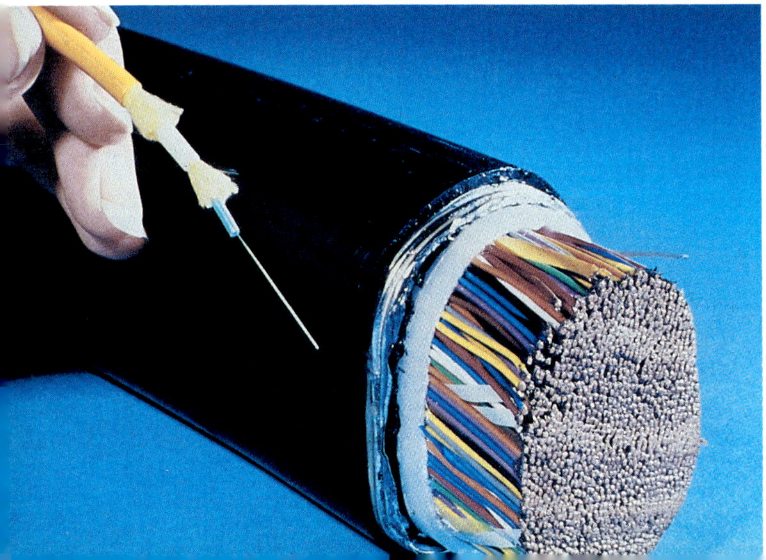

Figure 11–19 The strand of fiber optic cable being held in this picture can transmit the same amount of data as the multistrand copper cable also shown here.

technology is based upon the ability of smooth hair-thin strands of material to conduct light with high efficiency. The major advantages of fiber optics over wire cables include substantial weight and size savings and increased speed of transmission. A one and one-half pound fiber optic cable can transmit the same amount of data as thirty pounds of copper wire. A standard coaxial cable can carry up to 5,400 different voice channels, while a single fiber optic cable can carry up to 50,000 channels. Although fiber optics is not yet used on a large scale, it promises to dramatically increase data communication capabilities once it becomes widely installed.

Line configurations

There are several methods in which computer terminals, personal computers, and large computers can be connected to a host computer or to each other. The method used depends upon the amount of data being transmitted and the related cost of the transmission lines. The two major line configurations are: 1) Point-to-point lines; 2) Multidrop or multipoint lines.

A **point-to-point line** is a direct line between a terminal and a larger computer, a personal computer and a larger computer, or two larger computers (Figure 11-20). When a point-to-point line is used, no other terminals are on the line. A point-to-point line is used primarily when communication will be taking place on an almost continuous basis and fast response time is required; or when communication will take place only on occasion and the user can determine when to establish line contact. In many cases, point-to-point lines are used when large computers communicate with each other.

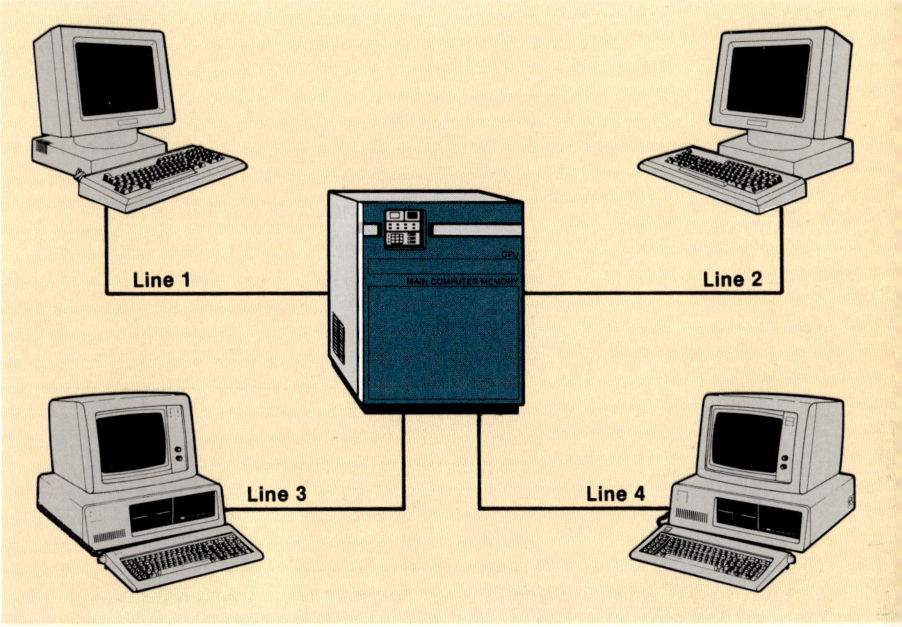

Figure 11-20 When a point-to-point line configuration is used, the terminals or personal computers are connected directly to the host computer. Only one terminal or personal computer is used for each line into the host computer.

A point-to-point line may be one of two types: 1) Leased line; 2) Switched line. A **leased line** is a permanent circuit to connect a personal computer, terminal, or larger computer with another computer. With a leased line, the device at one end of the line is always connected to the device at the other end of the line. Establishing contact between devices linked by a leased line is normally done by entering a control character or flipping a switch on the terminal, or by the host computer addressing a message to the appropriate leased line. Since the terminal or personal computer is always connected to the host computer via the leased line, the electronics of the systems are established so the host computer electronically listens for a request from the terminal or personal computer to send data for a period of time (usually much less than a second), and then the line is changed so the terminal listens for a request from the host computer to send data. In this way, merely touching a key can initiate contact between the host computer and the terminal or personal computer.

A **switched line** is so-called because it is established through the regular voice telephone network rather than a direct connection as found with a leased line. Each time a terminal or personal computer communicates with a host computer over a switched line, it can be using different circuits because the circuitry will be selected by the telephone company switching devices (hence the name). When using a switched line, the user initiates contact with the host computer by dialing the telephone number of the host computer. The modem for the line at the host computer site is assigned a telephone number just as if it were a regular telephone. When its number is dialed by the terminal or personal computer user, either manually or automatically, the modem answers the call and establishes the line connection. The modem also informs the terminal or personal computer, through the use of a control character sent down the line, that it is ready to receive data. The terminal can then begin sending data to the host computer.

The host computer can establish contact with any of the terminals or personal computers in the network by appropriate computer commands which dial the number of the terminal. The terminal modem then responds in the same manner as when the host computer modem is dialed. When a switched line is used, the terminal or personal computer and the host computer are connected only when data communications are occurring. When the user is finished communicating with the host computer, the connection is terminated. The next time the terminal or personal computer user wishes to communicate with the host computer, the line connection must again be made. Thus, using a switched point-to-point line is much like talking on the telephone.

The second major line configuration is called a **multidrop** or **multipoint line.** It has more than one terminal, personal computer, or larger computer on a single line connected to a host computer (Figure 11-21). When a multidrop line is used, only one terminal at a time can transmit to the host computer. More than one terminal on the line, however, can receive data at the same time. A multidrop line decreases line costs considerably because the line is used by many terminals. This line configuration is normally found in inquiry systems with multiple terminals because each terminal uses the line only a short period of time.

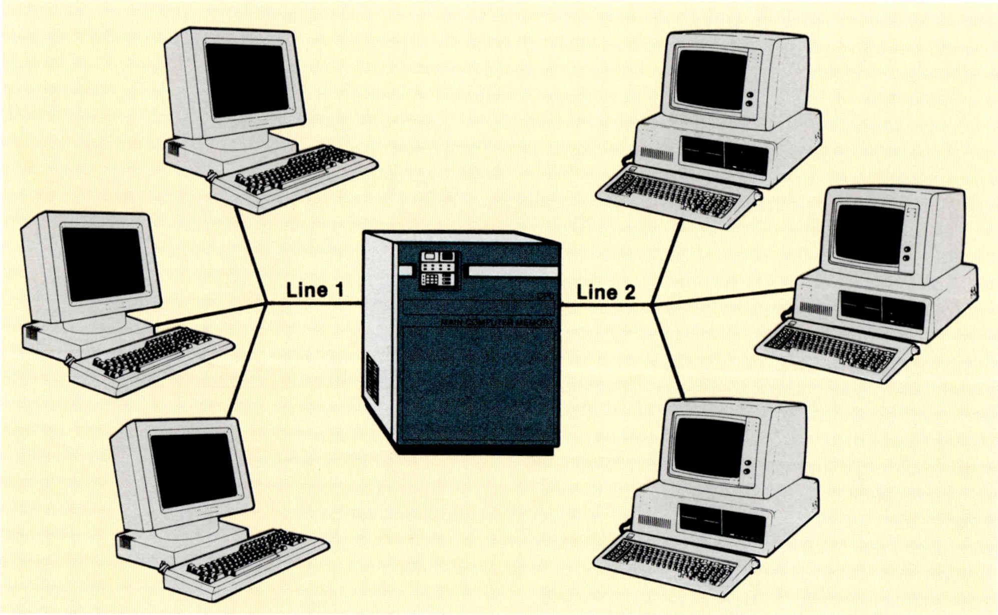

Figure 11-21 A multidrop line has more than one terminal or personal computer on a single line. In the example, there are three terminals on line 1 and three personal computers on line 2. On each line, only one personal computer or terminal at a time can transmit to the computer.

For example, an operator could use a CRT terminal to enter an inquiry. While the data is being transmitted to the host computer, other terminals on the line would not be able to send data. The time required for the data to be transmitted to the host computer, however, would most likely be less than one second. As soon as the inquiry is received by the computer, a second terminal could send an inquiry. Thus, it would appear to the terminal operator as if no other terminals were on the line, even though multiple terminals may be using the same line.

The number of terminals to be placed on one line is a decision made by the designer of the network based upon the amount of traffic which will be found on the line. For example, one hundred or more terminals could be contained on a single line, provided each of them was only going to be sending short messages, such as inquiries;

and each terminal was going to use the communication line only a few hours per day. On the other hand, if longer messages were required and the terminals were to be used almost continuously, the number of terminals on one line would have to be smaller.

A leased line is almost always used for multidrop line configurations. Contact is established between the terminals or personal computers and the host computer in one of two ways: 1) Polling; 2) Addressing. **Polling** is performed by the host computer and the associated communications control unit. The host computer asks each terminal or personal computer on the multidrop line if it has some data to send to the computer (Figure 11–22). The question is asked by special control characters which are transmitted to the terminal. If the terminal does not have data to send, it responds with negative control characters and the next terminal on the line is polled. If the terminal asked does have data to send, it gains control of the line and sends its data. Generally, once a terminal or personal computer gains control of the multidrop line, it has control until it relinquishes it, meaning that polling cannot continue. Thus, the danger exists that once a terminal gains control of a line, it can keep control for a long time. To overcome this condition, some systems include a programmed time-out which allows the terminal to control the line for a specified period of time and then breaks the connection so that other terminals on the line are not excluded from using the line.

The host computer can send data to a terminal or personal computer on a multidrop line by a technique called **addressing**. The host computer addresses the particular terminal on the line and sends the message to that terminal. Thus, even though multiple terminals are connected to one line, only the addressed terminal receives the message from the host computer.

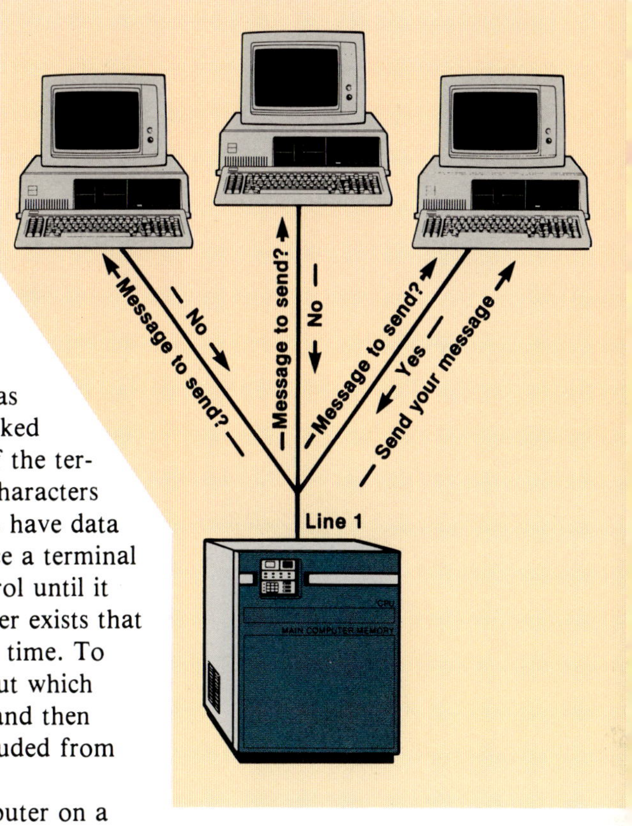

Figure 11–22 A host computer polls terminals or personal computers by asking if they have a message to send. If so, the host computer directs the personal computer or terminal to send its message.

Networks

The various elements of data communications which have been discussed thus far must normally be organized into a system, or **network**, in order to solve the problems for which they are used. Although a network can be defined as any system composed of two or more large computers, personal computers, and terminals, most networks are composed of multiple terminals and personal computers, and possibly multiple large host computers to enable the network to function most efficiently and productively. Many combinations can be used, but network design is usually categorized as one of two basic types: 1) Star network; 2) Ring network.

A **star network** (Figure 11–23) contains a central host computer and one or more

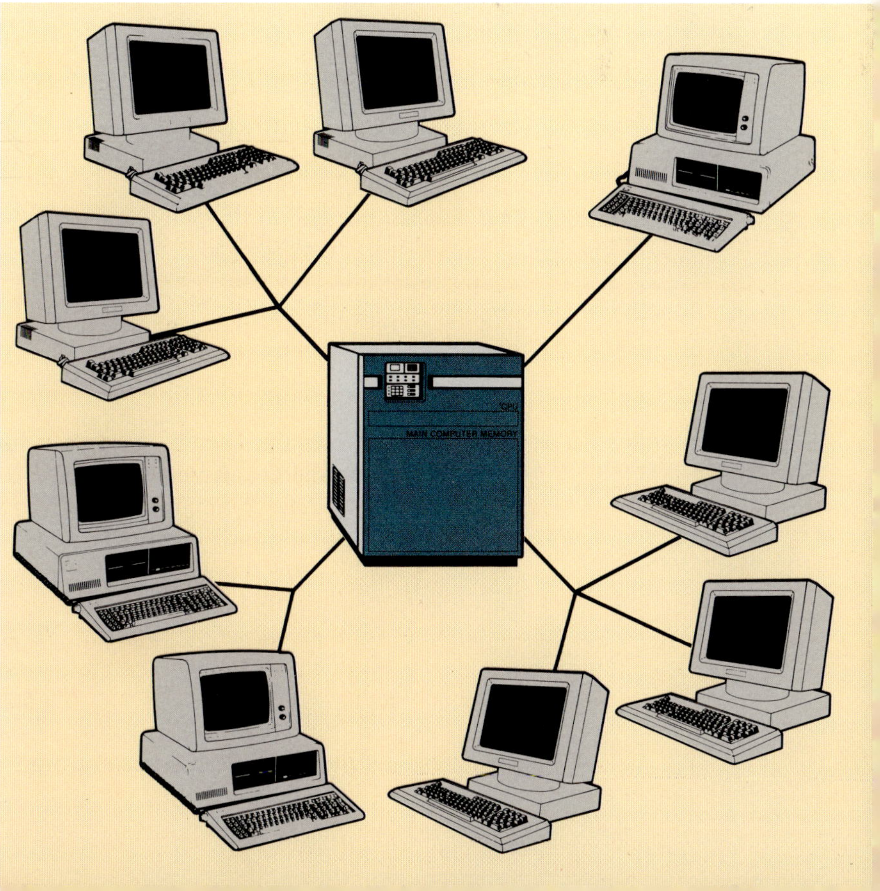

Figure 11–23 A star network contains a single, centralized host computer with which all the terminals or personal computers in the network communicate. Both point-to-point and multidrop lines can be used in a star network.

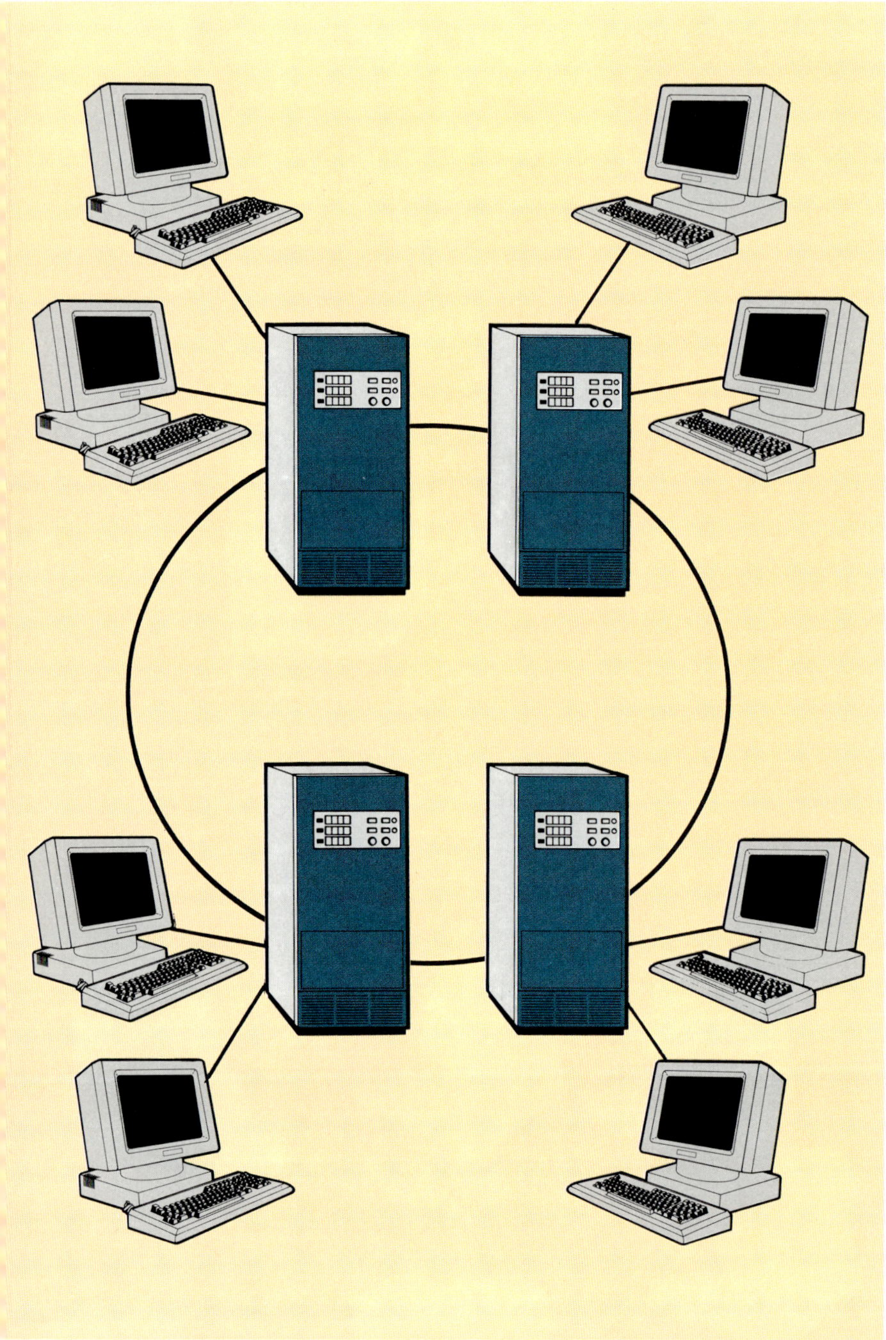

terminals or personal computers connected to it, forming a star. A pure star network consists of only point-to-point lines between the terminals and the host computer, but most star networks, such as shown in Figure 11-23, include both point-to-point lines and multidrop lines. A star network configuration is often used when the central host computer contains all of the data required to process the input from the terminals. For example, if inquiries are being processed in the data communications network, when a star configuration is used, all of the data to answer the inquiry would be contained in the data base stored on the central host computer.

While a star network can be relatively efficient and close control can be kept on the data processed on the network, its major disadvantage is that the entire network is dependent upon the centralized computer and the associated hardware and software. If any of these elements fail, the entire network is disabled. Therefore, in most large star networks, backup systems are available in case the primary system fails.

A **ring network** does not utilize a centralized host computer. Rather, a series of computers communicates with one another (Figure 11-24). A ring network can be useful when all of the processing is not done at a central site, but instead processing is accomplished at local sites. For example, computers could be located in three departments: the accounting department, the personnel department, and the shipping and receiving department. The computers in each of these departments could perform the processing required for each of the departments. On occasion, however, the computer in the shipping and receiving department, for example, could communicate with the computer in the accounting department to update certain data stored on the accounting department computer. Ring networks have not been extensively implemented for data communications systems which are used for long distance communication, but are used for more local commmunications.

Figure 11-24 In a ring network, computers are connected to one another as shown here. In many cases, minicomputers are used in a ring network.

Value added networks

The various networks and their elements discussed thus far are often designed and implemented individually by organizations. Several types of service organizations, however, offer data communications facilities and services which can be used in lieu of an independently designed network. These networks are often called **value added networks.** A value added network is a data communications network that is already established and which can be used by anyone subscribing to the service. Thus, arrangements can be made with the companies which offer value added network services to allow users and host computers to be tied into the networks. In most cases, the services offer switched networks.

The reason for value added networks is to save the user money and time. Rather than designing a large network and purchasing all the software and hardware necessary to implement the network, the user can merely tie into the already-existing value added network.

The companies which have developed these networks generally lease lines from the telephone company and other carriers such as satellite transmission services, and then use a multitude of minicomputers, switches, and interfacing devices to organize the lines into a nationwide network.

Within the network, the most unique aspect is that they use a technique called packet switching on very high speed synchronous lines. **Packet switching** is a technique whereby so-called packets of data, often consisting of 128 characters each, are transmitted across the network. The user is charged a certain rate based upon the number of packets transmitted, regardless of the distance the packets are transmitted. For example, a user transmitting 20,000 packets of data from New York to Los Angeles is charged the same as a user transmitting data from Dallas to Houston. The advantage is that the rates are reasonable, and the network is configured in such a way that it is virtually impossible for the network to become inoperable. Thus, if one line or group of lines becomes disabled, the network will merely reroute the data to its final destination.

Since data within a value added network and other networks as well must travel over a variety of channels, such as telephone lines, microwave signals, and satellite signals, a standardized set of procedures is required which specifies how electronic components, terminals, computers, and networks are designed. These standardized sets are called protocols.

A communications **protocol** is a formal set of rules governing the format and relative timing of message exchanges between two communicating devices. These can range from the electrical connections between two devices to the packet management specifications required for packet switching. A number of organizations and groups have established various protocols for data communications covering such subjects as the formatting of data on a line, error detection techniques, how users can gain access to transmission channels, and so on. Protocols that have been developed are of great value in allowing equipment from a variety of vendors to interact in a data communications environment.

Summary

The various aspects of data communications with relation to large computers communicating with large computers, as well as networks where smaller computers or terminals communicate with large computers, can become quite technically involved. In most cases, unless a person is going to be closely involved with the technical design and implementation of a data communications network, there is no need for a detailed understanding of all of these various technical areas. A familiarity with the topics presented thus far in the chapter, however, is beneficial.

SMALL COMPUTERS TO SMALL COMPUTERS

The third major combination found in data communications is small computers communicating with small computers. This combination can occur in basically two different ways: 1) Personal computer to personal computer over telephone lines or value added networks; 2) Personal computer or small computer to personal computer or small computer over local area networks. Each of these is explained in the following paragraphs.

Communicating with other personal computers

A type of data communications that is possible for those owning a personal computer is communicating with other personal computer users through the use of public telephone lines or through the use of value added networks. Both ends of the communication must have a personal computer, the appropriate software, and a modem (Figure 11-25).

Figure 11-25 Personal computers can communicate with other personal computers over telephone lines or value added networks. Public bulletin boards are easily accessible.

Today, many free sources of information can be accessed by users of personal computers. These information sources are called **public bulletin boards**. Public bulletin boards are computer users or clubs that have stored messages, public domain software, and other types of information on auxiliary storage of a personal computer. Through the data communications capabilities of personal computers, users can access the bulletin board information stored on auxiliary storage. In some cases, messages can be added to the bulletin board and then be accessed by other users, resulting in a form of electronic mail.

Local area networks

The second manner in which personal computers or small computers communicate with one another is through the use of a local area network. A **local area network** is a communications network that covers a limited geographic area, is privately owned and user administered, is mostly used for the internal transfer of information within a business, is normally contained within a single building or adjacent group of buildings, and transmits data at a very rapid speed.

The network consists of a communication channel that connects either a series of computer terminals together with a minicomputer or, more commonly, a group of personal computers to one another. Very sophisticated systems may connect a variety of pieces of office equipment, such as word processing equipment, computer terminals, video equipment, and personal computers, to form a network. In a local area network, many types of equipment might share the communication channels.

The three most important application areas of local area networks are: 1) Hardware resource sharing; 2) Information resource sharing; 3) Electronic mail and text transfer. **Hardware resource sharing** refers to placing certain expensive devices on the network to allow each personal computer on the network to use that device. For example, when a number of personal computers are used on the network, there may be a need for a letter quality printer, but each computer on the network does not require a letter quality printer all the time. Therefore, one daisy wheel printer could be purchased and be made a part of the network. Whenever a user of a personal computer on the network needed the printer, it could be accessed over the network.

To illustrate, the drawing in Figure 11–26 depicts a local area network. Although

Figure 11–26 A local area network consists of multiple personal computers or terminals connected to one another. The users can share hardware, information, and electronic mail.

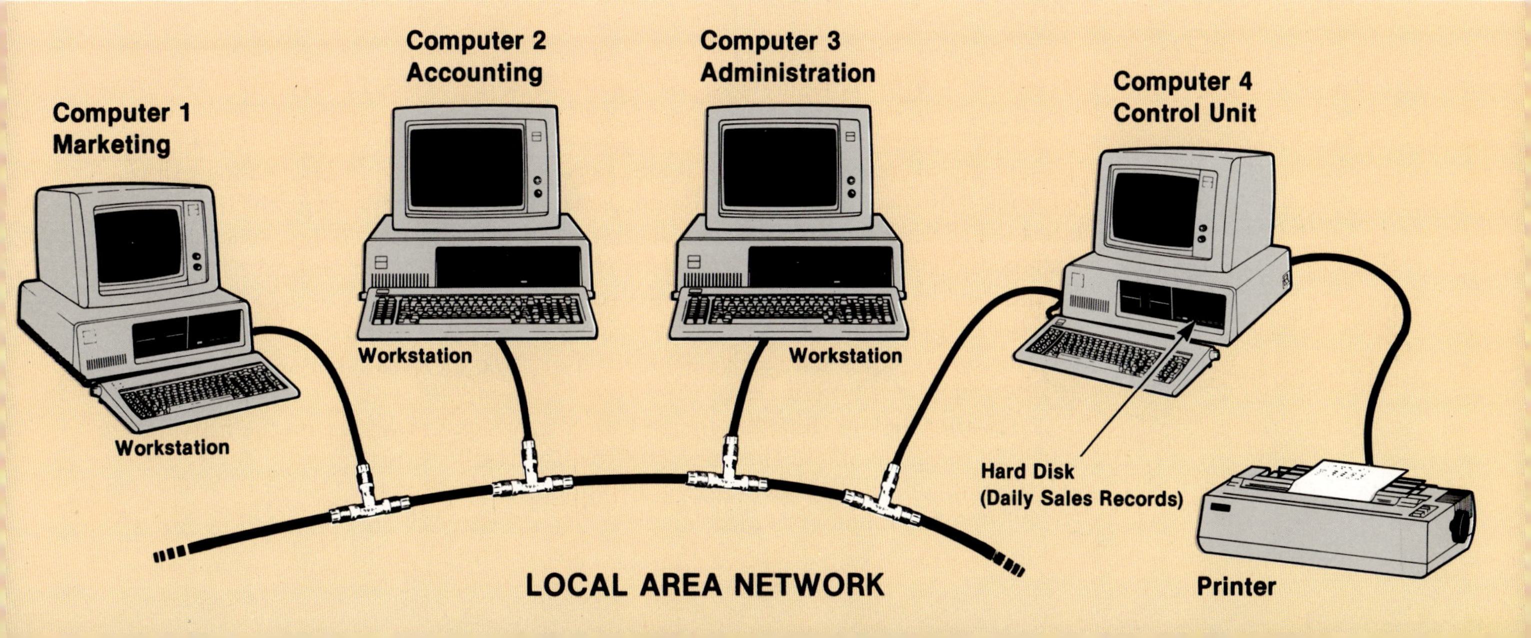

different network configurations are possible, this network consists of four personal computers linked together by a cable. Three of the personal computers (computer 1 in the marketing department, computer 2 in the accounting department, and computer 3 in the administration department) are **workstations**, and are available for use at all times. The fourth computer (computer 4) is used as a **control unit**, sometimes called a **server**. Many local area networks require that one of the computers be dedicated to handling the communications needs of the other computers in the network. The control unit computer contains the daisy wheel printer. Using the local network, all workstations and the control unit can use the printer attached to computer number 4. Thus, rather than having a printer for each personal computer, a single hardware resource (the printer) can be shared.

Information resource sharing allows anyone using a personal computer on the local area network to access data stored on any other computer in the network. In actual practice, hardware resource sharing and information resource sharing are often combined. For example, in Figure 11–26, the daily sales records could be stored on the hard disk associated with the control unit personal computer. Anyone needing access to the sales records could use this information resource. The ability to access and store data on common auxiliary storage is an important attribute of many local area networks.

Frequently used software is another type of resource that is often shared on a local area network. For example, if all users need access to word processing software, the software can be stored on the hard disk and accessed by all users as required. This is much more convenient and faster than having the software stored on a floppy disk and available at each workstation. For software written in-house, this is a common approach. It should be noted, however, that the licensing agreement from many software companies does not permit the purchase of a single software package for use by all the workstations in a network; therefore, it may be necessary to obtain a special agreement if a commercial software package is to be stored on hard disk and accessed by many users.

Electronic mail or **electronic text transfer** provides the ability to communicate directly with other users of the local area network. For example, using electronic mail a user can send a message from one computer to another on the communication network. The message would normally be stored on auxiliary storage of the receiving computer, and a message would be displayed on the screen of the receiving computer indicating the receipt of "electronic mail." The user could then display the message. When the message was displayed, the communications software could notify the sender that the message had been viewed. The message could also be printed.

Data communications and the local area network

An understanding of local area networks requires an understanding of the following basic data communications concepts: 1) Network topology, which is the term used to describe the physical organization of the network; 2) Transmission medium and method, which refers to the type of communication channel used and the method used to transmit signals over the communication channel; and 3) Network access, which identifies the procedures that allow each personal computer in the network to communicate and receive data. Each of these topics is discussed in the following paragraphs.

Network topology describes the pathways by which the devices on the network are connected to one another. The three most widely used local network topologies are the bus, the ring, and the star network.

When a **bus topology** is used, all devices in the network are connected to and share a single cable. Information is transmitted in either direction from any one personal computer to another. Any message can be directed to a specific work station. An advantage of the bus topology is that devices can be attached or unattached from the network at any point without disturbing the rest of the network. In addition, if one personal computer on the network fails, this does not affect the other users of the local area network. The network illustrated in Figure 11-26 is an example of a simple bus topology.

A **ring topology** has all devices in the network connected by a single communication cable that forms a circle (Figure 11-27). Messages are sent from one device to another around the ring. As the message moves around the ring, each terminal electronically detects whether the message is for it. If it is, the terminal processes the message. If not, the terminal or personal computer will normally boost the signal and transmit it to the next terminal or personal computer in the ring. A disadvantage of the ring topology is that the failure of a single terminal or personal computer within the ring can render the entire network inoperable.

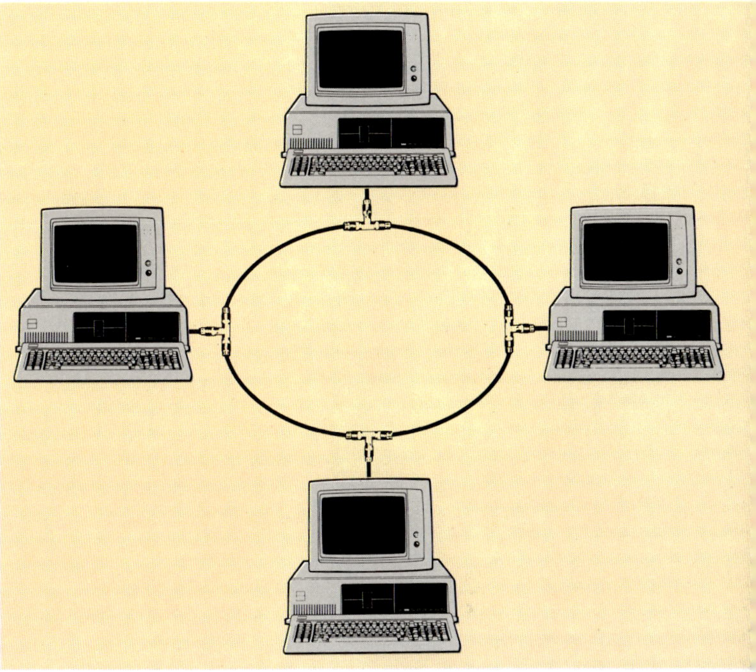

Figure 11-27 In a ring topology, computers are connected by a single cable that forms a ring.

When the **star topology** is used, each personal computer or terminal is connected through a central controlling communications unit (Figure 11-28). The central controlling unit handles the communication tasks of receiving and routing messages to the various stations. In the example shown in Figure 11-28, if computer 2 wants to send a message to computer 3, an indication is sent by computer 2 to the central controlling computer (computer 1) that transmission is to take place. Computer 1 then sends an electronic signal to computer 3 indicating that a message is to be sent from computer 2 and establishes the connection between the two.

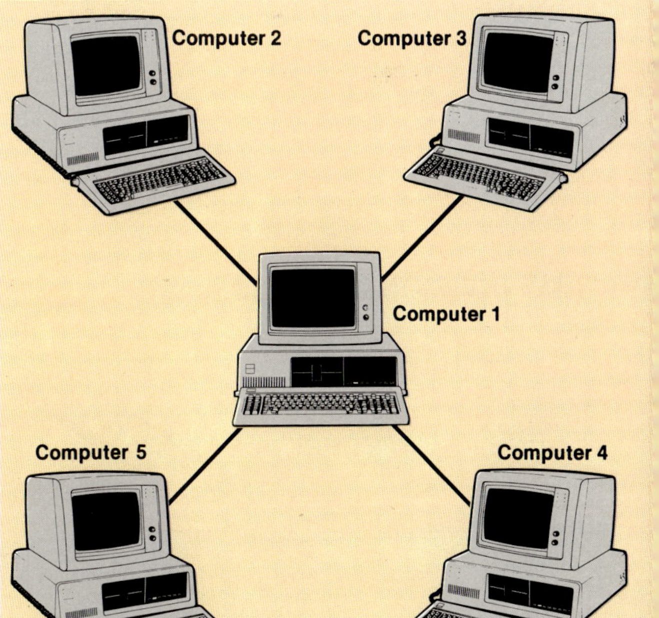

Figure 11-28 A star topology has a central controlling communications unit.

Transmission medium and transmission method

The second major concept with respect to local area networks is the transmission medium and the associated transmission method. The **transmission medium** is the type of communication channel or line used to interconnect personal computers or terminals in the local area network. The **transmission method** is the manner in which signals are transmitted over the medium. Generally, local area networks use twisted pair wire, coaxial cables, or optical fibers as the transmission medium.

Twisted pair wire is common telephone cord. It is an inexpensive transmission medium, and it can be easily strung from one location to another, but it has several major disadvantages. First, twisted pair wire is susceptible to outside electrical interference or noise such as generated by fans or air conditioners. This outside noise can garble the bits as they are sent over the line, causing transmission errors to occur. Second, the susceptibility to noise limits the distance that data can be transmitted.

Figure 11-29 These are a sample of the types of coaxial cable used with local area networks.

The farther the distance the weaker the signal and the more likely that transmission errors will occur. Twisted pair wire is most often used for low-cost, short distance local area networks that connect personal computers in a limited geographic area. On twisted pair wire, data can be transmitted at rates of up to one million bits per second at distances of 100-200 feet without using additional electronic devices to amplify the signal.

Coaxial cable is the most widely used transmission medium for local area networking. The coaxial cable used for local area networks is similar to the 75-ohm cable used with many television sets. It consists of a wire or central conductor, surrounded by a nonconducting insulator that is in turn surrounded by a woven metal shielding layer, and finally a plastic outer coating (Figure 11-29). Because of its construction, coaxial cable is not susceptible to electrical noise and can transmit data at higher data rates over longer distances than twisted copper wire.

There are two general types of coaxial cable, named for the transmission techniques they support: Baseband and broadband. **Baseband** coaxial cable carries one signal at a time. The signal, however, can travel very fast — in the area of ten million bits per second for the first 1000 feet. The speed drops off significantly as the length of cable is extended; therefore, boosters may be required periodically on the line to maintain transmission speed. For local area networks, baseband signals are always digital.

Since baseband signals are transmitted at a very high rate of speed, baseband transmission uses time-division multiplexing quite effectively. **Time-division multiplexing** means more than one personal computer or terminal can send a signal at the same time, and each terminal's signal is interspersed with other terminals' signals (Figure 11-30). Time-division multiplexing allows many terminals to use a baseband coaxial cable at essentially the same time. Baseband coaxial cable is normally best suited to small area networks with a relatively low number of users. Such a system is very fast, is relatively expensive, but is easy to install and maintain.

Broadband coaxial cable can carry many signals at one time, with each signal occupying a different frequency band on the cable. Up to 20 or 30 channels can be carried on a single cable, each with the capability of transmitting one to five million bits per second. It is similar to cable TV where a number of channels are available to the user from a single cable. A particular advantage of broadband channels is that data, audio, and video transmission can take place over the same line or within the same network. Therefore, a local area network using broadband coaxial cable can include not only personal computers, but video cameras for video conferencing, facsimile machines which transmit images, and even vocal communication.

The signal transmitted on broadband cable is an analog signal. Therefore, modems are required to convert the digital signal from a personal computer or terminal to an analog signal that can be transmitted over the coaxial cable.

Broadband networks are used for larger applications where numerous users have a need to transmit data, voice, and video over the same communication channel for a long distance. A broadband data network requires careful design and a significant amount of maintenance to keep it in working order.

Figure 11-30 When time-division multiplexing is used, each terminal's signal is interspersed with other terminals' signals.

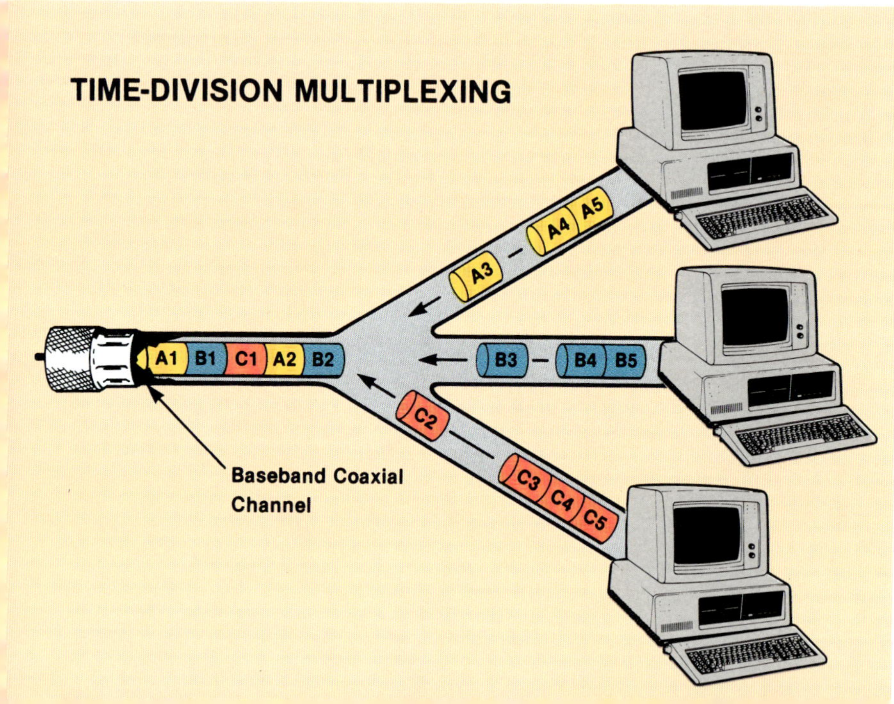

Network access

Network access identifies the procedures that allow each personal computer or terminal in the network to communicate and receive data. The two methods most often used are carrier sensed multiple access (CSMA) and token passing. These methods are explained below.

Carrier sensed multiple access (CSMA) is used on bus networks. It functions in the following manner. When a terminal has data to send, it first electronically listens to the network communication channel to determine if any other terminal or computer is transmitting data. If so, the terminal waits a short period of time (on the order of several hundred milliseconds) and again listens to the line. This process continues until the terminal finds the line free, at which time it transmits its message.

On occasion, the communication channel will be free and two terminals will begin sending data at the same time. This phenomenon is called a **collision**. When a collision occurs, no data can be transmitted because only one terminal can transmit at a time when CSMA is used. Therefore, both terminals cease transmitting, wait a random short period of time, and then attempt the transmission again. Since both terminals wait a different amount of time, as determined by an algorithm which is part of the hardware and software making up CSMA, a collision will not occur between the same two terminals two times in a row. Systems which operate in this manner are sometimes called carrier sensed multiple access/collision detection (CSMA/CD). This method for controlling traffic on a local area network has proved very popular and successful for bus networks.

A second access method called **token passing** can be used in bus or ring networks. A **token** is a string of bits that constantly travels around the network. Any terminal or personal computer which wishes to transmit data must wait until it receives the token from the previous station in the network. When the station receives the token, it transmits its data and then passes the token to the next station. In effect, possession of the token is permission to transmit.

A network's access method can significantly affect the performance of the network. Each access method functions differently under different kinds of traffic and on networks of different sizes. Performance on a CSMA/CD network degrades as the likelihood of a collision increases. Collisions are more likely when there are a large number of terminals on the network and when the terminals are sending a large number of short messages. Token passing networks perform better than CSMA/CD networks when there is uniform, heavy traffic on the network. Since each station has the right to send a message in turn as the token is passed from station to station, the more stations on the network, the longer a given station may have to wait prior to being able to transmit.

Summary — local area networks

Local area networks are used by many companies for hardware resource sharing, information resource sharing, and electronic mail. It is expected that many offices will use local area networks together with personal computers to fulfill a great deal of their computer processing needs. Hardware and software are also available which allow personal computers and terminals within a local area network to access large computers through the network. The computing needs of an organization are truly tied to communications capabilities.

CHAPTER SUMMARY

1. Communicating data over communication channels using computers is called data communications.

2. There are three basic combinations of computer systems used in data communications: a) Small computer or terminal to a large host computer; b) Large computers to large computers; c) Small computers to small computers in a local area network.

3. The basic components of a data communication system which allows access to a large computer and its data base are: a) A personal computer or terminal located at a site remote from the host computer; b) A modem at the personal computer or terminal site; c) The communication channel; d) A modem at the host computer site; e) The host computer.

4. A personal computer used in a data communications network requires software designed to allow data communications and a communications adapter with a serial interface.

5. The process of the large host computer transmitting data or software for storage on a personal computer is called downloading; when a personal computer transmits data to the host computer for storage, it's called uploading.

6. A communications adapter provides the hardware necessary to change parallel transmission to serial transmission required for data communications.

7. When bits are moved in groups, they are said to be moved in parallel; when bits are transmitted one bit after the other, serial transmission is being used.

8. A serial interface, or port, consists of a standard plug and socket with predefined connections.

9. The purpose of a modem is to change digital data consisting of bits into an analog signal that can be transmitted over telephone lines; or on the receiving end, to change the analog signal to digital.

10. An external direct connect modem is attached to a personal computer by a cable; an internal modem is installed internally in the personal computer.

11. An acoustic coupler is a modem that establishes connections by using a telephone headset.

12. The line speed most often used with personal computers is 300 bits per second.

13. An intelligent, or smart, modem contains a microprocessor that can automatically dial a telephone number or answer a call to the computer.

14. A communication channel is the medium over which data is sent. Telephone lines, microwave radio signals, and satellite transmissions are some of the available communication channels.

15. When asynchronous transmission is used, one character is transmitted at a time, identified by a start bit and a stop bit. Asynchronous transmission is relatively slow.

16. Synchronous transmission allows characters to be sent down the line as a group, without start-stop bits. The beginning and end of a character are determined by a timing mechanism in the modem.

17. A simplex channel allows data to be transmitted in one direction only. A half-duplex channel allows data transmission in either direction, but in one direction at a time. Full-duplex channels allow data to be transmitted in both directions at the same time.

18. A communications control unit interfaces between the modem and large host computer. Sophisticated control units, called front-end processors, can be programmed to edit records and control the network.

19. A coaxial cable is a high quality communication line that can transmit data much faster than telephone lines.

20. Fiber optics is based upon the ability of hair-thin strands of material to conduct light. It can carry a great deal more data than comparable sized coaxial cable. It is not used on a wide scale.

21. A point-to-point line is a direct line between a terminal and a larger computer.

22. A leased line is a permanent circuit to connect a personal computer, terminal, or larger computer with another computer. A switched line is established through the regular voice telephone network.

23. Contact is established on a switched line by calling the telephone number of the computer.

24. A multidrop or multipoint line has more than one terminal, personal computer, or larger computer on a single line connected to a host computer.

25. When polling is used, the host computer asks each terminal or personal computer on a multidrop line if it has a message to send. If the terminal responds yes, the terminal is requested to send the message.

26. A network is an organized system of all the elements of data communications.

27. A star network contains a central host computer and terminals or personal computers connected to it.

28. A ring network has a series of computers connected to each other in a ring.

29. A value added network is an established network that offers special services to data communications users.

30. Packet switching is a technique whereby packets of data are transmitted across a network.

31. A communications protocol is a formal set of rules governing the format and relative timing of message exchanges between two communicating devices.

32. A public bulletin board offers free sources of information available to the public.

33. A local area network is a communications network that covers a limited geographic area, is privately owned and user administered, is mostly used for the internal transfer of information within a business, is normally contained within a single building or adjacent group of buildings, and transmits data at a very rapid speed.

34. Hardware resource sharing is sharing expensive pieces of hardware in a network; information resource sharing is making certain information and software available to all persons using a network.

35. Network topology describes the pathways by which devices in a network are connected to one another. When bus topology is used, all devices are connected to and share a common cable. In a ring structure, all devices in the network are connected by a single cable that forms a circle; in a star topology, each personal computer or terminal is connected to a central controlling communications unit.

36. Twisted pair wire is common telephone wire. Coaxial cable is a wire in an insulated cable.

37. Baseband coaxial cable carries one signal at a time very fast.

38. Time-division multiplexing means more than one terminal can send a signal at the same time, and each terminal's signal is interspersed with other terminals' signals.

39. Broadband coaxial cable can carry multiple signals at one time.

40. Network access identifies the procedures that allow each personal computer or terminal in the network to communicate and receive data.

41. Carrier sensed multiple access with collision detection (CSMA/CD), used on bus networks, has each terminal listen to determine if the line is clear. If so, they transmit; if not, they wait and then try again.

42. A collision occurs when two terminals try to transmit at the same time using CSMA/CD.

43. When token passing is used, a token (a series of bits) is passed from one terminal to the next. When a terminal has the token, it can transmit; if it has nothing to transmit, it passes the token to the next terminal.

KEY TERMS

Acoustic coupler 11.5
Addressing 11.15
Asynchronous transmission 11.9
Baseband 11.22
Broadband 11.22
Bus topology 11.20
Carrier sensed multiple access (CSMA) 11.23
Coaxial cable 11.12, 11.22
Collision 11.23
Communication 11.1
Communication channel 11.6
Communications adapter 11.4
Communications control unit 11.11
Control unit 11.20
Data communications 11.1
Downloading 11.4
Electronic mail 11.20
Electronic text transfer 11.20
External direct connect modems 11.5
Fiber optics 11.12
Front-end processors 11.11
Full-duplex (channel) 11.10
Half-duplex channel 11.10
Hardware resource sharing 11.19
Information resource sharing 11.20
Intelligent (modem) 11.6
Internal modem 11.5
Leased line 11.13
Local area network 11.19
Modem 11.5
Multidrop (line) 11.14
Multipoint line 11.14
Network 11.15
Network access 11.23
Network topology 11.20
Packet switching 11.17
Parallel (transmission) 11.4
Point-to-point line 11.13
Polling 11.15
Port 11.5
Protocol 11.17
Public bulletin boards 11.19
RS-232C 11.5
Ring network 11.16
Ring topology 11.21
Serial interface 11.5
Serial transmission 11.4
Server 11.20
Simplex channel 11.9
Smart modems 11.6
Star network 11.15
Star topology 11.21
Switched line 11.13
Synchronous transmission 11.9
Time-division multiplexing 11.22
Token 11.23
Token passing 11.23
Transmission medium 11.21
Transmission method 11.21
Twisted pair wire 11.21
Uploading 11.4
Value added networks 11.17
Workstations 11.20

REVIEW QUESTIONS

1. What are the basic components of a data communication system that allows a small computer to access a large computer? Describe each component in some detail.
2. What is the role of communications software on a personal computer? What does a communications adapter do?
3. What is the difference between parallel and serial transmission?
4. Why is a modem used? Describe some of the types of modems available.
5. Describe asynchronous and synchronous transmission. What are the advantages and disadvantages of each?
6. What are simplex, half-duplex, and full-duplex lines? When is each of them used?
7. Draw a diagram and describe a typical network that could be used to allow a personal computer on the east coast of the United States to communicate with a large host computer on the west coast of the United States.
8. Describe the differences between point-to-point lines and multidrop lines.
9. What is a leased line? What is a switched line?
10. How does polling work? What is the difference between polling and addressing?
11. What is a local area network? What are the components of a local area network?
12. What are three reasons for using a local area network? Describe each of them.
13. Define network topology. What three topologies are used with local area networks?
14. Describe three media used for data transmission in a local area network.
15. What is the difference between baseband and broadband coaxial cable?
16. Describe network access using carrier sensed multiple access with collision detection (CSMA/CD). Describe access when a token passing system is used.

CONTROVERSIAL ISSUES

1. At a recent national convention of banking executives, a vice-president of a large midwestern bank flatly declared her bank will never offer home banking where users of personal computers can, by entering data on their computer at home, cause payments to be made, and generally conduct their banking business. She said they would not do this because the security of data sent over telephone wires is not good enough — it is too easy to tap the wire and make changes to the data. On the same panel, an official of the telephone company said this was nonsense. What do you think? Would you trust the telephone lines if you were sending data that could cause checks to be written for your bills? Could someone tap the line and alter the data so that the money would be transferred to their own account? Would this stop you from using the service?
2. A recent survey found three out of ten managers were reluctant to implement local area networks in their firm because of the possibility that individuals may have access to data they should not see. Is this possible? Should it stop the implementation of local area networks and information sharing?

RESEARCH PROJECTS

1. Many banks are beginning to offer home banking that can be performed from a personal computer at home. Obtain information from a bank in your area that offers this service, and prepare a report for your class.
2. A number of companies offer access to large data bases for home computer users. The services offered include access to airline schedules, entertainment schedules, electronic mail with other users, shopping services, stock market prices and quotations, and many others. Visit a local computer store and obtain information concerning one of these companies. Prepare a report for your class, including the services offered, the cost of the service, the personal computer hardware and software required to use the service, and how the service is used. If possible, sign on to the service at the store and report back to your class concerning your reaction.

Chapter Twelve

Application Software

Objectives

- ☐ Identify the two types of application software packages available for purchase
- ☐ List examples of specialized prewritten application software packages and generalized prewritten application software packages
- ☐ List and describe five guidelines for purchasing prewritten software packages
- ☐ Describe the user interface when using spelling checkers, electronic spreadsheets, and file management systems
- ☐ Specify the uses of fourth generation application development tools, their advantages, and their disadvantages

Application Software

Chapter Twelve

The previous chapters have explained the hardware components of a computer and the basic file organization and data base concepts. Another important area of study is application software. **Application software** refers to software which performs an application-related function on a computer. For example, applications such as managing home finances, billing millions of customers, or learning typing on a personal computer are all applications for which software is available on computers.

Application software can either be purchased or can be developed using application development tools. Two categories of application software can be purchased — specialized prewritten application software packages or generalized prewritten application software packages. **Specialized prewritten application software packages** perform application-specific tasks which fulfill the needs of the user. For example, a specialized prewritten application software package could be purchased to prepare the payroll for a firm. The package would perform all the tasks required by the user, including writing checks and preparing government reports.

The second category of application software packages, **generalized prewritten application software packages,** perform specific tasks, but can be used for many different applications. For example, a word processing application package can only be used to perform word processing functions. The letters and memos which are produced, however, can apply to any application. Thus, using the same word processing package, letters can be written by the accounting department to people who are late in their payments, by the marketing department to prospective customers, and by the president of the company to the stockholders.

Application software development tools allow the user or the professional information processing analyst or programmer to develop the application software. These application software development tools must be purchased. They fall into one of two categories: 1) Fourth-generation software development tools; 2) Programming languages.

This chapter will examine some of the specialized and generalized prewritten application software packages and some of the fourth generation software development tools which are available for large and small computers. Programming languages are discussed in Chapter Thirteen.

SPECIALIZED PREWRITTEN APPLICATION SOFTWARE PACKAGES

Thousands of specialized prewritten application software packages have been developed for computers of all sizes. These packages have been written so that once they are purchased or leased they can be immediately executed on the computer for which they were designed, although some software may have to be modified slightly to fulfill the particular requirements of a company. The following sections examine some of the specialized prewritten application software packages available for personal computers and larger computers.

Specialized prewritten application software packages for personal computers

While application packages are available for virtually any application imaginable, those developed for personal computers fall into two major categories: 1) Personal computer software for home and personal use; 2) Personal computer software for business use.

Personal computer software that is intended for home and personal use varies considerably, from games to sophisticated **personal financial management packages.** To illustrate a portion of a personal financial management package, the display screen shown in Figure 12–2 illustrates the main menu from the package. Note that the user has a number of choices for the activities to be performed. In this example, the user chose choice 1, Budget Analysis.

The Budget Analysis Submenu (Figure 12–3) gives the user further choices — the budget can be reviewed or changed, actual amounts can be entered, the budget and actual figures can be examined, or the user can exit back to the main menu. Assume the user chose number 4 — Compare Budget to Actual. The screen shown in Figure 12–4 would appear, showing each budget category, the budget amount, the actual amount, and the difference. From the main menu it can be seen that many more

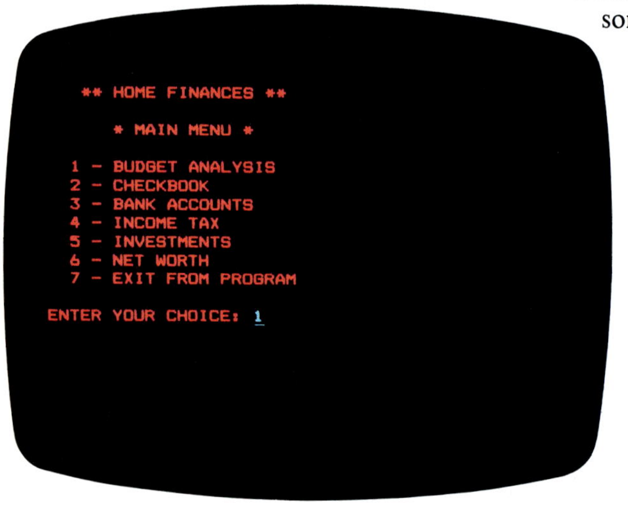

Figure 12–2 The main menu of the home finances software package presents the tasks which can be performed by the package. The user must choose one of the options. In this example, the user chose number 1, Budget Analysis.

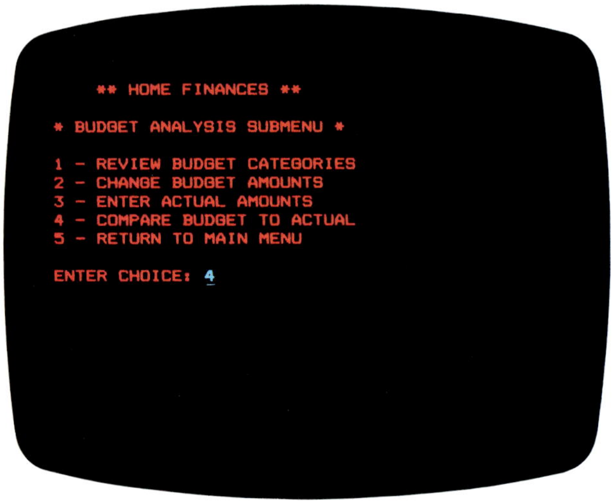

Figure 12–3 When budget analysis is chosen, a submenu is displayed which gives the user options. In this example, the user chose to compare the budget amounts to the actual amounts that had been entered.

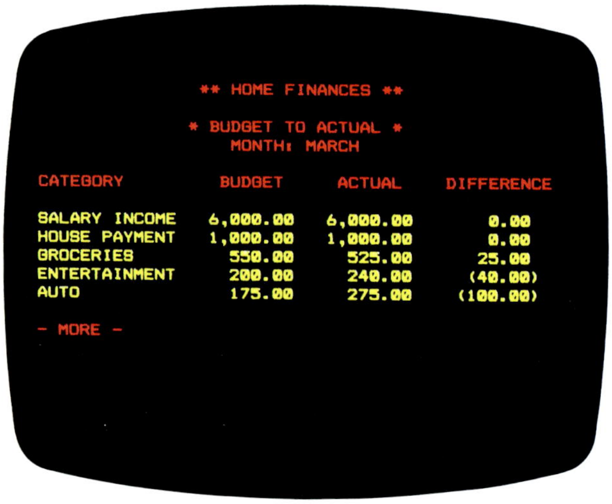

Figure 12–4 The budget to actual screen compares the budgeted amounts for both income and expenses to the actual amounts. Each category contains a budgeted amount. The actual amount is entered as the money is obtained or spent. The word — MORE — at the end of the page indicates there is more to view. The user would normally depress the space bar or the return key to view the next screen.

functions are available for the user. Application packages such as this one are quite involved and can cost from $100.00 to as much as $500.00.

Games and less sophisticated software for personal computers cost as little as $10.00 to a maximum of $100.00.

Specialized prewritten application software packages used on personal computers for business use include accounting software; inventory control software; materials requirements planning; specialized packages for such businesses as medicine, architecture, law, education, and real estate; and a wide variety of other packages as well. The business person must evaluate the needs of the company and then shop for those packages which fulfill the needs.

Specialized prewritten application software packages for large computers

A number of software vendors design and write application software packages for large computers. These packages usually are written for commonly found applications within business. Therefore, accounting applications, inventory applications, financial applications, and payroll applications are widely available (Figure 12–5). In many cases, large computer installations will purchase these packages rather than design and write the software in-house.

Software packages are also available for specific industries. For example, the publishing industry often uses large computers for specific applications such as accounting for the costs of producing books. This application, while specific to the publishing industry, is required by many companies in that industry. Therefore, application software packages are available to provide this service.

When purchasing software packages for large computers, there may be users from many different departments and with different needs. In addition, the software package may cost many thousands of dollars. Therefore, the procurement process for large computer software packages may involve many people and many months of study and evaluation prior to the actual purchase.

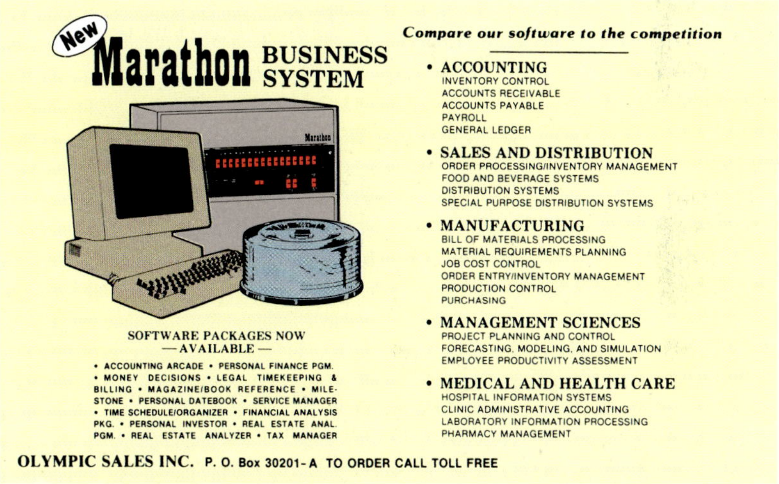

Figure 12–5 The business application packages shown in this advertisement are representative of the wide variety of application packages available on large computers.

GENERALIZED PREWRITTEN APPLICATION SOFTWARE PACKAGES

The second category of purchased software is generalized prewritten application software packages. The difference between these packages and the specialized packages is that these packages are used in many different application areas. The packages are available for both personal computers and large computers.

A typical generalized package that can be used in a large number of application areas is a word processing package and the associated spelling checker package. These

Figure 12–6 This list contains many of the features commonly found in word processing software packages.

WORD PROCESSING FEATURES	
INSERTION AND MOVING	**SEARCH AND REPLACE**
Insert character	Search and replace word
Insert word	Search and replace character strings
Insert line	
Move sentences	**PRINTING**
Move paragraphs	
Move blocks	Set top and bottom margins
Merge text	Set left and right margins
	Set tab stops
DELETE FEATURES	Print columns
	Single, double, triple space control
Delete character	Variable space control within text
Delete word	Right justify
Delete sentence	Center lines
Delete paragraph	Subscripts
Delete entire text	Superscripts
	Underline
SCREEN CONTROL	Boldface
	Condensed print
Scroll up and down by line	Enlarged print
Scroll by page	Special type fonts
Word wrap	Proportional spacing
Upper and lower case display	Headers
Underline display	Footers
Screen display according to defined format	Page numbering
Bold display	Print any page from file
Superscript display	
Subscript display	

packages can be used in any application where document preparation must occur.

As has been noted in previous chapters, word processing software allows the user to create, edit, change, save, and print documents. Word processing packages may have somewhat different capabilities and different ways of implementing their features, but most have similar features, such as those shown in Figure 12–6. Many vendors of personal computer software offer a word processing package for sale. These packages can cost from less than $50.00 to more than $500.00, depending upon the features available.

A software package often used in conjunction with a word processor is a **spelling checker**. Spelling checker software allows the user to check individual words in the text for correct spelling or to scan the entire text to ensure all words are correctly spelled. To check individual words, the user can position the cursor at the start of the word and depress a control key defined by the software to indicate that the word is to be checked. The word in the text will then be checked against a dictionary of words. Some spelling checker dictionaries contain over 100,000 words.

When scanning the text, each word in the text is checked for correct spelling. With one spelling checker, if a word is not recognized, the word is highlighted (Figure 12–7). A menu is then superimposed on the screen, giving the user the option of listing the possible spellings, ignoring the word, or adding the word to the dictionary. If the user requests a display of suggested spellings, the software will display one or more possible words which can be incorporated into the text.

Word processors and spelling checkers are just examples of generalized prewritten application software packages that can be purchased for both small and large computers. These packages provide functions which are often necessary in both personal applications and business applications.

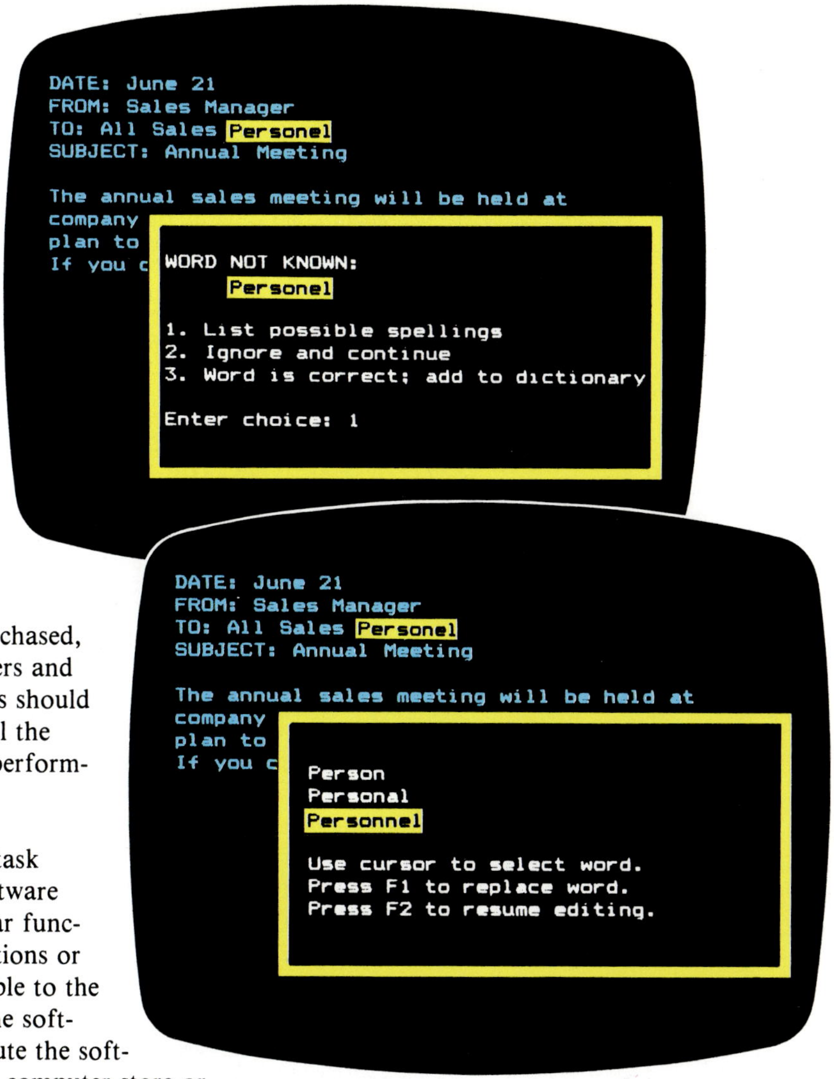
DATE: June 21
FROM: Sales Manager
TO: All Sales Personel
SUBJECT: Annual Meeting
The annual sales meeting will be held at
company
plan to
If you c
WORD NOT KNOWN:
Personel
1. List possible spellings
2. Ignore and continue
3. Word is correct; add to dictionary
Enter choice: 1
DATE: June 21
FROM: Sales Manager
TO: All Sales Personel
SUBJECT: Annual Meeting
The annual sales meeting will be held at
company
plan to
If you c
Person
Personal
Personnel
Use cursor to select word.
Press F1 to replace word.
Press F2 to resume editing.

Figure 12–7 In this example, the spelling checker, while checking the entire text for misspelled words, encountered the word Personel. Since it did not recognize this word, it gave the user the option of listing possible correct spellings, ignoring the word and continuing, or telling the speller it is a correct word and continuing. This latter choice is often used when a technical word or phrase that is not in the dictionary is properly used. Since the user chose option 1, a second screen asked the user to select the word to replace the misspelled word.

Guidelines for purchasing prewritten software packages

Whenever prewritten software is purchased, whether for small computers or large computers and whether for business use or personal use, steps should be taken to ensure that the software will fulfill the needs of the purchaser. This can be done by performing the following steps:

1. Verify that the software performs the task desired by the user. In some cases, software which is supposed to perform particular functions either does not perform the functions or performs them in a manner unacceptable to the user. The best method to verify that the software performs satisfactorily is to execute the software prior to purchase. Generally, the computer store or software vendor will allow the user to enter some data and process the data using the software to be purchased. If the software does not produce the desired results, or if the store or vendor will not allow the user to use the software, then the software package should not be purchased.
2. Verify that the software executes on the user's computer with the particular configuration owned or available to the user. The best way to verify this is to execute the software on a computer the same as the one available to the user. Such factors as the number of disk drives, whether the software can execute on a computer with a hard disk, the main memory requirements, the graphics capabilities, and other factors as well must be evaluated when the software package is purchased. For example, purchasing a word processing package that cannot use the printer attached to the user's computer is a worthless purchase.
3. Ensure that the software documentation is adequate. Even the best software may be unusable if the documentation is not adequate to describe what the software does, how it does it, what the user must do to use the software, how to recover from errors, how to back up data, and so on. A poorly documented software package not only might be unusable, it is also indicative that the organization which produced the software was not a quality-oriented organization.
4. Purchase the software from a reliable store, distributor, or vendor and verify that the company which developed the software is a reliable company. Regardless of the care taken, errors will often occur in software. A reliable software company will correct the errors and make the corrections available free of charge. In addition, many good companies offer telephone service so that a user can call to ask questions concerning the software.
5. Obtain the best price. Particularly with respect to personal computer software,

different stores or distributors will sell the same software package for different prices. So long as the store or dealer is reputable, there is no reason to pay more for the same product.

If these factors are kept in mind when buying prewritten application software packages, it is likely the software will perform as expected by the user.

APPLICATION SOFTWARE DEVELOPMENT TOOLS

Even though a great amount of generalized and specialized software has been developed for both small and large computers, many applications still remain for which software has not been developed. These applications may be so specialized that software manufacturers have decided it would not pay for them to write the software; or it could be that an organization requires software tailored exactly to their needs and no pre-written software package will suffice.

For whatever reasons there may be, many individual users and companies must or choose to develop their own software. When original software is developed, it can be done by the person who will actually use the results of the processing or it can be designed and written by professional analysts and programmers. There are advantages and disadvantages to each approach.

Professional programmers and analysts who work for an organization normally have assigned projects on which they work. In many installations, there are more projects than can be accomplished by the analysts and programmers, creating a backlog of projects waiting for design, programming, and installation. This backlog can be as much as three or four years. Obviously, with this type of backlog, the person submitting a project to the information systems department for implementation will wait a long period of time until the project is implemented unless schedules are changed to accommodate the request.

An option sometimes available if a backlog exists in the information systems department is to use consultants or other programmers and analysts who design and write programs for many different clients; or to use consulting firms which employ programmers and analysts who design systems and write programs for clients of the consulting firms.

Depending upon the application, the person who will use the output from the software may write the procedures required to generate the output. In most instances, if the task is large, the user will not write the procedures, but if the task is not large, this is a viable option. If the user decides to write the procedures, the task will usually be done in one of three ways: 1) From a terminal in the vicinity where the person works which is connected via data communications to a large computer; 2) On the personal computer which either will run the application or which will communicate with a larger computer that will run the application; 3) Using the facilities of the information center of an organization. In those instances where the software is being developed for implementation on a home personal computer, option 2 is normally the only option available.

Both professional programmers and users who develop their own application software have access to application software development tools which are commonly called **fourth generation software development tools**. These tools provide the ability to produce sophisticated programs and procedures with relatively little detailed programming knowledge and effort. The following sections discuss two of these tools which are available for personal computers (electronic spreadsheet software and file management software).

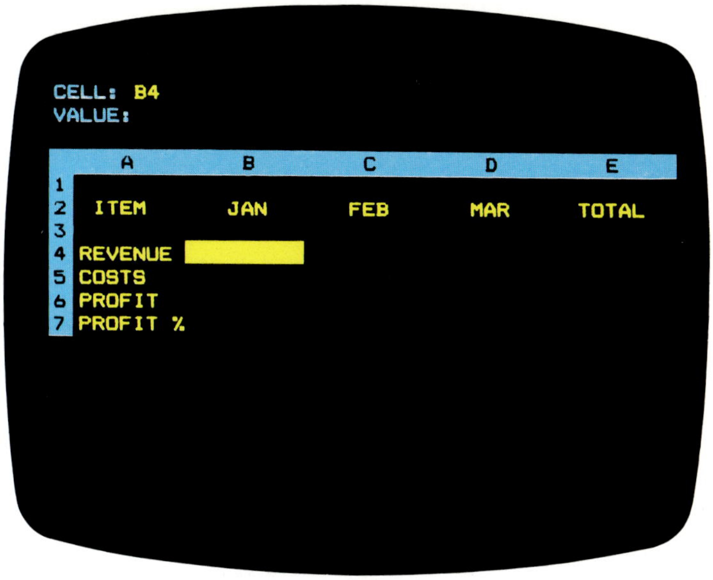

Figure 12–8, Screen 1

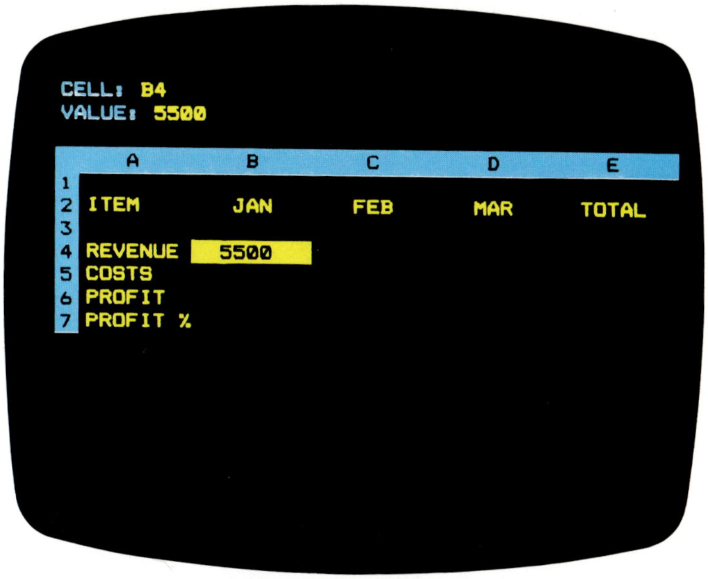

Figure 12–8, Screen 2

Electronic spreadsheet software

Electronic spreadsheet software is a software development tool which allows the user to develop a spreadsheet that contains both data and formulas. Calculations specified by the formulas are performed on the data in the worksheet. To illustrate a simple example of this powerful tool, the development of a spreadsheet shown in Chapter One will be examined.

The completed spreadsheet contains revenues, costs, profit, and profit percentage for three months and the totals for the three months. The labels used for the spreadsheet are illustrated in Figure 12–8, Screen 1. The spreadsheet is composed of rows and columns. The rows are identified by numbers, and the columns are identified by letters. Each intersection of a row and column is called a **cell**. Numbers, alphanumeric data, or formulas can be entered in the cells. In screen 1, the pointer, which is a reversed field on the screen, is located in cell B4. No value has been entered into the cell. The display at the top of the screen labelled CELL identifies the column and row being referenced, and the label VALUE identifies the value in the cell. Since the value field is blank, there is no value stored in cell B4.

Building the spreadsheet is performed by entering either data (numeric or alphanumeric) or formulas. In screen 2, the value 5500 has been entered and stored at cell B4. Note the entries in the display at the top of the screen, identifying what was entered into the cell. Screen 3 shows data entered in cell C4 and cell D4. In cell E4, a formula has been entered by the user. The formula specifies that the contents of cell E4 is to be the sum of the values in the cells B4, C4, and D4. On the spreadsheet itself, the numeric sum is displayed; in the prompt field at the top of the screen, however, the formula used to calculate the value is shown.

In screen 4, the sum of the values in cells B5, C5, and D5 is to be placed in cell E5.

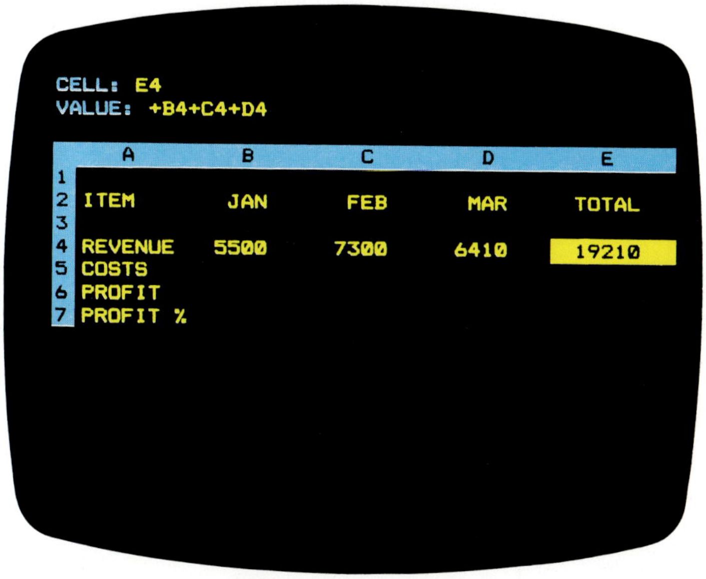

Figure 12–8, Screen 3

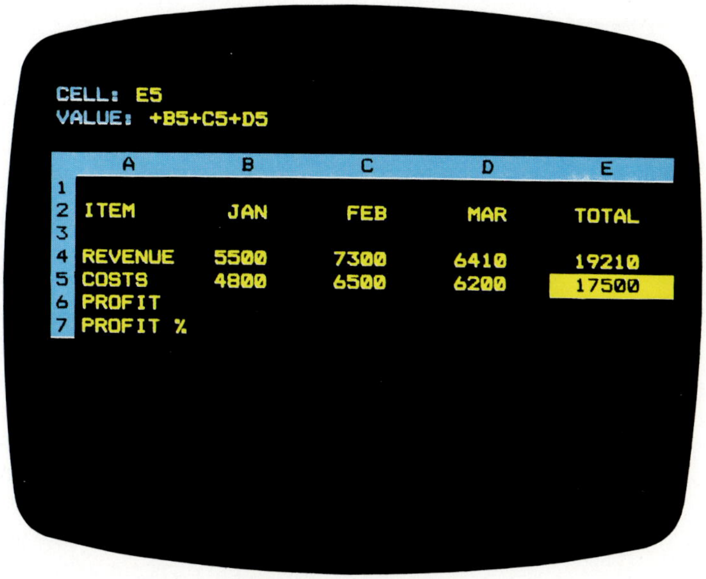

Figure 12–8, Screen 4

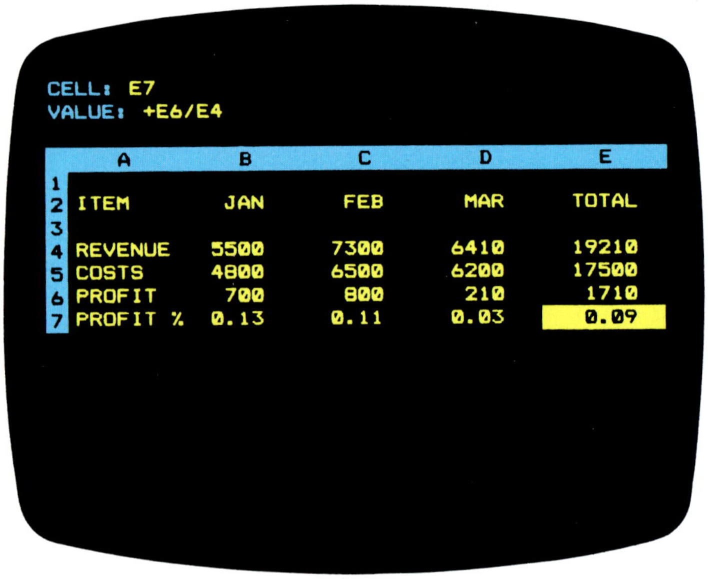

Figure 12-8, Screen 5

Figure 12-8 Screens 1-4 on page 12.7 and screen 5 here illustrate the development of an electronic spreadsheet.

Screen 5 shows the entire worksheet after it has been completed. The value in cell E7 is derived from the formula illustrated on the prompt line, which specifies the value in cell E6 is to be divided by the value in cell E4. The slash character indicates that division is to occur. Since the value in E6 is the total profit and the value in E4 is the total revenue, the result of the division operation is the profit percentage. Once the spreadsheet is complete, with all formulas entered, it can be stored on auxiliary storage for later use. Thus, once the spreadsheet is built, it can be used for many applications. In addition, different data can be entered and the formulas will be recalculated. For example, if the user entered the value 6000 in cell B4, the total in E4 would immediately be recalculated to 19710, the profit would be recalculated to a value 2210, and the profit percent is cell E7 would be recalculated to eleven percent. The profit total for January in cell B6 and the profit percentage in cell B7 would also be recalculated immediately. As can be seen, then, once it has been built, the spreadsheet allows the user to change values and still use the formulas. It is through this ability that spreadsheets can be used to perform "what if" simulations. For example, if the user wanted to know the effect on profits for the quarter if the costs in March were reduced to 4000, all that is necessary to determine the entire effect is to enter the value 4000 in cell D5.

Besides the abilities provided by spreadsheets, it is important to realize what has been accomplished. Using the application software development tool called an electronic spreadsheet, the user has constructed application software which will recalculate profits and profit percentages whenever required. Indeed, through just a few simple statements, a power piece of application software has been developed. This is indicative of the fourth generation application development packages — they require relatively few statements, each of which is reasonably simple, in order to develop sophisticated, powerful software.

File management application development software

A second software development tool that is quite useful is file management software. File management software is available on both personal computers and large computers. The purpose of **file management systems** (sometimes called **data base management systems**) is to allow users to define files, records within files, and data elements or fields within records in a relatively easy manner, and to provide a convenient method to access, update, and create reports from the data.

A file management system is a sophisticated software package that is used to create files that can be randomly accessed, retrieved, and updated. The user of the file management system is not concerned with computer instructions or logic, but rather responds to menus and prompts on the CRT screen that do not require a knowledge of computer hardware, file organization, or accessing techniques. One of the aspects of fourth generation software development tools is that the user need not be technically oriented in order to use them.

To show the use of a file management system, the screens in Figure 12-9 on page 12.9 are illustrated. They present the development of a personal checking account file and inquiry system using a file management system. The file management menu

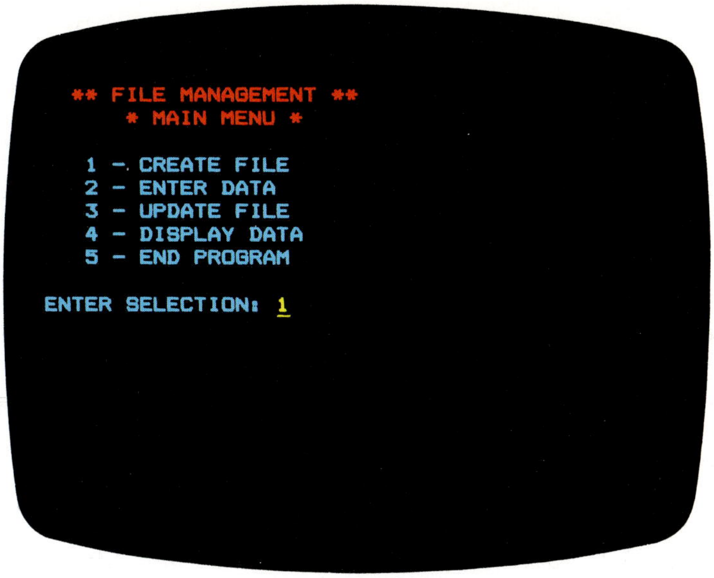

Figure 12–9, Screen 1

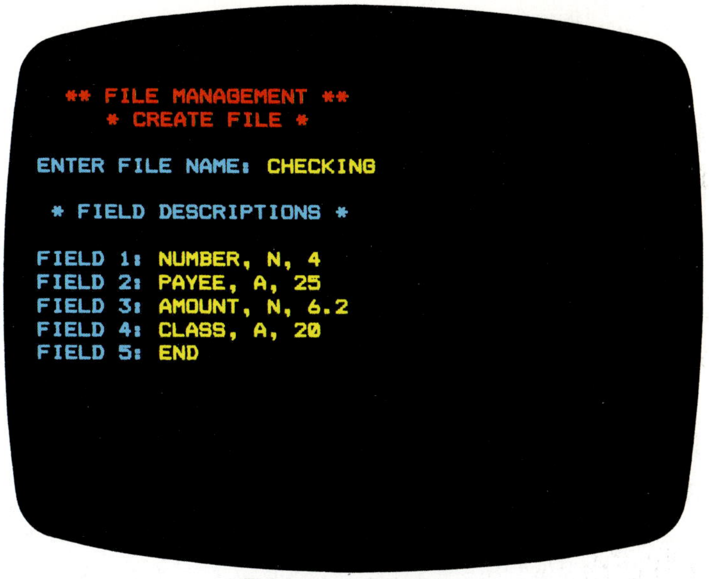

Figure 12–9, Screen 2

appears on screen 1. The user can create a file, enter data, update the file, display data, and terminate the processing of the file management system. In the example, the user selected the option CREATE FILE.

When option 1 is selected, the File Management Create File information in screen 2 is displayed. A prompt asks the user to enter a file name. The file name entered is the name under which the file being created will be stored on disk. In the example, the user entered the file name Checking.

After the file name is entered, the user is asked to enter field descriptions for each field in the records to be stored in the file. A field description consists of a field name, the type of data to be stored in the field (A for alphanumeric, N for numeric data), and the number of characters in the field. If, in a numeric field, digits are to appear to the right of the decimal point, the number of digits to the right are specified. Thus, for the amount field, the designation 6.2 means there are six numeric digits in the field with two of those digits to the right of the decimal point.

Once the fields in the records have been defined, data must be entered into the files. Therefore, the user would choose main menu entry number 2, Enter Data. The screen is shown in screen 3 of Figure 12–9. The file management system prompts the user to enter data for each record by placing the name of the field on the screen. The user merely enters the data to be stored in the field. Thus, after the file management system has displayed the field name NUMBER, the user enters the check number. Each field is completed in the same manner. The user would continue to enter data until all data is entered for the checking account file.

After the file has been defined and data has been stored in it, the user can use the file to produce information. Therefore the user would choose option 4, Display Data, from the main menu. The screen to display data is shown in screen 4 of Figure 12–9. The user is asked to enter the commands which specify what should be displayed and how the data should be

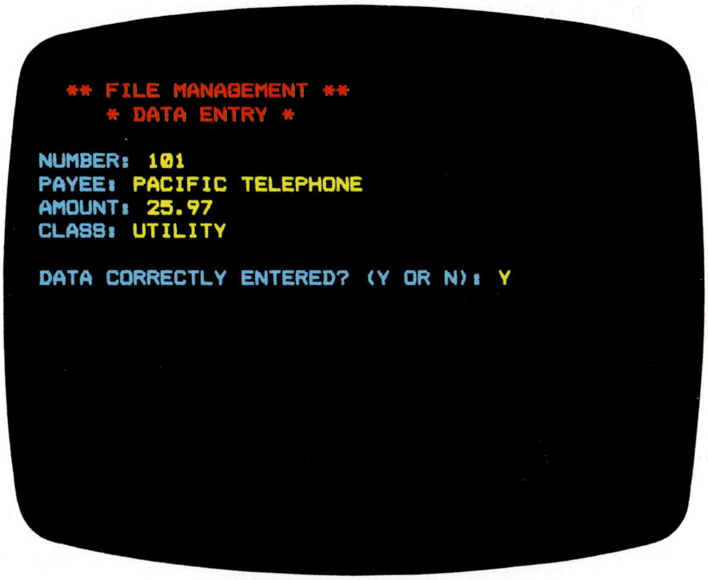

Figure 12–9, Screen 3

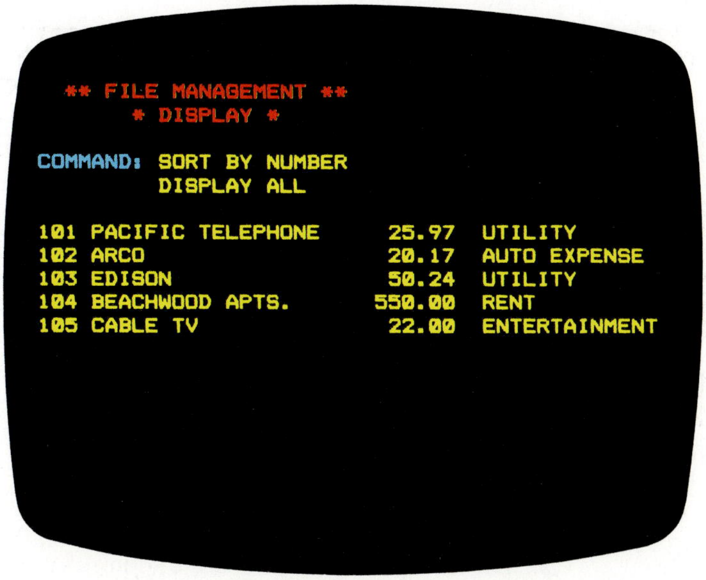

Figure 12–9, Screen 4

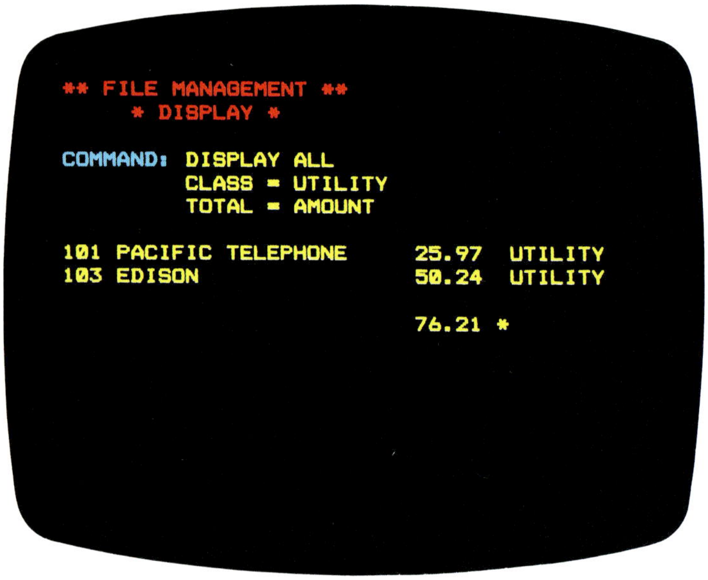

Figure 12-9, Screen 5

Figure 12-9 Screens 1 - 4 on page 12.9 and screen 5 here illustrate the use of a file management system.

processed prior to being displayed. In screen 4, the user stated the data should be sorted on the field called Number, and that all fields in the record should be displayed. As a result, the file management system produced the screen display shown.

In screen 5, the user again requested the display data option from the main menu. In this case, however, the system was directed to display only those records where the class is equal to UTILITY and a total is to be printed for the field Amount. As a result, the report shows only those records for which the classification is utility, and the values in the amount field are totaled and printed after all records have been processed.

Note again that when using this fourth generation application development tool, the user is not concerned with technical issues. These application development tools are designed to allow the user or the professional programmer to easily implement application software which in turn produces information for the user.

USE OF FOURTH GENERATION APPLICATION DEVELOPMENT TOOLS

With respect to the use of fourth generation application development tools, several issues must be examined. These include: 1) Who uses these tools; 2) Where are they used; 3) What systems and procedures must be developed for the tools.

To enable users to obtain the software they desire, many installations are making the fourth generation application development tools available to the users. In most cases, the tools will be available on a large computer and the user will have access to the tools through a terminal, personal computer, or the information center.

Increasingly it is being found that professional programmers should also make use of the tools. Historically, programmers have always used the programming languages explained in Chapter 13. But the use of these languages is viewed by some as an inappropriate solution to the backlog of application software. Noted authority James Martin has stated, "The way to change productivity is to avoid programming with languages of the level of COBOL or PL/I where possible." Thus, many installations direct their programmers to use fourth generation development tools to produce software.

When these tools are used, the systems and procedures associated with the software are as important as the systems and procedures associated with the software developed using programming languages. Sources of input, disposition of output, methods of making inquiries or updating data, and other aspects as well must be addressed. When users develop their own software using these tools, control must be exercised to ensure that the software is used appropriately and correctly. This includes control over the data which is used in the applications. For example, it has been found that individual users, after entering data for an application using a file management or data base management system, have tended to retain and update the data in their own files without sharing the updated data with other departments. This could result in data which is totally unreliable being used by people throughout a company.

As the development of application software changes, new procedures and approaches will be necessary to solve the emerging problems of a new method for producing application software.

CHAPTER SUMMARY

1. Application software refers to software which performs an application-related function on a computer.
2. Application software can be purchased or can be developed using application development tools.
3. Two categories of application software can be purchased — specialized prewritten application software packages or generalized prewritten application software packages.
4. Specialized prewritten application software packages perform application-specific tasks.
5. Generalized prewritten application software packages perform specific tasks but can be used for many different applications. Word processing software is an example.
6. Application software development tools allow the user or professional information processing analysts or programmers to develop the application software.
7. The two categories of application software development tools are: a) Fourth generation software development tools; b) Programming languages.
8. Specialized prewritten application software packages are written so that once they are purchased or leased, they can be immediately executed on the computer for which they were designed.
9. Personal computer specialized prewritten application software packages fall into two major categories: a) Personal computer software for home and personal use; b) Personal computer software for business use.
10. Specialized prewritten application software packages used on personal computers for business include accounting software, inventory control software, and software for specific businesses.
11. Specialized prewritten application software packages are available on large computers for both commonly found applications such as accounting and payroll, and for specific industries.
12. Spelling checker software allows the user to check individual words in a text for correct spelling or to scan the entire text to ensure all words are correctly spelled.
13. Whenever software is purchased, the following steps should be performed: a) Verify the software performs the task desired; b) Verify the software executes on the user's computer; c) Ensure the software documentation is adequate; d) Purchase the software from a reliable store, distributor, or vendor and verify the company which developed the software is a reliable company; e) Obtain the best price.
14. In many installations, there are more projects than can be accomplished by the analysts and programmers, creating a backlog of projects waiting for design, programming, and installation.
15. Fourth generation software development tools provide the ability to produce sophisticated programs or procedures with relatively little detailed programming knowledge and effort.
16. Electronic spreadsheet software allows the user to develop a spreadsheet that contains both data and formulas.
17. A spreadsheet is composed of rows and columns. Each intersection of a row and column is a cell.
18. Once the spreadsheet is complete, with all formulas entered, it can be stored on auxiliary storage.
19. Different data can be entered and a spreadsheet can be recalculated based upon the formulas.
20. File management systems (sometimes called data base management systems) allow users to define files, records, and fields; and provide a method to access, update, and create reports from the data.
21. Issues with respect to fourth generation application development tools are: a) Who uses these tools; b) Where are they used; c) What systems and procedures must be developed.

KEY TERMS

Application software 12.1
Application software development tools 12.1
Cell 12.7
Data base management systems 12.8
Electronic spreadsheet software 12.7
File management systems 12.8
Fourth generation software development tools 12.6
Generalized prewritten application software packages 12.1
Personal financial management packages 12.2
Specialized prewritten application software packages 12.1
Spelling checker 12.4

REVIEW QUESTIONS

1. What is application software? What is its significance to information processing?
2. How can application software be acquired?
3. What are two categories of purchased software? What are their similarities? What are their differences?
4. What are application software development tools? What are two categories into which these tools fall?
5. What are two categories for specialized prewritten application software packages for personal computers? Give some examples of software for each category.
6. Describe some of the activities that can be performed using personal financial management packages.
7. Identify several reasons specialized prewritten application software packages would not be available for large computer installations. When the packages are available, briefly describe procurement procedures.
8. What is a spelling checker? Describe a typical procedure when a misspelled word is found.
9. List the five steps which should be performed when purchasing software. Describe each of them.
10. What is an installation software backlog? What can a user do to overcome this backlog?
11. Describe fourth generation software development tools. Who can use these tools?
12. How are formulas entered on an electronic spreadsheet? How are "what if" questions asked when using an electronic spreadsheet?
13. Describe the capabilities provided by file management or data base management systems.
14. Why are users not concerned with technical issues when using fourth generation application development tools? What are the advantages and disadvantages to this approach?
15. Can professional programmers use fourth generation development tools? Why would they use them?

CONTROVERSIAL ISSUES

1. A veteran programmer, when asked about fourth generation development tools, replied that most of them were worthless. "The programs and procedures they produce," he said, "are inefficient and slow. Basically, they have no place in the arsenal of a competent application programmer." Others rebut this position by noting that programmers who do not use these tools are not very productive, and with three and four year software backlogs, these tools are the only way to produce timely software. What do you think? Should programmers use these tools?
2. Many articles have appeared in trade journals, academic research journals, and general magazines about the reliability of application software. Often the articles note that prewritten application software just is not reliable, does not do the job, and is overpriced. Is this a valid criticism? Should the information processing industry use software which has a reputation for unreliability?
3. "If you can't write my software, I'll do it myself," bellowed the accounting manager. "Go ahead, but it won't be any good!" shouted the programming manager. Does the accounting manager have this option? Who is right here?

RESEARCH PROJECTS

1. Visit a local installation, school computer laboratory, or computer store which has fourth generation development tools available. Study the documentation provided by the vendor until you understand the basics of the tool and then write a simple procedure. Write a report on your experience using the tool.
2. Choose a particular business or vocation, such as law, medicine, publishing, and so on. Research journals, stores and other sources to find software written for that specific business. Write a report on your findings.
3. Much has been written concerning the backlog in application software development. The articles note that users have been disappointed with the service they have been receiving from information systems departments. Read some of these articles and prepare a report on this problem, together with some of the suggested solutions.

Chapter Thirteen

Programming Languages

Objectives

- ☐ Define and describe a computer program
- ☐ Identify the attributes of the following languages: Assembler Language, FORTRAN, COBOL, PL/I, RPG, BASIC, Pascal, Ada, C, and Logo
- ☐ Describe the advantages and disadvantages of Assembler Language, FORTRAN, COBOL, PL/I, RPG, BASIC, Pascal, Ada, C, and Logo
- ☐ Specify the uses for the languages Assembler Language, FORTRAN, COBOL, PL/I, RPG, BASIC, Pascal, Ada, C, and Logo
- ☐ Identify some of the many languages which have been developed
- ☐ Differentiate between a well coded program and a poorly coded program

Programming Languages

Chapter Thirteen

As discussed in the previous chapter, a computer user can purchase pre-written specialized or generalized application software packages or can use fourth generation software development tools to assist in developing applications. Another method used to develop application software is for programmers to write application programs using one of the many programming languages available for computers of all sizes. The use of professional programmers is normally required when major application systems that are unique to a company are to be designed and implemented on a computer.

There are numerous application programming languages that may be used by the programmer. It is the purpose of this chapter to review some of the characteristics of widely used programming languages and point out the advantages and disadvantages of each language.

WHAT IS A COMPUTER PROGRAM?

It is important to understand the basic features of a computer program. A **computer program** contains a series of instructions which directs the computer to perform those tasks necessary to process data and produce a desired output.

To execute a program, the program must be loaded into main computer memory. The actual instructions which are executed must be in the form of **machine language**, which is a set of instructions the electronics of the computer can interpret and execute. In some cases, the instructions to be executed are stored in computer memory as machine language instructions. In other cases, the instructions are stored in the format written by the programmer and must be changed into machine language as the program is executed.

Although the instructions which are actually executed by the computer must be in a form called machine language, the programmer who writes the program does not normally write in machine language. Instead, the programmer uses a **source language**, which is designed to make it easier for a programmer to code a program. After the program is written in the source language, the instructions in the source language must be translated into machine language for actual execution on the computer.

There are numerous source languages for use by the programmer. Regardless of the source language used, most have program statements which fall into seven major categories. These categories are: 1) Statements to define data bases, files, and records which are to be processed by the program; 2) Statements to define other data within the program, such as total accumulators, headings which will appear on a screen, and other data required to produce the proper output from the program; 3) Statements which cause data to be read into main computer memory from input or auxiliary storage devices and statements which cause data to be written from main computer memory to output devices or auxiliary storage devices; 4) Statements which move data from one location in main computer memory to another; 5) Statements which cause arithmetic operations to occur; 6) Statements which cause data to be compared and perform alternative operations based upon the results of the comparison; 7) Statements which document the program.

It is the task of the computer programmer to utilize the capabilities of the programming language and develop the instructions that are necessary to process data and produce the required output.

Figure 13-2 Many individual operation codes comprise the instruction set of an assembler language. Some languages have over 100 individual instructions that can be used when writing a program.

FUNCTION	SYMBOLIC OPERATION CODE	MACHINE LANGUAGE OPERATION CODE
Add Decimal	AP	FA
Compare Decimal	CP	F9
Divide Decimal	DP	FD
Edit	ED	DE
Multiply Decimal	MP	FC
Subtract Decimal	SP	FB
Zero and Add	ZAP	F8
Branch and Link	BALR	05
Branch on Count	BCTR	06
Convert to Binary	CVB	4F
Convert to Decimal	CVD	4E
Insert Character	IC	43
Move	MVC	D2
OR	OR	16
Pack	PACK	F2
Store Character	STC	42
Start I/O	SIO	9C
Test Channel	TCH	9F
Test I/O	TIO	9D

PROGRAMMING LANGUAGES

Although it has been documented that there are over 400 different programming languages which have been developed during the past 40 years, many have been very specialized and have achieved limited use in industry, science, and education. Some of the programming languages which have played an important part in the development of the computer industry include Assembler Language, FORTRAN, COBOL, PL/I, RPG, BASIC, Pascal, Ada, C, and Logo.

The characteristics of these languages are explained in the following paragraphs.

Assembler language

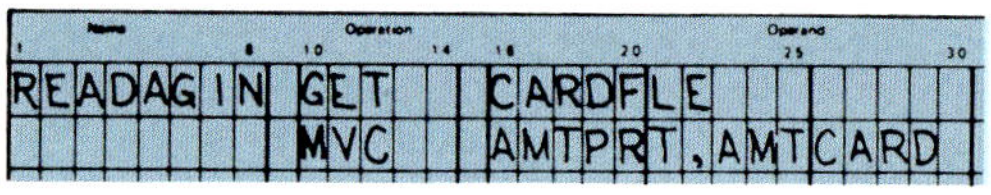

Figure 13-3 The two assembler language instructions above cause an input record to be read (GET), and a field to be moved (MVC). The GET statement is called a **macro**. From this single statement, a series of machine language instructions will be generated. Most assembler languages provide a limited number of macros to handle complex operations such as input/output processing. The MVC operation code generates a single machine language instruction to move data from one area to another.

The programming for the first stored program computers was performed in machine language. Since machine language programming was a difficult, burdensome, and error-prone task, programming languages were developed to facilitate the coding process.

The first programming languages were symbolic programming languages, commonly called **assembler languages**. These languages use symbolic notation to represent machine language instructions. Symbolic programming languages are closely related to machine language and the internal architecture of the computer on which they are used. They are called **low-level languages** since they are so closely related to the computer's internal design. Figure 13-2 illustrates a chart that contains a series of machine language operation codes, symbolic operation codes, and the functions performed by an assembler language for a widely used IBM computer.

An assembler language program consists of a series of individual statements or instructions which directs the computer to carry out the processing that is to occur. An assembler language statement consists of three parts: 1) A **label**; 2) An **operation code**; 3) One or more **operands**. Figure 13-3 shows an example of two assembler language statements.

Figure 13-4 The program listing of the assembler program contains both the source statements and the machine language instructions, called **object code**, generated from the source statements.

Machine Language — Assembler Language Instructions

```
  LOC    OBJECT CODE     ADDR1 ADDR2  STMT   SOURCE STATEMENT                PAGE   1
000068 0540                             45 BEGIN     BALR  4,0
00006A                                  46           USING *,4
                                        47           OPEN  CARDFLE,PRINT
                                        56 READAGIN  GET   CARDFLE
00008A 9240 40AA         00114          61           MVI   PRTOUT,X'40'
00008E D24E 40AB 40AA 00115 00114       62           MVC   PRTOUT+1(79),PRTOUT
000094 D205 40AF 407D 00119 000E7       63           MVC   EMPNOUT,EMPNO
00009A D218 40BE 405A 00128 000C4       64           MVC   NAMEOUT,NAME
                                        65           PUT   PRINT
0000AC 47F0 4014               0007E    70           B     READAGIN
                                        71 ENDOFJOB  CLOSE CARDFLE,PRINT
                                        80           EOJ
```

A segment of an assembler language program written for an IBM computer is illustrated in Figure 13–4.

Assembler languages are available for nearly all computers, including most home computers, personal computers, minicomputers, and large computers. All assembler languages for all computers are not the same, however. This is because the language is directly related to the internal architecture of the computer, and assembler languages are not designed to be machine independent.

Advantages and disadvantages of assembler language

The principal advantage of assembler language is that a program can be written which is very efficient in terms of execution time and main memory usage. This is because nearly every instruction is written on a one-for-one basis with machine language. In addition, assembler language has a full range of computer instructions that allow a programmer to manipulate individual records, fields within records, characters within fields, and even bits within bytes.

There are several significant disadvantages of assembler language. First, because assembler language reflects the architecture of the computer on which it is used, there is little compatibility between the assembler languages used with various computers. Thus, a program coded in assembler language for one computer will not run on a computer of a different manufacturer unless the internal design is exactly the same.

Additionally, an assembler language programmer will normally have to write a larger number of statements to solve a given problem than will a programmer using other high-level programming languages. Also, because of the concise symbolic notation used in assembler language, assembler language programs are often more difficult to write, read, and maintain than programs written in high-level languages.

Assembler languages are not normally used to write programs for generalized business application software such as payroll, accounts receivable, billing, and similar applications. Other languages are available that are more appropriate for programming these types of applications. Assembler language is commonly used where fast execution is essential. For example, with personal computers the actual prewritten application software to generate graphics on a screen is commonly written in assembler language.

FORTRAN

A programming language in which the program statements are not closely related to the internal characteristics of the computer is called a **high-level programming language**. As a general rule, one statement in a high-level programming language will develop a number of machine language instructions. This is in contrast to assembler languages, where one statement normally generates one machine language instruction. High-level programming languages were developed to make programming easier and less error-prone.

One of the earliest high-level programming languages was **FORTRAN** (FORmula TRANslation). FORTRAN, developed by IBM and released in 1957, was originally designed as a programming language to be used by scientists, engineers, and mathematicians. The language is noted for its ability to express mathematical expressions and equations easily.

When using FORTRAN (Figure 13–5), a programmer expresses mathematical

Figure 13–5 The FORTRAN arithmetic operators are used in statements to specify the calculations that are to occur.

SYMBOL	MEANING
+	Addition
-	Subtraction
*	Multiplication
/	Division
**	Exponentiation

```
TOTAL=HOURS*RATE-DED
```

Figure 13-6 The FORTRAN statement above will cause the data in the field referenced by the variable name HOURS to be multiplied by the data in the RATE field. The value in the DED field is subtracted from the multiplication result, and the final answer is stored in the TOTAL field. This type of notation in a programming language greatly simplified writing instructions of a mathematical nature.

operations through the use of arithmetic operators which are combined to form the expression. To form the expression, a variable name which identifies the field where the result of the operation is to be stored is written on the left side of an equal sign; and the arithmetic operation to be performed is written on the right of the equal sign (Figure 13-6). After the expression is evaluated, the answer is placed in the location in memory identified by the variable name on the left.

Although FORTRAN was originally developed by IBM and was not intended to be a universal language, by the early 1960's virtually all manufacturers of computers had either delivered or were committed to producing some version of FORTRAN. In May, 1962, a committee was established to develop a standard for FORTRAN which would specify those features of the language that should be available for all machines. In 1966, after nearly four years of development, FORTRAN standards were published through the auspices of the American Standards Association (now known as the **American National Standards Institute** or **ANSI**). The American Standards Association was the authority for establishing industrial standards in the United States. Thus, FORTRAN has the distinction of being the first programming language that was standardized. In 1977, further standards were published for FORTRAN.

A FORTRAN program is illustrated in Figure 13-7. The program is written on a

```
1 READ(1,2ØØ)NUMBER,SCOST,CCOST,REQ
  IF(NUMBER-999)2,3,3
2 EOQ=SQRT(2.0*(REQ*SCOST)/CCOST)
  IEOQ=EOQ
  IREQ=REQ
  WRITE(3,3ØØ)NUMBER,IREQ,SCOST,CCOST,IEOQ
  GO TO 1
3 STOP
  END
```

Figure 13-7 This FORTRAN program illustrates calculating an economic order quantity. Note in the calculation statement the entry SQRT. SQRT is one of many functions that are a part of the FORTRAN language. This entry causes the square root of the expression to be taken. Other functions available with FORTRAN can perform such tasks as determining the sin, cosine, or tangent of an angle; finding the cube root of a number, and finding the largest number in a list of many numbers.

special coding form that is designed to identify the columns where entries must be made.

As previously discussed, FORTRAN has been widely used as a programming language for mathematical and scientific types of problems on large computers for many years. The FORTRAN language is now also available for many personal computers, although the language is not often used in this area.

Advantages and disadvantages of FORTRAN

A significant advantage of FORTRAN is the easy expression of complex mathematical calculations through the use of arithmetic operators. In addition, because FORTRAN is a high-level language, the programmer can concentrate on the solution to the problem rather than the internal characteristics of the computer as is necessary when programming in assembler language.

The primary disadvantage of FORTRAN and many other high-level languages is that they do not have the versatility or capability of an assembler language in manipulating records, individual characters, or bits within a byte.

In addition, FORTRAN has several disadvantages when used as a business programming language. It has limited file processing capabilities, limited ability to define and effectively process alphabetic data, and limited ability to control the format of the printed report or CRT screen (such as printing commas and decimal points). For these reasons, FORTRAN is not widely used for business applications programming.

COBOL

One of the most widely used programming languages for business applications is **COBOL** (COmmon Business Oriented Language). COBOL was developed by a group of computer users and manufacturers and was released in 1960 as a high-level, business-oriented programming language.

One of the stated objectives was that the language was to be machine independent, meaning that a program written in COBOL should be able to be run on a variety of computers from a variety of manufacturers with little or no change. COBOL was also designed to be written in English-like form and to be self-documenting. Nearly every manufacturer of medium and large-scale computers has undertaken the implementation of COBOL. Some personal computer software developers have also implemented COBOL.

The success of COBOL can be credited to two major factors. First, in 1960, there was a definite need for a business-oriented high-level programming language as it was recognized that programming in a low-level language was difficult and error prone; and FORTRAN was not entirely suited for business applications. Secondly, there was strong pressure from the federal government for the establishment of a common language for business. Recognizing the need for a programming language that could be used on a variety of computers, the federal government in the early 1960's specified that if a company wanted to sell or lease computers to the federal government, it had to have COBOL software available unless it could demonstrate that COBOL was not needed for the particular class of problems to be solved. Since the federal government was the single largest user of computers, manufacturers quickly recognized the value of developing this software.

After going through a number of revisions, COBOL was officially approved as a United States standard in 1968. Subsequent revisions of the language led to the 1974 ANSI Standard COBOL, which is currently in use on most computers.

Writing instructions in COBOL

COBOL was designed to enable statements to be written in English-like form (Figure 13–8). Every effort was made to create formats for statements which could be easily written and understood. COBOL statements are composed of "verbs" to cause such functions as input/output, comparing, and calculations to be performed.

```
004180 A000-CREATE-POLICY-REPORT.                                 INSLIST
004190                                                            INSLIST
004200     OPEN INPUT  POLICY-INPUT-FILE                          INSLIST
005010          OUTPUT POLICY-REPORT-FILE.                        INSLIST
005020     READ POLICY-INPUT-FILE                                 INSLIST
005030           AT END                                           INSLIST
005040              MOVE "NO " TO ARE-THERE-MORE-RECORDS.         INSLIST
005050     PERFORM A001-FORMAT-PRINT-LINE                         INSLIST
005060           UNTIL ARE-THERE-MORE-RECORDS = "NO ".            INSLIST
005070     CLOSE POLICY-INPUT-FILE                                INSLIST
005080           POLICY-REPORT-FILE.                              INSLIST
005090     STOP RUN.                                              INSLIST
005100                                                            INSLIST
005110                                                            INSLIST
005120                                                            INSLIST
005130 A001-FORMAT-PRINT-LINE.                                    INSLIST
005140                                                            INSLIST
005150     MOVE SPACES TO POLICY-REPORT-LINE.                     INSLIST
005160     MOVE POLICY-NUMBER-INPUT TO POLICY-NUMBER-REPORT.      INSLIST
005170     MOVE NAME-INPUT TO NAME-REPORT.                        INSLIST
005180     MOVE AGENT-INPUT TO AGENT-REPORT.                      INSLIST
005190     MOVE INSURANCE-TYPE-INPUT TO INSURANCE-TYPE-REPORT.    INSLIST
005200     WRITE POLICY-REPORT-LINE                               INSLIST
006010           AFTER ADVANCING 1 LINES.                         INSLIST
006020     READ POLICY-INPUT-FILE                                 INSLIST
006030           AT END                                           INSLIST
006040              MOVE "NO " TO ARE-THERE-MORE-RECORDS.         INSLIST
```

Figure 13–8 The COBOL program consists of a series of English-like statements. COBOL was designed to be easy to read and, when properly written, should be easy to maintain.

Typical verbs in COBOL are Read, Write, If, Add, Subtract, Multiply, Divide, and Move. These verbs are utilized in COBOL sentences to express the operation to be performed. From the COBOL program illustrated in Figure 13-8, it can be seen that COBOL is a substantial improvement in terms of reading the program over programming in a low-level language such as assembler.

Most companies that have large mainframe computers utilize COBOL for programming business applications. COBOL is also available for use with personal computers but is not widely used for business application programming on personal computers.

Advantages and disadvantages of COBOL

COBOL as a business language has several important advantages. One of the most important is that COBOL is designed to be machine independent. A program written in COBOL can be run on any computer that supports the COBOL language, regardless of manufacturer, with very minor changes.

In addition, COBOL has strong file handling capabilities and supports sequential, indexed, and relative or direct files. Access to data base systems and data communications software is also available through COBOL. COBOL is relatively easy to write and, if properly written, can be easily understood by other programmers. Some observers consider the "wordiness" of COBOL a disadvantage, for more coding is required to produce a given result than is required, for example, with FORTRAN, which is noted for its concise notation.

It is important to recognize, notwithstanding the disadvantages, that many hundreds of thousands of programs have been written in COBOL during the past twenty-five years. It is apparent, therefore, that because of its widespread use, COBOL will remain an important language for many years to come.

PL/I

In the late 1950's, computer applications and computer classifications were clearly divided among the scientific community and the business community. Scientific users needed fast computational capability with limited input/output operations. Business users, on the other hand, needed decimal devices. As computers became more widely used in all application areas, there was a merging of the needs of the scientific and business user. Responding to this need, IBM began the development of a new programming language in the early 1960's. Their purpose was "to recommend a successor language for currently available FORTRAN's . . . while still remaining a useful tool to the engineer."

The design objectives were that the language should: 1) Be useful in a wide variety of application areas including engineering, business, and systems programming; 2) Be designed in such a way that the programmer could use virtually all of the power of a computer without resorting to assembler language; 3) Be designed in such a way that any programmer could easily use the elements of the language at his own skill level; 4) Be able to be written in free form with no prescribed columns for recording statements, which would assist in terminal operations; 5) Contain default options which provide for the language to select specifications required by the program if they are not explicitly specified by the programmer.

The language that was developed from these design specifications was called **PL/I.**

PL/I was released in 1966. The designers of the language used some of the computational concepts previously incorporated into FORTRAN and some of the file processing capabilities of COBOL. Thus, a PL/I program has some characteristics of FORTRAN and some characteristics of COBOL. PL/I has been primarily implemented on large computers and is used where there is a need for a general purpose programming language.

Advantages and disadvantages of PL/I

The strongest characteristics of PL/I are its breadth and detail. With the wide capabilities of PL/I, it is feasible to write applications and systems programs in any area without resorting to a lower-level programming language like assembler language. This characteristic may also be considered one of its weaknesses, however, because it is difficult to master all of the components of the language. PL/I also contains many of the characteristics necessary to write good structured programs.

RPG

RPG or Report Program Generator, was first widely implemented in the middle and late 1960's when small-scale business computers became readily available to a substantial number of users. Developed originally by IBM, RPG has become a "defacto" standard in the industry and is implemented on many different computers from different manufacturers.

RPG was originally developed to allow reports to be easily generated. To write a program in RPG, the programmer fills out a series of forms with the required entries in predetermined columns. The basic forms are called the File Description Specifications, Input Specifications, Calculation Specifications, and Output Specifications. A segment of a sample RPG program is shown in Figure 13-9. The entries on the forms are used

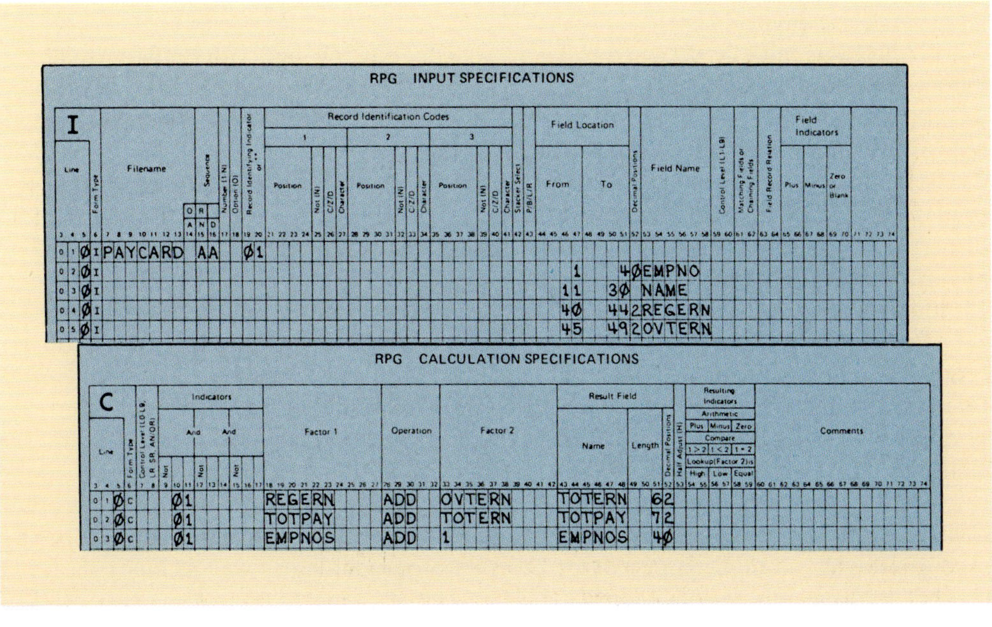

RPG INPUT SPECIFICATIONS

Line	Form Type	Filename	Record Identifying Indicator	From	To	Decimal Positions	Field Name
01Ø	I	PAYCARD AA	Ø1				
02Ø	I			1	4	Ø	EMPNO
03Ø	I			11	3Ø		NAME
04Ø	I			4Ø	44	2	REGERN
05Ø	I			45	49	2	OVTERN

RPG CALCULATION SPECIFICATIONS

Line	Form Type	Indicators	Factor 1	Operation	Factor 2	Result Field Name	Length	Decimal Positions
01Ø	C	Ø1	REGERN	ADD	OVTERN	TOTERN	6	2
02Ø	C	Ø1	TOTPAY	ADD	TOTERN	TOTPAY	7	2
03Ø	C	Ø1	EMPNOS	ADD	1	EMPNOS	4	Ø

Figure 13-9 When programming using RPG, the programmer must fill in the RPG forms with the entries required to generate the program.

to develop a program using a fixed program logic which is part of the programming language itself. When the source program is translated from the entries on the forms to an object program, this fixed logic is used to generate the sequence in which data will be processed. The intent, of course, is to free the programmer from the necessity of designing the logic required for processing the data.

Since the original announcement of RPG in the early 1960's, a number of enhancements have been added to the original language, including file processing capabilities for tape, disk, and data bases. In the early 1970's, RPG II was announced by IBM. **RPG II** has become a widely used language for machines from a number of manufacturers. **RPG III** was announced in 1979 and represents the latest revision to the language. Its main enhancement is the use of the language to process data stored in a data base.

RPG was originally developed for use on relatively small business computers. It has found great use in small companies that have need for a computer to process applications such as payroll, accounts receivable, billing, and similar types of applications. Today, it is also found in data base and data communications environments. RPG has not been developed for use with personal computers.

The principal advantage of RPG is the ability to generate routine business reports, screen handling, and inquiry reporting quickly and easily. In addition, the language can be relatively easily learned. Because of the fixed logic, however, programming problems which do not readily fit into the fixed logic can be difficult to program. As with most programming languages, the evolution of RPG has been that of changing from a rather limited language designed to produce reports to one with added capabilities which require the skills of a sophisticated programmer. Today RPG II and RPG III programmers are developing complex programs far beyond the capabilities originally intended when RPG was introduced.

BASIC

The most widely used programming language for personal computers is **BASIC**. BASIC, which stands for Beginner's All-purpose Symbolic Instruction Code, is a programming language that was developed at Dartmouth College in 1965 for use in an academic environment.

BASIC was initially designed to be a very concise language with limited capabilities. The intent was to have a programming language that could be learned quickly, so that students, with a limited amount of instruction, could write programs and utilize the computer as a tool for problem solving.

When microcomputers were developed in the 1970's, BASIC was selected as the primary language for use on these computers by all manufacturers. Thus, with millions of personal computers installed, BASIC is undoubtedly one of the most widely used programming languages in the world. A sample BASIC program is illustrated in Figure 13-10 on page 13.9

The primary advantage of BASIC is its ease of use. Part of the ease of use, of course, is because of its somewhat limited capabilities. In recent years, however, with extensions to the language, BASIC has become a more powerful language. The extensions have included the ability to create and access sequential and random files and the ability to create graphics by using the language.

As the extensions were added to the language, many minicomputer manufacturers began utilizing BASIC for business application programming. Thus, today, BASIC is used extensively on minicomputers for business programming as well as being the primary language on personal computers.

BASIC PROGRAM

```
100 REM PATIENTS                  MARCH 28                    SHELLY/CASHMAN
110                                                                      REM
120 REM THIS PROGRAM DISPLAYS THE ROOM NUMBER, PATIENT NAME,
130 REM AND DOCTOR NAME OF HOSPITAL PATIENTS.
140                                                                      REM
150 REM VARIABLE NAMES:
160 REM    N$....PATIENT NAME
170 REM    D$....DOCTOR NAME
180 REM    R.....ROOM NUMBER
190                                                                      REM
200 REM ***** DATA TO BE PROCESSED *****
210                                                                      REM
220 DATA "JOE RUIZ", "WARD", 213
230 DATA "TIM KREL", "NANCE", 112
240 DATA "MARY LEPO", "GOLD", 102
250 DATA "TOM PEP", "KING", 245
260 DATA "END OF FILE", "END", 999
270                                                                      REM
280 REM ***** PROCESSING *****
290                                                                      REM
300 PRINT "ROOM","PATIENT","DOCTOR"
310 PRINT " "
320                                                                      REM
330 READ N$, D$, R
340                                                                      REM
350 IF N$ = "END OF FILE" THEN 400
360   PRINT R, N$, D$
370   READ N$, D$, R
380 GOTO 350
390                                                                      REM
400 PRINT " "
410 PRINT "END OF PATIENT LIST"
420 END
```

Figure 13-10 BASIC, originally developed to be utilized in an academic environment, is now widely used on personal computers and small business computers as well.

Pascal

Pascal is a newer programming language which has gained wide acceptance. The name Pascal is not an abbreviation, but rather the language is named after the mathematician, Blaise Pascal (1623 - 1662), who developed one of the earliest calculating machines.

Pascal was one of the first major programming languages which provided statements to encourage using structured programming to implement programs. Structured programming is based upon the theory that all programming logic can be expressed using three basic logic structures. These structures are: 1) Sequence of operations; 2) Comparing logic structure; 3) Looping logic structure. The Pascal language allows these three logic structures to be easily expressed by the language statements.

The Pascal language was originally defined by **Niklaus Wirth**, a computer scientist at the Institut fur Informatik in Zurich, Switzerland, in 1968. The first Pascal compiler became operational in 1971.

Pascal provides for data names of any length, allows precise definition of various types of data, and contains statements that allow easy implementation of structured programming logic. Figure 13-11 illustrates a Pascal program.

Pascal is available for use on both personal computers and large computers. Because the Pascal language lends itself to developing programs using structured programming techniques, many colleges teach Pascal as the first programming language for students taking course work in computer programming. Pascal is also the language used for the Advanced Placement Test in computer programming administered nationally every year to high school students planning to study computer science in college.

Niklaus Wirth has made further improvements and extensions to the Pascal language. This language, called **Modula-2**, is now available on some computers.

Figure 13-11 Pascal is a general purpose programming language that contains statements that allow for the coding of structured programs.

```
(*========================================================*)
(*JUNE 14                AUTOEXPENSE            SHELLY/CASHMAN*)
(*========================================================*)

PROGRAM AUTOEXPENSE (INPUT, OUTPUT);     (*-PROGRAM NAME/FILES-*)

(*--THIS PROGRAM CALCULATES TOTAL MILES DRIVEN AND TOTAL EXPENSE
 BASED UPON USER INPUT. OUTPUT IS DISPLAYED ON A CRT SCREEN.--*)

(*------VARIABLES------*)

VAR
     BEGINNING_MILEAGE,
     ENDING_MILEAGE,
     MILES_DRIVEN    : INTEGER; (*-VARIABLES OF TYPE INTEGER-*)

     COST_PER_MILE,
     TOTAL_EXPENSE   : REAL;     (*-VARIABLES OF TYPE REAL-*)

(*------MAIN PROCESSING------*)

BEGIN
  WRITE ('ENTER BEGINNING MILEAGE: '); READLN (BEGINNING_MILEAGE);
  WRITE ('ENTER ENDING MILEAGE: '); READLN (ENDING_MILEAGE);
  WRITE ('ENTER COST PER MILE: '); READLN (COST_PER_MILE);
  WRITELN;
  MILES_DRIVEN:= ENDING_MILEAGE - BEGINNING_MILEAGE;
  TOTAL_EXPENSE:= MILES_DRIVEN * COST_PER_MILE;
  WRITELN ('BEGINNING MILEAGE = ', BEGINNING_MILEAGE: 2);
  WRITELN ('ENDING MILEAGE = ', ENDING_MILEAGE: 2);
  WRITELN ('TOTAL MILES DRIVEN = ', MILES_DRIVEN: 2);
  WRITELN ('TOTAL EXPENSE = $', TOTAL_EXPENSE: 3:2);
END.
```

Ada

Ada is a relatively new programming language which was developed under the direction of the U. S. Department of Defense. In the early 1970's, the Department of Defense became aware of the large software costs for defense department projects. Studies indicated annual software costs were in excess of $3 billion. It was further determined that a significant portion of these costs were related to software development and maintenance for programs which operated on embedded computer systems. Embedded computer systems are computers which are a part of other systems, such as airplanes, ships, tanks, and so on. The embedded computers control the operation of the systems in which they are embedded.

In 1975, a Department of Defense committee was formed to review and evaluate existing languages being used. They found that multiple languages were used for embedded systems. Whenever changes had to be made to the software, excess time and money were required because of the lack of uniformity. Further, it was determined that no existing language met the needs of the department. Therefore, it was recommended that a new language be developed, and that the new language should be based on existing languages such as PL/I and Pascal.

Contracts to design the language were opened to four vendors. The specifications of the language were revised to include not only the needs for embedded systems, but of all computer applications required at the Department of Defense. After three years of design and evaluation, a language developed by Honeywell was accepted in 1982. The name given to the language was Ada, named after Augusta Ada Byron, Countess of Lovelace, who in the 1800's worked on George Babbage's "difference engine" and who is considered by many to be the first computer programmer.

Ada was designed to facilitate the writing and maintenance of large programs that would be used over a long period of time, that would be developed by a team of programmers, and that would be subject to continual change. The Ada language encourages coding of readable programs that are portable, allowing them to be transferred from computer to computer.

The language can be used for writing operating systems, simulations, communications, industrial control applications, and other complex processing. Because of the influence of the Department of Defense, it is anticipated that Ada will be an important programming language.

The "C" programming language

The **C** programming language was developed at Bell Laboratories in 1972 by Dennis Ritchie. Originally designed as a programming language for writing systems software, it is now considered a general-purpose programming language featuring concise expression of functions to be performed, and a design that permits writing well structured programs. C has a small set of approximately 30 reserved words and is very portable, meaning that the language can easily be implemented on a wide variety of computers, varying from microcomputers to the largest of mainframes.

C first became widely recognized when the language was used to write the system control program called Unix for Bell Labs. Unix and its utilities consist of over 300,000 lines of C source code.

C provides very powerful, high-level statements and functions and also includes bit-manipulation operators, allowing for a wide range of uses for the language. The C language is available for a wide range of computers, including personal computers. Figure 13–12 illustrates a segment of a program in C.

```
MAIN()
{
        INT COUNT;

        COUNT = 1;
        WHILE (COUNT <= 5) {
            PRINTF("%D\N", COUNT*2);
            COUNT ++;
        }
}
```

Figure 13–12 The C programming language was originally designed to be used for systems programming, but is now used for general purpose programming as well.

The language for education — LOGO

Logo is a language that was developed by **Seymour Papert**, at MIT, for children to enhance their learning and problem solving skills. One of the features of Logo is that it allows the user to control a symbol, called a turtle, on the screen. High level commands move the turtle and draw pictures (Figure 13–13). In addition, Logo contains other powerful commands that allow the user to easily produce screen graphics, process data, and create files. As with most programming languages, Logo began as a relatively simple language and has grown to be considerably more complex in terms of the functions and features it offers.

Logo is widely used in lower school grades to teach programming and problem solving. It is argued by Logo advocates that children develop problem solving skills in all facets of education by learning to use Logo.

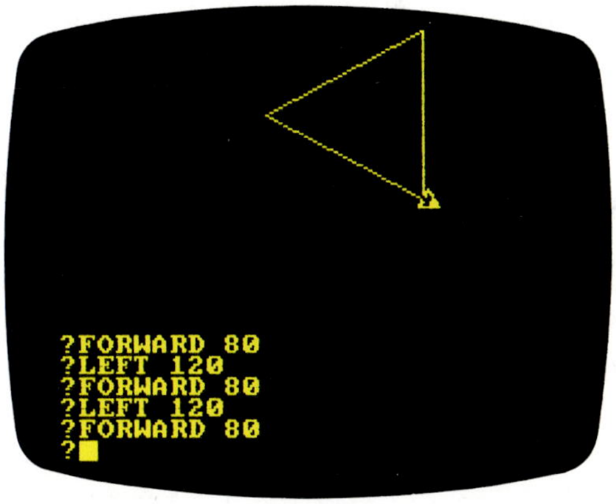
?FORWARD 80
?LEFT 120
?FORWARD 80
?LEFT 120
?FORWARD 80
?

Figure 13–13 Logo commands can be used to move the turtle (the arrow-like symbol) around the screen, drawing lines as it moves. Here, to draw a triangle, the command Forward moves the turtle 80 units in the direction the turtle is pointing. The command Left changes the direction the turtle is pointing by the number of degrees specified. As a result of the commands shown, the triangle is drawn.

Other programming languages

Numerous other programming languages have been developed over the past thirty-five years. Some of these languages with special names are nothing more than assembler languages that have been developed for specific computers. There have, however, been a number of specialized programming languages that have been implemented. These languages were developed, for example, to program manufacturing machines, to provide for authoring computer-assisted learning programs, and to allow special manipulation of alphabetic data for information retrieval applications. As specialized application areas are placed on the computer, specialized software is frequently developed to assist in the programming of the computer for these areas. A chart of some of the languages which have been developed in the past three decades is shown in Figure 13–14.

PROGRAMMING LANGUAGES

A–2 & A–3	COGENT	FORTRAN	MATHLAB	RTL–2
ADAM	COGO	FORTRANSIT	MATH–MATIC	Short Code
AED	COLASL	FSL	META 5	SIMSCRIPT
AESOP	COLOMGO	GAT	MILITRAN	SIMULA
AIMACO	COMIT	GPSS	MIRFAC	SNOBOL
ALGOL	Commercial	GRAF	MODULA–2	SOAP
ALTRAN	Translator	HALID	MORAL	SOL
AMBIT	CORAL	ICES	MUMPS	Speedcoding
AMTRAN	CPS	IPL–V	NEAT	SPL/I
APL	DEACON	IT	PASCAL	STRESS
ASSEMBLER	DYNAMO	JOSS	PEARL	TACPOL
AUTOCODER	473L Query	JOVIAL	PILOT	TMG
BACAIC	EASYCODER	LIS	PL/I	TRAC
BASIC	ECL	LISP	PRINT	TRANDIR
C	FACT	LOGO	Protosynthex	TREET
CBASIC	FLAP	MAD	QUIKTRAN	RNING
CLIP	FLOW–MATIC	MADCAP	RPG	UNICODE
CLP	FORMAC	Magic Paper	RPG II	
COBOL	FORTH	MAP	RPG III	

Figure 13–14 A partial list of the many languages developed for programming computers is shown here.

CODING QUALITY PROGRAMS

Regardless of the programming language being used, it is very important to produce a program which is easy to read and understand. Proper coding of a program can make the task of implementing and subsequently maintaining a program a relatively simple task, while an improperly coded program can be almost impossible to understand, correct, or modify.

The examples in Figure 13-15 illustrate poor coding and good coding to accomplish the same processing. The poor coding is very difficult to read. The good coding, on the other hand, uses remarks to document the program and utilizes blank spaces and indented statements to improve the readability of the program.

The principle of writing a legible, quality program applies to all programming languages, even though the example illustrates a program coded in BASIC. Standards can be established for all programming languages which will result in programs that are easy to read and understand. It is the responsibility of the programmer to write code in a clear, easily understood manner.

Figure 13-15 These two BASIC programs accomplish the exact same processing. The bad coding example, however, is quite difficult to read and understand while the good coding program is much more legible. This is a very small program; as programs increase in size, poorly coded programs become impossible to read and understand.

Bad coding

```
1 DATA 714, "749-2138", "SAM HORN"
2 DATA 213, "663-1271", "SUE NUNN"
3 DATA 212, "999-1193", "BOB PELE"
4 DATA 312, "979-4418", "ANN SITZ"
5 DATA 999, "999-9999", "END OF FILE"
6 READ A, T$, N$
7 IF N$= "END OF FILE" THEN 11
8 PRINT N$, A, T$
9 READ A, T$, N$
10 GOTO 7
11 PRINT " "
12 PRINT "END OF TELEPHONE LISTING"
13 END
```

Good coding

```
100 REM TELLIST              SEPTEMBER 22              SHELLY/CASHMAN
110                                                               REM
120 REM THIS PROGRAM DISPLAYS THE NAME, TELEPHONE AREA CODE
130 REM AND PHONE NUMBER OF INDIVIDUALS.
140                                                               REM
150 REM VARIABLE NAMES:
160 REM   A.....AREA CODE
170 REM   T$....TELEPHONE NUMBER
180 REM   N$....NAME
190                                                               REM
200 REM ***** DATA TO BE PROCESSED *****
210                                                               REM
220 DATA 714, "749-2138", "SAM HORN"
230 DATA 213, "663-1271", "SUE NUNN"
240 DATA 212, "999-1193", "BOB PELE"
250 DATA 312, "979-4418", "ANN SITZ"
260 DATA 999, "999-9999", "END OF FILE"
270                                                               REM
280 REM ***** PROCESSING *****
290                                                               REM
300 READ A, T$, N$
310                                                               REM
320 IF N$ = "END OF FILE" THEN 370
330   PRINT N$, A, T$
340   READ A, T$, N$
350 GOTO 320
360                                                               REM
370 PRINT " "
380 PRINT "END OF TELEPHONE LISTING"
390 END
```

CHAPTER SUMMARY

1. A computer program contains a series of instructions which directs the computer to perform those tasks necessary to process data and produce a desired output.
2. Machine language is a set of instructions the electronics of the computer can interpret and execute.
3. The programmer normally writes instructions using a source language.
4. Source language statements fall into seven categories: a) Statements to define data bases, files, and records; b) Statements to define other data within the program; c) Statements which cause data to be read into main computer memory or cause data to be written from main computer memory; d) Statements which move data in memory; e) Statements which cause arithmetic operations to occur; f) Statements which cause data to be compared and perform alternative operations based upon the results; g) Statements which document the program.
5. Assembler language is a symbolic language closely related to machine language and the internal machine architecture. Assembler language is called a low-level language.
6. The principal advantage of assembler language is that a program can be written that is very efficient in terms of execution time and main computer memory usage. Disadvantages are there is little compatibility between assembler languages for different machines, more statements must be written to solve a problem than with a high-level language, and assembler language programs are difficult to write, read, and maintain.
7. A programming language in which the statements are not closely related to the internal characteristics of the computer is called a high-level programming language.
8. FORTRAN was designed for use by scientists, engineers, and mathematicians. Its major advantage is the easy expression of complex mathematical calculations through the use of arithmetic operators.
9. COBOL is one of the most widely used programming languages for business application programming.
10. COBOL was designed to be able to be run on a variety of computers. It uses English-like statements containing verbs and sentences to cause operations to be performed and it has strong file handling capabilities.
11. The most important advantage of COBOL is that it is machine independent. COBOL is relatively easy to write and can be understood by other programmers. A disadvantage is its wordiness.
12. PL/I was designed by IBM as a general purpose programming language, but is not widely used.
13. RPG, which stands for Report Program Generator, allows reports, screen displays, and inquiry reporting to be generated by filling out a series of forms. RPG has been enhanced by the announcements of RPG II and RPG III.
14. BASIC was originally designed for use in an academic environment but is now widely used as the primary language on microcomputers. The primary advantage of BASIC is its ease of use.
15. Pascal was developed to provide statements which encourage the use of structured programming.
16. Ada is a programming language developed under the direction of the U. S. Department of Defense to facilitate the writing and maintenance of all programs used by the Department of Defense.
17. The C language was developed at Bell Laboratories to be used as a systems programming language.
18. Logo was developed by Seymour Papert at MIT for use by children to enhance problem solving skills.

KEY TERMS

ANSI 13.4
Ada 13.10
American National Standards Institute 13.4
Assembler languages 13.2
BASIC 13.8
C (Programming language) 13.10
COBOL 13.5
Computer program 13.1
FORTRAN 13.3
High-level programming language 13.3
Logo 13.11
Label 13.2
Low-level languages 13.2
Machine language 13.1
Macro 13.2
Modula-2 13.9
Object code 13.2
Operands 13.2
Operation code 13.2
PL/I 13.6
Seymour Papert 13.11
Pascal 13.9
RPG 13.7
RPG II 13.8
RPG III 13.8
Source language 13.1
Niklaus Wirth 13.9

REVIEW QUESTIONS

1. Define the term computer program.
2. Explain the difference between machine language and source language. Which form does a programmer use?
3. Identify and describe the seven major categories of program statements.
4. Describe the characteristics of an assembler language. What is a macro? An operand?
5. What is a low-level programming language? What is a high-level programming language? What are the advantages and disadvantages of each?
6. Why was FORTRAN developed? What is its historic significance?
7. What is COBOL? What are verbs and sentences in COBOL? List some of the verbs available in COBOL.
8. Explain some of the advantages and disadvantages of COBOL.
9. What does RPG mean? Explain how programming is accomplished using RPG. What are the newer versions of RPG?
10. Why was BASIC developed? What is its major use today?
11. What is Pascal? What is its major advantage? On what type of computers is Pascal used?
12. Why was Ada developed? What can it be used for?
13. What is the C programming language? What is its purpose?
14. Who developed Logo? Why was it developed? Where is Logo used?
15. For what purposes are specialized programming languages developed? Why do you suppose special purpose languages are developed instead of using one of the general purpose languages?
16. List some of the characteristics of a quality program.

CONTROVERSIAL ISSUES

1. Some developers of programming languages feel a programming language should be very concise, allowing the programmer to express the operations to be performed with as few lines of coding as possible. Others feel a language should allow the programmer to express the operations in English-like statements so the program can be easily understood by others. If you were designing a new programming language for business applications, what characteristics do you feel would be desirable for your language?
2. The American National Standards Institute has published standards for a number of programming languages, including FORTRAN and COBOL. Computer manufacturers and others implementing these languages are encouraged to follow the standards. Standards are supposed to allow the various languages to be essentially machine independent. Some argue that standards stifle language improvement because once standards are established, they are difficult to change. Most language developers add extensions to the language standards in an attempt to make their version of the language better. Are standards good? Do they help or hinder development of languages?

RESEARCH PROJECTS

1. Review the employment ads for computer programmers in a local newspaper. Prepare a report documenting which programming languages are required for employment in the various jobs.
2. In *Mindstorms: Children, Computers, and Powerful Ideas*, Seymour Papert explains the purpose and use of the Logo language. Prepare a book report on the purpose and use of Logo after reading *Mindstorms*.
3. Visit a local computer store and determine which programming languages are available on one of their widely sold personal computers. Report your findings to the class.
4. Choose two of the languages on the list in Figure 13–14 on page 13.11 that are not discussed in the chapter and prepare a report on them, explaining their use and how statements are written using the language.

Chapter Fourteen

Operating Systems and Systems Software

Objectives

- ☐ Write a definition of system software and an operating system
- ☐ Draw a diagram of main computer memory illustrating the memory allocation for an operating system
- ☐ Specify some of the utility programs available with an operating system and their functions
- ☐ Describe the processing that occurs when an interpreter is used
- ☐ List some of the currently available operating systems and their attributes
- ☐ Describe the processing that occurs in a concurrent program execution environment
- ☐ Identify the processing and output of a compiler

Operating Systems and Systems Software

Chapter Fourteen

The applications software discussed in Chapter Twelve and the application programs developed by using the programming languages examined in Chapter Thirteen must be augmented by systems software. **Systems software** consists of programs that start up the computer; load, execute, store, and retrieve application programs; store and retrieve files; and perform a series of utility functions. A part of the systems software available with most computers is the operating system. An **operating system** is a collection of programs which interfaces between the user or application programs and the computer hardware itself to control and manage the operation of the computer (Figure 14–2).

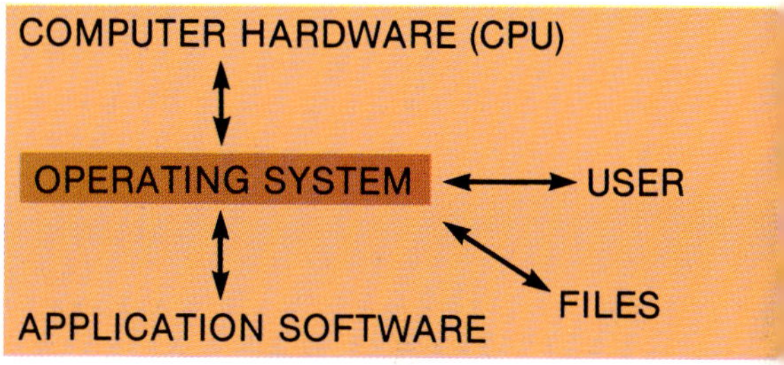

Figure 14–2 The software in an operating system communicates with application programs, the user, and the computer hardware.

Systems software and operating systems are available for both personal computers and larger computers such as minicomputers and mainframes. In all cases, they perform essentially the same functions. These functions include: 1) Booting, or starting, the computer operation; 2) Interface with users; 3) Resource management.

When a computer is turned on, the operating system is loaded into main computer memory by a set of instructions normally contained within ROM. This process is called **booting** or **initial program loading**. Once the operating system is in main computer memory, the user communicates with it to load application programs or to perform other functions. The operating system software controls access to disks, printers, CRT screens, and all other hardware resources available on the computer.

To illustrate this process, the example in Figure 14–3 shows the process that occurs when a personal computer is turned on and the operating system is booted into main computer memory. While this process is not identical to that used on large computers, the functions performed are virtually the same.

In the drawing in Figure 14–3, the following steps occur: 1) A floppy disk on which the operating system is stored is placed in the disk drive. It should be noted that the operating system could be stored on a hard disk as

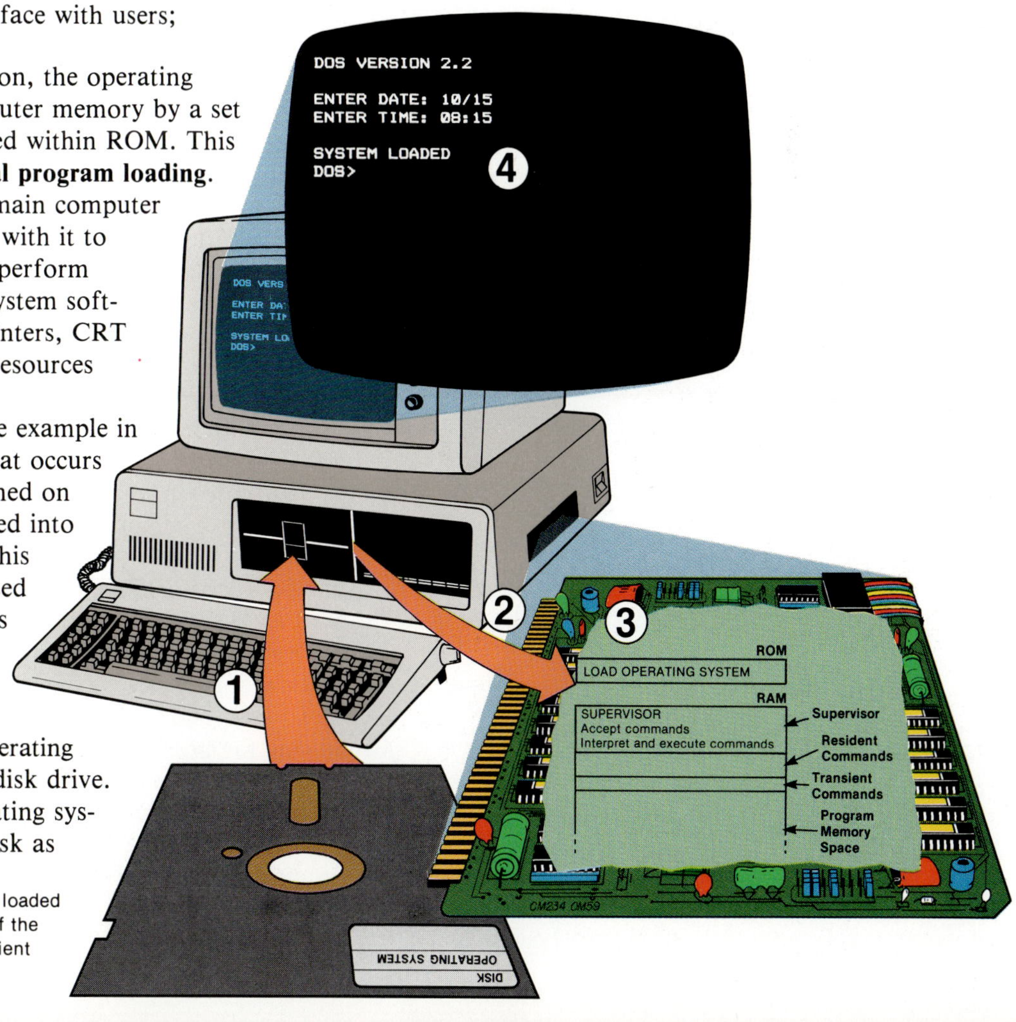

Figure 14–3 When an operating system is loaded into main computer memory, it consists of the supervisor, resident commands, and transient commands.

well. In that case, the floppy disk would not be used. 2) When the computer is turned on, the boot routine stored in ROM issues the commands to load the operating system into main computer memory. The operating system software is read from the floppy disk or hard disk into main computer memory. 3) When the operating system is loaded, a portion of main computer memory is used for it. The amount of memory required varies, depending upon the operating system being used. It can vary from as little as 4K to as much as 128K on personal computers. Operating systems on large computers may require as much as one megabyte of main computer memory. When stored in main computer memory, most operating systems are divided into three different sections: Supervisor, resident commands, and transient commands. The **supervisor** of an operating system contains instructions which communicate with the user, cause input/output operations to occur, and generally control the operations of the computer.

The **resident commands** portion of the operating system allows memory space for frequently used utility functions of the operating system that reside permanently in memory. For example, when a file is copied from one disk to another using an operating system utility program, the instructions to perform the copying are often stored in this portion of memory. These commands are always resident in memory.

The **transient commands** portion of memory is reserved for instructions which perform less frequently required functions, such as formatting a disk. When the user requires one of these functions to be performed, the instructions are loaded from the disk into this transient area and are executed. When another function is to be executed, that software is loaded into the area to overlay the previous instructions. Thus, the instructions are said to be transient because they are moved into the area in order to perform their function and then are overlayed with other instructions.

The remainder of main computer memory is not used by the operating system. Therefore, it is used for application programs.

4) After the supervisor is loaded into main computer memory, it is given control by the boot instructions which loaded it. In many cases, it will request the user to enter date and time information. After the user enters the requested information, the message System Loaded is displayed and the **operating system prompt** (in this example, DOS >) is displayed. This indicates to the user that the operating system is available for communication. The user needs merely to enter commands.

Figure 14-4 The directory of a disk contains the name of the file, the number of bytes the file occupies on the disk, the date the file was stored or last changed, and the time the file was stored or last changed.

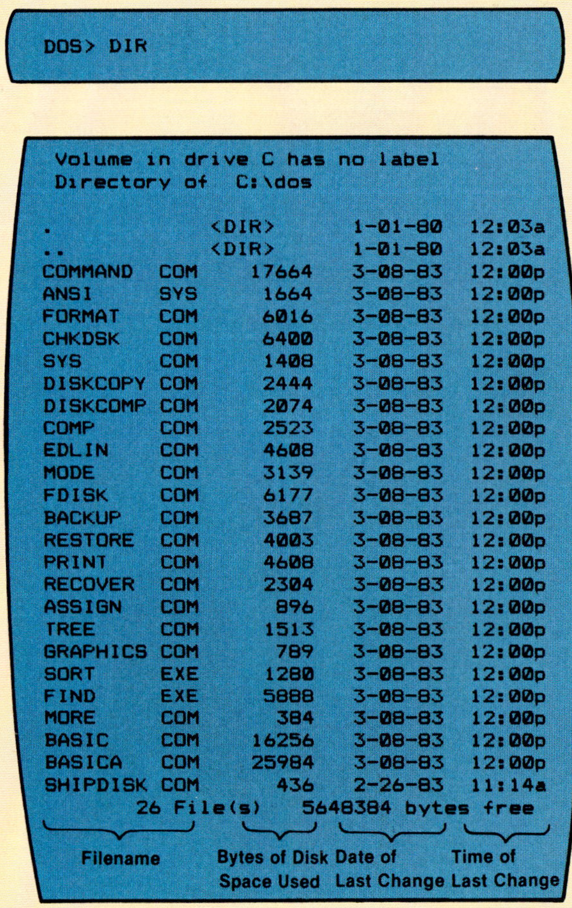

Communicating with the operating system

In order to communicate with the operating system, the user must enter commands which the supervisor portion of the operating system will interpret and act upon. For example, one of the functions of the operating system is to maintain a directory of all files and programs stored on a disk. To display the directory that is maintained by the operating system, many operating systems accept the command DIR, as illustrated in Figure 14-4). Note that the user entered the command DIR following the operating system prompt. The supervisor interpreted the command and displayed the directory.

In order to execute an application program, the user must enter a command which will cause the program to be loaded from disk into main computer memory. Some operating systems will execute a program if just the name of the program is entered by the user. Others require a command such as Run. Thus, the entry RUN SPREAD could cause the program to be loaded into main computer memory and be executed. The exact format and syntax of commands interpreted by an operating system depend upon the operating system itself, but it is important to note that all operating systems accept commands from the user and act upon the commands.

Program execution

When a program is loaded into main computer memory and executed, it performs whatever tasks it was designed to perform. When the program has completed processing, it issues a program instruction which causes control to be returned to the operating system. At that time, the user would again communicate with the supervisor portion of the operating system to cause the next operation to occur.

On some personal computer operating systems and virtually all operating systems used with large computers, operating system commands can be batched together and be read and executed independently of the computer operator or user. Thus, for example, a **batch file** which specifies that two, three, four, or more programs are to be executed could be prepared and stored on disk. The sequence of execution within the batch file is initiated when its name is entered in response to the operating system prompt. The first program in the sequence would be loaded into main computer memory and be executed. When the first program has completed processing, it returns control to the supervisor portion of the operating system which immediately causes the second program to be loaded into main computer memory. The second program is then executed. When it is complete, it returns control to the supervisory software which in turn causes the third program to be loaded and executed. This sequence would continue until all of the programs in the batch file had been executed. The ability to execute programs in a job stream of this type allows a great deal of program execution to occur independently of operator intervention. This technique is vital to large computers.

Utility programs

In addition to controlling the execution of application programs on a computer, the operating system contains a number of **utility functions** which it can perform. Some operating systems have 15 - 20 functions while others have several hundred. Those that are most commonly found on both small and large computer operating systems pertain to file management. **File management** includes formatting disks and diskettes, deleting files from a disk, copying files, renaming files, and other functions as well.

The following list provides a sampling of the types of utility programs and additional functions provided on most operating systems.

1. Enter date — This entry allows the operator to change the **system date** at any time. The system date is a date which the operating system uses to identify when files are written on a disk and for a variety of other tasks.
2. Enter time — The system time can be set with this command. The **system time** can be entered and the computer updates the time so that the correct time of day is always known. The time is written in the directory when the files are

created or changed (see Figure 14–4).

3. Display the directory — As noted before, the **directory** of a disk or diskette can be displayed by a utility program called by the command DIR.
4. Format a disk or diskette — It will be recalled from Chapter Nine that soft-sectored disks and diskettes must be formatted. A utility program in the operating system formats the disks and diskettes. **Formatting** a disk or diskette is an extremely important function of an operating system for two reasons. First, the disks cannot be used without formatting. Second, many operating systems format a disk using their own formatting criteria. In these cases, data stored on a disk formatted by one operating system cannot be read by a program running under another operating system. Effectively, then, the data stored on a disk from one operating system is incompatible with other operating systems. Users must be aware of this fact so that there are no expectations that files created under one operating system will be able to be read by programs running under another operating system.
5. Copy files — Files stored on hard disks or diskettes must often be copied. Frequently the reason is to create backup files. Utility programs associated with an operating systems perform this function. The **copy programs** are generally implemented through a console or keyboard command (Figure 14–5).
6. Rename files — Another utility function made available with operating systems is the ability to rename files. Thus, in Figure 14–5, the file copied onto drive B with the name DATAFILE.BAK could be renamed DATABACK.UP.
7. Delete files — Files can also be deleted from a disk or diskette through an operating system utility program. When a file is deleted from a disk, its name is removed from the disk directory, and the space it occupied on the disk is freed up so other files can be stored.
8. Copy an entire disk — In some instances instead of copying individual files for backup purposes, the entire disk is copied. The disk might be copied onto another disk, or it might be copied onto tape.
9. Compare the contents of disks — Frequently after an entire disk has been copied for backup purposes, the contents of the backup disk should be compared to the contents of the original disk just copied to ensure that no errors were made in copying the file. This utility program performs this function.

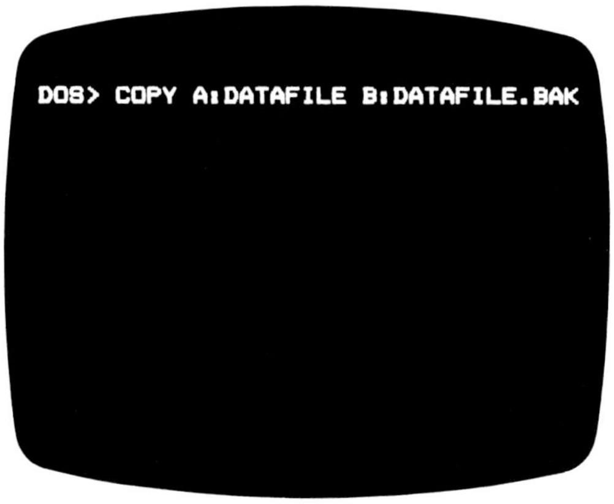
DOS> COPY A:DATAFILE B:DATAFILE.BAK

Figure 14–5 The command COPY causes the copy function of the operating system to copy one file to another. Here, the data in the file named DATAFILE is copied to the file with the name DATAFILE.BAK.

Utilities are a very important part of most operating systems.

BASIC interpreters

The BASIC programming language is widely used, particularly on personal computers. When a programmer writes a program using BASIC, the statements are written in a manner which can be understood by people. The statements used in the programming language, however, cannot be interpreted and executed by the electronics of the computer. The central processing unit, which actually executes the instructions, can understand only machine language. **Machine language** is a series of numbers and letters which the electronics of the CPU can interpret and execute. Since only machine language can be executed by the CPU, the BASIC statements written by the programmer must be translated into machine language prior to execution. On personal computers using BASIC, this is usually performed by a **BASIC interpreter.**

A BASIC interpreter is not normally considered a part of the operating system but it is a part of the systems software that is required on most computers where BASIC programs are to be written. The BASIC interpreter is usually stored on the same disk where the operating system utility programs are stored.

To write and execute a BASIC program, the BASIC interpreter must be loaded into main computer memory from the disk. After the interpreter is loaded, the programmer enters the program statements. Once all program statements have been entered, the programmer can indicate that the program should be executed by entering a command such as RUN. This command is given to the BASIC interpreter program. When the program is executed, the BASIC interpreter translates each program statement to machine language (Figure 14–6). The interpreter then sends the machine language instruction to the CPU where it is executed.

Each BASIC statement is interpreted and executed. Thus, an interpreter translates a program statement written by the programmer into a machine language statement that can be understood by the CPU each time the statement is to be executed. BASIC interpreters are normally a very important part of the system software.

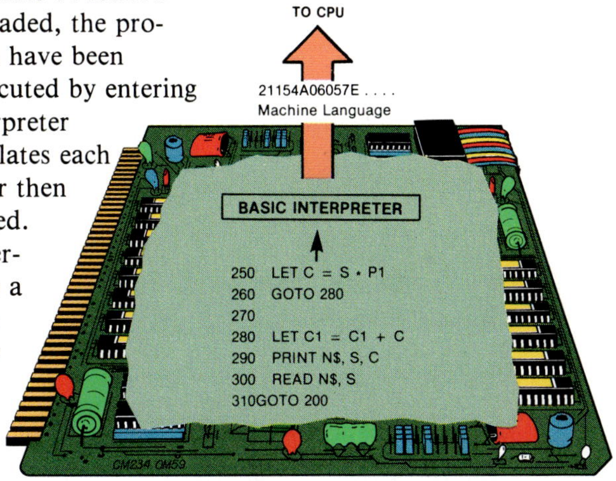

Figure 14–6 When a BASIC program is executed using a BASIC interpreter, each statement in the program is converted by the interpreter to a machine language instruction and then is immediately executed. Although this BASIC interpreter is shown in main computer memory as part of the system software, it should be noted that some BASIC's are stored in Read Only Memory (ROM) as part of the computer hardware.

Personal computer operating systems

A number of different operating systems have been developed for use on personal computers. These operating systems can be used on machines from different manufacturers, but are normally designed for use with a certain microprocessor. For example, an operating system that is used with the Intel 8088 chip can usually be used on any personal computer from any manufacturer which uses the Intel 8088 chip for its microprocessor. The following is a brief summary of a few of the operating systems available for personal computers.

CP/M was the first operating system developed for personal computers. It was designed and implemented by Gary Kildall. Kildall was one of the first people to recognize that operating systems were required for personal computers. CP/M (Control Program for Microprocessors) has been implemented for a number of different microprocessors. Newer versions include CP/M-86 and Concurrent CP/M. More than 15,000 application programs have been written to be run using CP/M.

AppleDOS (Disk Operating System) and **Apple ProDOS** are two operating systems which are used for all of the Apple II family of computers. Apple ProDOS is the newer operating system intended for use with hard disks. A very large amount of software has been written for execution under AppleDOS and ProDOS, although not every program that executes using Apple DOS will execute using ProDOS.

MS-DOS, also known as **PC-DOS**, is the operating system chosen for use with the IBM Personal Computer (hence the name PC-DOS). It is becoming a standard operating system in the industry because so many computers can now use it and because so much software is being developed that can run under MS-DOS.

Unix is an operating system developed by the Bell Laboratories for use on minicomputers, but in recent years it has been modified to run on personal computers. While performing all the functions of an operating system, Unix also offers a library of more than 200 utility programs which perform a multitude of useful programming tasks. It also offers a unique file structure which enables files to be manipulated in a way not available with other operating systems. Some experts are predicting that Unix will become the industry standard operating system in the future.

A number of other operating systems, such as TRSDOS, Pick, p-system, and others have also been developed. The decision concerning which operating system to use is largely dependent upon the computer and the available software.

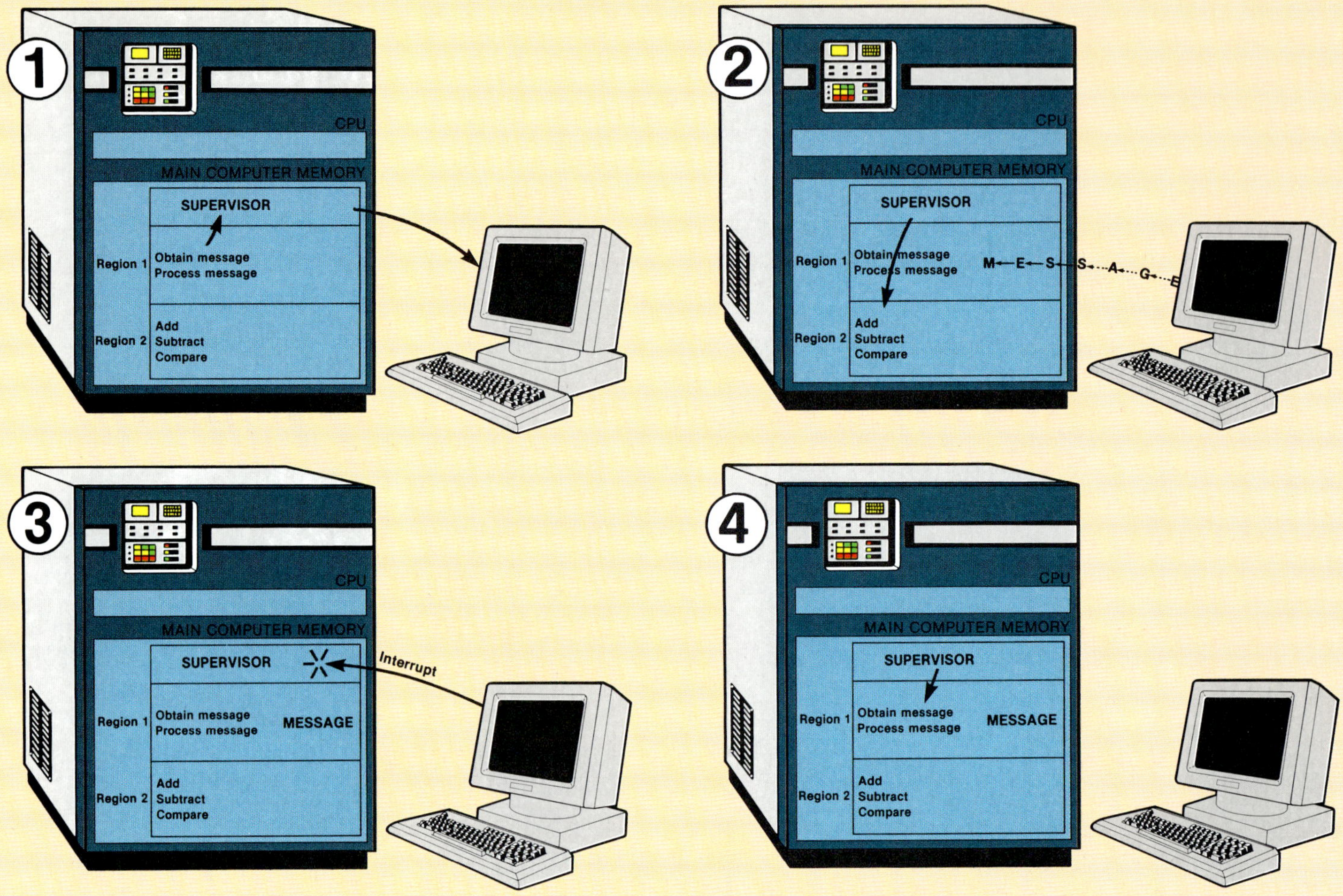

Figure 14–7 The use of an interrupt to allow multiprogramming is illustrated in this example. In step 1, the program in region 1 issues the command to obtain a message from the terminal. This command passes through the operating system. In step 2, while the message is being transmitted from the terminal to main computer memory, the program in region 1 can do no processing, so the operating system gives control to the program in region 2. When the message is in memory, an interrupt is sent to the operating system indicating the I/O operation is complete (step 3). The supervisor then determines that the region 1 program can process data (step 4), so control is passed back to the region 1 program.

LARGE COMPUTER OPERATING SYSTEMS

Operating systems on large computers perform many of the same functions as operating systems on personal computers. They are, however, larger and more complex since larger computers can perform more functions than personal computers. One function that large computer operating systems allow that is allowed on only several personal computer operating systems (Concurrent CP/M and Unix, for example), is **concurrent programming**, also known as **multitasking** or **multiprogramming**. These terms all refer to the concurrent execution of two or more computer programs on one computer. In order to understand how multiple programs can execute concurrently, it is helpful to examine the concept of an interrupt.

When a program issues an input/output command, the program is placed in a wait state until the execution of the command has been completed. When the transfer of data between main computer memory and the input/output device has been completed, the device generates an **interrupt**, which is a signal that the data has been transferred. The program may then continue processing. Multiprogramming is possible because of the time required to perform input/output operations. The example in Figure 14–7 illustrates the use of an interrupt to enable multiprogramming. The two programs in region 1 and region 2 are operating concurrently. When the program in region 1 requests the terminal to send a message, it cannot perform further processing until the message is received. Therefore, the operating system gives control to the program in region 2. When the message is sent, an interrupt is generated and control is given back to the program in region 1.

Another feature found on large systems which is not used too much on smaller systems is a compiler (Figure 14–8). As noted previously, source program statements must be translated to machine language before they can be executed. A **compiler** translates a source program into an **object program**, which is a program consisting

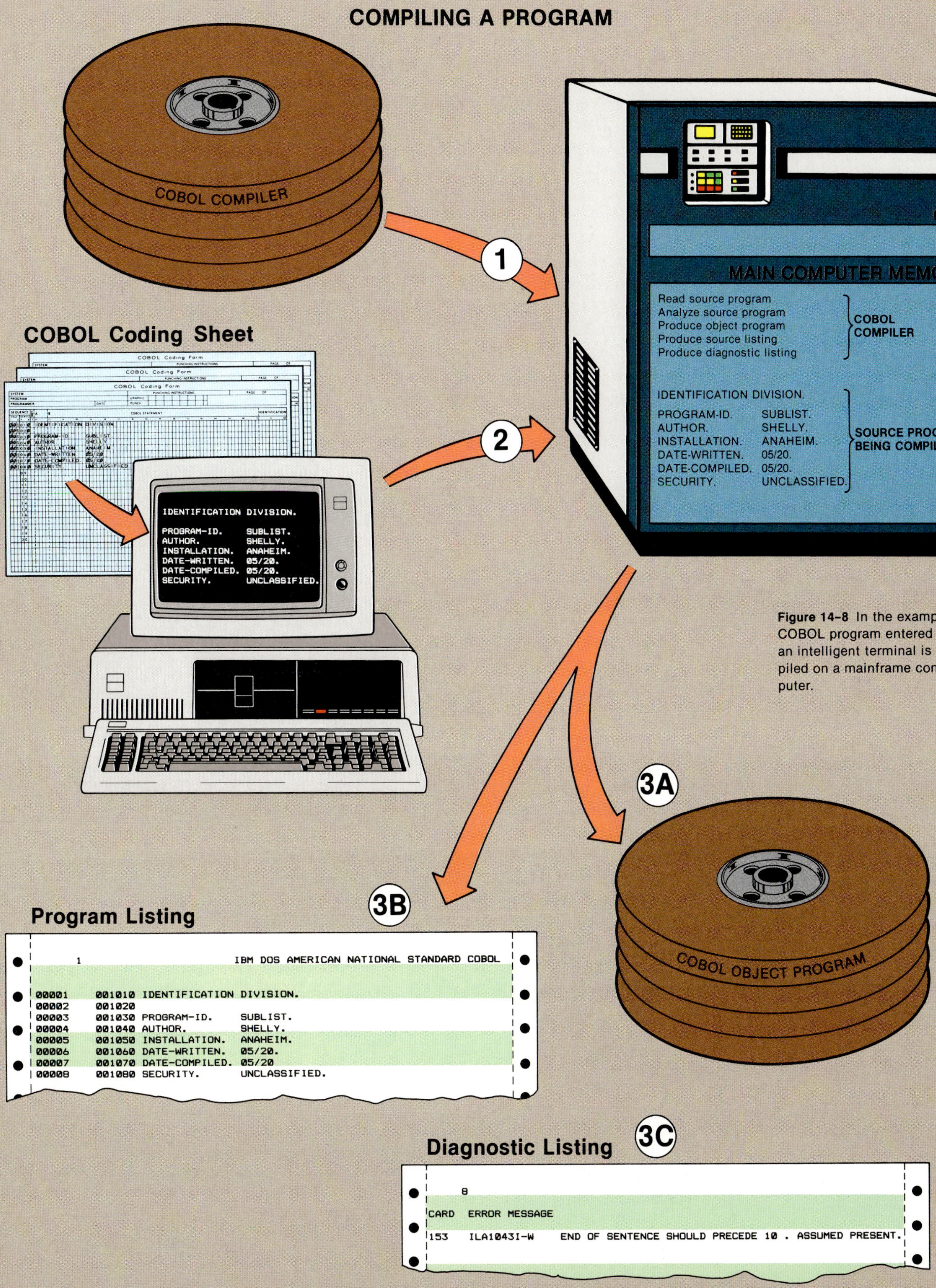

Figure 14–8 In the example, a COBOL program entered from an intelligent terminal is compiled on a mainframe computer.

only of machine language instructions. The object program is then executed. The processing performed by a compiler, as shown in Figure 14-8, includes the following: 1) The COBOL compiler is read into main computer memory; 2) The COBOL program is keyed on the personal computer and is transmitted to the mainframe; 3) The compiler analyzes each COBOL statement and produces the following output: a) The object program, which contains the machine language instructions; b) A source listing of the COBOL statements; c) A diagnostic listing of any errors in the usage of the language. The major advantage of a compiler over an interpreter is that each source statement need not be translated each time it is going to be executed; it is translated only one time when it is compiled. Therefore, the execution of an object program is much faster than the execution of an interpreted program.

Another difference between most personal computer operating systems and large computer operating systems is that the large systems are concerned with **memory management**. Memory management means that memory can be dynamically allocated to various programs at different times while the programs are executing. One example of memory management is **virtual storage systems**, where segments of a program which are not immediately required for processing are not stored in main computer memory but rather are stored on disk. Through control of the operating system and the memory management software, the portion of the program stored on disk is called into main computer memory when required.

In general, then, operating systems on small computers perform many of the same functions as operating systems on large computers, but large computer operating systems are more complex and offer additional features.

KEY TERMS

Apple ProDOS 14.5
AppleDOS 14.5
BASIC interpreter 14.5
Batch file 14.3
Booting 14.1
Compiler 14.6
Concurrent programming 14.6
Copy programs 14.4
CP/M 14.5
Directory 14.4
File management 14.3
Formatting (disk) 14.4
Initial program loading 14.1
Interrupt 14.6
Machine language 14.4
Memory management 14.8
MS-DOS 14.5
Multiprogramming 14.6
Multitasking 14.6
Object program 14.6
Operating system 14.1
Operating system prompt 14.2
PC-DOS 14.5
Resident commands 14.2
Supervisor 14.2
System date 14.3
System time 14.3
Systems software 14.1
Transient commands 14.2
Unix 14.5
Utility functions 14.3
Virtual storage systems 14.8

RESEARCH PROJECT

1. Choose one of the operating systems for personal computers mentioned in the text and either visit a computer store or write to the developer to obtain detailed information about the operating system. Prepare a paper on the operating system.

Chapter Fifteen

Systems Analysis And Design

Objectives

- ☐ Identify the three broad categories of systems and describe them
- ☐ List the six phases in the scientific approach to designing computer systems
- ☐ Describe each of the six phases in the scientific approach to designing computer systems in detail
- ☐ Describe the use of data flow diagrams, system flowcharts, display screen layout forms, and Gantt charts with respect to how they are used in systems analysis and design
- ☐ Describe the role of the user and of management in the development of a computer system

Systems Analysis And Design

Chapter Fifteen

Although the computer hardware, file organization methods, data bases, data communication facilities, and application software of modern computers are an important part of the information processing environment, the hardware devices and related software must all interact in the form of a system to produce useful output.

In any business organization, there are many systems. There are accounting systems, billing systems, inventory control systems, and many others. A **system** is a network of related procedures designed to perform some activity. **Procedures** are logical steps by which all repetitive actions are initiated, carried forward, controlled, and finalized. With the application of the computer to business problems, there is a need to precisely define a system because without a properly designed system, the most sophisticated hardware and software are virtually worthless.

Throughout this text, it has been emphasized that systems and procedures are critical to the successful use of computer processing. These systems and procedures must be developed for all applications, whether the software is developed in-house or whether the software is purchased. In this chapter, however, the emphasis is placed upon systems and the associated software which are developed in-house by the organization which will use the output of the system. The purpose of the chapter is to identify the major types of application systems and to provide an overview of the steps that occur when conducting a system project to ensure that a system is properly and efficiently designed and implemented in the business organization.

Types of business systems

Systems which are implemented using a computer fall into three broad classifications: 1) Operational systems; 2) Management information systems; 3) Decision support systems. An **operational system** is designed to process data that is generated by the day-to-day business transactions of a company. For example, in an order entry system, orders are received, the orders are processed, and output in the form of a shipping order and an invoice to the user is generated.

When computers were first used for processing business applications, the systems developed were primarily operational systems. The purpose was to "computerize" an existing manual system. This approach often resulted in faster processing, reduced clerical costs, and improved customer service.

It was soon realized, however, that computer processing could be used for more than computerizing existing manual systems. Those charged with the responsibility of designing systems recognized that with the computer's ability to perform rapid calculations, compare data, and produce large amounts of output, it was possible to use the computer to extract useful information for management from the data being processed by the computer. This led to the concept of management information systems.

Figure 15–2 Management information systems provide timely information for management.

Although the term management information system has been defined in a number of ways, today a **management information system (MIS)** refers to a computer-based system which not only processes the day-to-day transactions but also generates timely and accurate information for various levels of management. This information is most often presented in the form of printed reports or screen displays (Figure 15–2).

When the concept of management information systems was first developed a number of years ago, attempts were made to develop totally integrated systems for processing all data in an organization. The intent was to build this totally integrated system around a single data base that contained all of an organization's data so that management could acquire any information about the organization from a single data base. Very few totally integrated management information systems were ever developed because of the complexity of the task. In recent years, however, systems with related functions have been integrated through the use of data bases and other advanced software capabilities. For example, in a modern order entry system, when an order is filled, a reduction is made from the inventory data and an entry is made in the accounts receivable data. In the related management information system, sales reports and display screens can be used to view sales reports, inventory control information, balances in various customer accounts, and other information which is generated as a result of the processing of data in the system.

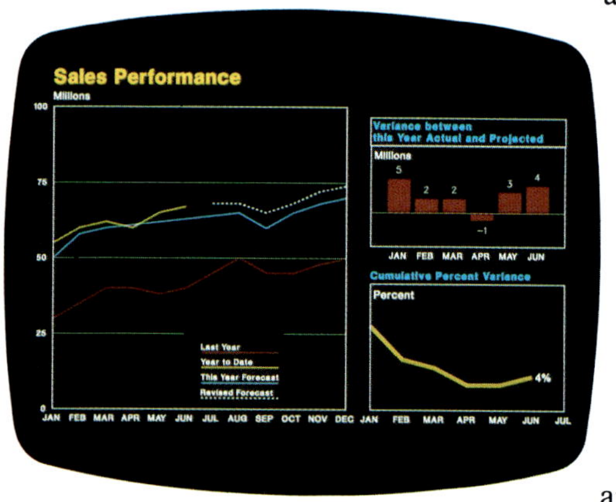

Figure 15–3 Decision support systems contain tools such as graphics which can be used to present information in the most efficient and useful manner.

Most management information systems provide information in a well-defined, structured manner, such as periodic reports or screen displays developed from day-to-day transactions. Management, however, has need for information in a less structured, more dynamic presentation method. For example, a vice-president of sales may need to know year-to-date sales performance and variances between actual and projected sales. This type of information is not generated on a routine basis by most day-to-day operations. To provide this information, decision support systems have been developed. Using fourth generation application development tools, data communications, graphics, and other tools as well, **decision support systems** allow a manager or officer of a corporation to ask questions that can be answered in a dynamic manner based upon data stored in data bases (Figure 15–3).

In addition, decision support systems allow business models and simulation exercises to occur. Thus, a top-level executive can use decision support systems to simulate what will happen to the business if certain strategic moves are made. One example of a decision support system is an electronic spreadsheet which allows the user to ask "what if" questions. Much more sophisticated modeling and simulation programs are also available. In most cases, the most powerful decision support systems must run on large computers because they access a great deal of data and the programs are quite large, requiring the main computer memory and processing speed of larger computers.

The three classifications of systems many times overlap. Operational and management information systems often perform many of the same functions. Decision support systems and management information systems often provide some of the same capabilities. The important fact to remember is that these systems are designed to provide important services to an organization. The methods used to develop them are quite critical, and are the subject of the remainder of this chapter.

INTRODUCTION TO SYSTEMS ANALYSIS AND DESIGN

Regardless of the classification of the information processing system to be designed, it is critical that the process to develop the system follow a well-defined scientific problem-solving approach. The approach can be broken down into a series of phases:

Phase 1 — Initiation of the system project and the preliminary investigation
Phase 2 — Detailed system investigation and analysis
Phase 3 — System design
Phase 4 — System development
Phase 5 — System implementation and evaluation
Phase 6 — System maintenance

Phase 1 — Initiation of the system project and the preliminary investigation

A system project can originate in several ways, but a common way is that the manager of a user department contacts the systems analysis and design group in the information systems department with a request for assistance. This request may be oral, but usually is made in writing using pre-established procedures. Within most organizations, the requests for new system projects exceed the capacity of the information systems department to implement them. Therefore, the manager of the systems department must review each request and make a preliminary determination as to the potential benefit for the company. Since many requests may be pending at the same time, the manager must prioritize the requests and schedule projects accordingly. When the manager determines that a request warrants further review, one or more analysts will be assigned to begin a preliminary investigation.

The purpose of the **preliminary investigation** is to determine if the request for assistance which has been communicated to the systems department warrants further detailed investigation and analysis. The most important aspect of the preliminary investigation is to identify if there is a problem and, if so, to uncover the true nature of the problem. Often the stated problem and the ''real'' problem are not the same. For example, a request for on-line inquiry into an accounts receivable data base because reports are not clear may not indicate the real problem in the accounting department. Instead, it may be that the data required for bad debt collection is not available in the accounts receivable data base. It is the purpose of the preliminary investigation to determine the real source of the problem.

A primary method of conducting the preliminary investigation is through the **personal interview**. The interviews are conducted with managerial and supervisory personnel who may have knowledge of the problem and system under study. These people may be able to provide the analyst with some insight as to whether further investigation and a commitment of people, time, and money is warranted. The analyst will also examine the documentation of the current system to help understand what is supposed to be happening in the system.

The duration of the preliminary investigation is usually quite short when compared to the remainder of the project. At the conclusion of the investigation, the analyst will present the findings to management and recommend the next course of action. If it is recommended to continue the project through a detailed investigation, the analyst will provide management with an estimate of the cost for the next phase in terms of dollars, manhours, and elapsed time.

Phase 2 — Detailed system investigation and analysis

If approval to proceed is obtained from management, the analyst will begin the **detailed investigation and analysis.** This phase of the system study is divided into two parts: 1) A detailed investigation in which the emphasis is on WHAT is taking place in the current system; 2) An analysis of what is taking place with an emphasis on WHY the procedures found are occurring, and what the user sees as the requirements for a new system.

The basic fact-gathering techniques used during the detailed system investigation are: 1) The interview; 2) Questionnaires; 3) Gathering the current system documentation and operating forms; 4) Personal observation of current procedures. During this fact-gathering phase of the system study, the analyst must develop a critical and questioning approach to each of the procedures within the system to determine what is actually taking place. Far too often in many organizations, operations are being performed not because they are efficient or effective, but because "they have always been done this way."

Specific steps undertaken at this time to gather the facts include: 1) Review the organizational chart of the structure of the company to determine who are the workers, supervisors, and management personnel associated with the system under study; 2) Conduct interviews with selected personnel to determine what is actually taking place in the current system, rather than what is supposed to take place according to the written rules of the company; 3) Obtain actual copies of operating documents; 4) Document and record all of the data flow within the currently existing system and the actual procedures which are followed.

Prior to analyzing the facts to determine why certain procedures are followed and what can be done to improve them, the facts as found must be documented. Although a number of methods exist to document what takes place within a system, one of the more effective is the data flow diagram (Figure 15-4). This **data flow diagram** illustrates

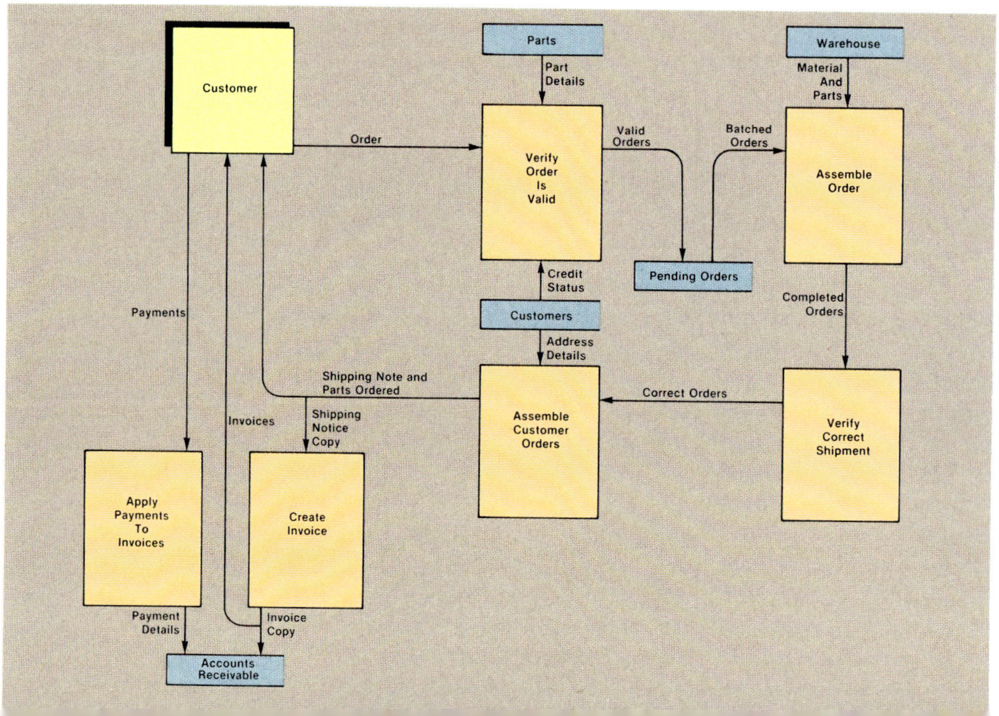

Figure 15-4 This data flow diagram is used to graphically illustrate the flow of data through a system. The shaded square is used to illustrate input to the system. The vertical rectangles show procedural steps. The open-ended boxes illustrate data which must be available to the particular procedure.

graphically the flow of data and the procedures used for an auto parts order entry system. By detailing the processing occurring in the present system in this manner, the analyst can examine each of the steps involved to determine exactly what happens in the present system.

Once the system has been documented, the analyst must review it. Each of the procedures should be analyzed as follows: 1) Who performs each of the procedures within the system; 2) What procedures are followed; 3) Where are the operations being performed; 4) When is a procedure performed; 5) How is the procedure performed. Within each of these questions, the analyst must ask WHY are things done this way?

This analysis is performed to detect any flaws or errors which are contained within the system. Since the present system is being reviewed in detail, there obviously were some problems in the system. It is the purpose of the analysis stage to find those problems and to develop some possible solutions.

After the current system has been documented and analyzed, the analyst must assist the user to identify the requirements for the new system. This analysis will include understanding the problems in the current system, planning for growth and change in the user department, understanding the personnel requirements and capabilities in the user department, and a number of other factors as well.

At the conclusion of this activity, the analyst should prepare a written and oral presentation of the findings which can be presented to both the user and to other management (Figure 15-5). As in the preliminary report, findings are presented, and recommendations are made. If it is recommended that the project proceed into the third phase, cost estimates of the system design are presented as well as the perceived benefits of the new system. Management weighs the relative costs and benefits and either approves or disapproves further action.

MEMORANDUM

DATE: April 1
TO: Management Review Committee
FROM: George Lacey, Manager, Systems
SUBJECT: Detailed Investigation and Analysis of Order Entry System

Introduction

A detailed system investigation and analysis of the order entry system was conducted as a result of approval given by the management review committee on March 1. The findings of the investigation are presented below.

Objectives of Detailed Investigation and Analysis

The study was conducted to investigate two major complaints of the wholesale auto parts order entry system. Complaints have been received that orders were not being shipped promptly, and customers were not notified of out of stock conditions for many days after sending in orders. The objective of this study was to determine where the problems existed and to develop alternative solutions.

Findings of the detailed investigation and analysis

The following problems appear to exist within the order entry system:

2. Place the order entry system on the computer. Computer terminals would be installed in the accounting department for order entry clerks. As orders are received, they would be entered into the computer. Orders could be immediately edited for proper part numbers, and checks could be made to determine if stock is available. Estimated costs: 1) Systems analysis and design - $26,000; 2) Programming and implementation - $40,000; 3) Training, new forms, and maintenance - $7,500; 4) Computer costs 1 year - $18,000.

The systems department recommends alternative 2 as offering the most effective solution to the order entry problem.

George Lacey

Figure 15-5 The report for the detailed system investigation and analysis should contain the results of the investigation and alternative solutions to the problem, together with the costs to implement the solutions.

Phase 3 — System design

Upon approval to proceed, the analyst must determine the best method for implementing a new system. The choices usually are: 1) Personnel in the information systems department design and implement the application; 2) The user, through the use of fourth generation application development tools or through the facilities offered by the information center, designs and implements the application; 3) A prewritten application software package is purchased which, with little or no modification, will perform the tasks required of the new system; 4) The systems department designs the system and then contracts with an outside organization to have the system programmed and implemented; 5) The entire project is contracted out to an outside organization that designs and implements the system.

The determination of which path to take depends upon a number of factors, such as: 1) The availability of prewritten software to perform the tasks required; 2) The costs of buying the software, contracting out the software, or building the software in-house; 3) The personnel within the information systems department and their availability for working on the project. In the remainder of this chapter, it is assumed that the choice was for personnel in the information systems department to design the system and write the programs.

When the system is designed by analysts in the information systems department, the following activities must be performed: 1) Design the system output; 2) Design the system input; 3) Design the files, data base, and processing methods; 4) Present the system design to management and users for approval. In addition, prior to and during these design activities, the analyst may develop a prototype system for testing by the user.

During the detailed system investigation and analysis, the analyst should have gained a thorough understanding of both the current system and the proposed new system. As a consequence, the analyst may want to, as the system design phase begins, develop a prototype of the new system. A **prototype** is a series of small programs that allows a few of the transactions which will be processed on the real system to be processed. The programs in the prototype system will present data on CRT screens as well. The reason for a prototype is to give the user a chance to preview the real system with the intent that the user can determine which screens and processing perform in the desired manner and which do not. As a result of the prototype system, the users will have an exact idea of how the system will behave when it is implemented, and the analysts are ensured that when the system is developed and implemented, the users will be satisfied.

When designing the **system output**, specific steps must be undertaken, including: 1) Define the output requirements for the new system; 2) Review the types of output media that might be useful; 3) Define the specific contents of the output that is to be produced; 4) Consider the methods for the disposition and handling of the output.

The output requirements and informational needs of a new system are defined jointly by the analyst and the user. During the design of the system output, the analyst must consider the various forms of output, including the printed report, computer output microfilm, CRT terminals for both text and graphics output, plotters, and audio response units. A determination must be made concerning the requirement of color, the quality of graphics if they are to be used, the volume of output to be produced as printed reports, and a number of other factors. Each of these must be considered so that not only the proper software, but also the required hardware will be available when the system is implemented.

To determine the format and specific content of each report and display screen for the new system, the analyst must consult with those who will be using the new

Display Screen Layout Sheet

COLUMN

```
        1—10        11—20        21—30        31—40        41—50        51—60
      1 2 3 4 5 6 7 8 9 0 1 2 3 4 5 6 7 8 9 0 1 2 3 4 5 6 7 8 9 0 1 2 3 4 5 6 7 8 9 0 1 2 3 4 5 6 7 8 9 0 1 2 3 4 5 6 7 8 9 0 1 2 3

01  MM/DD              ** ENTER ORDERS **
02                       - SCREEN 1 -
03
04  CUSTOMER NUMBER: XXXXXXX
05  ORDER NUMBER: NNNN
06
07  BILL TO: XXXXXXXXXXXXXXXXX  SHIP TO: XXXXXXXXXXXXXXXXX
08           XXXXXXXXXXXXXXXXX           XXXXXXXXXXXXXXXXX
09           XXXXXXXXXXXXXXXXX           XXXXXXXXXXXXXXXXX
10
11  ORDER DATE: MM/DD
12  TERMS: XXXXXXXXXX
13  SALESPERSON: XXXX
14  DISCOUNT %: .NNN
15
16  DEPRESS RETURN KEY TO CONTINUE:
```

ROW

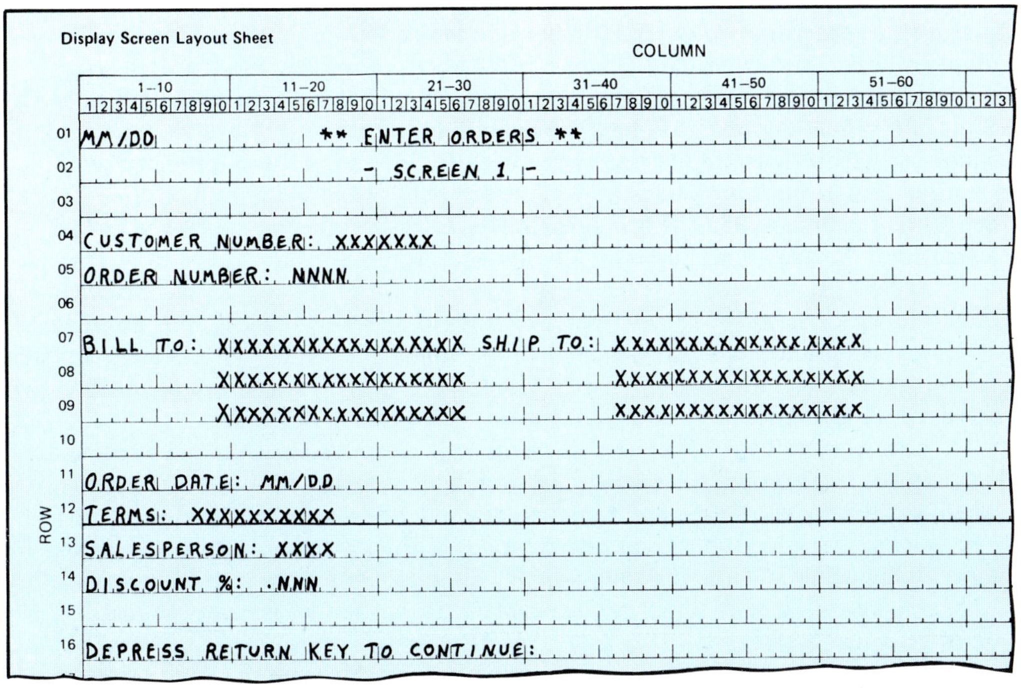

Figure 15-6 A display screen layout sheet can be used by the systems analyst to document the format of the screen which will be used in the system. Each row and column correspond to a row and column on the screen.

system. The parties must agree to screen formats, report formats, and the manner in which other output may be presented. The analyst must then document the agreed-upon formats. The example in Figure 15-6 illustrates a display screen layout sheet that is commonly used to document the format of a screen display. In addition to indicating the columns and rows where data is to be displayed, the analyst must specify what colors, if any, are to be used, which fields will be displayed in reversed type, and so on.

The design of the output from a system is critical to the successful implementation of the system because it is the output which provides the information to the users and is the basis for the justification of most computerized systems. The analyst, therefore, must spend considerable time and effort in determining what information must be produced from the system, the format in which it will be presented, and the methods to be used to place the output in the hands of the users.

Once it is determined what the output of a system will be, it then must be determined what data is necessary to generate the required output. As an additional consideration, the analyst must also define the method of data entry.

The method of data entry will depend to a large extent on whether batch processing or interactive processing is to be used. Typical questions which must be answered, depending upon the type of processing to be performed, include: 1) What media, if any, is to be used for storing input records; 2) How is the data to be entered; 3) Can the data be captured at its source; 4) What is the volume of input; 5) How often is it necessary to input the data; 6) What editing and safeguards must be provided to ensure valid input data; 7) If interactive processing is used, what response time is required; 8) Is hard-copy required for the interactive processing terminals.

Numerous factors must be considered when designing input records for batch processing systems. These factors include: 1) The length of the record; 2) The length of each field in the record and the type of field (alphanumeric or numeric); 3) The type of codes which might be incorporated into a field; 4) The editing which is required for each of the fields and the format which must be followed by the data in each of the fields.

The screen design and the procedures for entering data in an interactive system must be specified at this point in the system design. It is important that the analyst design these procedures with the terminal operator in mind, because the easier and more natural it is to enter data into the terminal, the less likely there will be errors made when the data is entered. The reliability of input data is one of the major concerns in a system on the computer. The analyst, therefore, must develop procedures which are less likely to cause errors when used for entering data into the computer.

The analyst must also, during the system design phase of the system project, determine the data which will be stored in files or data bases for use by the system. As a first step, the analyst will develop a data dictionary.

A **data dictionary** contains the following: 1) A list of the various data elements required for the system; 2) The attributes of the data, such as the length of the field; 3) The points in the system where the data is required; 4) The type of access required for the data (random or sequential); 5) The level of activity which can be expected for the data; 6) The amount of data which must be stored for the system.

The analyst will work with the data base administrator to determine what data may already be in a data base, what data will have to be added to a data base, whether the data base will support the activity and access speed requirements of the new system, and what other problems must be considered to solve the data requirements for the new system. The design of the data base and files, based upon elements which have been discussed in previous chapters, is critical to the successful implementation of a new system.

After the input data, the output information, and the data to be stored in files or a data base have been determined and designed, the analyst must determine how the system will operate in order to produce the information required.

There are several "tools" which can be used to accomplish the design of the processing within the system. The data flow diagram (shown previously in Figure 15–4) can be used to show the logical flow of data through the system. Another tool which is commonly used to illustrate the processing within the system is the **system flowchart**. The system flowchart should show all of the computer runs and their relationships, identify each file and/or data base, identify each report and each terminal site used in the system, indicate the number of programs to be written, and provide management with a means of reviewing the overall plans for the system.

Special symbols are commonly used for a system flowchart. These symbols are illustrated in Figure 15–7. A system flowchart for an order entry system is shown in Figure 15–8. Through the use of the flowchart symbols and the attached lines, the procedural flow through the system is illustrated.

The design of the system processing must continue until all processes have been

Figure 15–7 These system flowchart symbols are used to graphically illustrate the procedural steps and physical components of a system. The symbols representing the physical devices are drawn on the flowchart where they are used.

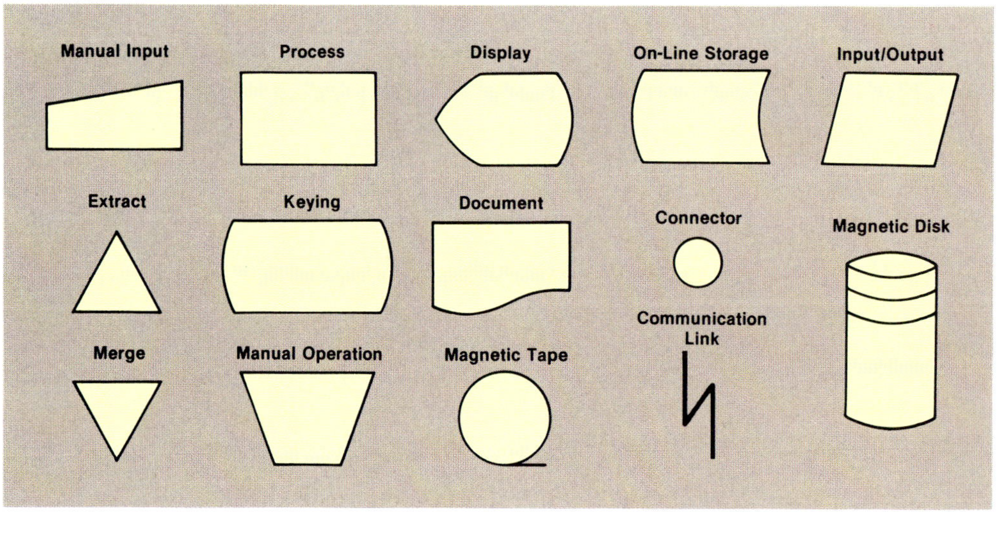

defined and documented. During the design of the processing, the analyst should be in constant contact with the users of the system to ensure that the system will accomplish what the user wants and that the procedures are compatible with the way the users conduct their work.

An important aspect of the design phase of the system project is the establishment of a comprehensive set of system controls. **System controls** are a plan to ensure that only valid data is accepted and processed, completely and accurately. Adequate controls must be established for two basic reasons: 1) To ensure the accuracy of the processing and the accuracy of the information generated from the system; 2) To prevent computer-related fraud.

There are four basic types of controls that must be considered by the systems analyst. These controls are: 1) Source document controls; 2) Input controls; 3) Processing controls; 4) Output controls.

There are many sources of input data in a business organization, such as sales orders, time cards, production statistics, etc. If management information is to be generated from this input, it is essential that all source documents are accounted for when the data is prepared for processing on the computer. Therefore, controlling the reliability of the information processing system should begin at the starting point — with source documents, the data which is entered from the source documents, and the sources of the data which is entered in interactive systems.

Source document controls include serial numbering input documents such as invoices and paychecks, document registers in which each input document is recorded and time stamped as it is received, and batch totaling and balancing to some predetermined totals to assure the accuracy of processing.

Input controls are established to assure the complete and accurate conversion of data from the source documents or other sources to a machine-processable form. Editing data as it enters the system is the most important form of input controls. With the widespread use of computer terminals and personal computers communicating with host computers in data communication systems, controlling access to the computers and data bases has become an increasingly important problem. A number of controls can be incorporated into a system to reduce unauthorized access to a computer and its data. These include: 1) Use of passwords to

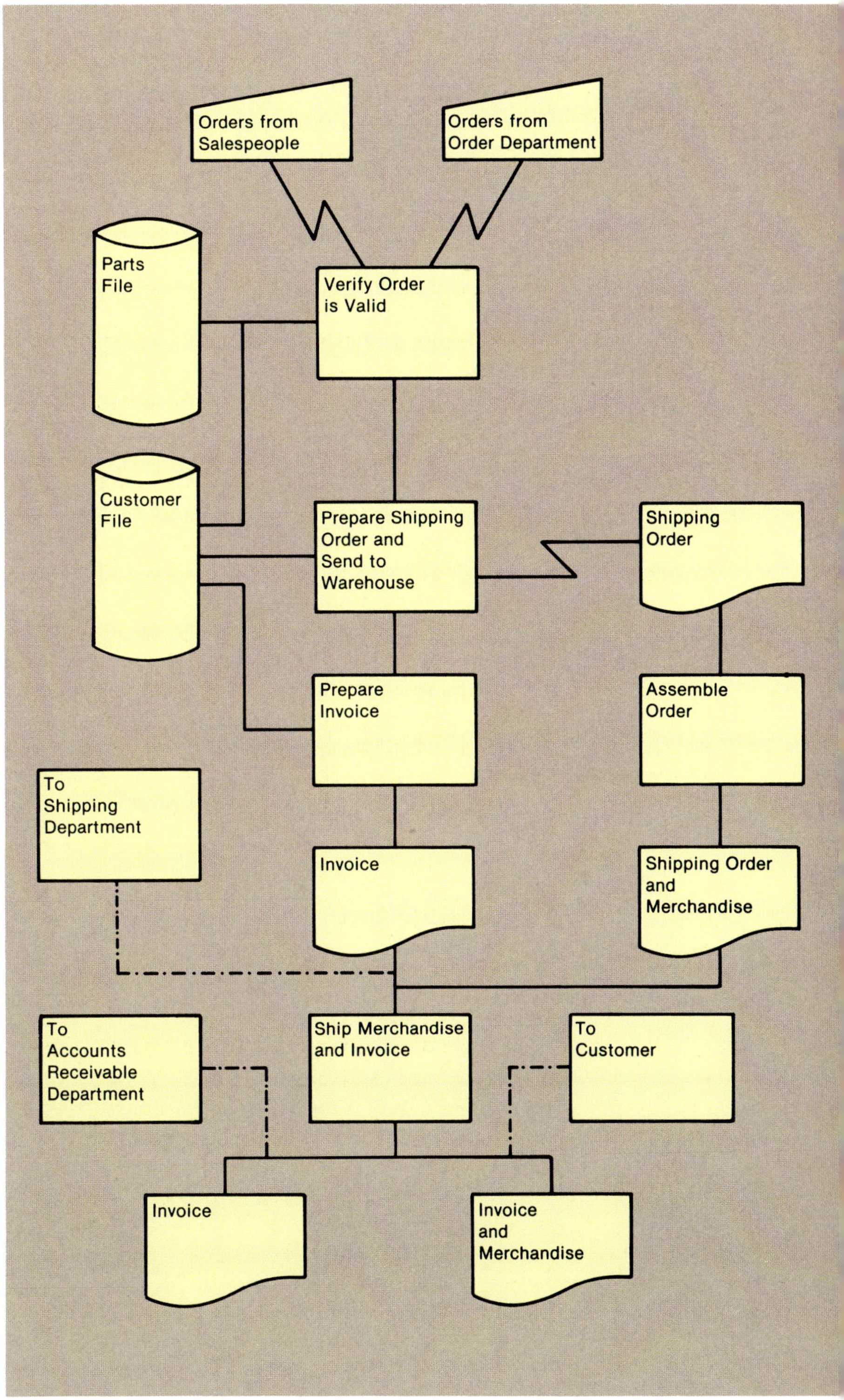

Figure 15-8 The system flowchart shows the actual steps which will occur in the system. This flowchart must be reviewed by the users to ensure the system will perform in the manner required.

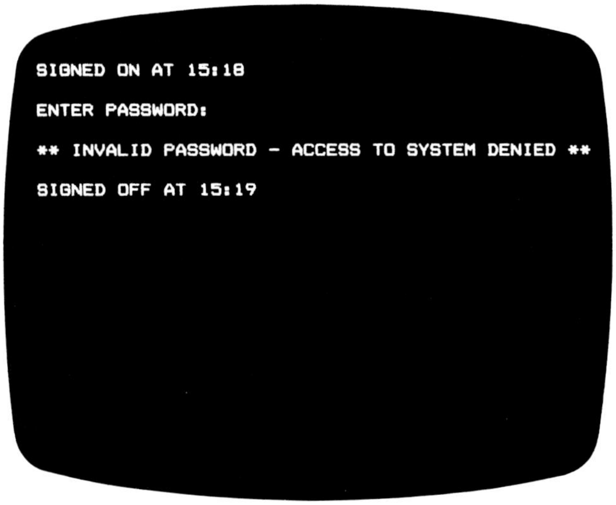

SIGNED ON AT 15:18
ENTER PASSWORD:
** INVALID PASSWORD - ACCESS TO SYSTEM DENIED **
SIGNED OFF AT 15:19

Figure 15-9 A password is a value unique to a user which identifies the user to the computer system, thus allowing the user to interact with the computer. In this example, the user entered a password and it was invalid, so the system denied the user access. The password entered by the user is not displayed on the screen. This is done so an onlooker cannot obtain a valid password to the system.

limit access (Figure 15-9); 2) Use of individual user identification codes; 3) Limiting certain terminals and users to selected portions of the data base.

Processing controls refer to procedures that are incorporated into computer programs within the system to assure the complete and accurate processing of the data throughout the system. Two types of processing controls are group controls and individual record checking. **Group controls** refer to those procedures used in batch processing systems where groups of data which have been processed are balanced to some manual totals to assure the accuracy of processing. For example, the totals for the invoices processed for the day could be balanced against manual totals taken for the same group of invoices. If the totals do not agree, the error must be found before processing proceeds.

Individual record checking includes editing the fields in input data for numeric data, blank fields, reasonable values, and other potential errors which may occur. These types of checks are performed in a batch system when the data is read into main computer memory. In interactive processing systems, the editing can be performed at the terminal if an intelligent terminal or personal computer is used, or on the main computer as the data is entered if a dumb terminal is used.

Another important form of control is the audit trail. An **audit trail** is designed to enable any input data or process executed on a computer to be traced back to the original source data. When data is stored electronically on auxiliary storage without careful consideration of controls, it may be possible to alter the data without leaving a visible track as to what caused the alterations to occur. Auditing is designed to make sure this does not happen.

Computer auditing has become a specialized accounting function. It can be an extremely difficult task, especially with interactive processing systems. Such controls as recording each transaction received from a terminal on auxiliary storage are usually built into interactive processing systems so that all transactions can be traced back to the terminal from which they were entered.

A further consideration when designing a system is computer and data backup, because in virtually every information processing system which is developed, the possibility exists that events may occur which accidentally alter or destroy data stored on auxiliary storage. This may occur because of natural disasters, such as fire, flood, or power outages; or it may occur through improper processing of the data.

It is essential, therefore, to provide a means to ensure that any lost data can be recovered. The most common method used is backup files. A **backup file** is merely a copy of a file, typically stored on magnetic tape. If for some reason the file or data base is destroyed or becomes unusable, the backup file can be used to recreate the file or data base.

Back up becomes extremely critical in interactive processing systems because updates to a data base or file can occur at any time. Therefore, most systems will provide for creating a backup file on a regular basis (sometimes every hour) and saving the transactions which occur to the file after the backup file is made. If the data base is rendered unusable, the data base can be recreated from the backup file and then the transactions which have been saved can be processed against the data base to bring it back to the status it had when it was destroyed.

Another consideration in interactive processing systems is the ability to restart if the computer or software ceases functioning. For example, if a transaction has been sent to a computer and has partially updated a data base when power is lost, it is necessary to both restore the data base and let the user know that the transaction was not processed. Various techniques are used to solve this type of problem, including backup files and messages sent to terminals asking them to resend those transactions which were not processed.

Since some on-line systems perform critical functions, such as controlling space flights or monitoring patients in a hospital, there may also be consideration given to having a backup computer. This computer could normally be used for other processing but when the computer controlling the on-line application goes down, the backup computer automatically takes over the processing. Although this type of arrangement is not common, it should be considered in those systems which perform critical applications.

The final step in the system design phase of the system project is the presentation of the system to management and the users. Although great efforts may have been expended in designing the new system, it is management's responsibility to give final authorization to enter the next phase of the system project — system development.

Three levels of management are normally involved in this approval — information systems department management, user department management, and corporate management. The information systems department management must concur that the system is feasible and can be implemented as designed. The user department management must approve the design as being responsive to their needs. Corporate management must weigh the costs of implementing the system versus the potential savings or increased availability of information.

Approval at all levels is extremely important because once the system enters the development and implementation phases, large sums of money may be involved, and the affected user departments must begin to prepare for the new information system.

Phase 4 — System development

Once the system design phase of the project has been completed and the design has been approved by management at all levels, the project enters the **system development** phase. The major tasks common to all system projects during the system development phase are: 1) Establish a project development and implementation plan; 2) Develop detailed programming specifications; 3) Program and test the system; 4) Prepare final documentation of the system.

One of the first steps in the system development phase is to develop a detailed schedule of each of the activities that is to be performed. These time schedules should include a week by week estimate of the time to be spent on each of the major tasks in the system development. Unless a realistic schedule is developed and followed, it is unlikely the project will be implemented on time. A method often used to document the schedule is the bar or **Gantt chart** (Figure 15–10).

The second step in the system development phase involves the development of detailed programming specifications by the systems analyst. These **programming specifications** should include: 1) A brief description of the system; 2) A systems flowchart; 3) A data flow diagram; 4) The format of the input, output, and files to be created

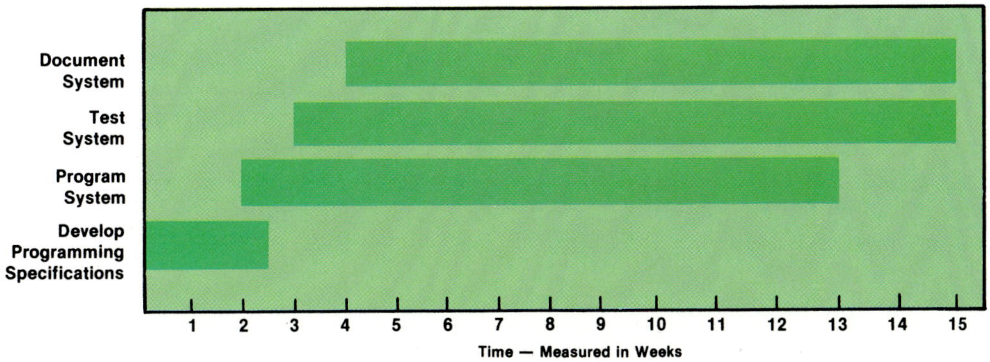

Figure 15–10 The bar or Gantt Chart is commonly used to graphically illustrate schedule deadlines and milestones. This Gantt Chart contains the schedule for the steps used in the system development phase of the system project.

and processed; 5) The format and content of any data bases to be used by the program (subschema); 6) A detailed description of the processing that is to take place in the program. The communication of the detailed specifications is one of the most vital steps in the entire process of systems analysis and design. Without clearly documented program specifications, the programmer will be unable to design and write a program which will fulfill the requirements of the system.

The process of producing a set of instructions for the computer from the detailed specifications that have been prepared by the systems analyst is the job of the computer programmer. This process involves: 1) Reviewing the program specifications; 2) Designing the program; 3) Coding the program; 4) Testing the program; 5) Documenting the program.

The first step in writing a program is to review the program specifications received from the systems analyst. The programmer must be absolutely sure that there are no questions or misunderstandings about what the program is to accomplish. Without a thorough understanding of the processing to be accomplished and the data to be processed, it is not possible to develop a program which will perform properly.

Program design entails the development of the structure of the program and then the development of the logic to solve the problem presented by the program. For many years, program flowcharts were used to assist programmers in the development of the logic for a program. These flowcharts are similar to system flowcharts but contain the detailed steps required for the solution to a problem. Today, a methodology called structured design is used to develop the structure of a program and the logic of the program is developed using the principles of structured programming.

After the program is designed, the programmer must code the program in a programming language. There are a variety of programming languages available to the programmer. The dominant language for medium and large-scale business applications is COBOL. Programs written for implementation on small computers and some medium-size computers are often written using the BASIC language.

After the program has been written by the programmer, it must be tested to ensure that it processes data properly and produces the required output. The first step usually involves removing any errors from the program caused by the improper use of the programming language. These errors are normally identified by the compiler which translates the program from source code to machine language. They are called to the attention of the programmer by diagnostic messages. After these errors have been removed from the program, it is tested by actual execution on the computer. Specially prepared test data is used to ensure that the program will process all data correctly under all circumstances. Preparation of test data and testing the program are vital parts of the system development process. Far too often programs are placed in production without being fully tested, resulting in erroneous output being produced and sent to the user.

After the programs in the system have been tested individually (commonly called **unit tests**), the entire system of programs must be tested as a whole. This process is called **system testing**. System testing includes not only further testing of the programs in the system, but also tests the procedures which have been established for users to interact with the system. Such things as screen layout, prompts which aid when entering data on a terminal, distribution of reports produced from the system, and a number of other elements of the system are tested during the system test. In this way, the system should be completely "debugged" when it is implemented in production.

A continuing part of both the system and program development is the **documentation** which must be developed. This documentation should include documentation for the programs that have been developed, documentation for operations personnel, and documentation for the users of the system. It is quite important that the documentation prepared for a system be accurate and adequate. If it is not, the users of the system will be adversely affected.

Phase 5 — Implementation and evaluation

After testing has been completed and the documentation prepared, the system is ready to be implemented on the computer and run in a production environment. **Conversion** refers to the process of making the change from the old system to the new system. The difficulty of conversion is directly dependent upon the complexity of the system being implemented. Two methods are direct conversion and parallel conversion.

With **direct conversion**, at a given date the old system ceases to be operational and the new system is placed into use. To those unfamiliar with converting large systems, this may seem a most logical approach. Direct conversion, however, can be risky, in spite of the great care which may have been taken in designing the system. In most complex systems, it is unlikely that the results for all processing will be exactly as planned because of the hundreds of variables that are found. Direct conversion, therefore, should normally be performed only with simple systems where, if an error occurs, it will not create an undue hardship within a company.

Direct conversion is, however, often implemented when a system prototype has been developed prior to or during the system design. Since the user has seen most of the screens that will be used, has given approval to most of the transaction processing which will take place in the system, and is generally quite familiar with the system, direct conversion may be successfully undertaken after a prototype has been used.

Parallel conversion consists of processing data on both the old and new systems simultaneously and comparing the results. If the output from both systems is identical, it indicates that the new system is functioning in the proper manner.

The major advantage of parallel conversion is that correct processing with the old system is taking place and, therefore, even if the new system does not work properly, the daily operation can continue. There are, however, several disadvantages which center around the fact that a complete duplication of effort is required in that both the old system and the new system must be run concurrently. This often increases costs because additional personnel are required, decreases efficiency because people may have to perform two different jobs (one for the old system and a similar one for the new system), and generally creates an atmosphere of anxiety. The result of parallel conversion, however, is normally a system which is well tested and which operates smoothly once the parallel operation is completed.

Regardless of the method of implementation used, it is important to conduct a formal post implementation evaluation of the system. This evaluation should consist of a careful analysis to determine if the system is performing as it was designed to do; if operating costs are as anticipated; and if any modifications are necessary to make the system operate effectively.

Phase 6 — System maintenance

An ongoing process after the system has been implemented is **system maintenance**. Maintenance consists of two major activities: 1) Changes to correct errors in the system; 2) Changes to give the system additional capabilities or to conform with government or company regulations.

Maintenance activities require a great deal of time for many programmers and analysts. Systems which are well documented and contain well designed programs are much easier to maintain than those which do not follow good documentation and coding standards.

CHAPTER SUMMARY

1. Hardware devices and related software must all interact in the form of a system to produce useful output.
2. A system is a network of related procedures designed to perform some activity.
3. Procedures are logical steps by which all repetitive actions are initiated, carried forward, controlled, and finalized.
4. Systems which are implemented using a computer fall into three broad classifications: a) Operational systems; b) Management information systems; c) Decision support systems.
5. An operational system is designed to process data that is generated by the day-to-day business transactions of a company.
6. A management information system (MIS) refers to a computer-based system which not only processes the day-to-day transactions but also generates timely and accurate information for various levels of management.
7. Most management information systems provide information in a well-defined, structured manner.
8. Decision support systems allow a manager or officer of a corporation to ask questions that can be answered in a dynamic manner based upon data stored in data bases.
9. Decision support systems allow business models and simulation exercises to occur.
10. The scientific problem-solving approach to systems analysis and design can be broken down into six phases: a) Initiation of the system project and preliminary investigation; b) Detailed system investigation and analysis; c) System design; d) System development; e) System implementation and evaluation; f) System maintenance.
11. The purpose of the preliminary investigation is to determine if a request for assistance which has been communicated to the systems department warrants further detailed investigation and analysis.
12. The most important aspect of the preliminary investigation is to identify if there is a problem and, if so, to uncover the true nature of the problem.
13. A primary method of conducting the preliminary investigation is through the personal interview.
14. The detailed investigation and analysis phase is divided into two parts: a) What is taking place in the current system; b) Why are the procedures taking place.
15. To gather facts, the analyst: a) Reviews organization charts; b) Conducts interviews; c) Obtains copies of operating documents; d) Records data flow through the current system.
16. A data flow diagram illustrates the data flow and the procedures used in a system.
17. Analyzing the current system involves asking: a) Who performs each procedure in a system; b) What procedures are followed; c) Where are the operations performed; d) When is a procedure performed; e) How is the procedure performed; and f) Why are things done this way.
18. The analyst must assist the user in determining the requirements for the new system.
19. At the conclusion of the detailed investigation and analysis phase, the analyst prepares a written and oral report with recommendations and, if required, cost estimates for further work.
20. The five ways to design and implement a new system are: a) Personnel in the information systems department design and implement the application; b) The user, using fourth generation application development tools or the facilities of the information center, designs and implements the system; c) A prewritten application software package is purchased; d) The systems department designs the system and outside people program and implement the system; e) An outside organization designs and implements the system.
21. The determination of how the system is designed and implemented depends upon: a) The availability of prewritten software; b) The cost of buying software, contracting out the software, or building the software in-house; c) The availability of personnel in the information systems department.
22. The activities which must be performed are: a) Design the system output; b) Design the system input; c) Design the files, data base, and processing methods; d) Present the design to management for approval.
23. A prototype is a series of small programs that allows a few of the transactions which will be processed on the real system to be processed.
24. When designing system output, the following steps are taken: a) Define the output requirements; b) Review output media; c) Define specific output content; d) Consider methods for disposition and handling.
25. Factors concerning system input include: a) What media is used for input records; b) How is data entered; c) Can data be captured at its source; d) Input volume; e) Timing; f) What editing is necessary; g) Terminal response time; h) Hard copy requirements.

26. A data dictionary contains the following: a) A list of data elements; b) Attributes of data; c) Points in the system where the data is required; d) Type of access required; e) Level of activity; f) Amount of data.

27. A tool commonly used to illustrate the processing within a system is the system flowchart.

28. System controls are a plan to ensure that only valid data is accepted and processed.

29. Four types of system controls are: a) Source document; b) Input; c) Processing; d) Output.

30. Input controls assure complete and accurate conversion from source documents to machine-processable form.

31. Processing controls assure complete and accurate processing of data throughout the system.

32. Group controls are procedures which ensure group data integrity.

33. Individual record checking includes editing input data to find potential errors.

34. An audit trail is designed to enable any input data or process executed on a computer to be traced back to the original source data.

35. A backup file is a copy of a file, typically stored on magnetic tape.

36. In interactive processing systems, a backup computer may be necessary.

37. After the system is designed, the analyst must make a presentation to information systems management, user department management, and corporate management.

38. In the system development phase, the tasks are: a) Establish a development and implementation plan; b) Develop detailed programming specifications; c) Program and test the system; d) Prepare final documentation.

39. A Gantt chart is used to graphically show a schedule.

40. Programming specifications include: a) Description of the system; b) Systems flowchart; c) Data flow diagram; d) Data formats; e) Data base subschemas; f) Detailed description of the processing.

41. The process of creating a program is: a) Review the program specifications; b) Design the program; c) Code the program; d) Test the program; e) Document the program.

42. Program design entails the development of the structure of the program and then the development of the logic to solve the problem presented by the program.

43. After a program is designed, it must be coded. COBOL and BASIC are widely used for business programs.

44. After the program is written, it must be tested. Individual program tests are called unit tests.

45. A system test tests the programs and procedures of a system.

46. Documentation should include material for the programs, for operations personnel, and for users.

47. Conversion refers to the process of making the change from the old system to the new system.

48. With direct conversion, at a given date the old system ceases to be operational and the new system is placed into use.

49. Direct conversion can be used for small, simple systems; or it can be used when a prototype is developed.

50. Parallel conversion consists of processing data in both the old and new systems simultaneously and comparing the results.

51. The major disadvantage of parallel conversion is the additional cost and personnel required.

52. System maintenance consists of two activities: a) Corrections to errors; b) Enhancements to the system.

KEY TERMS

Audit trail 15.10
Backup file 15.10
Conversion 15.13
Data dictionary 15.8
Data flow diagram 15.4
Decision support systems 15.2
Detailed investigation and analysis 15.4
Direct conversion 15.13
Documentation 15.12
Gantt chart 15.11
Group controls 15.10
Individual record checking 15.10
Input controls 15.9
Management information system (MIS) 15.2
Operational system 15.1
Parallel conversion 15.13
Personal interview 15.3
Preliminary investigation 15.3
Procedures 15.1
Processing controls 15.10
Program design 15.12
Programming specifications 15.11
Prototype 15.6
Source document controls 15.9
System 15.1
System controls 15.9
System development 15.11
System flowchart 15.8
System maintenance 15.13
System output 15.6
System testing 15.12
Unit tests 15.12

REVIEW QUESTIONS

1. Define a system. Define the term procedures. What is the relationship of a system to procedures?
2. What are the three broad classifications of systems? How do these systems overlap?
3. What capabilities does a manager have when using a decision support system?
4. List the six phases of the approach to developing a system.
5. What is the preliminary investigation? What is the most important aspect of the preliminary investigation? How is most of the information gathered during the preliminary investigation?
6. Briefly summarize the activities that take place during the detailed system investigation and analysis phase.
7. List four methods that are used to gather information during the detailed system investigation and analysis.
8. What is a data flow diagram? What is a system flowchart? How are they the same? How are they different?
9. What are the five ways in which to design and implement a new system? What factors determine which method is chosen?
10. What activities are performed during the system design phase?
11. What is a prototype? Why and when is a prototype used?
12. Specify the factors which are considered when the system output and the system input are designed.
13. What is a data dictionary? What is contained in a data dictionary?
14. For what purpose is an audit trail used?
15. Describe the four tasks which must be accomplished during the system development phase.
16. Discuss the two conversion methods most often used. Under what circumstances is each of them appropriate?
17. When is system maintenance required?

CONTROVERSIAL ISSUES

1. Large systems which require multiple computers, terminals, data communications, and many programs may take three to five years to design and implement. It is argued by some experts that undertaking such a task is ridiculous because the needs of the users and the technology change so much during the time it takes to implement the system that it is obsolete before it is implemented. Others point out that there are really no alternatives. What do you think? Would you approve a system project which would require 3 – 5 years to design and implement at a cost of several million dollars, knowing the rapid changes in technology and anticipating considerable growth and change within your company? What would be your alternatives?
2. "The difficulty in developing and implementing an information processing system is the user," proclaimed a senior analyst recently. "The users never know what they want. When they are shown what the system will do, they give their approval but when the system is implemented they are never happy. They always want changes. It's impossible to satisfy them." Is this a valid argument? Whose fault is this — the users or the analysts?

RESEARCH PROJECTS

1. As a member of a systems analysis and design team, you have been assigned the task of determining available software for the accounting applications of accounts receivable, accounts payable, and general ledger. The system is to be implemented on a mainframe computer. Determine sources of this software, obtain information from the sources concerning what the software can do and its price, and make a presentation concerning your findings.
2. A major problem facing systems analysts is documenting and defining the system so that it is readily understandable by programmers who must implement the system. An area of study called requirements analysis has been developed to deal with this problem. Prepare a research paper on the latest techniques of requirements analysis, including its availability and applicability to small and large systems alike.

Chapter Sixteen

Program Design, Coding, And Implementation

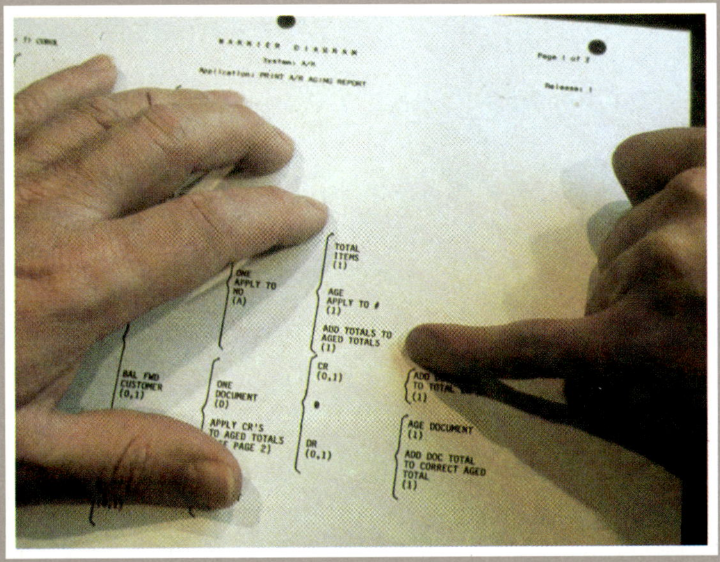

Objectives

- ☐ Identify the steps in the program development cycle
- ☐ Illustrate an understanding of the three control structures in structured programming by drawing flowcharts for the three structures
- ☐ Describe the need for program design and program walkthroughs
- ☐ Identify and describe three major techniques for developing modular programs
- ☐ Draw the logic for five commonly found design problems utilizing pseudocode and/or flowcharts
- ☐ Develop a decision table for a specified problem
- ☐ Identify the steps and procedures required to develop test data

Program Design, Coding, And Implementation

Chapter Sixteen

Approximately ten years ago Dr. Harlan Mills, a leading authority in the information processing industry, wrote, "Computer programming as a practical human activity is some 25 years old, a short time for intellectual development. Yet computer programming has already posed the greatest intellectual challenge that mankind has faced in pure logic and complexity."

As noted by Dr. Mills, the task of computer programming has posed some difficult challenges for programmers. Most programs used for business purposes will contain hundreds, and even thousands of individual statements. Each of these statements must be placed in exactly the right sequence for the correct output to be produced.

Problems in software design

When individuals first began programming computers, the process was very much an individual effort. Little was known about methods and techniques which could and should be used to design and write programs. Some people even considered programming an "art," and argued that the way the various computer instructions were utilized to produce the desired results should be left to the individual programmer.

Unfortunately, this approach has created a number of problems that, to a certain extent, still exist today with respect to the design and coding of computer programs. These problems include: 1) Programs are often unreliable; that is, they do not always produce the correct results. For example, newspapers have contained articles such as, "Computer sends homeowner $50,000 water bill" and "Computer error delays election results;" 2) Programs are often difficult to modify and maintain. When changes to software are necessary, it is often a very difficult task to determine what statements should be changed in the program and how they should be changed.

Because of the complexity of writing large business or scientific programs, it is important that the programmer approach writing a program in a systematic, disciplined manner. Toward this end, a **program development cycle** has been established. The program development cycle consists of five basic steps: 1) Review of program specifications; 2) Program design; 3) Program coding; 4) Program testing; 5) Program documentation. The purpose of this chapter is to review the steps in the program development cycle and to illustrate and explain the logic of some fundamental program design problems.

REVIEW OF PROGRAM SPECIFICATIONS

The first step in the program development cycle is a review of the system and

program specifications for the program to be written. These specifications normally contain record and screen formats, printer spacing charts, data base schemas and access requirements, system flowcharts and data flow diagrams, and a written narrative which provides a detailed description of the processing that is to occur.

It is extremely important that the programmer thoroughly understand all of the various aspects of the problem to be solved. These aspects include the output to be produced, the input that is available to produce the output, the data in the data base which is to be used in the production of the output, and the processing that must occur to produce the output.

It is the programmer's responsibility to directly implement the procedures defined in the programming specifications. Changes such as altering the format of a CRT screen because the programmer thinks it will improve the system should not be made at the programmer's discretion. If there are any questions, the programmer should discuss them with the systems analyst who designed the system.

At the end of the review of the system and program specifications, the programmer should completely understand what processing is to be performed, what data is to be processed, and how the output is to be derived from the data available to the program.

PROGRAM DESIGN

After the system and programming specifications have been carefully reviewed and all questions have been answered, the programmer begins the next phase of the program development cycle — designing the structure and logic of the program.

The design phase of the program development cycle is one of the most important; for if a program is properly designed, it will be easily implemented in code in the selected programming language. At the end of the design phase, the structure and logic of the program should be detailed in such a fashion that the resulting program code from the design will be efficient, and will always produce correct output **(reliable)**, will work under all conditions **(robust)**, and will be easily modified **(maintainable)**.

Figure 16-2 This "flowchart" by John von Neumann was used for the solution of a problem involving game theory.

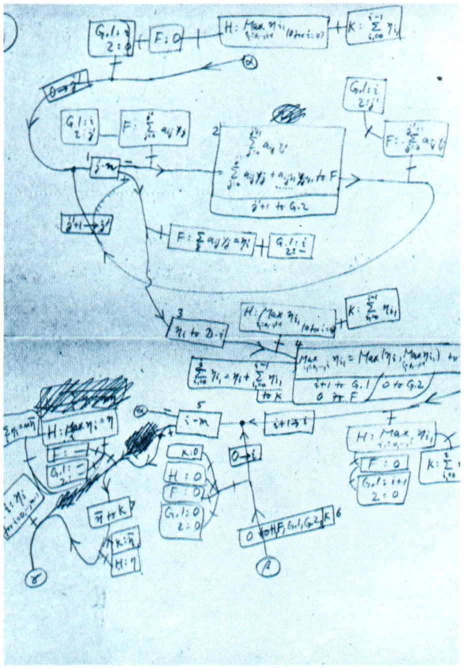

Early design methodologies

When the stored program concept proved to be a reality in the late 1940's, it soon became apparent that the task of writing instructions for a computer could be extremely complex, involving thousands of individual instructions. A programmer could not begin writing a program by immediately writing the first instruction, followed by the second instruction, and so on until the last instruction had been written. Some method was required to plan the program before the coding began.

To provide a means of expressing the logic which could solve a problem and to show the interrelationships of instructions within a program, symbols representing the logical solution to the problem were used. Using these symbols to show the logic of a program is called **flowcharting**. John von Neumann was one of the first people to use flowcharting (Figure 16-2).

For many years following von Neumann's early work, flowcharting the logic for a program prior to writing the code was the primary

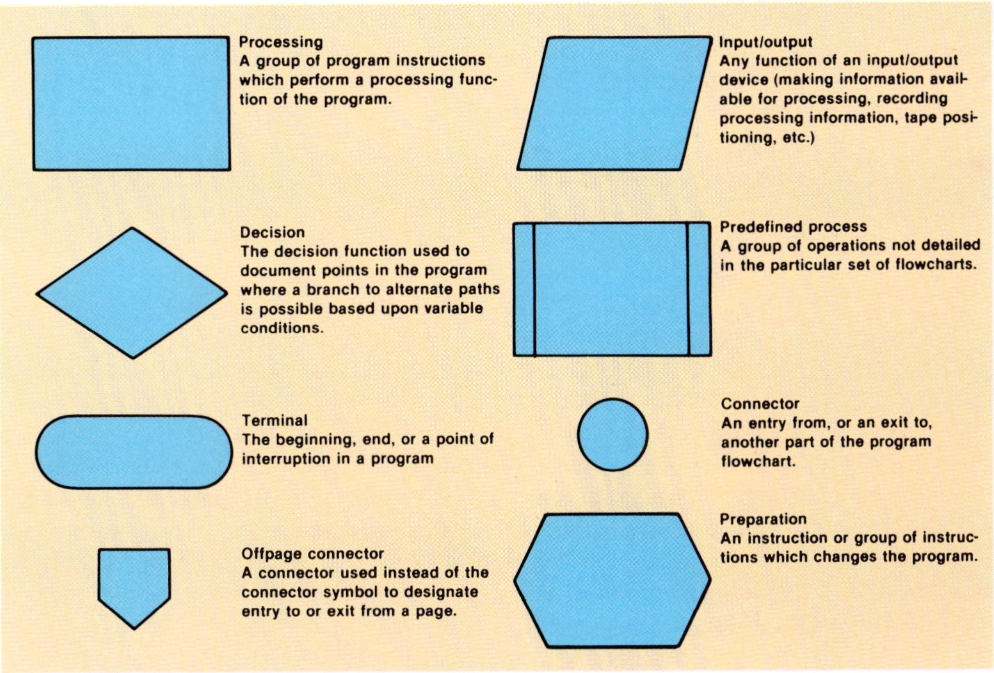

Figure 16–3 The ANSI flowchart symbols are used throughout the information processing industry when flowcharts are drawn.

means of program design. So important is its use that the American National Standards Institute (ANSI) published a set of flowcharting standards. These standards specify specially shaped symbols that should be used to represent the various operations that can be performed on a computer (Figure 16–3).

Flowcharting as a program design tool

When a program is designed through the use of flowcharting, the programmer normally begins by defining the precise sequence in which each operation is to be performed. The programmer must think through the individual steps required to solve the problem, including the input to be read, the calculations to be performed, the comparing operations or decisions to be made, the alternative actions to be taken based upon the results of the comparisons, and the output to be produced. Each of these individual steps is illustrated by means of one of the flowcharting symbols, which provide a graphic representation of the steps that are to occur in the program.

The value of a flowchart is that it graphically represents the steps in the solution of a problem. In flowcharts, symbols and words support one another. By placing a brief description within the symbols, the sequence of operations to be performed is apparent.

Problems with flowchart design

Although the flowchart is a valuable tool, it was found that programmers using a flowchart had little scientific theory on which to base the logic of the program. The programmers began the design of the program by recording the individual steps which appeared to be necessary, coping with each new combination of conditions as it was encountered. Thus, the programmer was not, in fact, aware of the overall design of the program until the flowchart was actually completed.

This method of program design led to programs which were not actually designed, but rather were more or less patched together to work. There was neither an organized structure to the program nor a methodology to approach the program design. Programmers could pass control to various parts of the program whenever necessary, leading to programs which were difficult to read, understand, and modify.

Development of structured programming

As the data processing industry matured in the 1960's, it was recognized that there was a need to develop design methodologies which would produce reliable and maintainable programs. Considerable research was undertaken by mathematicians and computer scientists aimed at changing program design from an "art" to a "science." It was necessary to change programming from an undisciplined, individualized expression of one's ideas for the solution of a logical problem to a disciplined approach using scientific techniques.

The first major breakthrough occurred in the mid-1960's, when research by computer scientists indicated that a technique called structured programming could help attain these goals. The earliest beginnings of structured programming theory can be traced to a paper presented by two mathematicians, Corrado Bohm and Guiseppe Jacopini, at the 1964 International Colloquium on Algebraic Linguistics and Automata Theory in Israel. Their paper proved that a few basic **control structures** could be used to express any programming logic, no matter how complex. These basic control structures are: 1) Sequence; 2) If-then-else; 3) Do while.

Structured programming is defined as a method of programming that uses these three control structures to form highly structured units of code that are easily read and are, therefore, easily maintained. The following paragraphs contain an explanation of these three control structures.

Sequence

When using the **sequence control structure**, one event occurs immediately after another. In Figure 16–4, the rectangular boxes represent a particular event that is to take place. For example, an event could be a computer instruction to move data from one location in main computer memory to another location. Each event takes place in the exact sequence specified, one event followed by another.

Figure 16–4 In the sequence control structure, one event occurs immediately after another.

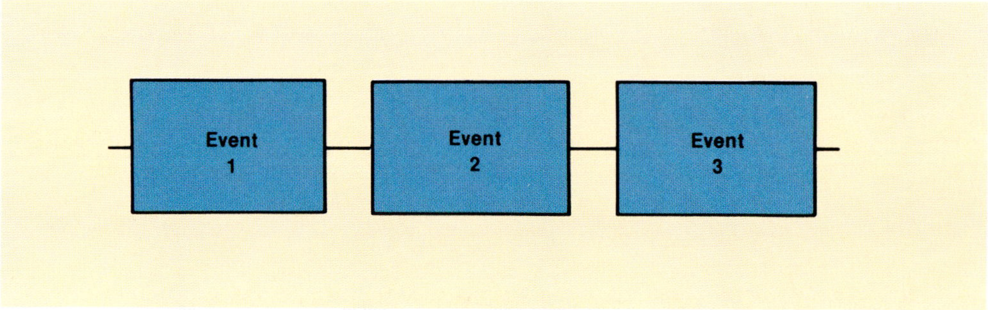

If-then-else

The second control structure is termed the **if-then-else structure** (Figure 16–5). This structure is used for conditional statements. The "if" portion of the structure tests a given condition. For example, the number of hours worked might be tested to determine if an employee worked overtime. The true portion of the statement is executed if the condition tested is true. For example, if the person did work overtime, the true portion of the statement would be executed.

The false portion of the statement is executed when the condition tested is not true. For example, if the employee did not work overtime, then the false portion of the statement would be executed. The term if-then-else was derived from the way the statement is read: If the condition is true, then perform the true processing else perform the false processing.

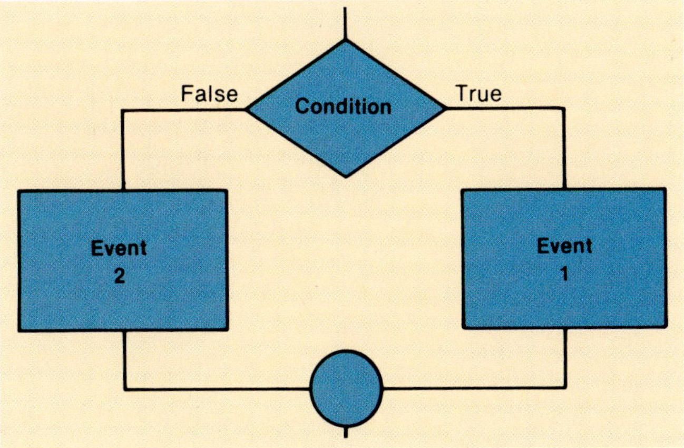

Figure 16–5 The if-then-else control structure is used for conditional statements. If the condition tested is true, event 1 takes place. If the condition is false, event 2 occurs.

Do while

The third logical structure, the **do while structure,** is used to allow program looping. **Looping** means that one or more events occur so long as a given condition remains true. In Figure 16–6, the condition is tested. If the condition is true, event 1 will take place. The same condition is again tested. If it is still true, then event 1 will occur again. This looping will continue until the condition being tested is not true. At that time, control will exit from the loop and subsequent processing will occur. In most cases, some processing in event 1 will change the condition being tested so it becomes not true, and the looping is terminated. As might be expected, this control structure is also referred to as the **looping structure**.

These three control structures, the sequence, the if-then-else, and the do while, can be used to solve any programming logic problem. They form the basis for a scientific approach to computer programming.

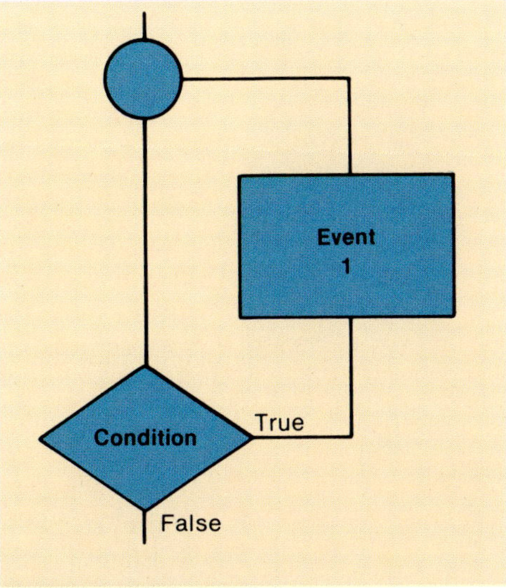

Figure 16–6 The do while, or looping, structure is used to control looping. If the condition is true, event 1 will be performed. The condition is then tested again. If it is still true, then event 1 will again be performed. This looping will continue until the condition is false when it is tested. At that time, control will exit from the loop.

Single entry/single exit

An **entry point** is the point where the control structure is entered. An **exit point** is the point where the control structure is exited. An important concept in structured programming is that there is but one entry point and one exit point in each of the three control structures. For example, in Figure 16–7 when the if-then-else

Figure 16–7 All three control structures used with structured programming have one entry point and one exit point. With this feature, it is easy to follow the logic in a program.

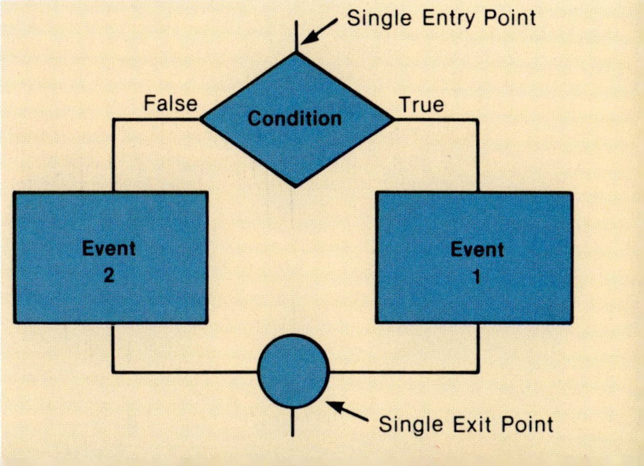

structure is used, control enters the structure at the point where the condition is tested. When the condition is tested, one event will be executed if the condition is true and one event will be executed if the condition is false. Regardless of the result of the test, however, the structure is exited at a common point.

This feature substantially improves the understanding of a program because, when reading the program, the programmer can be assured that whatever happens within the if-then-else structure, control will always exit at the common point. Prior to the use of structured programming, many programmers would pass control to other parts of a program without following the single entry-single exit rule. This practice led to programs which were extremely difficult to read and, therefore, to modify.

```
Open the files
Read a record
PERFORM UNTIL end of file
    Move employee number, name, regular pay, and
        overtime pay to the report area
    IF bonus code is alphabetic or not numeric
        Move error message to report area
    ELSE
        IF first shift
            Calculate total pay = regular pay +
                overtime pay
            Set bonus pay to zero
        ELSE
            IF second shift
                Calculate total pay = regular pay +
                    overtime pay + 5.00
                Set bonus pay to 5.00
            ELSE
                IF third shift
                    Calculate total pay = regular pay +
                        overtime pay + 10.00
                    Set bonus pay to 10.00
                ELSE
                    Move error message to report area
                ENDIF
            ENDIF
        ENDIF
    ENDIF
    Write a line
    Read a record
ENDPERFORM
Close the files
End the program
```

Figure 16-9 The pseudocode shown here implements the same logic as the flowchart in Figure 16-8. The major difference is that flowcharts use graphic symbols while pseudocode merely uses words to express the logic.

Sample flowchart

The use of flowcharting symbols to implement a program design using the three control structures is shown in Figure 16-8 on page 16.7.

Expressing logic using pseudocode

Flowcharting is used to graphically illustrate the logic which is to be implemented in a program to solve a problem. One of the requirements of flowcharting is to draw the graphic symbols required. It has been found that this requirement can be time-consuming and not conducive to complete program design because if an error is made when drawing the flowchart, the entire flowchart may have to be redrawn.

As an alternative to flowcharting, some authorities in program design advocate the use of pseudocode when designing the logic for a program. **Pseudocode** is nothing more than the logical steps to be taken in the solution of a problem written as English statements (Figure 16-9). The advantage of pseudocode is that a great deal of time need not be spent in drawing symbols and determining how to arrange the symbols on a sheet of paper while at the same time attempting to determine the program logic. The major disadvantage is that a graphic representation, which many people find useful when examining programming logic, is not available with pseudocode.

Designing large programs

Structured programming was a significant improvement in terms of specifying and structuring the logic for solving a problem on a computer, but a serious problem still remained in the design of large computer programs. The problem was that the programs were so large that it was virtually

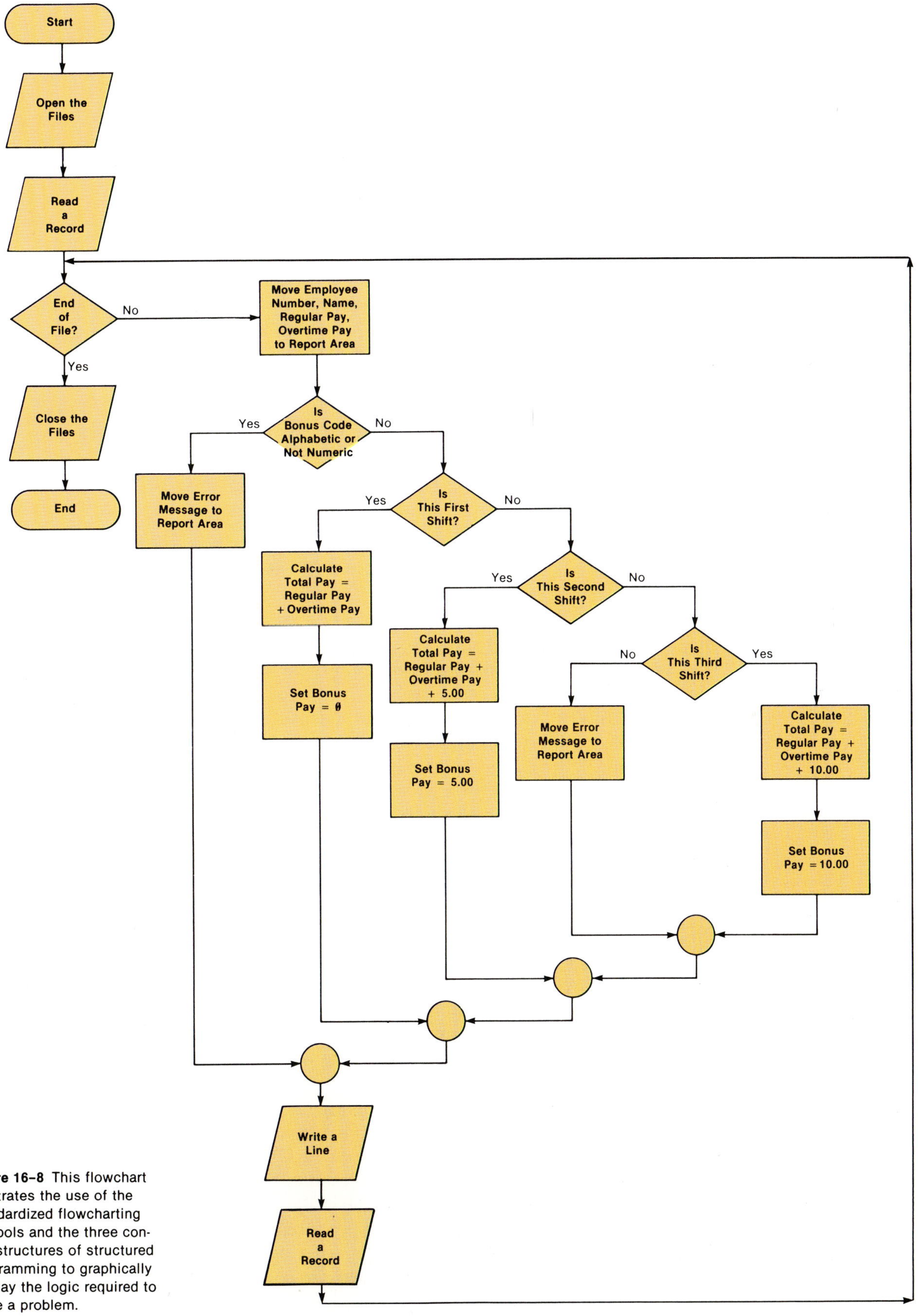

Figure 16–8 This flowchart illustrates the use of the standardized flowcharting symbols and the three control structures of structured programming to graphically display the logic required to solve a problem.

impossible to design the logic for the entire program with any kind of continuity and vision. The programs were just too complex to be well designed. Indeed, it is a tribute to programmers that these complex programs ever worked properly on computers.

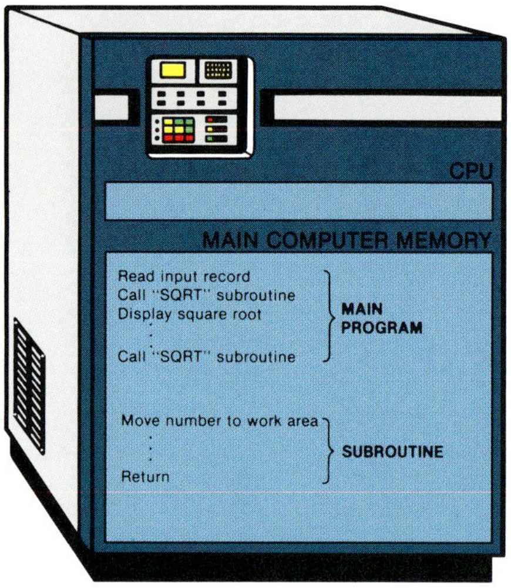

Figure 16-10 In this example, the square root subroutine named SQRT is used to compute the square root of a number given it. The subroutine is called from two different points in the main program. In each case, it returns control to the statement in the main program immediately following the statement which called it.

The subroutine

One of the early programming methods used to simplify programs was the subroutine. A **subroutine** is a series of computer instructions which, together, accomplish a given task. The subroutine can be "called" by other portions of the program to accomplish the task. For example, a subroutine could be written to take the square root of a number (Figure 16-10). When the square root of a number is required, the program can pass control to the subroutine which determines the square root. The subroutine will find the square root of the number and pass it back to the portion of the program which called it.

Structured design

Although subroutines help simplify programs, there was still a need for a methodology which would allow the overall structure of a program to be designed. The methodology should allow the program to be broken down into a series of small pieces for which the logic could easily be developed. Each small piece of the program should be easily understood by those who must read and understand the program.

Recognizing this need, in the late 1960's Larry Constantine, then employed by IBM, began to examine currently existing programs in an attempt to determine those attributes which made the program easy to read and understand and those attributes which made the program difficult to read and understand.

As a result of this investigation and similar work done by others, an article entitled "Structured Design," written by Wayne Stevens, Glenford Myers, and Larry Constantine was published in the *IBM Systems Journal* in 1974. This article described a design methodology called **structured design**, which when used resulted in a program consisting of many small portions of code called modules. A **module**, which is similar to a subroutine, performs one given task within the program.

The structured design methodology presented a technique whereby a large program could be decomposed into small modules, each of which performed a particular function in the program. The major benefit of this technique is that each of the modules is logically fairly simple, particularly when compared to the logic required for a very large program. By combining the processing of each of these small modules into a complete program, the program accomplishes the desired result.

There are several variations of methods for deriving the structure of a program. One of the most widely taught methods uses the IPO Chart as the primary design tool (Figure 16-11). The basic steps using this technique are: 1) The output, input, and major processing tasks for the first module in the program are defined. The output from the first module is the output to be produced by the program. The input to the module consists of the files and elements from a data base which are going to be used by the program. The **major processing tasks** are obtained by asking the question, "What tasks must be accomplished to obtain the given output from the given input?"

IPO CHART

PROGRAM: Produce Letters	PROGRAMMER Shelly/Cashman	DATE: May 20
MODULE NAME: Produce Letters	MODULE FUNCTION Produce Letters	

INPUT	PROCESSING	OUTPUT
1. User selection	1. Display the menu and obtain a user selection.	1. Menu
2. Data for letter	2. Determine the selection to be performed.	2. Instructions
3. Data for mailing labels	3. Display the instructions.	3. Letter
	4. Prepare and print the letter.	4. Mailing labels
	5. Print the mailing labels.	

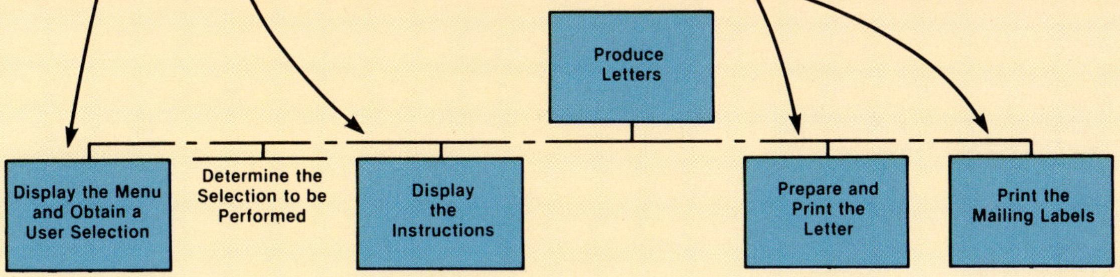

2) Once the tasks for the highest level module are determined, the program designer must ask if any of the tasks appears to require a significant number of programming statements to accomplish or does the task appear to require some complex logic. If either of these cases is true, then the task will appear in a separate module. It will not be accomplished in the module being analyzed. In the example in Figure 16–11, the tasks Display the menu and obtain a user selection, Display the instructions, Prepare and print the letter, and Print the mailing labels will be accomplished in separate modules. When the program decomposition is completed, the entire structure of the program is shown as a hierarchy chart which illustrates the relationship of each of the modules within the program (Figure 16–12).

This process continues until all of the program has been decomposed into small

Figure 16–11 Each major processing task defined in the IPO Chart which might be lengthy or which might contain complex logic will be accomplished in a separate module. Here, five separate modules will be used.

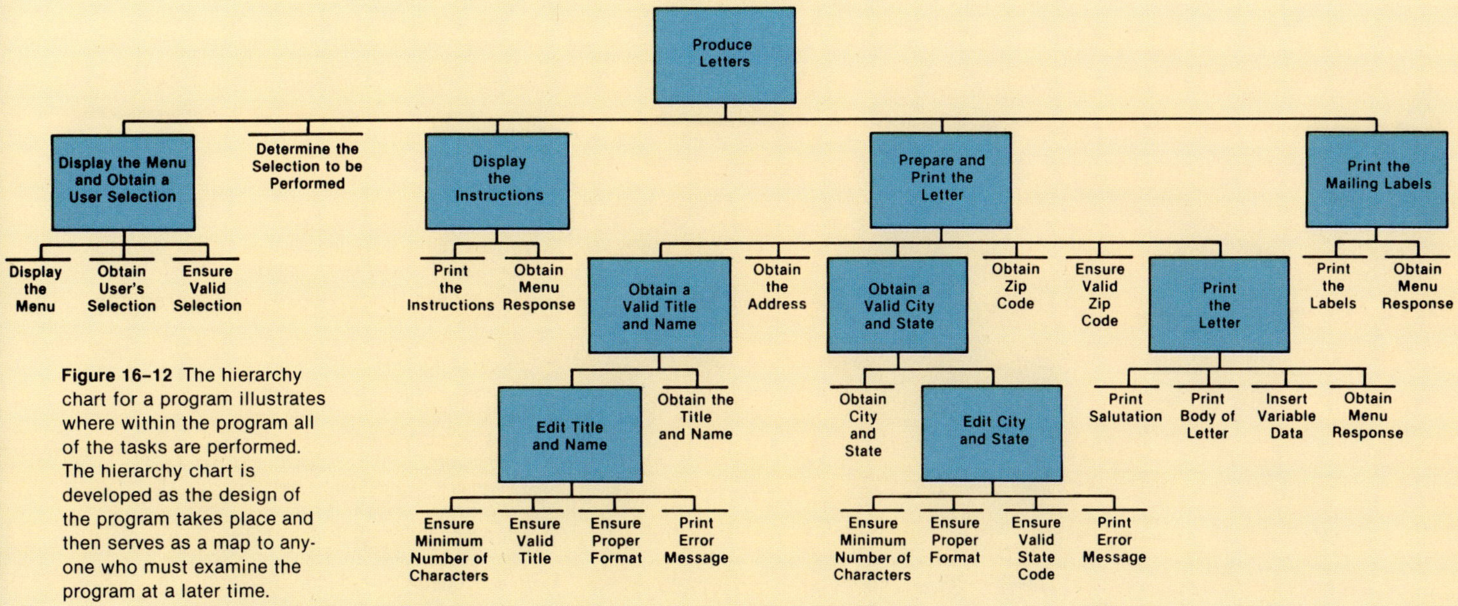

Figure 16–12 The hierarchy chart for a program illustrates where within the program all of the tasks are performed. The hierarchy chart is developed as the design of the program takes place and then serves as a map to anyone who must examine the program at a later time.

modules. The logic for each module is then designed. The logic can be designed using either flowcharts or pseudocode (Figure 16-13).

The logic for each program module is developed independently. Since each module accomplishes a specific task within the program, combining the modules will accomplish the function of the program.

Most programs which are written are not as small as the example illustrated in Figure 16-11, Figure 16-12, and Figure 16-13. Large programs may contain many individual modules.

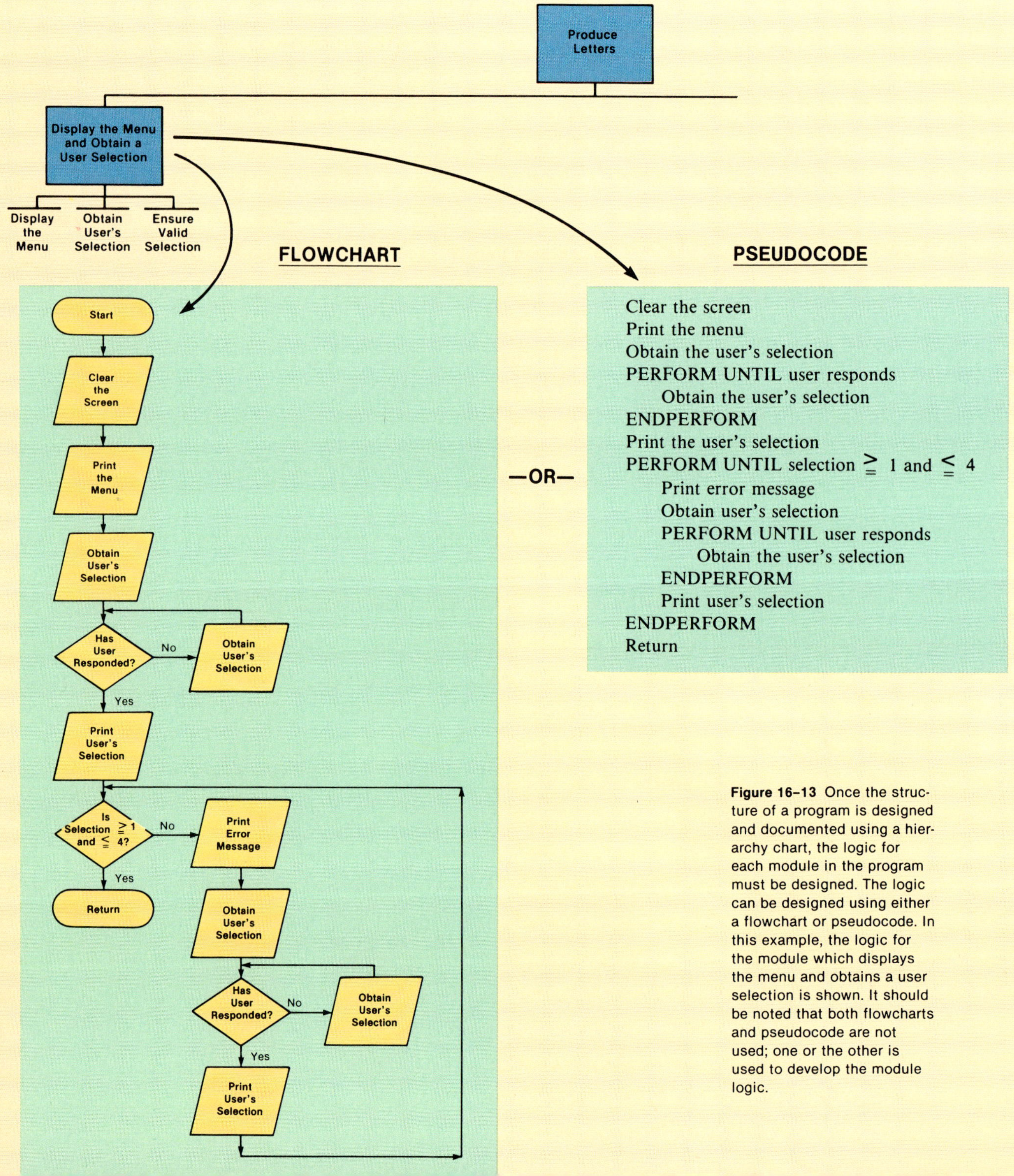
Produce Letters
Display the Menu and Obtain a User Selection
Display the Menu
Obtain User's Selection
Ensure Valid Selection
FLOWCHART
Start
Clear the Screen
Print the Menu
Obtain User's Selection
Has User Responded?
No
Obtain User's Selection
Yes
Print User's Selection
Is Selection ≥ 1 and ≤ 4?
No
Print Error Message
Obtain User's Selection
Has User Responded?
No
Obtain User's Selection
Yes
Print User's Selection
Yes
Return
—OR—
PSEUDOCODE
Clear the screen
Print the menu
Obtain the user's selection
PERFORM UNTIL user responds
Obtain the user's selection
ENDPERFORM
Print the user's selection
PERFORM UNTIL selection ≥ 1 and ≤ 4
Print error message
Obtain user's selection
PERFORM UNTIL user responds
Obtain the user's selection
ENDPERFORM
Print user's selection
ENDPERFORM
Return

Figure 16-13 Once the structure of a program is designed and documented using a hierarchy chart, the logic for each module in the program must be designed. The logic can be designed using either a flowchart or pseudocode. In this example, the logic for the module which displays the menu and obtains a user selection is shown. It should be noted that both flowcharts and pseudocode are not used; one or the other is used to develop the module logic.

Other design methodologies

At about the same time structured design was developed and distributed throughout the industry, several other design techniques were developed. The two other major methodologies are the **Jackson methodology** (named after Michael Jackson, its originator), and the **Warnier-Orr methodology** (named after Jean-Dominique Warnier and Kenneth Orr).

The Warnier-Orr methodology has become widely used. It is based upon analyzing the output to be produced from an application and developing modules based upon the processing that must be accomplished to produce the output. The example in Figure 16–14 illustrates a completed Warnier-Orr diagram for a checkbook balancing report program. Each bracket represents a module in the program. The statements within the brackets identify the processing that is to occur within the modules.

The Jackson methodology is based upon the data which is to be processed, under the theory that if the structure of the program mirrors the data which it processes, then the program will be easy to design and easy to read and understand.

All three design methodologies — structured design, the Jackson methodology, and the Warnier-Orr methodology — have their strengths and weaknesses; but all three have contributed significantly to the process of designing programs.

Figure 16–14 The Warnier-Orr diagram shown here illustrates the structural design for a program which balances a checkbook. This diagram not only shows the modules which are used in the program but also specifies some of the exact logic which will be used in the module.

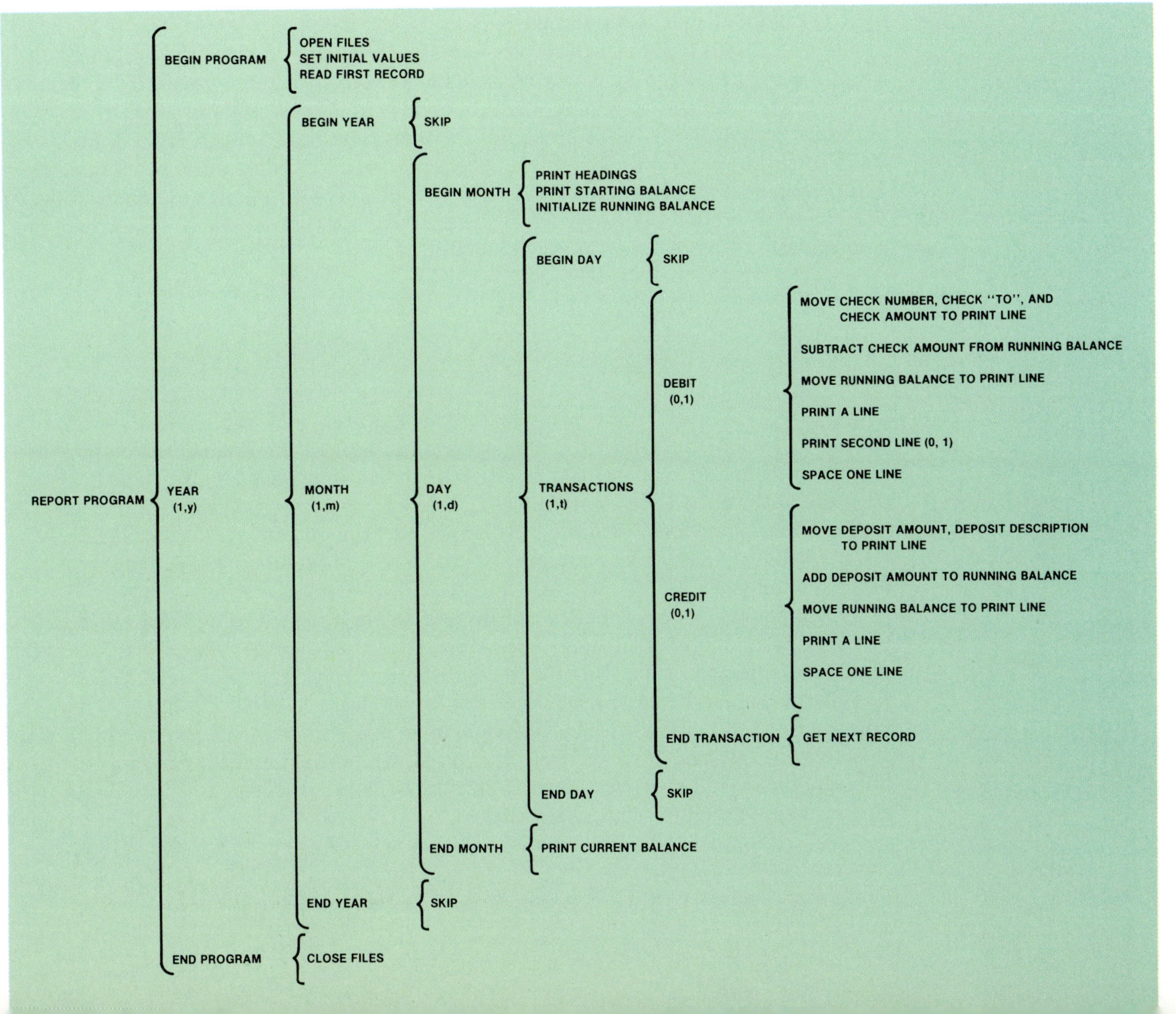

Egoless programming and structured walkthroughs

For many years, program design and program coding was thought by programmers to be an individual activity. Indeed, many programmers were protective of their programs, not allowing anyone to see their program design or program coding while they were performing these activities.

Recognizing that this attitude was not one to foster well-designed and well-coded programs, Dr. Gerald Weinberg of Weinberg and Weinberg, wrote a book in 1971 entitled *The Psychology of Computer Programming*. In his classic book, Weinberg criticized this attitude and proposed in its place an attitude he called "**egoless programming**." When egoless programming is practiced, the individual views his or her program not as an extension of themselves, but rather as a product which should be examined to make it better. As a result of Weinberg's work, as well as others, the concept of program reviews and structured walkthroughs emerged.

A **structured walkthrough** is an organized review of a program by other programmers. As a programmer designs and writes a program, it is important to approach the task with the idea that it will be done properly the first time, without any errors. On occasion, however, the programmer will inadvertently make an error in the program design or program coding. The intent of the walkthrough is to find any errors which have been made in the program — either errors in the use of a programming language or errors in the design of a program.

In order for a walkthrough to be successful, it is important for the programmer to adopt the attitude that a discovery of errors is welcome, since the program will be a valued asset to the company only when it contains no errors. The discovery of an error in a walkthrough is not an indictment of the individual programmer. Indeed, Weinberg states in his book, "We do know through our experiences with egoless programming that there is no particular reason why your friend cannot also be your sternest critic."[1] The review of program design is an important step in the development of a program, and should be a part of each programming project.

COMMON DESIGN PROBLEMS

When defining the logic of a program or a program module, there are a number of common logic problems that occur in business applications. These basic problems involve the logic to perform the following types of processing: 1) Basic input/output operations; 2) Basic calculating, counting records, and accumulating totals; 3) Basic comparing operations; 4) Interactive programming; 5) Arrays and array searching.

Each of these types of logic problems can be implemented using one or more of the three basic control structures — sequence, if-then-else, or do while. The flowcharts on the following pages illustrate the logic to solve each of these problems. These flowcharts contain the basic logic necessary for the solution to the problems. They do not contain such language dependent requirements as moving fields from an input area to an output area and space control. The intent of the structured flowcharts is to illustrate the overall approach taken to solve these basic problems using the three structured programming control structures.

1 Gerald M. Weinberg, *The Psychology of Computer Programming*, Van Nostrand Reinhold Company, 1971.

Basic input/output operations

One of the most basic operations that can be performed on a computer involves reading input data into computer memory from a device, such as a floppy disk, and producing output from that data such as printing a report or displaying output on a CRT screen.

The flowchart in Figure 16–15 illustrates the logic to read a series of input records containing an employee number, employee name, and a department name and displaying the output on a CRT screen. The input records are stored on floppy disk.

Figure 16–15 This flowchart shows the logic for basic input/output operations using sequential input files. The arrows within the loop would not be drawn by the programmer; they are used in this and subsequent illustrations merely to point out the control structures being used.

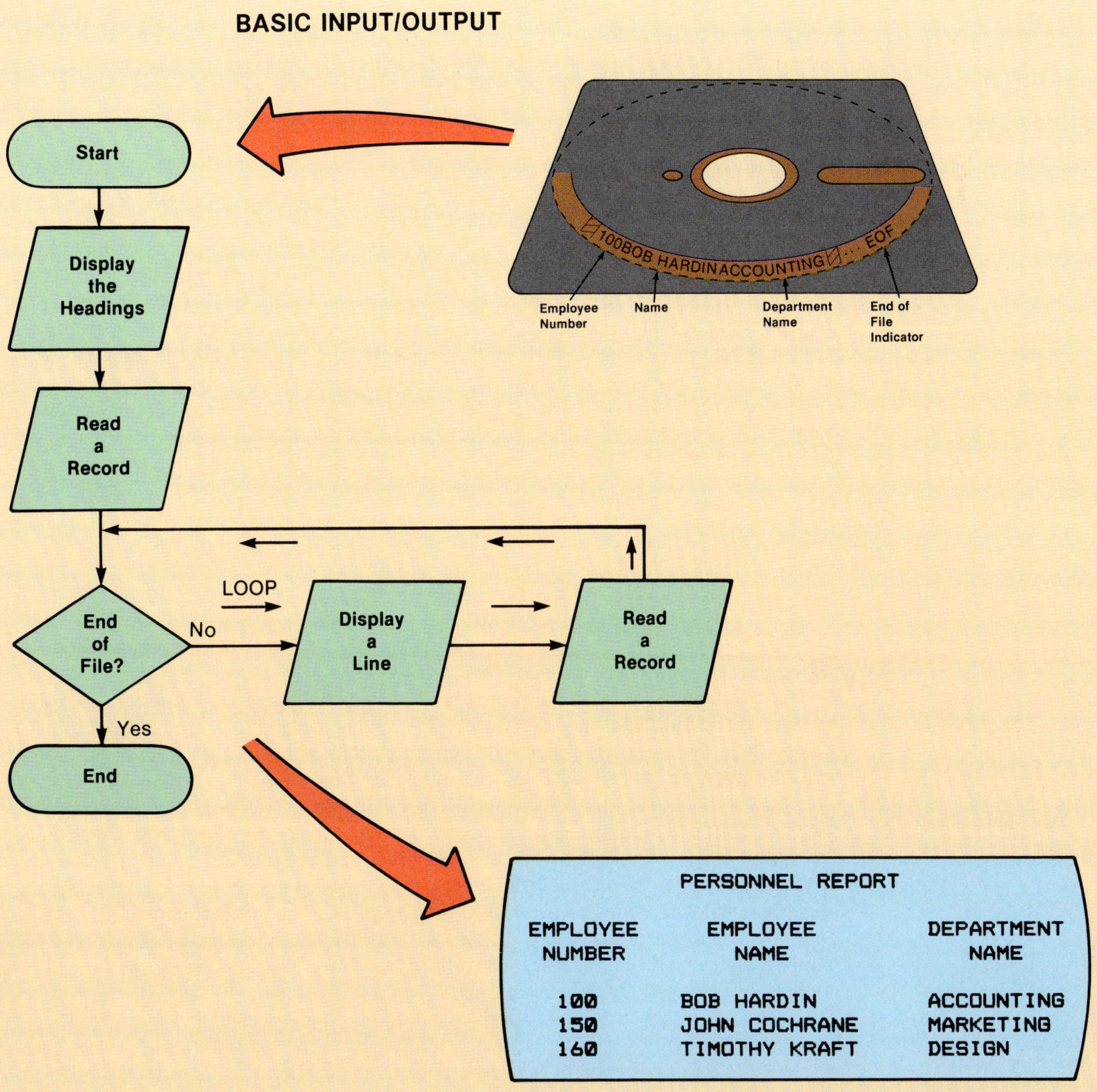

With all sequential input files, regardless of the medium on which they are stored, there must be an **end-of-file indicator** which indicates the end of the data in the file. This is accomplished by placing special end-of-file characters after the last data record in the file. In the example, the entry EOF is used to illustrate this end-of-file indicator.

The basic logic of the program consists of reading a record into main computer memory and then displaying a line on the CRT from the data that was contained in that record. This operation of reading and displaying continues until all records have been processed. The do while, or looping, logic structure, together with the sequence logic structure, are used to implement the logic of the program. The looping structure is used because reading input records and displaying data on the CRT screen must be done repeatedly (looping) until the end of file indicator is detected.

To identify the beginning of the flowchart, a special flowchart symbol containing the word Start is used. It is important to use the appropriate ANSI flowcharting symbols when drawing a flowchart. The next step, as illustrated by the input/output flowchart symbol, is to display the headings. After the headings are displayed, a record is read from the floppy disk into main computer memory.

After a record has been read into main memory, a check must be performed to determine if the record just read is the end-of-file record. This is indicated in the flowchart by the diamond shaped decision symbol containing the words End of File?. If it is not end of file, a line is displayed on the CRT screen, as indicated by the flowchart symbol containing the words Display a Line.

After a line is displayed, another record is read. Control is then returned to the decision step to check for end of file. The basic steps in this program, then, consist of checking to determine if it is end of file, displaying a line, and reading a record. This logic is implemented using the do while, or looping, logic structure. When a record is read that contains the entry EOF (end of file), there is an exit from the loop and execution of the program terminates.

The ability to loop is an important characteristic of computer programs because a single set of instructions can be written to process an unlimited number of input records in exactly the same way. The logic illustrated in this program should be thoroughly understood, for this logic forms the basis of most sequential file processing operations.

Counters, accumulators, and printing final totals

A variety of calculations can be performed by computer programs, including adding, subtracting, multiplying, and dividing. When calculations are involved in processing data, there is often a need to accumulate totals and print the totals after all input records have been processed. The totals are called **final totals**. In addition, it might be necessary to count the number of input records that have been read and processed.

To illustrate counting the number of input records processed and accumulating a final total, a payroll program will be designed. In this program, a report of gross pay is prepared. The input records, which are stored on floppy disk, contain the employee number, employee name, hours worked, and pay rate. The printed report contains these fields plus the gross pay for the employee, which is calculated by multiplying the hours worked times the pay rate. After all records have been processed, the total number of employees and the total payroll amount is printed.

The logic to produce the report is illustrated by the flowchart in Figure 16–16. The control structures used to implement the logic are the sequence and the do while structures. The major logic difference between this program and the previous program

COUNTERS, ACCUMULATORS, AND PRINTING FINAL TOTALS

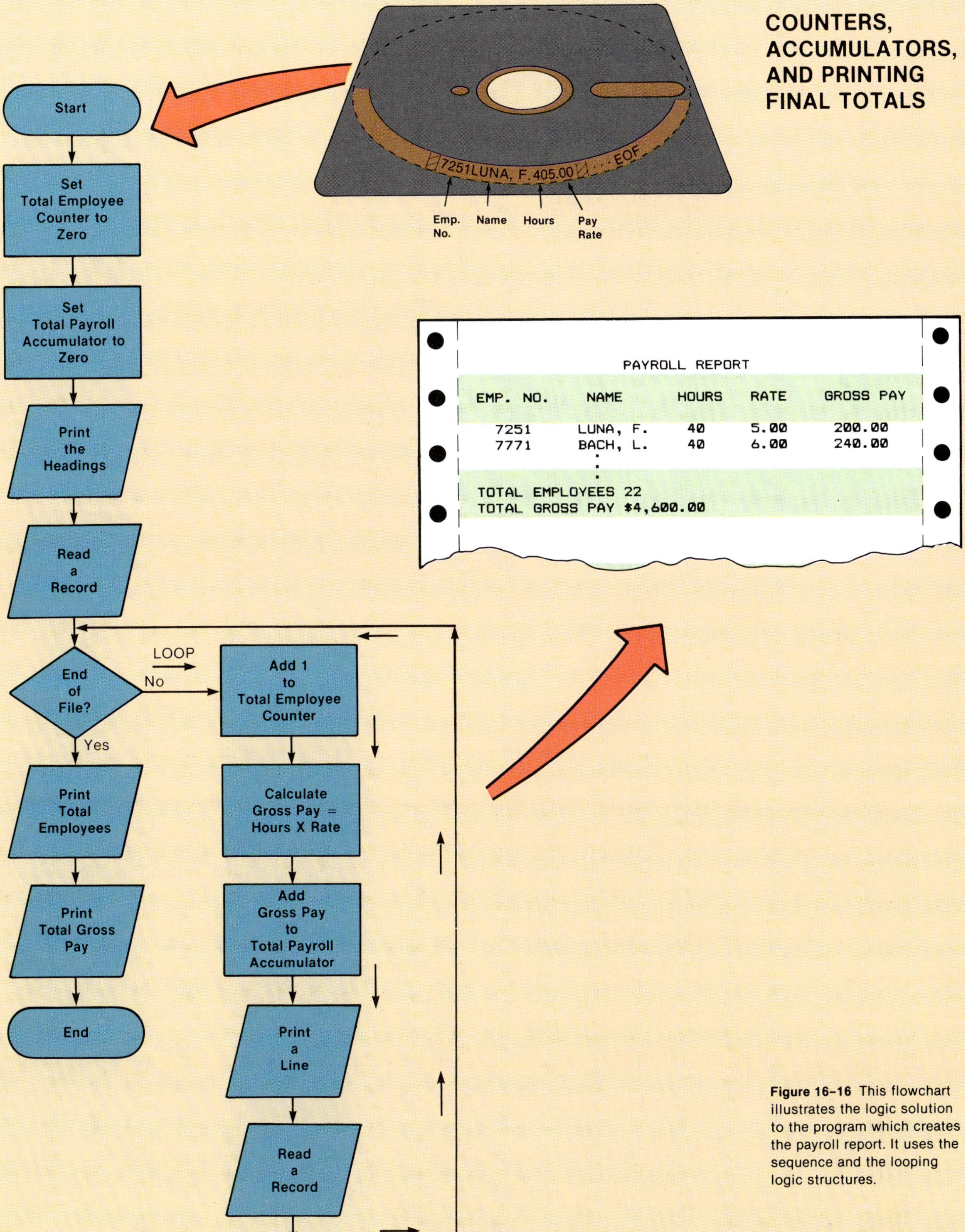

Figure 16–16 This flowchart illustrates the logic solution to the program which creates the payroll report. It uses the sequence and the looping logic structures.

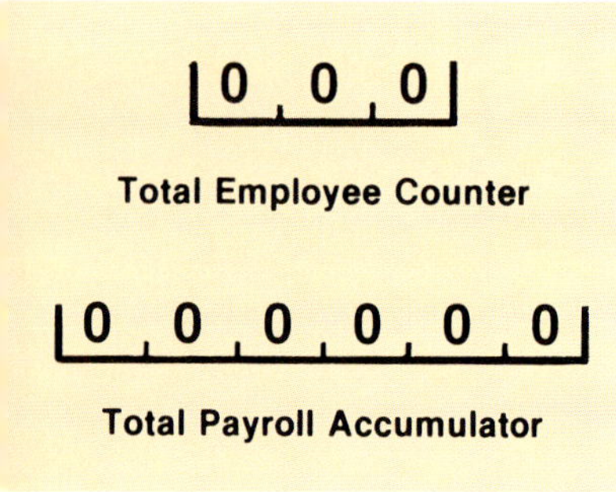

Figure 16–17 The total employee counter field and the total payroll accumulator field must be set to zero prior to processing any input records.

is the increased number of individual operations that must be performed.

To count the number of records processed and accumulate a final total, areas in main computer memory must be reserved for the totals. The area used to count records is called a **counter**. The area used to accumulate a final total is called an **accumulator**. These areas must be initialized to zero as one of the first steps in the program logic so that the total will be accumulated properly (Figure 16–17). The first two steps in the flowchart indicate that the total employee counter is to be set to zero, and the total payroll accumulator is to be set to zero.

The headings are then printed, and a record is read into main computer memory. When a record is read and it is not end of file, the main processing loop is entered. The first operation in the main processing loop is to add 1 to the total employee counter. Since the total employee counter was set to zero at the beginning of the program, the effect of this operation is to count the total number of employee records processed.

The gross pay is then calculated by multiplying the hours times the pay rate. The gross pay is then added to the total payroll accumulator. The total payroll accumulator was set to zero at the beginning of the program; therefore, the effect of adding the gross pay to the accumulator is to accumulate the total gross pay.

A line is then printed and another record is read. Control is then transferred to the decision step to determine if the end of file record was read. If not, the processing within the loop occurs again.

When the end of file record is read, the program exits from the loop. Upon exit from the loop, the total number of employees is printed and the total gross pay is printed. Execution of the program then terminates.

It is important to note that although this program accomplishes considerably more processing than the program illustrated in Figure 16–15, the basic logic structure of the program is the same; that is, a loop is entered when it is not end of file. This looping continues until all of the input records have been read and processed. At that time, the program exits from the loop.

Basic comparing

Another important characteristic of programs is their ability to compare the values stored in two fields and perform alternative operations based upon whether the value in one field is less than, equal to, or greater than the value in the other field. **Comparing** is implemented using the if-then-else control structure.

In order to illustrate the if-then-else control structure, a program which produces a sales report is illustrated in Figure 16–18. The input records to the program contain a salesperson number, a salesperson name, and a sales amount. The records are stored on a floppy disk. The report contains the salesperson number, the salesperson name, the sales amount, and the commission. The commission is calculated as follows: If the sales amount is greater than $500.00, then the commission is equal to the sales amount times 7%. If the sales amount is equal to or less than $500.00, then the commission is equal to the sales amount times 5%. After all input records have been processed, the total commissions paid to all sales people is printed.

The first step in the program is to set the total commission accumulator to zero. Headings are then printed and a record is read. If the end of file record is not encountered, the loop is entered.

The first step in the loop is to determine if the sales amount is greater than $500.00. This is done by comparing the sales amount in the input record to a constant value of $500.00 which would be defined by the program and be stored in main

BASIC COMPARING

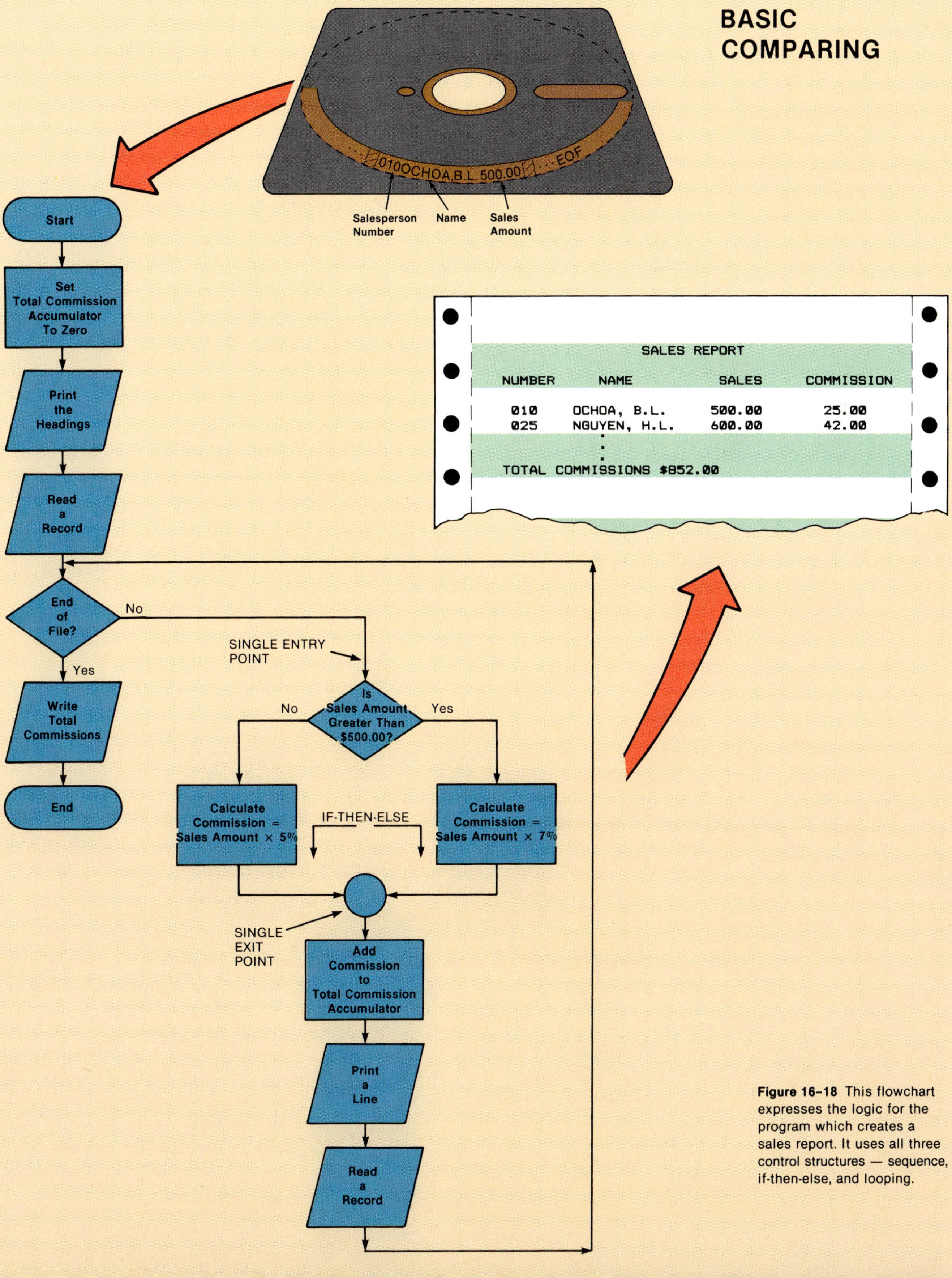

Figure 16–18 This flowchart expresses the logic for the program which creates a sales report. It uses all three control structures — sequence, if-then-else, and looping.

computer memory. If the sales amount is greater than $500.00, then the commission is calculated by multiplying the sales amount by 7%. If the sales amount is not greater than $500.00, the commission is calculated by multiplying the sales amount by 5%.

After the commission is calculated, it is added to the total commission accumulator, the line is printed on the report, and another record is read. The loop is then repeated so long as there are records to process.

It is important to note that there is a single entry point into the if-then-else control structure that determines the commission percentage. In addition, there is a single exit point from the structure after the commission is calculated. Thus, regardless of whether the commission percentage is 5% or 7%, the if-then-else structure exits at a common exit point. Using a single entry point and a single exit point greatly improves and simplifies the logic for programs and results in programs that are substantially easier to read, modify, and maintain.

After all records have been processed, the total commission for all employees is printed and processing is terminated.

Interactive programming

In many applications, the user communicates with the computer in an interactive mode to produce output. The flowchart in Figure 16–19 illustrates the logic for a program which uses interactive processing to prepare a rental charge chart for one week (7 days) based upon the charge for one day entered by the sales clerk or user.

On the first screen generated by the program, a message appears asking the user "DO YOU WANT TO PREPARE A RENTAL CHARGE CHART?" The user is asked to respond by entering the word YES or the word NO.

The program then edits the entry of the user to ensure that a proper response was made. The user can enter the value YES or the value NO. Any other response is not valid. In the example in Figure 16–19, the user entered a Y the first time. This caused an error message to be displayed and a request to the user to enter YES or NO.

The statement appearing on the next screen asks the user to "ENTER CHARGE FOR ONE DAY". Again, this data should be edited to assure that a reasonable value is entered. What is reasonable must be determined by the person designing the application system. In this example, the reasonable value has been established as a rental charge that is not greater than 99.99. Therefore, the program must ensure that the user does not enter a value greater than 99.99.

The output produced from the program is a rental charge report listing the charge for the rental of an item for one to seven days. The charges are calculated by multiplying the daily charge entered by the user by the number of days.

The first step in the flowchart is to set the maximum rental charge the user can enter to 99.99. This is to allow a comparison to be made in the program to ensure that the rental charge entered by the user is not greater than the maximum value. The number of days for which the charge is to be prepared is set to 7. This process of setting values at the beginning of a program is often called **program initialization**.

The CRT screen is then cleared of extraneous material (Clear Screen) and the message is displayed asking the user if they want to prepare a rental charge chart. The user must enter the word YES or the word NO. The logic for this segment is indicated by the decision symbol that contains the words Is Response = Yes or No? If the user did not enter either YES or NO (for example, if the user entered Y for the word YES), a loop is entered. Within the loop, an error message is displayed and the user is again requested to enter YES or NO. Control returns to the decision symbol where a check is made to determine if a valid entry has been made. If the user has entered either YES

INTERACTIVE PROGRAM DESIGN

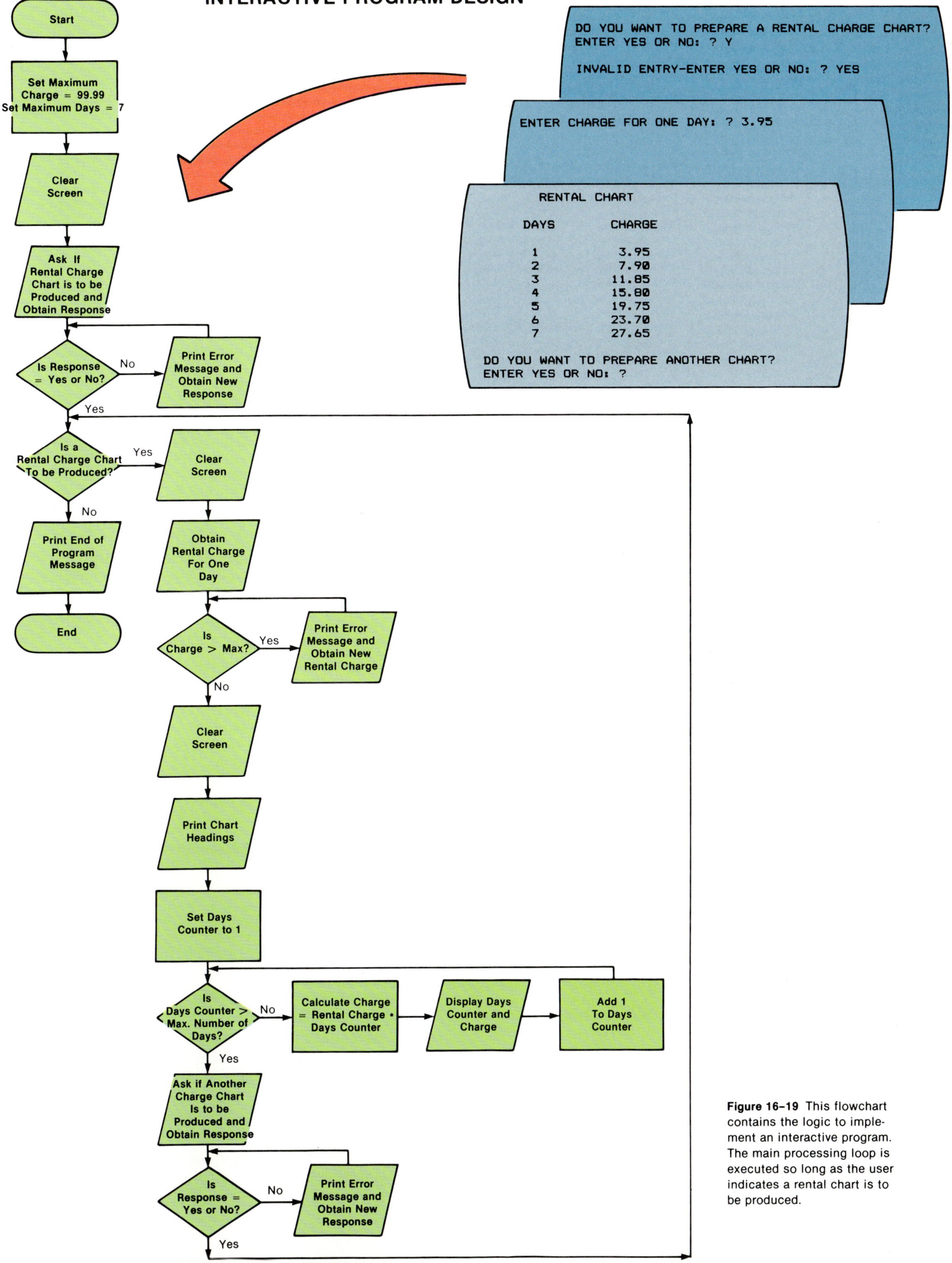

Figure 16–19 This flowchart contains the logic to implement an interactive program. The main processing loop is executed so long as the user indicates a rental chart is to be produced.

or NO, there is an exit from the loop. If not, the loop is entered again. This loop will continue until the user enters a valid value.

A check is then made to determine if the user entered the word YES by asking the question, Is a Rental Charge Chart to be Produced? If so, the main processing loop is entered. If not, processing is terminated.

When the main processing loop is entered, the screen is again cleared and the user is requested to enter the rental charge for one day. Since the charge must be not greater than 99.99, the value entered by the user is compared to the maximum value (99.99). If the value entered by the user is greater than the maximum value, a loop is entered, an error message is displayed, and the user must then enter a new rental charge.

When the user has entered a valid rental charge, there is an exit from the loop. The screen is again cleared. The chart headings are displayed, and the days counter is set to 1. A loop containing the processing steps to prepare the charges for one to seven days is then entered.

The entry to the loop is the decision symbol which asks if the days counter is greater than the maximum days (7). If not, the loop is entered and the rental charge is calculated by multiplying the rental charge entered by the user by the number of days in the days counter. The first time through the loop, the days counter contains the value 1. Therefore, the rental charge entered by the user is multiplied by the value 1. The value in the days counter and the calculated rental charge are then displayed. The value 1 is then added to the days counter. During the first pass through the loop, the days counter will be incremented to the value 2. A check is made to determine if the value in the days counter is greater than the maximum number of days (7). If not, the loop is again entered and the rental charges for the next day are calculated and displayed.

The looping will continue until the value in the days counter is greater than 7. At that time, since the charges for all seven days will have been calculated and displayed, there will be an exit from the loop.

After the exit from the loop, the next step is to determine if the user wants to prepare another rental charge chart. Therefore, the user is asked if another charge is to be prepared. As before, the user must enter the value YES or the value NO. When a valid entry has been made, control returns to the entry point of the main processing loop. The entry point of the main processing loop determines if the user entered YES. If so, the main loop is once again entered. If not, program execution is terminated.

The logic of this interactive program should be carefully reviewed since interactive programs are widely used in both personal and professional computing.

Arrays and array searching

The previous examples have illustrated processing a series of records stored on floppy disk and processing data on an interactive basis. Another important information processing concept is storing and processing data stored in **tables**, or arrays. An **array** consists of a series of related data items and fields stored in rows and columns.

Tables, or arrays, are used in many application areas. For example, there are height and weight tables, income tax tables, insurance tables, tables containing telephone numbers, and many others. When a table is used, it must be searched in order to extract the proper information.

Arrays play an important role when processing data on a computer. To illustrate the use of arrays, the logic for a program which accesses data stored in an array in main computer memory will be explained.

Figure 16–20 The array to be processed contains the item number, the item name, and the quantity on hand. When the item number is entered, the array is searched until an item number equal to that entered by the user is found. When it is, the corresponding item name and quantity on hand are extracted from the array and are displayed on the screen.

In the program, the user will enter an item number (Figure 16–20). When the user enters the item number, the item number field in the array will be searched until an equal condition is found. When an equal condition is found, the corresponding item name and quantity will be displayed. If the item number entered by the user is not found in the array, an error message will be displayed.

Subscripts

The entries in the array consisting of the item number, the item name, and the quantity on hand are called the **array elements**. To reference an element within the array, a subscript can be used (Figure 16–21). A **subscript** is a field which contains a value referencing a particular element within an array. For example, the value 1 in the subscript field would reference the first element in the array; the value 2 in the subscript field would reference the second element in the array, and so on. In the example, there are 49 elements in the array, although not all are shown.

Subscript	ITEM NUMBER	ITEM NAME	QUANTITY ON HAND
(1)	1001	PAPER	25
(2)	1009	RIBBON	75
(3)	2718	DISKETTE	60
(4)	3115	TEMPLATE	10
.	.	.	.
.	.	.	.
.	.	.	.
(49)	9292	LABELS	84

Figure 16–21 Subscripts are used to reference each element of an array. When the value in the subscript is 1, the first elements are referenced. When the value is 2, the second elements are referenced, and so on.

Program design

As with the previous interactive program, provision should be made to allow the user to indicate whether or not an inquiry is to be made and to allow for termination of the program. This is accomplished by displaying the message shown in Figure 16–22.

```
DO YOU WANT TO MAKE AN INQUIRY?
ENTER YES OR NO: ?
```

Figure 16–22 This message is displayed to ask if an inquiry is to be made. The user must enter the value YES or the value NO.

When the user enters YES the main processing will occur. If the user enters NO, program execution will terminate. No other response is valid.

The flowchart for the program is shown in Figure 16–23. The first step is to load the array. This may be accomplished by entering the data into the array through the use of the keyboard, by defining the data within the program, or loading the data into the array from a file stored on a diskette. Whichever method is used, after execution

Figure 16–23 This flowchart illustrates the logic to search an array.

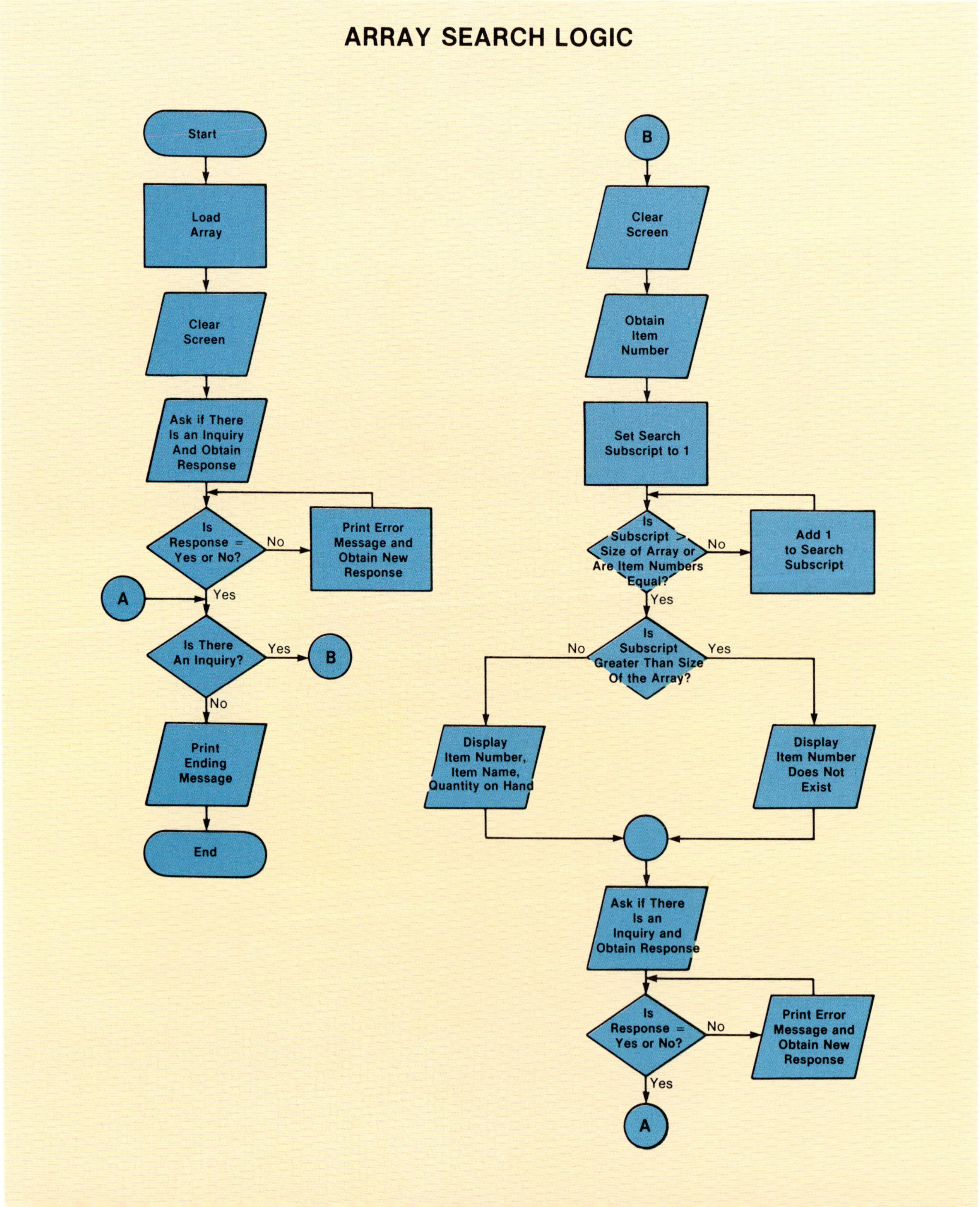

of this step, the data is stored in the array as illustrated previously in Figure 16–21.

The screen is then cleared, and a message is displayed on the screen asking the user if an inquiry is to be made. The user must answer YES or NO. When a valid response is obtained from the user, a check is performed to determine if the response entered was YES. If so, the main processing loop is entered. If not, the program is terminated.

The flowchart in Figure 16–23 makes use of the connector symbol, which is the small circle with the letter A or letter B in it. When an arrow points to the connector symbol, control is passed to the point in the program where the symbol has an arrow pointing away from it. Thus, when the response entered by the user is yes, control is passed to point B, which is at the top of the portion of the flowchart on the right. When that portion has completed processing, the arrow at the bottom points to a connector symbol with the letter A in it. At that point, control is passed to the connector for A, which is located in the flowchart on the left.

When the main processing loop is entered, the first step is to clear the screen. The user is then requested to enter the item number. Once the item number is entered, the array can be searched.

Prior to beginning the search, the search subscript is initialized to the value 1, so that the search will begin with the first element of the array. To perform the array search, a do while, or looping, control structure is used. The basic approach is to compare the item number entered by the user to the item number in the first element of the array. If they are equal, the corresponding item name and quantity on hand are displayed. If they are not equal, the item number entered by the user is compared to the item number in the second element of the array. If they are not equal, the item number entered by the user is compared to the third item number in the array, and so on. This continues until either an equal condition is found, at which time the appropriate data can be displayed, OR until all item numbers in the array have been examined. When all item numbers have been examined and there is not an equal condition, it means that the item number entered by the user was not in the array. In this case, a message is displayed noting the item number is not in the array.

The logic for this loop begins with the decision symbol which checks if the search subscript is greater than the size of the array or if the item numbers are equal. Since the value in the subscript is equal to 1 on the first pass of the loop, the item number entered by the user is compared to the item number in the first element of the array. If either condition is true, an exit from the loop will occur. If neither condition is true, the value 1 is added to the search subscript and control is returned to the decision symbol. Since the search subscript now contains the value 2, the second item number in the array will be compared to the item number entered by the user.

This looping continues until there is an exit from the loop. The exit from the loop will occur when either the value in the search subscript exceeds the size of the array or when the item number entered by the user is equal to an item number in the array.

The next step in the logic, then, must determine why an exit from the loop occurred. In the example, a check is performed to determine if the subscript is greater than the size of the array. If so, the item number entered by the user was not found in the array, and a message to that effect is displayed. If not, it is known that an equal condition caused the exit from the loop, and the item number, item name, and quantity on hand are displayed.

The final segment of the program logic asks the user if another inquiry is to be performed. When an appropriate response is entered by the user, control is returned to determine if the main processing loop should be entered or if the program should be terminated.

The use of arrays and array search logic is important in information processing. Each of the steps in the logic used for searching an array should be thoroughly understood.

		1	2	3	4	5	6	7	8
CONDITIONS	Account Current	Y	Y	Y	Y	N	N	N	N
	Purchase Within Credit Limit	Y	N	Y	N	Y	N	Y	N
	Payment Received Last 25 Days	Y	Y	N	N	Y	Y	N	N
ACTIONS	Unconditionally Approve	X							
	Approve, Subject to Credit Office			X					
	Deny, Subject to Credit Office		X		X	X	X	X	
	Send to Credit Office		X	X	X	X	X	X	
	Unconditionally Deny								X

Figure 16–24 The decision table identifies conditions that can occur and the actions which should be taken when the conditions do occur.

DECISION TABLES

In some applications, a number of conditions may occur within the program. It is often difficult to keep all of the conditions and the processing which is to occur as a result of these conditions in mind. Decision tables can be used to help clarify the actions which must be taken under certain conditions within the program.

A **decision table** is a graphical representation of the logical decisions that must be made concerning certain conditions which can occur within a program. In a decision table, both the conditions which must be tested and the actions which will be taken are graphically represented (Figure 16–24). The conditions which may occur are placed in the upper left-hand portion of the decision table (called the **condition stub**). The actions to be taken based upon the conditions are specified in the lower left-hand portion of the table (called the **action stub**).

The upper right portion of the table is called the **condition entry** part of the table. It is in this area that the different combinations of conditions which can occur are specified. In the example in Figure 16–24, the conditions pertain to an order entry system. The programmer has three criteria on which to base the approval of credit — account current, purchase within credit limit, and payment received in the last 25 days. The condition entry part of the decision table is used to indicate the various combinations of these three conditions that can occur.

There are five actions which can be taken — unconditionally approve; approve, subject to credit office; deny, subject to credit office; send to credit office; and unconditionally deny. The actions to be taken are indicated in the lower right portion of the table, which is called the **action entry** area.

The numbers across the top of the table are called the **rules,** and identify the vertical columns. Each vertical column gives the combination of conditions that can occur and the corresponding actions which should be taken. For example, Rule 1 says if the account is current (Y), the purchase is within the credit limit (Y), and a payment has been received within the last 25 days (Y), then the credit should be unconditionally approved. Rule 2 says that if the account is current (Y), the purchase is not within the credit limit (N), and payment has been received within the last 25 days (Y), then credit is denied, subject to review by the credit office. In Rule 2, two actions are taken — the credit is denied and the credit request is sent to the credit office for review. The other rules are read in a similar fashion.

Decision tables can be useful to systems analysts when they document the program specifications because decision tables can often be more clear than a narrative. In addition, they are useful to programmers when a combination of conditions must be checked to ensure that the proper processing will be included in the program.

STRUCTURED WALKTHROUGH — PROGRAM DESIGN

After a program has been designed, a formal structured walkthrough of the design should be scheduled with other programmers, the systems analyst, users, and any other parties who may be able to determine that an error has occurred in the program design. The purpose of the design walkthrough is to review the design and logic of the program to detect errors, and to improve the design so that the program will be efficient and easy to understand.

When the walkthrough is conducted, the individual who designed the program should explain the program design to others and be receptive to suggestions. The outcome of the design walkthrough should be an efficient, well designed program free of errors.

PROGRAM DEVELOPMENT

After the program has been designed, it must be coded, tested, and documented. The following paragraphs discuss these aspects of the program development cycle.

Coding the program

The programming language used to code a program will normally be determined by the systems analyst or project manager based upon the software available, the knowledge of the programming staff, and the standards established within the information systems department.

Coding begins after the program has been designed. Coding the program involves the actual writing of the detailed programming statements. The code in the program must implement the program which has already been designed. Therefore, the programmer must use the program design as the guide in coding the program.

Coding is a very exact skill. The programmer must not only implement the program design in code, but must also be precise in using the language. Each programming language has its own **syntax**, or coding rules, which must be followed. The programmer must follow these rules explicitly, or the program will not compile and execute as intended.

After the program has been coded (or in large programs, as the program is coded), a walkthrough of the coding should take place with other programmers. This walkthrough provides the opportunity for other programmers to review, on a line for line basis, the coding developed by the original programmer.

Particular attention should be paid to ensuring that the code implements the design logic as expressed by the flowchart or pseudocode, that the program is well documented, that the coding is free of errors, and that the coding is easy to read, leading to a program that is easy to modify and maintain. Upon completion of this walkthrough, the programmer should be confident that the program will execute properly the first time it is executed on the computer and will never fail subsequently.

Once it is agreed that the program code is well-written and correctly implements the design of the program, the source program must be prepared for processing on the computer. This requires that each line of the program be placed either on a machine-readable medium such as floppy disk using data-entry equipment or that it be entered directly into the computer via a terminal. When it is entered via terminal, the source program will normally be stored on disk for future processing. A program to be executed on a personal computer will always be entered directly into the computer and should be stored on disk after it is entered.

PROGRAM TESTING

After the program has been coded, it must be tested to ensure that it processes data properly and produces the correct output. The basic procedures for testing a program are:

1. Test data is created with which to test the program.
2. The program is compiled and all diagnostic errors are removed.
3. The program is tested. If an interpreter is used, steps 2 and 3 occur together.
4. Any errors which are found in the program are corrected, and the testing continues until the program is certified as error-free.
5. The program can be used in a system test to ensure that all programs within a system work properly together.

Creating test data

Creating test data with which to test a program is an important responsibility of a programmer. The development of adequate test data, together with good program design and coding, are the most important tasks accomplished by a computer programmer.

There are several elements to developing test data. These are: 1) What type of data should be developed? 2) Who should develop the test data? 3) Who will check the test data?

Test data should be designed to find errors in the program. Although it has been shown that testing — no matter how extensive — cannot be used to prove a program is entirely error-free, it has been found that properly designed test data can be used to show a high probability that errors do not exist.

Therefore, the task of developing test data should be approached with the same seriousness as designing or coding a program. Test data should be developed which requires the program to execute all the instructions within the program at least one time. To do this, test data will normally fall into two major areas: 1) Data which is in the correct format and which will cause the instructions processing correct data to be executed; 2) Data which contains predefined errors, causing the error routines within the program to be executed. For example, if a field is supposed to contain numeric data, one set of test data should have the correct numeric data in the field. Another set of test data, however, should place nonnumeric data in the field. In this way, both the normal processing routines and the error routines are tested, which ensures a complete test of the program.

Testing sequence

A program will not normally be tested by being executed just one time. The programmer should develop a test plan which, among other things, specifies the number of test runs to be executed, the portions of the program that are to be tested on each run, and the objectives of each test run. For example, a payroll program which calculates an employee's weekly earnings and prints the payroll check might first be tested to ensure that the payroll calculations were being performed properly, without regard to the ability of the program to print checks. After it is ensured that the calculations are performed correctly, the portion of the program which prints the checks can be tested.

Stub testing

Testing only a portion of a program to ensure that it works properly is normally good testing strategy. A variation of this is found when structured design is used for a program, and the program consists of a hierarchy of program modules. This strategy, called **stub testing**, allows a program to be partially coded and tested before the entire program is coded.

When using stub testing, one or more modules in the higher levels of the hierarchy of the program are coded. Those modules which are submodules will be coded as "stubs" when the program is tested. A stub contains merely a few statements of code which allow it to be referenced by those modules actually being tested. For example, in the hierarchy chart shown in Figure 16–25, there are ten modules in the program. Using stub testing techniques, the modules which produce the letters, display the menu and obtain a user selection, and prepare and print the letter could be coded and tested. The other modules could be coded as stubs. The important concept to be understood is that the programmer can test the three modules, ensure that the modules are operational, and know that an important portion of the program is completed.

Stub testing is an important testing technique in complex programs which may consist of hundreds of modules. Without stub testing, the entire program might have to be coded before testing could be started. With stub testing, testing can begin shortly after coding is begun; with the result that program testing is spread more evenly across the project time, and managment can review the progress of completed portions of the program.

Figure 16–25 This hierarchy chart illustrates a program with ten modules (the tasks identified within the rectangular boxes). The tasks under the horizontal lines are performed within the module itself, not by a separate module. To use stub testing, one or more of the higher level modules can be designed and coded. The lower level modules (stubs) contain just a few statements to allow them to be called.

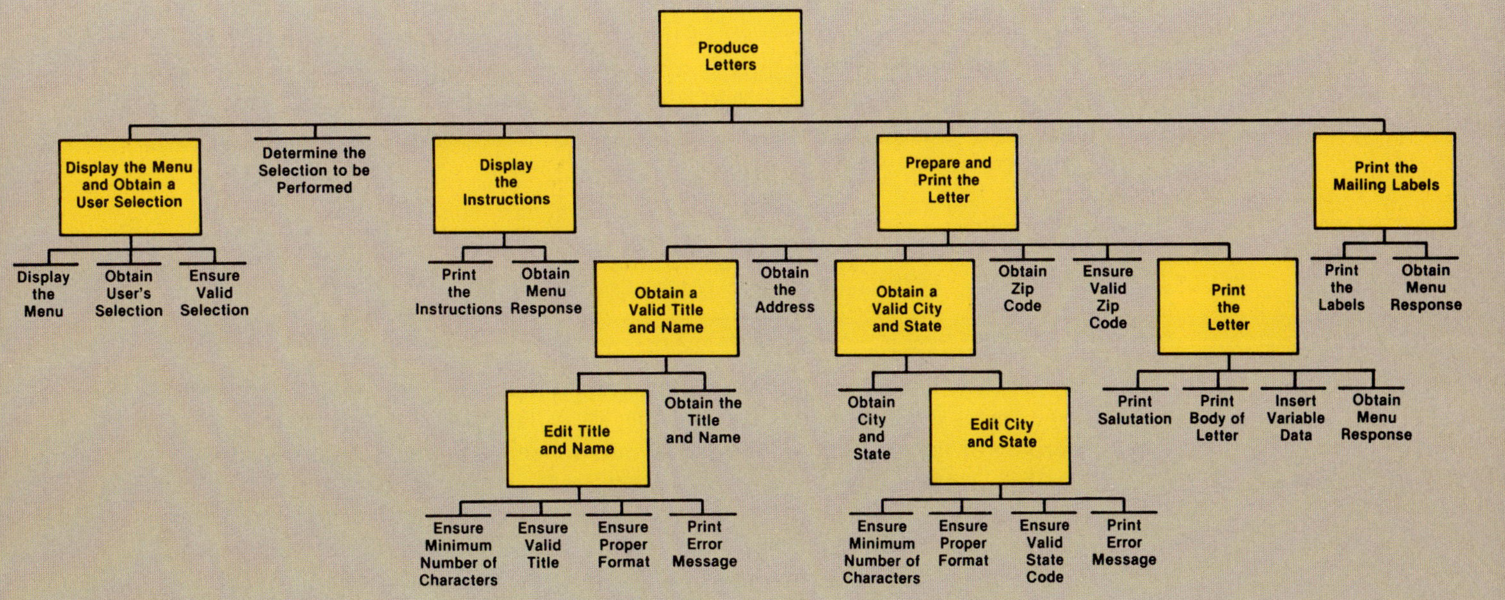

Assuring program correctness

There are several points in testing that must be recognized in order to have valid tests. First, the programmer who coded a program should not normally be the person who creates the test data. Many times the programmer who coded the program will not want, subconsciously, to find all the possible errors, and therefore, may not be completely diligent in preparing the test data.

Additionally, someone other than the programmer who coded the program should review the test results to determine if the correct output is produced. It has been found that when the person who coded the program checks the results, sometimes the programmer sees not what is there but what is supposed to be there. In large information systems departments, one group may be completely responsibile for testing all programs which are produced.

Program efficiency

Program efficiency consists of two elements: 1) The amount of main computer memory required to store the program when it is processing data; 2) The amount of time required by the program to process data. In some cases, program efficiency is not critical. For example, when a small program is written, the computer will always have enough memory for the program and the speed at which the program executes may not be important. In other programs, however, program efficiency could be extremely important. In very large programs, for example, there is the possibility that the computer may not contain enough memory to store the program. Indeed, in previous chapters it has been noted that some software packages require a certain amount of main computer memory in order to be executed.

With respect to execution speed, an efficient program can sometimes reduce the processing time for an application from hours to minutes. In some applications, as well, time is extremely critical. For example, when monitoring space flight, a program must react in very short periods of time in order to effectively perform its task.

Program efficiency is directly affected by program design and program coding. A well designed and coded program is not only understandable and easy to modify and maintain, it is also efficient with respect to the amount of main computer memory required and the speed with which it processes data.

PROGRAM DOCUMENTATION

The documentation of each program developed in an information systems department should include the following: 1) An abstract and general description of the purpose of the program; 2) Record layouts for report output, terminal output, files on auxiliary storage, user views of data bases used, and any other data which is necessary in the execution of the program; 3) A system flowchart, illustrating where the particular program fits within the system; 4) A detailed description of the processing which occurs within the program; 5) The structure or hierarchy chart of the modules within the program; 6) The logic utilized within each module of the program. This logic should be illustrated either through the use of flowcharts or through the use of pseudocode; 7) A listing of the source program; 8) A listing of the test data used to test the program and the results of the testing; 9) A console run form which includes the job control statements and any other information necessary to specify how the program is to be run on the computer; 10) A user guide on how to use the program. This guide may include what data is used in the system; the way to prepare source documents; and, in interactive programs, the manner in which to establish contact with the computer and interact with the program.

Programs written for use with home or personal computers quite often do not require quite the same amount of documentation as programs written in large information processing installations because their use will be limited. Many of the elements listed above, however, should be included. When software packages are purchased, the user should thoroughly examine the package documentation prior to purchase. In many cases, the documentation available with program can determine the success or failure of using the software.

Program documentation is an important but often neglected part of the programming process. In an organization with many hundreds or even thousands of programs, the lack of documentation can cause significant problems. Lack of good documentation on personal computer programs can lead to an inability on the part of the user to make effective use of the software.

Program maintenance

It is a truism in information processing that any program, regardless of size and regardless of whether it was written for the largest mainframe or the smallest personal computer, will be changed during its lifetime. Making these changes is called **program maintenance**. Emphasis has been placed in this chapter on good program design, good program coding, and good program documentation because each of these is required in order to be able to perform program maintenance.

Program maintenance can be required to correct errors in a program. It can also be required to make enhancements to a program, such as adding new features to a word processing program. When commercial software packages are changed, they often are given version numbers. For example, version 1.0 of a software package may be the first version. When changes are made, the version number may be changed to 1.1, 2.0, or some other value, depending on the vendor. Whenever purchasing software, the user should ensure that the latest version is purchased.

Summary — program design, coding, and implementation

The key to obtaining good programs in an information processing system is to perform good program design. The design of a program is, without question, the most important aspect of programming. By using the three control structures found in structured programming, together with a well-designed modular program derived using any of the major design methodologies, the programmer will develop a program which can subsequently be easily coded and implemented.

Coding a program, thoroughly testing it, and documenting it properly are all very important in obtaining understandable, maintainable programs. A failure in any of these areas will result in a poor program, notwithstanding the good design. Without good design, however, success in coding, testing, and implementation is unlikely.

CHAPTER SUMMARY

1. Problems with programs include: a) Unreliable programs; b) Programs are difficult to modify and maintain.

2. The program development cycle consists of five steps: a) Review of program specifications; b) Program design; c) Program coding; d) Program testing; e) Program documentation.

3. Program specifications contain all the documentation which specifies what a program is supposed to do and the formats of the data which the program is supposed to process.

4. It is the programmer's responsibility to implement the procedures defined in the program specifications.

5. A program should be designed so that it will be efficient, will produce the correct output (reliable), will work under all conditions (robust), and will be easily modified (maintainable).

6. Using symbols to show the logic of a program is called flowcharting.

7. The American National Standards Institute (ANSI) has developed flowcharting standards which indicate the operation represented by each specially shaped symbol.

8. The value of a flowchart is that it graphically represents the steps in the solution of a problem.

9. When using a flowchart, many programmers were not aware of the overall design of the program until the flowchart was actually completed. This led to programs which were difficult to read, modify, and maintain.

10. Structured programming is defined as a method of programming that uses three control structures — sequence, if-then-else, and do while (looping) — for all programming logic, no matter how complex.

11. When using the sequence control structure, one event occurs immediately after another.

12. The if-then-else control structure is used to compare two values and perform alternative operations based upon the results of the comparison.

13. The do while logic structure is used to allow program looping.

14. An entry point is where a control structure is entered.

15. An exit point is the point where a control structure is exited.

16. An important concept in structured programming is that each control structure has only one entry point and one exit point.

17. Pseudocode is the logical steps to be taken in the solution of a problem written as English statements.

18. Pseudocode is used as an alternative to flowcharting to develop the logic of a program.

19. The advantage of pseudocode is that a great deal of time need not be spent in drawing symbols and determining how to arrange the symbols on a sheet of paper while at the same time attempting to determine program logic.

20. A subroutine is a series of computer instructions which, together, accomplish a given task. A subroutine can be called by other portions of a program to accomplish the task.

21. Structured design is a program design methodology which results in a program consisting of many small portions of code called modules.

22. A module performs a given task within a program.

23. Major processing tasks are obtained by asking the question, "What tasks must be accomplished to obtain the given output from the given input?"

24. The Warnier-Orr design methodology is based upon analyzing the output to be produced from an application and developing modules based upon the processing that must be accomplished to produce the output.

25. The Jackson methodology is based upon the data which is to be processed.

26. When egoless programming is practiced, the individual views his or her program not as an extension of themselves, but rather as a product which should be examined to make it better.

27. A structured walkthrough is an organized review of a program by other programmers.

28. The intent of a walkthrough is to find any errors which have been made in a program.

29. Common design problems include: a) Basic input/output operations; b) Basic calculating, counting records, and accumulating totals; c) Basic comparing operations; d) Interactive programming; e) Arrays and array searching.

30. One of the most basic operations that can be performed on a computer involves reading data into main computer memory and producing output.

31. An end-of-file indicator indicates the end of the data in a sequential file.

32. The basic steps in a input/output program consist of checking to determine if end of file has been reached, displaying a line on the CRT screen, and reading an input record.

33. Totals which are accumulated and then displayed after all records have been processed are called final totals.

34. An area used to count records or other items is called a counter.
35. An area used to accumulate final totals is called an accumulator.
36. Comparing is implemented using the if-then-else control structure.
37. The process of setting values at the beginning of a program is called program initialization.
38. An array (or table) consists of a series of related data items and fields stored in rows and columns.
39. The entries in an array are called array elements.
40. A subscript is a field which contains a value referencing a particular element within an array.
41. A decision table is a graphical representation of the logical decisions that must be made concerning conditions that can occur in a program.
42. The conditions which may occur in a decision table are placed in the condition stub. The actions which may occur are placed in the action stub. Different combinations of conditions are placed in the condition entry part of the decision table. The actions to be taken are placed in the action entry area. The rules specify the combination of conditions that can occur and the corresponding action that should be taken.
43. The programming language used for a program will normally be determined by the systems analyst or project manager.
44. Coding a program involves the actual writing of the detailed programming statements.
45. The basic procedures for testing a program are: a) Test data is created; b) The program is compiled and diagnostic errors are removed; c) The program is tested; d) Errors are corrected until the program is error-free; e) The program is used in a system test.
46. The elements of creating test data are: a) What type of data should be developed? b) Who should develop the test data? c) Who will check the test data?
47. Test data should be designed to find errors in the program.
48. A test plan should specify the number of test runs to be executed, the portions of the program that are to be tested on each run, and the objectives of each test run.
49. When using stub testing, one or more higher-level modules are coded and tested without the remainder of the program being coded, allowing portions of a program to be completed without the entire program being done.
50. The programmer who coded a program should not be the person who creates test data or who determines if the output from a test run is correct.
51. Program efficiency consists of two elements: a) The amount of main computer memory required to store the program when it is processing data; b) The amount of time required by the program to process data.
52. Program documentation consists of a series of documents all intended to provide information concerning a program and how to use the program.
53. Making changes to a program is called program maintenance.

KEY TERMS

Accumulator 16.16
Action entry 16.24
Action stub 16.24
Array elements 16.21
Arrays 16.20
Comparing 16.16
Condition entry 16.24
Condition stub 16.24
Control structures 16.4
Counter 16.16
Decision table 16.24
Do while structure 16.5
Egoless programming 16.12
End-of-file indicator 16.14
Entry point 16.5
Exit point 16.5
Final totals 16.14
Flowcharting 16.2
If-then-else structure 16.5
Jackson methodology 16.11
Looping 16.5
Looping structure 16.5
Maintainable (program) 16.2
Major processing tasks 16.8
Module 16.8
Program development cycle 16.1
Program efficiency 16.28
Program initialization 16.18
Program maintenance 16.29
Program specifications 16.2
Pseudocode 16.6
Reliable (program) 16.2
Robust (program) 16.2
Rules (decision table) 16.24
Sequence control structure 16.4
Structured design 16.8
Structured programming 16.4
Structured walkthrough 16.12
Stub testing 16.27
Subroutine 16.8
Subscript 16.21
Syntax (program) 16.25
Tables 16.20
Warnier-Orr methodology 16.11

REVIEW QUESTIONS

1. What are the steps in the program development cycle? Briefly describe each of them.
2. What is the function of the program specifications? What is the result of these specifications?
3. What is a flowchart? What are its advantages and disadvantages?
4. Describe the three control structures found in structured programming. Draw a small flowchart illustrating each of them.
5. Define an entry point. Define an exit point. What is the single entry point/single exit point rule?
6. Define pseudocode. What is pseudocode used for? Describe its advantages and disadvantages.
7. Describe a subroutine. Give three examples of subroutines.
8. Explain the significance of structured design. Outline a basic methodology to develop the structure of a program.
9. What is egoless programming? What effect does it have on the programming process?
10. What is a walkthrough? What is the intent of a walkthrough? Who participates in a walkthrough? When should a walkthrough be conducted?
11. Identify five common program design problems. Draw a generalized flowchart for two of them.
12. Describe an array and flowchart the logic to search an array.
13. Describe the various elements of a decision table. Devise a logical problem, state the problem in narrative form, and then draw a decision table illustrating the solution to the problem stated.
14. What are the procedures for program testing? Who should prepare test data? Who should check test results?
15. Name the two elements of program efficiency. How can program efficiency affect the use of a program.?

CONTROVERSIAL ISSUES

1. Some veteran programmers who have been writing programs for many years claim that program design is largely a waste of time. Many argue that the logic for a program can be developed just as easily when writing code as when drawing a flowchart or writing pseudocode. Indeed, they say, there is really no difference between pseudocode and real program code. Others counter by saying that the heart of good programming is program design, and that if a program is well designed, anyone who knows a programming language should be able to implement the design in code. Which argument do you think is correct?
2. "Structured Programming — Another Programming Fad" was the title of a paper given at a major industry convention a few years ago. The author claimed that restricting the logic structures used in a program to just the sequence, if-then-else, and do while control structures restricted a programmer to the point that an efficient program could not be written. Further, argued the author, the use of structured programming removes the creativity which is so much a part of computer programming. Was this author correct?

RESEARCH PROJECTS

1. Different design methodologies, ranging from none at all to structured design, are used in information systems departments. Visit some large and small installations in your area and find out how they design their programs. Prepare a report on your findings for your class.
2. Obtain a copy of *The Psychology of Computer Programming* by Dr. Gerald M. Weinberg, published by Van Nostrand Reinhold Company. Pick a chapter in the book and prepare a written or oral report on the chapter. Include the major points that Weinberg makes, the anecdotes he uses to explain his points, and the reasons Weinberg feels as he does.
3. Research and prepare a report on one of the three major design methodologies described in this chapter.

Chapter Seventeen

Careers and the Computer Industry

Objectives

- ☐ Describe the hardware, software, and service elements of the information processing industry
- ☐ Identify job and career opportunities in information systems departments
- ☐ Specify job and career opportunities with respect to hardware manufacturers, software developers, retail stores, education, and other service areas
- ☐ Identify the three broad fields of study in the information processing industry and the career opportunities in each field
- ☐ Describe the professional associations available in the information processing industry
- ☐ Describe the need for professional standards and the role of certification in the information processing industry

Careers and the Computer Industry

Chapter Seventeen

Twenty-five years ago, the data processing industry consisted of the people and resources necessary to program and operate approximately 10,000 mainframe computers housed in centralized computer centers. Most of the computers were manufactured by a few dominant companies, including IBM and Sperry Univac. Computer programming and computer operations were considered new occupational areas which required highly trained technical specialists.

Since that time, the industry has changed dramatically and has experienced explosive growth. Many thousands of companies now manufacture computer hardware and peripheral devices. The design and development of software is a very large and important industry. Retail computer hardware and software stores are found in shopping malls to meet the needs of the owners of home and personal computers. Expenditures in the information processing industry for hardware, software, and personnel currently exceed 100 billion dollars annually. Information processing is one of the world's largest industries.

It is the purpose of this chapter to review the current status of the computer industry, and to describe some of the career opportunities available now and in the future in this dynamic field.

The hardware industry

Today, the hardware portion of the information processing industry includes personal computer manufacturers, small business computer manufacturers, minicomputer and mainframe manufacturers, and manufacturers of peripheral devices including computer terminals, disk drives, and printers (Figure 17–2). Data communications equipment, office automation equipment, and computer-assisted design and computer-assisted manufacturing hardware are an important part of the information processing industry as well.

IBM is the leading manufacturer of mainframe computers. Other major competitors include Sperry Univac, Burroughs, NCR, Control Data, and Honeywell. Although the term minicomputer is becoming difficult to define as the capabilities of

Figure 17–2 Manufacturing terminals is a big business, as shown here where ITT Courier terminals are made.

Figure 17–3 This announcement of a computer-controlled manufacturing machine drew an overflow crowd. Any product associated with computers draws wide attention.

all computers expand, companies that have traditionally been leaders in this area include Digital Equipment, Hewlett-Packard, Data General, and Wang. In the manufacture of personal computers, leaders include IBM, Apple, Tandy, Commodore, and Hewlett-Packard.

Business organizations specializing in specific phases of the information processing industry make product announcements almost daily (Figure 17–3). Companies such as Televideo, Convergent Technologies, Seagate, Tandom, and many others have been formed to meet specialized needs in the industry. Because of the dynamic nature of the industry, it is not unusual to find new companies being formed, achieving a high level of first year sales, and then disappearing from the industry because of a rapidly changing technology.

The software industry

When computers first became commercially available, the computer hardware and software were packaged and sold as a unit. The software supplied with the computer consisted primarily of the operating system and related programming language compilers. Utility programs and a few application programs were sometimes available free of charge from the manufacturer. Specialized applications were almost always designed and programmed in-house by a company's own staff of programmers.

In 1969, when IBM "unbundled" their software by separately pricing the hardware and software, opportunities opened up for independent software companies to design and write software for IBM computers, as well as for other machines. Since that time an entire new industry has emerged — the software industry. Today, many companies design and write software in virtually all application areas. In addition, designing and writing systems software such as data base management systems and data communications software has become a large part of the information processing industry.

Figure 17–4 Millions of personal computers have been sold for use by all members of society. Here, a student uses the Apple IIc to aid in completing homework assignments.

The personal computer has also given great impetus to the software industry. As millions of personal computers were sold (Figure 17–4), a tremendous demand was created for software of all types. The first software companies devoted their efforts to writing game programs for personal computers. As users of personal computers became more sophisticated, a need arose for software which accomplished a myriad of tasks. Thus, companies began specializing in particular application areas, such as educational software, business application software, word processing software, data base software, and graphics software.

Initially, the software industry was considered a "cottage industry"; that is, an industry that required little capital and could be conducted from one's home. The first software companies often consisted of one or two persons working at home and marketing their newly created programs through advertisements in personal computer magazines.

Very quickly, however, software production for personal computers became a very large and important industry. It was found that software packages could generate millions of dollars in revenues. For example, VisiCalc™, one of the first electronic spreadsheet programs for personal computers, has reportedly sold over 600,000 copies, generating more than 40 million dollars in revenues.

Lotus Development Corporation, which was founded in 1982 to develop and market an integrated software package for personal computers called Lotus 1-2-3™, reportedly spent over one million dollars for advertising. The result, however, was sales of over 50 million dollars in the first year! Personal computer software is indeed big business; and it even has its top ten sellers list (Figure 17–5).

Figure 17–5 This example of a software best selling list illustrates how widespread and important the personal computer software business has become.

THIS MONTH'S BUSINESS BEST SELLERS

RANK	PRODUCT	COMMENTS	COMPANY
1.	1-2-3	Combines spreadsheet with graphics and data base. This multifunctional product also includes limited word processing features.	Lotus Development Corp. Cambridge, Mass.
2.	Wordstar	The granddaddy of word processing programs. It's known for its sophisticated, sometimes complex features that can handle the most demanding scientific writing.	Micropro International Corp. San Rafael, Calif.
3.	Dbase II	This database program requires a lot of user interaction. Nevertheless, it's still leading the pack in this software genre.	Ashton-Tate Culver City, Calif.
4.	Multimate	A word processing package that has borrowed a few ideas from dedicated word processing minicomputers.	Softword Systems East Hartford, Conn.
5.	PFS:File	A data handler that allows you to set up a structured filing system of your own design.	Software Publishing Corp. Mountain View, Calif.
6.	Multiplan	Many believe this electronic worksheet is destined to become a classic.	Microsoft, Inc. Bellevue, Wash.
7.	PFS:Write	An easy-to-use word processing program that works well with the data handler program (and a host of others) offered by the same company.	Software Publishing Corp. Mountain View, Calif.
8.	Visicalc	The original electronic worksheet. It allows you to examine practically any "what if" situation a business is likely to encounter.	Visicorp San Jose, Calif.
9.	Wordperfect	An easy-to-use, moderately sophisticated word processing program that provides a full range of print formatting capabilities.	Satellite Software Int'l. Orem, Utah
10.	PFS:Report	A report generator designed to be used with PFS:File	Software Publishing Corp. Mountain View, Calif.

Now, hundreds of companies are producing thousands of software packages each year for personal computers. As large numbers of personal computers are sold, the demand for new software products should be even greater. It is predicted that the software industry will grow at a rate exceeding 25 percent for the next five years, with sales in excess of $30 billion expected.

Figure 17–6 In training courses such as this, executives with little knowledge of information processing can be taught the fundamentals by experienced, knowledgeable instructors.

Other areas of information processing

In addition to the hardware and software industries, there are many other specialized groups that, in total, make up the information processing industry. For example, office automation, which refers to an integrated collection of electronic devices used to increase office productivity, affects the more than 50 million people who currently work in offices. To meet the growing demand for new equipment, services, supplies, and training for office automation, an expenditure of close to $200 billion will be required in the next five years.

There are some companies in the information processing industry that own large and medium-sized computers to provide computing resources and services for other companies. These companies, often called **service bureaus**, receive data from their clients and then process their clients' payrolls, perform their billing, and perform other types of business functions as well, all for a fee. The client companies feel this approach is less expensive, more efficient, and less troublesome than having their own information systems department.

The widespread use of personal computers has led to the development of **retail computer stores**. More than 3,000 retail stores sell a variety of personal computers, computer supplies, and software. Retail computer hardware and software stores have become a multi-million dollar industry in the past few years.

Computer **education and training** has also evolved into a large industry. Numerous seminars, short courses, and workshops are offered in cities throughout the world to provide state-of-the-art training on the latest technological developments (Figure 17–6). Topics range from the use of word processing software to artificial intelligence. Cost of such instruction is in the range of $100 to $500 per day per person.

The information processing industry is touching the lives of almost every individual in every profession.

CAREERS IN INFORMATION PROCESSING

As might be imagined from the previous description of the projected growth in the information processing industry, numerous career opportunities in a wide variety of areas are available. In information systems departments, opportunities can range from such diverse jobs as data entry operators to business or scientific programmers. Those with an entrepreneurial flare will find opportunities in software development, consulting and education, and other areas as well as society scrambles to become computer literate and take advantage of the use of computers. Many opportunities exist in both small and large companies for those interested in pursuing a career in the information processing industry.

Career opportunities in information systems departments

Although it is difficult to generalize, the information systems department in many companies and governmental agencies can broadly be classified into five main groups: 1) Operations; 2) Data administration; 3) Systems analysis and design; 4) Programming; 5) Information center. These groups are commonly under control of a vice president of the information systems department (Figure 17-7). Opportunities in each of these areas are explained below.

Operations

Operations personnel are responsible for carrying out the day-to-day tasks that must be performed within the computer center of the information systems department to ensure that all processing occurs in a timely and reliable fashion. Tasks performed by operations personnel include operating the computer, preparing input data, checking and disbursing output data and materials, and scheduling the computer

Figure 17-7 This organization chart shows some of the positions that are available in a typical information systems department.

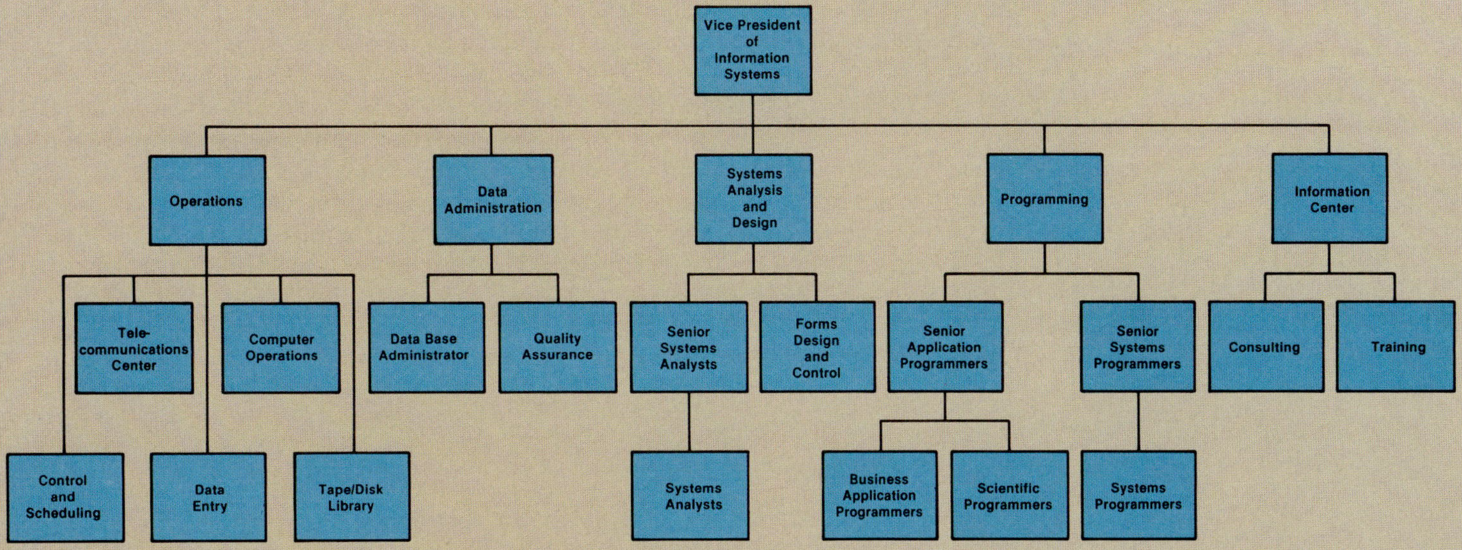

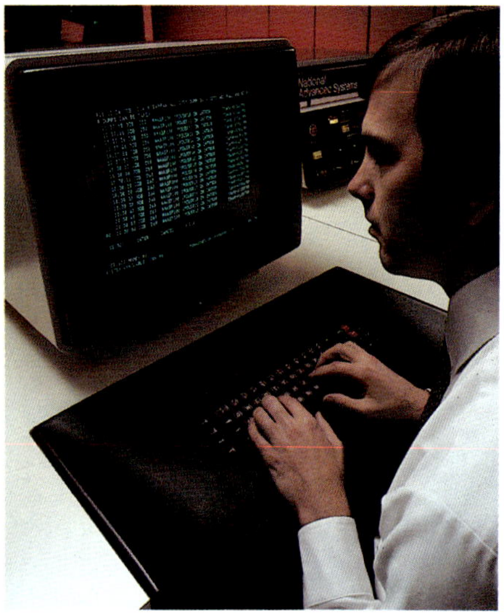

equipment. The operations section of the information systems department offers a number of entry level positions for those just beginning their careers.

One entry level job position in the operations section is computer operator. A **computer operator** runs the computer, ensuring that scheduled jobs are processed. Among the responsibilities of a computer operator are monitoring a CRT display to review current jobs being executed, mounting tapes and disks, loading printers with paper, removing printed reports from the printer after processing is completed, and similar tasks (Figure 17-8). Some two-year colleges and private business schools offer training in the area of computer operations. Computer operators earn approximately $15,000 to $25,000 a year.

A large number of support personnel work to ensure that computer operators can perform their jobs. One quite important group are those people who staff the **tape and disk libraries** (Figure 17-9). These people make sure the tape and disk files required for processing on the computer are available to the computer operators. A position in the tape library is normally an entry level position, with pay just a little less than computer operators.

Figure 17-8 (above) Computer operators are responsible for keeping the computer operating, which includes entering data and reacting to messages from the computer software.

Figure 17-9 (right) A tape/disk library is a busy part of the information systems department. All tapes and disks created on the computers within the department are stored in the library. Quite often, as in this picture, the storage locations of the tapes and disks are monitored using a small computer.

Figure 17-10 (below) The telecommunications center of a large information systems department must be staffed by people knowledgeable in both computing and data communications.

The **telecommunications center** of a modern information systems department requires people knowledgeable in both computers and data communications (Figure 17-10). The **data entry center** employs people who are responsible for keying large volumes of data, on a production basis, for mostly batch processing. This position of **data entry operator** requires accurate, rapid keying ability. The need for data entry operators, who are paid roughly $12,000 to $18,000 per year, has declined in recent years because many companies now require data to be keyed at its source by individuals working in the particular department where the data is generated.

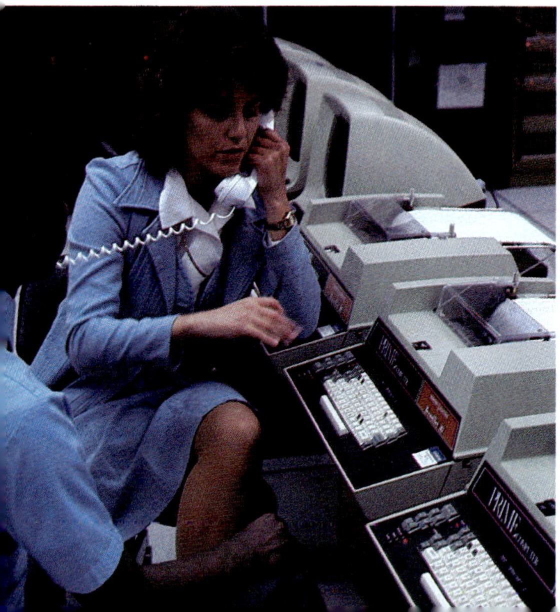

Control and scheduling personnel are responsible for scheduling computer time, ensuring that the input data required for processing is available, performing data editing using batch controls to verify valid data is entered into the computer, and similar tasks. These people must be knowledgeable in not only operation center activities but activities in the user departments as well.

Data administration

With the widespread use of data base systems, the task of data administration has become very important within an organization. The person most responsible in the data administration section of the department for data control is the **data base administrator**, who develops and maintains the data base, controls updating the data base, and often controls who within the business organization has access to the data base.

A data base administrator normally has at least a bachelor's degree and often a master's degree. The person is quite experienced in all aspects of information processing and must be knowledgeable about the business as well. The average salary range is $25,000 to about $40,000 per year, but some data base administrators earn as much as $70,000 per year.

Systems analysis and design

The systems analysis and design section of the information systems department is where new application systems are studied, defined, and developed. The individuals who perform these tasks are called **systems analysts** (Figure 17–11).

When designing a system, analysts work with management and the people within the company who will use the system to ensure that the output from the system will meet the needs of the user.

Most companies require systems analysts to have a minimum of four years of college, a strong business background, and a broad technical knowledge of both computer hardware and software. Many universities offer courses in the field of study called **management information systems** or **computer information systems.** These programs are designed to prepare individuals for entry into the information processing industry as systems analysts. Experienced systems analysts commonly earn $25,000 to $50,000 per year.

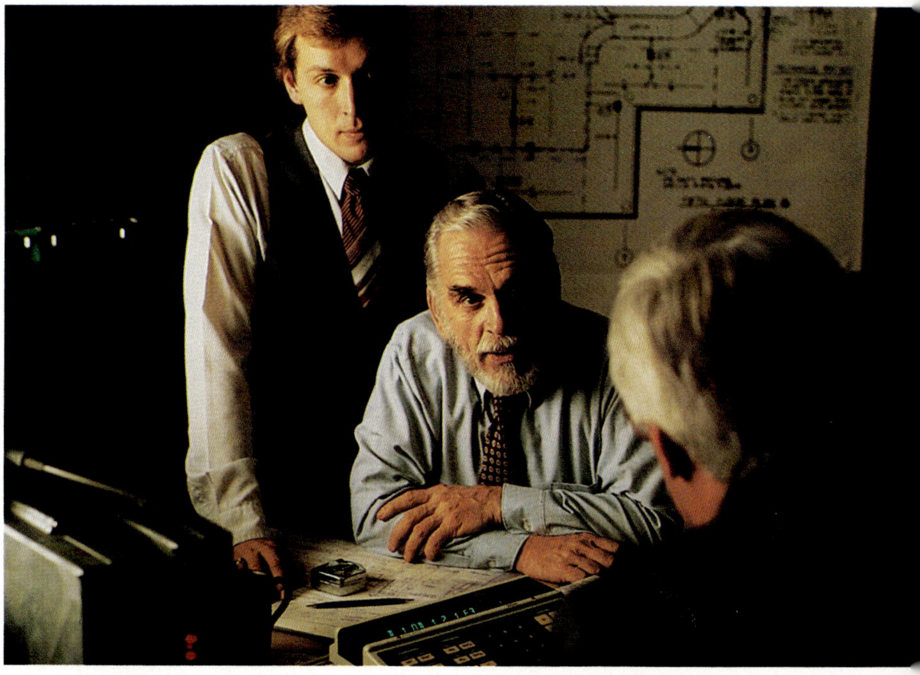

Figure 17–11 Systems analysts are the liason between the information systems department and the user. Therefore, as in this picture, analysts must quite often visit the user in the user's environment in order to ascertain the user's needs.

Computer programming

Computer programming also offers excellent job opportunities. There are three types of computer programmers generally found in information systems departments: 1) Business application programmers; 2) Systems programmers; 3) Scientific programmers. **Business application programmers** write programs which process business applications, such as payroll, accounts receivable, accounts payable, and inventory control. The programming language most often used for business application programming is COBOL, although a significant amount of business programming on small computers is done in BASIC. A business application programmer must be thoroughly trained in one or more programming languages and be capable of designing the logic to solve specific problems. A knowledge of accounting and business procedures is also valuable.

Many large companies require business application programmers to have a four-year college degree. Others will accept a two-year technical degree in computer programming. Many schools, both two-year and four-year, private and public, offer comprehensive training programs for individuals desiring to pursue business application programming as a career.

Business application programmers normally earn $16,000 to $36,000 per year, although individuals with special skills such as a knowledge of data communications programming might earn considerably more.

Systems programmers are responsible for maintaining the operating system utilized with the computer, making updates to the operating system as they are announced, ensuring that the data base and data communications software is operating properly, and generally ensuring the computer is operational from a software point of view. Systems programmers usually require an extensive technical background in assembler language for the specific computer upon which they are working.

Individuals who wish to become systems programmers frequently major in a field called **computer science** on the four-year college level. Computer science programs require considerable course work in mathematics and place emphasis upon such aspects of computer software as compiler and operating system design. Systems programming is one of the highest paid of the technical positions within the information systems department, with salaries for experienced systems programmers exceeding $40,000 per year.

Scientific programming, as the name implies, refers to programming computers for scientific or engineering activities. This might include such diverse activities as writing a program to control a nuclear reactor or a space vehicle, or to perform long range weather forecasting. Individuals who are scientific programmers normally have a bachelor's or master's degree in the area of mathematics or computer science.

Information center

As noted in Chapter One, the information center is an area within the information systems department containing hardware devices that are available for individuals within the company to use. The major reason for an information center is to give employees a simple, effective way to meet their own departmental and individual information processing needs. As an aid to employees using the information center, most companies provide teaching and consulting services.

The people who do the teaching and consulting in the information center are usually experienced programmers and analysts who are able to answer most questions and solve most problems of the employees. These people must be technically capable, patient and understanding, and highly motivated to make the user's experience as pleasant and useful as possible.

Information systems department management

Within the information systems department, management is required at all levels. Each of the sections, such as operations, systems analysis and design, and programming requires a manager. In addition, depending upon the size of the information systems department, additional management personnel may be required. For example, project managers may be in charge of the personnel committed to a particular project within a programming section. The project manager may report to the programming manager. Similarly, the data entry group may have a manager who reports to the operations manager. In most cases, management personnel are experienced people who have proven their abilities and skills in the information processing industry.

In addition, the entire department will have a manager or director. Many companies have established the position of Vice President of Information Systems, reporting directly to the President of the corporation (Figure 17–12). The individual in this position normally has many years of experience in the information processing industry, has at least a bachelor's degree, and in most instances, a master's or doctor's degree, and possesses management skills as well as technical skills.

Figure 17–12 The Vice-President of Information Systems (left) often reports directly to the President of the company (right).

The Vice President of Information Systems is responsible for overall operation of the information systems department. In some instances, this means the person is responsible for millions of dollars worth of computer equipment as well as many hundreds of employees and the well-being of the entire corporation, since information proceessing is so critical to the success of most companies. The salary for the Vice President of Information Systems varies considerably based upon the size and type of organization, but typically runs from a low of $40,000 to well over $100,000.

Summary — careers in information systems departments

Career opportunities and pay ranges vary considerably depending upon the part of the country in which one is working and the size of the company. In any case, however, the opportunities to work in the information systems department of a company are considerable. Most estimates of the growth of computing within companies show that jobs and opportunities will continue to be available for many years to come.

OTHER CAREER OPPORTUNITIES

The explosive growth of the information processing industry has led to career opportunities in many areas other than the information systems department of a company. Additional jobs may be found working for computer manufacturers, software companies, service and supplies companies, retail computer stores, and educational institutions. Some of these employment areas are discussed in the following sections.

Computer manufacturers

Companies that manufacture mainframes, minicomputers, and/or personal computers offer many job opportunities for individuals desiring to enter the profession. These jobs include such diverse tasks as sales representatives, systems engineers, computer technicians, computer engineers and designers, and research scientists.

Sales representatives, after comprehensive training by the company, call upon prospective customers with the intent of selling them the hardware the company

Figure 17–13 Testing components of computers is an important job that must be performed by personnel employed by computer manufacturing companies.

manufactures. Many such sales jobs are grouped into specialties. For example, a sales representative might be specially trained in banking applications and sell only to banks; others might be trained in hospital applications, and still others in city government. Such jobs may require substantial travel but can offer high financial rewards for the successful salesperson. A four-year college degree is normally required, with training in computers and business desirable.

Systems engineer is a term used by some companies to describe individuals who are technical specialists and serve as consultants to customers after the customer's computer has been installed. These individuals assist customers in both applications and systems programming, and attempt to ensure that the computer is operating effectively. These jobs commonly require a four-year degree with a high degree of technical knowledge in applications and systems programming.

For those interested in the electronics of the computer, jobs are available that vary from assembling computers, testing computers (Figure 17–13), and repairing computers at a customer's installation to designing and engineering new products (Figure 17–14). Assembling computers will require some training in electronics. Testing and repairing computers usually requires at least several years of technical training in electronics. Engineering and designing computers and the associated hardware requires at least a bachelor's degree in engineering, mathematics or an associated field, with a master's degree or a doctorate quite often a necessity. All of these areas offer excellent job opportunities for people interested in electronics.

Figure 17–14 Engineers employed by computer manufacturers are involved in many different areas of computer design and engineering. Here, an engineer reviews the design of a semiconductor chip.

Software companies

Many companies produce and sell software. These companies often specialize in a particular application area. For example, some companies specialize in designing and writing business accounting software, such as payroll, accounts receivable, and billing. These software companies will often tailor their generalized packages to the needs of the individual customer.

Other companies specialize in the development of operating systems software, data base management systems software, communications software, or special packages that make operating systems software supplied by the manufacturer more efficient.

Numerous companies have been formed to develop software for personal computers, such as games, educational software, and word processing, data base, or graphics packages.

Most software companies require highly skilled systems analysts and programmers to develop and write the actual software, but many of these companies also require people to perform the same tasks as are found in information systems departments, such as computer operations and data entry functions. Numerous job opportunities are available. One recent research study indicated that the typical software company had a six year backlog of projects waiting to be programmed.

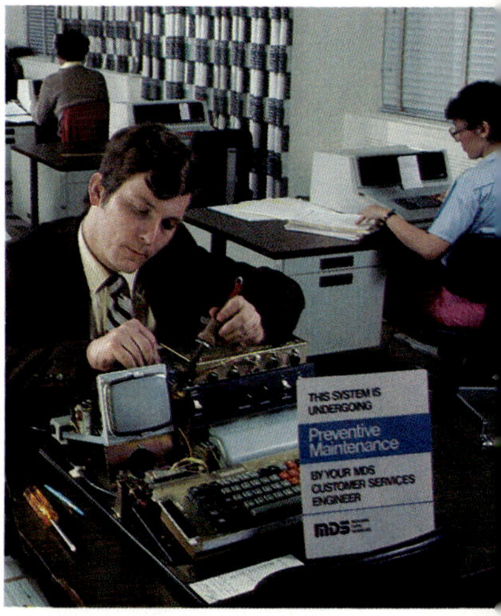

Figure 17–15 Preventive maintenance is the process of testing and repairing equipment on regularly scheduled intervals rather than when a piece of equipment fails. Generally, preventive maintenance saves a great deal of money. Both computer manufacturers and companies which specialize in computer maintenance offer preventive maintenance.

Service and supplies companies

In an industry as large as the information processing industry, a vast network of support companies is necessary in order to make available the supplies required by the industry. For example, millions of tons of paper are used each year by printers. Floppy disks are used by the millions on personal computers. Thousands of reels of tape are required each year on mainframe computers. These and many other supplies are required in the information processing industry. The companies which make and sell these products are an important part of the industry.

Companies which provide needed services, such as repairing computer hardware and performing preventive maintenance (Figure 17–15), are also an integral part of the industry. These companies and many more all require well-trained and highly motivated employees.

An exciting and interesting service industry is the magazine and publishing industry associated with information processing. Numerous magazines cover the field in detail, ranging from engineering magazines describing the latest in chips and semiconductor technology to home computer magazines demonstrating how to use the latest word processing software. Those who are interested in writing and computers will find ample opportunity to be part of the field.

Retail computer stores

For individuals particularly interested in the use and application of the personal computer in the home and business, working in retail computer stores could provide an employment opportunity. People seeking employment in retail computer stores should have a knowledge of the different types of personal computers and be interested and knowledgeable (or be willing to gain the knowledge) of application software.

In addition, most computer stores offer computer repair services, opening employment opportunities to those who enjoy working with electronics (Figure 17–16). There are now over 3,000 retail computer stores in operation, and many more are expected to open in the future.

Figure 17–16 Many computer retail stores offer computer repair services to their customers.

Teaching as a career

Individuals interested in both information processing and the field of education have unlimited teaching opportunities at all levels of education, from elementary school through college.

On the **elementary school** level, personal computers

are being used in all grades for computer-assisted instruction and even for teaching programming. The programming language Logo is usually taught in elementary schools. Many opportunities exist for not only teaching on this level, but also serving as a coordinator or consultant to the teachers in elementary schools. Job duties for coordinators and consultants include evaluating and selecting hardware and software suitable for the various grade levels, teacher training, curriculum development, and consulting. A degree in education is normally required, together with some course work in computers and an interest in educational technology.

Similar opportunities exist at the middle school level as well as in high schools (Figure 17–17). In some **high schools**, vocational courses are also taught. **Vocational courses** are designed to prepare students for entry level positions in the information processing industry.

Figure 17–17 The challenge and fulfillment of teaching about computers makes an attractive career opportunity. Here, an instructor aids a student using one of the many personal computers in the classroom.

Severe shortages of teachers exist on the community college level and the university level in the information processing field. **Community colleges** often require advanced degrees and some practical experience in the field. These schools are often quite willing to employ part-time instructors, however. Therefore, programmers and systems analysts who work for a company during the day may have the opportunity to teach during the evenings or on weekends.

At the **university** level, opportunities are available in computer science departments, management information systems or computer information systems departments, engineering departments, colleges of education, and other disciplines as well. The shortage of qualified individuals at the university level is acute. Most schools require a doctorate degree. The opportunity not only to teach but also to conduct research in a desired field is available at the university.

PREPARING FOR THE INFORMATION PROCESSING PROFESSION

Once an individual has decided to enter the information processing industry, the individual must obtain the proper education and training. What education is obtained and how it is obtained is generally determined by answering two basic questions: 1) What career opportunity is to be pursued? 2) How many years can be devoted to education?

The three broad fields of study in the information processing industry are (Figure 17–18): 1) Computer technology; 2) Business information processing; 3) Computer science. Within each of these fields are career opportunities and also study requirements. The paragraphs below discuss each of these fields with the intent of giving guidance in answering the two basic questions.

The field of **computer technology** deals to a great extent with computer hardware and the electronic components comprising computer hardware. Therefore, a person who pursues computer technology as a field of study should be interested in becoming a computer technician or computer design engineer, or entering a related field. Anyone studying in the computer technology area should be interested in the field of electronics.

An individual interested in the business aspects of the information processing industry should normally select the **business information processing** category. Course

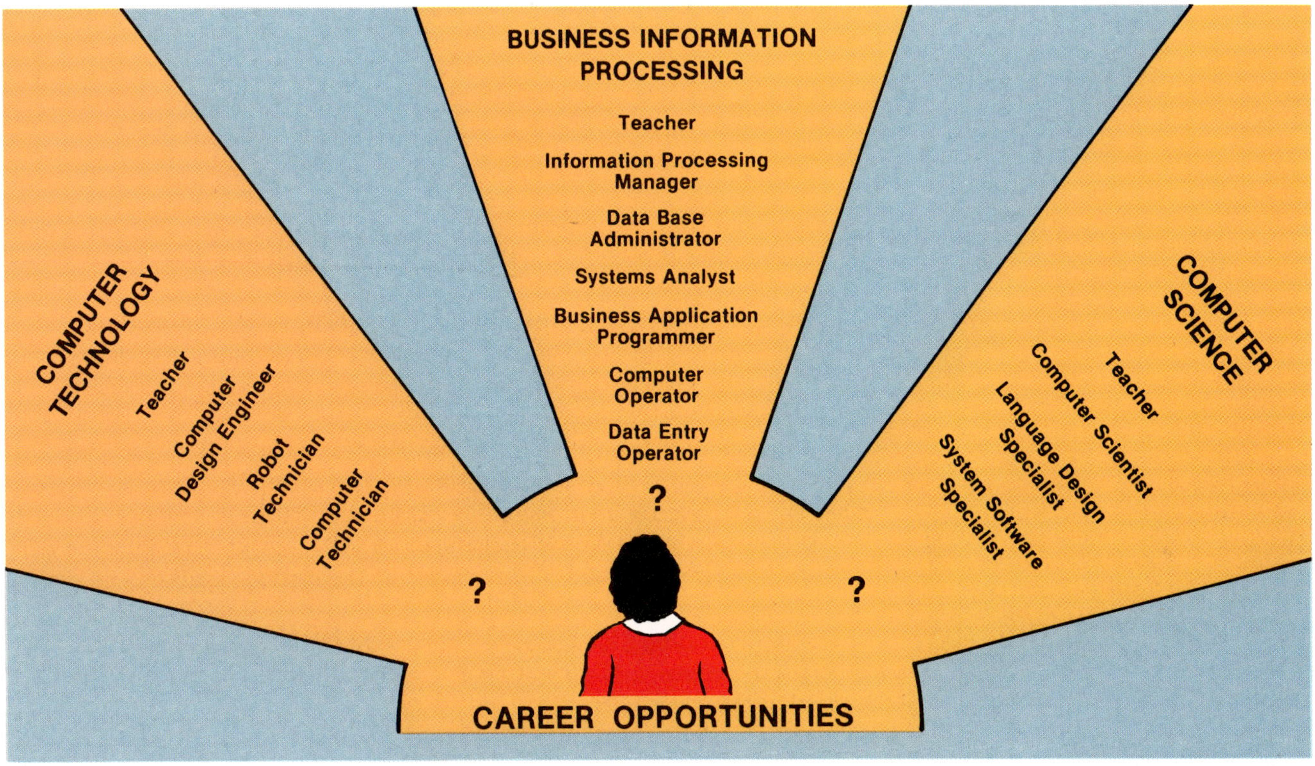

Figure 17–18 The three broad fields of study in the information processing industry are computer technology, business information processing, and computer science. In most cases, a person wishing to enter the profession must make a decision concerning which field of study to pursue.

work to prepare individuals for work as data entry operators, computer operators, and computer programmers is found in some high schools and most two-year colleges. Most four-year colleges and universities offer course work in the computer information systems department, or the school of business, to prepare people for employment as programmer/analysts, systems analysts, data base adminstrators, and information processing managers.

Those desiring to become software specialists or research computer scientists should pursue the **computer science** career field. Students in this career field take considerable course work in mathematics, the design and construction of compilers and operating systems, artificial intelligence, and similar topics. Most major universities offer comprehensive programs in computer science.

For some of the new emerging career opportunities in the information processing industry, such as a retail computer store owner, a broad educational background is desirable and should include some electronics training, some business course work, and some knowledge of computer science and business information processing.

PROFESSIONAL ACTIVITIES

Because of the rapid changes in the information processing industry, people entering the profession must be committed to life-long learning. This life-long learning may be accomplished by attending one- or two-day workshops that are offered by many companies to provide state-of-the-art training; by attending continuing education courses offered at many high schools, community colleges, and universities; by attending vendor training schools; by joining professional associations; by attending conferences and conventions; and by reading the many magazines, journals, and books produced about the industry each year.

Professional associations

Professional associations are formed when there is a group of people within a profession who have a common interest and desire to share knowledge. There are many professional associations in the information processing industry for virtually all areas of interest. Some of the associations which have been influential in the industry include:

Association for Computing Machinery (ACM) — An association composed of persons interested in computer science and computer science education. The association also has many special interest groups such as computer graphics, data base, and business.

Association of Information Systems Professionals — This association was originally aimed at word processing professionals, but now includes a much broader interest area, including office automation.

Association of Systems Management (ASM) — A group composed of individuals interested in the improvement of the systems analysis and design field.

Data Processing Management Association (DPMA) — A professional association composed of programmers, systems analysts, and information processing managers.

Institute of Electrical and Electronics Engineers (IEEE) and IEEE Computer Society — Organizations joined by engineers and computer scientists. Originally intended for hardware people, IEEE is now equally active in the software engineering field.

Each of the above associations has chapters throughout the United States (several throughout the world), and offers monthly meetings, sponsors workshops and seminars for members (Figure 17–19), sponsors national conventions, and publishes extensive lists of magazines, journals, and tutorial documents. Many have special interest groups within the organization for people with an interest in a specialized area. In addition, the organizations develop curriculum for all levels of educational institutions in an effort to ensure quality education.

February 14–16
■ **ACM Annual Computer Science Conference**
Philadelphia, Pa. Sponsor: Association for Computing Machinery. Conf. chm: Frank L. Friedman, Dept. of Computing and Information Science, Temple University, Computing Center Bldg. 303, Philadelphia, PA 19122; 215 787–1912.

February 16–17
■ **ACM SIGCSE Technical Symposium**
Philadelphia, Pa. Sponsor: ACM SIGCSE (Computer Science Education). Gen. chm: Richard H. Austing, Dept. of Computer Science, University of Maryland, College Park, MD 20742; 301 454–4245.

February 20–22
Office Automation Conference
Los Angeles, Calif. Sponsor: American Federation of Information Processing Societies contact: AFIPS, 1815 N. Lynn Street, Arlington, VA 22209; 703 558-3617.

March 6–8
International Zurich Seminar
Zurich, Switzerland. Sponsor: IEEE Switzerland Chapter on Digital Communication Systems. Contact: U. Bapst, IBM Research Lab., Saumerstrasse 4, CH-8803 Rüschlikon, Switzerland.

March 8–9
8th Conference on Programming Languages and Program Development
Zurich, Switzerland. Sponsors: Gesellschaft für Informatik and ACM Swiss Chapter. Conf. chm: U. Ammann, Contraves AG Abt. ESI, P.O. Box, CH-8052 Zurich, and H. Hinterberger, Inst. für Informatik ETH, CH-8092 Zurich.

March 19–21
■ **ACM Northeast Regional Conference**
Lowell, Mass. Sponsor: ACM Northeast Region. Conf. chm: Bryan Kocher, Northeast Region Rep., 250 Edge Hill Road, Sharon, MA 02067; 617 895-4700 or 784-3493.

March 21–23
■ **ACM SIGUCCS Computer Center Management Symposium**
St. Louis, Mo. Sponsor: ACM SIGUCCS. Conf. chm: William P. Heinbecker, Computer Center, 8001 Natural Bridge Road, St. Louis, MO 63121.

March 21–23
International Symposium on the Performance of Computer-Communication Systems
Zurich, Switzerland. Sponsors: IFIP WG7.3, IFIP TC6, ITC, INRIA, IBM. Contact: Werner Bux & Harry Rudin, IBM Zurich Research Laboratory, Saumerstrasse 4, CH-8803 Ruschlikon, Switzerland.

March 26–28
■ **Seventh International Conference on Software Engineering**
Orlando, Fla. Sponsors: ACM SIGSOFT, IEEE Com-

Figure 17–19 This list of conferences and seminars is representative of the types of activities found within the professional societies.

There are many other groups for nearly every area of interest, including Association of Women in Computing, Association of Records Managers, National Computer Graphics Association, Telecommunications Association, and many others.

Special interest groups exist for nearly every computer manufacturer and computer type. The personal computer industry has spawned computer clubs for users of Apple computers, Tandy computers, IBM computers, and others. Software users of particular packages have formed their own groups as well. These groups provide an excellent source of information for those just getting started in the computer field.

For anyone employed in or associated with the information processing industry, active participation in one or more professional associations is strongly recommended.

The need for professional standards

When a computer issues an inaccurate credit rating for a customer and the customer is denied credit, the computer is blamed for the error. Similarly, when a police officer stops a motorist for a traffic violation, makes an inquiry into a criminal network data base, receives a message that there are outstanding arrest warrants for the person, and places the person under arrest only to find out later that the message was in error, the computer receives the blame.

To those knowledgeable in information processing, it is obvious the computer was not to blame. Rather, the errors were made because of the incompetencies or carelessness of the programmers and systems analysts who did not provide safeguards to prevent these types of actions from occurring.

In each of the examples, an element of public safety and welfare was involved. In many areas of life where public safety and welfare is a consideration, society has seen fit to authorize governmental agencies to license personnel prior to allowing them to practice their profession. Thus, doctors must be licensed to practice medicine, attorneys to practice law, nurses to practice nursing, and others such as real estate agents and barbers must be licensed as well.

Some have suggested that because much of what is done in the information processing world has an effect on public safety and welfare, information processing professionals should be licensed by governmental agencies. This area is one that generates strong emotions and is still highly debated within the industry. Some of the issues are: should programmers and systems analysts be required to pass a rigid licensing examination before being allowed to practice their skills; or should programmers be required to carry malpractice insurance and be legally liable for errors in their programs that adversely affect public safety and welfare.

Should computer professionals be certified?

Although the industry does not have governmental certification at this time, the **Institute for the Certification of Computer Professionals (ICCP)** has been formed as a nonprofit organization for the purpose of testing and certifying the knowledge and skills of those in the computer profession.

The ICCP currently administers the **Certificate in Data Processing Examination** (Figure 17–20). This examination, which was originated by the Data Processing Management Association (DPMA) in 1962, contains five sections: 1) Computer equipment; 2) Computer programming and software; 3) Principles of management; 4) Accounting and quantitative methods; 5) Systems. To be eligible to take the examination, a person must have a minimum of five years' experience in the information processing industry. People who pass the examination are authorized to place the initials CDP after their name. The holder of the Certificate in Data Processing must subscribe to a code of ethics, conduct, and good practice.

The ICCP also administers the Certificate in Computer Programming (CCP) examination, which tests a common core of programming knowledge, and then provides three specialized tests in the areas of business programming, scientific programming, and systems programming.

The purpose of the certification movement is

Data Processing Management Association
DPMA
Be it known that George W. Abbott
has successfully completed all prescribed requirements and is hereby awarded by the Directors of the Association the professional
Certificate in Data Processing
In Witness whereof, we have subscribed our signatures under the seal of the Association this 4th day of September 1962
DATA PROCESSING MANAGEMENT ASSOCIATION DPMA 1951
EXECUTIVE DIRECTOR
INTERNATIONAL PRESIDENT

Figure 17–20 This is a copy of the first CDP certificate, granted to George W. Abbott, CDP, on September 4, 1962. The certificate was donated to the Smithsonian Institution by Abbott on October 12, 1977.

to upgrade the profession and recognize those in the industry who have attained a high level of competence. At this point in time, certification is voluntary and is offered through the profession itself.

Summary

The information processing industry has emerged as one of the world's largest industries, with sales of computer hardware, software, and services exceeding $100 billion annually. The growth in this industry has resulted in numerous job opportunities in many different categories with varying educational requirements. Career opportunities in computer technology, business information processing, and computer science offer challenges to individuals with a wide range of interests and abilities.

KEY TERMS

Association for Computing Machinery (ACM) 17.14
Association of Information Systems Professionals 17.14
Association of Systems Management (ASM) 17.14
Business application programmers 17.7
Business information processing 17.12
Certificate in Data Processing Examination 17.15
Community colleges 17.12
Computer information systems 17.7
Computer operator 17.6
Computer programming 17.7
Computer science 17.8, 17.13
Computer technology 17.12
Control and scheduling personnel 17.6
Data base administrator 17.6
Data entry center 17.6
Data entry operator 17.6
Data Processing Management Association (DPMA) 17.14
Education and training 17.4
Elementary school 17.11
High schools 17.12
IEEE Computer Society 17.14
Institute for the Certification of Computer Professionals (ICCP) 17.15
Institute of Electrical and Electronics Engineers (IEEE) 17.14
Management information systems 17.7
Retail computer stores 17.4
Sales representatives 17.9
Scientific programming 17.8
Service bureaus 17.4
Systems analysts 17.7
Systems engineer 17.10
Systems programmers 17.8
Tape and disk libraries 17.6
Telecommunications center 17.6
University 17.12
Vocational courses 17.12

RESEARCH PROJECTS

1. Salaries vary from place to place and year to year for jobs in the information processing industry. Many industry magazines contain national salary surveys on a yearly basis. Find a national salary survey in a magazine. Then, contact the personnel offices of some local businesses and determine the salaries paid for the same jobs as in the magazine. Create a chart showing the national salaries from the magazine versus the local salaries you discovered.

Chapter Eighteen

Computers in Our Society

Objectives

- ☐ Identify issues facing society as the computer era matures, including computer crime and the invasion of privacy
- ☐ Describe some of the moral issues facing society with respect to computers and information processing
- ☐ Demonstrate an understanding of the ethical problems facing the information processing industry by taking concrete positions on certain ethical questions

Computers in Our Society

Chapter Eighteen

"If every computer in the world were to suddenly go dead, planes would not fly, trains would not run, traffic lights would not change, banks would have to close, space projects would be aborted, and department stores and grocery stores would not be able to sell . . . . if computers were suddenly silenced the world would be thrown into instant chaos . . ." There is little doubt, as expressed by this paragraph from the booklet, *The Computers Are Coming*, by David W. Webber, that the computer is an integral part of the world's activities. With millions of computers in the office, in manufacturing plants, in schools, and in homes, it is easy to stand in awe of the tremendous technological achievements which have been made during the last forty years.

It is now apparent that experience with computers must be a part of the education of all members of society. An individual cannot fully understand our emerging culture and be a productive citizen without a first-hand knowledge of how to use and apply computers to the solution of everyday problems.

It cannot be assumed, however, that the computer together with other technological advancements will be the solution to all of the world's problems. Some social scientists have begun to question whether technology and the remarkable advances in the computer industry will ultimately contribute to the quality of life for the next generation. Is it possible, they ask, that the misuse of the computer will threaten many basic freedoms which people enjoy, result in mass unemployment, and alter our lifestyle in a negative manner?

Paul V. Galvin, in a commencement address at Loyola University in Chicago, stated, "In human society there is moral as well as material need. Great technical advances do not preclude for one moment the all important requirement of moral order. Regardless of the technical marvels, affairs of human beings must be managed by people with justice, wisdom, honesty, and ability."

It is the purpose of this chapter to review some of the important social issues facing a society which is undergoing rapid technological change, and to pose as yet unanswered questions concerning the use of the computer in this society.

The computer and information revolution

Social scientists who study the way people live and how societies change have observed that the world is rapidly changing from what has been called the "industrial age" to a "computer or information age."

In the industrial age, brought about by the industrial revolution over 200 years ago, profound changes took place in society. There was a shifting of population from the farm to the city. A shift occurred in the types of jobs people performed and the way in which people worked. Large numbers of individuals changed from agricultural workers to factory workers. Hand-crafted goods were replaced by machine produced goods. The use of machinery required new job skills, and the structure of business organizations changed. Businesses employing hundreds of workers were created in large industrial centers.

It is now apparent that major societal changes are again taking place. These changes, brought about by the computer, are dramatically altering the way people live and work. Social scientists predict that these changes are as significant to this generation as the industrial revolution was to earlier generations. Through the use of the computer and the electronic processing of information, the manner in which people play, the way they communicate, how they learn, where they learn, and where they work will be substantially changed in the years to come. Computerized games, computerized banking and shopping, computerized access to newspapers and other information sources, and computerized robots to automate factory processes are but a part of today's emerging lifestyle.

THE IMPACT OF THE PERSONAL COMPUTER ON SOCIETY

In 1977, the first fully assembled personal computer appeared on the market. Today, there are nearly ten million personal computers in use in the home, in elementary schools, high schools, colleges and universities, and businesses. It is predicted that by 1990, as many as 50 million personal computers will be in use. The personal computer is dramatically altering the way we learn, the way we receive and communicate information, and the way decisions are made in businesses.

The need for computer literacy

With the widespread use of the personal computer, many authorities in the field of education have pointed out the need for computer literacy. Some authorities have even indicated that basic skills for survival in modern society include reading, writing, arithmetic, and a knowledge of computers.

Unfortunately, there is no universal agreement as to what the term "computer literacy" means. Some feel computer literacy means knowing how to make the computer "compute"; that is, knowing how to program computers in one or more programming languages. These individuals advocate teaching computer programming beginning in elementary schools, and continuing this education throughout all grade levels. Upon graduation from high school, the computer literate student will be able to direct the computer to solve nearly any required problem, they argue.

Others feel that knowing how to program is merely a small segment of computer literacy. These people claim the major emphasis in schools should be on teaching how to effectively use the many software packages that are available, so that students will be knowledgeable in using word processing systems, home accounting systems, and similar software packages that will allow them to be more productive citizens in their personal and professional lives. Some folks argue computer literacy is a study of social issues.

Still others suggest that computer literacy education is not required. These individuals suggest that computers are being so rapidly integrated into our society that using a computer will be as common as using a telephone or a video tape recorder, and that special education will not be necessary.

Regardless of one's definition of computer literacy, it is recognized by most that learning to use a computer is indeed an important skill in modern society.

The personal computer in the home

With the increased use of personal computers in the home and the ability of personal computers to communicate with other computers, some authorities predict a dramatic change in lifestyle for a large segment of our population. The term "electronic cottage" has been used to describe a society in which the home becomes the central focal point for education, entertainment, and even working.

With the ability to use computer-assisted instruction in the home and the ability to access large data bases such as information contained in libraries, some futurists maintain that much of the education now taking place in schools could just as well take place in the home. The computer and related video games can and do serve as a source of entertainment.

Today, millions of people travel millions of miles to work each day. Could not many of the jobs performed at one's company be performed at home using a personal computer communicating with other computers? Couldn't computer programmers just as easily work at home? Won't many executives perform their tasks while traveling? (Figure 18-2). Couldn't word processing operators and others using computers in their daily job activities complete many of their tasks at home?

Home banking, home shopping, and voting in public elections using a computer in the home are all technologically possible. Do these activities reflect the world of tomorrow?

Figure 18-2 The executive riding a train to work in the morning can now prepare memos and other documents required for the day while traveling. Portable computers are significantly changing the times and places people can use computers.

The effect of computers on people in their work environment

Much has been written about how computers can improve productivity in businesses at all levels — in the office, in the warehouse, in design and manufacturing, and in the executive office. Little research has been done in the past, however, on the effects the computer is having on people, their attitudes, and feelings in this new computerized environment. It is now being recognized that computers do more than just improve productivity. Computers are causing fundamental changes to occur in the business organization. Job duties are changing, job titles are changing, and even more importantly, the nature of the work is changing. Some jobs will disappear and new job titles and responsibilities will appear.

A vice president of a large office equipment manufacturer stated, "Office automation will enable American business to create 20 million new jobs before the end of the century." The local leader of a service employees union countered, "There are 20 million people in this country whose jobs will be put at risk in one way or another by office automation." Regardless of which statement one accepts as being factual, almost all authorities agree that the use of computers will radically change the way work is done.

It is often the case that when computers are utilized in a system, those jobs requiring the fewest job skills are the jobs that are replaced. Thus, if individuals are to remain employed, their job skills must be upgraded. For example, in the factory, routine assembly jobs are being replaced by robots. In the office, routine filing and typing are being replaced by file management and word processing systems using the computer.

Does this mean there will be few or no job opportunities for individuals incapable or lacking the opportunity to learn higher level job skills such as might be required to control a robot or to utilize a file managment or word processing system? Does this mean mass unemployment for a segment of the population that desperately needs the opportunity to become productive citizens in our society?

The change from physical to mental labor

The use of the computer is changing the very nature of many jobs that exist within a business. In the industrial revolution, tools were developed to assist in improving production, but much work still involved physical labor. The information revolution has brought about another change — a change from physical labor to mental labor. Many so-called blue collar jobs now require demanding, mental concentration to properly perform the job duties.

One study conducted by a psychologist consisted of interviewing workers before and after the installation of a robot. The robot was used to control a machining process of stamping and assembling metal parts. Prior to the installation of the robot, much of the work was done by skilled machinists. After installation, the robot did the work, but the workers controlled the robot through a control panel. The results of the study indicated that the workers praised the robot for eliminating the physical labor and fatigue of the manual operation, but complained of more and continued stress. Prior to installation of the robot, there was time for daydreaming, talking, or short periods of relaxation between jobs, it was reported. Now, however, because of the speed of the robot, there was a need for constant scanning and monitoring of the operations being performed by the robot. Has the installation of the robot created a better work environment? Has the change from physical labor to mental stress resulted in an improved quality of life, a better society? Much additional research is necessary (Figure 18–3).

Pressure on the computer worker can be great. Whether operating a robot, running a computer, or programming a computer, a single error can be disastrous. The smallest error, for example, could conceivably misdirect an airline, disrupt delivery schedules, or cost millions of dollars. Such pressures are undoubtedly felt by workers in many areas.

Rapid technological changes place tremendous pressures on the worker to keep up with the changes. There must be constant learning in order to apply this new technology. In some cases people have become so involved with learning and using computers that social interaction decreases and a type of "marriage" between the individual and the machine occurs, completely altering the individual's lifestyle. Is such devotion to technology bad? Is this devotion to technology becoming an increasingly large part of the lifestyles of more and more people in our society? Will "computer widows" and "computer widowers" become a norm in society? Are family interactions being threatened by the computer? Or is this merely a reflection of the desires of a few individuals?

Figure 18–3 (opposite page) The newspaper headlines in this collage vividly illustrate the concern shown by society as computers and computer-controlled machines become a factor in the workplace.

Union Files Complaint Objecting to Robot

PITTSBURGH, Pa. — A potentially precedent-setting case concerning the rights of workers replaced by robots...

bots
Labor
New
Th
Clou
the A
ment

quires the union to represent all workers at the facility, Clougherty explained. The four workers have been assigned to other jobs, but Clougherty is concerned about what

unskilled workers, not whether the robot can do the job better, he said.

Because of the publicity surrounding the case, Clougherty expects

ner." He said the union will ask that the robot be "retired" and the workers given back their jobs until MSHA and union officials c a reach

Technology Seen Reshaping Labor Movement

Blakely said.
• Giving advance notice to workers displaced by work nology and providump-sum payments f service in addition nt compensation. a shorter workweek available jobs

ers who are displaced by technology for other positions.
• Providing retraining and continuing education programs at the work site to provide greater accessibility for employees, part prepare those

man resources," Blakely said.
Among the suggested govern alternatives were:
• Crea

NYPD bomb squad using robots in life-threatening situations

NEW YORK — It's become a cliche at the ideal tasks for robots are ose that are either too tedious or o dangerous for humans. The New ork Police Department (NYPD) now ilizes three strictly mechanical, rete-controlled robots in

In early January, bots were loaned Y., police departm oot-out that left ad and two others unmen were cornered ent, and police eventu bot device "to go in a e suspects were dead, an for the Elmira police id. He declined to discu vices.

Nor would NYPD discu e the device in Elmira.

them for six years.

Detective Frank Guerra, training officer for the bomb squad department uses times

College Trustees Almost Cancel Robot Course

HAVERHILL, Mass. — The fear at robotics threatens American rs' jobs almost caused the government of a state junior college ard of funding for training emerging technol munity Col ocation cer

program that very morning.

On the second vote the board voted seven to three to accept the grant. One trustee who changed her vote in favor, Carolyn Whittaker, reportedly stressed that she "philosophically" opposes robotics and will not vote to continue the course next year.

The program is funded by $54,000 in U.S. Department of Edu funds that are awarded throug state education department. I vides for a 12-month certifica riculum comprised of several c using on hydraulics, mathe mmed devices and the obotics equipment. imitry, in an int d, said the a degr

ing estimates that many currently furloughed auto industry workers may never be rehired. A native of Detroit himself, Dimitry said he deplores such a situation but realizes that American industry has been built on the continued development of "labor-saving devices."

The college, with a total enroll f 8,800 students in day and

area, which for years has suffere from dependence on the declini textile industry.

In the adjoining town of No Andover is a Western Electric p employing more than 6,000 w the Lowell headquarters of V Laboratories, Inc. is within eas muting distance; and Haverhi is currently seeking federal uld unable Wang to

Robots to be sold to jail for use as guard devices

NEWS

RN, Mass. — Robots are e off the factory floor plan of a two t recently 20 mo

by human bodies.

The robot will be progra speak as many as 10 diffe tences, including warning prisoners, "You have been c

Encased in an armored be two Motorola, Inc. 680 processors, "vast amount dom-acce and son program read-on (Eprom ton sai

ill not
it

'Bill of Rights' Serves as Guide To Technology

WASHINGTON, D.C. — The International Association of Machinists d Aerospace Workers (IAMAW) is forerunner in the labor movent's bid to come to grips with the roduction of technology into the rk place and its potentially negae impact on workers.

n November 1982, representaes of the IAMAW ratified a 10nt "Technology Bill of Rights" at union's Electronics and Technol Conference in Seattle. The bill of hts has been dist als as a guide to tract negotiation The union has al government co delines and plan "rights" into con tly be negotiati ines.

'Not Against N

George Poulin, r e-president of the e are the only one hnology Bill of R er unions do hav nt programs." H ons are "not again " but rather belie should be used panywide, leadi ment, instead of oulin, who is b ned that the g

Senator Requests Study of Computer Use Effect

Claims They Upset Federal Balance of Power

By Jake Kirchner
CW Washington Bureau
INGTON, D.C. — A U.S. committee chairman has re congressional study to de ether computers are up balance of powers legislative and execu of government. ent this month hnology A liam V. of the Se Committ iophisti

'clearinghouse' for information to help state and local licensing officials stay current of-state offer in a man federe

applicants' out been 'updated' ould give the trol over the n between licensing

nal committees — not to mention Congress as a whole."
The Senate Governmental A Committee has been activ two years in loo late

Course to Cover Use of Micros In Corporations

WHEATON, Ill. — A seminar on the use of personal computers in the corporate environment is being offered to individual data centers by

SPECIAL **REPORT**

Middle managers feeling automation ax

The implementation of today's more sophisticated factory automation systems often results in job displacement among the middle managers required to implement them. These middle managers are faced with a difficult choice. If they strive to implement the new system successfully, they may end up losing

this information becomes available faster and often more accurately, directly from the factory floor.

The successful implementation of advanced MIS as part of an overall factory automation project resulting in computer-integrated manufacturing can lead to the displacement of

middle managers compete with each other for the few remaining jobs. Sometimes this competition is encouraged to an extreme. Here the problem is that the implementation period usually lasts several years. Few organizations can survive several years of intense back-stabbing

there for years and perhaps came up through the ranks?

Knowing the future job opportunities and being able to train for them can go a long way toward encouraging middle managers to cooperate enthusiastically in the implementation of advanced factory automation projects that may result in the elimination of their present jobs.

This same approach should be

Without the cooperation of the middle manag-

Are computers hazardous to your health?

With computers and CRT terminals becoming a part of the work environment for millions of employees, the question of the health and safety of individuals working with these devices has become an important area of study. More than one survey of CRT display terminal users has revealed that the users suffered from more visual problems, headaches, muscle strain, backaches, stress, and other ills than nonusers.

Reporting to a congressional subcommittee conducting hearings on employee safety and health, a representative of a service employees union described the working environment in an insurance company by stating that individuals, "Work from eight to ten hours a day, sitting in long rows at impersonal workstations dominated by video display terminals processing insurance claims." She added, "I have noticed the deterioration of our vision since working on the terminals . . . . my eyes frequently tear and sting." The individual went on to say there was little doubt that VDT (video display terminal) use causes long term, serious health problems, including danger to working women who are pregnant.

Representatives of the American College of Obstetricians and Gynecologists and the American College of Ophthalmology told the subcommittee investigating VDT safety that "scientific evidence proves there is no reproduction or vision danger from using VDT's." They further stated that there was no reason for VDT operators to request transfers to other jobs during pregnancy or to demand periodic eye examinations, as some proposed legislation had suggested.

These contradictory statements are sure to be a subject of debate for many years to come.

COMPUTERS — A THREAT TO PRIVACY?

One of the more pressing issues facing society is that modern computers have made it technically and economically feasible to store large volumes of data about citizens. This data can be readily accessed and analyzed. Some feel that the establishment of data banks containing information about people offers a great potential for the loss of privacy and that misuse of this data threatens many of the basic freedoms in society. Others feel that data banks are a natural extension of our technological society and can be of great benefit.

Data banks

In the early 1970's, a national data bank was proposed. The national data bank, it was reasoned, could be developed to serve as a central repository for as much information as could be obtained about the citizens of the country. It would contain such information as the name, address, marital status, income, medical history, education, credit rating, criminal records, social security information, tax data, and other types of information about each individual living in this country. This information is available in a number of separate data bases. Why not, it was asked, have a single data base containing all of the information.

With this national data bank, economists, social workers, the FBI, or other authorized users could make inquiries to determine information such as the average income in New York City, the divorce rate in California, or the average age of the people in Texas. In order to implement this data bank, a universal identifier would be assigned at birth. It would serve as a personal identification number for medical records, school records, social security purposes, payroll records, criminal records, and even, it was suggested, as a personal telephone number.

The outcry was strong, both from those within the information processing profession and from other concerned citizens. The potential for misuse of such information was very great. Who would have access to this data? How was access to this data to be controlled? Because of these and other problems, a national data bank has never been implemented; however, data about citizens has been gathered and stored in computerized files at an astounding rate (Figure 18–4).

Figure 18–4 The data banks shown in this illustration represent the many hundreds of thousands which have been developed over the years.

THE MAIN DATA BANKS

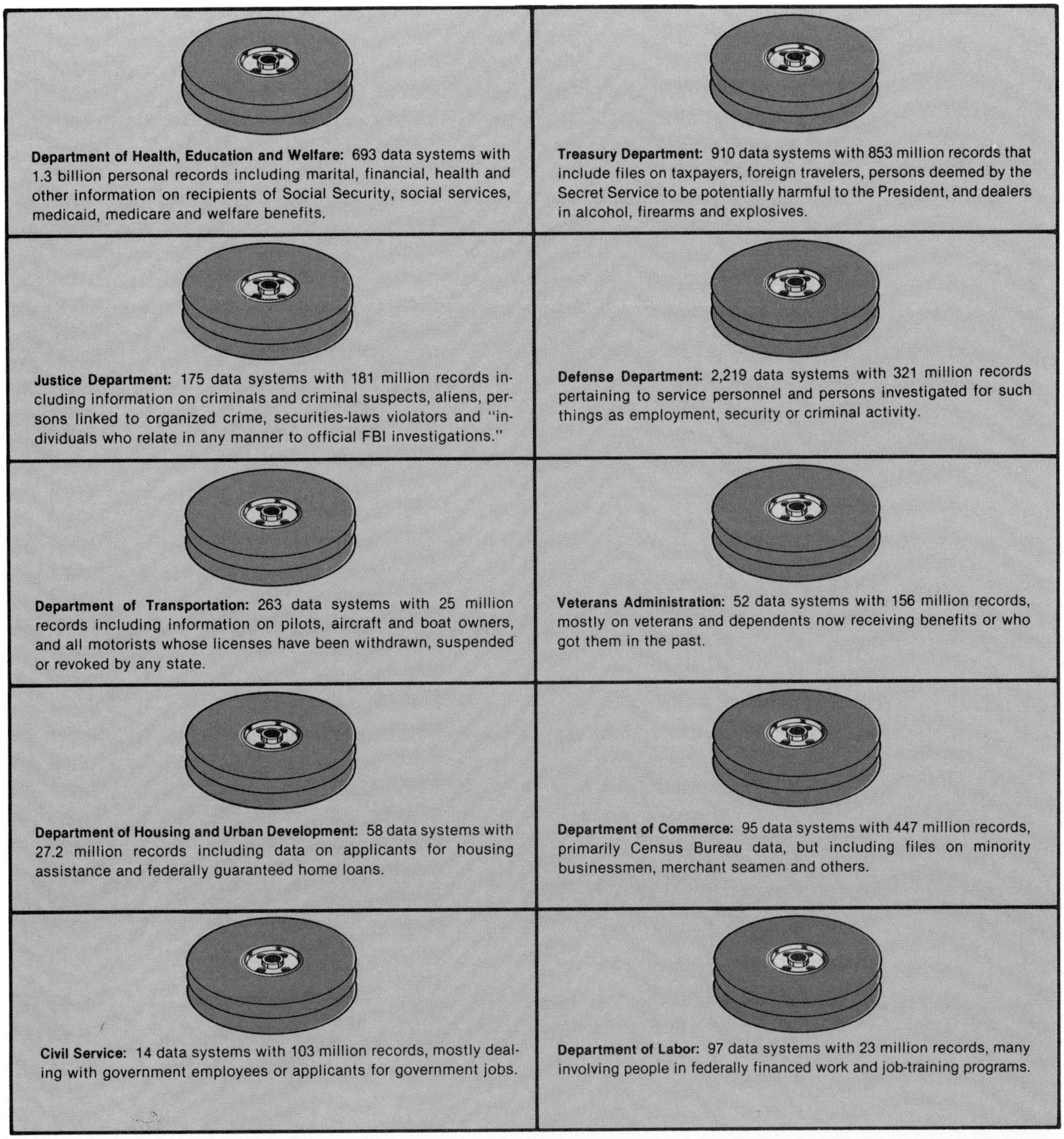

Department of Health, Education and Welfare: 693 data systems with 1.3 billion personal records including marital, financial, health and other information on recipients of Social Security, social services, medicaid, medicare and welfare benefits.
Treasury Department: 910 data systems with 853 million records that include files on taxpayers, foreign travelers, persons deemed by the Secret Service to be potentially harmful to the President, and dealers in alcohol, firearms and explosives.
Justice Department: 175 data systems with 181 million records including information on criminals and criminal suspects, aliens, persons linked to organized crime, securities-laws violators and "individuals who relate in any manner to official FBI investigations."
Defense Department: 2,219 data systems with 321 million records pertaining to service personnel and persons investigated for such things as employment, security or criminal activity.
Department of Transportation: 263 data systems with 25 million records including information on pilots, aircraft and boat owners, and all motorists whose licenses have been withdrawn, suspended or revoked by any state.
Veterans Administration: 52 data systems with 156 million records, mostly on veterans and dependents now receiving benefits or who got them in the past.
Department of Housing and Urban Development: 58 data systems with 27.2 million records including data on applicants for housing assistance and federally guaranteed home loans.
Department of Commerce: 95 data systems with 447 million records, primarily Census Bureau data, but including files on minority businessmen, merchant seamen and others.
Civil Service: 14 data systems with 103 million records, mostly dealing with government employees or applicants for government jobs.
Department of Labor: 97 data systems with 23 million records, many involving people in federally financed work and job-training programs.

Computer record matching

Although a national data bank has never evolved, the ability of computers to communicate with one another and readily exchange and compare data has resulted in new concerns and benefits in recent years.

Computer matching involves comparing data in two or more separate data bases. In one program, the federal government matched the computerized records of ten million governmental employees against a computerized list of student loan defaulters. The efforts resulted in the identification of 47,000 governmental employees with loans in default. The federal government indicated that it would garnishee the wages of those identified.

In another case, the department of public welfare submitted computer tapes with the social security numbers of welfare recipients to over 100 banks. These tapes were matched with records of bank balances to determine if recipients had more money in their bank accounts than allowed by law.

Advocates support computer record matching as a means of detecting fraud and carrying out the law. Those against computer matching point out the threat to the privacy of individual citizens.

To provide for some degree of privacy, fair information practices have been implemented, and federal and state statutes have been developed regarding storing and accessing computerized data. Basic practices include the following: 1) Information collected and stored about individuals should be limited to what is necessary to carry out the function of the business and governmental agency collecting the data; 2) Once collected, provision should be made to restrict access to that data to those within the organization who need access to it to perform their job duties; 3) Personal information should be released outside the organization collecting the data only when the person has agreed to its disclosure; 4) When information is collected about an individual, the individual should know that data is being collected and have the opportunity to assure the accuracy of the data.

One authority has stated, "While the potential for the proper use of the computer is beyond our imagination, the potential for misuse threatens the foundation of a free society."

Electronic funds transfer systems

There has been much discussion about the cashless society, where money would not be needed, and all goods and services would be bought through the use of a universal cash card. On payday, the amount of an individual's paycheck would be electronically transferred from the company's account to the employee's account. To purchase groceries, gasoline, or any other products or services, the universal cash card would be used to transfer money from the purchaser's account to the vendor's account.

The benefits are obvious. At the end of the month, a complete record of each individual's expenditures would be available; there would be a tremendous reduction in paperwork; and bad checks would be eliminated. Today, under the term Electronic Funds Transfer (EFT), this concept is being implemented in what may become one of the largest communications networks in existence. Many banks have begun to offer home banking to those who have home computers. One bank offers more than 600 companies to which checks can be sent by merely making an entry on one's home computer.

The issues presented by EFT are similar to those of national data banks with respect to individual privacy — who is to have access to this financial information, and what protection do citizens have in ensuring their rights of privacy.

Some authorities feel that EFT offers one of the greatest threats to freedom that currently exists in society. For, when carried to its fullest extent, EFT would provide governmental agencies with a complete record of every facet of each person's life. Little could be done, from eating to traveling, without a record's being entered in a computer data base. Some feel that a system such as this could lead to complete governmental control over society.

Others argue, however, that the benefits far outweigh the possible dangers; and all that is needed are safeguards built into the legal system that will protect individual rights and freedoms in the emerging computerized society.

COMPUTER CRIME AND ETHICS

A worker in an insurance company files fictitious dental claims which cause the computer to issue phony insurance benefit checks to relatives in the amount of $8,000. A computer programmer, while working for a governmental agency, writes an unauthorized program that allows issuance of $17,000 in checks payable to himself. Included in the program are instructions to erase all evidence of the transactions. A disgruntled computer programmer fired from his position adds to an existing program instructions that erase the company's accounts receivable records on disk. A bank teller electronically transfers funds from an inactive savings account to a fictitious account and then withdraws the funds for personal use. An employee takes from his employer a copy of the company payroll program stored on magnetic tape and starts a computer service bureau processing other companies' payrolls. A former employee, using a computer terminal, gains access to his former employer's computer and uses the computer for personal use. Each of these examples illustrates true stories of a growing threat posed by the use of computers — computer crime.

It is estimated that over $100 million per year is lost through computer related crime activities throughout the United States.

Software piracy

With the widespread use of personal computers, thousands of software packages have been developed. These software packages, commonly stored on a single floppy disk, can range in price from a few dollars to over $500.00. A serious problem facing the personal computer software industry is what is commonly called software piracy, that is, the illegal duplication of this software. It has been estimated that of each copy of a software package sold, at least four additional copies are illegally made. The loss to the industry is estimated to be in excess of $100 million. An important question facing the industry is how to copy protect software to prevent this illegal copying.

In most cases, packages are not copied to be sold again. Rather, they are copied so other people can use the package without paying the price. For example, in one company, a word processing package was purchased and the floppy disks on which the software was stored were copied for the 142 secretaries in the company. Additional confusion has occurred because the primary laws used to protect software are federal copyright laws, and they are not explicit about the rights of software producers.

Many software manufacturers contend they are not selling the software to a buyer but rather are licensing the buyer to use the software on only one computer. Therefore, if the user uses the software on two different machines, the software license has been violated. This policy has created significant problems in schools, where a software package is purchased for use with all the computers in a classroom.

Policies regarding these issues are yet to be agreed upon by the software producers and the buyers of software. It is expected that these issues will continue to be debated in the years to come.

What is computer crime?

Although some examples of fraud and misuse of the computer can readily be recognized as being crimes, other types of activities involving computers are not as easily classified. One of the difficulties related to the topic of computer crime is answering the question, "What is a computer crime?"

For example, is it a computer crime for the sales clerk in a department store to access a data base containing the credit rating of a neighbor when this information is not needed in the performance of the job? Is it a computer crime for a student to obtain access to the school's grade reports stored on disk and look at other students' grades? The term "hacker" has been used to describe individuals, usually very technically knowledgeable, who routinely use remote computer terminals and communications lines to gain unauthorized access to restricted data bases. Often, access is not malicious with the intent to destroy information, but merely one of curiosity. Should this unauthorized access be a crime?

Professional ethics

Today, society is becoming increasingly concerned with the ethics of the information processing profession and with the relationship between ethical behavior and criminal behavior with respect to information processing. The attitude test in Figure 18-5 illustrates some of the ethical/criminal considerations which those in the information processing profession must encounter daily. Take the test, being able to justify each answer.

Computer crime laws

In an attempt to answer the question, "What is a computer crime?", both federal and state laws are being developed. Legislation in one state defines first-degree computer fraud as accessing any computer system to obtain goods and services illegally or to execute a scheme to defraud. Altering, destroying, or preventing access to a computer system is also considered first degree computer fraud. These types of activities are punishable with a fine up to $20,000 and a maximum of five years in jail.

Figure 18-5 (opposite page) The Attitude Test — Ethics of Information Processing is representative of the types of ethical issues facing the information processing industry.

Second degree computer fraud is defined as simply accessing a computer system or data base without authority. This law is aimed at discouraging "hackers."

Computer crime, its definition, and the emerging laws are an important area that

ATTITUDE TEST
ETHICS OF INFORMATION PROCESSING

Instruction: Place a check in the space provided which best reflects your opinion.

1. A computer operator runs a program at work for a friend and uses 10 minutes of computer time. The program was run when the computer was idle; that is, not being used for company business.

   Ethical _______ Unethical _______ Computer Crime _______

2. A student gives out a password to another student not enrolled in a computer class for which a laboratory fee is charged. The password allows access to the school computer. The unauthorized student uses 3 hours of computer time in a timesharing environment.

   Student enrolled in class: Ethical _______ Unethical _______ Computer Crime _______
   Unauthorized student: Ethical _______ Unethical _______ Computer Crime _______

3. A copy of a payroll program developed by a programmer on the job is given to a friend at a different company.

   Ethical _______ Unethical _______ Computer Crime _______

4. Utilizing a terminal, an individual breaks a security code and reviews confidential company salaries of corporate executives. No use is made of the information . . . . "I was just curious" is the response when caught.

   Ethical _______ Unethical _______ Computer Crime _______

5. A bank teller electronically transfers money from a relatively inactive customer account to his own personal account and then transfers the money to a credit card account to pay current credit card charges. On pay day, money is deposited into his personal account, and then he electronically transfers the money back to the customer's account. No money changes hands, and no interest is lost to the customer's account.

   Ethical _______ Unethical _______ Computer Crime _______

6. An individual buys a special program that can duplicate a word processing program, even though the manufacturer built in a copy protect feature. The individual uses the copied program as a backup disk only.

   Ethical _______ Unethical _______ Computer Crime _______

7. A programmer is asked to write a program which she knows will generate inaccurate information for stockholders of the company. When she questions her manager about the program, she is told she must write it or lose her job. She writes the program.

   Company: Ethical _______ Unethical _______ Computer Crime _______
   Programmer: Ethical _______ Unethical _______ Computer Crime _______

8. A marketing manager uses her electronic spreadsheet program on a personal computer in the accounting department even though the licensing agreement that came with the software when she purchased it indicates use of the software is authorized only for her personal computer in the marketing department. The manager argues she should not have to buy a $395.00 software package each time she moves from one computer to another.

   Ethical _______ Unethical _______ Computer Crime _______

will influence the way our society functions in the future.

The future — artificial intelligence

Are there any areas where it is not appropriate to use a computer?

> "This person has a real urge to suffer, and does things so as to bring suffering on herself . . . . she hasn't learned to get satisfaction in life in any better way."

The above quotation was written by a computer that interpreted the answers given on a personality assessment test. Is this a valid use of a computer? Traditionally, the interpretation of personality tests has been done by someone trained in psychology or test interpretation. Now computers are frequently used. More and more often, computers are used for applications traditionally thought to be the domain of human beings because the activity performed required reasoning and judgment.

Artificial intelligence, a field of study that has traditionally included natural language processing and computer vision, has made considerable progress in the use of computers to simulate the thought process of human experts in narrowly defined subjects. Programs that simulate human brainpower are called "expert systems." The artificial intelligence exhibited by expert systems includes not only the ability to recall data stored in memory but heuristic knowledge as well. Heuristic knowledge consists of intuitions, judgment, and inference that, used in conjunction with factual knowledge about a subject, allow intelligent problem solving behavior.

One authority in artificial intelligence has stated, "Technology is changing the computer from a fantastically fast calculating machine to a device that can see, touch, smell, recognize spoken commands, and answer in plain English. Such machines mull over problems, make judgments, acquire additional learning, and eventually may even acquire emotions."

Summary — computers in our society

From the statements in this chapter, it is apparent that society is about to enter a new era full of exciting developments and challenges. The problem of using computer power for beneficial purposes must be addressed and solved as the entire world becomes affected by the marvel of the twentieth century.

CONTROVERSIAL ISSUES AND RESEARCH PROJECTS

1. As noted above, artificial intelligence is an important discipline which will become even more important in the years to come. Indeed, the Japanese have proclaimed a fifth generation of computers and software largely based on artificial intelligence principles. Research this area of computing, and write a paper which not only describes the activities that are taking place in artificial intelligence but also takes a moral and philosophical position concerning artificial intelligence.

Appendix A — PROGRAMMING IN BASIC

The purpose of this appendix is to provide an introduction to the principles of program design and computer programming using the BASIC language. The approach taken to teach this material is to present a series of applications that can be processed using a computer. The input data, the output to be produced, and the processing that is to occur is carefully explained. The program design and logic are then illustrated through the use of a flowchart.

This is followed by an explanation of the BASIC statements required to implement the logic. The complete BASIC program is then illustrated. This program, when entered into main computer memory and executed, will produce the output from the input specified. At the end of each section, student programming assignments are presented that should be designed, coded, entered, and executed on a computer.

The sample problems illustrated and explained in this appendix include: Basic input/output operations; Arithmetic operations and accumulating final totals; Comparing; Interactive programming and looping; and Arrays and array searching.

The programming concepts presented in each of the sample problems should provide an insight into the programming process and develop an understanding of the basic techniques of program design and computer programming. An understanding of these concepts will establish a firm foundation for further study in the field of information processing and computer programming.

The programming process

Computer programs can vary significantly in size and complexity. A simple program may contain only a few statements. A complex program can contain hundreds and even thousands of statements. Regardless of the size of the program, it is extremely important that the task of computer programming be approached in a professional manner, for computer programming is one of the most precise of all human activities.

Learning computer programming should not be approached as a trial-and-error type of activity. By carefully reviewing the sample problems, the program design, and the BASIC coding presented within this appendix, the student should be able to write well-designed programs that produce correct output when executed on a computer.

Computer programming is not "naturally" an error-prone activity. Errors will enter into the design and coding of the computer program only through carelessness or lack of understanding the programming process. With careful study and attention to detail, errors can be avoided. Just as it is the job of the accountant, the mathematician, the engineer, and the scientist to produce correct results, so too it is the job of the computer programmer to produce a program that will be reliable and give accurate results.

As noted previously in this book, the actual programming process involves the following activities: 1) Analyze the problem for understanding; 2) Design the structural and logical approach to solving the problem; 3) Write the code to implement a solution to the problem; 4) Execute and test the program to ensure it produces correct output.

It has been found that when using a careful approach to program design and coding, there is no reason why programs cannot be developed that will execute the first time on the computer and will never fail subsequently.

PROBLEM 1 — BASIC INPUT/OUTPUT OPERATIONS

The most fundamental of all operations performed on a computer are basic input/output operations. A common application of this type involves reading input records and displaying the records on an output device.

The first sample program that is designed and coded in this appendix illustrates the input/output operation by reading hospital patient records and creating a listing of the patients on the CRT display screen. The input, output, flowchart, and the program are explained on the following pages.

Input

The input data to be processed consists of a series of input records. Each input record contains a patient name, a doctor name, and a room number. The chart below illustrates the input records to be processed.

PATIENT NAME	DOCTOR NAME	ROOM NUMBER
JOE RUIZ	WARD	213
TIM KREL	NANCE	112
MARY LEPO	GOLD	102
TOM PEP	KING	245
END OF FILE	END	999

Figure A–1

The data taken as a group is called a file. The data about a single individual is called a record. Each unit of data within the record is called a field. Thus, the input data consists of a file of hospital patient records. Each record contains a patient name field, a doctor name field, and a room number field.

In the list of records in Figure A–1, the last record contains the words END OF FILE in the patient name field, the word END in the doctor name field, and the numbers 999 in the room number field. This record is called a trailer record. It is used to indicate when all of the records have been processed. When the record that contains the words END OF FILE in the patient name field is read, the program can determine that all of the data records have been processed. Execution of the program can then be terminated.

Output

The output to be produced is a listing of each record in the input file on a CRT display screen. The output listing is shown in Figure A–2.

```
ROOM          PATIENT           DOCTOR

 213          JOE RUIZ          WARD
 112          TIM KREL          NANCE
 102          MARY LEPO         GOLD
 245          TOM PEP           KING

END OF PATIENT LIST
```

Figure A–2

The output includes the room number, the patient name, and the doctor name for each record. Note that the sequence of the fields displayed on the CRT screen is different from the sequence of the fields in the input record. Column headings identify each field. After all records have been processed, the message END OF PATIENT LIST is displayed.

Program flowchart

The flowchart, BASIC program, and output for the sample problem are shown in Figure A–3. The flowchart in Figure A–3 illustrates a simple looping structure. After the headings are printed, a record is read. A test is then performed to determine if the record just read was the trailer record containing the words END OF FILE. If so, all of the data records have been read and processed. If not, then more records remain to be processed. It is this decision that determines if the loop is entered. If end of file has not been reached, the loop is entered. There, the record just read is printed (displayed on the CRT screen) and another record is read. A return is then made to the decision portion of the loop. As long as the end of file record has not been read, the looping will continue.

When the trailer record is read, that is, when the words END OF FILE are found in the patient name field, there is an exit from the loop. An end of list message is printed, and execution of the program terminates.

This basic logic is appropriate for all applications which involve reading input records and printing the fields from the input record on an output device.

Program Flowchart

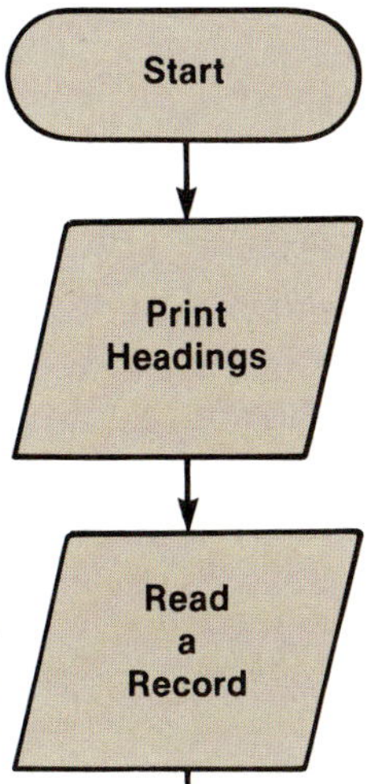

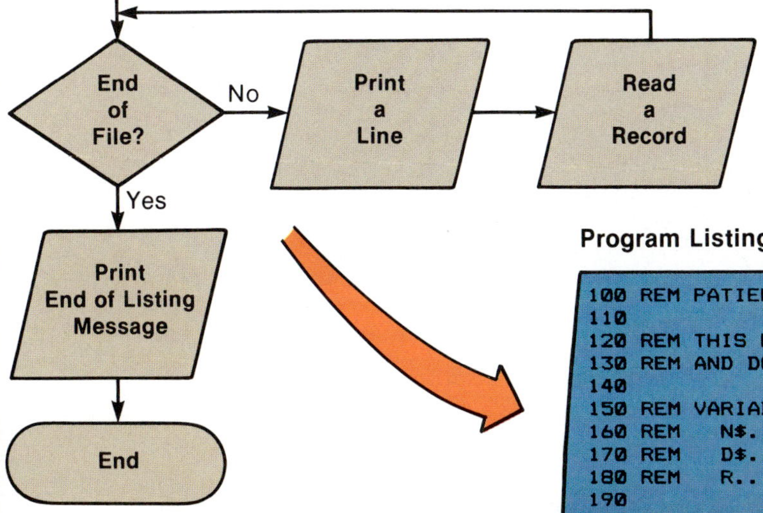

Program Listing

```
100 REM PATIENTS                MARCH 28                SHELLY/CASHMAN
110                                                                REM
120 REM THIS PROGRAM DISPLAYS THE ROOM NUMBER, PATIENT NAME,
130 REM AND DOCTOR NAME OF HOSPITAL PATIENTS.
140                                                                REM
150 REM VARIABLE NAMES:
160 REM    N$....PATIENT NAME
170 REM    D$....DOCTOR NAME
180 REM    R.....ROOM NUMBER
190                                                                REM
200 REM ***** DATA TO BE PROCESSED *****
210                                                                REM
220 DATA "JOE RUIZ", "WARD", 213
230 DATA "TIM KREL", "NANCE", 112
240 DATA "MARY LEPO", "GOLD", 102
250 DATA "TOM PEP", "KING", 245
260 DATA "END OF FILE", "END", 999
270                                                                REM
280 REM ***** PROCESSING *****
290                                                                REM
300 PRINT "ROOM","PATIENT","DOCTOR"
310 PRINT " "
320                                                                REM
330 READ N$, D$, R
340                                                                REM
350 IF N$ = "END OF FILE" THEN 400
360   PRINT R, N$, D$
370   READ N$, D$, R
380 GOTO 350
390                                                                REM
400 PRINT " "
410 PRINT "END OF PATIENT LIST"
420 END
```

Output

```
ROOM          PATIENT        DOCTOR

 213          JOE RUIZ       WARD
 112          TIM KREL       NANCE
 102          MARY LEPO      GOLD
 245          TOM PEP        KING

END OF PATIENT LIST
```

Figure A–3

The BASIC program

It is important when writing computer programs to approach the task in a professional manner. Programs should be well documented, easy to read, easy to understand, and easy to modify and maintain. For these reasons, programming standards have been developed to guide the beginning programmer in the task of writing programs. These standards are illustrated and explained in all sample programs shown in this appendix. They should be followed when completing programming tasks for school, personal, or business use.

A program written using the BASIC language consists of a series of statements which serve one of three functions: 1) Document the program; 2) Define data; 3) Cause processing to occur. All BASIC language statements begin with a line number followed by the operation to be performed. The line numbers, which serve to identify each statement, are assigned in an ascending sequence by the programmer. Line numbers can begin with the number 1 and be incremented by 1. The programs in this textbook always begin with the number 100, and the statement numbers are always incremented by 10 for each of the subsequent statements in the program. This is done to provide for uniformity in coding and for readability. Incrementing by 10 allows statements to be inserted in the program at a later time and still retain the ascending sequence of statements within the program (Figure A–4).

Line Numbers→

```
100 REM PATIENTS                    MARCH 28               SHELLY/CASHMAN
110                                                                   REM
120 REM THIS PROGRAM DISPLAYS THE ROOM NUMBER, PATIENT NAME,
130 REM AND DOCTOR NAME OF HOSPITAL PATIENTS.
140                                                                   REM
150 REM VARIABLE NAMES:
160 REM   N$....PATIENT NAME
170 REM   D$....DOCTOR NAME
180 REM   R.....ROOM NUMBER
190                                                                   REM
```

Figure A–4

A quality program is well documented. This means the program contains information which helps a reader of the program understand it. Documentation within the program should include a program identification, the date the program was written, an author identification, and a brief description of the program. The first segment of the program illustrated in Figure A-4 contains the BASIC statements to document the program.

Documentation within a BASIC program is accomplished through the use of the remark (REM) statement. The remark statement consists of a line number and the entry REM. Following the entry REM, the programmer may include any characters, numbers or words required to document the program.

The first statement in the program (line number 100) is a remark statement. The line number 100 is followed by a blank space and then the word REM. REM identifies the entire statement as being a remark. Following the REM entry is a single blank space and then the name of the program. This programmer-chosen name should be the name under which the program will be saved on auxiliary storage. The rules for forming the name vary from computer to computer. Some computers require the name to begin with a letter of the alphabet and be comprised of eight characters or less. In the example, the name chosen is PATIENTS. This entry is followed by the date the program was written, centered on the line, and the name of the author(s) in the rightmost positions.

Line 110 contains a REM statement in the rightmost positions of the line. The REM is used in this manner to give the appearance of a blank line between entries. The use of the blank line is to improve readability. Lines 120 and 130 contain REM statements. These lines are used to give a brief description of the program. The REM statement on line 140 provides a blank line.

The REM statements on lines 150 through 180 document the variable names used in the program. Variable names are names assigned by the programmer to fields in main computer memory which will be referenced by statements within the program. In the sample program, a variable name must be assigned for the patient name, the doctor name, and the room number. The entry 150 REM VARIABLE NAMES: is used to identify this portion of the program. The entries on lines 160, 170, and 180 document the various names chosen by the programmer. Note how the entries are indented two space. These spacing standards should be followed exactly.

Variable names assigned to fields referenced in a BASIC program must conform to certain rules defined by the developer of the language. All BASIC interpreters allow variable names according to the following rules:

1. Names assigned to reference fields that contain numeric data are called numeric variable names. Numeric variable names must begin with a letter of the alphabet (A – Z). The names can be one or two characters in length. If a second character is used, this character must be numeric (0 – 9). Valid numeric variable names include R, N, R1, N9, and A4.
2. Names assigned to reference fields that contain alphabetic data, alphanumeric data, or fields that contain any nonnumeric character are called string variable names. String variable names must begin with a letter of the alphabet (A – Z) and be followed by a dollar sign. Valid string variable names include N$, D$, and R$.

From the coding in Figure A–4, it can be seen that the variable name assigned to the patient name field is N$. The name assigned by the programmer to the doctor name field is D$, and the room number field is assigned the numeric variable name R.

Statement 190 uses the REM statement to create a blank line. This blank line separates the introductory remarks from the rest of the statements in the program.

Documenting the program as illustrated is fundamental to writing a quality program. The proper use of remarks, blanks, and indentations can substantially improve the readability of the program. It is suggested that the format illustrated in the sample program be used when coding all BASIC programs.

The data statement

The next section of the program is used to define the data that will be processed. The portion of the coding in the sample program which defines the data is illustrated below.

```
200 REM ***** DATA TO BE PROCESSED *****
210                  Patient Name   Doctor Name                          REM
220 DATA "JOE RUIZ", "WARD", 213 <-- Room Number
230 DATA "TIM KREL", "NANCE", 112
240 DATA "MARY LEPO", "GOLD", 102
250 DATA "TOM PEP", "KING", 245
260 DATA "END OF FILE", "END", 999
270                                                                      REM
```

Figure A–5

The rem statement on line 200 is used to indicate that the next section of the coding contains the definition of the data which will be processed by the program.

In this program, the data to be processed is defined through the use of data statements. In Figure A–5, the first data statement on line 220 defines the data to be processed as the first input record. The second data statement defines the data to be processed as the second input record, and so on. A data statement begins with a line number, followed by a space, and then the word DATA. The word DATA is followed by a single space. The data to be defined is specified next. The data statement on line 220 contains the patient name (JOE RUIZ), the doctor name (WARD), and the room number (213). Each of the various fields must be separated by a comma. The patient name and the doctor name are enclosed in quotation marks.

In BASIC, if a field contains alphabetic data, alphabetic data and numeric data combined, or if the field contains any nonnumeric character, the data in the field is called string data. String data specified in a data statement is normally enclosed in quotation marks. In the data statement on line 220, both the patient name (JOE RUIZ), and the doctor name (WARD) are enclosed in quotation marks because the names are string data. The room number field contains all numbers. Data with just numbers is called numeric data. Numeric data is not enclosed within quotation marks in a data statement.

The data statements on lines 220 through 260 are used to define each of the input records to be processed in the program. The last data statement is the trailer record. When a trailer record is used in this manner, it is necessary to include an entry in each field. In the example, the words END OF FILE were included for the patient name, the word END was included in place of the doctor name, and the value 999 was included for the room number. These values, of course, will not be included on the screen display. Data statements are used in BASIC to define the data which will be processed by the program.

The read, if, print, goto, and end statements

After the documentation of the program is complete and the data to be processed by the program has been defined, the statements which will implement the logic specified in the flowchart and execute the data must be written.

```
280 REM ***** PROCESSING *****
290                                                          REM
300 PRINT "ROOM", "PATIENT", "DOCTOR"
310 PRINT " "
320                                                          REM
330 READ N$, D$, R
340                                                          REM
350 IF N$ = "END OF FILE" THEN 400
360   PRINT R, N$, D$
370   READ N$, D$, R
380 GOTO 350
390                                                          REM
400 PRINT " "
410 PRINT "END OF PATIENT LIST"
420 END
```

Figure A–6

This segment of the program consists of six types of statements: rem statements, print statements, read statements, the if statement, the goto statement, and the end statement. The rem statement on line 280 is used to identify the main processing portion of the program. Line 290 contains a rem statement to cause the blank line.

The print statement causes data to be displayed on a CRT screen. The print statement consists of a line number, one or more spaces, the word PRINT, one or more spaces, and then the words, numbers, or variable names of the fields to be displayed on the screen. To display the column headings on the screen, the print statement on line 300 is used. To print string constant data such as the words ROOM, PATIENT, and DOCTOR, each of the words must be enclosed in quotation marks following the word PRINT.

In the example, each word to be printed in the heading is enclosed in quotation marks and is separated by a comma from the other words to be printed. When the fields specified in the print statement are separated by commas, the fields will be displayed in predefined columns called zones on the CRT screen. These zones vary in size depending upon the computer being used. In the sample program, the word ROOM prints beginning in column 1, the word PATIENT beginning in column 15, and the word DOCTOR beginning in column 29 because these are the predefined zones on the computer used to execute the program (see Figure A–2 for the screen format).

The statement on line 310 is a print statement followed by a blank space enclosed within quotation marks. A print statement written in this form will cause one blank line to be displayed. The purpose of printing this blank line is to separate the column headings by one vertical space from the patient data to be printed.

To transfer data from the data statements to an area in main computer memory where the data can be referenced, the read statement is used. The read statement consists of a line number, one or more spaces, the word READ, and one or more spaces followed by one or more variable names. The variable names must be separated from each other by commas. The read statement causes data defined in a data statement to be placed in the fields in main computer memory identified by the variable names N$ (patient name), D$ (doctor name), and R (room number). The variable names must be specified in the order in which the data is recorded in the data statements.

Upon execution of this read statement, the first constant in the first data statement (line 220) is placed in the main memory field identified by the first variable name in the read statement. Thus, the first constant in the data statement (JOE RUIZ) is placed in the field identified by the first variable name (N$). The second constant in the data statement, which is the doctor's name (WARD), is placed in the field identified by the second variable name (D$). Likewise, the third constant (213) is placed in the third field, which has the variable name R. After the read statement has been executed, an instruction referencing the variable name N$ will reference the value JOE RUIZ. Similarly, the use of the variable name D$ will reference the value WARD; and the variable name R will reference the numeric value 213.

After the read statement on line 330, there is a rem statement used to generate a blank line. The purpose of this blank line is to separate the first read statement from the statements that comprise the main program loop.

After the first read statement has been executed, a check must be performed to determine if end of file has been reached. A test for end of file should always immediately follow the reading of data. In the sample program, this test is implemented using the if statement on line 350. An if statement is a comparing statement that allows numeric constants and variables or string constants and variables to be compared. Based upon the results of the comparison, alternative statements can be executed.

On line 350, the if statement compares the data in memory referenced by the variable N$ (patient name) to the string constant "END OF FILE" to determine if the fields are equal. A string constant such as END OF FILE must be enclosed in quotation marks when it appears in a statement. The equal sign indicates the comparison is to determine if the fields are equal. If, when the if statement is executed, the value in the field identified by the string variable N$ is equal to the constant END OF FILE, the statement at the number specified following the word THEN (statement 400) would be executed. The statements beginning at 400 are used to display the end of patient listing message and terminate processing. If the data referenced by N$ is not equal to the words END OF FILE, the next statement in sequence is executed. This is the print statement on line 360. In summary, then, the if statement is used to determine if the trailer record has been read. It implements the logic indicated by the decision symbol on the flowchart in Figure A–3.

If the end of file record has not been read, the print statement on line 360 is executed. This print statement contains the variable names of the fields in main computer memory. These variable names are specified in the sequence in which they are to be printed. Each name is separated by a comma from the other names; thus, the various fields will print in the predefined zones on the CRT screen. The fields are not printed in the same sequence as they are specified in the data statements.

After a line is printed, the logic of the program as illustrated in the flowchart in Figure A–3 specifies that another input record should be read. This is accomplished by the read statement on line 370. Since this is the second time a read statement has been executed, the data in the second data statement (line 230) would be transferred to the fields defined in the read statement (N$, D$, and R).

After a record has been read, the logic specifies that the next task is to transfer control back to the decision step to check if the end of file record was just read. To transfer control to a particular statement in a BASIC program, the goto statement is used. The goto statement consists of a line number and then the word GOTO followed by a statement number. When executed, the goto statement causes control to be passed to the statement whose number is specified in the statement. On line 380 of the sample program, the goto statement will cause control to be transferred to statement 350, which is the if statement that determines if the end of file record has been read.

The statements on lines 350 to 380 implement the looping logic illustrated in the flowchart in Figure A–3. The indentation of the statements on lines 360 and 370 is used to improve the readability of the program, and to make it easy to see the scope of the looping operation.

When a record is read that contains the words END OF FILE in the patient name field, the if statement on line 350 specifies that control should be transferred to statement 400. The print statement on line 400 will cause a blank line to appear on the display screen, separating the body of the report from the ending message. The print statement at line 410 will cause the message END OF PATIENT LIST to be displayed.

The last statement in the program is the end statement. This statement consists of a line number and the word END. It is used to terminate execution of the program.

It is important to review both the flowchart logic and the coding techniques utilized to implement this logic. The coding techniques illustrated in this program should be used whenever personal or business programs are written.

The complete BASIC program and the output produced are again illustrated in Figure A-7.

BASIC Program

```
100 REM PATIENTS                    MARCH 28                SHELLY/CASHMAN
110                                                                    REM
120 REM THIS PROGRAM DISPLAYS THE ROOM NUMBER, PATIENT NAME,
130 REM AND DOCTOR NAME OF HOSPITAL PATIENTS.
140                                                                    REM
150 REM VARIABLE NAMES:
160 REM   N$....PATIENT NAME
170 REM   D$....DOCTOR NAME
180 REM   R.....ROOM NUMBER
190                                                                    REM
200 REM ***** DATA TO BE PROCESSED *****
210                                                                    REM
220 DATA "JOE RUIZ", "WARD", 213
230 DATA "TIM KREL", "NANCE", 112
240 DATA "MARY LEPO", "GOLD", 102
250 DATA "TOM PEP", "KING", 245
260 DATA "END OF FILE", "END", 999
270                                                                    REM
280 REM ***** PROCESSING *****
290                                                                    REM
300 PRINT "ROOM", "PATIENT", "DOCTOR"
310 PRINT " "
320                                                                    REM
330 READ N$, D$, R
340                                                                    REM
350 IF N$ = "END OF FILE" THEN 400
360   PRINT R, N$, D$
370   READ N$, D$, R
380 GOTO 350
390                                                                    REM
400 PRINT " "
410 PRINT "END OF PATIENT LIST"
420 END
```

Output

```
ROOM          PATIENT       DOCTOR

 213          JOE RUIZ      WARD
 112          TIM KREL      NANCE
 102          MARY LEPO     GOLD
 245          TOM PEP       KING

END OF PATIENT LIST
```

Figure A-7

STUDENT PROGRAMMING ASSIGNMENT 1
Basic Input/Output Operations

Instructions: A list of employees, their department numbers, and their pay rates is to be prepared. A program should be designed and coded in BASIC to produce the list.

INPUT Input consists of records that contain the employee name, department number, and pay rate. The input data is illustrated below.

NAME	DEPT. NO.	PAY RATE
SUE LONG	10	4.25
CHIN SONG	12	5.15
MARY LOPEZ	14	4.75
JAN HONIG	14	3.85
END OF FILE	99	9.99

OUTPUT Output is a list of the input records containing the department number, employee name, and the employee's pay rate. The format of the output is illustrated below. Spacing between fields should be based upon the standard zones provided by the BASIC language being used. Column headings should be printed. After all records have been processed, the message END OF PERSONNEL LIST should be printed.

```
DEPT.          NAME           PAY RATE

 10            SUE LONG         4.25
 12            CHIN SONG        5.15
 14            MARY LOPEZ       4.75
 14            JAN HONIG        3.85

END OF PERSONNEL LIST
```

STUDENT PROGRAMMING ASSIGNMENT 2
Basic Input/Output Operations

Instructions: A list of individuals, including their birthdates and ages, is to be prepared. A program should be desiged and coded in BASIC to produce the list.

INPUT Input consists of records that contain the individual's birthdate, age, and name. The input data is illustrated below.

BIRTHDATE	AGE	NAME
DECEMBER 7	41	SUTHERLIN
MARCH 16	38	WACHTEL
JUNE 9	27	HATHAWAY
AUGUST 6	25	SCOTT
END OF FILE	99	END

OUTPUT Output is a list containing the name, birthdate, and age of each individual. Each piece of information about the individual should be printed on a separate line, and each piece of information should be labeled. The spacing between the label and the field of information should be based upon the standard zones provided by the BASIC language being used. After all records have been processed, the message END OF LIST should be printed. A sample of the output is illustrated below.

```
NAME:              SUTHERLIN
BIRTHDATE:         DECEMBER 7
AGE:                41

NAME:              WACHTEL
BIRTHDATE:         MARCH 16
AGE:                38

NAME:              HATHAWAY
BIRTHDATE:         JUNE 9
AGE:                27

NAME:              SCOTT
BIRTHDATE:         AUGUST 6
AGE:                25


END OF LIST
```

PROBLEM 2 — BASIC ARITHMETIC OPERATIONS AND ACCUMULATING FINAL TOTALS

Many applications require arithmetic operations to be performed on the input data to produce the required output. To perform the basic arithmetic operations of addition, subtraction, multiplication, division, and raising a value to a power, a series of BASIC arithmetic operators are provided. These operators are similar to those used in ordinary mathematics. The operators and an example of their use in a let statement are illustrated in the chart below.

MATHEMATICAL OPERATIONS	BASIC ARITHMETIC OPERATOR	EXAMPLE
Addition	+	100 LET T = D1 + D2
Subtraction	–	100 LET P = S - 5.95
Multiplication	*	100 LET G = H * R
Division	/	100 LET A = D / 5
Raising to a Power	↑	100 LET M = A ↑ 4

Figure A-8

To perform arithmetic operations, the let statement is used. As shown in Figure A-8, the first entry in a let statement is a line number. This entry is followed by one or more blank spaces and then the word LET. The remainder of the let statement contains the entries to accomplish the arithemtic. Addition is accomplished by the plus (+) arithmetic operator, subtraction by the minus (–) arithmetic operator, multiplication by the asterisk (*), division by use of the slash (/), and raising to a power by the up arrow (↑).

When performing arithmetic operations, the calculations to be performed are specified on the right side of the equal sign by using the appropriate arithmetic operators together with the variable names of the fields containing the data and/or data constants that are to be used in the operation. The variable name of the field where the answer is to be stored is specified on the left side of the equal sign.

In the first example in the Figure A-8, the statement 100 LET T = D1 + D2 will cause the value in the field referenced by the variable name D1 to be added to the value in the field referenced by the variable name D2. The answer will be stored in the field referenced by the variable name T. The contents of the fields in main memory before and after execution are illustrated in the diagram below.

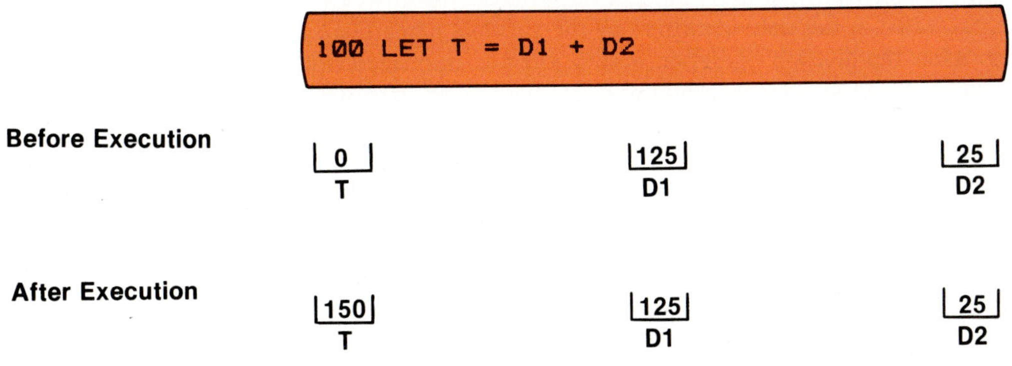

Figure A-9

In the example in Figure A-9, the value in the field identified by the variable name T is zero prior to the execution of the let statement. When the statement is executed, the value in D1 (125) is added to the value in D2 (25) and the answer (150) is placed in the field identified by the variable name T. The values stored in the fields identified by the variable names D1 and D2 have not been altered.

In addition to variable names, actual numeric values, called numeric constants, can be specified in let statements that implement an arithmetic operation. In the second example in Figure A-8, 100 LET P = S − 5.95, the value 5.95 is a numeric constant. This let statement would cause the value 5.95 to be subtracted from the value in the field identified by the variable name S, and the answer would be stored in the field identified by the variable name P. Numeric values used in this manner may consist of numbers, a decimal point, and a plus or minus sign. No special characters such as a comma or dollar sign can be included in a numeric constant.

The next two examples in Figure A-8 illustrate the use of the multiplication and division arithmetic operators. In the last example in Figure A-8, the exponential arithmetic operator (↑) is specified in the statement 100 LET M = A ↑ 4. If the field identified by the variable name A contains the value 2 when the statement is executed, the answer stored in M would be 16, which is 2 raised to the 4th power (2 * 2 * 2 * 2).

Arithmetic operators can be combined to perform more complex operations. For example, to calculate a new balance in an account (N) by adding the old balance (O) and purchases (P) and subtracting the payments (P1), the following statement could be used:

```
210 LET N = O + P - P1
```

Figure A-10

As can be seen, BASIC provides a very convenient way of expressing any arithmetical calculations that must be performed.

Hierarchy of operations

When multiple arithmetic operations are included in a single let statement, such as when addition and division take place in the same statement, the sequence in which the calculations are performed is determined in accordance with the following hierarchy of operations rules: 1) First, exponentiation is performed; 2) Second, multiplication and division are performed; 3) Third, addition and subtraction are performed; 4) Within each of these three steps, calculations are performed left to right.

```
450 LET A = M + T + W + H + F / 5
```

Figure A-11

In the example above, the hierarchy of operations rules specify that division would occur before any addition operations occur. Therefore, the value in the field identified by the variable name F would be divided by the constant value 5 as the first step. After the division operation occurs, the addition steps would take place from left to right, one at a time. The effect of the let statement in Figure A-11, then, is to first divide the value in F by 5 and then add that result to the values in the fields identified by the variable names M, T, W, and H.

Although the results obtained using the hierarchy of operations rules might be satisfactory, there is the possibility they may be incorrect in some applications. For example, in the example in Figure A-11, if the values in each of the variable fields represented total sales for each day of the week, and if the object of the calculation was to determine the average daily sales, then the calculation in Figure A-11 would be incorrect. The operation that should have transpired was to add all the values together and then divide the sum by 5.

To control the sequence in which operations are performed, parentheses can be used in the let statement. When an expression is placed in parentheses, it is evaluated prior to any other operations being performed. Thus, to find the average daily sales for the week, the addition operations should be placed within parentheses. In this manner, the addition will take place prior to the division operation. The statement to calculate the average sales is shown in Figure A–12.

```
450 LET A = (M + T + W + H + F) / 5
```

Figure A–12

In the example above, the addition operations specified within the parentheses would be performed first. The resulting value would then be divided by 5, giving the average daily sales for the week. In most cases, it is advisable to use parentheses around multiple arithmetic operations in an arithmetic expression even if the hierarchy of operations will produce the correct answer. In this way, the sequence of operations is explicitly clear.

Sample problem 2

To illustrate the BASIC statements and the logic to perform calculations and to accumulate totals in a program, a sample problem involving the preparation of an auto expense report will be explained.

Input

Input consists of auto expense records that contain an employee name, the license number of the employee's car, the beginning mileage for the employee's car, and the ending mileage for the car. The input records used in the sample program are shown below.

NAME	LICENSE	BEGINNING MILEAGE	ENDING MILEAGE
T. ROWE	HRT-111	19100	19224
R. LOPEZ	GLD-913	21221	21332
C. DECK	LIV-193	10001	10206
B. ALEK	ZRT-904	15957	16419
END OF FILE	END	99999	99999

Figure A–13

Output

The output of the program is a report which will be displayed on a CRT screen. The report contains the employee name, the automobile license number, the total mileage, and the expense. The total mileage is calculated by subtracting the beginning mileage from the ending mileage. The expense is calculated by multiplying the mileage by 22 cents. The format of the output is shown in Figure A–14.

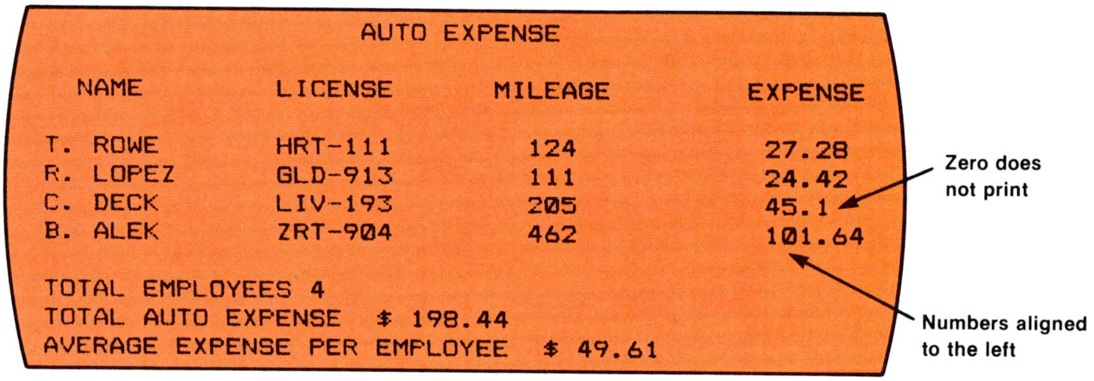
AUTO EXPENSE
NAME LICENSE MILEAGE EXPENSE
T. ROWE HRT-111 124 27.28
R. LOPEZ GLD-913 111 24.42
C. DECK LIV-193 205 45.1
B. ALEK ZRT-904 462 101.64
TOTAL EMPLOYEES 4
TOTAL AUTO EXPENSE $ 198.44
AVERAGE EXPENSE PER EMPLOYEE $ 49.61
Zero does not print
Numbers aligned to the left

Figure A–14

The output listing above contains both report headings and column headings. After all records have been processed, the total number of employees and total auto expenses are printed. In addition, the average expense per employee is calculated by dividing the total auto expense by the total number of employees. The average expense per employee is then printed.

When using the BASIC print statement, insignificant zeroes to the right of a decimal point are not printed. In addition, when printing decimal numbers, the numbers are aligned to the left rather than on the basis of the decimal point. Both of these factors are illustrated in the output in Figure A–14.

To change this method of printing decimal values, additional programming is required. Some BASIC interpreters, however, provide a statement which allows fields to be edited and printed in a variety of formats. This statement is called the print using statement. Its use is illustrated in the last pages of this section.

Program flowchart

The flowchart for the sample program which produces an auto expense report and accumulates and prints final totals is illustrated in Figure A–15.

When counting records and accumulating totals, it is necessary to reserve fields in main computer memory for these totals. In most cases, these fields, called counters and accumulators, must contain the value zero prior to processing the first input record. In addition, prior to beginning the main processing, a variable name should be assigned to constant numeric values such as the auto cost per mile value (22 cents). This variable name is then used whenever the auto cost per mile is required in a calculation. The process of establishing total fields, setting them to zero, and assigning variable names to constants is called initialization. The initialization steps required for the sample program are indicated in the flowchart by the rectangle following the start symbol. The rectangle contains the notation "Initialize Variables."

The next flowchart symbol specifies that the headings are to be printed. A record is then read, and a test is performed to determine if the record read was the end of file record. If the end of file record was not read, the value 1 is added to the total employees counter. The purpose of this operation is to count the number of records (employees) so that the total employees may be printed out after all records have been processed.

After the total employees counter is incremented, the beginning mileage is subtracted from the ending mileage, giving the mileage driven by the employee. The auto expense is then calculated by multiplying the mileage driven times the auto cost per mile (.22). The auto expense is then added to the total auto expense accumulator. This accumulator was set to zero initially. A line is then printed, and another record is read. Control then returns to determine if the end of file record was read. This looping operation continues until the end of file record is read.

When the end of file record is read, the total number of employees is printed, the total auto expenses are

Program Flowchart

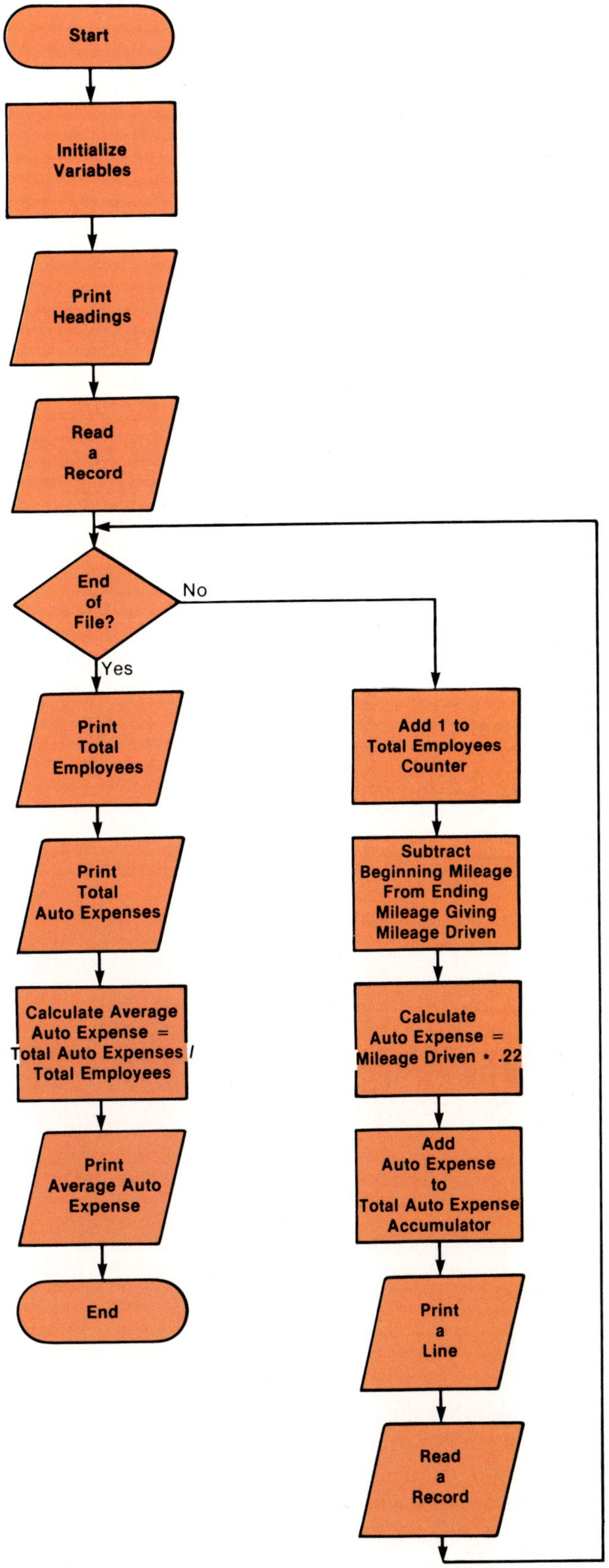

Figure A–15

printed, the total auto expenses are divided by the total employees to give the average auto expense, and the average auto expense per employee is printed. Execution of the program is then terminated.

The BASIC program

The first sections of the BASIC program to prepare the auto expense report are illustrated below. This coding illustrates the beginning documentation and the data statements for the data records processed in this program.

```
100 REM AUTOEXP                  MARCH 28                  SHELLY/CASHMAN
110                                                                    REM
120 REM THIS PROGRAM PREPARES AN AUTO EXPENSE REPORT. MILEAGE
130 REM EXPENSE IS CALCULATED BASED UPON AN AUTO COST OF 22
140 REM CENTS PER MILE. AFTER ALL DATA IS PROCESSED, THE TOTAL
150 REM EMPLOYEES AND TOTAL AUTO EXPENSE WILL BE PRINTED. THE
160 REM AVERAGE EXPENSE PER EMPLOYEE WILL THEN BE CALCULATED
170 REM AND PRINTED.
180                                                                    REM
190 REM VARIABLE NAMES:
200 REM   N$....EMPLOYEE NAME
210 REM   L$....AUTO LICENSE NUMBER
220 REM   B.....BEGINNING MILEAGE
230 REM   E.....ENDING MILEAGE
240 REM   M.....MILEAGE DRIVEN
250 REM   C.....AUTO COST PER MILE
260 REM   X.....AUTO EXPENSE
270 REM   T1....FINAL TOTAL - TOTAL EMPLOYEES
280 REM   T2....FINAL TOTAL - AUTO EXPENSE
290 REM   A.....AVERAGE AUTO EXPENSE PER EMPLOYEE
300                                                                    REM
310 REM ***** DATA TO BE PROCESSED *****
320                                                                    REM
330 DATA "T. ROWE", "HRT-111", 19100, 19224
340 DATA "R. LOPEZ", "GLD-913", 21221, 21332
350 DATA "C. DECK", "LIV-193", 10001, 10206
360 DATA "B. ALEK", "ZRT-904", 15957, 16419
370 DATA "END OF FILE", "END", 99999, 99999
380                                                                    REM
```

Figure A-16

Initialization of variables

The first section of coding following the program documentation and the data statements is used to initialize the variables. These statements are illustrated in Figure A-17.

The statements on lines 410 and 420 set the total employees counter (T1) and the total expense accumulator (T2) to zero. When these let statements are executed, the zeroes on the right side of the equal sign will be placed in the fields referenced by T1 and T2. Counters and accumulators should always be set to zero at the beginning of a program.

```
390 REM ***** INITIALIZATION OF VARIABLES  *****
400                                                              REM
410 LET T1 = 0
420 LET T2 = 0
430 LET C = .22
440                                                              REM
```

Figure A-17

When the let statement on line 430 is executed, the value .22 specified on the right side of the equal sign will be placed in the field referenced by the variable name C. The field identified by the variable name C can then be used in those statements within the program which require the numeric value .22 (the auto cost per mile). The purpose of using a field referenced by a variable name rather than the constant .22 is to facilitate any future changes in the program. For example, if the auto cost per mile were changed from .22 to .25, the constant value in the statement on line 430 could be changed to .25. All references in the program to the field identified by the variable name C would then reflect this change. Numeric constants should normally not be used in the program statements that perform calculations. Instead, good programming practice dictates that numeric constants be assigned to variable names in the section of the program used for the initialization of variables.

Print the report headings

The first statements in the processing section of the program, beginning on line 450, are used to print both the report and column headings. This section of the program is illustrated in Figure A-18.

```
450 REM ***** PROCESSING *****
460                                                              REM
470 PRINT TAB(20) "AUTO EXPENSE"
480 PRINT " "
490 PRINT "  NAME          LICENSE        MILEAGE          EXPENSE"
500 PRINT " "
510                                                              REM
```

Figure A-18

The print statement on line 470 is used to print the report heading. It uses the tab function. The tab function specifies the column in which a constant or value in a field is to begin printing. In the print statement in Figure A-18, the tab function is used to indicate that the constant AUTO EXPENSE is to be printed beginning in column 20 of the report. The tab function must be written by specifying the word TAB and, immediately following the word TAB with no intervening spaces, the column number within parentheses.

The print statement on line 480 causes a blank line to appear after the report heading. The print statement on line 490 causes the column headings to be printed. The words in the constant within the print statement are positioned so they will print over the columns of data which will print in the predefined zones of the CRT screen. The statement on line 500 causes a blank line to be printed following the column headings.

Reading and processing records

The statements to read and process the auto mileage records are illustrated in Figure A-19 on page A.18.

```
520 READ N$, L$, B, E
530                                                      REM
540 IF N$ = "END OF FILE" THEN 630
550   LET T1 = T1 + 1
560   LET M = E - B
570   LET X = M * C
580   LET T2 = T2 + X
590   PRINT N$, L$, M, X
600   READ N$, L$, B, E
610 GOTO 540
620                                                      REM
```

Figure A–19

The read statement on line 520 will transfer the first four items in the first data statement in the program to the name field (N$), the auto license number field (L$), the beginning mileage field (B), and the ending mileage field (E). After these fields have been transferred, a check is performed by the if statement on line 540 to determine if the value END OF FILE is in the name (N$) field, signifying the end of file record. If so, control is transferred to the statement on line 630.

If end of file has not been detected, the statements beginning on line 550 are executed. The let statement on line 550 is used to count the number of records processed. Each time the statement is executed, the value 1 will be added to the value in T1. Since T1 was initially set to zero (see Figure A–17), the value in T1 after the first execution of the statement will be equal to 1. After the statement is executed a second time, the value in T1 will be equal to 2 because the value 1 is being added to the value 1 already in T1. This counting will continue while all of the records are read and processed. When end of file is detected, the value in T1 will be equal to the number of records processed.

The let statement on line 560 calculates the mileage the automobile was driven (M) by subtracting the beginning mileage (B) from the ending mileage (E). On line 570, the let statement calculates the auto expense (X) by multiplying the miles the automobile was driven (M) by the value in the field identified by the variable name C. The value .22 was placed in the C field in the initialization section of the program (see Figure A–17). Thus, multiplying the value in M (miles driven) by the value in C (.22) calculates the auto expense.

The let statement on line 580 adds the auto expense (X) to the final total auto expense accumulator T2. The field referenced by the variable name T2 was set to zero in the initialization section of the program. When this let statement is executed the first time, the auto expense is added to the value zero. When the statement is executed the second time, the auto expense for the second record is added to the auto expense for the first record. The effect of this let statement, then, is to accumulate the auto expenses in the final total accumulator identified by the variable name T2.

The print statement on line 590 prints the name (N$), license number (L$), mileage driven (M), and the auto expense (X). The read statement on line 600 transfers data from the next data statement to the fields defined in the read statement. The goto statement then transfers control to the if statement on line 540. Note that statements 550 through 600 have been indented two spaces. This is done so that those statements within the loop can easily be seen in the coding of the program. The looping operation continues until the end of file record is read, at which time control is transferred to the end of file routine beginning at line 630.

End of file processing

After all records have been processed, control is transferred to the print statement on line 630 (Figure A–20), which prints a blank line. The next print statement prints the total number of employees (T1). Note the manner in which the print statement is written to print both a constant and a variable. The words TOTAL EMPLOYEES are enclosed within quotation marks. After the right quotation mark, a semicolon is written in the statement. A semicolon in the print statement is used to control horizontal spacing. When a semicolon follows a

```
630 PRINT " "
640 PRINT "TOTAL EMPLOYEES"; T1
650 PRINT "TOTAL AUTO EXPENSE  $"; T2
660 LET A = T2 / T1
670 PRINT "AVERAGE EXPENSE PER EMPLOYEE  $"; A
680 END
```

Figure A–20

string constant (such as the words TOTAL EMPLOYEES), string data specified following the semicolon will be displayed immediately adjacent to the string constant. When numeric data follows a semicolon, such as in this example where the numeric variable T1 follows the semicolon, room is always provided for printing a minus sign. If the number is positive, a blank space will appear before the numeric value. No blank spaces follow the word EMPLOYEES in the string constant. The result is that the word EMPLOYEES and the positive numeric value in the T1 field are separated by a single blank space when the line is printed (see Figure A–14).

A review of the output in Figure A–14 also indicates that a dollar sign is to be printed for the total auto expense and average expense per employee dollar amounts. Although there are a number of programming techniques that can be used to print the dollar sign, the method used in the sample program is to include the dollar sign in quotation marks as part of the string constant identifying the amounts printed (lines 650 and 670 in Figure A–20). It will be noted from Figure A–14 as well that a single space appears between the dollar sign and the numeric amounts (198.44 for auto expense and 49.61 for average expense). The reason is that, as explained above, when a numeric value follows a semicolon in a print statement, the first position will be blank when the numeric value is positive, as in this case. Thus, using this technique, there is no way for the dollar signs to print immediately adjacent to the numeric values.

The last statement in the program is the end statement which terminates execution of the program.

The BASIC program

The complete BASIC program for the sample problem which produces the auto expense report is illustrated in Figure A–21 and Figure A–22.

BASIC Program (1 of 2)

```
100 REM AUTOEXP                    MARCH 28                 SHELLY/CASHMAN
110                                                                    REM
120 REM THIS PROGRAM PREPARES AN AUTO EXPENSE REPORT. MILEAGE
130 REM EXPENSE IS CALCULATED BASED UPON AN AUTO COST OF 22
140 REM CENTS PER MILE. AFTER ALL DATA IS PROCESSED, THE TOTAL
150 REM EMPLOYEES AND TOTAL AUTO EXPENSE WILL BE PRINTED. THE
160 REM AVERAGE EXPENSE PER EMPLOYEE WILL THEN BE CALCULATED
170 REM AND PRINTED.
180                                                                    REM
190 REM VARIABLE NAMES:
200 REM   N$....EMPLOYEE NAME
210 REM   L$....AUTO LICENSE NUMBER
220 REM   B.....BEGINNING MILEAGE
230 REM   E.....ENDING MILEAGE
240 REM   M.....MILEAGE DRIVEN
250 REM   C.....AUTO COST PER MILE
260 REM   X.....AUTO EXPENSE
270 REM   T1....FINAL TOTAL - TOTAL EMPLOYEES
280 REM   T2....FINAL TOTAL - AUTO EXPENSE
290 REM   A.....AVERAGE AUTO EXPENSE PER EMPLOYEE
```

Figure A–21

BASIC Program (2 of 2)

```
300                                                              REM
310 REM ***** DATA TO BE PROCESSED *****
320                                                              REM
330 DATA "T. ROWE", "HRT-111", 19100, 19224
340 DATA "R. LOPEZ", "GLD-913", 21221, 21332
350 DATA "C. DECK", "LIV-193", 10001, 10206
360 DATA "B. ALEK", "ZRT-904", 15957, 16419
370 DATA "END OF FILE", "END", 99999, 99999
380                                                              REM
390 REM ***** INITIALIZATION OF VARIABLES  *****
400                                                              REM
410 LET T1 = 0
420 LET T2 = 0
430 LET C = .22
440                                                              REM
450 REM ***** PROCESSING *****
460                                                              REM
470 PRINT TAB(20) "AUTO EXPENSE"
480 PRINT " "
490 PRINT "  NAME          LICENSE        MILEAGE          EXPENSE"
500 PRINT " "
510                                                              REM
520 READ N$, L$, B, E
530                                                              REM
540 IF N$ = "END OF FILE" THEN 630
550   LET T1 = T1 + 1
560   LET M = E - B
570   LET X = M * C
580   LET T2 = T2 + X
590   PRINT N$, L$, M, X
600   READ N$, L$, B, E
610 GOTO 540
620                                                              REM
630 PRINT " "
640 PRINT "TOTAL EMPLOYEES"; T1
650 PRINT "TOTAL AUTO EXPENSE  $"; T2
660 LET A = T2 / T1
670 PRINT "AVERAGE EXPENSE PER EMPLOYEE  $"; A
680 END
```

Output

```
                    AUTO EXPENSE

   NAME          LICENSE          MILEAGE            EXPENSE

T. ROWE          HRT-111            124              27.28
R. LOPEZ         GLD-913            111              24.42
C. DECK          LIV-193            205              45.1
B. ALEK          ZRT-904            462              101.64

TOTAL EMPLOYEES 4
TOTAL AUTO EXPENSE   $ 198.44
AVERAGE EXPENSE PER EMPLOYEE   $ 49.61
```

Figure A-22

Report editing

Information displayed on a report or CRT screen should be in a format which is easy to read and understand. For example, numeric values should normally be aligned on the decimal point and, when dollars and cents are printed, both numbers to the right of the decimal point should print. Placing information in a format such as this is called report editing.

Many BASIC interpreters provide a statement called the print using statement that can be used for report editing. Through the use of the print using statement, operations such as suppressing the printing of leading zeroes in a field (for example, printing 124 instead of 00124), printing an amount field with the decimal point, comma, and dollar sign if appropriate, and aligning fields based upon the decimal point can take place.

Report editing with the print using statement is accomplished using special characters to format the data. These special characters, which are specified either as a constant in the print using statement or as a string constant placed in a field identified by a string variable name, indicate where zero suppression is to occur, where decimal points, commas, and dollar signs are to be printed, and where string constants are to be printed.

To illustrate the use of the print using statement, the sample program which creates the auto expense report will be modified. The report to be produced by the modified program is illustrated in Figure A-23.

```
                AUTO EXPENSE

   NAME        LICENSE    MILEAGE EXPENSE

T. ROWE        HRT-111        124     27.28
R. LOPEZ       GLD-913        111     24.42
C. DECK        LIV-193        205     45.10
B. ALEK        ZRT-904        462    101.64

TOTAL EMPLOYEES    4
TOTAL AUTO EXPENSE $198.44
AVERAGE EXPENSE PER EMPLOYEE    $49.61
```

Figure A-23

Note that the dollar and cents values in the expense field are aligned on the decimal point. In addition, the total auto expense and the average expense per employee dollar fields are printed with the dollar sign immediately adjacent to the leftmost digit in the number. This is known as a floating dollar sign.

To control the printing that is to take place with the print using statement, a print using format must be written by the programmer. This format, which is a string constant, indicates how data is to be printed on the report. In the sample program, let statements are used to place the print using formats into fields identified by string variable names. The following example illustrates a let statement together with the print using format used for the detail line of the report as it corresponds to the line on the report.

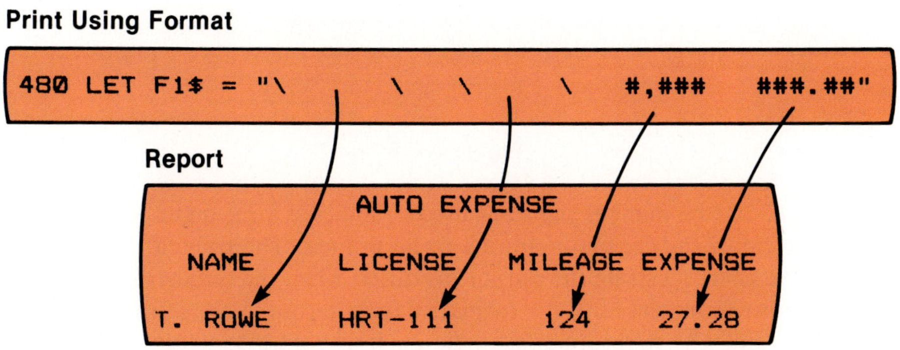

Figure A-24

In the example in Figure A–24, the print using format, enclosed within quotation marks, is placed in a field identified by the string variable name F1$ by the let statement on line 480. Some BASIC interpreters, such as the one used to execute the programs in this book, allow a string variable name with an alphabetic character followed by a numeric value and then the dollar sign, such as F1$.

The print using format specifies how the data is to appear on the report line. The backward slashes (\ ) indicate where string fields are to be placed in the report line. The first backward slash indicates the first character position in the string field, and the second backward slash indicates the last character position in the field. Therefore, in the name field, room for eight characters is defined — the two backward slashes and the six spaces between them.

The license number field is also a string field. It is defined as seven characters in length by the two backward slashes and the five spaces between them. Numeric fields are defined through the use of the number sign (#). Each occurrence of a number sign corresponds to a numeric digit in the field. Punctuation is placed in the format where it is to occur in the actual output. For the mileage field, the comma is placed where it will print — to the left of the third numeric digit so that the number is easier to read. Since the mileage in the first line of the report is less than 1,000, the comma is not printed. Similarly, a decimal point is placed in the format where it is supposed to print. In the expense field, the format ###.## specifies that there will be three digits to the left of the decimal point and two digits to the right of the decimal point in the printed output. Thus, the field prints as a dollars and cents field.

To print the output line illustrated in Figure A–24, the print using statement is used. This statement, as used in the sample program, is shown in Figure A–25.

```
670   PRINT USING F1$; N$, L$, M, X
```

Figure A–25

Following the line number and the words PRINT USING is the variable name (F1$) that identifies the field where the print using format is stored. This variable name is followed by a semicolon, and then the names of the fields to be printed are specified. The following chart illustrates further examples of the print using statement.

EXAMPLE	DATA TO BE EDITED	PRINT USING FORMAT	PRINTED RESULTS
1	125.62	###.##	125.62
2	005.76	###.##	5.76
3	.65	###.##	0.65
4	1208.78	#,###.##	1,208.78
5	986.05	#,###.##	986.05
6	34.87	$$#,###.##	$34.87
7	3579.75	$$#,###.##	$3,579.75
8	561.93	$##,###.##	$ 561.93

Figure A–26

In example 1 in Figure A–26, the number signs are used to indicate three digits to the left of the decimal point and two digits to the right of the decimal point are to be printed. The printed results indicate this. The second and third examples in the chart illustrate the output produced when the number of characters to be printed is less than the number of number signs placed in the format. Excess zeroes to the left of the decimal point in the number to be printed will normally be suppressed (example 2). In the third example, however, when there are no digits to the left of the decimal point in the number to be edited, a single zero will be printed to the left of the decimal point.

In the fourth and fifth examples, a comma is included in the print using format. The format as written will cause a comma to print if there are more than 3 digits to the left of the decimal point in the number to be printed (example 4). If not, the comma is not printed (example 5).

The last three examples illustrate a print using format that will print dollar signs. If two dollar signs are placed in the format, a floating dollar sign will be printed. If one dollar sign is specified in the print using format (example 8), the dollar sign will print in the fixed position specified.

Constants can be included in the print using format. The print using format and the output generated for the total auto expense are illustrated in Figure A-27.

```
500 LET F3$ = "TOTAL AUTO EXPENSE $$##.##"
```

```
TOTAL AUTO EXPENSE $198.44
```

Figure A-27

In the example above, the constant to be printed (TOTAL AUTO EXPENSE) is included within the print using format. Both constants and the formats of variable fields can be included in the print using format.

Many other variations of print using formats are available. Those presented here, however, provide significant flexibility when writing programs which produce output that is easy to read and understand.

The coding in Figure A-28 and Figure A-29 illustrates the program which produces the auto expense report with report editing. Particular attention should be paid to lines 480 - 510 which contain the print using formats; line 670, which contains the print using statement for the detail line; and statements 720, 730, and 750, which are the print using statements that print the total lines.

BASIC Program (1 of 2)

```
100 REM AUTOEXP                    MARCH 28               SHELLY/CASHMAN
110                                                                   REM
120 REM THIS PROGRAM PREPARES AN AUTO EXPENSE REPORT. MILEAGE
130 REM EXPENSE IS CALCULATED BASED UPON AN AUTO COST OF 22
140 REM CENTS PER MILE. AFTER ALL DATA IS PROCESSED, THE TOTAL
150 REM EMPLOYEES AND TOTAL AUTO EXPENSE WILL BE PRINTED. THE
160 REM AVERAGE EXPENSE PER EMPLOYEE WILL THEN BE CALCULATED
170 REM AND PRINTED.
180                                                                   REM
190 REM VARIABLE NAMES:
200 REM    N$....EMPLOYEE NAME
210 REM    L$....AUTO LICENSE NUMBER
220 REM    B.....BEGINNING MILEAGE
230 REM    E.....ENDING MILEAGE
240 REM    M.....MILEAGE DRIVEN
250 REM    C.....AUTO COST PER MILE
260 REM    X.....AUTO EXPENSE
270 REM    T1....FINAL TOTAL - TOTAL EMPLOYEES
280 REM    T2....FINAL TOTAL - AUTO EXPENSE
290 REM    A.....AVERAGE AUTO EXPENSE PER EMPLOYEE
300 REM    F1$...PRINT USING FORMAT FOR THE DETAIL LINE
310 REM    F2$...PRINT USING FORMAT FOR TOTAL EMPLOYEES LINE
320 REM    F3$...PRINT USING FORMAT FOR TOTAL AUTO EXPENSE LINE
330 REM    F4$...PRINT USING FORMAT FOR AVERAGE EXPENSE LINE
340                                                                   REM
```

Figure A-28

BASIC Program (2 of 2)

```
350 REM ***** DATA TO BE PROCESSED *****
360 REM
370 DATA "T. ROWE", "HRT-111", 19100, 19224
380 DATA "R. LOPEZ", "GLD-913", 21221, 21332
390 DATA "C. DECK", "LIV-193", 10001, 10206
400 DATA "B. ALEK", "ZRT-904", 15957, 16419
410 DATA "END OF FILE", "END", 99999, 99999
420 REM
430 REM ***** INITIALIZATION OF VARIABLES  *****
440 REM
450 LET T1 = 0
460 LET T2 = 0
470 LET C = .22
480 LET F1$ = "\       \   \       \   #,###    ###.##"
490 LET F2$ = "TOTAL EMPLOYEES ###"
500 LET F3$ = "TOTAL AUTO EXPENSE $$##.##"
510 LET F4$ = "AVERAGE EXPENSE PER EMPLOYEE $$##.##"
520 REM
530 REM ***** PROCESSING *****
540 REM
550 PRINT TAB(13) "AUTO EXPENSE"
560 PRINT " "
570 PRINT "  NAME      LICENSE   MILEAGE EXPENSE"
580 PRINT " "
590 REM
600 READ N$, L$, B, E
610 REM
620 IF N$ = "END OF FILE" THEN 710
630   LET T1 = T1 + 1
640   LET M = E - B
650   LET X = M * C
660   LET T2 = T2 + X
670   PRINT USING F1$; N$, L$, M, X
680   READ N$, L$, B, E
690 GOTO 620
700 REM
710 PRINT " "
720 PRINT USING F2$; T1
730 PRINT USING F3$; T2
740 LET A = T2 / T1
750 PRINT USING F4$; A
760 END
```

Figure A-29

STUDENT PROGRAMMING ASSIGNMENT 1
Basic Arithmetic Operations

Instructions: A payroll report is to be prepared listing all employees, their hourly pay rates, and their weekly pay. A program should be designed and coded in BASIC to produce the payroll report.

INPUT Input consists of records that contain the employee name and hourly rate of pay. The input data is illustrated below.

EMPLOYEE NAME	HOURLY PAY RATE
LOMAX	7.70
MANN	6.05
ORR	8.10
SIMMS	9.50
ZANG	12.00
END OF FILE	99.99

OUTPUT Output is a CRT display listing all employees, their hourly pay rates, and their weekly pay. It is assumed that all employees work 40 hours per week. Weekly pay is calculated by multiplying the hourly pay by 40 hours. The total number of employees and the total weekly pay of all employees will be displayed at the bottom of the listing. Headings should be included. The print using statement should be used if available. A sample of the output is illustrated below.

```
                PAYROLL REPORT

EMPLOYEE          HOURLY          WEEKLY
  NAME              PAY             PAY

  LOMAX             7.70          308.00
  MANN              6.05          242.00
  ORR               8.10          324.00
  SIMMS             9.50          380.00
  ZANG             12.00          480.00

TOTAL EMPLOYEES     5
TOTAL WEEKLY PAY $1,734.00
```

STUDENT PROGRAMMING ASSIGNMENT 2
Basic Arithmetic Operations

Instructions: A CRT report is to be prepared listing students and their test scores for the current period. The report will include each student's test scores and the average of each student's scores. A program should be designed and coded in BASIC to produce the list.

INPUT Input consists of records that contain the student name and the test scores for the current period. The input data is illustrated below.

STUDENT NAME	TEST 1 SCORE	TEST 2 SCORE
BANKS	70	78
DAVIS	92	94
GOMEZ	88	84
KATZ	78	82
END OF FILE	99	99

OUTPUT Output consists of a CRT display listing the student's name, the test scores, and the average of each student's test scores. The average of each student's test scores is calculated by adding the score for test 1 and the score for test 2 and dividing by 2. After all records for all students have been processed, the total number of students and the class average on all tests should be displayed. To obtain a true class average, add all test scores into an accumulator and divide by the number of tests taken. Headings should be included. The print using statement should be used if available. A sample of the output is illustrated below.

```
                 TEST SCORES

STUDENT       TEST 1      TEST 2       AVERAGE

BANKS           70          78           74
DAVIS           92          94           93
GOMEZ           88          84           86
KATZ            78          82           80

TOTAL STUDENTS    4
CLASS AVERAGE 83.25
```

PROBLEM 3 — COMPARING

The ability to compare numbers or letters of the alphabet and perform alternative operations based upon the results of the comparison is one of the more powerful features of computers that can be implemented using a programming language. When comparing, six types of operations can be performed. These operations include comparing to determine if: 1) One value is equal to another; 2) One value is less than another; 3) One value is greater than another; 4) One value is less than or equal to another; 5) One value is greater than or equal to another; 6) One value is not equal to another.

Relational operators

When using the BASIC language, six relational operators are used with the if statement to perform comparing operations. Relational operators are symbols that are used to express the relationship being tested for. The chart below illustrates the relational operators, their meanings, and an example of their use.

RELATIONAL OPERATOR	INTERPRETATION	EXAMPLE
=	equal to	300 IF D = M THEN 420
<	less than	300 IF M < 100 THEN 630
>	greater than	450 IF F > J THEN 870
<=	less than or equal to	450 IF Q <= P THEN 510
>=	greater than or equal to	470 IF L >= A THEN 620
<>	not equal to	500 IF M <> T THEN 580

Figure A-30

When using the relational operators with the if statement, if the condition tested is true, then the statement referenced by the line number following the word THEN is executed. If the condition is false, the next statement in sequence is executed. In the first example above, the data referenced by the variable name D is compared to the data in the field referenced by M. If an equal condition occurs, statement 420 will be executed. If the value in D is not equal to the value in M, the statement following statement 300 will be executed. The other examples illustrate the various comparing operations that can be performed.

Comparing string data

String data can also be compared using the if statement. To compare string data, a string variable or a string constant is placed to the left of the relational operator. Another string variable or string constant is placed on the right side of the relational operator. The values are then compared based upon the relational operator. This is illustrated in the two examples below.

Example 1:

```
200 IF N$ = A$ THEN 560
```

Example 2:

```
400 IF N$ = "END OF FILE" THEN 800
```

Figure A-31

In example 1, if the data in the area referenced by the string variable N$ is equal to the data in the field referenced by A$, then control will be passed to the statement referenced by line 560; otherwise, the next statement in sequence will be executed. The if statement in example 2 compares the value in the field referenced by the variable name N$ to the string constant END OF FILE. If the data in N$ is equal to the constant, control will be passed to statement 800; otherwise, the next statement in sequence will be given control.

Sample problem 3

To illustrate a comparing operation, a program which prepares a report listing the charges for video rental will be designed and coded in BASIC. In this application, if the video tape is rented for three days or less, the charge is $2.49 per day. If the video tape is rented for more than three days, the charge is $2.49 for the first three days and $3.49 per day for each day over three days.

Input

Input consists of records containing the title of the video tape rented and the number of days the tape was rented. A sample of the input is illustrated below.

VIDEO TITLE	DAYS RENTED
LOST IN SPACE	1
TOGETHER AGAIN	3
THE LAST DAY	5
SUNDAY MORNING	4
END OF FILE	9

Figure A–32

Output

The output is a video rental summary report that lists the title of the video tape rented, the number of days the tape was rented, and the charge for the rental. After all records have been processed, the total number of tapes rented and the total of the charges are to be printed. The format of the output is illustrated below.

```
     V I D E O   R E N T A L S

   TITLE              DAYS     CHARGE

LOST IN SPACE           1        2.49
TOGETHER AGAIN          3        7.47
THE LAST DAY            5       14.45
SUNDAY MORNING          4       10.96

TOTAL VIDEOS RENTED    4
TOTAL CHARGES    $35.37
```

Figure A–33

Program flowchart

The flowchart below illustrates the logic required to produce the video rentals report.

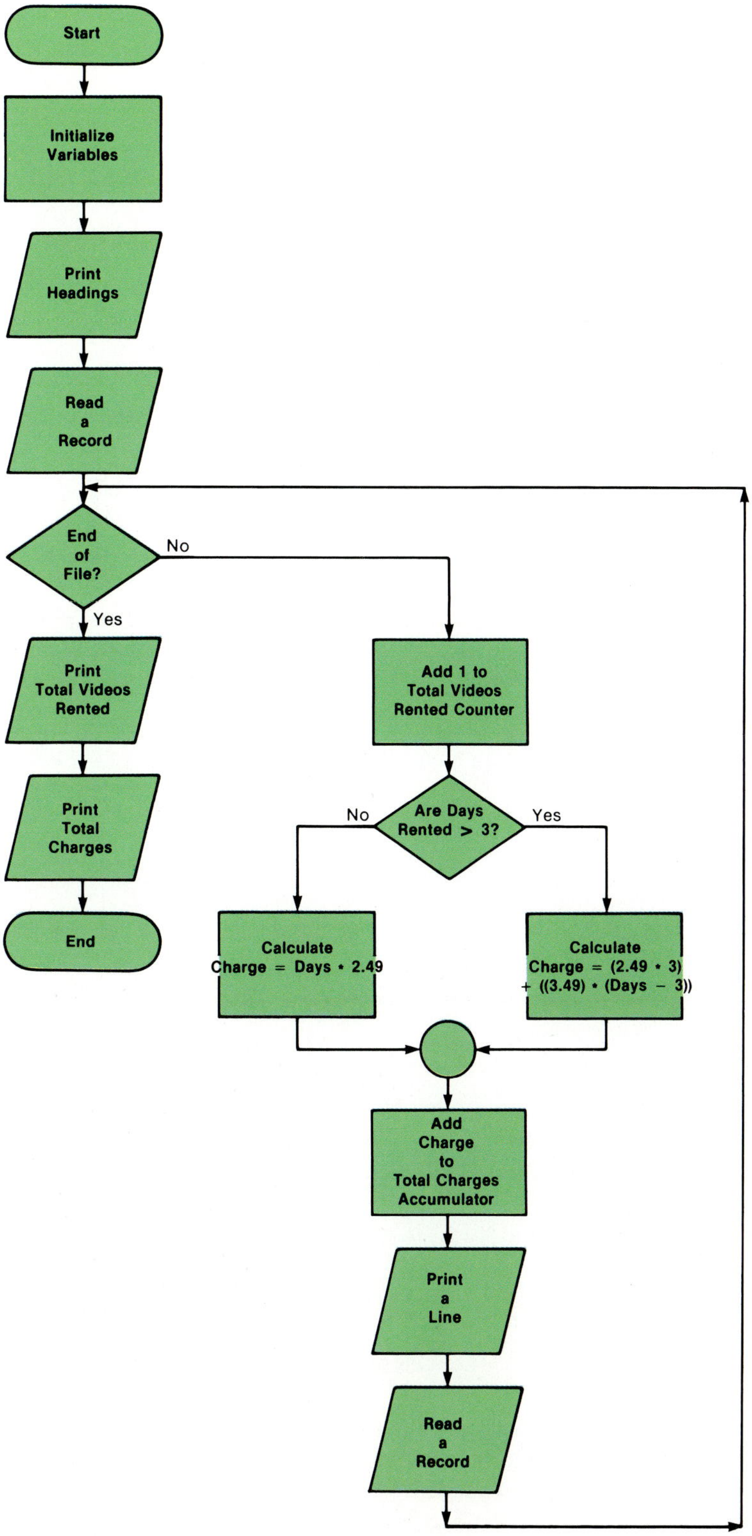

Figure A–34

The BASIC program

The documentation and the first portion of the BASIC program is illustrated in Figure A-35 below.

```
100 REM RENTALS                    MARCH 28                   SHELLY/CASHMAN
110                                                                      REM
120 REM THIS PROGRAM CALCULATES VIDEO RENTAL CHARGES BASED UPON
130 REM A RATE STRUCTURE THAT HAS ONE CHARGE PER DAY FOR THE
140 REM FIRST THREE DAYS AND A HIGHER CHARGE PER DAY FOR EACH
150 REM DAY THEREAFTER. TOTAL VIDEOS RENTED AND TOTAL CHARGES
160 REM ARE PRINTED AFTER ALL RECORDS HAVE BEEN PROCESSED.
170                                                                      REM
180 REM VARIABLE NAMES:
190 REM    T$....TITLE OF VIDEO
200 REM    D.....DAYS RENTED
210 REM    R.....RENTAL CHARGE - CALCULATED BY PROGRAM
220 REM    N.....NUMBER OF DAYS FOR LOWER CHARGE - 3 DAYS
230 REM    C1....CHARGE PER DAY FOR FIRST THREE DAYS
240 REM    C2....CHARGE PER DAY FOR EACH DAY MORE THAN 3 DAYS
250 REM    T1....FINAL TOTAL - TOTAL VIDEOS RENTED
260 REM    T2....FINAL TOTAL - TOTAL CHARGES
270 REM    F1$...PRINT USING FORMAT FOR DETAIL PRINT LINE
280 REM    F2$...PRINT USING FORMAT FOR TOTAL VIDEOS LINE
290 REM    F3$...PRINT USING FORMAT FOR TOTAL CHARGES LINE
300                                                                      REM
310 REM ***** DATA TO BE PROCESSED *****
320                                                                      REM
330 DATA "LOST IN SPACE", 1
340 DATA "TOGETHER AGAIN", 3
350 DATA "THE LAST DAY", 5
360 DATA "SUNDAY MORNING", 4
370 DATA "END OF FILE", 9
380                                                                      REM
390 REM ***** INITIALIZATION OF VARIABLES *****
400                                                                      REM
410 LET T1 = 0
420 LET T2 = 0
430 LET N = 3
440 LET C1 = 2.49
450 LET C2 = 3.49
460 LET F1$ = "\                 \     ##        ###.##"
470 LET F2$ = "TOTAL VIDEOS RENTED ###"
480 LET F3$ = "TOTAL CHARGES $$##.##"
490                                                                      REM
```

Figure A-35

The first lines of coding are used to document the program and define the data to be processed. The entry on line 410 sets the final total counter for the total number of videos rented to zero, and the let statement on line 420 sets the final total accumulator for the total charges to zero.

Although constants can be used in calculations and if statements, as noted previous in this appendix, it is a better programming technique to assign the constants to fields identified by variable names and use the variable names in the calculation and if statements. Therefore, in the sample program, the number of days which are used for the charge of $2.49 (3 days) is placed in the field identified by the variable name N (line 430). The variable name N will then be used in subsequent statements.

Similarly, the entries on lines 440 and 450 place the charge per day for the first three days (2.49) and the charge per day for each day after three days (3.49) into fields identified by the variable names C1 and C2, respectively. The statements on lines 460, 470, and 480 are used to define the print using formats of the various lines that will be printed. These entries will be referenced in the print using statements.

The portion of the program to display the headings, read and process the data, and print the final totals is illustrated in Figure A-36.

```
500 REM ***** PROCESSING *****
510                                                     REM
520 PRINT TAB(7) "V I D E O   R E N T A L S"
530 PRINT " "
540 PRINT "    TITLE                  DAYS     CHARGE"
550 PRINT " "
560                                                     REM
570 READ T$, D
580                                                     REM
590 IF T$ = "END OF FILE" THEN 730
600   LET T1 = T1 + 1
610   IF D > N THEN 650
620     LET R = D * C1
630     GOTO 680
640                                                     REM
650     LET R = (C1 * N) + ((C2) * (D - N))
660     GOTO 680
670                                                     REM
680   LET T2 = T2 + R
690   PRINT USING F1$; T$, D, R
700   READ T$, D
710 GOTO 590
720                                                     REM
730 PRINT " "
740 PRINT USING F2$; T1
750 PRINT USING F3$; T2
760 END
```

Figure A-36

The statements on lines 520 through 550 print the headings. A record is then read and a check is performed to determine if the END OF FILE record was read. If not, the videos rented counter (T1) is incremented by one. The if statement on line 610 compares the days rented (D) to the number of days for the lower charge, which is the value 3 stored in the field identified by the variable name N. If the days rented are greater than the value in N, control is passed to the let statement on line 650. If the days rented are less than or equal to the value in N, statement 620 will be executed.

The let statement on line 620 multiplies the days (D) by the value in C1 (2.49) and stores the answer in the field identified by the variable name R. Control is then transferred to line 680, where the rental charge (R) is added to the total rental charge accumulator (T2). A line is then printed and another record is read.

When the days rented are greater than three, the let statement on line 650 is executed. This statement calculates the rental charge by determining the charge for three days (C1 * N) and adding the result to the charge for all days greater than three ((C2) * (D − N)). Control is then transferred to line 680, where the rental charge (R) is added to the total rental charge accumulator (T2). A line is printed and another record is read.

Control is then passed to statement 590, which checks for end of file. When it is end of file, the final totals are printed and program execution is terminated.

The complete BASIC program to produce a video tape rental report is illustrated in Figures A-37 and A-38.

BASIC Program (1 of 2)

```
100 REM RENTALS                  MARCH 28                  SHELLY/CASHMAN
110                                                                   REM
120 REM THIS PROGRAM CALCULATES VIDEO RENTAL CHARGES BASED UPON
130 REM A RATE STRUCTURE THAT HAS ONE CHARGE PER DAY FOR THE
140 REM FIRST THREE DAYS AND A HIGHER CHARGE PER DAY FOR EACH
150 REM DAY THEREAFTER. TOTAL VIDEOS RENTED AND TOTAL CHARGES
160 REM ARE PRINTED AFTER ALL RECORDS HAVE BEEN PROCESSED.
170                                                                   REM
180 REM VARIABLE NAMES:
190 REM   T$....TITLE OF VIDEO
200 REM   D.....DAYS RENTED
210 REM   R.....RENTAL CHARGE - CALCULATED BY PROGRAM
220 REM   N.....NUMBER OF DAYS FOR LOWER CHARGE - 3 DAYS
230 REM   C1....CHARGE PER DAY FOR FIRST THREE DAYS
240 REM   C2....CHARGE PER DAY FOR EACH DAY MORE THAN 3 DAYS
250 REM   T1....FINAL TOTAL - TOTAL VIDEOS RENTED
260 REM   T2....FINAL TOTAL - TOTAL CHARGES
270 REM   F1$...PRINT USING FORMAT FOR DETAIL PRINT LINE
280 REM   F2$...PRINT USING FORMAT FOR TOTAL VIDEOS LINE
290 REM   F3$...PRINT USING FORMAT FOR TOTAL CHARGES LINE
300                                                                   REM
310 REM ***** DATA TO BE PROCESSED *****
320                                                                   REM
330 DATA "LOST IN SPACE", 1
340 DATA "TOGETHER AGAIN", 3
350 DATA "THE LAST DAY", 5
360 DATA "SUNDAY MORNING", 4
370 DATA "END OF FILE", 9
380                                                                   REM
390 REM ***** INITIALIZATION OF VARIABLES *****
400                                                                   REM
410 LET T1 = 0
420 LET T2 = 0
430 LET N = 3
440 LET C1 = 2.49
450 LET C2 = 3.49
460 LET F1$ = "\              \     ##       ###.##"
470 LET F2$ = "TOTAL VIDEOS RENTED ###"
480 LET F3$ = "TOTAL CHARGES $$##.##"
490                                                                   REM
500 REM ***** PROCESSING *****
510                                                                   REM
520 PRINT TAB(7) "V I D E O   R E N T A L S"
530 PRINT " "
540 PRINT "    TITLE                DAYS     CHARGE"
550 PRINT " "
560                                                                   REM
570 READ T$, D
580                                                                   REM
590 IF T$ = "END OF FILE" THEN 730
600   LET T1 = T1 + 1
610   IF D > N THEN 650
620     LET R = D * C1
630     GOTO 680
640                                                                   REM
```

Figure A-37

BASIC Program (2 of 2)

```
650      LET R = (C1 * N) + ((C2) * (D - N))
660      GOTO 680
670                                                    REM
680    LET T2 = T2 + R
690    PRINT USING F1$; T$, D, R
700    READ T$, D
710 GOTO 590
720                                                    REM
730 PRINT " "
740 PRINT USING F2$; T1
750 PRINT USING F3$; T2
760 END
```

Figure A–38

STUDENT PROGRAMMING ASSIGNMENT 1
Comparing

Instructions: A program is to be designed and written using the BASIC language that will produce a student registration report. The report will be a CRT display which will include the student name, the number of units being registered, the fee charged, and the student status.

INPUT Input consists of records that contain the student name and the number of units for which registration is desired. The input records to be used in the program are shown below.

STUDENT NAME	UNITS
T. BOWLS	14
B. DAVIS	18
J. SLATT	16
T. WONG	11
END OF FILE	99

OUTPUT Output consists of a CRT display listing the student name, the number of units, the fee charged to the student for the units, and the student status (part time or full time). The registration fee for students taking less than 16 units is $75.00. They are considered part time students. The registration fee for full time students (16 units or more) is $5.00 per unit. The total number of students and the total fees should be accumulated and printed at the bottom of the listing. A sample output listing is illustrated below.

```
              STUDENT REGISTRATION

  STUDENT      UNITS       FEE       STATUS

 T. BOWLS       14        75.00     PART TIME
 B. DAVIS       18        90.00     FULL TIME
 J. SLATT       16        80.00     FULL TIME
 T. WONG        11        75.00     PART TIME

 TOTAL STUDENTS  4
 TOTAL FEES $320.00
```

STUDENT PROGRAMMING ASSIGNMENT 2
Comparing

Instructions: A computer usage report is to be prepared. The report will be displayed on a CRT screen. A program should be designed and coded in BASIC to produce the report.

INPUT Input consists of records that contain the company name, the number of hours, and the number of minutes of computer time used. The input data is shown below.

COMPANY	HOURS	MINUTES
ACME INC.	2	0
HITEK	2	50
FLOLINE	5	10
DECOY CO.	1	15
END OF FILE	9	99

OUTPUT The output consists of a CRT display listing the company name, the hours of computer usage, the minutes of computer usage, and each company's charge for the total time used. The cost for computer usage is as follows: For less than two hours, the cost is $50.00; for computer usage equal to or greater than two hours, the cost is .50 per minute. A summary of all computer time used and all charges should be printed at the end of the listing. A sample output listing is illustrated below.

```
                 COMPUTER USAGE

COMPANY        HOURS    MINUTES    CHARGES

ACME INC.        2          0        60.00
HITEK            2         50        85.00
FLOLINE          5         10       155.00
DECOY CO.        1         15        50.00

TOTAL HOURS 11.25
TOTAL CHARGES $350.00
```

PROBLEM 4 — LOOPING AND INTERACTIVE PROGRAMMING

The previous programs have illustrated applications in which looping was used to process input records until end of file was detected. There are many other types of applications where looping is the basis of the processing that occurs. The looping logic structure is used in any problem which requires repetitive processing until a given condition occurs. BASIC language statements called the for statement and the next statement are used to implement looping for certain types of problems. The use of the for-next loop will be explained in this section.

With the widespread use of interactive processing, a need exists for a BASIC statement that allows input data to be accepted from the computer keyboard. The input statement is used for this purpose. The input statement is also explained in this section.

The input statement

To enable data to be entered into main computer memory from the computer or terminal keyboard, the input statement is used. The input statement causes the program operation to halt until the user has entered data from the keyboard. After the user enters data from the keyboard, program operation continues.

When the input statement is executed, a question mark appears on the CRT screen, indicating to the user that data is to be entered. When the data is entered by the user, it is displayed on the screen and stored in main computer memory for processing. An example of this process is illustrated in Figure A-39.

Figure A-39

As can be seen from Figure A–39, the input statement consists of a line number and the word INPUT followed by a numeric variable name (G). When the statement is executed, a question mark appears on the screen. The user enters a value, and the value is stored in memory in the field identified by the variable name specified in the input statement. In the example, the number 50 was entered on the keyboard. This number is displayed on the screen and is stored in the field with the variable name G.

When a numeric variable name is specified in an input statement, the value entered can consist of a number, a decimal point, and a plus or minus sign. Entering other characters such as a comma or dollar sign as a part of the number will cause an error message to be displayed.

String variable names can also be specified in the input statement. When a string variable name is included in the input statement, the user can enter any values desired. The data entered will be displayed on the CRT screen and stored in the field identified by the string variable name specified in the input statement.

Prompts

When data is entered by the user from a keyboard, prompts are frequently displayed to assist the user. A prompt is a message displayed on the screen that provides information and instructions to the user regarding some entry to be made or action to be taken. String constants can be specified in the input statement to display prompts. The example below illustrates the use of a prompt.

Figure A–40

A prompt message is included in an input statement by placing the message in quotation marks following the word INPUT. This entry is followed by a semicolon, and then the variable name of the field where the data entered is to be stored. In the example in Figure A-40, when the input statement is executed, the message ENTER COST OF ONE ITEM: is displayed on the screen. This message is followed by a question mark indicating that the computer is ready to accept data from the user. In the example, the user entered the value 1.25. This value was displayed on the CRT screen and stored in the field identified by the variable name C.

When longer prompts are to be displayed, the print statement is often used in conjunction with the input statement. The example in Figure A-41 illustrates the BASIC statements to display a prompt on the screen to ask the user if a cost chart is to be prepared.

```
360 PRINT "DO YOU WANT TO PREPARE AN ITEM COST CHART?"
370 INPUT "ENTER YES OR NO: "; R$
```

```
DO YOU WANT TO PREPARE AN ITEM COST CHART?
ENTER YES OR NO: ? YES
```

Figure A–41

When the print statement is executed, the first line of the prompt is printed. When the input statement is executed, the second line of the prompt is displayed, and the data can then be entered.

Multiple input variables

More than one numeric variable name or string variable name may be specified in an input statement. If more than one variable name is included in an input statement, the variable names must be separated by commas. The following example illustrates the use of two string variable names in an input statement.

```
190 INPUT "ENTER DATE AND NAME: "; D$, N$
```

Figure A–42

On most computers, when the input statement in Figure A–42 is executed, a question mark will appear on the screen. The user should then enter the date, a comma, and a name.

The input statement is widely used in interactive programming and can be used in all applications where it is necessary or desirable to enter data from the keyboard into main computer memory.

Sample problem 4

The sample program in this chapter illustrates the preparation of an item cost chart that contains the cost of one to ten items. The operation begins by asking the user if a cost chart is to be prepared. The user must enter on the keyboard either the word YES or the word NO.

If the user enters NO, the program is terminated. If the user enters the word YES, a message appears on the CRT asking the user to enter the cost of one item. The cost of one item must be less than $1,000.00. After the cost of one item is entered, a chart will be prepared listing the cost of one through ten items. The sequence of screens which will appear when the program is executed is shown in Figure A–43.

```
DO YOU WANT TO PREPARE AN ITEM COST CHART?
ENTER YES OR NO: ? YES
```

```
ENTER COST OF ONE ITEM: ? 1.25
```

```
ITEM COST CHART FOR    $1.25

ITEMS                  COST
-----                  ----
  1                    $1.25
  2                    $2.50
  3                    $3.75
  4                    $5.00
  5                    $6.25
  6                    $7.50
  7                    $8.75
  8                   $10.00
  9                   $11.25
 10                   $12.50

DO YOU WANT TO PREPARE ANOTHER ITEM COST CHART?
ENTER YES OR NO: ? NO

END OF ITEM COST CHART
```

Figure A–43

Program flowchart

The flowchart for the sample problem which produces the item cost chart for one to ten items is illustrated in Figure A–44. To begin the program, variables are initialized. When the CRT screen is used for messages and prompts, it is desirable to clear the screen of any command or control codes that might be on the screen. This step is indicated in the flowchart by the Clear Screen entry.

The user is then asked if an item cost chart is to be produced. The user must enter either the word YES or the word NO. Any other response is invalid. The logic to ensure a valid response uses the looping logic structure. If the user does not enter the value YES or the value NO, the loop is entered. Within the loop, an error message is printed, and the user is requested to enter a new answer. The looping continues until the user enters either YES or NO.

When the user enters either YES or NO, a check is performed to determine which entry was made. If the value NO was entered, an ending message is printed and the program is terminated. If the value YES was entered, indicating that an item cost chart is to be prepared, the main loop is entered.

The first statement clears the screen and then the user is requested to enter the cost of one item. The cost

Flowchart

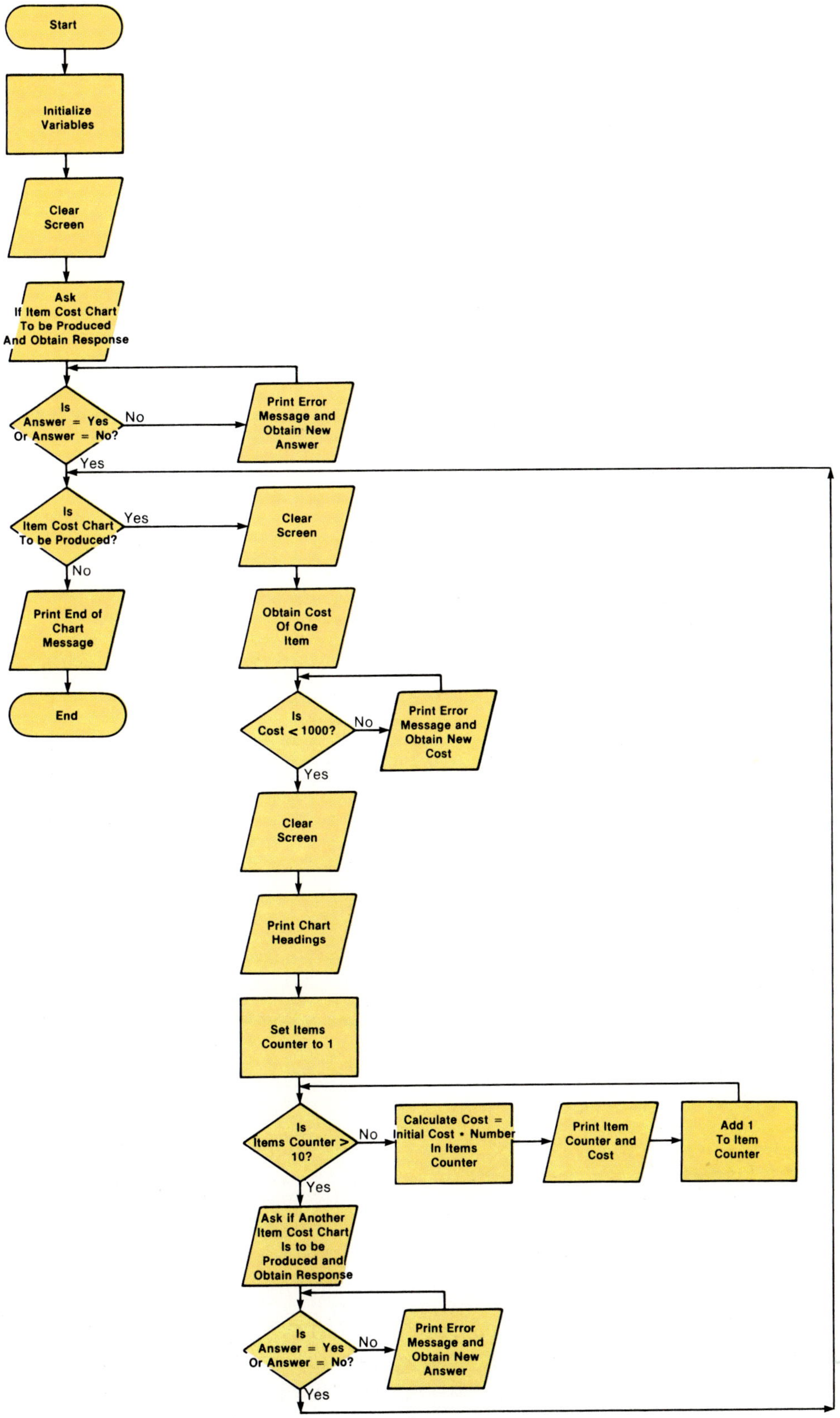

Figure A–44

of the item must be less than 1000.00. A check is performed to determine if the cost entered was less than 1000.00. If not, a loop is entered until the user enters a valid cost.

Once a valid cost has been entered, the screen is cleared, the headings are printed, a counter is initialized to one, and a loop is entered. The statements in the loop will be executed ten times in order to calculate the cost of one to ten items. After the costs have been calculated for all ten items, there is an exit from the loop, and the user is asked if another item cost chart is to be produced. The user must then respond with either YES or NO. When a valid response has been entered, control returns to the decision portion of the main processing loop. When the user enters the value YES, indicating that another cost chart is to be prepared, the main processing loop is entered again; otherwise, the end of job processing takes place.

Input editing

Whenever users enter data from a keyboard, the data entered should be edited; that is, statements should be included within the program to assure that valid data is entered. The definition of valid data is found in the programming specifications.

In the sample problem, the user must enter the words YES or NO in response to the question, "Do you want to produce an item cost chart?" A segment of the flowchart and the coding which ensures that a valid entry is made is illustrated in Figure A–45.

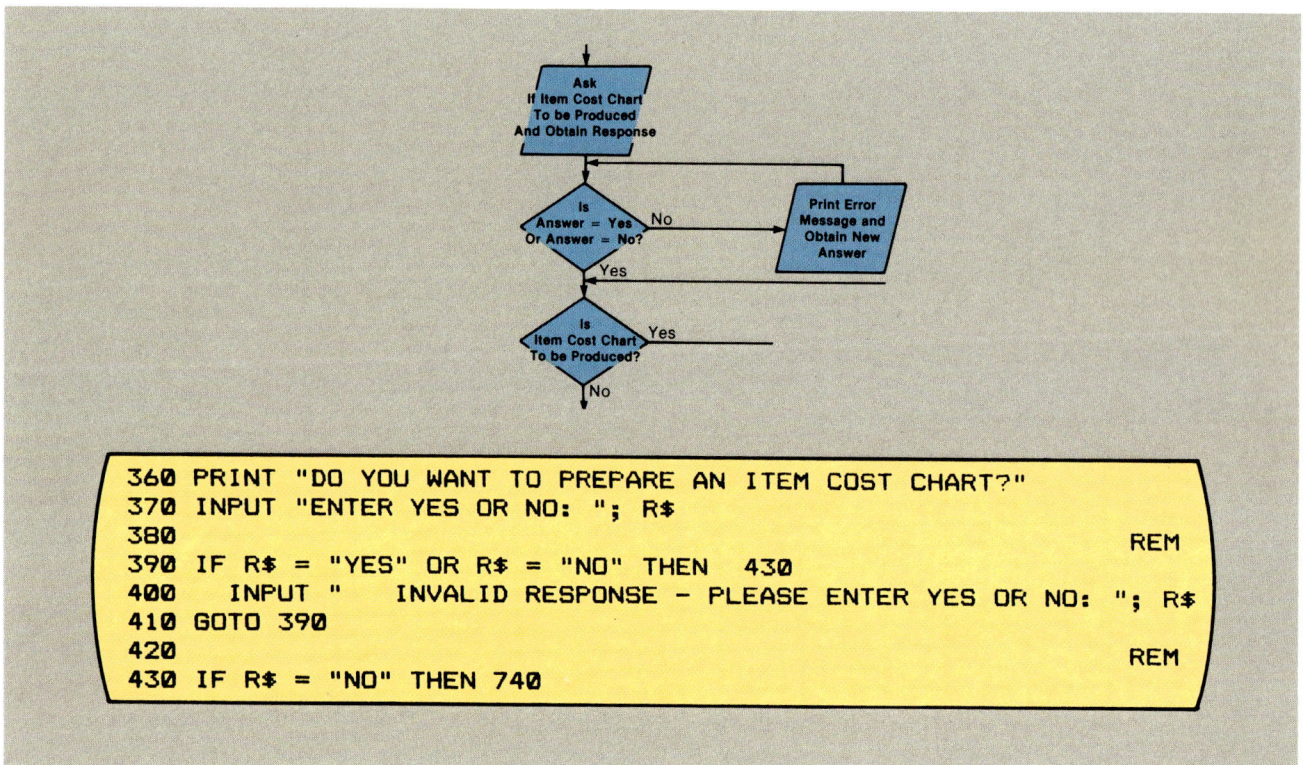

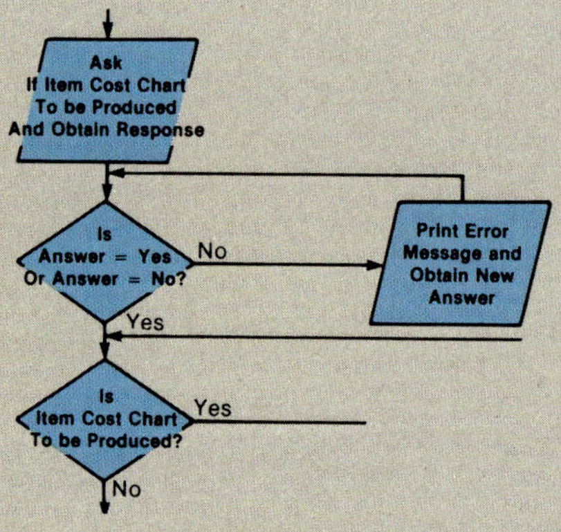


```
360 PRINT "DO YOU WANT TO PREPARE AN ITEM COST CHART?"
370 INPUT "ENTER YES OR NO: "; R$
380                                                    REM
390 IF R$ = "YES" OR R$ = "NO" THEN  430
400   INPUT "   INVALID RESPONSE - PLEASE ENTER YES OR NO: "; R$
410 GOTO 390
420                                                    REM
430 IF R$ = "NO" THEN 740
```

Figure A–45

On line 360 the print statement displays the question "DO YOU WANT TO PREPARE AN ITEM COST CHART?". The input statement on line 370 asks the user to enter the word YES or NO. Only the word YES or the word NO are valid responses — any other response, such as Y or N, are not valid. The response from the user is stored in the field identified by the variable name R$.

The if statement on line 390 tests if the value entered and stored in R$ is equal to YES or is equal to NO.

The statement is the first statement in a loop. It illustrates the use of the OR logical operator. The OR logical operator is used in an if statement to combine conditions. If either of the conditions tested is true, then the entire condition is considered true, and the statement on line 430 will be given control. If both of the conditions are false, that is, if the value in R$ is neither YES nor NO, then the statement on line 400 is given control.

When the response entered by the user is not equal to YES or NO, an invalid entry has been made. The input statement on line 400, which is then executed, prints a prompt indicating an invalid response has been entered and asks the user to make another entry. After the input statement is executed, the goto statement on line 410 returns control to the if statement on line 390 where the entry made by the user is again checked to determine if the user entered either YES or NO. This looping continues until a valid response has been entered.

When control is transferred to the statement at line number 430 by the if statement on line 390, it is known that a valid response (YES or NO) was entered by the user. A check must then be performed to determine which response was given. The if statement on line 430 checks if the response was equal to NO. If the response was equal to NO, indicating the user does not desire to prepare an item cost chart, control is passed to the statement on line 740, which prints an ending message and terminates the program. If the answer is YES, the main processing loop of the program is entered.

Editing for reasonableness

In most interactive applications, it is desirable to check that the data entered by the user is reasonable; that is, the value entered is not greater than or less than a given value that might cause incorrect output to be produced. In the sample program, it has been determined that the cost for one item entered by the user must be less than 1000.00. The coding in the program to ensure that the item cost is less than 1000.00 is shown below.

```
440   CLS
450   INPUT "ENTER COST OF ONE ITEM: "; C
460                                                           REM
470   IF C < M THEN 530
480     PRINT "    COST ENTERED IS TOO HIGH"
490     PRINT "    PLEASE ENTER A COST LESS THAN"; M;
500     INPUT C
510   GOTO 470
520                                                           REM
```

Figure A-46

In the coding above, the input statement on line 450 asks the user to enter the cost of one item. The value entered is stored in the area referenced by the variable name C. The if statement on line 470 compares the value stored in C to the value stored in the field referenced by the variable name M. The value 1000 was placed in the field identified as M in the initialization of variables section of the program. The effect of the if statement, then, is to determine if the value entered by the user is less than 1000.

If the value in C is less than the value in M, the user entered a value less than 1000, which means the entry is valid. Therefore, control is passed to the statement on line 530, where statements are executed to prepare the item cost chart.

If the value in C is not less than the value in M, the value 1000 or more was entered by the user. Since invalid data has been entered, the statements on line 480 and 490, which are executed next, print an error message informing the user that an amount has been entered that is too high, and request that an amount less than M (1000) be entered. The input statement on line 500 allows the user to make another entry. Control is then returned to the if statement at line 470 by means of the goto statement on line 510. This looping will continue until the user enters a value less than 1000.

Editing data is an important part of the programming process. Data editing should be incorporated into all programs in an attempt to ensure that the program processes valid data only.

For and next statements

The if and goto statements have been utilized in previous examples to implement the looping logic structure. The if statement determines whether the loop should be entered, and the goto statement transfers control back to the if statement after each processing pass through the loop.

In some applications, it is desirable to execute a loop a specific number of times based upon a value in a counter. When a loop is to be executed a specific number of times based upon the value in a counter, the for and next statements provide a convenient and easy to use method for controlling the execution of the loop. A for-next loop executes the statements between the word FOR and the word NEXT a specific number of times as controlled by the entries in the for statement. The segment of the sample program which calculates the cost of one to ten items is implemented using a for-next loop. The flowchart and coding for this portion of the program is illustrated in Figure A-47.

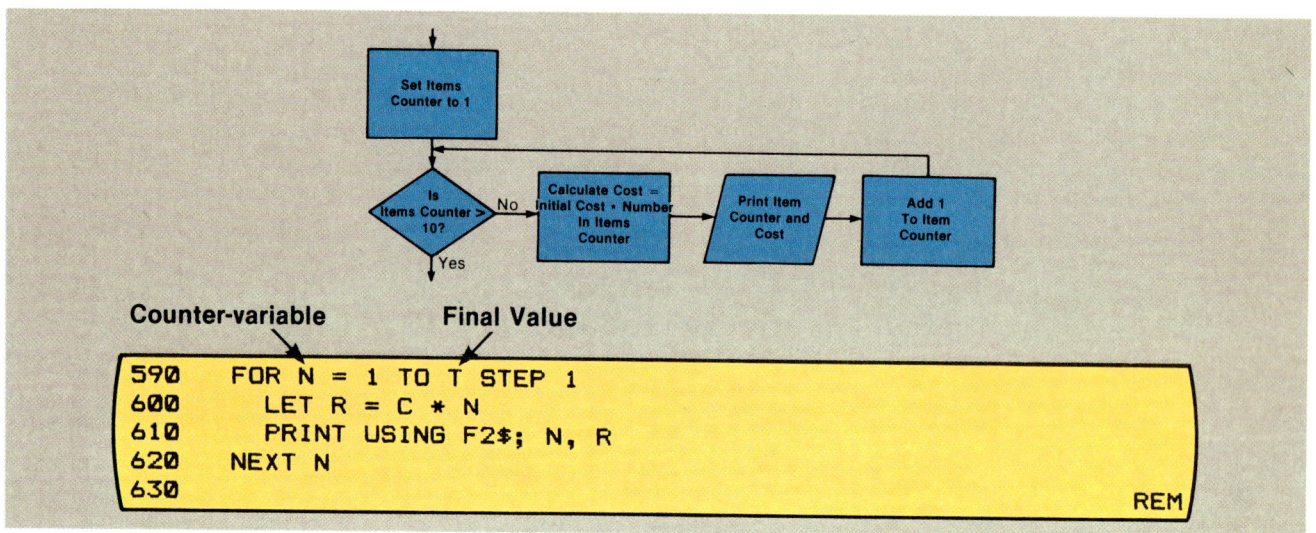

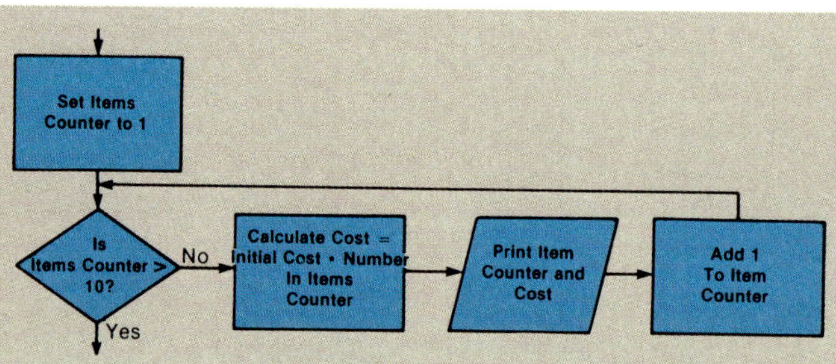

Counter-variable **Final Value**

```
590    FOR N = 1 TO T STEP 1
600       LET R = C * N
610       PRINT USING F2$; N, R
620    NEXT N
630                                                    REM
```

Figure A–47

The logic illustrated in the flowchart above is used to calculate and print the cost of one to ten items. This logic follows the standard looping logic structure. The first step is to initialize a counter to 1. This counter is used to keep track of the number of times the loop has been executed. A test is then performed to determine if the loop should be entered. The loop will be entered when the value in the counter is not greater than the number of times the loop is to be executed (in this example, ten). When the loop is entered, the cost of one item is calculated and printed. The counter is then incremented by 1, and control is returned to the decision step to determine if the statements within the loop have been executed the required number of times. Because the looping operation is based upon the value in a counter, the for and next BASIC statements are used to implement it.

The for statement begins with a line number and then the word FOR. The word FOR is followed by an entry consisting of a variable name, an equal sign, and a value. The field identified by the variable name is called the counter-variable. In the example, the field identified as N is the counter-variable. The entry in the for statement is N = 1. This entry sets the value in the counter-variable field N to 1 and implements the first step in the flowchart, "Set Items Counter to 1." The counter-variable can be initialized to any value required for the application.

The word TO is specified next, followed by a variable field which contains the final value. The final value must be exceeded by the value in the counter-variable in order for the loop to be terminated. In the example, the field containing the final value is referenced by the variable name T. The field T contains the number 10, which was placed in the field in the initialization section of the program. Following the name of the field containing the final value is the step entry. The word STEP is followed by the value which will be added to the value in the counter-variable field after each execution of the for-next loop. In the sample program, the counter-variable will be incremented by 1 after each pass through the loop. The counter-variable can be incremented by any value required by the application.

When the for-next loop is entered, the value in the counter-variable is set to the value specified in the for statement. In the example in Figure A-47, the value will be set to 1. The BASIC statements between the word FOR and the word NEXT will then be executed. After they have been executed one time, the value in the counter-variable will be incremented by the value specified in the step entry of the for statement. In this example, the counter-variable will be incremented by 1, giving the value 2 in the counter-variable field N. The value in the counter-variable N will then be compared to the final value (10) stored in T. If the value in the counter-variable is greater than the final value, the loop will be terminated. Otherwise, the instructions within the loop will be executed again, and the same process will occur.

After ten executions of the instructions within the loop, the value in the counter-variable field N will be equal to 11 when the comparison to the final value takes place. Therefore, the loop will be exited. Note that the loop was executed ten times because the initial value in the counter-variable field was one, the value in the counter-variable field was incremented by one, and the final value was ten.

The for-next loop as implemented using the for and next statements is commonly used whenever a loop is going to be executed a given number of times based upon the value in a counter.

Clear screen statement

At several different points in the sample program, there is a need to clear the CRT screen of extraneous data in order to make the information on the screen as legible as possible. On many computers, the clear screen statement is used for this purpose. It completely blanks the screen and places the cursor in the upper left hand corner of the screen. The use of the clear screen statement is illustrated below.

```
440    CLS
```

Figure A-48

The clear screen statement consists of the letters CLS. On some computers, this statement is not available. In those cases, the programmer should check the appropriate reference manual to determine the statement which can be used to clear the screen.

The sample program

The complete program to accept the cost of one item from the user via the computer keyboard, and prepare an item cost chart for one to ten items is illustrated below and on the following page.

BASIC Program (1 of 2)

```
100 REM ITEMCOST                    MARCH 29                    SHELLY/CASHMAN
110                                                                        REM
120 REM THIS PROGRAM PREPARES AN ITEM COST CHART. THE USER
130 REM ENTERS THE COST OF ONE ITEM AND THE PROGRAM CALCULATES
140 REM THE COST OF 1 THRU 10 ITEMS.
150                                                                        REM
160 REM VARIABLE NAMES:
```

Figure A-49

BASIC Program (2 of 2)

```
170 REM   C.....ITEM COST - ENTERED BY USER
180 REM   M.....ITEM COST ENTERED MUST BE LESS THAN THIS VALUE
190 REM   N.....COUNTER USED TO INCREMENT NUMBER OF ITEMS
200 REM   R.....VARIABLE TO HOLD THE RESULT OF CALCULATION
210 REM   R$....RESPONSE AREA FOR YES OR NO ENTRY
220 REM   T.....NUMBER OF ITEMS FOR WHICH TO CALCULATE COST
230 REM   F1$...PRINT USING FORMAT FOR THE TITLE LINE
240 REM   F2$...PRINT USING FORMAT FOR THE DETAIL LINE
250                                                                     REM
260 REM ***** INITIALIZATION OF VARIABLES  *****
270                                                                     REM
280 LET T = 10
290 LET M = 1000
300 LET F1$ = "ITEM COST CHART FOR $$##.##"
310 LET F2$ = " ##                  $$,###.##"
320                                                                     REM
330 REM ***** PROCESSING *****
340                                                                     REM
350 CLS
360 PRINT "DO YOU WANT TO PREPARE AN ITEM COST CHART?"
370 INPUT "ENTER YES OR NO: "; R$
380                                                                     REM
390 IF R$ = "YES" OR R$ = "NO" THEN  430
400   INPUT "   INVALID RESPONSE - PLEASE ENTER YES OR NO: "; R$
410 GOTO 390
420                                                                     REM
430 IF R$ = "NO" THEN 740
440   CLS
450   INPUT "ENTER COST OF ONE ITEM: "; C
460                                                                     REM
470   IF C < M THEN 530
480     PRINT "   COST ENTERED IS TOO HIGH"
490     PRINT "   PLEASE ENTER A COST LESS THAN"; M;
500     INPUT C
510   GOTO 470
520                                                                     REM
530   CLS
540   PRINT USING F1$; C
550   PRINT " "
560   PRINT "ITEMS                    COST"
570   PRINT "-----                    ----"
580                                                                     REM
590   FOR N = 1 TO T STEP 1
600     LET R = C * N
610     PRINT USING F2$; N, R
620   NEXT N
630                                                                     REM
640   PRINT " "
650   PRINT "DO YOU WANT TO PREPARE ANOTHER ITEM COST CHART?"
660   INPUT "ENTER YES OR NO: "; R$
670                                                                     REM
680   IF R$ = "YES" OR R$ = "NO" THEN 720
690     INPUT "   INVALID RESPONSE - PLEASE ENTER YES OR NO: "; R$
700   GOTO 680
710                                                                     REM
720 GOTO 430
730                                                                     REM
740 PRINT " "
750 PRINT "END OF ITEM COST CHART"
760 END
```

Figure A–50

STUDENT PROGRAMMING ASSIGNMENT 1
Looping and Interactive Programming

Instructions: A pay chart listing hourly pay and the corresponding weekly pay is to be prepared. Design and write the BASIC program to produce the pay chart. The for and next statements should be used in the program.

INPUT Input will be the user's responses to prompts. The prompts ask the user if a pay chart is to be prepared and the beginning hourly pay rate that should be used.

OUTPUT Output is three different screens which communicate with the user. These screens are illustrated below. The program should begin with a question to the user asking if a pay chart is to be prepared. Only the answers yes and no are valid. If the answer is no, the program should be terminated. If the answer is yes, the second screen which asks the user to enter the beginning pay rate should be displayed. The user should then enter a pay rate greater than $1.00 per hour and less than $25.00 per hour. Any other entries are invalid. To produce the pay chart, the beginning hourly and weekly pay are displayed, and then the hourly pay is incremented by .50 per hour. The chart contains ten entries. The weekly pay is calculated by multiplying the hourly pay by 40. When the user indicates no when asked if another pay chart is to be prepared, the ending message should be printed, and the program terminated.

```
DO YOU WANT TO PREPARE A PAYROLL CHART?
ENTER YES OR NO:? YES
```

```
ENTER BEGINNING PAY RATE: ? 5.00
```

```
            PAY CHART

HOURLY                 WEEKLY
 PAY                    PAY
------                 ------
 5.00                 $200.00
 5.50                 $220.00
 6.00                 $240.00
 6.50                 $260.00
 7.00                 $280.00
 7.50                 $300.00
 8.00                 $320.00
 8.50                 $340.00
 9.00                 $360.00
 9.50                 $380.00

DO YOU WANT TO PREPARE ANOTHER PAY CHART?
ENTER YES OR NO: ? NO

END OF PAY CHART
```

STUDENT PROGRAMMING ASSIGNMENT 2
Looping and Interactive Programming

Instructions: A meter conversion table displaying meters, yards, feet, and inches is to be prepared. Design and write the BASIC program to produce the meter conversion table. The for and next statements should be used in the program.

INPUT Input will be the user's responses to prompts. The prompts ask the user if a meter conversion table is to be prepared, the number of meters to be converted, and the meter increment which will be used in the calculations.

OUTPUT Output is three different screens which communicate with the user. These screens are illustrated below. The program should begin with a question to the user asking if a meter conversion table is to be prepared. The only valid answers are yes and no. If the answer is no, the program should be terminated. If the answer is yes, the user should then be asked to enter the number of meters to be converted and the increment number. The valid range for the number of meters that can be entered is 1 to 1500. The valid range for the increment values is 1 to 100. The output should contain ten different meter lengths (beginning with the number of meters entered by the user and incremented by the increment number entered by the user) and their equivalent yards, feet, and inches. The conversion factors are: 39.37 inches in one meter; 3.28 feet in one meter; 36 inches in one yard. In the example below, the number of meters entered by the user is 100, and the meter increment is 10.

```
DO YOU WANT TO PREPARE A METER CONVERSION TABLE?
ENTER YES OR NO:? YES
```

```
ENTER NUMBER OF METERS (MAX. 1500): ? 100

ENTER METER INCREMENT (MAX. 100): ? 10
```

```
      METER CONVERSION TABLE

 METERS     YARDS     FEET     INCHES
 ------     -----     ----     ------
 100.00    109.36    328.00    3937.00
 110.00    120.30    360.80    4330.70
 120.00    131.23    393.60    4724.40
 130.00    142.17    426.40    5118.10
 140.00    153.11    459.20    5511.80
 150.00    164.04    492.00    5905.50
 160.00    174.98    524.80    6299.20
 170.00    185.91    557.60    6692.90
 180.00    196.85    590.40    7086.60
 190.00    207.79    623.20    7480.30

DO YOU WANT TO PREPARE ANOTHER CONVERSION TABLE?
ENTER YES OR NO: ? NO

END OF METER CONVERSION
```

PROBLEM 5 — ARRAYS AND ARRAY SEARCH

Tables are commonly used to look up information or to extract values for use in calculations. For example, one might use a table of distances between various cities when making a trip. Income tax tables, insurance tables, or sales tax tables may be used when extracting a value for use in a calculation. When a table is used, it must be searched in order to extract the proper information.

Tables also play an important role in computer programming. When tables are used in computer programming, they are often called arrays. Arrays are used to store data which can be extracted based upon given information. The example in Figure A-51 below illustrates a banking application in which the account number, name of the account holder, and account balance of individuals who have savings accounts are stored in arrays in main computer memory. When required, the bank teller can enter an account number. The array containing the account numbers in main computer memory is then searched for the number entered by the bank teller. When the account number is located in the arrays, the related name and account balance will be retrieved from the arrays containing the name and balance. The name and balance retrieved from the arrays can be displayed on the CRT screen.

Figure A-51

In the example above, when the teller enters account number 20013, the account number array is searched to find an equal account number. When the equal account number is found, the corresponding name (DARLA SIMMONS) and the corresponding balance (932.49) are extracted from the arrays and are displayed on the screen.

Sample problem 5

The sample problem in this section illustrates the design and coding of a program to implement the banking application just shown. Figure A-52 contains the various displays that will appear.

```
DO YOU WANT TO MAKE AN INQUIRY?
ENTER YES OR NO: ? YES
```

```
ENTER ACCOUNT NUMBER: ? 20013
```

```
ACCOUNT NUMBER: 20013
ACCOUNT NAME: DARLA SIMMONS
ACCOUNT BALANCE:    $932.49

DO YOU WANT TO MAKE ANOTHER INQUIRY?
ENTER YES OR NO: ? NO

END OF INQUIRY
```

Figure A-52

The first display asks if the user wants to make an inquiry. If the answer is no, an ending message is printed, and the program execution is terminated. If the answer is yes, the user is requested to enter the account number. After the account number is entered by the user, the account number array is searched. If the account number is found in the array, the account number, account name, and the account balance are displayed. If the account number is not found, an error message will be displayed. In the sample program, five different account numbers and the related fields are used.

The flowchart illustrating the logic for the program is shown in Figure A-53 on page A.49. It follows the same logic explained in Chapter 16.

Arrays

One of the first steps in the sample program is to reserve areas in main computer memory for the elements within the arrays. An element is a single entry in an array. This is accomplished through the use of the dim statement (DIMension statement). The dimension statement used in the sample program is shown in Figure A-54.

```
400 LET N = 5
 .
 .
 .
450 DIM A(N), N$(N), B(N)
```

Figure A-54

The dimension statement begins with a line number, followed by the word DIM. The next entry consists of one or more variable names. The variable names are used to assign names to the arrays that are defined by the dim statement. Immediately following each variable name, with no intervening spaces, are sets of parentheses. Within the parentheses is a numeric value or numeric variable name which indicates the number of elements in each array. In the example in Figure A-54, the numeric variable name N is specified with each array variable name. Since the value 5, representing the five account numbers and related fields, was placed in the field identified by the variable name N in the initialize variables section of the program, each of the arrays will have five

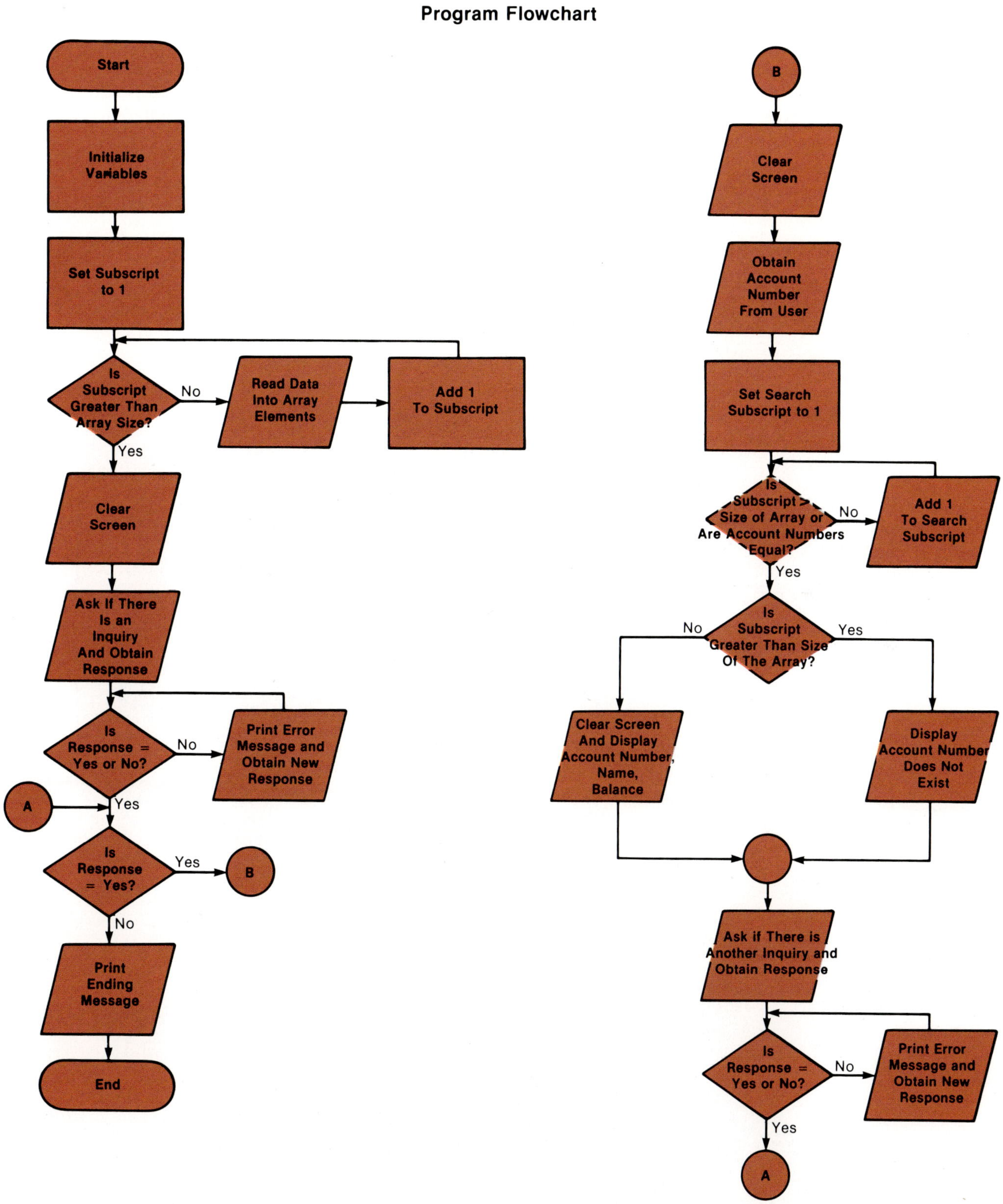

Figure A-53

elements. Thus, the numeric array A will have five elements for the account numbers. The string array N$ will have five elements for the name of account holders, and the numeric array B will have five elements for the account balance.

Each of the elements in the array is referenced through the use of the array name and a subscript. A subscript is a numeric value or variable name representing a numeric value that is contained within parentheses. For example, the entry A(1) represents the first element in the account number array. The entry B(5) represents the fifth element in the account balance array.

Some BASIC interpreters begin numbering elements within an array with the subscript of zero; therefore the entry DIM F(5) would reserve space for six elements in the F array. The first element would be referenced by the entry F(0). In the examples in this book, the first element is referenced by a subscript of 1. In addition, some BASIC interpreters do not require a dimension statement if the array contains fewer than 10 elements. It is suggested that dimension statements always be included in BASIC programs to specify the number of elements in each array.

Loading the arrays

The dimension statement defines the arrays in memory, but it does not place any data in the arrays. Therefore, after one or more arrays have been defined using the dimension statement, data must be placed in each

```
300 REM ***** DATA TO BE LOADED INTO ARRAY *****
310                                                     REM
320 DATA 10093, "THOMAS LANG", 100.51
330 DATA 20013, "DARLA SIMMONS", 932.49
340 DATA 70014, "MARY BURNS", 1555.19
350 DATA 93197, "TY RIDER", 571.88
360 DATA 97111, "TED DAVIS", 2752.12
 .
 .
 .
430 REM ***** DEFINE AND LOAD ARRAYS *****
440                                                     REM
450 DIM A(N), N$(N), B(N)
460                                                     REM
470 FOR S1 = 1 TO N STEP 1
480   READ A(S1), N$(S1), B(S1)
490 NEXT S1
```

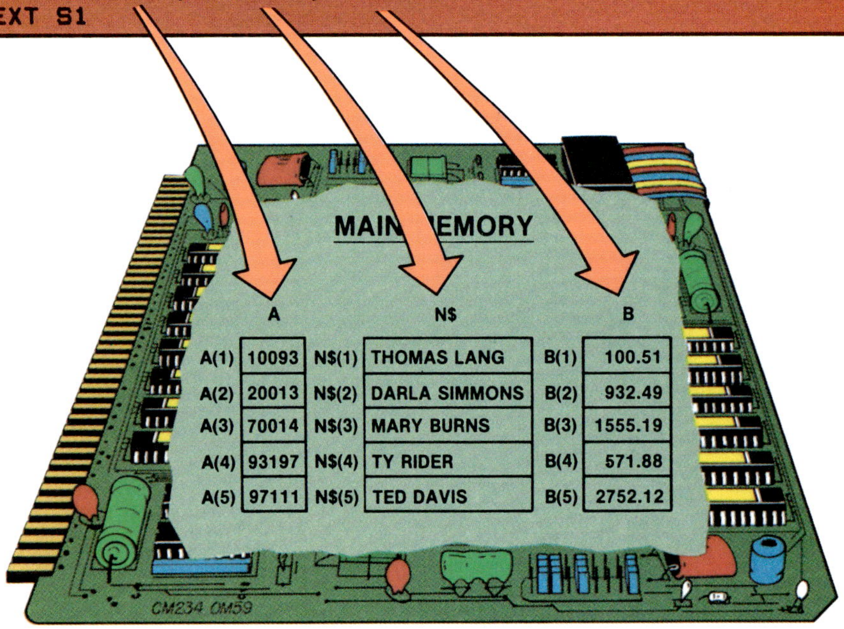

Figure A-55

of the elements. A for-next loop, together with the read and data statements, is often used to load data into arrays. The for-next loop used in the sample program to load data into the account number array, the account name array, and account balance array are illustrated in Figure A–55 on page A.50.

The data statements on lines 320 through 360 contain the data to be placed in each array. The for-next loop on lines 470 through 490 contains the statements necessary to transfer the data from the data statements into the various elements of the arrays.

The for statement on line 470 initializes the counter variable S1 to 1. This counter variable is used to keep track of the number of times the loop is executed. The final value, which is stored in the field referenced by N, has been set to the value 5 in the initialization portion of the program. Upon each execution of the loop, the counter variable will be incremented by 1.

The first statement in the loop is the read statement on line 480. When it is executed, the data from the first data statement on line 320 will be read into the fields specified following the word READ. The fields are A(S1), N$(S1), and B(S1). These are the names of the arrays together with the subscript S1. Since the value in S1 is 1 (the value was set by the for statement) the first time the loop is executed, the data from the data statement on line 320 will be read into the first element of each of the arrays specified. Thus, the account number 10093 will be read into the array element A(1), the name THOMAS LANG into N$(1), and the account balance 100.51 into array element B(1).

When the next statement on line 490 is encountered, control is passed back to the for statement on line 470. The value in S1 is incremented by 1 and is compared to the final value contained in N. Since the value in S1 is now 2, and 2 is less than the final value 5, the loop is again entered. The data from the data statement on line 330 will be read into element 2 of the various arrays because the value in S1 is used as the subscript for the array names in the read statement. This process continues until all of the data in the data statements has been loaded into the five elements of the arrays.

Coding the array search

After the data has been loaded into the arrays and it has been determined that the user wants to make an inquiry, the next segment of the program accepts an account number from the user and searches the account number array for the number entered by the user. If it is found, the account number, account name, and account balance are displayed. If the account number is not found in the array, an error message is displayed. The coding to implement this logic is illustrated below.

```
640   INPUT "ENTER ACCOUNT NUMBER: "; A1
650   LET S2 = 1
660                                                   REM
670   IF S2 > N THEN 720
680   IF A1 = A(S2) THEN 720
690     LET S2 = S2 + 1
700   GOTO 670
710                                                   REM
720   IF S2 > N THEN 790
730     CLS
740     PRINT "ACCOUNT NUMBER:"; A(S2)
750     PRINT "ACCOUNT NAME: "; N$(S2)
760     PRINT USING F1$; B(S2)
770     GOTO 830
780                                                   REM
790     PRINT " "
800     PRINT "**ACCOUNT NUMBER"; A1; "DOES NOT EXIST"
810     GOTO 830
```

Figure A–56

The input statement on line 640 obtains the account number from the user and stores it in the field identified by the variable name A1. The value in the field identified by the variable name S2 is set to 1. This field is used as the subscript in the search loop.

The if statement on line 670 checks if the value in the subscript field S2 (which now contains a 1) is greater than the size of the arrays (which is 5) as specified by the value in the field identified by the variable name N. When the subscript field is greater than the size of the arrays, the entire account number array has been searched and an equal account number has not been found. This condition will occur when an account number has been entered that is not contained within the array.

If the value in S2 is not greater than the value in N, the if statement on line 680 is executed. This if statement determines if the account number entered by the user (referenced by the variable name A1) is equal to the account number in the element of the array referenced by the entry A(S2). Since S2 contains the value 1, the account number in the first element of the array is compared to the number entered by the user. If the numbers are equal, control is transferred to the statement on line 720. If the numbers are not equal, the statement on line 690 is executed. This statement adds 1 to the subscript value in S2. S2 now contains the value 2. The goto statement on line 700 then returns control to the if statement on line 670.

A check is again performed to determine if the value in S2 is greater than the size of the array. Since it is not, the value entered by the user is compared to the second element in the account number array. This looping operation continues until an equal condition is encountered (the number entered by the user is equal to a number in one of the elements of the account number array) or until all of the elements in the array have been compared.

Upon exit from the search loop, statement 720 compares the value in the subscript S2 to the size of the arrays stored in N. If the value in S2 is greater than the value in N, it means no equal account number was found in the account number array. When this occurs, control is transferred to statement 790, where an error message is printed.

When the if statement on line 720 determines that the value in the subscript is not greater than the size of the arrays, it means an equal account number has been located in the account number array. The value in S2 will identify which element within the account number array was equal. The value in S2 can then be used to reference the corresponding elements in the account name array and the account balance array. The statements beginning on line 730 clear the screen and display the account number, the account name, and the account balance from the respective arrays using the value in S2 as the subscript.

Array search logic is widely used in many application areas, and both the logic and coding should be carefully reviewed.

The coding below and on the following page illustrates the complete program for the sample problem.

BASIC Program (1 of 2)

```
100 REM INQUIRY                MARCH 29                   SHELLY/CASHMAN
110                                                                  REM
120 REM THIS PROGRAM LOADS ACCOUNT NUMBERS, NAMES, AND BALANCES
130 REM INTO ARRAYS. THE USER CAN THEN PERFORM AN INQUIRY BY
140 REM ENTERING AN ACCOUNT NUMBER. BASED UPON THE ACCOUNT
150 REM NUMBER, THE PROGRAM DISPLAYS THE NAME OF THE ACCOUNT
160 REM HOLDER AND THE BALANCE IN THE ACCOUNT.
170                                                                  REM
180 REM VARIABLE NAMES:
190 REM   A()...ACCOUNT NUMBER ARRAY
200 REM   N$()..NAME ARRAY
210 REM   B()...ACCOUNT BALANCE ARRAY
220 REM   N.....NUMBER OF ELEMENTS IN THE ARRAY
230 REM   A1....ACCOUNT NUMBER - ENTERED BY USER
240 REM   S1....SUBSCRIPT TO LOAD ARRAYS
250 REM   S2....SUBSCRIPT TO SEARCH THE ACCOUNT NUMBER ARRAY
260 REM         AND REFERENCE ALL ARRAYS WHEN THE SEARCH IS
270 REM         SUCCESSFUL
280 REM   R$....RESPONSE AREA FOR ANSWER TO PROMPT QUESTION
290                                                                  REM
300 REM ***** DATA TO BE LOADED INTO ARRAY *****
310                                                                  REM
320 DATA 10093, "THOMAS LANG", 100.51
330 DATA 20013, "DARLA SIMMONS", 932.49
```

Figure A–57

BASIC Program (2 of 2)

```
340 DATA 70014, "MARY BURNS", 1555.19
350 DATA 93197, "TY RIDER", 571.88
360 DATA 97111, "TED DAVIS", 2752.12
370                                                            REM
380 REM ***** INITIALIZATION OF VARIABLES *****
390                                                            REM
400 LET N = 5
410 LET F1$ = "ACCOUNT BALANCE: $$,###.##"
420                                                            REM
430 REM ***** DEFINE AND LOAD ARRAYS *****
440                                                            REM
450 DIM A(N), N$(N), B(N)
460                                                            REM
470 FOR S1 = 1 TO N STEP 1
480   READ A(S1), N$(S1), B(S1)
490 NEXT S1
500                                                            REM
510 REM ***** PROCESSING *****
520                                                            REM
530 CLS
540 PRINT "DO YOU WANT TO MAKE AN INQUIRY?"
550 INPUT "ENTER YES OR NO: "; R$
560                                                            REM
570                                                            REM
580 IF R$ = "YES" OR R$ = "NO" THEN 620
590   INPUT "     INVALID RESPONSE - PLEASE ENTER YES OR NO: "; R$
600 GOTO 580
610                                                            REM
620 IF R$ = "NO" THEN 930
630   CLS
640   INPUT "ENTER ACCOUNT NUMBER: "; A1
650   LET S2 = 1
660                                                            REM
670   IF S2 > N THEN 720
680   IF A1 = A(S2) THEN 720
690     LET S2 = S2 + 1
700   GOTO 670
710                                                            REM
720   IF S2 > N THEN 790
730     CLS
740     PRINT "ACCOUNT NUMBER:"; A(S2)
750     PRINT "ACCOUNT NAME: "; N$(S2)
760     PRINT USING F1$; B(S2)
770     GOTO 830
780                                                            REM
790     PRINT " "
800     PRINT "**ACCOUNT NUMBER"; A1; "DOES NOT EXIST"
810     GOTO 830
820                                                            REM
830   PRINT " "
840   PRINT "DO YOU WANT TO MAKE ANOTHER INQUIRY?"
850   INPUT "ENTER YES OR NO: "; R$
860                                                            REM
870   IF R$ = "YES" OR R$ = "NO" THEN 910
880     INPUT "     INVALID RESPONSE - PLEASE ENTER YES OR NO: "; R$
890   GOTO 870
900                                                            REM
910 GOTO 620
920                                                            REM
930 PRINT " "
940 PRINT "END OF INQUIRY"
950 END
```

Figure A–58

STUDENT PROGRAMMING ASSIGNMENT 1
Arrays and Array Search

Instructions: An interactive inquiry program to allow a user to enter a person's name and obtain the person's telephone number is to be prepared. Design and write the BASIC program to accomplish this.

INPUT The input consists of responses to prompts and individual's names which are entered by the user.

ARRAY DATA The data containing the individual's name and telephone number is to be stored in an array. The data to be used in the program is shown below.

NAME	TELEPHONE NUMBER
MILLER	(213) 430-2865
FLAMING	(213) 866-9082
FUQUA	(714) 925-3391
BINGLE	(805) 402-3376
COURSE	(213) 423-7765

OUTPUT The screens to be used in the program are shown below. Data entered by the user should be edited. The programmer should design error messages when the user does not enter the values YES or NO or when the name entered by the user is not found in the name array.

```
DO YOU WANT TO FIND A PHONE NUMBER?
ENTER YES OR NO: ? YES
```

```
ENTER NAME OF PERSON: ? BINGLE
```

```
NAME........... BINGLE

PHONE NO....... (805) 402-3376

DO YOU WANT TO MAKE ANOTHER INQUIRY?
ENTER YES OR NO: ? NO

END OF PHONE INQUIRY
```

STUDENT PROGRAMMING ASSIGNMENT 2
Arrays and Array Search

Instructions: An interactive inquiry program that allows users to find their desirable weight based upon their height and sex is to be prepared. Design and write the required BASIC program.

INPUT The input consists of responses to prompts and the sex and height of the individual making the inquiry.

ARRAY DATA The data containing the height and weight is stored in arrays. The data to be used is shown below.

MEN

HEIGHT	SMALL FRAME	MEDIUM FRAME	LARGE FRAME
66	124-133	130-143	138-156
67	128-137	134-147	142-161
68	132-141	138-152	147-166
69	136-145	142-156	151-170
70	140-150	146-160	155-174
71	144-154	150-165	159-179
72	148-158	154-170	164-184
73	152-162	158-175	168-189
74	156-167	162-180	173-194

WOMEN

HEIGHT	SMALL FRAME	MEDIUM FRAME	LARGE FRAME
62	102-110	107-119	115-131
63	105-113	110-122	118-134
64	108-116	113-126	121-138
65	111-119	116-130	125-142
66	114-123	120-135	129-146
67	118-127	124-139	133-150
68	122-131	128-143	137-154
69	126-135	132-147	141-158
70	130-140	136-151	145-163

OUTPUT The screens to be produced by the program are illustrated below. When the sex and height are entered, the program should obtain the appropriate weights for small frame, medium frame, and large frame people. If a word other than YES or NO, a sex other than M or F, or a height not contained in the arrays is entered, an error message should be displayed. The programmer should design the error message.

```
DO YOU WANT TO FIND YOUR DESIRABLE WEIGHT?
ENTER YES OR NO: ? YES
```

```
ENTER YOUR SEX (M/F): ? M
ENTER HEIGHT (INCHES): ? 68
```

```
              SMALL      MEDIUM      LARGE
HEIGHT        FRAME      FRAME       FRAME
------        -----      ------      -----
  68         132-141    138-152     147-166

DO YOU HAVE ANOTHER INQUIRY?
ENTER YES OR NO: ? NO

END OF WEIGHT INQUIRY
```

Appendix B — Number Systems

Data is stored in main computer memory as a series of bits being "on" or "off," symbolically represented as a "1" or "0." As these bits can only assume one of two possible states, the representation of data in main computer memory is based upon the binary number system — a number system in which only two symbols are used to represent values.

Although not required for a general understanding of how computers operate and store data, an understanding of the binary number system provides added insight into the operation of computers.

The decimal number system

A review of some of the basic concepts of the decimal number system is often useful in understanding other number systems.

The decimal system utilizes ten symbols to represent values. These symbols are: 0, 1, 2, 3, 4, 5, 6, 7, 8, and 9. Through the use of these ten symbols, any quantity can logically be represented.

To represent quantities greater than 9, two or more symbols must be used. The proper utilization of these symbols to represent quantities is based upon the concept of place values.

In the decimal number system, each place position from right to left is as follows: ones, tens, hundreds, thousands, etc. These place values are obtained by using a base of 10 (because there are ten symbols in the decimal number system) and raising this base to the next highest power each position to the left.

The example below illustrates the concept of place values and how decimal numbers derive their meaning.

0	1	1	0	
THOUSAND	HUNDRED	TEN	ONE	Place Value
10^3	10^2	10^1	10^0	Base

Figure B-1

In the example above, the number one hundred and ten is represented by the digits 110. The number 110 in the decimal number system derives its value from the place value of each digit. Thus, the number 110 in the decimal system really means 1 - one hundred, 1 - ten, and 0 - ones. Any decimal number can be analyzed in a similar manner. The place value concept can be applied to a number system with any base. The remainder of this appendix will examine number systems with a base 2 (binary) and a base 16 (hexadecimal).

The binary number system

In the binary number system, 0 and 1 are the only digits used. Thus, the binary number system uses a base of 2 to establish the place value for each digit. In the binary number system, each place position is assigned the following values: one, two, four, eight, etc. The place value is established by raising the base of 2 to the next highest power each place position to the left. The following charts illustrate the place values for the first four positions in the binary number system and the decimal numbers 1, 2, and 3 represented in the binary number system.

	0	0	0	1	
NUMBER 1 =	EIGHT	FOUR	TWO	ONE	Place Value
	2^3	2^2	2^1	2^0	Base

	0	0	1	0	
NUMBER 2 =	EIGHT	FOUR	TWO	ONE	Place Value
	2^3	2^2	2^1	2^0	Base

	0	0	1	1	
NUMBER 3 =	EIGHT	FOUR	TWO	ONE	Place Value
	2^3	2^2	2^1	2^0	Base

Figure B–2

As can be seen from the illustration above, the decimal number 1 is represented in binary as 0001, the decimal number 2 as 0010, and the decimal number 3 as 0011.

The following chart summarizes the binary equivalents of the decimal numbers 0 - 9.

Decimal	Binary
0	0000
1	0001
2	0010
3	0011
4	0100
5	0101
6	0110
7	0111
8	1000
9	1001

Figure B–3

By relating these binary numbers to the place value chart, it is easy to see how these zeros and ones derive their related decimal values.

The diagram from Chapter 8 illustrating the decimal number 2053 stored in a binary format is shown in Figure B–4. Note the use of the place values to derive the decimal value.

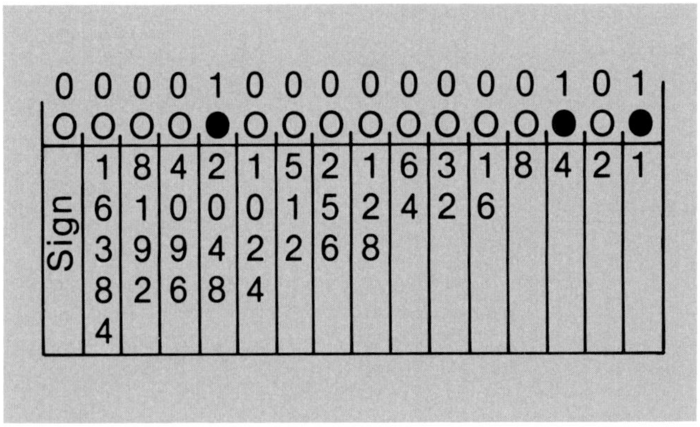

Figure B–4

The hexadecimal number system

On some computers, machine language instructions, memory locations, and data in main computer memory are referenced in a number system using the base 16. This number system is called the hexadecimal number system.

The hexadecimal number system represents the decimal values 0–15 by means of 16 individual symbols. The representation of the digits 0–9 are the same in the hexadecimal number system as in the decimal number system. To represent the decimal values 10–15, however, the hexadecimal system uses the letters of the alphabet A–F. Thus, the decimal value 9 is represented in hexadecimal as 9, the decimal value 10 is represented in hexadecimal as the character A, the decimal value 11 as the character B, etc. The chart below illustrates the decimal values 0–15 and their equivalent hexadecimal notation.

DECIMAL VALUE	HEXADECIMAL NOTATION	DECIMAL VALUE	HEXADECIMAL NOTATION
0	0	8	8
1	1	9	9
2	2	10	A
3	3	11	B
4	4	12	C
5	5	13	D
6	6	14	E
7	7	15	F

Figure B–5

Understanding the use of the hexadecimal number system requires an understanding of the place value concept as it relates to hexadecimal numbers. The hexadecimal number system uses the base 16 with sixteen different symbols. By raising the base 16 to the next highest power when moving from right to left, the place values become 1, 16, 256, 4096, and so on.

The diagram in Figure B-6 illustrates the first four place positions of the hexadecimal number system, with the digits one and zero recorded in the first 2 positions.

0	0	1	0	
4096	256	16	1	**Place Value**
16^3	16^2	16^1	16^0	**Base**

Figure B-6

Using the place value chart, it can be seen that the rightmost position represents the units position. Thus, a 1 recorded in this position would represent the decimal value 1. An A recorded in this position would represent the decimal value 10 because the symbol A in hexadecimal represents the decimal quantity 10. The symbol F represents the decimal value 15, which is the highest value that can be represented by a single character in hexadecimal. In order to represent the decimal value 16, two digits are required. The entry 10 in hexadecimal represents the value 16 in decimal. This is because in hexadecimal, the 1 in the second place position to the left represents the decimal value 16. In hexadecimal, the value 11 would represent the decimal value 17, hexadecimal 12 the decimal value 18, and so on. The chart below summarizes the representation of the decimal values 0–47 in hexadecimal.

DECIMAL	HEXADECIMAL	DECIMAL	HEXADECIMAL	DECIMAL	HEXADECIMAL
0	0	16	10	32	20
1	1	17	11	33	21
2	2	18	12	34	22
3	3	19	13	35	23
4	4	20	14	36	24
5	5	21	15	37	25
6	6	22	16	38	26
7	7	23	17	39	27
8	8	24	18	40	28
9	9	25	19	41	29
10	A	26	1A	42	2A
11	B	27	1B	43	2B
12	C	28	1C	44	2C
13	D	29	1D	45	2D
14	E	30	1E	46	2E
15	F	31	1F	47	2F

Figure B-7

Use of hexadecimal number system

As previously mentioned, on some machines memory addresses and data in main computer memory are referenced in a hexadecimal form. This is done because a representation in binary form is difficult to interpret.

For example, the number 5 recorded in main computer memory in the extended binary coded decimal interchange code would be displayed in a binary form as 11110101. This type of notation is difficult to interpret, especially if long sequences of digits were to be read.

If, however, the binary notation 11110101 is separated into four bits and each of the four bits is converted to a hexadecimal value, the results would appear as illustrated in Figure B-8.

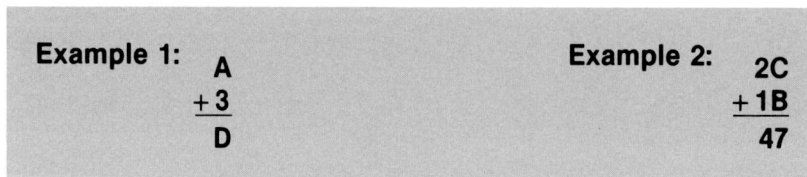

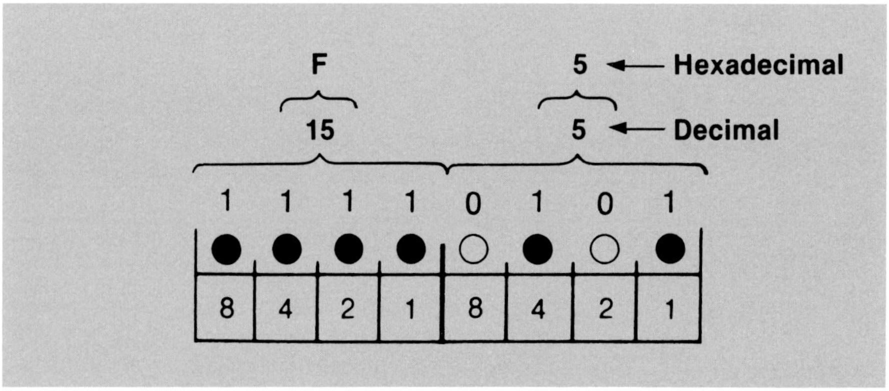

Figure B-8

In the drawing above, the leftmost four bits contain a binary 1111. This is the equivalent of decimal value 15, which is represented in hexadecimal as an F.

The next four bits contain 0101. This is a decimal 5 and a hexadecimal 5. Thus, the number 5 in the extended binary coded decimal interchange code recorded in a binary form as 11110101 is displayed in hexadecimal as F5.

Addition using hexadecimal numbers

Data is often displayed for use by the programmer in hexadecimal form. This includes machine language instructions, memory addresses, and the data in memory. Because of this fact, it is sometimes necessary to add and subtract hexadecimal numbers. A simplified technique for adding and subtracting hexadecimal values is explained in the paragraphs below.

The following examples illustrate typical problems.

Example 1:

```
  A
 +3
 --
  D
```

Example 2:

```
  2C
 +1B
 ---
  47
```

Figure B-9

An easy way to add hexadecimal numbers is to mentally convert the hexadecimal value to decimal, add in decimal, and then mentally convert the answer back to hexadecimal. Using this technique, the mental reasoning to add the hexadecimal values above would be as follows:

Example 1: Hexadecimal A is added to hexadecimal 3: 1) Hexadecimal A is equivalent to decimal 10; 2) Hexadecimal 3 is equivalent to decimal 3; 3) Decimal 10 plus decimal 3 is equal to decimal 13;

4) Decimal 13 is equivalent to hexadecimal D; therefore, the answer is hexadecimal D.

Example 2: Hexadecimal 2C is added to hexadecimal 1B: 1) Hexadecimal C is equivalent to decimal 12; 2) Hexadecimal B is equivalent to decimal 11; 3) The sum of decimal 12 and decimal 11 is decimal 23; 4) The sum 23 is 7 greater than decimal 16, which is the base of the hexadecimal number system. Therefore, the result is hexadecimal 7 with a carry of 1; 5) The value 2 plus the value 1, plus 1 carry equals 4. Thus, the answer is hexadecimal 47.

Subtraction using hexadecimal numbers

A similar approach is taken when subtracting hexadecimal values. Several examples are illustrated below.

Example 1:		Example 2:	
	4F		C1E
	-1D		-2F
	32		BEF

Figure B-10

To subtract, each hexadecimal value should be converted to its decimal value, subtraction should take place, and the answer should be converted back to hexadecimal.

Example 1: Hexadecimal 1D is subtracted from hexadecimal 4F: 1) Hexadecimal F is equivalent to decimal 15; 2) Hexadecimal D is equivalent to decimal 13; 3) Decimal 13 subtracted from decimal 15 is equal to 2; thus, 2 becomes the rightmost digit in the answer; 4) Hexadecimal 1 is subtracted from hexadecimal 4, giving a 3. Thus, the final answer is hexadecimal 32.

Example 2: Hexadecimal 2F is subtracted from hexadecimal C1E: 1) Hexadecimal E is decimal 14 and hexadecimal F is decimal 15, so a one must be borrowed. Therefore, the first two characters of the minuend C1E become C0. When a 1 is borrowed in hexadecimal, it is in reality the decimal value 16. Therefore, the total value becomes 30 (E + 16 = decimal 30); 2) Decimal 15 from 30 leaves a value of decimal 15 or a hexadecimal value of F. Hence, the rightmost value in the answer is F; 3) The problem now becomes C0 minus 2; 4) Once again, a 1 must be borrowed from the digit to the left (the C). Decimal 2 is subtracted from decimal 16, and the answer is decimal 14 which is hexadecimal E; 3) When the 1 was borrowed from the hexadecimal C, it became hexadecimal B. The final answer is, therefore, hexadecimal BEF.

Using this approach, hexadecimal values can be added and subtracted rapidly and accurately.

Index/Glossary

–A–

Atanasoff, Dr. John V. Designed and built the first electronic digital computer, called the ABC. 2.1
Audit trail A control designed to enable any input data or process executed on a computer to be traced back to the original source data. 15.10
Automatic programming Writing a computer program in a notation other than machine language. 2.8
Auxiliary storage The storage of data and instructions not being used in main computer memory on either magnetic tape or magnetic disk. 3.10, 9.1
Auxiliary storage devices Devices used to store data and instructions when they are not being used in main computer memory. Common types are magnetic tape and magnetic disk. 1.7, 3.2
Availability (of data) Data required for an application can be obtained in a manner which ensures the integrity of the data. 4.9

-B-

BASIC (Beginner's All-Purpose Symbolic Instruction Code) A programming language developed by Dr. John Kemeny, initially used by Dartmouth College students, and today being used on millions of personal computers. 2.14, 13.8, A.1
BASIC interpreter A systems software program which translates a BASIC statement into machine language and then causes the instruction to be executed immediately. 14.4
Backorder An order for which the item ordered is not in inventory. 5.14
Backup file A copy of a file, typically stored on magnetic tape. 9.10, 15.10
Backus, John Headed a small group of IBM employees who together developed FORTRAN. 2.9
Band printers A printer that utilizes a horizontal, rotating band containing characters to print. 6.11
Bar charts A type of display chart that represents data by vertical or horizontal bars. 6.20
Baseband Coaxial cable that carries one signal at a time. 11.22
Batch controls The comparison of totals produced manually prior to data entry to totals produced by the computer. 5.4
Batch file A file which can contain statements to cause multiple programs to execute without operator intervention. 14.3
Batch processing A mode for processing data on a computer whereby data records are accumulated and are processed as a group when all of the required records have been gathered. 2.13, 4.2
Bidirectionally The ability of a printer to print while the print head moves from left to right and also right to left. 6.4
Binary digit The basic unit for storing data in main computer memory. 8.1
Bit An abbreviation for binary digit — the basic unit for storing data in main computer memory. 8.1
Bit-mapped displays Display monitors, also called dot-addressable displays, used for graphics 6.17
Bits per inch (bpi) A measurement of the recording density of a diskette. 9.3
Blinking A feature of a screen that allows characters or words to blink. 5.9
Blocked records Placing two or more logical records into a block to form a physical record. 9.16
Bold A feature of a CRT screen that allows some characters or words to be displayed at a greater brightness level. 5.9
Booting The process of loading an operating system into main computer memory. 14.1
Broadband Coaxial cable that carries many signals at one time, with each signal occupying a different frequency band on the cable. 11.22
Bubble memory Memory composed of small magnetic domains, or bubbles, formed on a thin single-crystal film of synthetic garnet. 9.17
Buckets The location within a direct file into which a record will be stored and from which the record can be retrieved. 10.5
Bus topology All devices in a local area network are connected to and share a single cable. 11.20
Business application programmers Individuals who write programs which process business applications, such as payroll, accounts receivable, accounts payable, and inventory control. 17.7
Busses The lines along which bits are transmitted. 8.16
Byte A location in main computer memory consisting of eight adjacent bits. 8.2

-C-

C (Programming language) A general purpose, portable programming language featuring concise expression of functions to be performed, and a design that permits writing well structured programs. 13.10
CAD/CAM An abbreviation for computer-assisted design (CAD) and computer-assisted manufacturing (CAM). 6.21
COBOL (COmmon Business Oriented Language) A widely used machine-independent business programming language that allows programs to be written in an English-like fashion. 2.10, 13.5
CPM The first operating system developed for personal computers. 14.5
CPU An abbreviation for Central Processing Unit. 1.6, 8.1
Carrier sensed multiple access (CSMA) The terminal electronically listens to the bus network communication channel until it is determined that data is not being transmitted by another terminal or computer, at which time the terminal sends its message. 11.23
Cashless society A society in which money would not be needed, and all goods and services would be bought through the use of a universal cash card. 18.8

Cassette tape Auxiliary storage used on the first personal computers to store data and programs sequentially. 9.10
Cathode ray tube (CRT) An output unit with a TV-like screen used to display information from a computer. 1.6
Cell Each intersection of a row and a column on an electronic spreadsheet. 12.7
Central processing unit (CPU) The electronic circuits which, as a part of the processor unit, cause processing to occur by interpreting and executing instructions and controlling the input, output, and storage operations. 1.6, 3.1, 8.1
Centralized data entry The entry of data from source documents by trained personnel located in the centralized data entry section of the information systems department. 5.24
Certificate in Data Processing Examination An examination administered by the ICCP that tests the areas of computer equipment, computer programming and software, principles of management, accounting and quantitative methods, and systems. 17.15
Chain printer An impact printer, also called a train printer, containing numbers, letters of the alphabet, and selected special characters on a rotating chain. 6.10
Check digit A means of detecting transcription and transposition errors. 5.26
CLEAR SCREEN statement A BASIC statement used to clear the CRT screen of extraneous data. A.43
Coaxial cable A high quality communication line consisting of a multitude of wires within a cable enclosure. 11.12, 11.22
Collision The generation of the same disk address by using a hashing technique on different keys. 10.6
Collision (Local area networks) An attempt by two terminals to send data at the same time over a network that only allows one terminal to transmit at a time. 11.23
Command query language The most basic type of query language using preselected words which direct the software to perform a certain function. 7.18
Communication channel The communication line which allows a personal computer or terminal to communicate with a host computer. 11.6
Communications adapter A circuit board that changes data from a parallel form to a serial form for transmission. 11.4
Communications control unit A device that assembles the bits received from the modem into characters for transmission to the main computer memory of the host computer. 11.11
Comparing The ability of a program to compare the values stored in two fields and perform alternative operations based upon whether the value in one field is less than, equal to, or greater than the value in the other field. 3.7, 16.16, A.27
Compiler A program, often called an translator, that interprets computer programs written in a high-level language and converts them to machine language. 2.9, 14.6
Composite video monitor A color monitor that uses a single electron signal to turn on the color phosphors within the pixel. 6.18
Computer An electronic device, operating under the control of instructions stored in its own memory unit, which can accept and store data, perform arithmetic and logical operations on that data without human intervention, and produce output from the processing. 1.1
Computer-assisted design (CAD) The use of the computer in the design process. 5.31, 6.21
Computer-assisted instruction (CAI) Computer software which helps a student learn by asking questions and evaluating the answers given by the student. 2.21
Computer-assisted manufacturing The use of the computer in the manufacturing process. 6.21
Computer-assisted retrieval The automatic data lookup feature available on some microfilm readers. 6.25
Computer crime Crime in which a computer is used. 18.9
Computer graphics Displaying information in the form of charts, graphs, or pictures so the information can easily and quickly be understood. 6.19
Computer hardware The input, processor, output, and auxiliary storage units which process data. 1.6
Computer literacy The ability to recognize an application in which the use of a computer is appropriate and the ability to use the computer for that application. 2.25, 18.2
Computer matching Comparing data in two or more separate data bases. 18.8
Computer operator An individual in the operations section of the information systems department who runs the computer, ensuring that scheduled jobs are processed. 17.6
Computer output microfilm (COM) An output technique that records output from a computer as microscopic images on roll or sheet film. 6.24
Computer plotter An output device that can create drawings, charts, diagrams, and similar types of graphic output. 6.23
Computer program A series of instructions which directs a computer to perform input, arithmetic, logical, output, and storage operations. 1.8, 13.1
Computer programmers People who design, write, test, and implement programs on a computer. 1.18, 17.7
Computer science A field of study on the four-year college level for individuals who wish to become systems programmers, software specialists, or research computer scientists. 17.8, 17.13
Computer software A series of instructions, also called programs, which directs a computer to perform input, arithmetic, logical, output, and storage operations. 1.8, 3.1

Computer technology A field of study that deals with computer hardware and the electronic components comprising computer hardware. 17.12
Computer users People who directly use the computer or who benefit from the output of computer processing. 1.19, 4.11
Conceptual file A file that contains record keys and the fields in the records. 10.9
Conceptual (view of data) The logical organization of data within a data base, and how the data can be retrieved. 10.7
Condition entry The portion of a decision table located in the upper right area that contains the different combinations of conditions which can occur. 16.24
Condition stub The upper left-hand portion of a decision table that contains the conditions which may occur. 16.24
Continuous form paper Paper used on computer printers that has each page connected for continuous flow through the printer. 6.6
Control and scheduling personnel Individuals responsible for scheduling computer time, ensuring that the input data required for processing is available, performing data editing using batch controls to verify valid data is entered into the computer, and similar tasks. 17.6
Control break report A report in which unique processing will be performed when the value in a control field within a record changes. 4.14
Control structures The three basic structures — sequence, if-then-else, and do while — that can be used to express any programming logic. 16.4
Control unit A component of the central processing unit that directs and coordinates the activities of the entire computer. 8.14
Control units (Local area networks) A computer, also called a server, dedicated to handling the communications needs of the other computers in a local area network. 11.20
Conversion The process of making the change from the old system to the new system. 15.13
Copy programs Programs which are part of the operating system that copy files. 14.4
Counter An area in main computer memory reserved for a count total, such as a count of the number of records processed. 16.16, A.14
Counter-variable The variable used in a FOR statement to count the number of times the loop controlled by the FOR statement is executed. A.42
Cursor (CRT screen) A symbol which indicates where on the screen the next character will be entered. 5.10, 7.3
Cursor (digitizers) A device which can translate the coordinates read from the lines on a drawing to coordinates which computer software can duplicate. 5.30
Cylinder A collection of tracks which can be referenced by one positioning of the access arm. 9.13
Cylinder method A method of organizing data on a disk in which the cylinder number, recording surface number, and record number is used to reference a record on the disk. 9.13

–D–

DIM statement A BASIC statement used to reserve area in main computer memory for the elements of an array. A.48
Daisy wheel printer A letter quality, impact printer that consists of a type element that contains raised characters, resembling the structure of a flower, which strikes the paper through an inked ribbon. 6.7
Data Numbers, words, and phrases which are suitable for processing in some manner on a computer. 1.4, 3.3
Data banks Large collections of information about thousands of individuals, stored on auxiliary storage devices. 2.17
Data base A collection of data organized in a manner which allows retrieval and use of that data. 1.22, 10.7
Data base administrator The person who develops and maintains the data base, controls updating the data base, and often controls who within the business organization has access to the data base. 1.19, 17.6
Data base management system Software packages, also called file management systems, that allow users to define files, records within files, and data elements or fields within records in a relatively easy manner, and to provide a convenient method to access, update, and create reports from the data. 10.11, 12.8
Data base schema All of the owner-coupled sets and relationships established for a given network data base. 10.10
Data collection devices Devices used for obtaining data at the site where the transaction or event reported upon takes place. 5.23
Data communications Electronic communication and transfer of data from one computer to another. 1.23, 11.1
Data dictionary A list of the data elements, the attributes of the data, the type of access required for the data, the level of activity, and the amount of data which must be stored for a system. 15.8
Data editing The process of comparing the data entered to predetermined values to ensure that the data entered conforms to the predetermined criteria. 4.9
Data entry center An area of the information systems department that employs people who are responsible for keying large volumes of data, on a production basis, for mostly batch processing. 17.6
Data entry device An input unit that allows fast and accurate entry of data and storage of data on disk for eventual transfer to magnetic tape for entry into a computer. 1.14
Data entry operator An individual who is required to possess accurate, rapid keying ability. 17.6

Data flow diagram A manner of graphically documenting the flow of data and the procedures used within a system. 15.4
Data integrity An attribute of data which determines the confidence a user can have in the processing of that data. Data integrity is composed of the three primary elements: 1) Data accuracy; 2) Reliable data entry; 3) Timeliness. 4.8
Data item A piece of data required in the information processing cycle, but normally only useful after being combined with other data items or after a relationship between data items is established. 3.3
Data management Techniques and procedures which ensure that the data required for an application will be available in the correct form and at the proper time for processing. 4.10
Data management system A group of programs, also called a file management system, that performs the actual physical process of reading data from a file stored on disk or tape or writing a record into a file. 10.2
Data security and control Systems and procedures developed for a computer application that allow only authorized personnel to access the data stored in a data base. 4.10
Data Processing Management Association (DPMA) A professional association composed of programmers, systems analysts, and information processing managers. 17.14
DATA statement A BASIC statement used to define the data to be processed. A.5
Data transfer rate The time required to transfer data from disk to main computer memory and vice versa. 9.6
Decision support systems Systems developed using fourth generation application development tools, data communications, graphics, and other tools, to allow questions to be asked that can be answered in a dynamic manner based upon data stored in data bases. 1.20, 15.2
Decision table A graphical representation of the logical decisions that must be made concerning certain conditions which can occur within a program. 16.24
Default data Data, appearing on a screen, which is assumed correct but which can be changed. 5.16
Deleting a record Removing a record from auxiliary storage when the record becomes obsolete. 3.14
Desktop screen A screen containing icons which indicate the application programs that can be selected and other functions that can be performed, displayed on the screen in such a way as to resemble tasks sitting on the desk. 7.16
Destructive read in The process of reading data into memory replacing previous data at the same location or moving data from one location to another, replacing the data at the second location. 8.9
Detail report A printed report in which each line on the report usually corresponds to one input record that has been read. 6.14
Detailed investigation and analysis A phase of the system study that includes a detailed investigation of WHAT is taking place in the current system, analysis of WHY the procedures found are occurring, and what the user sees as the requirements for a new system. 15.4
Digit portion of the byte The rightmost four bits of an eight-bit byte. 8.9
Digitizer A graphical input device that converts points, lines, and curves from a sketch, drawing, or photograph to digital impulses and transmits them to a computer. 5.31
Direct access storage devices (DASD) Magnetic disk devices that can randomly store and retrieve data stored on disk. 9.11
Direct conversion The process of ceasing to use the old system and placing the new system into use on a given date. 15.13
Direct file A file in which records are stored in relative locations within the file and can be randomly retrieved. 10.5
Disk cartridge Auxiliary storage that contains one or more hard disks housed in a cartridge that can be inserted and removed from the disk drive. 9.9, 9.12
Diskette An oxide-coated plastic disk, also called a floppy disk, commonly used on personal computers which stores data as magnetic spots. 1.7, 9.1
Distributed data entry The entry of data from various locations within an organization. 5.5
Do while structure A control structure, also called the looping structure, used to allow program looping. 16.5
Documentation Written words, drawings, and screen messages which tell a person the exact procedures for all activities associated with a system. 4.11, 15.12
Documentation (program) Statements placed within a program that contain information which helps a reader of the program understand it. A.4
Dot-addressable displays Display monitors, also called bit-mapped displays, used for graphics. 6.17
Dot matrix printer An impact printer that uses a movable print head containing small pins that when struck against a ribbon and paper cause small dots which form characters to be printed. 6.4
Double density (DD) Diskettes and drives that record approximately 5,876 bits per inch. 9.3
Double-sided (drives) Diskette drives designed so that data can be recorded on both sides of the diskette. 9.3
Double size A feature of a screen that allows certain characters or words to be displayed at twice the size of normal characters and words. 5.9
Double track drives Diskette drives that record data in 80 tracks on the diskette. 9.4
Downloading Transferring large amounts of data from a data base on the host computer to the personal computer for storage on auxiliary storage. 11.4
Drum plotter A pen plotter that uses a rotating drum or cylinder over which drawing pens are mounted and moved to the left and right as the drum rotates to create images. 6.23

Dumb terminals A computer terminal, sometimes called a limited function terminal, that does nothing more than pass data keyed by an operator over some type of communication line to the computer. 5.6

-E-

EBCDIC An abbreviation for Extended Binary Coded Decimal Interchange Code. 8.9, 9.4

EDSAC (Electronic Delay Storage Automatic Calculator) Developed by Maurice V. Wilkes, it was the first computer using the stored program concept to be operational. 2.4

EDVAC (Electronic Discrete Variable Automatic Computer) An early computer developed by John von Neumann that utilized the stored program concept. 2.4

ENIAC (Electronic Numerical Integrator and Computer) The first large-scale electronic digital computer, developed by Dr. John W. Mauchly and J. Presper Eckert, Jr. 2.3

EPROM An abbreviation for erasable programmable read only memory. 8.13

Eckert, J. Presper, Jr. Together with Dr. John W. Mauchly developed the ENIAC, the first large-scale electronic digital computer. 2.2

Egoless programming Computer programming in which the programmer views his or her program not as an extension of themselves, but rather as a product which should be examined to make it better. 16.12

Electro-mechanical machines Punched card machines used by business for almost 40 years to process large volumes of data prior to the invention of more sophisticated computing devices. 2.6

Electro-sensitive printers Impact printers, also called thermal printers, that require the use of special sensitized paper to form images on the page. 6.3

Electronic cottage A society in which the home becomes the central focal point for education, entertainment, and working. 18.3

Electronic data processing (Also called information processing) The production of information by processing data on a computer. 1.5

Electronic Funds Transfer (EFT) The concept of a cashless society. 18.8

Electronic mail (Electronic text transfer) A software package that gives computer users the ability to send messages in the form of letters and memos to other personal computers connected in a network. 1.23, 11.20

Electronic spreadsheet software A software development tool which allows the user to develop a spreadsheet that contains both data and formulas. 1.9, 12.7

Electronic text transfer (Electronic mail) The ability to communicate directly with other users of the local area network. 11.20

Electrostatic plotter A plotter that produces drawings through the use of a row of styli across the width of the paper. 6.24

Element A single entry in an array. A.48

END statement A BASIC statement used to terminate execution of the program. A.7

End-of-file indicator Special characters placed after the last data record in a sequential input file to indicate the end of the data in the file. 16.14

End users Those individuals who directly use computers to help in the performance of their jobs. 7.1

Entry point The point where a control structure is entered. 16.15

Ergonomics The study of characteristics that need to be considered in designing and arranging things that are used in order that people and the things will interact most efficiently. 5.11

Erasable programmable read only memory Semiconductor memory in which the user can erase the data stored in memory using special ultraviolet devices and store new data. 8.13

Exception report A printed report that draws attention to "exceptional" information needed in order to make decisions or take specific action. 6.14

Executive workstations Units, sometimes called integrated workstations, that provide both telephone and computer terminal capabilities within a single unit by allowing both voice and data communication. 5.13

Exit point The point where a control structure is exited. 16.5

Expert systems Programs that simulate human brainpower. 18.12

Extended Binary Coded Decimal Interchange Code A commonly used coding scheme for mainframes. 8.9

External access Access to a data base for users to enter inquiries. 10.12

External direct connect modems A modem located adjacent to the personal computer and connected to the computer by a cable that plugs directly into a standard telephone jack to allow communication over telephone lines. 11.5

External report A printed report that is used outside the business organization. 6.13

-F-

Fair information practices Practices implemented to guard against the threat to the privacy of individual citizens caused by computers. 18.8

Fiber optics A communication line consisting of smooth hair-thin strands of material that conduct light. 11.12

Field A group of numbers or letters entered into memory as a unit of data. 3.3, 8.7, 10.1
File A collection of records. 1.22, 3.3, 10.1
File management Tasks performed by operating system programs, including formatting disks and diskettes, deleting files from a disk, copying files, renaming files, and other functions. 14.3
File management system (data base) Software packages, also called data base management systems, that allow users to define files, records within files, and data elements or fields within records in a relatively easy manner, and to provide a convenient method to access, update, and create reports from the data. 12.8
Final totals Totals which are accumulated and then are printed after all input records have been processed. 16.14
Fixed block architecture A method of organizing data on a disk, also called the sector method, in which the sector number is needed to reference data on disk. 9.13
Fixed disk A magnetic disk that is not removable from the disk drive. 1.16, 9.12
Flatbed plotters A pen plotter whose pen or pens are moved down to the flat drawing surface and whose movement is then directed to create images. 6.23
Floppy disk An oxide-coated plastic disk, also called a diskette, commonly used on personal computers which stores data as magnetic spots. 1.7, 9.1
Flowcharting The use of symbols to represent the logical solution to a problem. 16.2
Flying heads The movement of the read/write heads in and out over the surface of the disk. 9.8
FOR statement A BASIC statement used in connection with the NEXT statement to implement the looping structure. A.42
For-next loop The BASIC statements used to implement the looping structure. A.42
Formatting the diskette The process of defining the number and size of sectors on a soft-sectored diskette. 9.5, 14.4
FORTRAN (FORmula TRANslation) A high-level programming language designed for scientists, mathematicians, and engineers. 2.9, 13.3
Fourth generation of computer systems A classification of computers, including the IBM System/370, designed using large scale integration (LSI). 2.16
Fourth generation software development tools Tools that provide the ability to produce sophisticated programs and procedures with relatively little detailed programming knowledge and effort. 12.6
Friction feed mechanisms A paper feed mechanism that moves single sheets of paper through the printer by pressure on the paper and the carriage. 6.7
Front-end processors Communications control units that can be programmed by the user. 11.11
Front striking A technique of printing used by impact printers where a printing mechanism containing a solid character or a series of pins which can form a character strikes a ribbon against paper to form an image. 6.2
Full-duplex (channel) A communication channel that allows the transmission of data in both directions at the same time. 11.10
Function keys Keys on a terminal keyboard that can be programmed to accomplish certain tasks. 5.11
Function support The use of computers by people to perform their jobs faster, more efficiently, and cheaper. 1.20

-G-

Gantt chart A chart used to document a schedule for each of the major tasks in the system development. 15.11
Generalized prewritten application software packages Software which performs specific tasks, but can be used for many different applications. 12.1
Gigabytes A measurement of storage capacity. One gigabyte equals one billion bytes. 9.12
GOTO statement A BASIC statement used to transfer control to a particular statement in the program. A.7
Graphic output Output, appearing graphically, such as line, pie, and bar charts. 1.22
Graphics tablet A graphical input device similar to the digitizer which also contains unique characters and commands which can be called out by the person using the tablet. 5.31
Group controls Procedures used in batch processing systems in which groups of data that have been processed are balanced to some manual totals to assure the accuracy of processing. 15.10

-H-

Hacker Individuals, usually very technically knowledgeable, who routinely use remote computer terminals and communication lines to gain unauthorized access to restricted data bases. 18.10
Half-duplex (channel) A communication channel that allows the transmission of data in either direction, but in only one direction at a time. 11.10
Half-height drives Floppy disk and hard disk drives which are half the height of a full-size drive. 9.9
Hammer striking A technique of printing used by impact printers where a ribbon and paper are struck against the character by the hammer to form the image on the paper. 6.2
Hard disk Oxide-coated metal platters, sealed in a dust-free housing, which store data as magnetic spots. 1.7, 9.7
Hard-sectored diskette A diskette on which the number and size of sectors is determined by a hole located in front of each sector. 9.4

Instruction register An area of memory within the control unit of the CPU which can store a single instruction at a time. 8.15
Integer A whole number. 8.12
Integrated software Software packages that combine functions such as word processing, electronic spreadsheet, and graphics into a single easy-to-use program.1.23
Integrated workstations Units, sometimes called executive workstations, that provide both telephone and computer terminal capabilities within a single unit by allowing both voice and data communication. 5.13
Intelligent (modem) A modem, also called a smart modem, that contains a microprocessor which controls many functions, allowing easier and more flexible use of data communications. 11.6
Intelligent terminals A display terminal, also called a programmable terminal, that has substantial processing capabilities, is programmable, and can be used for extensive data editing. 5.7
Interactive processing A mode for processing data on a computer whereby a data field or group of fields is processed immediately and output is produced immediately. 2.14, 4.2
Interblock gap The blank space that separates records on magnetic tape. 9.16
Internal access Access to a data base by programs which are written in an installation. 10.12
Internal modem A modem consisting of a printed circuit board, with the related electronics, that is installed internally in a personal computer. 11.5
Internal report A printed report that is used within the business organization. 6.13
Interrupt A signal that data has been transferred from main compuer memory to a device or from a device to main computer memory. 14.6

-J-

Jackson methodology A design methodology based upon the data which is to be processed, under the theory that if the structure of a program mirrors the data which it processes, then the program will be easy to design and easy to read and understand. 16.11

-K-

Kemeny, Dr. John Developed time-sharing software for use on a computer and implemented the BASIC programming language. 2.14
Key A value in a record which defines the sequence in which data is stored in sequential files. 3.10, 10.2
Key-to-disk shared processor systems A number of keying stations, under control of some type of processor, where data is temporarily stored on disk, then transferred to tape for input to the main computer. 5.18
Key verification The process in which data is first keyed into the system and then is rekeyed and compared. 5.20
Keypunch A machine that contains a keyboard and punching mechanism used to punch holes representing numbers, letters of the alphabet, and special characters in a card. 5.1

-L-

Label A symbolic notation within an assembler language statement that identifies the address of the instruction to be executed. 13.2
Large scale integration (LSI) Placing large numbers of circuits on a single microcomputer chip. 2.16
Laser printer A nonimpact printer that converts data from the computer into a beam of laser light that encodes an organic photoconductor with the data, forming the images to be printed. 6.9, 6.12
Latency The time it takes for a sector containing data to rotate under the read/write head of a diskette drive. 9.6
Leased line A point-to-point line that is a permanent circuit to connect a personal computer, terminal, or larger computer with another computer. 11.13
Letter quality A printed character that is a fully formed, solid character that is easy to read. 6.5
Light pen A graphical input device used directly on the display screen to create or modify graphics. 5.31
Limited function terminals A computer terminal, sometimes called a dumb terminal, that does nothing more than pass the data keyed by an operator over some type of communication line to the computer. 5.6
Line charts A type of display chart that represents data relationships by a continuous line across the chart. 6.20
Line printers Printers, also called high speed printers, that print from 300 to 3,000 lines per minute. 6.3
Liquid crystal displays An output display consisting of a liquid crystal material deposited between two sheets of polarizing material, which when exposed to an electrical current, creates an image. 6.22
Local area network A communications network that covers a limited geographic area, is privately owned and user administered, is mostly used for internal transfer of information within a business, is normally contained within a single building or adjacent group of buildings, and transmits data at a very rapid speed. 11.19
Logical input/output systems A group of programs that performs the job of establishng the indexes when records are stored in an indexed file, retrieving records either sequentially or randomly when requested by a program, and adding records and modifying the index accordingly when records are added. 10.5

Logical operations Operations performed on a computer that compare data stored in main computer memory and determine if one value is less than, equal to, or greater than another value. 1.4, 3.7
Logical records Individual records stored on magnetic tape. 9.16
Logical (view of data) The logical organization of data within a data base and how the data can be retrieved. 10.7
Logo A programming language designed to enhance the learning and problem solving skills of children. 13.11
Looping The occurrence of one or more events so long as a given condition remains true. 3.7, 16.5, A.3
Looping structure A control structure, also called the do while structure, used to allow program looping. 16.5
Low-level languages Programming languages, also called assembler languages, that use symbolic notation to represent machine language instructions and are closely related to the internal architecture of the computer on which they are used. 13.2
Low speed printers Printers, also called serial printers, that print from 15 to 600 characters per second. 6.3

–M–

MS-DOS The operating system chosen for use on the IBM Personal Computer. 14.5
Machine language A set of instructions that the electronics of the computer can interpret and execute. 2.8, 13.1, 14.4
Machine language instruction An instruction which the electronic circuits in the CPU can interpret and execute. 8.15
Macro An assembler language statement from which a series of machine language instructions will be generated. 13.2
Magnetic core memory Small, ring-shaped pieces of metal that could be magnetized, or polarized, in one of two directions and be used for main computer memory. 8.12
Magnetic disk Oxide-coated platters that are used to store data as electronic spots. 1.16
Magnetic ink character recognition (MICR) A method used almost exclusively in the banking industry to encode and read checks. 5.22
Magnetic tape Oxide-coated tape, usually one-half inch in width, used on large computers to store data as electronic impulses. 1.16, 9.13
Main memory Electronic components which, as a part of the processor unit, store data and instructions that control processing. 1.6, 3.1, 8.1
Mainframe A large centralized computer, with more processing capabilities than a minicomputer, which is able to store large volumes of data and provide access by numerous users. 1.12
Maintainable (program) Program code that can be easily modified. 16.2
Major processing tasks The tasks that must be accomplished to obtain given output from given input. 16.8
Management information system (MIS) A computer-based system that not only processes the day-to-day transactions but also generates timely and accurate information for various levels of management. 15.2
Management support Activities carried out within a company to supply management with information on which decisions can be made and actions taken. 1.19
Mark reader A device that can read carefully placed pencil marks on specially designed documents. 5.22
Mauchly, Dr. John W. Together with J. Presper Eckert, Jr. developed the ENIAC, the first large-scale electronic digital computer. 2.2
Member An element of a network data base that is linked to one or more owner elements. 10.9
Memory address A number that identifies each byte of main computer memory. 8.6
Memory management Managing memory on a large computer to allow memory to be dynamically allocated to various programs at different times while the programs are executing. 14.8
Menu A display on a CRT screen that allows a user to make a selection from multiple alternatives. 7.12
Microcomputers Small computers, also called personal computers, with memory capacity and speeds less than the larger mainframes and minicomputers. 1.1
Microfiche Sheet film used when recording information using computer output microfilm. 6.24
Microfloppy disks Diskettes that vary in size from 3¼ inches to approximately 4 inches in diameter. 9.7
Microprocessor A central processing unit stored on a single silicon chip smaller than a fingernail. 2.20
Microseconds Millionths of a second. 8.13
Minicomputer A large centralized computer introduced by Digital Equipment Corporation, with less processing capabilities than a mainframe, which is able to store large volumes of data and provide access by numerous users. 1.12, 2.15
Modem A device which changes digital data to an analog signal which can be sent over communication channels and changes analog data to digital data on the receiving end of the transmission. 11.5
Modula-2 A programming language containing further improvements and extensions to the Pascal language. 13.9
Module A small portion of code that performs one given task within a program. 16.8
Monochrome A CRT screen that displays one color on a black background. 6.16
Movable print head A printing mechanism used by dot matrix printers that contains small pins that when struck against a ribbon and paper causes small dots which form characters to be printed. 6.4
Mouse A small, light-weight device that can easily fit in the palm of one's hand and be moved across a flat surface to control the movement of the cursor and select menu choices. 7.6

Multidrop (line) A communication line, also called a multipoint line, which has more than one terminal, personal computer, or larger computer connected to a host computer. 11.14
Multipoint line A communication line, also called a multidrop line, which has more than one terminal, personal computer, or larger computer connected to a host computer. 11.14
Multiprogramming The concurrent execution of two or more computer programs on one computer. 14.6
Multitasking The concurrent execution of two or more computer programs on one computer. 14.6

-N-

Nanoseconds Billionths of a second. 8.13
National data bank A proposed data bank to serve as a central repository for as much information as could be obtained about the citizens of the country. 18.6
Natural join relational operation An operation that joins two different relations based upon the common field found in each relation and produces a new relation. 10.11
Natural language communication Communication with a computer in a natural language like English. 7.19
Network Any system composed of two or more large computers, personal computers, or terminals. 11.15
Network access The procedures that allow each personal computer or terminal in a local area network to communicate and receive data. 11.23
Network data base A data base in which a child element (member) can have more than one parent element (owner). 10.9
Network topology The pathways by which the devices on a local area network are connected to one another. 11.20
NEXT statement A BASIC statement used in connection with the FOR statement to implement the looping structure. A.42
Nonimpact printing A form of printing in which printing occurs without having characters striking against a sheet of paper. 6.2
Numeric constants Actual numeric values. A.12
Numeric variable names Names assigned to reference fields that contain numeric data. A.5

-O-

Object code The machine language instructions generated from source language statements. 13.2
Object program A program consisting only of machine language instructions. 14.8
Off-line data entry The device from which the data is being entered is not connected directly to the computer which will process the data. 5.3
Office automation An integrated collection of electronic devices which are used to increase office productivity. 2.27
On-line The device from which the data is being entered for interactive processing is connected directly to the computer. 5.2
Operands A symbolic notation within an assembler language statement that identifies the address of the data to be processed. 13.2
Operating system A collection of programs which interfaces between the user or application programs and the computer hardware itself to control and manage the operations of the computer. 14.1
Operating system prompt A display from the operating system which indicates the operating system is available for communication. 14.2
Operation code A unique value which is typically stored as the first byte in a machine language instruction that indicates to the computer electronics what operation is to occur. 8.15, 13.2
Operations manager Person responsible for all operational aspects of the information systems department. 1.19
Operator's console Normally a computer terminal consisting of a keyboard and CRT screen, attached to the processor unit, used to monitor the activities of a computer system. 1.15
Operational system A system designed to process data that is generated by the day-to-day business transactions of a company. 15.1
Optical character reader (OCR) A device that reads typewritten, computer-printed, and in some cases hand-printed characters from ordinary documents. 5.21
Optical disk systems Devices that utilize a laser reading and writing optical disk device to store large amounts of unchanging data on 12-inch disks. 9.17
Optical mark readers (OMR) A device that can read marked documents. 5.22
Order entry The process which is followed when an order is received from a customer. 5.14
Output Information produced by transferring data stored in main computer memory to a medium or device which can be used by people. 3.9
Output operations The operations which make information generated from processing data on the computer available for use. 1.4
Output devices Devices which make information generated by a computer available for use. 1.6, 3.2
Owner An element of a network data base that is linked to, or points to, member elements. 10.9
Owner-coupled set A set of owner records and member records from the conceptual files in a CODASYL data base. 10.9

-P-

PC-DOS The operating systems used on the IBM Personal Computer. 14.5

PL/I A programming language designed with some of the computational concepts of FORTRAN and some of the file processing capabilities of COBOL. 13.6

PROM An abbreviation for programmable read only memory. 8.13

Packet switching A technique whereby so-called packets of data, often consisting of 128 characters each, are transmitted across a network. 11.17

Page printers Printers, also called very high speed printers, that print in excess of 3,000 lines per minute. 6.3

Paging A feature of a CRT screen that allows two or more pages of data to be stored and displayed. 5.9

Papert, Seymour Developer of the Logo programming language. 13.11

Parallel conversion The process of processing data in both the old and the new systems simultaneously and comparing the results until the new system is functioning in the proper manner. 15.13

Parent-child relationship The relationship of data within a hierarchy data base in which parent elements point to child elements, and each child element has only one parent element. 10.8

Parallel (transmission) The movement of groups of bits along a communication channel. 11.4

Pascal A programming language which provides statements to encourage the use of structured programming. 13.9

Password A value, such as a word or number, which is associated with the user and used to gain access to the computer. 7.21

Pen plotters A type of plotter that creates images on paper by the movement of one or more pens over the surface of the paper or by the movement of the paper under the tip of the pens. 6.23

Personal computer network A series of personal computers, joined together with a cable, making communication among the personal computers possible. 1.22

Personal computers Small computer systems, also called microcomputers, with memory capacity and speeds less than the larger mainframes and minicomputers. 1.1

Personal Electronic Translator (PET) The first microcomputer assembled in a single housing, built by Commodore Ltd. 2.21

Personal interview Interviews conducted with managerial and supervisory personnel during the preliminary and detailed investigations. 15.3

Phosphor-coated screen A CRT screen coated with phosphors making the illumination of the screen possible. 6.17

Photolithography A technique by which circuits are drawn, photographed, reduced and etched on a silicon wafer. 2.19

Physical organization The organization of data stored on auxiliary storage consisting of fields, records, and files. 10.1

Physical record A group of logical records placed together on magnetic tape. 9.16

Picture element Each addressable dot, also called a pixel, that can be illuminated on the display screen. 6.17

Pie chart A type of display chart used to depict data that may be expressed as a percentage of a whole. 6.19

Pixel Each addressable dot, also called a picture element, that can be illuminated on the display screen. 6.17

Plasma screen An output display consisting of a grid of conductors sealed between two flat plates of glass containing a gas which, when excited, creates an image. 6.22

Point of sale terminal An input device used for retail sales. 4.7, 5.29

Point-to-point line A direct communication line between a terminal and a larger computer, a personal computer and a large computer, or two larger computers. 11.13

Pointing device A device which is used to move the cursor around on the screen and make selections based upon the options on the screen. 7.6

Polling The host computer and the associated communications control unit ask each terminal or personal computer on a multidrop line if it has some data to send to the computer. 11.15

Port A standard plug and socket with predefined connections, also called a serial interface, needed to transmit a serial stream of bits in and out of the computer. 11.5

Portable teleprinters Small, lightweight terminals consisting of a standard size keyboard and a built-in printing device that combine both input and output capabilities. 5.12

Preliminary investigation An investigation to determine if the request for assistance which has been communicated to the systems department warrants further detailed investigation and analysis. 15.3

Preprinted form A form containing fixed information which is printed on the form prior to its being used on the computer printer. 6.15

Prime number A number that is divisible by only itself and one. 10.5

PRINT statement A BASIC statement that causes data to be displayed on a CRT screen. A.6

PRINT USING statement A BASIC statement used for report editing. A.21

Printed reports A form of computer output generated by a printing device. 6.1

Printer An output unit used for printing information from a computer. 1.6

Privacy Act of 1974 A congressional act requiring justification to be shown by federal agencies whenever a data bank was to be established or accessed, and allowing access by an individual to the store of information concerning that individual. 2.18

Procedure A series of logical steps by which all repetitive actions are initiated, carried forward, controlled, and finalized. 4.10, 15.1
Processing controls Procedures that are incorporated into computer programs within the system to assure the complete and accurate processing of the data throughout the system. 15.10
Processor unit The hardware unit which stores data and instructions and contains the electronic circuitry to process data. It consists of main memory and the central processing unit (CPU). 1.6, 3.1, 8.1
Production data entry The entry of large amounts of data by a terminal operator whose only job is to enter the data. 5.3
Program development cycle A systematic, disciplined approach to writing computer programs consisting of the review of program specifications, program design, program coding, program testing, and program documentation. 16.1
Program efficiency The amount of main computer memory required to store a program when it is processing data and the amount of time required by the program to process data. 16.28
Program initialization The process of setting values at the beginning of a program. 16.18
Program maintenance Making changes to a computer program. 16.29
Program specifications A set of documents that contains record and screen formats, printer spacing charts, data base schemas and access requirements, system flowcharts and data flow diagrams, and a written narrative which provides a detailed description of the processing for a computer program. 15.11
Programmable read only memory Semiconductor memory in which the user can store data in the memory prior to assemblying it with the computer and can read but not alter the data. 8.13
Programmable terminals Display terminals, also called intelligent terminals, that have substantial capabilities built into them. 5.7
Programming manager Person responsible for all programmers in the information systems department. 1.19
Programs A series of instructions, also called computer software, to direct a computer to perform input, arithmetic, logical, output, and storage operations. 3.1
Projection relational operation An operation that selects specified columns from a given relation, removes any duplicate records, and produces a new conceptual file. 10.10
Prompt A message displayed to the user which provides information or instructions to the user regarding some entry to be made or action to be taken. 7.11, A.36
Protocol A formal set of rules governing the format and relative timing of message exchanges between two communicating devices. 11.17
Prototype A series of small programs that allows a few of the transactions which will be processed on the real system to be processed 15.6
Pseudocode The logical steps to be taken in the solution of a problem written in the form of English statements. 16.6
Public bulletin boards Computer users or clubs that have stored messages, public domain software, and other types of information on auxiliary storage or a personal computer. 11.19
Pull-down menu A type of menu which is pulled down to view. 7.16
Punched cards A computer input media capable of storing data in the form of punched holes. They were used primarily for entering data into batch processing systems. 2.6

–Q-R–

Query languages The methods used to enter data for the purpose of inquiry. 7.18
RAM An abbreviation for random access memory. 8.13
REM statement A BASIC statement used to document a program. A.4
RGB monitor A color monitor that uses three signals to turn on the required phosphors within the pixel. 6.19
ROM An abbreviation for read only memory. 8.13
RPG A programming language designed to allow reports to be easily generated using fixed program logic. 13.7
RPG II An early 1970's enhancement to RPG that included file processing capabilities. 13.8
RPG III A 1979 enhancement to RPG II that included the use of the language to process data stored in a data base. 13.8
RS-232C A widely used type of standardized serial interface. 11.5
Random access memory Semiconductor memory that allows data to be stored and extracted using instructions within a computer program. 8.13
Random retrieval The retrieval of any record from magnetic disk regardless of the order in which it is physically stored. 3.11
Raster-scan CRT screens A type of CRT screen that projects an electron beam onto a phosphor-coated screen to form an image. 6.16
READ statement A BASIC statement used to transfer data from the data statements to an area in main computer memory where the data can be referenced. A.6
Read/write heads The mechanism on a disk drive that reads data stored on disk or writes data on disk. 9.8
Read only memory Semiconductor memory in which data is recorded when the memory is manufactured and can be read but not altered. 8.13
Record A collection of related data items, or fields. 3.3, A.2

Recording density The number of bits that can be recorded on a diskette in a one-inch circumference of the innermost track on the diskette. 9.3
Redundant data The same data stored in more than one file. 10.7
Refreshed The process of scanning the CRT screen with an electron beam anywhere from 30 to 60 times per second causing the phosphors to remain lit. 6.17
Relational data base A data base in which the relationships among data can be determined dynamically at the time the user requests information from the data base. 10.10
Relational operators Symbols used with the IF statement to perform comparing operations. A.27
Relative cursor movement The user must locate the current cursor position and then specify the movement required to move from the current location to the desired location. 7.3
Relative file A file, also called a direct file, in which records are stored in relative locations within the file and can be randomly retrieved. 10.5
Reliable data entry An element of data integrity guaranteeing the user's confidence in the result of data processing by assuring that the data to be entered is entered correctly. 4.9
Reliable (program) Program code that produces correct output. 16.2
Removable disks A magnetic disk pack that is removable from the disk drive. 1.16, 9.11
Report editing The process of displaying information on a report or CRT screen which is easy to read and understand. A.21
Resident commands Commands which are stored in the resident command area occupied by the operating system. 14.2
Response time The time that elapses between the instant a user enters data and the instant the computer responds to the entry. 7.21
Retail computer stores Retail stores that sell a variety of personal computers, computer supplies, and software. 17.4
Reverse video The process of reversing the normal display on the CRT screen. 5.8
Rigid disks Magnetic disk packs, also called fixed disks, that are not removable from the disk drive. 9.8
Ring network A series of computers communicating with one another and without a centralized host computer. 11.16
Ring topology All devices in a local area network are connected by a single communication cable that forms a circle. 11.21
Robots Machines, operating under the control of a computer and related software, that are designed to perform repetitive manufacturing and operational tasks. 2.8
Robust (program) Program code that will work under all conditions. 16.2
Rules (decision table) The numbers across the top of the decision table that identify the combination of conditions that can occur and the corresponding actions that should be taken. 16.24

-S-

Scientific programming Programming computers for scientific and engineering activities. 17.8
Scrolling A feature of a CRT screen that allows lines displayed on the screen to be moved up or down by one line. 5.9
Second degree computer fraud Accessing a computer system or data base without authority. 18.10
Second generation A classification of computers designed exclusively with transistors that replaced the use of vacuum tubes in previous computers. 2.11
Sector method A method of organizing data on a disk, also called fixed block architecture, in which the sector number is used to reference data stored on disk. 9.13
Selection relational operation An operation that selects certain records from a single relation and places them in a new relation, based upon the criteria specified for building a new relation. 10.10
Selective report A report generated on a computer in which selected data is listed. 4.14
Semiconductor memory Main computer memory manufactured from silicon or other semiconductor metal that is placed on a chip in layers. 8.12
Sequence control structure A control structure where one event occurs immediately after another. 16.4
Sequential file organization The organization of records within a file one after the other, normally in a prescribed sequence based upon a key. 10.2, 9.16
Sequential retrieval The retrieval of data from auxiliary storage one record after another based upon the sequence in which the data is stored on auxiliary storage. 10.1
Serial interface A standard plug and socket with predefined connections, also called a port, used to transmit a serial stream of bits in and out of the computer. 11.5
Serial printer Printers, also called low speed printers, that print from 15 to 600 characters per second. 6.3
Serial transmission The movement of one bit after another along a communication channel. 11.4
Server A computer, also called a control unit, dedicated to handling the communications needs of the other computers in a local area network. 11.20
Service bureaus Companies that receive data from their clients and process the data for a fee. 17.4
Settling time The time required for the read/write head to be placed in contact with the disk. 9.6
Simplex channel A communication channel that allows the transmission of data in one direction only. 11.9
Single density (SD) Diskettes and drives that record approximately 2,768 bits per inch. 9.3

Single-sided drives Diskette drives designed so that data can be recorded on only one side of the diskette. 9.3
Smart modems Modems, also called intelligent modems, that contain a microprocessor which controls many functions, allowing easier and more flexible use of data communications. 11.6
Smart terminals Computer terminals that have some processing capabilities built into them. 5.6
Soft-sectored diskettes A diskette on which the number and size of sectors is determined by the formatting of the diskette. 9.5
Software packages Computer programs available for purchase from computer stores and software vendors. 1.9
Software piracy The illegal duplication of software packages. 18.9
Solid logic technology (SLT) The technology of storing electronic components on small chips rather than transistors and diodes on a board. 2.13
Sorting The process of examining the records in a file and placing them in an ascending or descending sequence based upon the value in a field or fields within the record. 4.14
Source data collection The process of entering data as the event or transaction is occuring at the location where the event is occurring. 5.25
Source document Documents used primarily with batch processing which contain the data to be processed and from which data is punched in cards or placed on magnetic tape. 4.4, 5.3
Source document control Controls that include serial numbering input documents, using a document register to record the time an input document was received, and batch totaling. 15.9
Source language A programming language designed to make the coding of a program by a programmer easier than using machine language. 13.1
Specialized prewritten application software packages Software which performs application-specific tasks. 12.1
Spelling checker A software package used in conjunction with a word processor that allows the user to check individual words in the text for correct spelling or to scan the entire text to ensure all words are correctly spelled. 12.4
Star network A single, central host computer and one or more terminals or personal computers connected to it, forming a star. 11.15
Star topology Each personal computer or terminal in a local area network is connected through a central controlling communications unit. 11.21
STEP entry An entry in the FOR statement to control incrementing the counter-variable. A.43
Streaming cartridge-tape drive A device that is used to back up fixed, hard disks onto ¼ inch tape. 9.10
String variable names Names assigned to reference fields that contain alphabetic data, alphanumeric data, or fields that contain any nonnumeric character. A.5
Structured design A design methodology which when used results in a program consisting of many small portions of code called modules. 11.8
Structured programming A method of programming that uses the sequence, if-then-else, and do while control structures to form highly structured units of code that are easily read and maintained. 16.4
Structured walkthrough An organized review of a program by other programmers. 16.12
Stub testing Partially coding and testing a program before the entire program is coded. 16.27
Stylus A graphical input device used to enter commands to change or modify the graphics on the screen. 5.31
Submenus Menus which further define operations that can be performed. 7.14
Subroutine A series of computer instructions which accomplishes a given task. 16.8
Subschemas The definition of those owner-coupled sets in a data base available to a given user. 10.10
Subscript A numeric value or variable name representing a numeric value used to reference an element in an array. 16.21, A.50
Summary report A report that contains totals for certain values which can be accumulated. 4.14, 6.14
Supervisor A resident portion of the operating system which communicates with the user, causes input/output operations to occur, and generally controls the operations of the computer. 14.2
Switched line A point-to-point line that is established through the regular voice telephone network. 11.13
Synchronous transmission The transmission of groups of characters over a communication line without start or stop bits. 11.9
Synonyms The two record addresses generated when the hashing technique is used on different keys and a collision occurs. 10.6
Syntax (program) The coding rules used in a programming language. 16.25
System A network of related procedures designed to perform some activity. 4.10, 15.1
System/360 computer system A family of six computers, all compatible, with a variety of input/output devices and memory sizes, designed for both scientific and business use. 2.12
System controls A plan to ensure that only valid data is accepted and processed, completely and accurately. 15.9
System date The date which the operating system uses to identify when files are written on a disk, when files are changed, and a variety of other tasks. 14.3

System development A phase of the system project that establishes a project development and implementation plan, develops detailed programming specifications, programs and tests the system, and prepares final documentation of the system. 15.11
System flowchart A tool used to show the computer runs and their relationships, identify each file and/or data base, identify each report and terminal site used, indicate the number of programs to be written, and provide management with a means of reviewing the overall plans for the system. 15.8
System maintenance The ongoing process of making changes to correct errors in a system and making changes to give the system additional capabilities or to conform with government or company regulations. 15.13
System output The output produced by a system. 15.6
System testing The testing of the entire system of programs as a whole. 15.12
System responses Messages and other actions taken by the computer when a user enters data into a computer. 7.21
System time The time of day written by the operating system in the directory when files are created or changed. 14.3
Systems analysts People who review current operations within a company and design new systems. 1.18, 17.7
Systems engineers Individuals who are technical specialists and serve as consultants to customers after the customer's computer has been installed. 17.10
Systems manager Person who oversees activities in the systems analysis and design area of the information systems department. 1.19
Systems programmers Individuals responsible for maintaining the operating system utilized with the computer, making updates to the operating system as they are announced, ensuring that the data base and data communications software is operating properly, and generally ensuring the computer is operational from a software point of view. 17.8
Systems software Programs that start up the computer; load, execute, store, and retrieve application programs; store and retrieve files; and perform a series of utility functions. 14.1

–T–

TAB function A function used with the PRINT statement that specifies the column in which a constant or value in a field is to begin printing. A.17
Table A series of related data items or fields, also called an array, stored in rows and columns. 10.10, 16.20, A.47
Tape and disk libraries An area in the information systems department where magnetic tapes and disks are stored. 1.16, 17.6
Tape density The number of characters or bytes which can be stored on an inch of tape. 9.14
Telecommunications center An area of the information systems department that requires people knowledgeable in computers and data communications. 17.6
Teleprinters A general purpose interactive terminal consisting of a keyboard and a low-speed printer. 5.12
Text editing The ability to add, delete, or change characters, words, and lines after the data has been entered. 5.6
Thermal printers Impact printers that require special sensitized paper to form images on the paper. 6.3
Third generation of computers A classification of computer systems designed with solid logic technology (SLT). 2.12
Time-division multiplexing More than one personal computer or terminal can send a signal at the same time, and each terminal's signal is interspersed with other terminals' signals. 11.22
Time-sharing Attaching many terminals to a central computer and allowing each terminal fast access to the computer. 2.14
Timeliness The data to be processed has not lost its usefulness or accuracy because time has passed. 4.9
Token A string of bits that constantly travels around the network. 11.23
Token passing The transmission of a token from one computer to the next computer in a bus or ring local area network that gives the receiving computer permission to transmit. 11.23
Touch screens Screens that allow users to touch areas of the monitor screen to enter data. 7.8
Track A very narrow recording band forming a full circle around the diskette. 9.2
Tracks per inch A measurement of the number of tracks a diskette drive can record. 9.4
Tractor feed mechanisms A paper feed mechanism that transports continuous form paper through the printer by using sprockets which fit into holes on each side of the paper. 6.7
Trailer record The last record in a file used to indicate when all of the records have been processed. A.2
Train printer An impact printer, also called a chain printer, containing numbers, letters of the alphabet, and selected special characters on a rotating chain. 6.10
Transaction-oriented processing A special form of interactive processing in which all data pertaining to a complete business transaction is entered, and then processing for that particular transaction is performed. 2.17, 4.3
Transcription error An error in data entry made in copying the values from a source document. 5.26
Transient commands Commands which are stored in the transient command area occupied by the operating system. 14.2
Transistor Electronic components that either block electrical current or allow the current to pass, thus representing a bit being "off" or being "on." 2.10, 8.13
Translator A program, also called a compiler, that interprets computer programs written in a high-level language and converts them to machine language. 2.9
Transmission medium The type of communication channel or line used to interconnect personal computers or terminals in the local area network. 11.21

Transmission method The manner in which signals are transmitted over a transmission medium. 11.21
Transposition error An error in data entry made by switching two numbers. 5.26
Tuple A record within a conceptual file. 10.10
Turn-around document A document which is prepared by computer output, sent to a consumer or an organization, and then returned for reading by an OCR device. 5.22
Twisted pair wire Common telephone cord. 11.21

-U-

UNIVAC I (UNIVersal Automatic Computer) The first electronic computer dedicated to business applications. 2.5
Underlining A feature of a CRT screen that allows characters, words, lines, or paragraphs to be underlined. 5.29
Unit tests The tests performed on each individual program within a system. 15.12
Universal cash card A card used to purchase all goods and services in a cashless society. 18.8
Universal Product Code A special set of bar code characters which are printed on retail products. 5.29
Unix An operating system developed by Bell Laboratories for use on minicomputers but which has been modified to run on personal computers. 14.5
Uploading The transmission of data from files on the personal computer to data bases on the host computer. 5.7, 11.4
User friendly Software that can be easily used by individuals with limited training. 7.2
User interface The combination of hardware and software that allows a user to communicate with and control the functional aspects of an information system. 7.1
Utility functions Functions performed by the operating system, many of which pertain to file management. 14.3

-V-

Value added networks A data communications network that is already established and which can be used by anyone subscribing to the service. 11.17
Variable names Names assigned by the programmer to fields in main computer memory which will be referenced by statements within the program. A.5
Very high speed printers Printers, also called page printers, that print in excess of 3,000 lines per minute. 6.3
Vice President of Information Systems A title often given to the information systems department manager. 1.19
Video display terminals (VDT) Another term for CRT terminals. 5.29
Virtual storage systems Systems in which segments of a program that are not immediately required for processing are not stored in main computer memory but rather are stored on disk and are loaded into main computer memory when required. 14.8
VisiCalc The first electronic spreadsheet program, designed by Dan Bricklin and Bob Frankston. 2.21
Vocabulary (voice input) The collection of words which can be entered and stored for use during voice input. 7.9
Voice input The ability to enter data and issue commands to the computer with spoken words. 7.9
Voice output A form of output consisting of spoken words which are conveyed to the computer user from the computer. 6.25
Voice recognition A system which understands human speech regardless of the speaker or the words which are spoken. 7.9
Voice synthesizer A type of voice generation which can transform words stored in main computer memory into speech. 6.25
von Neumann, Dr. John Prepared the first written documentation of the stored program concept. 2.4

-W-

Warnier-Orr methodology A design methodology based upon analyzing the output to be produced from an application and developing modules based upon the processing that must be accomplished to produce the output. 16.11
Wilkes, Maurice V. Developed the EDSAC, the first computer using the stored program concept to be operational. 2.4
Window A portion of the CRT screen that is used to display information. 1.23
Winchester disk A type of hard, fixed disk often used with personal computers. 9.7
Wirth, Niklaus A computer scientist who originally defined the Pascal language. 13.9
Word processing A software package that allows users to prepare letters and memos using the computer. 1.20
Workstations Personal computers connected to a local area network that are available for use at all times. 11.20

-X-Y-Z-

Zone portion of the byte The leftmost four bits of an eight-bit byte. 8.9